Lecture Notes in Computer Science 730

Edited by G. Goos and J. Hartmanis

Advisory Board: W. Brauer   D. Gries   J. Stoer

David B. Lomet (Ed.)

Foundations of
Data Organization
and Algorithms

4th International Conference, FODO '93
Chicago, Illinois, USA, October 13-15, 1993
Proceedings

Springer-Verlag

Berlin Heidelberg New York
London Paris Tokyo
Hong Kong Barcelona
Budapest

Series Editors

Gerhard Goos
Universität Karlsruhe
Postfach 69 80
Vincenz-Priessnitz-Straße 1
D-76131 Karlsruhe, Germany

Juris Hartmanis
Cornell University
Department of Computer Science
4130 Upson Hall
Ithaca, NY 14853, USA

Volume Editor

David B. Lomet
Digital Equipment Corporation, Cambridge Research Lab
One Kendall Square, Building 700, Cambridge, MA 02139, USA

CR Subject Classification (1991): E.1-2, F.2.2, H.2-5

ISBN 3-540-57301-1 Springer-Verlag Berlin Heidelberg New York
ISBN 0-387-57301-1 Springer-Verlag New York Berlin Heidelberg

© Springer-Verlag Berlin Heidelberg 1993
Printed in Germany

Typesetting: Camera-ready by author
Printing and binding: Druckhaus Beltz, Hemsbach/Bergstr.
45/3140-543210 - Printed on acid-free paper

Message of the General Chairman

It has been my great pleasure to organize The Fourth International Conference on Data Organization and Algorithms (FODO'93) in Evanston. FODO has from its inception been an international conference. First in Warsaw (1981), then in Kyoto (1985), and Paris (1989), the conference has brought researchers together to share ideas and friendship. The 1981 conference concentrated on the consecutive retrieval property; the following meetings broadened the focus to include general access methods. FODO'93 reflects the maturing of the database field which has been driven by the enormous growth in the range of applications for database systems. The "non-standard" applications of the not-so-distant past, such as hypertext, multimedia, scientific, and engineering databases, now provide some of the central motivation for the advances in hardware technology and data organization and algorithms.

We were very fortunate to have a group of dedicated people who have worked enthusiastically to make this conference happen. I would like to thank first the steering committee, and Yahiko Kambayashi in particular, for keeping the spirit of FODO alive. My sincere appreciation goes to David Lomet and Katsumi Tanaka, the Program Chairs, and their Program Committees for an outstanding job in selecting high quality papers. Thanks too, to Edward Omiecinski for publicity, to Kathi Davis for registration, Aris Ouksel for finances, Chris Clifton for local arrangements, and to our international coordinators.

The proceedings bring together twenty-two contributed papers as well as invited talks by David Maier, Yahiko Kambayashi and C. Mohan. The talks by Maier and Kambayashi present stimulating ideas on data organizations for new hardware technology, specifically continous-media and flash memory. The talk by Mohan presents an integrated view of many of the implementation issues of large databases. I thank them for their fine contributions. Additional highlights are the panels, "Highways and Jukeboxes" and "Scientific Databases". I thank Margaret Murphy, our panel chair, for her help in organizing these. The conference has been preceded by tutorials on "Mobile Computing and Database Problems" by Tomacz Imielinski and "Audio/Video Databases" by Simon Gibbs and Christian Breiteneder. Tutorials and panels complement the paper sessions by presenting challenges for data organization and algorithms in new domains.

I would like to express my gratitude to the industrial and university sponsors without whom FODO'93 could not have happened: DEC, HP, Kyoto University, Matsushita and Northwestern University.

I hope that FODO will continue to serve the database community as a conference at the forefront between emerging technology and fundamental data organizations and algorithms.

Peter Scheuermann
FODO'93 General Chair

Message from the Program Committee Chairs

FODO'93 continues the FODO tradition of focusing on the data organizations and how systems use them to support data management. This year's call-for-papers explicitly emphasized not only traditional concerns but also called attention to physical storage and new application areas. The number of submissions and the quality of the accepted papers document the progress within the FODO scope, including these new areas.

The 1993 FODO program is a strong one. This reflects well on the authors of the papers. FODO has successfully attracted strong participants in the data organizations and algorithms community. The review process scoring was based on the standards of the VLDB and SIGMOD conferences. The scores for the accepted FODO papers are comparable to those of these pre-eminent database conferences. Some of the papers received outstanding scores. We wish to thank all authors for their submissions as it is the quality of the technical program that determines the value of a conference.

The strength of this year's program is a tribute to the program committees. The ability of conferences like FODO to attract quality submissions depends on the quality and credibility of the program committee. This year's FODO committees were outstanding. It is a pleasure to report also on the excellent cooperation and communication between the committees. We wish to thank the distinguished database experts who served on the FODO program committees for their efforts. The quality of the submissions made for tough choices.

The technical program is both focused on data organizations and quite diverse in coverage. The session on access methods applies these methods to new forms of data and system configurations. The text retrieval section contrasts signature and index trie methods. Multimedia considerations are addressed from the user interface level to data storage. The physical storage session deals directly with disk storage considerations. The query processing session emphasizes data organization and management aspects. A "new directions" session captures some of the more recent trends, OO, hypertext, multiversioned objects. The industrial papers session is of special interest, with two papers describing work that commercial enterprises expect to impact the marketplace. We hope you learn from and enjoy this fine proram.

Our message would be incomplete without further acknowledgements. Thanks particularly to conference chair Peter Scheuermann, whose vision and determination brought FODO'93 to fruition. Peter deserves credit also for recruiting our outstanding invited speakers. Thanks also to Michelle Gillespie of DEC's Cambridge Research Lab, who formatted the proceedings front material and handled PC correspondence.

David Lomet and Katsumi Tanaka
FODO'93 Program Co-chairs

FODO'93 Conference

General Chairman:	Peter Scheuermann Northwestern University
Steering Committee:	Claude Delobel, Altair, France Sakti Ghosh, IBM, USA Yahiko Kambayashi, Kyoto University, Japan

ORGANIZING COMMITTEE:

American Coordinator:	Clement Yu, University of Illinois at Chicago, USA
Asian Coordinator:	Yoshifumi Masunaga, ULIS, Japan
European Coordinator:	Gerhard Weikum, ETH, Switzerland
Treasurer:	M. Aris Ouksel, University of Illinois at Chicago, USA
Publicity:	Edward Omiecinski, Georgia Institute of Technology, USA
Local Arrangements:	Chris Clifton, Northwestern University, USA
Registration:	Kathy Hogshead Davis, Northern Illinois University, USA

SPONSORED BY: Northwestern University

IN COOPERATION WITH:

Association for Computing Machinery (ACM)
Special Interest Group on Management of Data (SIGMOD)
Institute of Electrical and Electronic Engineers (IEEE)
Technical Committee on Data Engineering (TCDE)

SUPPORTED BY:

Digital Equipment Corporation
Hewlett-Packard Labs
Kyoto University
Matsushita Electric, Ltd.

FODO'93 Program Committee

America/Europe Committee

David Lomet (chair)
DEC Cambridge Research Lab
USA

Stavros Christodoulakis
Technical University of Crete
GREECE

Jim Gray
DEC San Francisco Systems Center
USA

Laura Haas
IBM Almaden Research Center
USA

Rivka Ladin
DEC Cambridge Research Lab
USA

Witold Litwin
University of Paris
FRANCE

J. Eliot Moss
University of Massachusetts, Amherst
USA

Frank Olken
Lawrence Berkeley Laboratory
USA

Thomas Ottmann
University of Freiburg
GERMANY

M.V. Ramakrishna
Michigan State University
USA

Betty Salzberg
Northeastern University
USA

Hans Schek
ETH Zurich
SWITZERLAND

Asia/Pacific Committee

Katsumi Tanaka (chair)
Kobe University
JAPAN

David Abel
CSIRO
AUSTRALIA

Hideto Ikeda
Hiroshima University
JAPAN

Yoshihiko Imai
Matsushita Electric, Ltd.
JAPAN

Yasushi Kiyoki
Tsukuba University
JAPAN

Hongjun Lu
National University of Singapore
SINGAPORE

Akifumi Makinouchi
Kyushu University
JAPAN

Shojiro Nishio
Osaka University
JAPAN

A. Ohori
OKI Electric
JAPAN

Maria E. Orlowska
University of Queensland
AUSTRALIA

Kyu-Young Whang
KAIST
KOREA

Masatoshi Yoshikawa
Kyoto Sangyo University
JAPAN

Table of Contents

External Referees

Berndt Amann	INRIA, France
Masatoshi Arikawa	Kyoto University, Japan
Fritz Augenstein	University of Freiburg, Germany
Guangyi Bai	Kyushu University, Japan
Anthony Berglas	University of Queensland, Australia
Andrew Black	Digital Equipment Corp., USA
Yuri Breitbart	University of Kentucky, USA
Jae-Woo Chang	Chun-Pook University, Korea
Andrew E. Deacon	ETH Zurich, Switzerland
Sam DeFazio	Digital Equipment Corp., USA
David DeWitt	University of Wisconsin, USA
Gisbert Droege	ETH Zurich, Switzerland
Juergen Eckerle	University of Freiburg, Germany
Doo-Hun Eum	Duk-Sung Women's University, Korea
Cathy Ewald	University of Queensland, Australia
Jay Feenan	Digital Equipment Corp., USA
Tetsuya Furukawa	Kyushu University, Japan
Stephane Grumbach	INRIA France
Alois Heinz	University of Freiburg, Germany
Edmund Ihler	University of Freiburg, Germany
Yannis Ioannidis	University of Wisconsin
Bin Jiang	Union Bank of Switzerland
Yoki Kusumi	Matsushita Electric, Ltd., Japan
Steve Langdon	Digital Equipment Corp., USA
Dick Loveland	Digital Equipment Corp., USA
Xuemin Lin	University of Queensland, Australia
Bo-jiang Liu	Osaka University, Japan
Akifumi Makinouchi	Kyushu University, Japan
Moira Norrie	ETH Zurich, Switzerland
Beng-Chin Ooi	National University of Singapore
Young-Chul Park	Kyung-Pook University, Korea
Werner Schaad	ETH Zurich, Switzerland
Craig Schaffert	Digital Equipment Corp., USA
Juergen Schoening	University of Freiburg, Germany
Stefan Schroedl	University of Freiburg, Germany
Sven Schuierer	University of Freiburg, Germany
David Shertleff	Digital Equipment Corp., USA
Amit P. Sheth	Bellcore, USA
Ian Smith	Digital Equipment Corp., USA
Kazutoshi Sumiya	Matsushita Electric, Ltd., Japan
Wolfgang Weck	ETH Zurich, Switzerland
Peter Zabback	ETH Zurich, Switzerland
Yanchun Zhang	University of Queensland, Australia
Xiaofang Zhou	University of Queensland, Australia

Storage System Architectures for Continuous Media Data*

David Maier, Jonathan Walpole, and Richard Staehli

Department of Computer Science and Engineering
Oregon Graduate Institute of Science & Technology
20000 N.W. Walker Rd.
PO Box 91000
Portland, OR 97291-1000, USA

Abstract. Data storage systems are being called on to manage continuous media data types, such as digital audio and video. There is a demand by applications for "constrained-latency storage access" (CLSA) to such data: precisely scheduled delivery of data streams. We believe that anticipated quantitative improvements in processor and storage-device performance will not be sufficient for current data management architectures to meet CLSA requirements. The need for high-volume (but high-latency) storage devices, high-bandwidth access and predictable throughput rates mean that standard latency-masking techniques, such as buffering, are inadequate for the service demands of these applications.

We examine the ways in which storage system architectures must change in order to provide CLSA on continuous media, taking into account operating system and network support as well as database management. Particular points we cover include

- changes in the form of requests and responses at the application-database and database-OS interfaces
- new kinds of abstractions and data independence that data mangement systems will need to supply, such as quality-of-service requests and mapping of domain events to OS events
- effects of CLSA demands on query optimization, planning and evaluation, including the need for accurate resource estimates and detailed schedules
- new information requirements for the database system, such as better characterizations of storage subsystem performance and application patterns.

We illustrate the problems and new demands of continuous media access with application requirements of an all-digital television production studio of the future. We conclude by presenting a storage architecture we are pursuing that we believe will support "scripted" CLSA to shared data.

---

* This research is supported by NSF Grant IRI-9117008 and by funds from Tektronix, Inc. and the Oregon Advanced Computing Institute.

1 Introduction

Does incorporating new multimedia types into a data storage system make much of a difference as far as database system architecture is concerned? One might take the view of Negroponte that multimedia is a misnomer and what we are managing is "unimedia", that "bits are bits" [7]. Modern computer and network technology is indeed at the point where nearly every data type, including audio and video, can be captured faithfully in digital form—as bits rather than analog signals. The basic storage support for new multimedia types may indeed be the same as for conventional database types such as records. However, the kinds of data manipulations and application interfaces needed, especially for continuous media types, are vastly different from those found in conventional data processing. We believe that addressing these differences will require significant changes in storage system architectures, both for database management systems and for the underlying operating system and network facilities.

For continuous media, the mode of delivery of data is all important. The human eye, and more so the human ear, are sensitive to shifts and skips in the time domain, so rates of presentation are significant. Most continuous media presentations will combine more than one data stream, so there are also synchronization demands. The data storage volumes demand tertiary storage, which introduces seconds of latency on some accesses. Data rates are high enough (80Mbps for uncompressed NTSC color video) relative to hardware capabilities that buffering of data in the storage system or application memory is only suitable for overcoming very small latencies or time shifts. Getting data too early becomes as much a problem as getting data too late. The schedule with which data is delivered to an application becomes critical. We use the term *Constrained Latency Storage Access* (CLSA) for the requirement for read access to a store larger than main memory without the latency of secondary storage access [12]. We have concentrated our work on multimedia types with CLSA requirements, though we acknowledge not all multimedia types have this characteristic. For the moment, we are further restricting our attention to *scripted access*, where fairly large sequences of retrieval requirements are known in advance.

Most current multimedia systems leave these issues of latency, synchronization and scheduling almost entirely under application control. The application programmer is responsible for initiating requests and managing resources explicitly. Aside from being a major programming hassle, we do not believe this application-responsibility approach will work for large, shared systems. An application programmer may have enough control over system performance in a dedicated computing environment, such as a personal computer. We argue in later sections, however, that a single application will not have enough global information or control in a distributed, shared environment to reliably schedule data accesses to give acceptable service. Even if one could write an application to properly schedule a multimedia presentation, the resulting program would necessarily have wired-in information on data location, data layout and device performance. It would not have the kind of device and physical data independence that we expect from a database system, and could not be moved from one environment to another without recoding.

One answer is to over-engineer the computing, storage and network environment so that all conceivable simultaneous requests can be handled on demand. In nearly all cases, the cost of such a solution will be prohibitive. The approach we favor is for the storage system—the combination of database, operating system and network services working on data access and manipulation—to handle most of the details of scheduling data delivery. However, providing such a capability will require rethinking both the application's interface to the data management system and the interface of the DBMS to the lower system layers.

Relational data manipulation languages demonstrate the utility of letting the application specify *what* is wanted, and letting the database plan *how* to retrieve it. We believe that multimedia data managers will need DMLs that also allow the application to say *when* (and possibly *where*) the answer to a request should be delivered. Of course, one must indicate how precisely the "when" must be met— what are the tolerances on the requested delivery schedule. This constraint on delivery is one example of a *quality-of-service* (QOS) based interface. In general, with multimedia requests, there may be other service qualities to specify, and one would want to express preferences on which qualities to exchange for others. One would like the ability to make different trade-offs on jitter, synchronization, latency, drop-out, resolution, start time, color accuracy, and so forth for different data sets or different applications. Of course, QOS interfaces provided by the database will in turn require resource reservation and QOS guarantees from the OS and network interfaces.

Obviously there is not always a retrieval plan for a particular query that meets a requested QOS level. Thus, part of the interaction with a continuous media storage system is *acceptance testing*, where a request is examined for feasibility. This gating function might give a simple go/no-go response, or it may respond with choices on which QOS parameters can be relaxed. For example, "Requested data can be provided at reduced resolution R or with delayed start time D."

One should ask why current database systems will not suffice. One difficulty is with how the application-programming interface to a DBMS generally works. Typically a query is submitted, and a cursor bound to the result, with the application having to explicitly request the next data item. For the CSLA applications we envision, we would want the database to initiate the transfer of result data. Furthermore, the size of result will typically be such that the DBMS cannot compute the answer in its entirety and then begin delivery to the application. Rather, the result will have to be sent to the application while the query is still running. (We have heard of relational systems in which the first batch of tuples is returned to the application before the the entire query result is computed.) A more fundamental flaw with current database architectures is that there is really no notion of requested delivery schedule that goes along with request processing. Real-time databases [11] do not solve the problem. In the first place, most rely on keeping the database in memory to avoid the indeterminacy in secondary storage access. Clearly, the data volumes in continuous media are too large for that approach. Second, real-time databases work in terms of deadlines by which the entire answer must be delivered. With continuous media, such a guarantee is not sufficient. A 30-second video clip delivered all at the 30th second is of no use. Even if delivery is specified for the 1st second of playback, the application has no place to put the data until it is time to display it. The application really needs the data delivered at a particular rate. Conceivably, the application could break the single request into multiple requests with different deadlines, such as a separate request for each frame of video. But now the scheduling problem has been shifted back onto the application, which we were trying to shield from such responsibilities. We believe there is a clear need to rethink database system architecture to support CLSA.

In the remainder of the paper we examine what the requirements are on CLSA architectures. We start by looking at what the storage management demands are for a hypothetical all-digital television production studio. We then review current approaches to multimedia storage access and consider the data manipulation needs of the TV studio example. In light of the example, we consider what has to change in a storage system to support it. We conclude with a brief description of our own approach and research plans.

2   Motivating Example: A Digital Television Studio

Advances in computer and network technology have the potential to revolution-ize the TV production industry by providing integrated support for the functions that are supported separately in traditional analog production studios. The digital television studio, which we will refer to as simply the studio, provides the functionality of analog studios, but with a single high-bandwidth data network replacing many separate dedicated data and control channels, and specialized software replacing expensive hardware for special effects and control.

The architecture of the studio, as sketched in Figure 1, consists of multiple disk servers connected to editing and control workstations via an ATM switch network. Media input and output connections are made through workstation I/O devices, possibly on dedicated I/O servers. Software on each machine provides bandwidth guarantees for real-time inter-process communication.

The digital TV studio allows many users to work concurrently, sharing access to the database of continuous media. The primary functions of the studio consist of loading input media, editing presentations and controlling live output. The format and access characteristics of the input data are summarized below. A more detailed description of the editing and controlling operations for production of a television program is given in Section 4.

An NTSC color video signal can be digitized using 8-bit samples at three times the color subcarrier frequency to yield an 80Mbps data stream. This fig-ure is a reasonable estimate of the bandwidth requirements for a production studio, since compressing the data by an order of magnitude will introduce visi-ble artifacts with today's compression technology. When data is loaded into the database from live sources, it must be captured and written at this rate.

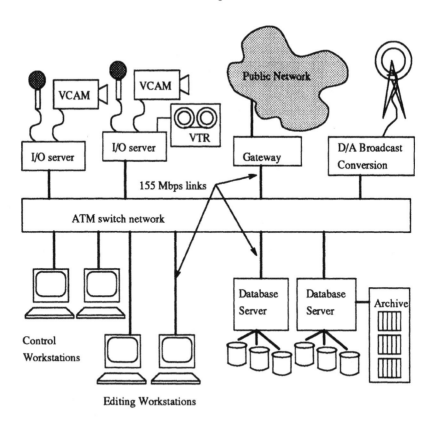

Fig. 1. Proposed architecture for a digital television studio.

A single day's newsfeeds will constitute 10 hours of video which require up to 360GB of storage. The studio can be expected to have many terabytes of archival video on site. A single user may be interested in only an hour of video data and thus might be able to work effectively with a 35 GB partition of the database.

Once in the database, video data is immutable. This constraint simplifies sharing of the data, since the same segment of a video may be included by reference in independent presentations without making independent copies. Playback processes can require the simultaneous presentation of multiple video segments with one or more audio tracks. The first time a user requests such a presentation, the database will need to concurrently retrieve all the data streams. The aggregate bandwidth will be the sum of the bandwidths required for each individual stream.

Input capture must occur concurrently with editing and production in the studio. In particular, live feeds must be captured, even as they are passed through for broadcast, so that important events that occur during other stories or commercial interruptions are not lost and can be played back from storage.

Video tape recorders include time codes with every frame that tell the time at which the frame was captured. The information from these timecodes must be preserved when the data is loaded into the database, though it may be more useful to use them for indexing rather then leaving them embedded in the data stream. These time codes can be used to automatically resynchronize video with its associated sound track. Similarly, when multiple cameras are recording the same proceedings, the timecodes provide a way to accurately cut between cameras on playback without losing audio synchronization. In addition to the time codes, video data will have annotations such as title, author and location of shoot. These annotations can be used to query the database for appropriate video segments.

Editors need to retrieve useful video footage, load new data, interactively view the data, and compose selected segments into new video presentations. Interactive viewing includes manual fast forward and reverse control to find visual and audio cues. A precise playback rate is not as important during this interactive search as it is during normal speed presentation, but it does require that full frames be retrieved without reading the entire data stream serially from storage, since the latter might need up to 100 times the normal bandwidth.

Composition operators include serial cuts from one data stream to another, parallel compositions such as lip-synched audio or voice-over narration, spatial layout of multiple regions of a display, and combination of inputs, including transitions such as wipes and fades.

For reviewing the compositions, playback must be real-time with broadcast quality signal reproduction and synchronization of media elements. The products of the editing process are scripts, that is, data structures that describe the media selections and compositions to be performed for playback. In contrast to the raw input media, these scripts are viewed as mutable data that are updated in place. After creation of a script, committed versions may be viewed as immutable in order to facilitate sharing among editors. Eventually, a script may be replaced by copying the data referenced into a contiguous space: a process sometimes referred to as "flattening" a script. However, flattening results in the loss of the original context of the component media segments.

It is important to distinguish between large and small multimedia systems. Small multimedia applications can be easily supported with simple operating systems and dedicated hardware resources. Examples of small multimedia systems can be found in the entertainment and educational software on personal computer platforms. Multimedia applications for personal computers often assume control of data layout and local disk resources. We claim that the digital television studio is representative of large multimedia systems which are characterized by networked computing resources and multi-user execution environments. Real-time constraints are harder to meet in such systems because of the greater number of factors that contribute to delay, including network communications and contention for resources between competing users. The studio requirements for concurrent multi-user access to stored video data argues for a global name space and shared storage resources. Because the video data consumes large amounts of bandwidth and storage, it is not possible to replicate the entire database for each user. At the same time, it will almost certainly be necessary to do some caching of data when a user may need to interactively search through the data many times without interference from other users.

Database technology to search for and retrieve data is needed in the digital television studio. However, the studio's requirements for timing guarantees during presentation are not well met by today's database systems.

3 Review of Current Approaches

Existing approaches to managing multimedia storage access vary widely in their effectiveness and applicability to different types of system [12]. These approaches can be grouped into three broad categories according to the type of architecture they are most suitable for: personal-computer-oriented approaches, approaches geared towards small-scale but shared systems, and approaches oriented towards large-scale systems.

3.1 Personal-Computer-Oriented Approaches

Personal-computer-based systems usually leave the problems of storage access latency and throughput variability to the application programmer. Applications typically employ a greedy prefetching algorithm [5], which prefetches the next data item into a FIFO buffer as soon as buffer space becomes available. After an initial start-up delay, during which the buffer is filled, reads by the application directly trigger prefetch operations to fill the newly freed buffer. Start-up latency is not hidden using this approach, despite the fact that data access sequences must be known in advance. If these data access sequences are derived solely from information relating to object types, then the approach will not be able to support certain inter-object synchronization operations. Note also that this approach must allocate and fill enough buffers to be able to satisfy demand during the worst-case interval in which the consumption exceeds prefetching. This constraint is reasonable in dedicated environments, but can be difficult to quantify when systems are shared. In particular, because greedy prefetching retrieves data in demand order, it is inappropriate when the demand sequence could cause thrashing on the storage devices.

Two common alternatives to greedy prefetching are to either presequence the data into a single contiguous data file or to rehearse the presentation and generate a prefetch script [10]. This latter approach is referred to as scripted prefetching [12]. The first approach aims to eliminate seek and startup latency between segments by placing the data sequentially in storage. However, it requires space and time to copy the data. The time spent laying out data for efficient access may be justified for presentations that are mastered on CD-ROM, but it is likely to be inappropriate for more interactive applications involving an edit-playback cycle.

Rehearsing a presentation is useful when the author of a presentation can observe synchronization errors due to storage latency and compensate for them by adjusting the prefetch script. In this context, the script is used to specify fetch times rather than display times, and the presentation of data is driven by ready events from the storage system. There are several limitations of this approach: it is not practical for the end user, it requires dedicated resources at the display site that are identical to those at the authoring site, and it can be difficult to determine a feasible prefetch sequence that avoids disk thrashing.

All of the approaches above assume that data access patterns are known in advance. For interactive applications, where data access patterns are at best probabilistic, prefetching becomes more complicated. One approach, described by Ghandeharizadeh et al. [6], is to prefetch the start of several possible data streams before the user has selected which will be needed. In this way, the system gains enough of a head-start to satisfy presentation demands while the remainder of the stream is being fetched following the decision.

3.2 Shared Storage Architectures

When storage resources are shared with competing applications, latency and throughput become functions of the policies used to schedule applications and allocate resources. Consequently, such policies must offer guaranteed real-time access. An emerging approach is to define quality-of-service based interfaces and to use resource reservation in conjunction with admission testing.

For example, the Continuous Media File System (CMFS) [1] supports multiple concurrent real-time audio and video sessions by reserving sufficient resources for each session's throughput requirements. For applications and data types with simple periodic access patterns and uniform throughput, resource reservation is relatively straight-forward and QOS requirements can be derived solely from the type of data being retrieved. Admission testing is performed before sessions are established to determine whether sufficient resources are available. In this way, work is rejected during admission testing, before the system becomes over-loaded, rather than allowing the QOS for existing sessions to degrade.

Once sufficient resources have been reserved, the CMFS uses round-robin scheduling between sessions and greedy prefetching within each session to hide storage access latency. Hence, resource reservations are used to provide dedicated resources, which are then managed in a similar manner to PC-based systems. Non-real-time file access is handled during slack time between cycles.

The approaches above must be extended for more complicated applications in which multiple streams are combined and synchronized. Admission tests must consider complex scripts for which groups of resources must be reserved atomically. They must also consider resource requirements to cover start-up latency for streams. The approach is complicated yet further when data access patterns are only known probabilistically. We are not aware of any existing systems that handle this level of complexity.

3.3 Large-Scale Storage Architectures

Large-scale systems have all the problems of shared architectures discussed above (because they are invariably shared), but they also introduce additional problems [4, 13]. First, the extremely large volume of data forces the use of tertiary storage devices such as automatic tape libraries and optical disk jukeboxes. These devices introduce media loading delays of several seconds or more and tape drives involve very long search times. Integrating archival tertiary storage with regular storage is a fairly well-explored research topic [3]. However, supporting guaranteed real-time access in such an environment remains a difficult research problem.

Christodoulakis, et al. describe the Object Virtual Machine (OVM), which manages a three-level multimedia store consisting of main memory, magnetic disks and tertiary storage (i.e., optical disks) [4]. OVM separates descriptive information, used for query evaluation and data location, from the raw data of multimedia objects. This separation allows raw data to be stored on tertiary storage or distributed across files on independent devices in order to achieve parallelism, and thus higher throughput. However, OVM does not support automatic prefetching to hide storage access latency: multimedia object values are only brought into main memory upon the user's explicit demand.

Second, large scale storage architectures are typically distributed [2]. Therefore, network resources are introduced into the data access path and hence contribute to data access latency and throughput limits. QOS-based interfaces and protocols are a hot topic in networking research [8]. However, the integration of these into a QOS-based storage architecture is still unexplored territory.

Examples of large-scale storage architectures include medical information systems, on-line multimedia libraries and TV production studios.

4 Data Manipulation and Storage Requirements

Current approaches to multimedia storage system design have significant limitations for large-scale applications such as the digital TV studio. This section focuses on the specific database-related requirements of such an application and illustrates these by studying an example scenario.

4.1 Digital Television Studio Operations

The operation of a studio is based on multiple concurrent retrieve, edit, store, and broadcast cycles. Initially, a large collection of video and audio objects is brought into a local central data repository from archival storage. Current analog systems require manual retrieval of working sets of data from their archives in advance. However, we expect future systems to support a more integrated approach to accessing local and remote archival storage in real time. Once the audio and video data has been retrieved from archives, the model of accessing it is similar to that of accessing and mixing live feeds from cameras and microphones. That is, there is an expectation that data can, at least, be accessed with negligible latency and guaranteed throughput. Additional characteristics are expected of stored data, such as the ability to display it in fast-forward mode and to search for a specified location.

Once archive retrieval has been performed, the central local repository of data serves as the basis for composing and editing new presentations. New composite objects are produced by combining parts of raw data objects and parts of existing composite objects. The composition operators correspond to the various synchronization operations between continuous media streams [9]. Components are identified by referencing an object (which is typically a video or audio clip) and then identifying the required part of that object via a range of time codes or frame numbers. Current analog systems use short, semantically meaningful labels to identify stored clips and then use time codes to specify the desired portions of those clips. A database for such a system should support composite objects and efficient data retrieval based on names, time codes and frame numbers.

The retrieval and display of data during the editing phase is likely to be at multiple data rates and resolutions. For example, it is common to review clips in fast and slow-motion as well as at the normal rate. Similarly, it is often acceptable to retrieve lower-resolution data during the early stages of editing and only use high resolution data during the later stages. Consequently, buffering and prefetching strategies must anticipate switches between data rates during interactive editing. This requirement complicates prefetching considerably because both slowing down and speeding up presentations can render the current contents of a buffer useless.

A possible solution to this problem involves a multi-buffer prefetching strategy for each data stream. In this scheme, each buffer would be used to anticipating a different data rate for the object. Information regarding the different possible data rates would originate in the application's QOS requirements. QOS information of this type could potentially be complex, therefore, we would expect the system to define a small number of standard QOS categories for use by applications, for example, editing QOS and broadcast QOS. During broadcast the presentation must be at high resolution and the accuracy of normal presentation is important. Since broadcast entails a new QOS specification for the same data item, the database should not simply associate a single QOS specification with each data type or item.

During the interactive-editing phase, the exact composition of a presentation is likely to change frequently. Therefore, it is inappropriate to copy or presequence the presentation in storage. A more suitable approach is to perform composition "by reference", leaving the original data in place. This approach is particularly appealing given the high volume and read-only nature of the raw data. However, it further complicates prefetching strategies. In this environment, prefetching must be based on scripts that describe the presentation object's synchronization points and component objects. Since multiple editing and broadcast sessions are taking place concurrently on shared storage resources, an approach based on resource reservation and admission testing is also required. Hence, the application script must be translated to obtain the information necessary for reserving the appropriate resources.

Once the editing phase is complete, the resulting presentation is ready for broadcast. At this stage the presentation is stored permanently in the studio's database. The presentation object could be stored either as a composite object (a collection of references to other permanent objects), or as a new "raw" object. In the latter case, the data would be copied into one contiguous place to simplify resource scheduling for the final broadcast. Broadcast can be complicated by the need to integrate live feeds into the presentation. A common requirement is for a live feed to be buffered in, and accessed through, the storage system. In this case, the database must be able to support the notion of a continuous media object with a continually moving start and end.

Each of these requirements is illustrated below in the context of a real-world example, where we also sketch a scripting structure to meet video editing needs.

4.2   Example Scenario: Editing a News Story

Producing a television news story involves three steps: 1) identifying components from original source media, 2) specifying composition relationships between them and 3) mixing and presentation of the data. An example of such a news story is a network report on President Clinton's Northwest Forest Summit, held in Portland during April 1993. The source videos include video of the summit proceedings from multiple cameras, a single sound track from the summit, archival footage of logging operations, plus an on-site reporter's intro and commentary. The goal of the editor is to provide some introductory context, show highlights of the proceedings including a major portion of the President's closing statement, and to close with the reporter's comments.

In constructing this news story, the author first queries the database for videos with keywords logging OR clearcut OR (forests AND aerial) in the text annotations that were shot in the 1980s when the controversy became news. The query returns only the titles, dates and keyframes for each video (and associated audio) that matches. The editor identifies two of the titles that sound promising and assigns each to a separate playback window. Each playback window accepts independent commands to start, pause and reposition a playback cursor. The editor first chooses to start playback of both videos at normal speed. The database must guarantee that the data for successive frames is retrieved in time to maintain the correct frame display rate. The first video is familiar to the editor and he thinks that the most interesting part is near the end. To search ahead, the he selects this video for interactive control and fast forwards the playback cursor by spinning a knob on the keyboard. This action causes both the video and audio display to speed up, skipping frames as necessary to keep up with the cursor. This interactive playback control is called jog-mode and requires quick response from the system, on the order of 1/10th of a second, but need not meet the strict synchronization requirements for normal-rate playback.

We define a script as a mapping from presentation events to time intervals, where all times are relative to the start of presentation. A presentation satisfies a

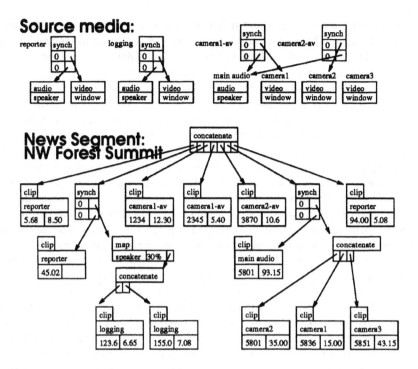

Fig. 2. Script composed of archival footage and video from the forest summit.

script if the actual time of each presentation event, such as the display of a video frame, falls with in the interval specified by the script. Some other multimedia scripting languages allow programmed responses to user interaction and other computations, that increase the scripting language's power but also complicate analysis. We restrict the scripting language to specifying synchronization relative to the start so that we can determine resource requirements prior to playback. A QOS specification may be associated with a script to define how much data may be lost or omitted while still satisfying the script.

Each media object in the database has a default script that specifies the display resolution, frame rate (for continuous media) and a logical output channel. The resolution and frame rate are QOS parameters that affect the data bandwidth requirements of the script. The logical output channel defines additional quality of service parameters such as the allowable bit error rate and jitter. More complex scripts can be composed from subscripts using operators that specify remapping of output channels, clipping, synchronization and concatenation. In our example, each logging segment is retrieved from the database as a script that specifies the natural synchronization between audio and video streams that were captured together.

Having found some good footage of logging operations, the editor uses the cursor control knob to locate and define a start and end frame for each "clip" that is to be used. These clips can be played back with accompanying audio and behave as if they were cut out from the original source data, except that the user does not have to wait for the data to be physically copied. The editor creates one more clip from the same source to be shown immediately after the first.

References to the other source videos are retrieved from the database by name via a browser that lists the day's newsfeeds. To assemble an introduction to the forest summit, the author concatenates a clip from the on-site reporter's introduction to the front of the logging footage. Another clip of audio from the on-site reporter is used for voice-over narration during the logging scenes. The audio from the logging videos is attenuated to 30% to avoid drowning out the narration. Figure 2 shows the resulting script. The voice-over clip is initially 1.3 seconds longer than the logging clips. To pad the video presentation, the author chooses to trim the start of the first logging clip by -1.3 seconds. This operation depends on the existence of more data in the source segment and having a reference to that segment. Note that subtracting 1.3 seconds from the starting offset in the clip definition applies to both the audio and video components.

Scripts specify only the timing of display events and not duration. For example, text display will persist until overwritten or moved by another operation. A video display script specifies painting each frame over the previous at the same rate as they were recorded. The last frame of video displayed by a script will also persist until overwritten. The timing constraint for video can be expressed as a frame rate r such that the presentation of frame n should occur within the interval $[n/r, n+1/r)$ relative to the start of the clip. A real-time clock is needed to meet this constraint. Elementary types also have defaults for display parameters such as volume and resolution. A special type, called the Null type, performs no display operations but allows specification of the end of a previous display operation. Continuous media types such as video are always null terminated so that a concatenation of two clips begins the display of the second exactly one frame interval after the last frame of the first. For example:

```
cat(synch[(0,f1),(5,Null)],synch[(0,f2),(3,Null)])
= synch[(0,f1),(5,f2),(8,Null)]
```

The editor composes the main section of the program by concatenating three clips of highlights from the proceedings, including the President's closing statement. During audio playback for the closing statement, the video cuts between several cameras to provide varied viewpoints and reaction shots. Since the cameras are all naturally synched to the single audio stream, the editor needs to specify only the point at which to cut rather than independent stop and start frames for each video clip. Such cuts are made easy for the author by providing simultaneous, synchronized playback of the video from each camera (called a *synch roll*) on the editing workstation.

To confirm that the resulting composition is acceptable, the editor may request broadcast-quality playback of the script and will likely do so several times with minor adjustments to the script between playback requests. Broadcast quality requires full-screen resolution with imperceptible synchronization errors and loss of data.

5   What Has to Change

We point out here some of the ways that we believe storage system architecture must change in order to support requirements such as those illustrated in the previous section. We consider in turn the application-database interface, the database-OS interface, and finally database system internals.

5.1   Application-Database Interface

As pointed out in the introduction, requests for continuous media will need to specify the manner of delivery as well as what is wanted. While several multimedia scripting languages have been proposed to deal with the "what", we have not seen many worked-out proposals on how to specify CLSA and other QOS requirements. Should timing requests be in absolute terms or relative to other events? For example, in showing two video streams of the same scene (say a main shot and and an inset reverse-angle view), the synchronization of the two streams is more important than the absolute delivery schedule of the individual streams. Video has an inherent internal frame structure that provides obvious synchronization points, but specifying synchronization at the granularity of audio samples seems too fine. How should timing requirements on audio be indicated? Life gets more complex when the application might want to flip between two modes of playback, such as fast-forward and normal playback speed, where lower resolution is tolerable during fast forward. There are then two QOS specifications that will alternate at query evaluation time, and possibly a third specification to say how quickly the storage system must be able to switch between them.

The interfaces for getting the results of a database request need to change as well. Results may take the form of multiple streams, and a cursor-like polling of the storage system by the application may be inappropriate. More likely what we want is for the application to specify destination buffers (possibly owned by other processes) and have the database initiate data delivery. That is, result transfer occurs in a data-driven rather than demand-driven fashion. There will likely be some need for flow control by the application, or provision for synchronization signals. The latter would be needed to compensate for cumulative drift of the application over time. If the application is running a few percent slow, and the database blindly delivers results at the requested rate, it will eventually overrun the application's buffer space. It could also be useful if the data delivery interface for live data were the same as that for retrieved data, giving an application some independence over the origin of the data.

5.2 Database-Operating System Interface

If the database is going to meet timing and other QOS demands from applications, it needs to be able to reserve system resources in preparation for query execution. The kinds of resources needed include memory, device access, CPU and bus bandwidth for data transfer and even CPU time for the database's own internal processing. During query evaluation, the database needs real-time service capabilities from the OS, so that events such as disk accesses, data transfers and database computations can be predictably scheduled. Also, there must be ways of avoiding system layers when they would add unacceptable latency or indeterminacy. An example is routing the result of a secondary storage fetch directly onto the network, rather than having it copied up through various levels of file system, OS and application, then back down through OS and communication layers.

5.3 Database Internals

The database system itself is called upon to provide new abstractions and mappings. We are now expecting it to mask latency. It is being asked to translate CLSA and QOS demands from domain terms (frame rates, jitter, resolution) to OS terms (resource reservations, prefetches). The job of query planning and evaluation is thus more complex than in conventional database systems. More information is needed and more information must be developed in the planning process. The query planner needs more knowledge of the execution environment, such as accurate information on subsystem performance (time to fetch a page, time to transfer a message over the net) and resource availability (amount of buffer space available, unreserved network bandwidth). The query planner needs to come up with a schedule of activities, not just an access plan. This schedule will need to include execution of database routines as well as calls on subsystems. Also, the environment in which planning and evaluation takes place is a constantly shifting target in a shared system, as resource availability changes. Thus, some part of query planning and scheduling will need to take place very near to query execution time.

In normal query optimization, it is not that critical that execution cost estimates be accurate in absolute terms. Rather, the important aspect is that estimated costs stand in the same relationship as actual costs. That is, the plans with the lowest estimates are the ones that actually have the smallest execution times. For acceptance testing in a continuous media database, however, the DBMS must be able to compute fairly exact resource requirements, not just relative costs.

Query processing will differ also in that there will be additional phases. One is a prepare phase, in which data staging and resource reservations occur. Another activity is figuring out how to reorganize or copy data in order to meet timing or QOS requests that cannot be met with the current data organization.

There will undoubtedly need to be new data formats and access methods. Consider data compression. Compression rates on video vary during a segment depending on scene complexity and the amount of change from one frame to the next. Thus, reading compressed data from storage at a constant rate will not result in a uniform rate of uncompressed data. In order to schedule reads of compressed data to get a constant rate of uncompressed data, one could create a "compression index". This auxiliary structure would record the compression rates at points throughout the segment, so that an appropriate amount of storage could be read to give a fixed amount of uncompressed data.

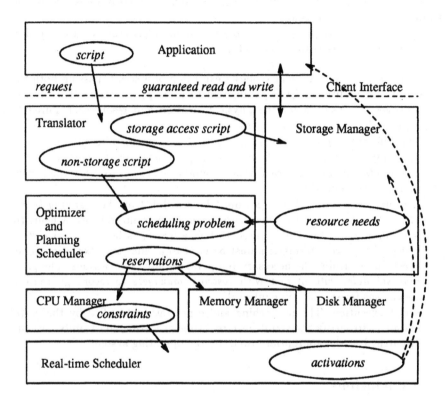

Fig. 3. Architecture for translating script requirements into execution guarantees.

6   Our Work

We intend to use the digital TV studio application to guide the design and refinement of our architecture and interfaces for a continuous media storage system with scripted access and QOS guarantees. We first need to better characterize and quantify TV studio access needs in order to develop requirements on QOS information and the script language. We then will consider alternative data layout and resource scheduling approaches to see which can best exploit script and QOS information for admission testing and resource reservation. Once we have selected a basic approach, we will develop the algorithms to map requests from the storage-system interface to OS and network interfaces, and determine where those interfaces need to be extended to meet storage-system needs. To test our concepts and gain operational insight, we will build a prototype video storage, access and composition environment using conventional hardware, software and an existing scripting language.

Figure 3 illustrates one possible storage system architecture we are considering. The key features of this architecture are:

- Script translation. A client requests execution of a script, passing both the script and additional QOS parameters to a *script translator*. The storage manager is consulted for the physical location and resources required to retrieve the data named in the script.
- Schedule optimization. The *script optimizer* compares alternative ways of satisfying the script, given the resource requirements for storage access. The *script optimizer* must interact with a *planning scheduler* to determine delays that a given plan will incur.
- Resource reservation. Resources must be scheduled by the *planning scheduler* so that they do not conflict with currently guaranteed tasks. A heuristic scheduling algorithm will be used to find a feasible schedule. Device state and performance information must be used to predict task execution times and help determine the necessary temporal resource reservations. The *planning scheduler* will interact with *resource managers* to record guaranteed allocations for specific time intervals.
- Script execution. The prefetching and other tasks identified by the *script optimizer* to satisfy the script have real-time execution constraints, and are dispatched at the appropriate times by the operating system.

7 Conclusions

We are far from a complete solution on CLSA for continuous media types. Our initial architectures and prototypes will undoubtedly leave a fair amount of responsibility with the application programmer, and fail sometimes to find feasible schedules when such exist. Also, we are restricting our attention to scripted access, which is likely the easiest case. Interactive presentation and browsing interfaces to continuous media will be more challenging. We have not dealt much yet with processing inputs to the database, although there is a real need for that capability in the television studio application. Adequate performance may have to wait for new OS and network interfaces, and perhaps better hardware. However, we feel anything that can be provided to simplify the construction of multimedia applications will be well received, even if it does not solve the whole problem.

Acknowledgements. We would like to thank Mayer Schwartz, Don Craig and Guy Cherry of Tektronix, Inc., for sharing their expertise on digital studio requirements, and to Scott Daniels and Bill Trost for reading a draft of this paper.

References

1. D.P. Anderson, Y. Osawa, R. Govindan: A File System for Continuous Media. ACM Transactions on Computer Systems, Vol. 10, No. 4, November 1992, pp. 311-337.
2. P.B. Berra, C.Y.R. Chen, A. Ghafoor, C.C. Lin, T.D.C. Little, D. Shin: Architecture for Distributed Multimedia Database Systems. Computer Communications [UK] Vol. 13, No. 4, May 1990, pp. 217-231.
3. M.J. Carey, L.M. Haas, M. Livny: Tapes Hold Data, Too: Challenges of Tuples on Tertiary Store. 1993 ACM SIGMOD Intl. Conf. on Management of Data, pp. 413-417.
4. S. Christodoulakis, N. Ailamaki, M. Fragonikolakis, Y. Kapetanakis, L. Koveos: An Object Oriented Architecture For Multimedia Information Systems. Data Engineering Vol. 14, No. 3, September 1991, pp. 4-15.
5. J. Gemmell, S. Christodoulakis: Principles of Delay-Sensitive Multimedia Data Storage and Retrieval. ACM Transactions on Information Systems, Vol. 10, No. 1, January 1992, pp. 51-90.
6. S. Ghandeharizadeh, L. Ramos, Z. Asad: Object Placement in Parallel Hypermedia Systems. in Proceedings of the 17th International Conference on Very Large Data Bases, September 1991, pp. 243-253.
7. B. Kantrowitz, J.C. Ramo: An Interactive Life. Newsweek, Vol. 121, No. 22, May 31, 1993, pp. 42-44.
8. A. Lazar, G. Pacifici: Control of Resources in Broadband Networks with QOS Guarantees. IEEE Communications Magazine, October 1991.
9. T.D.C. Little, A. Ghafoor: Network Considerations for Distributed Multimedia Object Composition and Communication. IEEE Network Magazine , November 1990, pp. 32-49.
10. Microsoft Windows multimedia authoring and tools guide: Microsoft Press, Redmond, WA, 1991, pp. 9-4.
11. M. Singhal: Issues and Approaches to Design of Real-Time Database Systems. SIGMOD Record, Vol 17, No. 1, March 1988, pp. 19-33.
12. R. Staehli, J. Walpole: Constrained-Latency Storage Access. Computer, Vol. 26, No. 3, March 1993, pp. 44-53.
13. H. Vin, P.V. Rangan: Designing a Multi-User HDTV Storage Server. Tech. Rept. CS92-225, University of California, San Diego, January 1992.

Physical Storage Organizations for Time-Dependent Multimedia Data*

Huang-Jen Chen and T.D.C. Little

Multimedia Communications Laboratory
Department of Electrical, Computer and Systems Engineering
Boston University, Boston, Massachusetts 02215, USA
{*huangjen,tdcl*} *@buenga.bu.edu*

Abstract. Multimedia computing requires support for heterogeneous data types with differing storage, communication and delivery requirements. Continuous media data types such as audio and video impose delivery requirements that are not satisfied by conventional physical storage organizations. In this paper we describe a physical organization for multimedia data based on the need to support the delivery of multiple playout sessions from a single rotating-disk storage device. Our model relates disk characteristics to the different media recording and playback rates and derives their storage pattern. This storage organization guarantees that as long as a multimedia delivery process is running, starvation will never occur. Furthermore, we derive bandwidth and buffer constraints for disk access and present an approach to minimize latencies for non-continuous media media stored on the same device. The analysis and numerical results indicate the feasibility of using conventional rotating magnetic disk storage devices to support multiple sessions for on-demand video applications.

Keywords: Multimedia, physical data organization, file systems, data clustering, time-dependent data.

1 Introduction

Files comprised of multimedia data are different from conventional data files in many respects. As shown in Table 1, multimedia data, and hence files, consume enormous space and bandwidth relative to text of program files. For example, a single feature-length JPEG-compressed movie can require over 2 gigabytes of memory for digital storage. Because multimedia data are also sensitive to timing during delivery, a multimedia file system must satisfy timing constraints of some data and not others. When a user *plays-out* or *records* a time-dependent multimedia data object, the system must consume or produce data at a constant, gap-free rate. This means that the file system must ensure the availability of

---

* This work is supported in part by the National Science Foundation under Grant No. NRI-9211165.

sufficient data buffer space for the playback or recording process. For example, to maintain a continuous NTSC-quality video playback, a file system must deliver data at a rate of 30 frames/s. Moreover, the delivery mechanism must also satisfy the intermedia synchronization requirement among related media (e.g., the lip synchronization between audio, video, and subtitles).

Table 1. Properties of multimedia data

Data Type	Buffer/Bandwidth
Voice-quality audio (8 bits @ 8 KHz)	64 Kb/s
CD quality audio (stereo @ 44.1 KHz)	1.4 Mb/s
NTSC-quality video (uncompressed @ 512 × 480 pixels, 24 bits/pixel)	5.9 Mb/frame (177 Mb/s)
JPEG-compressed NTSC video	≈ 7 Mb/s – 3.5 Mb/s
MPEG-I-compressed NTSC video	≤ 1.5 Mb/s
MPEG-II-compressed NTSC video	≤ 10 Mb/s
HDTV-quality video (uncompressed @ 1248 × 960 pixels, 24 bits/pixel)	28.7 Mb/frame (863 Mb/s)

A storage subsystem accesses data by positioning its read heads at the desired location for a data block. A random allocation approach, regardless of the time-dependency for multimedia data, increases the head and seek switching frequency and resultant access latency. In addition, the electromechanical nature of secondary-storage devices requires the use of scheduling disciplines modified to meet the throughput and real-time requirements of multimedia data delivery. When a multimedia file system transfers data from a disk, it must guarantee that multimedia data arrive at the consuming device on time. It must also meet the timing requirements of the multimedia object; however, this task is difficult due to the unpredictability of disk seek latencies. Furthermore, in a multitasking system, more than one user can request multimedia or non-real-time services, thereby requiring multiple session management. In contrast, the data allocation and scheduling strategies for conventional file systems are only concerned about the throughput, latency, and storage utilization for random access to files.

Our objective is to provide real-time behavior for a set of multimedia *sessions* originating from a single, conventional rotating-disk magnetic storage device. Since conventional file systems can not satisfy the real-time requirements for multimedia applications, we propose a new file system to support multimedia applications.

A number of related works exist in this area. The problem of satisfying timing requirements for multimedia data has been studied as a conceptual database problem [7], as an operating system delivery problem [1, 10, 17, 9], and as a physical data organization and performance problem [3, 4, 5, 11, 8, 16, 18].[2] Rangan et al. [13] propose a model for storing real-time multimedia data in file systems. The model defines an interleaved storage organization for multimedia data that permits the merging of time-dependent multimedia objects for efficient disk space utilization. In a related work, Rangan et al. [12] develop an *admission control* algorithm for determining when a new concurrent access request can be accepted without violating the real-time constraints of existing sessions. Polimenis [11] shows that the hard requirement for the acceptance of a set of real-time sessions is the availability of disk bandwidth and buffer space. Gemmell and Christodoulakis [5] establish some fundamental principles for retrieval and storage of time-dependent data. A theoretical framework is developed for the real-time requirements of multimedia object playback. Storage placement strategies for multichannel synchronized data are also examined. P. Yu, Chen, and Kandlur [8] present an access scheme called the *grouped sweeping scheme* (GSS) for disk scheduling to support multimedia applications by reducing buffer space requirements. C. Yu et al. [16, 18] describe approaches to interleaving time-dependent data to support constant playout rates.

In this paper, we propose a physical data organization for multimedia data. We interleave different media objects within a block so as to maintain temporal relationships among those objects during retrieval (Fig. 1). We also define an allocation policy based on the contiguous approach to prevent frequent head movement that can cause significant seek latencies and can support editing on multimedia files. The behavior of a conventional magnetic rotating-disk storage device is analyzed with respect to the mean and variance of the seek latency.

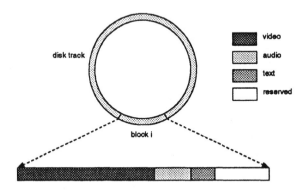

Fig. 1. Physical storage organization for a rotating disk device

A round-robin scheduling discipline is chosen for the service of multimedia sessions as in other work [9, 11, 14], permitting the disk to switch alternately be-

---

[2] The communications view is not applicable here.

tween multimedia tasks and other non-real-time tasks. We show the constraints which must be satisfied to permit the acceptance of a set of multimedia sessions including bandwidth and buffer considerations. We also evaluate the impact of the disk latency and establish a probabilistic model for our disk access schedule to guarantee that the frequency of starvation will be less than a specified rate.

The remainder of this paper is organized as follows. In Section 2, we describe the storage organization and allocation policy for multimedia objects to facilitate disk bandwidth utilization. In Section 3, we analyze the probabilistic behavior of seek latency for a disk. In Section 4, we show an access schedule for the disk and present a periodic service discipline for multimedia objects based on a probabilistic model of a disk, and show how this schedule reduces the required buffers and increases the number of supported multimedia sessions. Section 5, concludes the paper.

2 Storage Organization for Multimedia Objects

Most existing storage server architectures employ random allocation of blocks on a disk. This type of organization is not sufficient to meet the real time requirements for multimedia applications because the disk latency between blocks of a media object is unpredictable [14]. The file system cannot guarantee satisfaction of the deadline for the retrieval of multimedia data.

We view a multimedia object as consisting of components of any data type. Without loss of generality, we model a typical multimedia object as being comprised of audio, video and text. These three components can be viewed as distinct even though they are simultaneously recorded, and as input, arrive at the file system as three different streams [14]. During retrieval, these three streams are sent to three output queues for playout and ultimately are experienced by the user. From a timing perspective, the data streams can arrive at the file system with specific implied timing (e.g., live audio) or can arrive at the file system arbitrarily. For example, live video and audio can be recorded at the same time while subtitles are recorded later.

This leads us to the issue of data interleaving for maintaining intermedia synchronization. The advantage of interleaving multiple data streams into a single layout is the preservation of timing between related steams. The penalty with this scheme is the overhead associated with data combination and redistribution. These layouts are also called *homogeneous* (non-interleaved) and *heterogeneous* (interleaved) layouts [14]. The homogeneous layout stipulates storage of single medium data in blocks without interleaving. Of course, for this layout scheme timing relationships between media are not implicitly stored with the interrelated media.

In the homogeneous approach, each medium requests a session in a round-robin schedule. When retrieving a multimedia object, the file system must switch between sessions which can consume additional disk bandwidth and degrade throughput. There is no such problem in the heterogeneous approach. We merge different media data within a block based on their temporal relationships and can treat the aggregation of data as a single media object. Therefore, there is only one session for each multimedia object for the heterogeneous approach. For this reason we use the heterogeneous layout approach in this work. In our approach, multiple media streams being recorded are stored within the same block and the length of each object is proportion to its consumption rate.

In terms of *intramedia* timing, interleaving of data becomes important to maintain smooth, gap-free playout. In the extreme case, contiguous space allocation yields the highest effective bandwidth from a disk, but with a penalty for costly reorganization during data insertions and updates:

1. With the interleaved policy, multimedia data are stored on disk in a interleaved fashion [13, 14, 16, 18]. This approach can guarantee continuous retrieval and smooth the speed gap between disk and multimedia devices. Therefore, it can reduce the buffer requirement significantly. Usually, it can be applied on optical disks or in a single user environment.
2. With the contiguous policy, multimedia data are stored on a disk contiguously. This policy can also provide continuous retrieval, but entails enormous copying overhead during insertions and deletions [13]. However, it is the most efficient way for bandwidth utilization [11]. This approach can be used for data that is seldom modified (read-only) such as digital motion picture archives which do not need deletion and insertion.

In our approach, we refine the contiguous scheme using a two-tiered structure. On the first level, we propose a doubly-linked list which is built based on the temporal relations of a multimedia object [7]. Each item in the list contains a pointer which points to the disk address of a media block. The reason for the doubly-linked list structure is to support the ability to provide reverse playback of multimedia objects. On the second level, we store the multimedia data that are indicated in the first level, permitting the reversal of a multimedia presentation at any moment. Basically, multimedia objects are stored sequentially on the disk. Subsequent media blocks are put on adjacent, unoccupied blocks. If a disk track or cylinder becomes full (or the next block is occupied) this policy places the multimedia data in the next nearest available block.

3 Disk Latency and Bandwidth

Multimedia data require large file sizes and consumption rates. The file system must organize the multimedia data on the disk for efficient use of the limited available space and bandwidth. To reach the highest bandwidth, a disk system must read (or write) contiguously. A discontinuous disk access can result in diminished disk bandwidth due to additional seek and rotational latencies involved in each discontinuity.

In our approach, there are two classes of disk latencies. The first one is caused by fragmentation inside the multimedia file. The file system can trace the file index and calculate the latencies. The second one is task switching latency. In our scheduling approach, the disk switches alternately to different multimedia

Table 2. Disk parameters and derived statistical behavior

Symbol	Identification	Value	Units
S_{dt}	Size of a single track	54,900	bytes
N_{head}	Number of tracks in a cylinder (number of disk heads)	15	tracks
T_{hh}	Time to change head to the another surface	2,000	μs
T_{tt}	Time to cross a track	21	μs
T_{start}	Seek start-up time	11,000	μs
T_{rot}	Rotation time for a disk	16,700	μs
R_t	Data transfer rate within a track	3.29	Mbyte/s
c	Number of cylinders per disk	2,107	cylinders
$T_{latency}$	$= T_{cross} + T_{switch} + T_{rotate}$		ms
$E(T_{cross})$	$\cong \frac{1}{3} c \times T_{tt} + T_{start}$	25.7	ms
σ^2_{cross}	$\cong \frac{c^2}{18} T^2_{tt}$	108	ms^2
σ_{cross}	$\cong \frac{c}{\sqrt{18}} T_{tt}$	10.4	ms
$E(T_{switch})$	$= \frac{N_{head}-1}{N_{head}} T_{hh}$	1.86	ms
σ^2_{switch}	$= T^2_{hh} \frac{N_{head}-1}{N^2_{head}} \cong \frac{T^2_{hh}}{N_{head}}$	0.27	ms^2
σ_{switch}	$\cong \frac{T_{hh}}{\sqrt{N_{head}}}$	0.51	ms
$E(T_{rotate})$	$\cong \frac{1}{2} T_{rot}$	8.35	ms
σ^2_{rotate}	$\cong \frac{1}{3} T^2_{rot}$	92.96	ms^2
σ_{rotate}	$\cong \frac{1}{\sqrt{3}} T_{rot}$	9.64	ms
$E(T_{latency})$	$\cong \frac{1}{3} c \times T_{tt} + T_{start} + \frac{N_{head}-1}{N_{head}} T_{hh} + \frac{1}{2} T_{rot}$	35.9	ms
$\sigma^2_{latency}$	$\cong \frac{c^2}{18} T^2_{tt} + \frac{T^2_{hh}}{N_{head}} + \frac{1}{3} T^2_{rot}$	201.6	ms^2

tasks. Because one can *pause, stop* or *reverse* a multimedia presentation at any moment, and a multimedia object can be allocated anywhere in the disk, there are unpredictable and significant latencies during retrieval. In this section, we determine these disk latencies and their distributions through analysis for a typical hard disk storage unit suitable for a Unix workstation [15]. Parameters characterizing such a device are summarized in Table 2 using symbols adopted and extended from Kiessling [6].

3.1 Seek Delay Latency

When a user edits the multimedia file or the file system schedules another process to access the disk, the next block to be retrieved can be arbitrarily located anywhere on the device. The disk head must start up and cross a number of tracks, switch to a recording (write) surface and rotate to the indicated block. Assuming that the location of the desired block is uniformly distributed on the whole disk, then the total latency is $T_{latency} = T_{cross} + T_{switch} + T_{rotate}$, where T_{cross} is the arm positioning time for disk head move to the correct track, T_{switch}

is the delay to switch the head to the other surface, and T_{rotate} is the delay for disk rotation. We have derived various statistical disk performance behaviors from these base parameters [2], and summarize them in Table 2.

3.2 Disk Bandwidth Normalization

In an ideal disk storage organization, data can be accessed without latencies, and the data transfer rate (or bandwidth) is dependent only on the disk rotational speed. In a real disk, latencies are introduced due to track and platter switching, and disk rotation. These latencies are determined by the layout of data on the disk and the scheduling policy for their access. We can normalize the data transfer rate based on a complete disk scan policy as follows: once the head reaches and retrieves the first block of an object, it retrieves the adjacent block in the same track. If the whole track has been retrieved, it switches to the next surface but remains on the same cylinder. If the whole cylinder has been retrieved, the disk arm crosses to the next track. We normalize the disk bandwidth by considering each of these head motions in the complete scan as:

$$R = \frac{1}{\frac{1}{R_t} + \frac{1}{S_{dt}}T_{hh} + \frac{1}{S_{dt} \times N_{head}}[T_{start} + T_{tt}]} \tag{1}$$

Therefore, we can use this derived value as the maximum effective bandwidth for data transfer from the disk.

4 Disk Access Scheduling

In this section we show the constraints for the acceptance of a set of multimedia sessions and the requirements for buffer size and disk bandwidth.

4.1 Layout Model

In the layout model of Polimenis [11], a working period T_{period} is defined for a set of multimedia tasks and other non-real-time tasks as shown in Fig. 2.

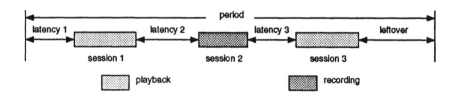

Fig. 2. Layout model

During a working period, the schedule switches among all multimedia sessions. It carries enough data into the buffer for the ith session to keep task i busy until its term is active in the next working period. If R is the whole disk bandwidth that we derived in (1), then each session i shares an interval $T(i)$ proportional to its consumption rate $R^c(i)$. The amount of data accessed during $T(i)$ is equal to the amount consumed during the period T_{period}. Thus, we have $T(i) = \frac{R^c(i)}{R} T_{period}$.

In this equation, $R^c(i)$ represents the bandwidth requirement for session i. Let the ith session contain k different media data (video, audio, text, etc.). Each medium j requires $R^c_j(i)$ of bandwidth. Thus, the total bandwidth requirement $R^c(i)$ for session i is $\sum_{j=1}^{k} R^c_j(i)$. For viable multimedia data delivery, the bandwidth lost due to task switching latencies plus the bandwidth consumed by each multimedia session must be less than the normalized disk bandwidth (where the period is fixed unless we change the number of sessions).

4.2 Bandwidth Requirements

In this section, we derive the bandwidth constraint. Let $n(i)$ be the number of bytes accessed for medium i during a working period T_{period}. The total number of bytes n to be read during a period T_{period} is then $\sum_{i=1}^{m} n(i)$. Because the time interval $T(i)$ for each media is proportional to its bandwidth requirement and $n(i) = T(i) \times R$. Thus, we have $n(i) = T_{period} \times R^c(i)$.

As shown in Fig. 2, the total interval used for multimedia sessions plus the disk seek latency should be less than the working period T_{period} in order to have enough bandwidth for other non-real-time tasks. On the other hand, the period T_{period} must be greater than the time needed in the worst case to transfer data from (or to) the disk for all sessions. Suppose we have m multimedia sessions. Let R be the total disk bandwidth and $T_{latency}(i)$ be the task switching latency between sessions $i-1$ and i. Then,

$$\frac{n}{R} + \sum_{i=1}^{m} T_{latency}(i) < T_{period} = \frac{n(i)}{R^c(i)}, \qquad (2)$$

where $\frac{n(i)}{R^c(i)}$ should be equal to T_{period} to maintain a steady-state. This means that the amount of data read from the disk for each session i during a period is exactly equal to the amount of data consumed by the ith consumer process. Thus, by (2),

$$R > \frac{n}{\frac{n(i)}{R(i)} - \sum_{i=1}^{m} T_{latency}(i)} = \frac{1}{\frac{n(i)}{n} \frac{1}{R(i)} - \frac{\sum_{i=1}^{m} T_{latency}(i)}{n}}.$$

Since, $\frac{n(i)}{n} = \frac{R^c(i)}{\sum_{i=1}^{m} R^c(i)}$, then

$$R > \frac{1}{\frac{R^c(i)}{\sum_{i=1}^{m} R^c(i)} \frac{1}{R(i)} - \frac{\sum_{i=1}^{m} T_{latency}(i)}{n}} = \frac{1}{\frac{1}{\sum_{i=1}^{m} R^c(i)} - \frac{\sum_{i=1}^{m} T_{latency}(i)}{n}}.$$

The right hand side of the above equation can be divided into two parts. The first part is the bandwidth requirement of all multimedia sessions. The second part is the factor due to the seek latency between any two sessions. Thus,

$$R > \sum_{i=1}^{m} R^c(i) + \frac{(\sum_{i=1}^{m} R^c(i))^2 \times \sum_{i=1}^{m} T_{latency}(i)}{n - \sum_{i=1}^{m} R^c(i) \times \sum_{i=1}^{m} T_{latency}(i)}. \qquad (3)$$

The last term of this equation describes the bandwidth wasted, or lost, when the disk head is moved, or seeked, between sessions.

4.3 Buffer Requirements

In Section 4.1, we showed the bandwidth requirements for a set of multimedia sessions without considering their acceptability in terms of buffer utilization. In the layout model, each session i shares only part of a period (Fig. 2). Each session must carry enough data into the buffer to keep the process i busy until it is reserviced. Otherwise, the process starves. Therefore, the second condition to accept a set of multimedia sessions is the availability of sufficient buffer space. As illustrated in Fig. 3, session i shares a duration $T(i)$ in a disk access.

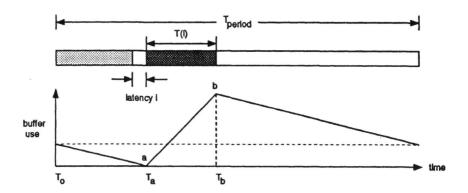

Fig. 3. Buffer consumption

When session i is active, its buffer size increases at a rate $R - R^c(i)$. Outside this duration, the buffer size shrinks at a rate $R^c(i)$. Let $B(i)$ be the buffer requirement for session i. Then $B(i) > (R - R^c(i)) \times T(i)$, or $B(i) > R^c(i) \times (T_{period} - T(i))$. If we let B be the total buffer requirement, then $B > \sum_{i=1}^{m}[(R - R^c(i)) \times T(i)]$. Rewriting, we get:

$$B > \sum_{i=1}^{m}[R^c(i) \times (T_{period} - T(i))] \qquad (4)$$

Therefore, we have defined the buffer constraint that can be applied to determine the feasibility of adopting additional multimedia sessions.

4.4 Length of Period T_{period}

In Fig. 2 and (2), we show that the period T_{period} must be greater than the sum of all individual session periods in order to transfer data from (or to) disk for all sessions. Let D be the leftover duration as shown in Fig. 2. For each period, the disk spends $T_{transfer}$ to transfer data, where, $T_{transfer} = T_{period} - \sum_{i=1}^{m} T_{latency}(i) - D$. In a period, session i shares $T(i)$ duration based on its consuming rate $R^c(i)$. Therefore,

$$T(i) = [T_{period} - \sum_{i=1}^{m} T_{latency}(i) - D] \times \frac{R^c(i)}{\sum_{i=1}^{m} R^c(i)}$$

To maintain a steady-state for the system, the data read from the disk during $T(i)$ for session i must be equal to the amount consumed during the period T_{period}. Otherwise, the buffer can starve or grow without bound. Thus,

$$T_{period} \times R^c(i) < [T_{period} - \sum_{i=1}^{m} T_{latency}(i)] \times \frac{R^c(i)}{\sum_{i=1}^{m} R^c(i)} \times R$$

$$T_{period} > \sum_{i=1}^{m} T_{latency}(i) \times \frac{R}{R - \sum_{i=1}^{m} R^c(i)} = T \tag{5}$$

In (5), $T_{latency}(i)$ represents the seek latency when the disk switches the service from session $i-1$ to session i. Because the next retrieval data for session i can be allocated anywhere on the disk, the latency $T_{latency}$ is a random variable. In Section 3, we derive the average seek latency and the variance of the seek latency. Let $E(T_{latency})$ be the average seek latency and $\sigma^2_{latency}$ be the variance of seek latency (Table 2). The expectation $E(T)$ and variance $\sigma^2(T)$ of T in (5) are as follows:

$$E(T) = m \times E(T_{latency}) \times \frac{R}{R - \sum_{i=1}^{m} R^c(i)}$$

$$\sigma^2(T) = m \times \sigma^2_{latency} \times \frac{R}{R - \sum_{i=1}^{m} R^c(i)}$$

By the above equations, we know T is also a random variable, so we cannot assign T to be the lower bound of the period T_{period}^{min}. Let p be the probability of starvation that can be tolerated for the mth session, by Chebychev's Inequality we have $P[|T_{period}^{min} - E(T)| > k] \leq \frac{\sigma^2(T)}{k^2} = p$, and therefore,

$$T_{period}^{min} \geq E(T) + \frac{\sigma(T)}{\sqrt{p}} \tag{6}$$

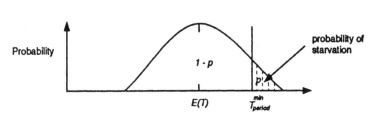

Fig. 4. Distribution of T

This means that if the lower bound T_{period}^{min} is chosen, the probability for the mth session can be accepted successfully is greater than $1 - p$.

By (6), if we chose T_{period} equal to the lower bound $E(T) + \frac{\sigma(T)}{\sqrt{p}}$, we can guarantee that the starvation rate for session m will be less than p. Equation 6 is always true; however, it does not mean that the starvation rate is equal to p. In the heavy load situation, when the number of multimedia sessions m is very large, by the Law of Large Numbers, the starvation rate will approach p. In the light load case, the starvation rate can be much lower than p. Conversely, we can use a shorter period T_{period} to keep the starvation rate under p.

A period T_{period} for a set of multimedia sessions must meet two hard requirements. In Section 4.2, we derived the bandwidth requirement, but it was not sufficient to accept a set of multimedia sessions. The system must provide enough buffer for each multimedia session. In the light load situation, there are always enough resources to allocate to multimedia sessions. Thus, we are more interested in the heavy load case. Let us assume the number of multimedia sessions m is large. Then, comparing with the period T_{period}, the duration $T(i)$ assigned to each multimedia session is small. We simplify (4) by ignoring the $T(i)$ and the result is still valid:

$$B \cong T_{period} \times \sum_{i=1}^{m} R^c(i) \tag{7}$$

By the equation above, we find that the buffer requirements are dependent on the length of period T_{period}. Let B_{max} be the maximum buffer space that is available. Obviously, there is a upper bound T_{period}^{max} for the period that can be accepted for a set of multimedia sessions. Otherwise, the total buffer requirements will exceed the available buffer space B^{max}. From (7), we have:

$$T_{period}^{max} = \frac{B^{max}}{\sum_{i=1}^{m} R^c(i)} \tag{8}$$

Eqs. (6) and (8) derived above are for the general case where the consumption rates for multimedia sessions have different values. In real applications, the disk bandwidth requirements for multimedia sessions can have the same value. In the following example, we assume, for simplicity, that the consumption rates for all multimedia sessions are the same and evaluate the buffer consumption and number of sessions supported.

Example 1 Let us assume all multimedia sessions request the same disk bandwidth. Each multimedia session includes video data at a rate of 1.92 Mb/frame @ 30 frames/s with a 20:1 compression ratio, and audio data at a rate of 1.4 Mb/s with a 4:1 compression ratio. Each multimedia session consumes disk bandwidth at a rate of 0.4 Mbyte/s. Using the same disk parameters as in Table 2, the average disk latency $E(T_{latency})$ is equal to $35,965\mu s$ and the standard division $\sigma_{latency}$ is equal to $14,212\mu s$. In (6) we let p be 0.05. We then derive the lower bound for different numbers of supported sessions using (6) assuming that there are 16 Mbytes of main memory that can be assigned for buffering. The upper bound of a period is determined by (8).

Table 3. File system performance for Example 1

	100 % Bandwidth Utilization		100 % Buffer Allocation	
N	T_{period}^{min} (ms)	Buffer Allocation (bytes)	T_{period}^{max} (ms)	Bandwidth Utilization
1	86	29,000	40,000	16.35 %
2	213	143,000	20,000	32.88 %
3	385	386,000	13,333	49.58 %
4	706	946,000	10,000	66.48 %
5	1,577	2,641,000	8,000	83.75 %
6	14,013	* 28,163,000	6,667	* 100.80 %

* Insufficient memory.

Let N be the number of multimedia sessions and T_{period}^{min} be the lower bound for the period. In this example we assume all multimedia sessions request the same disk bandwidth R^c. If T_{period}^{min} is chosen then there is no disk bandwidth left. By (4) we know that the buffer requirement is minimized. By (4), we have

$$B = \sum_{i=1}^{N}\{R^c(i) \times [T_{period}^{min} - \frac{R^c(i)}{R}T_{period}^{min}]\} = N \times R^c \times T_{period}^{min} \times (1 - \frac{R^c}{R})$$

The results of this analysis are summarized in Table 3. The third column presents the buffer requirement for N multimedia sessions when we chose T_{period}^{min}. The fourth column indicates the upper bound for period. In this case, the whole 16 Mbytes of memory are assigned for buffering. This allows us to use the least amount of disk bandwidth.

In our layout model, a period T_{period} is equal to the sum of all durations assigned multimedia sessions and the disk latency for switching service between multimedia sessions plus the leftover used for other non-real-time process (Fig.

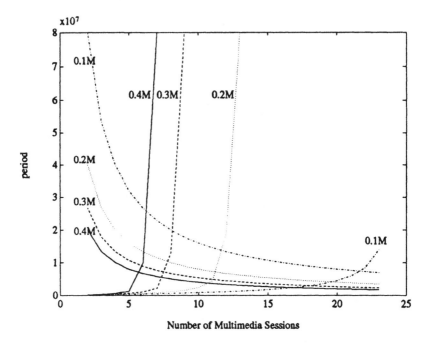

x10⁷

Fig. 5. Number of sessions vs. period length

2). The percentage P of disk bandwidth consumed by multimedia sessions can
be considered as the interval assigned to multimedia session, plus disk latency
lost in task switching between multimedia sessions, divided by the length of the
period:

$$P = \frac{\sum_{i=1}^{N} T(i) + \sum_{i=1}^{N} T_{latency}(i)}{T_{period}^{max}} = \frac{N \times T_{period}\frac{R^c}{R} + N \times T_{latency}}{T_{period}^{max}}$$

In the fifth column, we show the percentage of disk bandwidth consumed by
the multimedia sessions when the upper bound T_{period}^{max} is chosen.

In Fig. 5, when we increase the number of supported sessions, the buffer
requirement for lower bound and disk bandwidth requirement for upper bound
increases. If there are five multimedia sessions accessing the file system, the
system can perform within these constraints, but it cannot accept additional
multimedia sessions. An additional session causes the request for a 28,163,000
byte buffer and 100.8% of disk bandwidth, both of which exceed the capacity of
the system.

Fig. 5 also shows the effect of varying the compression rate to reduce the
bandwidth required for any (video) session and increase the number of multi-

media sessions supported per device. For video data, a compression ratio in the range of 1:10 to 1:100 is not unreasonable.

4.5   Consideration for Choosing a Period

Two hard requirements must be met when choosing the length of a period, otherwise the system cannot work. A period must be greater than T_{period}^{min} to meet the bandwidth requirement and less than T_{period}^{max} to meet the buffer requirement. These constraints are summarized as:

$$T_{period}^{max} > T_{period} > T_{period}^{min} \qquad (9)$$

A new multimedia session can be accepted only it satisfies this relationship. Fig. 5 illustrates the ranges of sessions supported that satisfy these constraints. The region enveloped by the lower bound and upper bound is safe. In Table 3 for the sixth session the lower bound of period T_{period}^{min} is $14,013$ ms, the upper bound T_{period}^{max} is $6,667$ ms. Since $T_{period}^{min} > T_{period}^{max}$, we know the file system can not accept six multimedia sessions at the same time.

We estimate the upper and lower bound very conservatively (due to the large m assumed). The real upper bound can be larger and the lower bound can be lower than we derived. However, when the number of sessions increases, our estimates approach the real upper and lower bounds. There are two reasons to support our assumption. First, in the light load case, there are always enough resources for use. We are more concerned about the heavy load situation when the number of multimedia sessions m is large. Second, it is not necessary or wise to chose a period T_{period} close to either the upper or lower bound because of the degradation of the throughput of other non-real-time data transfers. For a general-purpose machine, a multimedia file system not only has to meet the hard requirements above, but also must leave enough bandwidth for these other non-real-time transfers. Let $A = D/T_{period}$ be the the percentage of disk bandwidth used to carry data from disk for non-multimedia job during every period T_{period}. For a set of multimedia sessions, we have the maximum value of A when $T_{period} = T_{period}^{max}$ [11]. This means if we increase the period T_{period} we can have more disk bandwidth left for the non-multimedia task.

From a memory perspective, a multimedia file system must minimize its buffer utilization to provide more free memory for other system tasks. By (7), when period $T_{period} = T_{period}^{min}$, the buffer requirement is minimized. By the above two results, we intend to increase the period to have more disk bandwidth left for non-multimedia traffic but minimize the period to get more free memory for non-multimedia tasks. In the extreme case, if we minimize the T_{period} value, we minimize the buffer requirement and maximize free memory for other non-multimedia tasks. At the same time, the leftover for disk bandwidth is zero. Similarly, maximizing the T_{period} can free the maximum disk bandwidth for other non-multimedia processes to use but will also result in complete memory consumption. In this case, even if the disk has ample bandwidth available, no non-multimedia process can use it. Thus, these two soft requirements are in conflict.

To improve the response time for non-multimedia processes, we can change the period T_{period} dynamically with feedback from operating system to balance the resources allocation. For example, if there are tasks suspended due to disk bandwidth shortage and there is free memory space available, the file system can extend the period T_{period} in order to have more disk bandwidth to assign to the non-multimedia processes. On the other hand, if there are non-multimedia processes waiting for memory space and the disk is idle during the leftover interval. The file system can shrink the period T_{period} in order to free more memory space and to load more processes in the memory.

For a multimedia on-demand server, the file system need only provide service to multimedia processes. In this situation, we chose the lower bound to achieve the highest disk utilization. Given the physical disk characteristics, we can determine the buffer requirements. By Fig. 3 and (4), we know the buffer consumed is dominated by the period length T_{period}. By (5), the period length depends on the sum of random variables $T_{latency}(i)$. We assume the worst case, take the maximum value for for all task switching latencies $T_{latency}(i)$, and decide the period length. This assumes that starvation can never happen, when in practice it will only rarely happen. In a refined model, we define an acceptable rate $q = 1 - p$ of non-starvation, and derive the period length which guarantees a set of multimedia session can be accepted with at least a value of q for the probability of not starving. For example, we define $q = 95\%$. In this case, if there are five multimedia sessions in the system we can save 20.8% of available memory.

5 Conclusion

When a multimedia file system transfers data from a disk, it must guarantee that multimedia data arrive at the playout device with a minimum latency. It must also satisfy the timing requirements implied by the nature of the multimedia object (e.g., intermedia synchronization among media). However, disk seek latency is very significant and can be unpredictable in a general-purpose file system.

In this paper we presented a physical data organization for supporting the storage of time-dependent multimedia data. We interleaved different media objects within a block to maintain timing among the objects during data storage and retrieval. We also refined existing contiguous allocation approaches to maximize disk bandwidth utilization and to prevent the enormous copying overhead during editing. Furthermore, we introduced a probabilistic model as a refinement of the round-round scheduling discipline that supports concurrent multimedia processes. Moreover, it reduces the amount of required buffering. We showed the acceptance conditions for additional multimedia sessions which include bandwidth and buffer constraints, and a means for balancing these two parameters to support the largest number of multimedia sessions originating from a single device.

References

1. Anderson, D.P., Homsy, G.: A continuous media I/O server and its synchronization mechanism. Computer 24 (1991) 51-57
2. Chen, H.J. Little, T.D.C.: A file system for multimedia applications. Tech. Rept. 12-09-1992, Multimedia Communication Laboratory, Boston University (1992)
3. Christodoulakis, S., Faloutsos, C.: Design and performance considerations for an optical disk-based, multimedia object server. Computer 19 (1986) 45-56
4. Ford, D.A., Christodoulakis, S.: Optimal placement of high probability randomly retrieved blocks on CLV optical disks. ACM Trans. on Information Systems 9 (1991) 1-30
5. Gemmell, J., Christodoulakis, S.: Principles of delay-sensitive multimedia data storage and retrieval. ACM Trans. on Information Systems. 10 (1992) 51-90
6. Kiessling, W.: Access path selection in databases with intelligent disc subsystems. The Computer Journal 31 (1988) 41-50
7. Little, T.D.C., Ghafoor A.: Interval-based conceptual models for time-dependent multimedia data. To appear in IEEE Trans. on Data and Knowledge Engineering (1993)
8. Yu, P.S., Chen, M.S., Kandlur, D.D.: Design and analysis of a grouped sweeping scheme for multimedia storage management. Proc. 3rd Intl. Workshop on Network and Operating System Support for Digital Audio and Video, San Diego (1992) 38-49
9. Lougher, P., Shepherd, D.: The design and implementation of a continuous media storage server. Proc. 3rd Intl. Workshop on Network and Operating System Support for Digital Audio and Video, San Diego (1992) 63-74
10. Nakajima, J., Yazaki, M., Matsumoto, H.: Multimedia/realtime extensions for the mach operating system. Proc. Summer 1991 Usenix Conf., Nashville, Tennessee (1991) 183-198
11. Polimenis, V.G.: The design of a file system that supports multimedia: ICSI Tech. Rept. TR-91-020 (1991)
12. Rangan, P.V., Vin, H.M., Ramanathan, S.: Designing an on-demand multimedia service. IEEE Communications Magazine 30 (1992) 56-64
13. Rangan, P.V., Kaeppner, T., Vin, H.M.: Techniques for efficient storage of digital video and audio. Proc. Workshop on Multimedia Information Systems, Tempe, Arizona (1992) 68-85
14. Rangan, P.V., Vin, H.M.: Designing file systems for digital video and audio. Proc. 13th Symposium on Operating Systems Principles (SOSP'91), Operating Systems Review 25 (1991) 81-94
15. Seagate Technology: Seagate Wren 8 ST41650N product manual (volume 1). Publication No. 7765470-A (1991)
16. Wells, J., Yang, Q., Yu, C.: Placement of audio data on optical disks. Proc. Intl. Conf. on Multimedia Information Systems, Singapore (1991) 123-134
17. Wolf, L.C.: A runtime environment for multimedia communications. Proc. 2nd Intl. Workshop on Network and Operating Support for Digital Audio and Video, Heidelberg, Germany (1991)
18. Yu, C., Sun, W., Bitton, D., Yang, Q., Bruno, R., Tullis, J.: Efficient placement of audio data optical disks for real-time applications. Communications of the ACM 32 (1989) 862-871

User Interface Management System Embedded in a Multimedia Document Editor Framework[*]

Takashi Ohtsu[1] and Michael A. Harrison[2]

[1] Information Systems Research Lab., Matsushita Electric Industrial Co., Ltd.,
1006 Kadoma, Kadoma, Osaka 571 Japan
[2] Computer Science Division, University of California at Berkeley,
571 Evans Hall, Berkeley, CA 94720 U.S.A.

Abstract. This paper describes *Duma: a Data-based User interface management system for Multimedia Application*, which is embedded in a multimedia document editor framework (MMDEF). MMDEF is the core of a multimedia document editor, which can adapt to externally defined media types and operations, and enables the user to work on documents composed of multimedia objects, including objects of newly defined types, through a coherent user interface. Duma introduces an extensible data model called *interactor* that abstracts the user interaction between application semantics and user interface components. Also, Duma's *data-based UIMS architecture* embodies an interactive UI design environment in which interfaces to the interactor model are given.

1 Introduction

Remarkable advances in CPU performance and system software enable recent desktop computers to process and present non-textual objects with relatively inexpensive cost. Accordingly, in the field of document processing, a number of DTP systems have started incorporating capabilities to let non-professional users author *multimedia documents* that combine not only text objects but multiple kinds of non-textual media objects. An example of such systems is Microsoft's Word which is equipped with the 'plug-in' capability that allows externally-defined media objects and their subeditors to be hooked up to its main editor. Meanwhile, most of these DTP systems treat foreign media objects as special textual objects that inherit features of text in terms of presentation and editing. Therefore, in editing a multimedia document, users have to explicitly go back and forth between the main editor for textual media and other medium-specific editors as shown in Fig. 1(A). We observe that this type of user interfaces (UI's) will become unacceptable for users when the number of foreign media explodes, since users will have to take care of the differences of all media incorporated in documents.

---

[*] This research has been sponsored in part by the Defense Advanced Research Projects Agency (DARPA) under Contract N00039-88-C-0292, monitored by Space and Naval Warfare Systems Command, and under Grant MDA972-92-J-1028. The content of the information in this paper does not necessarily reflect the position or the policy of the U.S. Government.

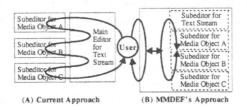

(A) Current Approach   (B) MMDEF's Approach

Fig. 1. Editing Environment for Multimedia Documents

To deal with this problem, we have been designing and implementing a multimedia document editor called *Ensemble*. Ensemble, whose appearance is shown in Fig. 2, is built on our research framework called MMDEF (MultiMedia Document Editor Framework). MMDEF is the core of a tightly integrated multimedia document editor that adapts to different media. Ensemble uses a novel architecture to utilize common services unlike a system like Quill [3] which is a collection of subeditors. The user of Ensemble may have the illusion that s/he is in a subeditor when editing a MODULA program. For the integrated multimedia document editor on MMDEF, all of the available media are adapted. In other words, the differences among media are taken care of by MMDEF instead of by users as shown in Fig. 1(B).

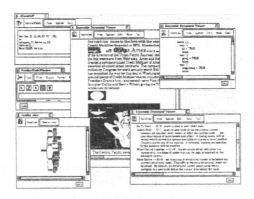

Fig. 2. A Screen Dump of Ensemble based on MMDEF

We claim that MMDEF plays the role of a user interface management system (UIMS). In addition, MMDEF should offer software repository of UI's that can be shared among adapted media at runtime. The repository might store diverse models of user interaction that can be reused rapidly by newly adapted media.

In this paper, we describe the design and the implementation of *Duma* [7]: an embedded data-based UIMS in MMDEF, that provides users, UI designers, and AP designers with coherent UI's. Duma's achievement is characterized by the following two medium-independent services. First, Duma introduces an extensible data model called *interactor* that abstracts runtime user interaction between applications (AP's) on MMDEF and UI widgets. Secondly, Duma's *data-based UIMS architecture* embodies an interactive UI design environment in which both UI and AP designers are given interfaces to the interactor model by means of a UI specification language and coherent tools provided by MMDEF. Fig. 3 shows the architecture of Ensemble consisting of MMDEF and Duma.

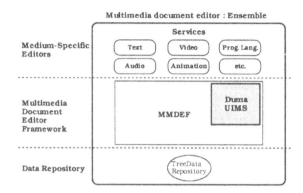

Fig. 3. Ensemble Architecture

In the following chapters, we discuss the data-based UIMS followed by the architecture of MMDEF. Then, we introduce the interactor model, the UI design layers we adopted into Duma, and the Duma prototype we have implemented. Finally, we discuss our conclusions and our plans for future work.

2 Related Work

2.1 Graphical UIMS Architecture

Since the Seeheim model [10] calls for three components in a UIMS – presentation, semantic interface, and dialog control – a number of UIMS architectures have been proposed. Recently, as window applications proliferate, the role of UI widgets in terms of graphical UIMS's is getting more important. On the other hand, we observe that currently available graphical UIMS's such as Motif, Open-Look, and ET++ [11] are still primitive and do not clarify the border between UI's and AP's.

For example, to switch a set of radio buttons into a menu, one must replace lines of code statically written in the AP and recompile it because s/he has to verify compatibilities of these UI widgets by hand. We observe that problems mentioned above arise because most traditional UIMS's have been focusing on the sequence of users' events rather than the semantics of user interaction between UI's and AP's.

2.2 Data-based UIMS Architecture

Depicting universal semantics of user interaction is unrealistic; but considering the fact that most interactions using typical UI components like buttons and panels contributes to transfer certain data objects to/from AP's/users, representing the user interaction as data types that encapsulate two concepts is realistic and effective in reducing AP/UI designers' chores. The two concepts are: the class of the data to be transferred, and the scenario that demonstrates the detailed runtime manner of user interaction. In this paper, we define a *data-based UIMS* as one that explicitly supports such abstract data types of user interaction. The design of Duma is based on this UIMS architecture.

The ITS architecture [12] is considered to be a data-based UIMS architecture. In ITS, data values to be passed among application semantics and UI's are stored in data tables. User interaction of ITS is represented by two models of communication: one between the data tables and the application semantics, and another between the tables and the UI widgets. As for the style specification, ITS adopts if-then rules. The if part specifies a pattern of attributes. The then part specifies an attribute environment in which the UI is presented. These rules are compiled statically and produce runtime objects that keep the UI consistency defined by the rules. However, neither users, nor the UI designers, nor the AP designers can interactively edit the rules at runtime.

Selectors [6] are widgets used in the ACE environment that enhances the ITS architecture. Selectors are classified according to semantics of interaction rather than their appearances. Though this idea is close to what we would like to have, we pursue the following three properties in addition to those of the Selectors: the rapid adaptability of new UI objects to the application and the UIMS, the extensibility of abstraction for runtime interaction, and the interactivity of UI design environment.

3 MMDEF Architecture

MMDEF treats each multimedia document as an object instantiated from a certain document class. A document class can be composed of multiple media while a document class itself is also considered to be one composite medium. Please notice that we use the term *medium* (or *media* in plural form) in a slightly different way from the general usage. Common examples of media, such as Text and Video, can not be decomposed, therefore, we call them *primitive media*.

The research goal of MMDEF is to clarify medium-independent services for multimedia document processing and to guarantee the adaptability of externally defined document class to its multimedia document editor. MMDEF should coordinate editing protocols and UI's of media objects of multimedia documents so that their boundaries could be virtually hidden. We claim MMDEF to be composed of several well-organized modules each of which serves as a medium-independent abstraction for a certain purpose. We call such a module a *mediator*. MMDEF consists of five mediators in its initial design: *tree data mediator, structure mediator, presentation mediator, editor mediator,* and *UI mediator.* Fig. 3

shows the Ensemble architecture including Duma and MMDEF. The architectural goals of Duma meet those of the UI mediator of MMDEF. In the following, we briefly discuss each mediator.

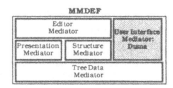

Multimedia Document Editor Framework

Fig. 4. MMDEF Architecture

3.1 Tree Data Mediator

The fundamental information regarding documents in MMDEF such as their logical structure have the form of trees, which are stored in the tree data repository shown in Fig. 3. The tree data mediator provides interfaces to effective operations on those tree-formed data.

One distinguished service of the tree mediator is its *virtual tree service* which is for multiple clients who share the same logical tree data simultaneously. In our design, a virtual tree class takes an essential tree as a *base tree* and derives multiple virtual trees whose structures are, at first, the same as that of the base tree. Structural modifications of the base tree are reported to each virtual tree immediately. On the other hand, modifications to virtual trees are not propagated to the base tree and other derived trees. This mechanism allows clients to annotate the same tree as they please without affecting the underlying data structure. Clients will use virtual trees for their own transitory data representations. To maintain the integrity of such tree-structured data, the tree data mediator also provides transaction services in terms of a database management system to ensure atomic editing operations on trees.

3.2 Structure Mediator

The structure mediator maintains the structural consistency of documents. In other words, according to requests to modify the structures of documents, the structure mediator examines whether the requests are acceptable or not by applying a set of rules to the logical structure of the document. The set of rules is called a *structure schema*, which is given to each document class and is stored as an external ASCII file. An example of the structure schema for the memo document class is shown in Fig. 5(A).

The logical structure tree of a document, which is maintained by a certain structure schema, is called a *document tree*. An example of the document tree which is derived from the **memo** structure schema is shown in Fig. 5(B).

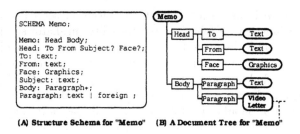

```
SCHEMA Memo;

Memo: Head Body;
Head: To From Subject? Face?;
To: text;
From: text;
Face: Graphics;
Subject: text;
Body: Paragraph+;
Paragraph: text | foreign ;
```

(A) Structure Schema for "Memo"   (B) A Document Tree for "Memo"

Fig. 5. Structure Schema and Document Tree for **Memo**

3.3 Presentation Mediator

The presentation mediator supports the management of multi-media document presentation [4]. In the first place, the presentation mediator accepts a document tree, maps a set of rules to it, and derives a *presentation tree* that includes the structural information regarding its presentation. Finally, the presentation tree is formatted to various kinds of physical devices such as printers for page-oriented documents, bitmap displays for graphics, speakers for audible objects, and so on.

The set of rules called *presentation schema* are stored as an external ASCII file. Each document class may have more than one presentation schemas, which implies that the documents of the class might have several presentations simultaneously. An example of the presentation schema for memo document class is shown in Fig. 6.

```
MEDIUM text;                                  RULES
                                                Memo :
PRESENTATION memo FOR memo;                       BEGIN
                                                    Width = 432;
DEFAULT                                             HorizPos: Left = 72;
  BEGIN                                             VertPos: Top = 36;
    Width = AllChildren . Width;                    FontFamily = "schoolbook";
    Height = AllChildren . Height;                  LineSpacing = 1.2;
    VertPos: Top = LeftSib . Bottom;                Size = 14;
    HorizPos: Left = Parent . Left;                 Justify = LeftJustify;
    Justify = Parent . Justify;                      END;
    FontFamily = Parent . FontFamily;         To :
    Bold = No;                                    BEGIN
    Italic = No;                                    HorizPos: Left = RightSib . Left;
    Size = Parent . Size;                           Italic = Yes;
    LineSpacing = Parent . LineSpacing;             END;
    Indent = 0;                               From :
    Visible = Yes;                                BEGIN
    RightMargin = 504;                              HorizPos: Left = RightSib . Left;
    END;                                            Italic = Yes;
                                                    END;
```

Fig. 6. Presentation Schema for **Memo**

3.4 Editor Mediator

The editor mediator receives editing requests on multimedia documents and interprets them as a set of procedural commands on involving different media. Then, it invokes appropriate services with those commands.

For example, with an editing request on objects presented in a view, the editor mediator functions as follows. First, the editor mediator specifies objects on documents to which the request is issued by both the locational information from the presentation mediator and the structural information from the structure mediator. Then, it finds services corresponding to the objects. Finally, the editor mediator interprets the request as a sequence of commands and dispatches them. The editor mediator should also take care of multiple users' requests on the same logical document, since one logical document may be viewed with different presentations simultaneously.

3.5   UI Mediator: Goals of Duma

The UI mediator offers a medium-independent UI model to AP's such as services and viewers, and embodies a UI development environment where highly interactive design and customization are possible. Our goal here is to make UI's adaptable to MMDEF as well as externally defined document classes so that newly adapted document classes can reuse and share UI's. This adaptability must take two forms. First, it must be relatively easy to define new UI's. Secondly, it must be possible to register these new UI's with MMDEF without having to directly modify the code. To explore the adaptability of UI's, the medium-independent UI model of the UI mediator utilizes the model of user interaction which was introduced in the data-based UIMS architecture. We call the model that we discuss in detail in the next section the *interactor model*.

At runtime where particular interaction is requested, the UI mediator deploys a UI agent who binds the AP to UI widgets by examining the data types of the user interaction. Then, AP and UI widgets are allowed to communicate with each other through the agent. The characteristics of the agent include understanding which class of values should be transferred and which UI widgets are valid to effect the user interaction in exchanging the values of the class.

The ultimate goal of the UI mediator is to provide MMDEF with the user interaction models and UI widgets as one media type. By doing so, the UI mediator can utilize the full set of services given by MMDEF to edit, author, and customize UI specifications. We expect that the UI mediator will make it possible to embed UI components in documents as well as other media objects. We are looking at the Embedded Buttons architecture [2] as the first step. In the long run, the UI guideline itself will be produced as one multimedia document on MMDEF.

4   Interactor Model

The interactor is the fundamental model that the Duma adopts in order to combine AP's with UI's under the data-based UIMS architecture. As introduced in section 2.2, we represent user interaction as the transfer of primitive/composite objects and the scenarios that describe the detailed manner of interaction. For example, suppose we have an interaction 'get one full-name of an employee of the company'. In this case, an employee object, whose name attribute is Takashi_Ohtsu, will be transferred and its scenario might be 'to select one highlighted name from the employees listed sequentially in a scrollable window pane widget'.

Therefore, the interactor model also represents both the scenario and the class of media objects to be transferred in a common model to all the media supported in MMDEF. An interactor consists of the following three objects: *virtual interactor*(VI) that provides interfaces to the interactor with AP's, *interactor widget*(IW) that provides interfaces to the interactor with UI's, and *real interactor*(RI) that connects a virtual interactor and an interactor widget. An interactor is represented by one of the following tuples:

```
1) (a VI, a IW, a RI)
2) (a VI, a RI)
3) (a RI, a IW)
```

Most interactors are represented by 1). Interactors defined of the form of 2) and 3) are called *application-defined interactor* and *user-defined interactor* respectively. AP's can not access the user-defined interactor, while UI's can not access the application-defined interactor.

In the following, we discuss each object in detail.

4.1 Virtual Interactor

The virtual interactor is an object that manages data to be passed to/from users and represents the essential interaction method which is completely independent of detailed behaviors and appearances of UI's. In Duma, AP's communications with UI widgets are substituted by communications with virtual interactors.

Each virtual interactor is typed by an *interactor type*. The interactor type is represented by a decision tree that consists of classes of media objects to be transferred in interaction and partial interaction scenarios which are independent of the appearences of UI widgets. Schematic examples of the interactor types are shown in Fig. 7.

In Fig. 7, each leaf of an interactor type is a *basetype* that represents a class name of the media object adapted to MMDEF. We assume that the basetypes have a class hierarchy. In Fig. 7(A), a basetype FONTNAME is shown, which may have values of Helvetica, Courier, or Schoolbook. Meanwhile, internal nodes of an interactor type are instances of the CHOICE function, which takes a single argument k representing the number of choices that can be made simultaneously. The value of k may be a positive number or either of the two special values, ANY and EVERY. The semantics of the CHOICE function make it pointless for an internal node to have a single internal node child. The semantics of the CHOICE function depend on the type(s) the of node's child(ren). Namely, if the CHOICE function has a single base child, k is the maximum number of basetype values that may be selected, while if it has multiple internal children, k is the maximum number of subtrees whose decision points can be selected. A value of ANY indicates that any number of subtrees are selectable while a value of EVERY indicates that a value should be obtained for every subtree.

In Fig. 7(A), k is equal to one. Accordingly, the interactor type shown in Fig. 7(A) has the semantics of choosing one of the known fontnames. Meanwhile, in order to get a font size from the user, s/he will define an interactor type GETFONTSIZE as shown in Fig. 7(B). Fig. 7(C) shows the font face style selection that we often see in commercial products such as Microsoft's Word. The value of OTHERTYPEFACE is either Bold, Italic, Underline, Shadow, or Outline, while the NORMALTYPEFACE takes the value Normal only.

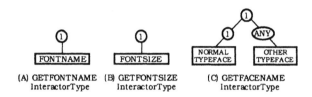

(A) GETFONTNAME   (B) GETFONTSIZE   (C) GETFACENAME
InteractorType   InteractorType   InteractorType

Fig. 7. Interactor Types

4.2 Interactor Widget

The interactor widget is an object that embodies one well-organized widget set composed of more than one primitive widget component such as buttons and panes, which behaves as one integrated UI component. Selectors widgets are thought to be categorized in these interactor widgets. We show the appearances of interactor widgets in Fig. 8. Like the virtual interactor, the interactor widget is given a type by the interactor type except that the interactor type for the interactor widget has only two nodes, a root and a leaf, where the CHOICE(x) function represents how many media object values of the basetype could be selectable at most by the user, where x could be a natural number or ANY. The basetype of the leaf is the type of the media object that the interactor widget can manipulate. In our approach, interactor widgets are UI guideline independent, namely, file selection boxes of Motif and OpenLook are treated equally regardless of their different policies.

In Fig. 8, each interactor widget has a CHOICE(1) function where (A) has the basetype FONTNAME, (B) has the basetype IMAGE, and (C) has the basetype STRING. A simple string label and an icon are considered to have CHOICE(0) function.

4.3 Real Interactor

The real interactor mediates between a virtual interactor and an interactor widget. It assigns a virtual interactor to an interactor widget once it verifies the compatibility of their interactor types at runtime. The algorithm applied to this verification is shown in Fig. 9. It first checks whether all the basetypes of the

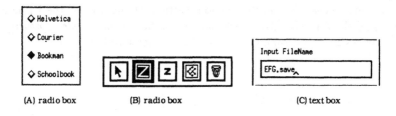

(A) radio box   (B) radio box   (C) text box

Fig. 8. Interactor Widgets

interactor type are "compatible" with the basetype of the interactor widget. We define a type **A** to be *compatible* with a type **B** if **A** is defined as a subclass of **B**.

Since a font name is expressible by a string, the basetype **FILENAME** is defined as a subclass of **STRING**. Therefore, according to the algorithm, the interactor type **GETFONTNAME** in Fig. 7(A) not only matches the sophisticated file selection box, but also matches a simple interactor widget as we show in Fig. 8(C). Cf. [5] for a more elaborate design of a file browser for Ensemble.

```
CheckTypesOf(ITV:InteractorType of a VirtualInteractor,
             ITW:InteractorType of an InteractorWidget){
  // check all base types
  for (all leaves of ITV){
    if(basetype of leaf is not compatible the base
       type of ITW) return ERROR;
  }
  // check CHOICE types
  for (traverse ITV){
    if(current node is CHOICE(x) node){
      if(children are base types)
        currentnode.maxchoice = x;
      if(children are CHOICE nodes)
        currentnode.maxchoice =
          maximum selectable items at this level
          considering x and the maxchoice of each child;
    }
  }
  Node node = rootNode of ITV;
  if(node.maxchoice <= y ) // where ITW  has a type
                           // of CHOICE(y)
    return AGREE;
  else
    return ERROR;
}
```

Fig. 9. Compatibility Checking Algorithm

5 Data-based UIMS Architecture in Duma

Duma's data-based UIMS architecture provides a UI design environment for window-oriented AP's such as services and viewers on MMDEF according to the interactor model described in the previous section. Duma divided the UI design process into the following five layers: *medium action, dialog, style composition, layout composition,* and *command dispatcher* as shown in Fig. 10.

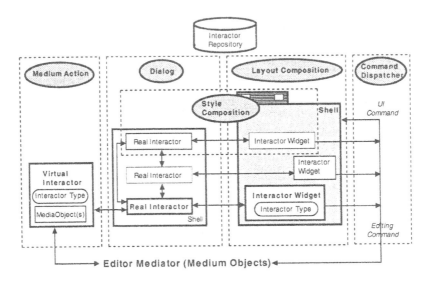

Fig. 10. UIMS Architecture in Duma

Medium Action Layer The medium action layer provides interfaces to design interactor types by means of basetypes adapted to MMDEF. Please note that the design of interactor types is a process independent from the AP semantics and interactor widgets. At runtime, AP's instantiate virtual interactors according to the interactor type defined in this layer. For now, as soon as a virtual interactor is instantiated, a real interactor is also instantiated and bound to it. Then, the real interactor waits for requests to bind interactor widgets.

Dialog Layer The dialog layer provides interfaces to group semantically related interactors into one object called a *shell.* The shell is considered a container object whose constituent elements are interactors. It gives one scope in the sense of programming language to those interactors. The shell is one of interactors and is assigned to an interactor widget whose appearance is an window. An interactor may belong to more than one shell. The constraints among interactors are described as behaviors of shell objects.

For example, suppose we design a dialog that prompts for several font properties such as name, size, and face style at a time. The application designer might define a shell object called `FontSelectDialog` with real interactors whose interactor types are `GETFONTNAME`, `GETFONTSIZE`, and `GETFACENAME`.

Style Composition Layer The style composition layer provides interfaces to assign interactor widgets to interactors according to the compatibility checking described in section 4.3. Since this assignment is performed at runtime, UI designers can easily prototype interactor widgets on the fly. Also, UI designers may search for interactor widgets compatible with the interactors from the tree data repository.

Layout Composition Layer The layout composition layer provides runtime formatters for interactor widgets according to a certain layout policy that the user can specify. The examples of the layout policies are the simple hierarchical model, the constraint based model, and the TEX's box and glue model. The fundamental services of the formatters should be similar to that of the presentation mediator of MMDEF. For now, the layout composition layer has its own formatters.

UI designers may append user-defined interactor widgets to the shell and lay them out as well as the usual interactor widgets. These widgets are the user-defined interactor widgets, which are, in fact, not bound to any AP's semantics. However, they can work as assistants that guide the user's operations by offering informative messages.

As an example of layout results, the appearance of a shell window derived from the shell object **FontSelectDialog** we mentioned earlier is shown in Fig. 11. The layout policy we adopted here is a simplified box and glue model.

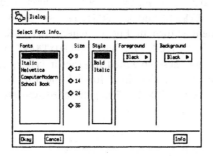

Fig. 11. The Appearance of a Shell **FontSelectDialog**

Command Dispatcher Layer The command dispatcher layer provides interfaces to assign commands to command-dispatchable interactor widgets such as menus, buttons, and keys. The commands are acceptable either by Duma or system services adapted to MMDEF. Duma has a built-in basetype called **COMMAND** for the interactors that dispatch commands. In other words, menus and buttons are considered to have interactor types whose basetypes are **COMMANDS**, and they dispatch commands by users' operations at runtime to the editor mediator of

MMDEF. Commands that are acceptable by the editor are called *editing commands* and commands acceptable by Duma's objects are called *UI commands*. Commands that open/close windows are examples of UI commands.

6 Duma Prototype

The current Duma prototype is implemented as a module of Ensemble, which is written in C++ using the GNU C++ library and the OSF/Motif X11 toolkit on Sun SparcStations. At the time of this writing, our group is near completion of the interactor model and the data-based UIMS architecture with a limited number of primitive media provided by MMDEF.

Interactive UI specification in the Duma prototype is done through a human-readable declarative language, or *USPEC*. USPEC specification can be loaded at any time while the MMDEF is running, and its modifications are promptly reflected in the UI design of the AP's. For now, USPEC specifications are edited through a text editor of Ensemble.

All the objects of interactors designed by USPEC have their own identifiers. The identifiers are unique. At runtime, AP's and UI's can access these objects by querying the built-in **INTERACTOR** class with identifiers.

In the following, we introduce several UI specification examples that have been implemented.

Virtual/Real Interactor Specification In the current implementation, interactor type specification is done by naive C++ description. For example, the interactor type **GETFONTNAME** and **GETFONTSIZE** we mentioned earlier are defined with the fragment shown in Fig. 12 where **IDT_ONE**, **IBT_FONTNAME**, and **IBT_FONTSIZE** represent **CHOICE(1)**, a basetype **FONTNAME** and a basetype **FONTSIZE**, respectively. Then, using these specified interactor types, interactors are generated as shown in Fig. 13. In the third line of the Figure, an interactor **size** whose interactor type is **GETFONTSIZE** is generated and stored in the tree data repository.

```
new InteractorType("GETFONTNAME", IDT_ONE, IBT_FONTNAME);
new InteractorType("GETFONTSIZE", IDT_ONE, IBT_FONTSIZE);
```

Fig. 12. Interactor Type Specification

```
1     registerInteractor("body",   "LABEL");
2     registerInteractor("fonts",  "GETFONTNAME");
3     registerInteractor("size",   "GETFONTSIZE");
4     registerInteractor("style",  "GETFACENAME");
5     registerInteractor("bgcolor", "GETCOLOR");
6     registerInteractor("fgcolor", "GETCOLOR");
```

Fig. 13. Virtual/Real Interactor Specification

Shell and Interactor Widget Specification In Fig. 14, we show the USPEC specification of the shell object **FontSelectDialog** that consists of the six inter-actors previously specified in Fig. 13. At the same time, the Figure shows which interactor widget is assigned to each interactor. For example, in the third line of Fig. 14, the real interactor *body* is assigned the interactor widget of the class **SIMPLE_LABEL**, which is a label widget whose the interactor type is **CHOICE(0)** of **STRING**. The rest of interactor widgets used by this dialog have class names beginning with **ONE_OF_M** indicating the type **CHOICE(1)** of **STRING**. The compat-ibility checking is done when this specification is loaded. If the checking fails, an appropriate interactor widget is chosen as default from the tree data repository.

```
1       DIALOGSET FontSelectDialog
2       BEGIN
3           PARTS = (%body,    SIMPLE_LABEL),   // label
4                   (%fonts,   ONE_OF_M_LIST),  // list selection box
5                   (%size,    ONE_OF_M_RBTN),  // radio button
6                   (%style,   ONE_OF_M_LIST),  // list selection box
7                   (%fgcolor,ONE_OF_M_PBTN),   // push button
8                   (%bgcolor,ONE_OF_M_PBTN);   // push button
9       END
```

Fig. 14. Interactor Widget Style Specification for a Shell **FontSelectDialog**

Layout Specification Currently, layout specification in Duma is based on a tree structured presentation whose internal nodes have one of two types, *VPack* or *HPack*. A VPack node implicitly specifies that its children should be packed vertically. An HPack node implies horizontal packing.

Fig. 15 shows the part of the USPEC that defines the tree structure of the shell window **FontSelectDialog**. This specification defines a presentation tree using a function-call-like notation.

```
DIALOGSET FontSelectDialog
BEGIN
  STYLE = VPack(%body,Sep(),
          HPack(VPack(SLabel("Font"), %fonts),Sep(),
              VPack(SLabel("Size"),%size), Sep(),
              VPack(SLabel("Style"),%style),Sep(),
              VPack(SLabel("Foreground"),%fgcolor),Sep(),
              VPack(SLabel("Background"),%bgcolor)));
END
```

Fig. 15. Layout Specification

Command Dispatcher Specification The specifications in the command dis-patcher layer are for keyboard commands and pulldown/popup menus, which are written in USPEC. Fig. 16 shows an example for popup-menu and menubar specification where Fig. 17 shows the generated hierarchy of the menubar from Fig. 16.

```
MENUSET Default BEGIN
  MENUBAR   (View, Edit(Insert, Delete));
  POPUPMENU (Insert, Delete);
  DEFINE View BEGIN
    LABEL="View"; MEDIUM= TextEd;
    ITEMS=("Open","editor SuperEditor OpenDocument"),
          ("Save","editor SuperEditor SaveDocument"),
          ("Export","editor TextEd ExportDocText"); END
  DEFINE Insert BEGIN
    LABEL="Insert"; MEDIUM= TextEd;
    ITEMS=("Node","editor StructEditor InsertNode"),
          ("Query","editor StructEditor QueryInsert");END
  DEFINE Delete BEGIN
    LABEL="Delete"; MEDIUM= TextEd;
    ITEMS=("Atom","cursor DeleteAtom"),
          ("AtomBack","cursor DeleteAtomBack"),
          ("Word","cursor DeleteWord");              END
  DEFINE Edit BEGIN
    LABEL="Edit"; MEDIUM= ;
    ITEMS=("Redraw","editor StructEditor Repaint"); END
END
```

Fig. 16. Command Dispatcher Specification for Menus

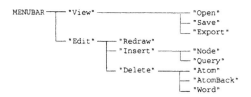

Fig. 17. Complete Menu Structure for a Menubar

7 Conclusion and Future Work

We have designed and implemented Duma as the UI mediator of the integrated multimedia document editor, Ensemble, on MMDEF. Duma adopts the interactor model and the data-based UIMS architecture to realize a highly extensible UI design environment. Though the number of available media given by MMDEF is currently limited, all windows of Ensemble including the control panel, the document viewers, and the dialog panels shown in Fig. 2 are built by Duma. Most of the UI features are customizable by Duma through the USPEC description, while the detailed settings such as what X resources do are not fully supported. Currently, Ensemble on MMDEF exceeds 90,000 lines of code of which the UI mediator occupies about 15%.

Our future work is to eliminate all C++-style UI specifications and implement direct manipulative editors for UI design. Furthermore, Duma should have multi-view interactive editors for UI design. The two-view approach is proposed by FormsVBT [1] and we extend their idea by incorporating MMDEF's multi-presentation services. At this point, the tree-structured data viewer *realize* [9] is attached to MMDEF and gives fundamental interactive features.

We also plan to enrich interactor types and interactor widgets so that the interactor object model could support a wider range of media objects. The very first step is to review the decision tree representation of the interactor type. We currently consider attributes to be annotated on the CHOICE function. Moreover, we consider the runtime command interpreter on the interactor object model. This enriches the semantics of the events to be passed to interactors. For that reason, we are planning to incorporate the Tcl/Tk [8] architecture with the interactor model soon.

References

1. Gideon Avrahami, Kenneth P. Brooks, and Marc H. Brown. A two-view approach to constructing user interfaces. *Computer Graphics*, 23(3):137–146, July 1989.

2. Eric A. Bier. EmbeddedButtons: Documents as user interfaces. In *proceedings of the ACM SIGGRAPH Symposium on User Interface Software and Technology*, pages 45–53, November 1991.

3. Donald D. Chamberlin, Helmut F. Hasselmeier, Allen W. Luniewski, Dieter P. Paris, Bradford W. Wade, and Mitch L. Zolliker. Quill: An extensible system for editing documents of mixed type. In *Proc. of the 21st Hawaii International Conference on System Sciences*, pages 317–326, Kailua-Kona, Hawaii, Jan 5–8 1988.

4. Susan L. Graham, Michael A. Harrison, and Ethan V. Munson. The Proteus presentation system. In *ACM SIGSOFT symposium on software development environments*, pages 130–138, Tyson's Corner, VA, 1992.

5. Michael A. Harrison and Thomas A. Phelps. The next best thing in file browsers. In *Proceedings of the TCL/Tk Workshop*, pages 110–112, Berkeley, CA, June 1993. Computer Science Division, University of California at Berkeley.

6. Jeff Johnson. Selectors: Going beyond user-interface widgets. In *proceedings of CHI '92 Conference: Human Factors in Computing Systems*, pages 273–279, NY, May 1992.

7. Takashi Ohtsu. Duma: a data-based user interface management system for multimedia application. Master's thesis, Computer Science Division, University of California, Berkeley, Berkeley, CA 94720, October 1992.

8. John K. Ousterhout. An X11 toolkit based on the tcl language. In *USENIX Summer Conference Proceedings*, pages 105–115, 1991.

9. John L. Pasalis. Realize: An interactive graphical data structure presentation and rendering system. Master's thesis, Computer Science Division, University of California, Berkeley, Berkeley, CA 94720, 1992.

10. Gunther E. Pfaff, editor. *User Interface Management Systems.* Spring-Verlag, Berlin, 1985.

11. Andre Weinand, Erich Gamma, and Rudolf Marty. ET++ – an object-oriented application framework in C++. In *OOPSLA 1988 Proceedings*, pages 46–57, September 1988.

12. Charles Wiecha, William Bennett, Stephen Boies, John Gould, and Sharon Greene. ITS: A tool for rapidly developing interactive applications. *ACM Transactions on Information Systems*, 8(3):204–236, July 1990.

Management of Physical Replicas in Parallel Multimedia Information Systems*

Shahram Ghandeharizadeh and Cyrus Shahabi

Department of Computer Science
University of Southern California
Los Angeles, California 90089

Abstract. Multimedia information systems have emerged as an essential component of many application domains ranging from library information systems to entertainment technology. However, most implementations of these systems (based on a workstation) cannot support a continuous display of multimedia objects and suffer from frequent disruptions and delays termed *hiccups*. This is due to the low I/O bandwidth of the current disk technology, the high bandwidth requirement of multimedia objects, and the large size of these objects which requires them to be almost always disk resident. One approach to resolve this limitation is to decluster a multimedia object across multiple disk drives in order to employ the aggregate bandwidth of several disks to support its continuous retrieval (and display). To support simultaneous display of several multimedia objects for different users, the system can replicate data across multiple groups of disk drives in a *virtual* manner. This paper describes techniques to manage the replicas of objects in a parallel multimedia information system. These techniques are general and can be customized by the database administrator to satisfy the constraints of an application. We quantify the tradeoffs associated with these strategies using a simulation study.

1   Introduction

During the past decade, information technology has evolved to store and retrieve multimedia data (e.g., audio, video). Multimedia information systems utilize a variety of human senses to provide an effective means of conveying information. Already, these systems play a major role in educational applications, entertainment technology, and library information systems. A challenging task when implementing these systems is to support a "real-time" display of multimedia objects. By "real-time", we mean a continuous retrieval of an object at the bandwidth required by its media type. This is challenging because certain media types, in particular video, require very high bandwidths. For example, the bandwidth required by NTSC[2] for "network-quality" video is about 45 megabits

---

* This research was supported in part by NSF IRI-9110522, and NYI IRI-9258362.

[2] The US standard established by the National Television System Committee.

per second (mbps) [10]. Recommendation 601 of the International Radio Consultative Committee (CCIR) calls for a 216 mbps bandwidth for video objects. A video object based on HDTV (High Definition Television) requires approximately a 700 mbps bandwidth. Compare these bandwidth requirements with the typical 10 mbps bandwidth of a magnetic disk drive[3], which is not expected to increase significantly in the near future [12]. Presently, there are several ways to support a real-time display of these objects: 1) sacrifice the quality of the data by using either a lossy compression technique (e.g., predictive [1], frequency oriented [11], importance oriented [9], etc.) or a low resolution device, 2) employ the aggregate bandwidth of several disk drives by declustering an object across multiple disks [8], and 3) use a combination of these two techniques. Lossy compression techniques encode data into a form that consumes a relatively small amount of space, however, when the data is decoded, it yields a representation similar to the original (some loss of data). While it is effective, there are applications that cannot tolerate loss of data. As an example consider the video signals collected from space. This information may not be compressed using a lossy compression technique [3]. Otherwise, scientists who later uncompress and analyze the data run the risk of either observing phenomena that may not exist due to a slight change in data or miss important observations due to some loss of data[4].

The focus of this study is on parallel multimedia information systems and applications that cannot tolerate loss of data. In order to simplify the discussion, we assume a shared-nothing [14] architecture (or a multicomputer) as our hardware platform[5]. Briefly, a shared-nothing architecture consists of a number of processors interconnected by a high speed communication network such as a hypercube or a ring. A processor consists of a CPU, a disk drive, and some random access memory. Processors do not share disk drives or random access memory and can only communicate with one another by sending messages. Furthermore, we assume that the stations used to display objects are independent of the backend processors that contain the data. In this study, we focus on the I/O bottleneck phenomena, and assume that the bandwidth of both the network and the network device driver exceeds the bandwidth requirement of an object. This assumption is justified considering the current technological trends. **In this paper, the term processor is used to imply a node of the shared-nothing architecture consisting of a CPU, some RAM, and one disk drive.**

Assuming a fixed bandwidth for each disk (B_{Disk}) in the system, in order to support a real-time display of an object with bandwidth requirement $B_{Display}$, an object is declustered into M pieces (termed **fragments**) where

---

[3] The developed concepts are applicable to other secondary storage devices.

[4] There are also *lossless* compression techniques (e.g., Huffman, Lempel Zev, etc.). While a good estimate for reduction in size with these techniques is anywhere from a factor of 2 to 10, with lossy techniques it ranges from a factor of 50 to 1000 [4]. Consequently, lossless compression techniques are generally regarded as ineffective.

[5] However, the extension of our techniques to a multi-disk architecture (e.g., RAID [12]) should be straightforward.

$M = \lceil \frac{B_{Display}}{B_{Disk}} \rceil$ [7, 8]. One approach to enable the system to support simultaneous display of multiple objects to different users is *virtual data replication*[6]. This technique extends the shared-nothing architecture with a tertiary storage

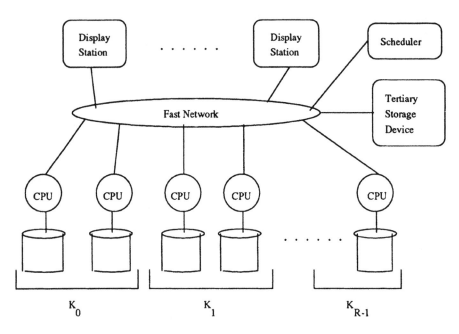

Fig. 1. Virtual data replication

device that is accessible to all the processors in the system (see Figure 1). The database resides *permanently* on the tertiary storage device. Assuming that all objects belong to a single media type (each object has M as its degree of declustering), this technique organizes a P processor system into R processor partitions ($R = \lfloor \frac{P}{M} \rfloor$). A partition stores objects transiently (i.e., reads objects from the tertiary storage device as the need arises and deletes objects when its storage capacity is exhausted). This technique is named virtual data replication because: 1) logically, the database is replicated R times, and 2) each replica is virtual (i.e., cached in from the tertiary storage device on demand). We use the following terminology for the rest of this paper. All partitions contain a *virtual* replica of an object (say o_x). Once a partition materializes o_x from the tertiary storage device, it is said to contain a *physical* replica of o_x. A partition can display o_x only if it has a physical replica of o_x.

We assume a processor in the system is designated as the centralized scheduler[7]. This site maintains the availability of each partition and the objects that are

---

[6] An alternative approach is disk multitasking [7].

[7] We are aware that the centralized scheduler may become a bottleneck and limit the capability of the system to scale to a large number of processors. As discussed

Term	Definition
$B_{Display}$	Bandwidth required to display an object
B_{Disk}	Bandwidth of a single disk drive
$B_{Tertiary}$	Bandwidth of the tertiary storage device
M	Degree of declustering for an object, $M = \lceil \frac{B_{Display}}{B_{Disk}} \rceil$
P	Number of processors in the system
R	Number of partitions in the system, $R = \lfloor \frac{P}{M} \rfloor$
$heat(o_x)$	Frequency of access to object o_x
$size(o_x)$	Size of object o_x
NOW	The current time
$T_{Display}(o_x)$	Time to display o_x, $T_{Display}(o_x) = \frac{size(o_x)}{B_{Display}}$
$T_{Materialize}(o_x)$	Time to Materialize o_x from tertiary storage, $T_{Materialize}(o_x) = \frac{size(o_x)}{B_{Tertiary}}$
$FDT(o_x)$	Future Display Time of o_x, $FDT(o_x) = heat(o_x) \times T_{Display}(o_x)$
$Usage(K_i)$	Future usage time of partition K_i
$AT(K_i)$	Specifies when partition K_i will be available to service another request

Table 1. List of terms used repeatedly in this paper and their respective definitions

stored on each of the R partition. All requests are first directed to the central-ized scheduler. When a user requests an object o_x, the scheduler determines those idle partitions that contain a physical replica of o_x. If such partitions exist, it employs one of them to service the request. Otherwise, the scheduler determines the busy partitions that contain a physical replica of o_x. Either there exist at least one or none of the partitions has a physical replica of o_x. Consider each case in turn:

- If one or more partitions contain a physical replica of o_x, the scheduler has two possible choices. It can either 1) queue the request and wait for the partition with the least wait time to become available or 2) utilize an idle partition that does not contain a physical replica of o_x (say K_1) to materialize o_x and then display it. In the second case, if the storage capacity of K_1 has been exhausted, then the scheduler should also determine which objects of this partition should be deleted in order to provide sufficient space for o_x. The decision between these two alternatives has an impact on both the response time of the system and the frequency of access to the tertiary storage device.
- If none of the partitions contains a physical replica of o_x, the scheduler chooses an idle partition (say K_2) to both materialize a replica of o_x, and display o_x once it is materialized. If the storage capacity of K_2 has been exhausted, then the scheduler also determines which objects of this partition should be deleted in order to provide sufficient storage space for o_x.

---

in Section 6, we intend to replace the centralized scheduler with novel distributed scheduling policies.

This paper formalizes the problems associated with managing replicas. It describes policies employed by the centralized scheduler to determine the partition that should service a request in order to maximize the performance of the system. These policies are general and employ several parameters to enable the database administrator (DBA) to customize them to satisfy the requirements of an application.

These policies are novel and different than those described in the operating system (or database system) literature designed to manage the frames of a buffer pool due to two novel features of our system: 1) when a partition is employed to either materialize an object from the tertiary storage device or service a request, the physical replica of its other objects become unavailable, and 2) in certain cases, it might be advantageous to materialize a frequently accessed object on several partitions in order to avoid a partition from becoming the bottleneck for the system.

1.1 Overview

In this study, we assume:

1. The size of each object in the database is smaller than the storage capacity of a partition. A partition may contain the physical replica of several different objects, however, it contains at most one physical replica of an object.
2. The database consists of a single media type with bandwidth requirement $B_{Display}$ (i.e., the degree of declustering is M for all objects).
3. The bandwidth of the tertiary storage device is lower than the bandwidth requirement of an object ($B_{Tertiary} < B_{Display}$), hence, its bandwidth is lower than that of a partition (recall that $B_{Display} \simeq M \times B_{Disk}$).
4. The frequency of access and the size of each object is provided (termed $heat(o_x)$ and $size(o_x)$ respectively [2]).

Using assumption 4, we define the expected Future Display Time of an object o_x as:

$$FDT(o_x) = heat(o_x) \times T_{Display}(o_x) \tag{1}$$

where $T_{Display}(o_x)$ is the time required to display o_x. Assuming that a partition (say K_i) contains the physical replica of q objects, its future usage time is:

$$Usage(K_i) = \sum_{j=1}^{q} FDT(o_j) \tag{2}$$

In order to maximize the processing capability of the system, the $Usage$ of each of its partitions should be almost identical.

Once a request for object o_x is issued, the scheduler can reach five different states:

A: One or more idle partitions contain a physical replica of o_x.
B: One or more busy partitions contain a physical replica of o_x.

C: There is one or more idle partitions with sufficient storage space to materialize o_x (these partitions do not contain a physical replica of o_x).

D: There is one or more idle partitions with **insufficient** storage space to materialize o_x (these partitions do not contain a physical replica of o_x).

E: No partitions is idle and no partition contains a physical replica of o_x.

Both the transition from one state to another and the decisions made at each state depends on the requirements of an application. In this study, the policies developed for each state can be tailored to achieve the following goals:

1. Minimize the frequency of access to the tertiary storage device in order to reduce its probability of becoming a bottleneck for the system.
2. Minimize the response time of the system.
3. Distribute the workload of the system evenly across the partitions in order to avoid the formation of hot spots and bottleneck partitions [6].

A customized policy can be further fine tuned to achieve its goal for either the pending request (termed $Gpresent_i$) or the future requests (termed $Gfuture_i$). This choice is due to: 1) our knowledge of the expected frequency of access to each object, 2) the assumption that a partition may contain the physical replica of multiple objects, and 3) once a partition is employed to either display an object or materialize it from the tertiary storage device, the physical replica of other objects stored on this partition become unavailable for the duration of this operation. The choice between $Gpresent_i$ (Gp_i) and $Gfuture_i$ (Gf_i) depends on: 1) the accuracy of $heat(o_x)$, and 2) the requirements of an application. The present and future impact of each goal is as follows:

Gp_1 Minimize the probability of access to the tertiary storage device for the pending request.

Gf_1 Service the pending request with the objective to minimize the frequency of access to the tertiary storage device for the future requests.

Gp_2 Service the pending request as soon as possible.

Gf_2 Service the pending request with the objective to minimize the response time for future requests.

Gp_3 Service the pending request to approximate an even distribution of the load for the present.

Gf_3 Service the pending request in order to evenly distribute the load for the future requests.

In general, to satisfy Gp_1, we service a request by utilizing a partition that contains a physical replica of o_x (if available). To satisfy Gp_2, a request is serviced using the partition with the least wait time. To satisfy Gp_3, a request is serviced using the partition with the longest idle time. As we assume no prior knowledge of the sequence of requests for the objects, in order to satisfy Gf_1, Gf_2, and Gf_3, a request is serviced by employing the partition with the least future expected $Usage$. This distributes the workload of an application evenly across the partitions, avoiding the formation of hot spots that have an adverse impact on Gf_1, Gf_2, and Gf_3. Due to this similarity, these goals are combined into one, termed Gf.

The rest of this paper is organized as follows. Section 2 describes the data structures maintained by the centralized scheduler. Section 3 describes techniques for decision making at each state in order to implement the alternative goals. Section 4 describes the alternative state transition diagrams for the system to visit the different states. Section 5 evaluates the alternative decision making policies and state transition diagrams using a simulation study. Our conclusion and future research directions are contained in Section 6.

2 Scheduler and its Data Structures

The scheduler maintains: 1) the status of the tertiary storage device and its queue of request, 2) the availability of each partition and the physical replica of objects stored on that partition (using a partition table), and 3) the different objects in the system and the partitions containing their physical replicas (using an object table).

The scheduler maintains when the tertiary storage device would be available to service a request (termed Available at Time, AT(tertiary)). Using this variable and the current time (termed NOW), the scheduler can compute the wait time for this device (if NOW $> AT(tertiary)$ then $wait\_time(tertiary) = 0$, otherwise $wait\_time(tertiary) = AT(tertiary) - NOW$).

For each partition K_i $(0 \le i < R)$, the **partition table** maintains a list of objects currently materialized on K_i, when K_i would be available to service another request $(AT(K_i))$, the total time that K_i has been idle since the system generation time, and the storage space available on K_i. Once a request for an object o_x is issued, if the scheduler employs an idle partition (say K_1) to service this request, then its idle time is adjusted as follows:

$$Idle\ Time(K_1) = Idle\ Time(K_1) + (NOW - AT(K_1)) \tag{3}$$

If K_1 has a physical replica of o_x, then its AT is adjusted as follows:

$$AT(K_1) = NOW + T_{Display}(o_x) \tag{4}$$

If K_1 does not contain a physical replica of o_x and is required to materialize it from the tertiary storage device, then:

$$AT(K_1) = NOW + wait\_time(tertiary) + T_{Materialize}(o_x) + T_{Display}(o_x) \tag{5}$$

where $T_{Materialize}(o_x)$ is the time required to read object o_x from the tertiary storage device. In this case, the scheduler ensures that its available storage space is greater than the size of o_x.

For each object o_x, the **object table** maintains a list of partitions containing a physical replica of o_x, size(o_x), and heat(o_x). This table is used to determine the candidate partitions that contain the physical replica of a requested object.

3 Decisions Made at Each State

Given a request for object o_x, the decisions made at each state are as follows:

A: Choose one of several idle partitions with a physical replica of o_x.

B: Choose one of several busy partitions with a physical replica of o_x.

C: Choose one of several idle partitions to materialize and display o_x.

D: In addition to choosing one of several idle partitions to materialize o_x, the scheduler decides which object of this partition should be deleted to provide sufficient space for o_x.

E: No decisions are made. The request is queued, and once a partition becomes available, the scheduler services this request by starting from state A (see Section 4 for the alternative state transition diagrams).

We start by describing how state B makes its decision. Next, Section 3.2 describes a technique to choose between the available partitions. This technique is utilized by states A, C, and D. Due to lack of space, we describe neither how the system chooses objects to be replaced nor explain how the disk space is managed to avoid the fragmentation of its space (refer to [5] for a complete description of these techniques). Both topics are important as they have a significant impact on the performance of a system that employs virtual data replication.

3.1 Best Partition for State B

Once at state B, the scheduler determines the busy partitions that contain a physical replica of o_x. Next, it chooses one of these partitions to service the pending request. This decision impacts Gp_2 and Gf (and has no impact on Gp_1 and[8] Gp_3). If the objective is to minimize the response time of the pending request (Gp_2), the request should be queued at the partition with the minimum wait time (minimum $AT(K_i)$). However, if the objective is to satisfy Gf, this request should be queued at the partition with the minimum future usage time (minimum $Usage(K_j)$) in order to free other partitions with a higher future usage time to service other requests.

The DBA may want to customize state B to assign a different weight with each goal. To achieve this, AT and $Usage$ of each candidate partition should be compared using the specified weight. There are two problems associated with this. First, these two variables are in terms of different units: AT is units of time while $Usage$ is in terms of both time and heat. Second, these variables are based on different scales. Our solution to both problems is to normalize each component as follows:

$$AT_{Normalized}(K_i) = \frac{AT(K_i)}{AT_{Avg}} \qquad (6)$$

---

[8] Once at state B, all candidate partitions are busy. Consequently, Gp_3 is meaningless. Moreover, Gp_1 is already satisfied as the system will not access the tertiary storage device.

$$Usage_{Normalized}(K_i) = \frac{Usage(K_i)}{Usage_{Avg}} \tag{7}$$

Both AT_{Avg} and $Usage_{Avg}$ are computed by considering only those partitions that satisfy the constraints of state B (and NOT all the partitions in the system). Next, state B queues this request at partition K_i with minimum value for:

$$Usage_{Normalized}(K_i) + \frac{Gp_2}{Gf} AT_{Normalized}(K_i) \tag{8}$$

Both Gp_2, and Gf are positive real numbers, ranging in value from zero to one. By choosing a value close to one for Gp_2 and a small value for Gf (close to zero), state B services this request by employing the partition with the least wait time (approximates Gp_2).

Once the system decides to enter state B, this request is queued at the chosen partition (say K_x), and $AT(K_x)$ is incremented with $T_{Display}(o_x)$.

3.2 Best Partition for States A, C, and D

At each state A, C, and D, the scheduler might be required to choose between several partitions that satisfy the constraints of that state. For example, once at state A, there might be m idle partitions that contain a physical replica of o_x, and the system must choose one of these partitions.

For each state, the decision between the available partitions has an impact on Gp_3 and Gf (and no impact on either Gp_1 or Gp_2). To satisfy Gp_3, the scheduler should employ the partition with the largest idle time (maximum Idle Time(K_j)). However, in order to satisfy Gf, the scheduler should employ the partition with the least expected future usage time (minimum Usage(K_i)).

Once again, the DBA can customize each state to give each goal a different weight. In order to make the idle time and future usage of a partition comparable, we normalize each component (see Section 3.1), and utilize the partition with the minimum value for:

$$Usage_{Normalized}(K_i) - \frac{Gp_3}{Gf} Idle\ Time_{Normalized}(K_j) \tag{9}$$

Both Gp_3 and Gf are positive real numbers ranging in value from zero to one.

Note that we subtract the two normalized components from each other because their objectives conflict (*maximum* idle time vs. *minimum* future usage).

4 Alternative State Transition Diagrams

In this section we describe three alternative state transition diagrams for visiting the different states. We use the following terminology. Once at a state (e.g., A), if no partitions satisfy the constraints of that state (e.g., no partition is idle), the state has *failed*. Once a state fails, the system proceeds to test the constraints of another state. This section describes: 1) the state that initiates the transition, and 2) the order in which the different states are visited (i.e., the *state transition diagram* employed by the scheduler).

Different transition diagrams satisfy different goals. In this section, we describe three alternative transition diagrams: 1) Minimum Tertiary Access transition diagram (MTA) to satisfy Gp_1, 2) Minimum Response Time transition diagram (MRT) to satisfy Gp_2, 3) FleXible Transition diagram (FXT) to approximate Gf. We do not describe a state transition diagram for Gp_3 because, at this point in time, we consider it unrealistic for a system.

4.1 MTA (*pessimistic*)

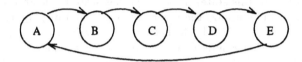

a) MTA state transition diagram

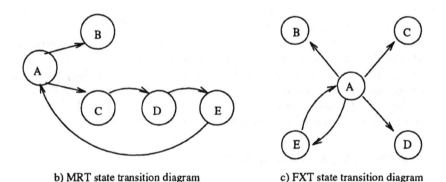

b) MRT state transition diagram   c) FXT state transition diagram

Fig. 2. Three state transition diagrams

Figure 2.a shows the state transition diagram for Gp_1 (minimum frequency of accesses to the tertiary storage device). Once a request is issued, it visits state A. If A fails, state B is the next best choice because the objective is to service this request without accessing the tertiary storage device (even if it results in a long wait time). If B fails, the subsequent states are C and D which result in an access to the tertiary storage device. When D fails, the request is queued until a busy partition becomes available (state E). Once a partition becomes available, the scheduler services this request by starting from state A. This enables the scheduler to determine if another request has materialized o_x on a different partition, and if so, utilizes this partition to service the pending request.

MTA is pessimistic because it allows at most one physical copy of each object in the system. If an object is accessed very frequently, the partition containing its physical copy may become hot and the bottleneck for the entire system. This is a consequence of visiting state B before C and D. Moreover, state B makes no decisions because at most one busy partition contains the physical replica of o_x.

4.2 MRT (*optimistic*)

Figure 2.b contains the transition diagram that minimizes the service time of a request. Given a request, the system starts its traversal with state A. If A fails, it decides between states B and C. This is done as follows. It probes state B for the busy partition that will service this request. B returns either K_B or -1 (-1 indicates the failure of this state). Next, it probes state C for an idle partition that will be used to materialize the requested object and display it. This state also returns either K_C or -1. If both states return a valid partition, the system determines the state that results in a lower response time and proceeds to that state (i.e., if $AT(K_B) < T_{Materialize}(o_x) + wait\_time(tertiary)$ then go to state B, otherwise go to state C). If C returns -1 and B returns a candidate partition, then the system proceeds to state B. If B returns -1, the system proceeds to state C. In this case, if state C also fails, the system enters state D. Finally, if D also fails, the request is queued at state E. Once a partition becomes available, the system tries to service this request by starting from state A.

MRT is optimistic because it uses the tertiary storage device to materialize additional physical replicas of o_x, risking the possibility of: 1) the additional replicas not getting accessed in the future, and 2) a request during $T_{Materialize}(o_x)$ accessing the tertiary storage device and waiting for a longer interval of time. Note that the decision making policy employed by states B and C (see Sections 3.1 and 3.2) impacts the decision between these two states.

4.3 FXT(*A Flexible Version of MRT*)

Figure 2.c shows the state transition diagram for Gf (termed FXT). It is almost identical to MRT, except that it is more optimistic. Once state A fails, FXT decides between states B, C, and D. It probes each state for a candidate partition. Assuming that each state succeeds and returns a valid partition (termed K_B, K_C, and K_D respectively), the scheduler determines if it is faster to wait for a busy partition that contains a physical replica of the requested object to become available (state B) or to materialize the requested object (either state C or D). If it is faster to proceed to state B, then it does so. Otherwise, it decides between states C and D based on the expected usage time of each candidate partition. If Usage(K_C) < Usage(K_D), it proceeds to state C, otherwise, it proceeds to state D. The justification for this is as follows. K_C could have many frequently accessed objects (a high usage time) while K_D contains many objects with a low frequency of access. In this case, FXT replace the least frequently accessed objects with those that are accessed more frequently.

FXT is more optimistic than MRT because, if the deleted object is accessed in the near future, it must be materialized from the tertiary storage device. This would result in both a high response time and a low system throughput. Moreover, the tertiary storage device may become a bottleneck for the system, diminishing the overall processing capability of the system. Once again, the DBA's choice of values for input parameters of states C and D impacts the candidate partition produced by each state and the overall decision to visit either state C or D.

5 Performance Evaluation

We quantified the performance tradeoffs associated with the alternative state transition diagrams and parameters using a simulation model of a parallel information system and a general purpose workload. This model is implemented using the CSIM [13] simulation language. We start by describing the simulation model. Next, we present the performance results obtained from the system.

5.1 Simulation Model

Our simulation model consisted of five main elements: the **Display Station, Centralized Scheduler, Interconnection Network, Processor**, and **Tertiary Storage**. Each Display Station consists of a terminal which generates the workload of the system. Each Processor consists of a CPU, some RAM, and a single disk drive with a 10 megabit per second bandwidth ($B_{Disk} = 10$ mbps). The Tertiary Storage device provides a 20 megabit per second bandwidth ($B_{Tertiary} = 20$ mbps). The Interconnection Network models a fully connected network with a one millisecond latency time. The Centralized Scheduler consists of an Object Manager, a Partition Manager, and a Tertiary Manager. These components maintain the data structures described in Section 2.

Each Display Station's request is first dispatched to the Centralized Scheduler. The Scheduler services this request based on its customized: 1) state transition diagram (MTA, MRT, FXT), and 2) the value of parameters Gp_2, Gp_3, and Gf.

A user employs a display station to request an object. We assume that a display station can display only one object at a time. In our experiments, we varied the number of display stations from one to 64 in order to vary the system load. We assumed a closed system where once a display station issues a request, it does not issue another until the first one is serviced. We also assume a zero think time between the requests. This parameter was chosen in order to stress the system and investigate its limitations.

The database consisted of a single media type. The bandwidth requirement of this media type is 50 megabits per second ($M = 5$). The system consisted of 125 processors ($P = 125$), resulting in 25 partitions ($R = 25$). Attached to each processor is a one gigabyte disk drive. The total storage capacity of the system is 125 gigabytes. In all experiments, we assumed equi-sized objects and did not analyze the impact of this variable[9]. Using this assumption, state D replaces objects based on their frequency of access with the least frequently accessed objects being replaced first.

The experimental design of this study was three dimensional. Its axes where: 1) the multiprogramming level of the system, 2) the size of the database, and 3) the distribution of access to the objects in the database (uniform vs. exponential). The multiprogramming level of the system is controlled using the number of display stations. In this study, we analyzed two different database sizes: small, and large. The size of the small database is 80% of the total storage capacity of the system and can be materialized on the disks (across the different partitions), rendering the tertiary storage device redundant. The size of the large database is five times that of the storage capacity of the system. We analyzed these two different database sizes in order to understand the tradeoffs associated with our policies. In particular, we wondered whether our policies are redundant for a database that is small enough to become disk resident. As demonstrated in Section 5.2, it is beneficial to use the tertiary storage device even for small databases.

5.2 Performance Results

We present our performance results for each database size in turn. Unless stated otherwise, states A, B, and C were customized to give a higher priority to the present instead of the future (i.e., $Gp_2 = Gp_3 = 1$, $Gf = 0.0001$). For the large database, we analyze the impact of using different values for these parameters. Due to the general nature of our workload, these parameters do not have an impact on the overall performance of the system.

In all experiments, we use the throughput of the system to compare the alternative transition diagrams.

Small Database: In this experiment, the database consisted of 250 objects, each 400 megabytes in size ($T_{Display} = 64$ seconds). The total size of the database was 80% of the storage capacity of the system. We analyzed the throughput of the system as a function of the number of users in the system for two different distributions of access: skewed and uniform (see Figure 3). In these experiments, we tried to simulate a system that has been operating for a while with the entire database already materialized on the disk drives. To achieve this, we employed a greedy algorithm that assigns the objects with the objective to evenly distribute the workload of an application across the partitions[10]. The maximum theoretical processing capability of the system is 23.5 displays per minute. This is a theoretical upper bound because it assumes: 1) no access to the tertiary storage device, and 2) a uniform distribution of access to the partitions in the system.

---

[9] This is a part of our future research direction.

[10] This algorithm is as follows: 1) it sorts the objects based on their frequency of access, 2) assigns one object at a time to the partitions in a round-robin manner.

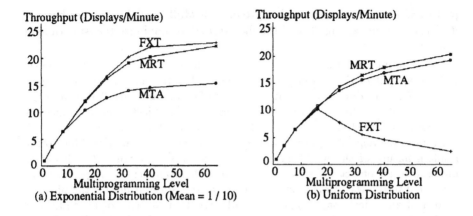

Fig. 3. Small database (Mean is a fraction of the number of objects in the database)

With an exponential distribution of access to the objects (mean = $\frac{1}{10}$ of the number of objects in the database, i.e., 25), MRT and FXT outperform MTA because, at multiprogramming levels higher than 8, these two techniques utilize the remaining 20% of each disk drive to materialize the frequently accessed objects on several partitions. By doing so, they avoid a single partition from becoming the bottleneck for the entire system, maximizing the overall performance of the system. MTA cannot utilize the remaining 20% of the system's storage capacity because it avoids the scheduler from accessing the tertiary storage device. Consequently, the original assignment of objects to partitions remains unchanged, and the partition containing the most frequently accessed object becomes a bottleneck. At high multiprogramming levels, FXT outperforms MRT. Because it replaces the least frequently accessed objects with those that are accessed more frequently in order to maximize the useful utilization of the disk space. MRT cannot behave this way because, once the storage capacity of the system is exhausted (causing state C to fail), it enters state B at all times and avoids both state C and D.

At high multiprogramming levels, the throughput of the system with MRT and FXT is 23 displays. These strategies do not attain the maximum processing capability of the system (23.5) because the bandwidth of the tertiary storage device is lower than that of a partition; consequently, when a partition is required to materialize the frequently accessed object, it sits idle for some duration of time.

With a uniform distribution of access, MTA results in a performance almost identical to MRT[11]. This access pattern distributes the workload of the application evenly across the partitions and minimizes the probability of a bottleneck

---

[11] Indeed, the throughput of MTA with a uniform distribution of access is higher than that with an exponential distribution (compare Figure 3.a with 3.b).

partition. The performance of the system with MRT is slightly higher because it utilizes the remaining 20% of the disk storage to minimize the wait time at state B.

At high multiprogramming levels, FXT exhibits a thrashes behavior, causing the throughput of the system to drop. The explanation for this behavior is as follows. FXT decides between states B, C, and D. Similar to MRT, it utilizes the remaining 20% of the disk storage to replicate several objects multiple times (by visiting state C). At some point, the storage capacity of the system is exhausted. Once multiple requests collide and compete for the same partition (due to the random nature of the workload), FXT enters state D because it is faster to materialize an object on an idle partition with insufficient storage device as compared to the wait time at state B. Once at this state, it deletes the physical replica of an object (say o_y) from an idle partition in favor of an additional replica of the requested object (o_x). If this is the only **physical** replica of o_y in the system, then deleting it is clearly a mistake because o_y will be accessed at some point in the future (due to a uniform distribution of access). In this case, once o_y is accessed, the system has to materialize it from the tertiary storage device (which is slow), degrading the overall performance of the system. As we increase the multiprogramming level, state D becomes more attractive because when a partition (say K_i) materializes o_y, the requests referencing the physical replica of other objects stored on K_i wait for a longer interval of time (at state B). This causes the system to service a larger fraction of requests by materializing objects from the tertiary storage device, reducing the overall throughput of the system.

Large Database: In this experiment, the database consisted of 5000 objects, each 125 megabytes in size ($T_{Display} = 20$ seconds). The total size of the database was five times the storage capacity of the system. We analyzed the impact of both the alternative state transition diagrams and parameters on the overall performance of the system. We do not present all the obtained results because they show the same observation repeatedly. Instead, we present the results for two different system loads: a light system load (multiprogramming level = 15), and a heavy system load (multiprogramming level = 50). For each system load, we analyze the throughput of the system for the alternative transition diagrams and parameters as a function of the degree of skew to the objects in the database. We analyzed four different degrees of skews simulated using an exponential distribution with the following means: $\frac{1}{5}$, $\frac{1}{50}$, $\frac{1}{500}$, and $\frac{1}{5000}$ of the number of objects (5000) in the database (i.e., the mean was varied from 1000 to 1). As the mean of this distribution becomes smaller, the access to the objects becomes more skewed. Figure 4 compiles the obtained results in two different graphs. Each graph corresponds to a different system load. The x-axis of these graphs corresponds to the mean of the exponential distribution (i.e., degree of skew). These experiments were conducted assuming a system whose disk drives contain the physical replica of no objects (the greedy algorithm of Section 5.2 was not employed).

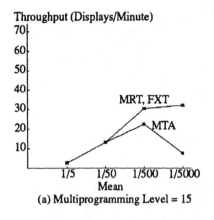
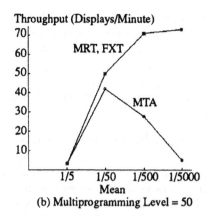

Fig. 4. Large database (Mean is a fraction of the number of objects in the database)

Unlike the small database, the large database forces the alternative state transition diagrams to visit both states C and D. A general trend in these figures is that MRT, FXT and MTA result in an identical performance when the distribution of access to the objects is close to uniform ($\frac{1}{5}$). As the distribution becomes more skewed, MRT and FXT outperform MTA by a wider margin. Consider each case in turn. With a low degree of skew ($\frac{1}{5}$), most of the requests cause the alternative state transition diagram to enter state D in order to materialize the requested object, resulting in a high frequency of access to the tertiary storage device. Consequently, the tertiary storage device becomes a bottleneck and determines the full processing capability of the system. If every request resulted in an access to the tertiary storage device, the throughput of the system would have been 0.8 displays per minute[12]. We observed a throughput of 3 displays per minute (for all system loads) because every now and then a request observes a hit (i.e., finds the requested object disk resident).

With a high degree of skew ($\frac{1}{5000}$), both MRT and FXT outperform MTA because MTA allows at most one physical replica of an object in the entire system (it tries to minimize the frequency of access to the tertiary storage device). The partition containing the most frequently accessed object becomes a bottleneck, and determines the full processing capability of the system (the processing capability of a partition is at most 3 displays per minute). MRT and FXT replicate this object on several different partitions, maximizing the overall processing capability of the system.

In general, MTA provides a better performance with a moderate degree of skew ($\frac{1}{500}$) as compared to either a high or a low degree of skew ($\frac{1}{5000}$). This is because state D materializes the frequently accessed objects on different partitions,

---

[12] If none of the requests accessed the tertiary storage device, the maximum processing capability of the system would have been 75 displays per minute.

resulting in a more even distribution of the load across the partitions.

We analyzed the performance of the system with various values for Gp_2, Gp_3, and Gf. More specifically, we analyzed values that either enable or disable a certain functionality. Due to the general nature of our workload, these choices have a marginal impact on the overall throughput of the system (and the obtained results are almost identical to that of Figure 4).

6   Conclusion and Future Research Directions

In this paper we described virtual data replication as a technique to support simultaneous display of several multimedia objects to different users. We developed novel techniques to manage the physical replica of multimedia objects. These techniques determine the partition employed to materialize and display an object.

Once a request for an object is issued, we identified five possible states in the system and a flexible decision making policy for each of these states. In addition, we developed three state transition diagrams for the scheduler (MTA, MRT, and FXT). Both the decision making policies and the state transition diagrams approximate different objectives, enabling the database administrator to customize the system to satisfy specific requirements of an application.

We used a simulation study to quantify the tradeoffs associated with the alternative state transition diagrams and policies. Due to the general nature of our workload, the alternative decision making policies at each state have marginal impact on the overall performance of the system (i.e., these policies are appropriate for a specific application and not an arbitrary workload). However, the alternative state transition diagrams have a significant impact on the overall performance of the system. In general, our results demonstrate that MRT is a superior strategy as compared to both MTA and FXT. Moreover, while at first glance one might be convinced that both the tertiary storage device and the policies developed in this study are redundant for a small database, as demonstrated in Section 5.2, MRT can transform a static system into a dynamic one that maximizes the utilization of the disk space and enhances the overall performance of the system.

Virtual data replication is a promising area of research that enables parallel database management systems to support real-time display of multimedia data. We intend to extend this study in several ways. First, when the system resources are committed (i.e., the number of requests exceeds the number of partitions), we intend to design scheduling policies that analyze the queue of requests and reserve partitions in a manner that maximizes the overall performance of the system (this should minimize the impact of the thrashing behavior for FXT, and further enhance the performance of the system for both MRT and MTA). Second, we intend to investigate the following optimization techniques: 1) use a partition to service multiple requests for an object (by multiplexing the stream of data to different terminals), 2) use a variation of the first optimization to overlap the display of a frequently accessed object with its materialization on a different partition (since the bandwidth of the tertiary storage is lower than that of a partition). Third, for a system with hundreds and thousands of processors, the centralized scheduler may become a bottleneck. It was essential to assume a centralized scheduler in this study in order to understand the tradeoffs associated with the alternatives state transition diagrams. We intend to replace the proposed centralized policies with novel distributed scheduling algorithms.

References

1. Daniel R. Benigni, editor. *Digital Video in the PC Environment*. McGraw-Hill, 1991.
2. G. Copeland, W. Alexander, E. Boughter, and T. Keller. Data placement in bubba. In *SIGMOD*, pages 100–110. ACM, 1988.
3. J. Dozier. Access to Data in NASA's Earth Observing System. Keynote address, *SIGMOD 1992*, page 1, ACM, 1992.
4. E. A. Fox. Advances in Interactive Digital Multimedia Sytems. *IEEE Computer*, pages 9–21, October 1991.
5. S. Ghandeharizadeh. Management of disk space with virtual data replication. Unpublished manuscript, June 1993.
6. S. Ghandeharizadeh and D. DeWitt. A multiuser performance analysis of alternative declustering strategies. In *Proceedings of International Conference on Database Engineering*, 1990.
7. S. Ghandeharizadeh and L. Ramos. Continuous retrieval of multimedia data using parallelism. August 1993.
8. S. Ghandeharizadeh, L. Ramos, Z. Asad, and W. Qureshi. Object Placement in Parallel Hypermedia Systems. In *proceedings of the International Conference on Very Large Databases*, 1991.
9. J. Green. The evolution of dvi system sotftware. *Communications of the ACM*, 35(1), January 1992.
10. B. Haskell. International standards activities in image data compression. In *Proceedings of Scientific Data Compression Workshop*, pages 439–449, 1989. NASA conference Pub 3025, NASA Office of Management, Scientific and technical information division.
11. A. Lippman and W. Butera. Coding image sequences for interactive retrieval. *Communications of the ACM*, 32(7), July 1989.
12. D. Patterson, G. Gibson, and R. Katz. A case for Redundant Arrays of Inexpensive Disks (RAID). In *Proceedings of the 1988 ACM SIGMOD Int'l Conf.*, May 1988.
13. H. Schwetman. CSIM: A C-Based Process-Oriented Simulation Language. Technical Report PP-080-85, Microelectronics and Computer Technology Corporation, 1985.
14. M. R. Stonebraker. The case for Shared-Nothing. In *Proceedings of the 1986 Data Engineering Conference*. IEEE, 1986.

Efficient Similarity Search In Sequence Databases

Rakesh Agrawal and Christos Faloutsos* and Arun Swami

IBM Almaden Research Center, 650 Harry Road, San Jose, CA 95120-6099

Abstract. We propose an indexing method for time sequences for processing similarity queries. We use the Discrete Fourier Transform (DFT) to map time sequences to the frequency domain, the crucial observation being that, for most sequences of practical interest, only the first few frequencies are strong. Another important observation is Parseval's theorem, which specifies that the Fourier transform preserves the Euclidean distance in the time or frequency domain. Having thus mapped sequences to a lower-dimensionality space by using only the first few Fourier coefficients, we use R^*-trees to index the sequences and efficiently answer similarity queries. We provide experimental results which show that our method is superior to search based on sequential scanning. Our experiments show that a few coefficients (1-3) are adequate to provide good performance. The performance gain of our method increases with the number and length of sequences.

1 Introduction

Sequences constitute a large portion of data stored in computers. There have been several efforts to model time-sequenced data, to design languages to query such data, and to develop access structures to efficiently process such queries (see [28] for a bibliography). Most of the work, however, has focussed on "exact" queries. New emerging applications, particularly database mining applications [1], require that databases be enhanced with the capability to process "similarity" queries. The following are some examples of the similarity queries over sequence databases:

- Identify companies with similar pattern of growth.
- Determine products with similar selling patterns.
- Discover stocks with similar movement in stock prices.
- Find if a musical score is similar to one of the copyrighted scores.

Similarity queries can be classified into two categories:

---

* On sabbatical from the Dept. of Computer Science, University of Maryland, College Park. This research was partially funded by the Systems Research Center (SRC) at the University of Maryland, and by the National Science Foundation under Grant IRI-8958546 (PYI), with matching funds from EMPRESS Software Inc. and Thinking Machines Inc.

a. *Whole Matching.* The sequences to be compared have the same length n.

b. *Subsequence Matching.* The query sequence is smaller; we look for a subsequence in the large sequence that best matches the query sequence.

We concentrate on whole matching, and present an indexing technique that can be used to efficiently process such queries. Within the whole matching case, we consider the following problems:

a1. *Range Query.* Given a query sequence, find sequences that are similar within distance ϵ.

a2. *All-Pairs Query* (or 'spatial join'). Given N sequences, find the pairs of sequences that are within ϵ of each other.

The parameter ϵ is a distance parameter that controls when two sequences should be considered similar. It could be either user-defined, or determined automatically (eg., $\epsilon=10\%$ of the 'energy' of the query sequence; see Eq. 3 for the definition of 'energy').

Approximate matching has been attracting increasing interest lately. Motro described a user interface for vague queries [20]. Shasha and Wang [27] proposed an indexing method that uses the triangular inequality and some precomputed distances to prune the search. However, the space overhead of the method seems quadratic on the number of objects, which may make it prohibitive for large databases. Aurenhammer [5] surveyed recent research on Voronoi diagrams, along with their use for nearest neighbor queries. Although Voronoi diagrams work well for approximate matches in 2-dimensional spaces, they need intricate transformations to work for a 3-d space, and they do not work at all for higher dimensionalities. Jagadish [17] suggested using a few minimum bounding rectangles to extract features from shapes and subsequently managing the resulting vectors using a spatial access method, like k-d-B-trees, grid files, etc. Related efforts, but not directly applicable to numerical sequences, include algorithms for approximate string searching [30, 6] with full text scanning, approximate searching methods for DNA sequences [4], and clustering algorithms in information retrieval and library science [24].

For numerical sequences, we propose extracting k features from every sequence, mapping it to k-dimensional space, and then using a multidimensional index to store and search these points. The multidimensional indexing methods currently in use are R^*-trees [7] and the rest of the R-tree and k-d-Btree family [13, 16, 18]; linear quadtrees [25]; and grid-files [21]. There are two subtle problems with this approach that must be addressed:

- *Completeness of feature extraction*: How to extract features, and how to guarantee that we do not miss any qualifying object (time sequence, in our case). To guarantee no "false dismissal", objects should be mapped to points in k-dimensional space such that the Euclidean distance in the k-dimensional space is *less than or equal* to the real distance between the two objects.
- *Dimensionality "curse"*: Most multidimensional indexing methods scale exponentially for high dimensionalities, eventually reducing to sequential scanning. For linear quadtrees, the effort is proportional to the hyper surface of

the query region [15]; the hyper surface grows exponentially with the dimensionality. Grid files face similar problems, since they require a directory that grows exponentially with the dimensionality. The R-tree based methods seem to be most robust for higher dimensions, provided that the fanout of the R-tree nodes remains > 2. Experiments [23] indicate that R^*-trees work well for up to 20 dimensions. The feature extraction method should therefore be such that a few features are sufficient to differentiate between objects.

We propose to use the *Discrete Fourier Transform* [22, 14] for feature extraction. Given a sequence, we transform it from the time domain to the frequency domain. We then index only on the first few frequencies, dropping all other frequencies. This approach addresses the two problems cited above as follows:

- *Completeness of feature extraction:* Parseval's theorem [22], discussed in Section 2, guarantees that the distance between two sequences in the frequency domain is the same as the distance between them in the time domain.
- *Dimensionality curse:* As we discuss in subsection 3.3, a large family of interesting sequences exhibit strong amplitudes for the first few frequencies. Using the first few frequencies then avoids the dimensionality problem, while still introducing few *false hits*. The false hits are removed in a post-processing step.

The organization of the rest of the paper is as follows. Section 2 gives some background material on the Discrete Fourier Transform, and introduces Parseval's theorem that provides the basis for the indexing technique we propose. A resume of our indexing technique is given in Section 3. We also justify our choice of similarity measure and the selection of DFT for feature extraction in this section. Section 4 contains performance experiments that empirically show the effectiveness of our technique. We conclude with a summary in Section 5.

2 Discrete Fourier Transform

We start with a brief overview of the Discrete Fourier Transform (DFT). The importance of the DFT is the existence of a fast algorithm, the *Fast Fourier Transform (FFT)*, that can calculate the DFT coefficients in $O(n \log n)$ time. Further information on the Fourier transform can be found in any digital signal processing textbook, for example, [22, 14].

The n-point *Discrete Fourier Transform* [22] of a signal $\mathbf{x} = [x_t]$, $t = 0, \ldots, n-1$ is defined to be a sequence $\mathbf{X}$ of n complex numbers X_f, $f = 0, \ldots, n-1$, given by

$$X_f = 1/\sqrt{n} \sum_{t=0}^{n-1} x_t \exp\left(-j2\pi f t/n\right) \quad f = 0, 1, \ldots, n-1 \tag{1}$$

where j is the imaginary unit $j = \sqrt{-1}$. The signal $\mathbf{x}$ can be recovered by the inverse transform:

$$x_t = 1/\sqrt{n} \sum_{f=0}^{n-1} X_f \exp\left(j2\pi f t/n\right) \quad t = 0, 1, \ldots, n-1 \tag{2}$$

X_f is a complex number (with the exception of X_0, which is a real, if the signal **x** is real). There are some minor discrepancies among books: some define $X_f = 1/n \sum_{t=0}^{n-1} \dots$ or $X_f = \sum_{t=0}^{n-1} \dots$. We have followed the definition in (Eq 1), for it simplifies the upcoming Parseval's theorem (Eq 4).

Definitions: For a complex number $c = a + jb = A\exp(j\phi)$

- $A \equiv |c|$ is said to be the *amplitude* and ϕ to be the *phase* of the number c.
- The *conjugate* c^* of c is defined as $a - jb$.
- The *energy* $E(c)$ of c is defined as the square of the amplitude ($E(c) \equiv |c|^2 \equiv c\,c^*$).
- The *energy* $E(\mathbf{x})$ of a sequence **x** is defined as the sum of energies at every point of the sequence:

$$E(\mathbf{x}) \equiv \| \mathbf{x} \|^2 \equiv \sum_{t=0}^{n-1} |x_t|^2 \tag{3}$$

A fundamental observation for this paper is Parseval's theorem [22]:

Theorem 1 (Parseval) *Let* **X** *be the Discrete Fourier Transform of the sequence* **x**. *Then we have*

$$\sum_{t=0}^{n-1} |x_t|^2 = \sum_{f=0}^{n-1} |X_f|^2 \tag{4}$$

That is, the energy in the time domain is the same as the energy in the frequency domain.

The Discrete Fourier Transform inherits the following properties from the continuous Fourier transform. Let '$\Longleftrightarrow$' indicate Fourier pairs, i.e.,

$$[x_t] \Longleftrightarrow [X_f] \tag{5}$$

means that $[X_f]$ is the Discrete Fourier Transform of $[x_t]$. The Discrete Fourier Transform is a *linear transformation*: If

$$[x_t] \Longleftrightarrow [X_f]; [y_t] \Longleftrightarrow [Y_f] \tag{6}$$

then

$$[x_t + y_t] \Longleftrightarrow [X_f + Y_f] \tag{7}$$

$$[ax_t] \Longleftrightarrow [aX_f] \tag{8}$$

Also, a shift in the time domain changes only the phase of the Fourier coefficients, but not the amplitude.

$$[x_{t-t_0}] \Longleftrightarrow [X_f \, \exp(2\pi f t_0 j/n)] \tag{9}$$

Given the above, Parseval's theorem gives

$$\| \mathbf{x} - \mathbf{y} \|^2 \equiv \| \mathbf{X} - \mathbf{Y} \|^2 \tag{10}$$

The latter implies that the Euclidean distance between two signals $\mathbf{x}$ and $\mathbf{y}$ in the time domain is the same as their Euclidean distance in the frequency domain.

We believe that for a large number of time sequences of practical interest, there will be a few frequencies with high amplitudes. Thus, if we index only on the first few frequencies, we shall have few *false hits*. This is *a key observation* for our proposed method.

3 Proposed Technique

We propose using the square root of the *sum of squared differences* as the distance function between two sequences. Specifically, the distance $\mathcal{D}(\mathbf{x}, \mathbf{y})$ between two sequences $\mathbf{x}$ and $\mathbf{y}$ is the square root of the energy of the difference:

$$\mathcal{D}(\mathbf{x}, \mathbf{y}) \equiv (\sum_{t=0}^{n-1} |x_t - y_t|^2)^{1/2} \equiv (E(\mathbf{x} - \mathbf{y}))^{1/2} \tag{11}$$

If this distance is below a user-defined threshold ϵ, we say that the two sequences are similar.

The importance of Parseval's theorem (Eq 4) is that it allows to translate the query from the time domain to the frequency domain. Coupled with the conjecture that few Fourier coefficients are enough, it allows us to build an effective index with a low dimensionality.

The following is a resume of our proposed technique:

1. Obtain the coefficients of the Discrete Fourier Transforms of each sequence in the database.
2. Build a multidimensional index using the first f_c Fourier coefficients, where f_c stands for 'cut-off frequency'. Thus, each sequence becomes a point in a $2f_c$-dimensional space (recall that the Fourier coefficients are complex numbers). We discuss in subsection 3.3 why f_c can be taken to be small (< 5). As discussed earlier, we recommend the R^*-trees as the indexing structure, since it has been shown to work well for at least up to 20 dimensions [23]. This index will be called 'F-index' henceforth.
3. For a range query, obtain the first f_c Fourier coefficients of the query sequence. Use the F-index to retrieve the set of matching sequences that are at most ϵ distance away from the query sequence.
4. For an all-pairs query, we do a spatial join using the F-index. The result of the join will be a superset of the answer set.
5. The actual answer set is obtained in a post-processing step in which the actual distance between two sequences is computed in the time domain and only those within ϵ distance are accepted.

The 'completeness' of this method is based on the following lemma:

Lemma 1. *The F-index introduces no false dismissals.*

We only give the proof for range queries; the proof for 'all-pairs' queries is very similar. Suppose we want all sequences **x** that are similar to a query sequence **q**, within distance ϵ, *i.e.*:

$$\mathcal{D}(\mathbf{x}, \mathbf{q}) \leq \epsilon \tag{12}$$

or, equivalently:

$$\| \mathbf{x} - \mathbf{q} \|^2 = \sum_{t=0}^{n-1} |x_t - q_t|^2 \leq \epsilon^2 \tag{13}$$

Using Parseval's theorem (Eqs. 4, 10), we want all **X** such that

$$\| \mathbf{X} - \mathbf{Q} \|^2 = \sum_{f=0}^{n-1} |X_f - Q_f|^2 \leq \epsilon^2 \tag{14}$$

Keeping only the first $f_c < n$ coefficients, we have

$$\sum_{f=0}^{f_c-1} |X_f - Q_f|^2 \leq \sum_{f=0}^{n-1} |X_f - Q_f|^2 \leq \epsilon^2 \tag{15}$$

Thus, equation (14) implies the following condition

$$\sum_{f=0}^{f_c-1} |X_f - Q_f|^2 \leq \epsilon^2 \tag{16}$$

In other terms, the condition of (Eq. 16) will retrieve all **X** that are in the answer, plus some false hits. Thus, our index acts as a filter that returns a superset of the answer set.

∎

3.1 Choice of Similarity Measure

The similarity measure is clearly application-dependent. Several similarity measures have been proposed, for 1-d and 2-d signals. In a recent survey for images (2-d signals), Brown [8](p. 367, sect. 4.2) mentions that one of the typical similarity measures is the cross-correlation (which reduces to the Euclidean distance, plus some additive and multiplicative constants). We have chosen the Euclidean distance, because (a) it is useful in many cases, as is (b) it can be used with *any* other type of similarity measure, as long as this measure can be expressed as the Euclidean distance between feature vectors in some feature space.

In fact, the Euclidean distance is the optimal distance measure for estimation [12], if signals are corrupted by Gaussian, additive noise. Thus, if **q** is our query and **x** is a corrupted version of it in the database, a searching method using the Euclidean distance should produce good results.

A valuable feature of the Euclidean distance is that it is preserved under orthonormal transforms. Other distance functions, like the L_p norms

$$L_p(\mathbf{x}, \mathbf{y}) = (\sum |x_t - y_t|^p)^{1/p} \tag{17}$$

do not have this property, unless $p = 2$ (because $L_2 \equiv$ Euclidean distance).

3.2 Using DFT

Having decided on the Euclidean distance as the distance measure, we would like a transform that (a) preserves the distance (b) is easy to compute and (c) concentrates the energy of the signal in few coefficients.

The distance-preservation requirement is met by any *orthonormal transform* [11], DFT being one of them. Orthonormal transforms form two classes: (1) the data-dependent ones, like the Karhunen-Loeve (K-L) transform, which need all the data signals to determine the transformation matrix and (2) the data-independent ones, like the DFT, Discrete Cosine (DCT), Harr, or wavelet transform, where the transformation matrix is determined a-priori.

The data-dependent transforms can be fine-tuned to the specific data set, and therefore they can achieve better performance, concentrating the energy into fewer features in the feature vector. Their drawback is that, if the data set evolves over time, e.g., a recomputation of the transformation matrix may be required to avoid performance degradation, requiring expensive data reorganization. We, therefore, favor data-independent transforms.

Among them, we have chosen the DFT because it is the most well known, its code is readily available and it does a good job of concentrating the energy in the first few coefficients, as we shall see next. In addition, the DFT has the attractive property that the *amplitude* of the Fourier coefficients is invariant under shifts (Eq. 9). Thus, using Fourier transforms for feature extraction has the potential that our technique can be extended to finding similar sequences ignoring shifts.

Note that our approach can be applied with *any* orthonormal transform. In fact, our response time will improve with the ability of the transform to concentrate the energy: the fewer the coefficients that contain most of the energy, the faster our response time. Thus, the performance results presented next are just pessimistic bounds; better transforms will achieve even better response times.

3.3 Using a Few Fourier Coefficients for Indexing

Using a small value for the number of Fourier coefficients retained f_c does not affect the correctness — the F-index is a filter that returns a superset of the answer set. However, our proposed technique will not be very effective if the choice of a small f_c results in a large number of false hits.

The worst-case signal for our method is *white noise*, where each value x_t is completely independent of its neighbors x_{t-1}, x_{t+1}. The energy spectrum of white noise follows $O(f^0)$ [26], that is, it has the same energy in every frequency. This is bad for the F-index, because it implies that all the frequencies are equally important. However, we have strong reasons to believe that real signals have a skewed energy spectrum. For example, *random walks* (also known as *brown noise* or *brownian walks*) exhibit an energy spectrum of $O(f^{-2})$ [26], and therefore an amplitude spectrum of $O(f^{-1})$. Stock movements and exchange rates have been successfully modeled as random walks (e.g., [9, 19]). Figure 1 illustrates a synthetically generated random walk and its amplitude spectrum in doubly logarithmic plot — notice the close approximation of the $1/f$ line.

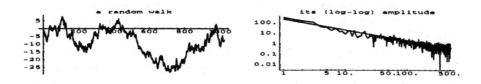

Fig. 1. A random walk; amplitude of its Fourier coefficients; the $1/f$ line

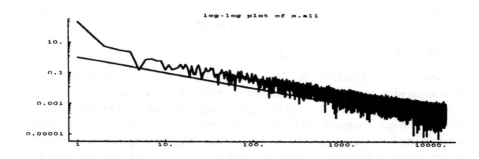

Fig. 2. (Log-log) amplitude of the Fourier transform of the Swiss-franc exchange rate, along with the $1/f$ line

The movement of the exchange rate between the Swiss franc and the US dollar starting August 7, 1990 to April 18, 1991 (30,000 measurements) is available through ftp from *sfi.santafe.edu*. Using this data set Figure 2 shows the amplitude of the Fourier coefficients as well as the $1/f$ line, in a doubly logarithmic plot. Observe that the amplitude of the Fourier coefficients follow the $1/f$ line, in the same way that the artificially generated random walk of Figure 1 does.

Our mathematical argument for keeping the first few Fourier coefficients agrees with the intuitive argument of the Dow Jones theory for stock price movement (see, for example, [10]). This theory tries to detect *primary* and *secondary* trends in the stock market movement, and ignores *minor* trends. Primary trends are defined as changes that are larger than 20%, typically lasting more than a year; secondary trends show 1/3-2/3 relative change over primary trends, with a typical duration of a few months; minor trends last roughly a week. From the above definitions, we conclude that primary and secondary trends correspond to strong, low frequency signals while minor trends correspond to weak, high frequency signals. Thus, the primary and secondary trends are exactly the ones that our method will automatically choose for indexing.

In addition to the above, it is believed that several other families of real signals are not white noise. For example, 2-d signals, like photographs, are far from white noise, exhibiting a few strong coefficients in the lower spatial frequencies. The JPEG image compression standard [29] exactly exploits this phenomenon, effectively ignoring the high-frequency components of the Discrete Cosine Transform, which is closely related to the Fourier transform. If the image consisted of white noise, no compression would be possible at all. Birkhoff's theory [26] claims that *'interesting'* signals, such as musical scores and other works of art, consist of *pink noise*, whose energy spectrum follows $O(f^{-1})$. The theory argues that white noise with $O(f^0)$ energy spectrum is completely unpredictable, while brown noise with $O(f^{-2})$ energy spectrum is too predictable and therefore boring. The energy spectrum of pink noise lies in-between. Signals with pink noise also have their energy concentrated in the first few frequencies (but not as few as in the random walk). There is another group of signals, called *black noise* [26]. Their energy spectrum follow $O(f^{-b})$, $b > 2$, which is even more skewed than the spectrum of the brown noise. Such signals model successfully, for example, the water level of rivers as they vary over time [19].

4   Performance Experiments

To determine the effectiveness of our proposed method (the *F-index* method), we compared it to a *sequential scanning* method. We used the R^*-tree for the index. For range queries, the sequential scanning method computes the distance between the query sequence and each data sequence. In our effort to do the best possible implementation for the sequential scanning, we stop the test as soon as the square of the distance exceeds ϵ^2, and we declare the two sequences to be dissimilar. Thus, a data sequence is fully scanned only if it is similar to the query sequence. For 'all-pairs' queries, each sequence in the database is tested against every other sequence, for a total of $N(N-1)/2$ tests.

We investigated the following questions in these experiments:

- How to choose the number of Fourier coefficients to be retained (cut-off frequency f_c) in the F-index method. A larger f_c reduces the false hits but at the same time increases the dimensionality of the R^*-tree, and hence the search time.

- How does the search time grow as a function of number of sequences in the database?
- How does the length n of the sequences affect the performance?

4.1 Experimental setup

We generated synthetic sequences for the experiments. Each sequence $\mathbf{x} = [x_t]$ was a random walk:

$$x_t = x_{t-1} + z_t \tag{18}$$

where z_t ($t = 1, 2, \ldots$) are independent, identically distributed (IID) random variables. For implementation convenience, each z_t variable is uniformly distributed in the range (-500, 500). The probability distribution of each z_t is immaterial; the results would be the same had we chosen a gaussian distribution, or a fair, random coin. For each set S of N sequences, queries were generated by creating a distorted copy $[\tilde{x}_t]$ of each sequence $[x_t]$ in S. This was accomplished by adding a small amount of noise to every x_t, i.e.,

$$\tilde{x}_t = x_t + p\, w_t \tag{19}$$

where $p=0.05$ and w_t ($t = 1, 2, \ldots$) are IID random variables, each following a uniform distribution in the range (-500,500).

Let Q be the set of distorted sequences, which we shall use as queries. For range queries, we search S for sequences within distance ϵ for every distorted sequence in Q. For all-pairs queries, we concatenate S and Q, and ask for all sequence pairs within ϵ distance. The execution time for the F-index method includes both the search time in the R^*-tree and the post-processing time.

Each experiment was replicated 10 times by generating 10 sequence sets with different seeds, and averaging the execution times for the replicates. Table 1 summarizes the parameters of the experiments.

Parameter	Symbol	Values	Default value
# Fourier coefficients kept	f_c	1, 2, 3, 4	2
# sequences in S	$|S|$	50, 100, 200, 400	400
Length of each sequence	n	256, 512, 1024, 2048	1024
Distance (tolerance)	ϵ	sqrt(1000 × n)	

Table 1. Summary of experimental settings

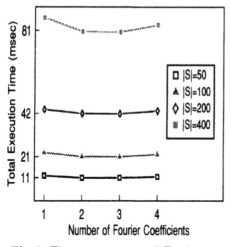

Fig. 3. Time per query vs. # Fourier coefficients f_c, for range queries

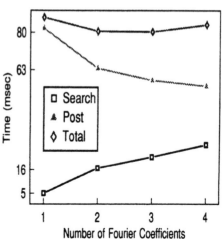

Fig. 5. Breakup of the execution time, for range query ($|S| = 400$)

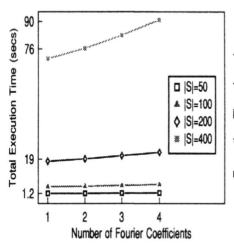

Fig. 4. Time per query vs. # Fourier coefficients f_c, for all-pairs queries

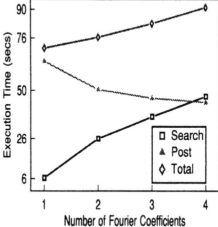

Fig. 6. Breakup of the execution time, for all-pairs query ($|S| = 400$)

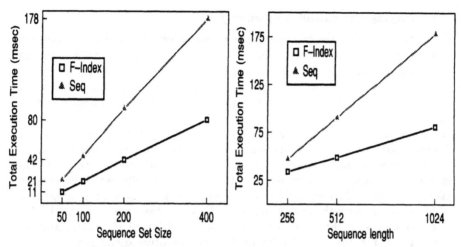

Fig. 7. Time per query varying # sequences $|S|$, for range queries

Fig. 9. Time per query varying the sequence length n, for range queries

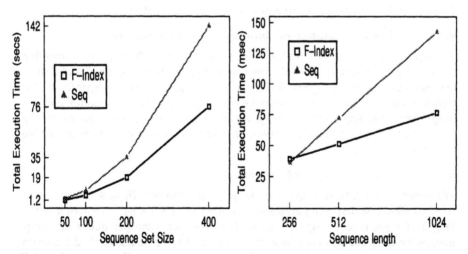

Fig. 8. Time per query varying # sequences $|S|$, for all-pairs queries

Fig. 10. Time per query varying the sequence length n, for all-pairs queries

4.2 Varying the cut-off frequency f_c

Figures 3 and 4 show the execution time per query for range and all-pairs queries respectively, for different number of sequences in S. Figures 5 and 6 give the the the total execution time by the F-index method for the two types of queries, broken into (a) search time in the R^*-tree and (b) post-processing time (where the 'false hits' are eliminated). The latter two graphs have been plotted for $|S| = 400$ sequences in S.

As the number of Fourier coefficients ('cut-off frequency' f_c) increases, the dimensionality of the R^*-tree increases. Recall that each Fourier coefficient, being a complex number, increases the dimensionality of the R^*-tree by 2. The increase in dimensionality results in better index selectivity, which gives fewer false hits. This reduction in false hits is reflected in the post-processing time, which decreases with the cut-off frequency. However, the time to search the R^*-tree increases with the dimensionality, because the fanout is smaller, and the tree is taller. Figures 5 and 6 validate the above intuitive arguments.

Given the trade-off between the tree-search time and the post-processing time, it is natural to expect that there is an 'optimal' f_c. Indeed, the total execution time of our method shows such a minimum, as illustrated in Figures 3 and 4. Notice that this minimum is rather flat, and, more importantly, it occurs for small values of the cut-off frequency f_c. This experiment confirms our early conjecture that we can effectively use a small number of Fourier coefficients for indexing sequences. For the rest of the experiments, we kept $f_c=2$ Fourier coefficients for indexing resulting in a 4-dimensional R^*-tree.

4.3 Varying the number of sequences in the database

The next experiment compares the F-index method with the sequential scanning method for increasing number of sequences in the database. Figures 7 and 8 show the execution time per query for range and all-pairs queries respectively, for different values of the number of sequences in $|S|$. Clearly, the F-index method outperforms the sequential scanning. As the number of sequences increases, the gain of the F-index method increases, making this method even more attractive for large databases.

4.4 Varying the length of sequences

We varied the length of sequences, keeping the number $|S|$ of sequences in S fixed to 400. The distance parameter ϵ was set to $(1000 \times n)^{1/2}$ (where n is the length of a sequence). Figure 9 shows the execution time per query for range queries for different sequence lengths. The gain of the F-index method increases with n. Figure 10 shows the results of the experiments for all-pairs queries. The trends are similar to the trends for range queries.

4.5 Discussion

The major conclusions from our experiments are:

- The minimum execution time for both range and 'all-pairs' queries is achieved for a small number of Fourier coefficients ($f_c = 1-3$). Moreover, the minimum is rather flat, which implies that a sub-optimal choice for f_c will give search time that is close to the minimum.

- Increasing the number of sequences in the database results in higher gains for our method.
- Increasing the length of the sequences n also results in higher gains for our method.

Thus, the experiments show that the proposed F-index method achieves increasingly better performance, as the volume of the data increases.

Finally, we also examined whether a 'naive' feature extraction method would work as well. For example, consider a method that keeps the first few values of each time sequence, and indexes on them. We carried out an experiment in which we indexed on the first 10 values of each time sequence. The performance of this method was very poor compared to the F-index method; there were many false hits, resulting in a large post-processing time. Judging that further details are of little interest, we omit the experimental results.

5 Summary

We proposed a method to index time sequences for similarity searching. The major highlights of this method are:

- The use of an orthonormal transform, and specifically, the Discrete Fourier Transform, to extract features from a sequence. The attractive property of the DFT is that the Euclidean distance in the time domain is preserved in the frequency domain, thanks to Parseval's theorem. Thus, the DFT fulfills the "completeness of feature extraction" criterion. In addition, the DFT is fast to compute ($O(n \log n)$).
- The recognition that a large family of sequences have only a few (f_c) strong Fourier coefficients. For example, random walks, stock price movements, exchange rates, exhibit an amplitude spectrum of $O(1/f)$. Ignoring the weak coefficients, we introduce a few false hits, but no false dismissals. The importance of this observation is that it avoids the "dimensionality curse" at the expense of a modest post-processing cost. Keeping the first f_c coefficients, each sequence becomes a point in a $2f_c$–dimensional space (recall that the Fourier coefficients are complex numbers).
- The use of spatial access methods, and specifically R^*-trees, to index those points. We believe that R^*-trees are more robust than their competitors, for medium dimensionalities.

Extensive empirical evaluation demonstrated the effectiveness of the proposed method. We generated random walks, which model well stock price movements. The conclusions from our experiments are the following: (a) the execution time of our method shows a rather flat minimum for a small cut-off frequency ($f_c \approx$ 1-3) (b) compared to sequential scanning, our method achieves better gains with increasing number of sequences and increasing length. Thus, our method will be more and more attractive, as the volume of the database increases.

Although we have made certain choices (Euclidean distance between sequences in time domain for similarity measure, DFT for feature extraction, and R^* tree for maintaining indexes), our technique can be trivially adapted for

- any similarity measure that can be expressed as the Euclidean distance between feature vectors in some feature space
- any distance-preserving (eg., orthonormal) transform (the more the energy is concentrated in a few coefficients, the faster the response time)
- any multi-dimensional index that performs well for the number of features indexed.

Future work could examine the following issues

- Examination of other orthonormal transformations, in addition to the Discrete Fourier Transform.
- Extensions of our approach to 2-d and higher-dimensionality signals (e.g., images), in addition to 1-d signals (time sequences) that we have examined.

The work reported in this paper has been done in the context of the Quest project [1] at the IBM Almaden Research Center. In Quest, we are exploring the various aspects of the database mining problem. Besides the problem of queries over large sequences, some other problems that we have looked into include the enhancement of the database capability with the classification queries [2] and with "what goes together" kinds of association queries [3]. The eventual goal is to build an experimental system that can be used for mining rules embedded in massive databases. We believe that database mining is an important application area, combining commercial interest with intriguing theoretical questions.

Acknowledgements: We thank Myron Flickner for several constructive comments and for his help with Parseval's theorem. We thank Harpreet Sawhney for pointing out the optimality of the Euclidean distance as the similarity measure under Gaussian, additive noise.

References

1. R. Agrawal, T. Imielinski, and A. Swami, "Database Mining: A Performance Perspective", *IEEE Transactions on Knowledge and Data Engineering*, Special issue on Learning and Discovery in Knowledge-Based Databases, (to appear).
2. R. Agrawal, S. Ghosh, T. Imielinski, B. Iyer, and A. Swami, "An Interval Classifier for Database Mining Applications", *VLDB 92*, Vancouver, August 1992.
3. R. Agrawal, T. Imielinski, and A. Swami, "Mining Association Rules between Sets of Items in Large Databases", *ACM SIGMOD*, Washington D.C., May 1993.
4. S.F. Altschul, W. Gish, W. Miller, E.W. Myers and D.J. Lipman, "A Basic Local Alignment Search Tool" *Journal of Molecular Biology*, 1990.
5. F. Aurenhammer, "Voronoi Diagrams - A Survey of a Fundamental Geometric Data Structure" *ACM Computing Surveys* 23(3):345-405, Sept. 1991.
6. Ricardo Baeza-Yates and Gaston H. Gonnet, "A New Approach to Text Searching", *Comm. of ACM*, **35** 10, Oct. 1992, 74-82.

7. N. Beckmann, H.-P. Kriegel, R. Schneider, and B. Seeger, "The R*-tree: an efficient and robust access method for points and rectangles", *ACM SIGMOD*, pages 322–331, May 1990.
8. L. G. Brown, "A Survey of Image Registration Techniques", *ACM Computing Surveys*, 24(4), pages 325–376, December 1992.
9. C. Chatfield, *The Analysis of Time Series: an Introduction*, Chapman and Hall, London & New York, 1984, Third Edition.
10. R. D. Edwards and J. Magee, *Technical Analysis of Stock Trends*, John Magee, Springfield, Massachusetts, 1966, 5th Edition, second printing.
11. K. Fukunaga, *Introduction to Statistical Pattern Recognition*, Academic Press, 1990, 2nd Edition.
12. A. Gelb, *Applied Optimal Estimation*, MIT Press, 1986.
13. A. Guttman, "R-trees: a dynamic index structure for spatial searching", *Proc. ACM SIGMOD*, pages 47–57, June 1984.
14. Richard Wesley Hamming, *Digital Filters*, Prentice-Hall Signal Processing Series, Englewood Cliffs, N.J., 1977.
15. G. M. Hunter and K. Steiglitz, "Operations on images using quad trees", *IEEE Trans. on PAMI*, PAMI-1(2):145–153, April 1979.
16. H. V. Jagadish, "Spatial search with polyhedra", *Proc. Sixth IEEE Int'l Conf. on Data Engineering*, February 1990.
17. H. V. Jagadish, "A retrieval technique for similar shapes", *Proc. ACM SIGMOD Conf.*, pages 208–217, May 1991.
18. D. Lomet and B. Salzberg, "The Hb-Tree: a Multiattribute Indexing Method with Good Guaranteed Performance", *ACM TODS*, 15(4), pages 625–658, December 1990.
19. B. Mandelbrot. *Fractal Geometry of Nature*, W.H. Freeman, New York, 1977.
20. A. Motro, "VAGUE: A User Interface to Relational Databases that Permits Vague Queries," *ACM Trans. on Information Systems (TOIS)*, 6(3), pages 187–214, July 1988.
21. J. Nievergelt, H. Hinterberger, and K. C. Sevcik, "The grid file: an adaptable, symmetric multikey file structure", *ACM TODS*, 9(1):38–71, March 1984.
22. A. V. Oppenheim and R. W. Schafer, *Digital Signal Processing*, Prentice-Hall, Englewood Cliffs, N.J., 1975.
23. M. Otterman, "Approximate Matching with High Dimensionality R-trees", M.Sc. scholarly paper, Dept. of Computer Science, Univ. of Maryland, College Park, MD, 1992.
24. G. Salton and M.J. McGill, *Introduction to Modern Information Retrieval*, McGraw-Hill, 1983.
25. H. Samet, *The Design and Analysis of Spatial Data Structures*, Addison-Wesley, 1989.
26. M. Schroeder, *Fractals, Chaos, Power Laws: Minutes From an Infinite Paradise*, W.H. Freeman and Company, New York, 1991.
27. D. Shasha and T-L. Wang, "New techniques for best-match retrieval", *ACM TOIS*, 8(2):140–158, April 1990.
28. R. Stam and R. Snodgrass, "A Bibliography on Temporal Databases", *IEEE Bulletin on Data Engineering*, 11(4), Dec. 1988.
29. G. K. Wallace "The JPEG Still Picture Compression Standard", *CACM*, 34(4):31–44, April 1991.
30. Sun Wu and Udi Manber, "Text searching allowing errors", *Comm. of ACM (CACM)*, 35(10):83–91, October 1992.

Filtered Hashing

Ilsoo Ahn

AT&T Bell Laboratories
Columbus, Ohio 43213, U.S.A.

Abstract. *Filtered hashing* is a new method of hashing that can maintain the benefits of hashing even when there are many overflow records. When an overflow occurs, a bucket is split into two and its address is stored in the *overflow filter*. When an underflow occurs, two buckets can be merged into one to reduce the file size. As long as the overflow filter fits in the main memory, the number of disk accesses to retrieve a record is guaranteed to be just one. The cost of inserting or deleting a record is also bounded by between 2 and 4 disk accesses. If the overflow filter grows too big due to excessive growth, the file can be reorganized with a bigger address space at a convenient time to achieve the optimal performance of static hashing, and can still adapt to dynamic changes later on.

1. Introduction

Most computer applications involve retrieving data from a file or a database stored on random access disk drives. There exists a gap of many orders of magnitude between the CPU speed and the disk access time, and the gap keeps growing wider as the technologies advance. Therefore, it is important in real-time or on-line systems to minimize the number of disk accesses for retrieving data.

Hashing is a classic technique to map the key of a record to a storage address through a hash function. In a static environment where the number of records is fixed, the upper bound to the number of disk accesses for retrieving a record can be just one with a good hash function and a reasonable space utilization [1] [2] [3]. In a dynamic environment where the number of records is unknown or keeps growing over time, more records than the capacity will be mapped to a bucket, resulting in an overflow.

There are two major categories of schemes for handling the overflows: *fixed-size* and *variable-size*. In the fixed-size hashing schemes, the size of the primary address space remains the same as determined by the range of the hash function. Various methods have been proposed to handle overflows for this category: such as *linear probing*, *rehashing*, and *coalesced chaining*. These methods can handle a small number of overflows reasonably well, but the performance of data retrieval tends to deteriorate to $O(n)$, where n is the number of records, if there are many overflows.

In contrast, the variable-size hashing schemes allow the size of the primary address space to grow or shrink as overflows or underflows occur. Many such schemes have been proposed, which can be classified as *directory* or *directoryless* [4]. Directory schemes such as *dynamic hashing*, *extendible hashing*, and their variations can be considered as a combination of hashing and indexing. Directoryless schemes such as *virtual hashing* and *linear hashing* with several variations handle dynamic changes without maintaining a directory. We compare these methods in more details in Section 5.

We propose a new method of variable-size hashing, called *filtered hashing*, which combines useful characteristics of both the directory and the directoryless schemes. Until there occurs an overflow, filtered hashing works in the same way as conventional fixed-size hashing, like a directoryless scheme. When an overflow or an underflow occurs, a bucket is split into two or merged with another, like a directory scheme. Unlike a directory scheme, filtered hashing does not require index entries for every bucket in the file. Only a list of overflow addresses, termed *overflow filter*, is maintained to represent the history of the file evolution.

Since the overflow filter contains only the addresses of the buckets that encountered overflows, it is usually small enough to reside in the main memory even for a high degree of volatility. Hence the number of disk accesses to retrieve a record is guaranteed to be just one, which is often difficult with other variable-size hashing schemes. The cost of inserting or deleting a record is also bounded by between 2 and 4 disk accesses, and address calculation with the overflow filter is very simple and efficient.

If the overflow filter grows too big due to excessive changes, the same hashing scheme can be applied recursively to the filter itself for a rapid access (*recursive filtered hashing* or *filtered hashing with a filter-hashed filter*). It is also possible to reorganize the file with a bigger address space at a convenient time to achieve the optimal performance of a static hashing and still adapt to future dynamic changes.

We implemented the algorithm of filtered hashing in the C language, ran various tests, and measured the performance. In this paper, we first describe the concepts as an overview, and illustrate the algorithm with a series of examples for inserting and deleting records. Next we describe the performance characteristics in terms of space utilization, access time, and the size of the overflow filter. Then we compare the expected values with the results measured from the actual tests. We also compare the characteristics of filtered hashing with other variable-size hashing schemes, and discuss several ways to make further enhancements.

2. Overview

Filtered hashing works in the same way as conventional fixed-size hashing without any overhead, until there occurs an overflow. Each record is first hashed on the key through a hash function h_0, whose range is $\{1, 2, ..., n_0\}$ where n_0 is the number of buckets initially allocated for the file. When a record needs to be inserted into a bucket which does not have sufficient space, resulting in an overflow, a new bucket is appended to the end of the file. Then the overflowed bucket is split into two by moving some of its records to the new one according to a *split function* s_i, $i > 0$, where i, termed the *depth* of overflow for the bucket, is the number of overflows that had occurred on the path to locate the bucket including the latest one. The split function s_i has the range of $\{0, 1\}$, and determines whether a record stays in the original bucket or is moved to the new bucket. Hence, the hash function h_0 and the split functions s_i should satisfy the constraints:

$$h_0 : K \rightarrow \{1, 2, ..., n_0\}$$

$$s_i : K \rightarrow \{0, 1\} \quad \text{for } i \geq 1$$

where K is an arbitrary key, and n_0 is the initial file size in buckets.

At this time, the address of the overflowed bucket is stored into a list, called the *overflow filter*, which is initially empty. The *overflow filter* is simply a list of addresses where overflows occurred, but it also represents information on the *depth* of overflow for a bucket, and where a new bucket was added upon an overflow. Such information maintained by the overflow filter is in fact sufficient to retrieve a record at the cost of exactly *one* bucket access, given the key of the record.

To determine the address of the bucket for a given key K, h_0 is first applied to K. If $h_0 (K) = a_0$, where $1 \leq a_0 \leq n_0$, a_0 is called the *initial* address. If a_0 is not an active member of the overflow filter, it becomes the *final* address of the bucket for K. Otherwise, determine the position p_0 of a_0 in the overflow filter, and temporarily check off a_0 from the filter. Then depending on whether $s_1 (K)$ is 0 or 1, the next *intermediate* address a_1 becomes a_0 or $n_0 + p_0$, respectively. Now if a_1 is not an active member in the overflow filter, it becomes the *final* address of the bucket for K. If a_1 is again an active member of the overflow filter, then repeat the steps similar to those for the case of a_0 being a member of the overflow filter, except that each subscript of p_0, a_0, s_1, a_1 is incremented by 1 respectively on each iteration. Note that the subscripts are determined by the *depth* of overflow for the bucket in question, which is the number of overflows which had occurred along the path to the bucket. The final address of the bucket for K is determined when a_i is found not to be an active member of the overflow filter. At that moment, all inactive members of the overflow filter are checked on again.

Once the final address of the bucket for K is determined, retrieving a record with such a key needs only to search the corresponding bucket. Whether the search is successful or not, its cost is just one bucket access, assuming that the overflow filter can be kept in main memory.

To insert a record with a key K, the bucket at the final address for the key is checked if it has sufficient space to receive the record. If so, the record is simply put into the bucket. Otherwise, a new bucket is appended to the end of the file, the original bucket is split into two, and the address of the original bucket is added to the overflow filter, as mentioned earlier. The cost of an insertion is one or two bucket accesses depending on whether it involves an overflow.

To delete a record with a key K, the record is searched in the bucket at the final address. If it is not found, the request fails. Otherwise, the record is deleted from the bucket. It is also possible to merge the bucket with another if certain conditions are met as discussed in Section 3.3.

3. Examples and Terminologies

This section first illustrates the procedures of inserting records with a series of examples. Then several terminologies are defined for further discussions, followed by examples for deleting records and merging buckets. Detailed algorithms to insert, delete, and retrieve records are given in the next section.

3.1 Insertions

Let's assume that the initial file size n_0 is 3, and that the hash function h_0 and the split functions s_i are:

$$h_0 (K) = K \bmod n_0 + 1$$
$$s_i (K) = \frac{K}{2^{i+1}} \bmod 2 \text{ for } i \geq 1$$

Some of the split functions are:

$$s_1 (K) = \frac{K}{2^2} \bmod 2$$
$$s_2 (K) = \frac{K}{2^3} \bmod 2$$
$$s_3 (K) = \frac{K}{2^4} \bmod 2$$

Note that the split functions can be computed very efficiently by a *bit-shift* and an AND operations. For example, $s_3 (K) = (K \gg 4)$ & 1 in C. It becomes even simpler if we test whether the result is 0 or just positive. Then we compute the split function by a single AND operation. $s_3 (K)$ becomes equivalent to (K & 0x10) in C.

We also assume that each bucket can hold up to three records, and call a record with n as the key simply record n. When records 12, 29, 37, 30, 13, 34 are inserted in sequence, the overflow filter remains empty. So far, filtered hashing works in the same way as conventional fixed-size hashing without any overhead.

To insert record 10 next, $h_0 (10) = 10 \bmod 3 + 1 = 2$. Since bucket 2 is already full, an overflow occurs. So a new bucket is appended as bucket 4, and records 37, 13, 34 are rehashed through s_1. Since $s_1 (34) = 0$ and $s_1 (37) = s_1 (13) = 1$, record 34 stays in the original bucket 2, and records 37 and 13 are moved to the new bucket 4. The new record 10 is now put into bucket 2, since $s_1 (10) = 0$. The file now looks like Fig-1(a), and the overflow filter becomes <2>. Note that the line between bucket 2 and bucket 4 is only conceptual, and does not denote any physical link.

For record 64, $h_0 (64) = 2$. But address 2 is at the position 1 of the overflow filter, which is now temporarily checked off. Since $s_1 (64) = 0$, its next intermediate address is still 2. There is no active member with the address 2 in the overflow filter, so the final address for record 64 is 2. The record is put into bucket 2, and the member 2 of the overflow filter is checked on again.

To insert record 22, $h_0 (22) = 2$. Since bucket 2 is at the position 1 of the overflow filter, and $s_1 (22) = 1$, its next intermediate address is $n_0 + p_0 = 3 + 1 = 4$. There is no member with address 4 in the overflow filter, so the final address for record 22 is 4.

To insert record 40, h_0 (40) = 2. But there is the address 2 at the position 1 of the overflow filter, which is now temporarily checked off. Since s_1 (40) = 0, its next intermediate address is still 2. There is no more active member with address 2 in the overflow filter, so the final address for record 40 is 2. But bucket 2 is already full. Thus a new bucket is appended as bucket 5, and records 34, 10, 64 are rehashed through s_2. Since s_2 (34) = s_2 (64) = 0 and s_1 (10) = 1, records 34 and 64 stay in the original bucket 2, and record 10 is moved to the new bucket 5. The new record 40 is now put into bucket 5, since s_2 (40) = 1. The file now looks like Fig-1(b), and the overflow filter is <2, 2>.

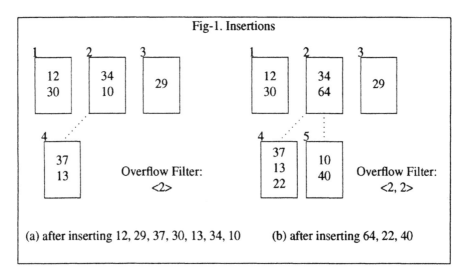

Fig-1. Insertions

(a) after inserting 12, 29, 37, 30, 13, 34, 10   (b) after inserting 64, 22, 40

If we insert record 28 next, h_0 (28) = 2. Since bucket 2 is at the position 1 of the overflow filter, and s_1 (28) = 1, its next intermediate address is $n_0 + p_0 = 3 + 1 = 4$. There is no member with address 4 in the overflow filter, so the final address for record 28 is 4. But bucket 4 is already full, so a new bucket is appended as bucket 6, and records 37, 13, 22 are rehashed through s_2. Since s_2 (37) = s_2 (22) = 0 and s_2 (13) = 1, records 37 and 22 stay in the original bucket, and record 13 is moved to the new bucket. Now record 28 is put into bucket 6, since s_2 (28) = 1, and the overflow filter now becomes <2, 2, 4>. Inserting records 46 and 49 next results in Fig-2(a).

To insert record 16 as a final example, h_0 (16) = 2. There is the address 2 at the position 1 of the overflow filter, which is now temporarily checked off. Since s_1 (16) = 0, the next intermediate address is 2. But there is still the address 2 at the position 2 of the overflow filter, which is also temporarily checked off. Now s_2 (16) = 0, so the next intermediate address is still 2. Bucket 2 is no longer an active member of the overflow filter, so the final address becomes bucket 2. Since bucket 2 is already full, a new bucket is appended as bucket 7, and records 34, 64, 49 are rehashed through s_3. Since s_3 (34) = s_3 (64) = 0 and s_3 (49) = 1, records 34 and 64 stay in the original bucket, and record 49 is moved to the new bucket. The new record 16 is put into the new bucket, since $s_3(16) = 1$. The result is Fig-2(b), and the overflow filter now becomes <2, 2, 4, 2>.

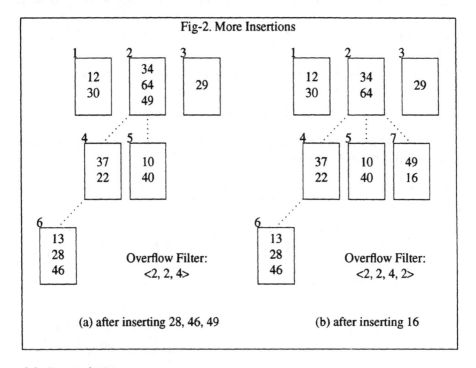

Fig-2. More Insertions

(a) after inserting 28, 46, 49

Overflow Filter:
<2, 2, 4>

(b) after inserting 16

Overflow Filter:
<2, 2, 4, 2>

3.2 Terminologies

Now we define some terminologies for filtered hashing before describing the deletion procedures. When an overflow occurs to a bucket, and a new bucket is added as a result, we call the original bucket the *parent* bucket, and call the new one the *child* bucket. Children with the same parent are called *siblings*, and a bucket without a child is called a *leaf*.

The *depth* of overflow for a bucket, or simply the depth of a bucket, is the number of overflows that had occurred along the path to locate a record in the bucket. It is identical to the order of the split function to be used to determine the final address of a record in the bucket. Now the depth of a bucket can be defined as the number of buckets corresponding to its *ancestors*, its *elder* siblings, and its *own* children. Note that younger siblings are not counted.

In Fig-2(b), for example, bucket 2 is the parent of buckets 4, 5 and 7. The depth of buckets 1 and 3 is 0. Bucket 2 has 3 children, so its depth is 3. Bucket 4 has one ancestor and one child, so its depth is 2. The depth of bucket 5 and 6 is also 2, since the former has an ancestor and an elder sibling, while the latter has two ancestors. Bucket 7 has an ancestor and two elder siblings, so its depth is 3.

The children of a bucket can be found by locating all occurrences of the bucket number in the overflow filter. If the bucket number is found at a position p_i of the overflow filter, the address of the child bucket corresponding to the position is $n_0 + p_i$, where n_0 is the initial file size. Bucket 2 in Fig-2(b) occurs at positions 1, 2 and 4 of the overflow filter. Since $n_0 = 3$, the children of bucket 2 are buckets 4, 5 and 7.

The parent p_i of a bucket a_i can also be determined from the overflow filter.

$$p_i = \begin{cases} none & \text{if } a_i < n_0 \\ OF[a_i - n_0] & otherwise \end{cases}$$

where $OF[k]$ denotes the k-th member of the overflow filter. The parent of bucket 6 in Fig-2(b) is bucket 4, since $OF[6 - n_0] = OF[3] = 4$.

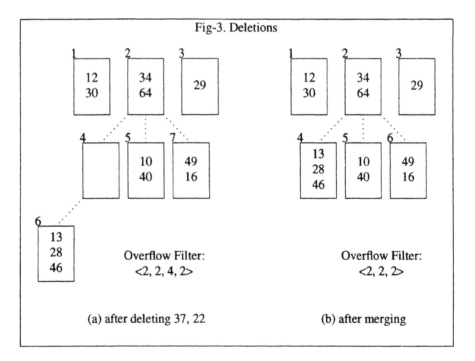

Fig-3. Deletions

(a) after deleting 37, 22

(b) after merging

3.3 Deletions

It is also possible to delete a record, and merge two buckets into one if space permits. To delete a record with a key K, the bucket at the final address is retrieved. If there is no such record, the request fails. Otherwise, such a record is removed from the bucket. At this point, we can check the possibility of merging the bucket with its parent or its child.

If a bucket to be merged is both a leaf and the youngest child, and if space permits, then the bucket can be merged easily into its parent bucket. This happens when a record is deleted from a parent bucket whose youngest child is a leaf, or when a record is deleted from a bucket which is both a leaf and the youngest child. In this case, the address of the parent bucket is removed from the overflow filter, and the addresses of buckets added after the child bucket are decremented by one each.

For example, deleting records 37 and 22 from Fig-2(b) results in Fig-3(a). Since bucket 6 is a leaf and the youngest (only) child of bucket 4, we can merge bucket 6 into bucket 4 and remove the address 4 from the overflow filter, as shown in Fig-3(b). Note that we do not merge bucket 4 with bucket 2, though they are also in the parent-child relationship.

Merging a bucket which is not the youngest child or not a leaf is more complex. For example, deleting records 13 and 46 from Fig-3(b) results in Fig-4(a). Bucket 4, which is not the youngest child, can be merged into bucket 2, moving record 28 to the parent bucket. But we can't remove the address 2 from the position 1 of the overflow filter, because it contains information on the depth of split functions for its younger siblings. Thus we mark such an address by negating it, as in Fig-4(b). Bucket 4 is released to the storage pool, and can be reused later. Note that we have used the scheme to count addresses from 1, not 0.

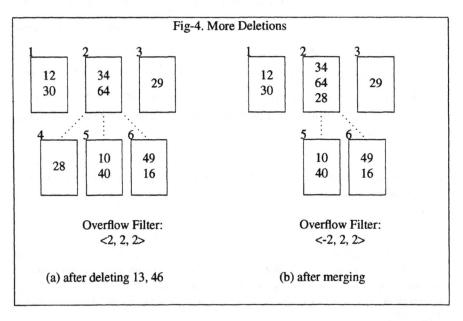

Fig-4. More Deletions

Overflow Filter:
<2, 2, 2>

(a) after deleting 13, 46

Overflow Filter:
<-2, 2, 2>

(b) after merging

Merging a bucket which is the youngest child but not a leaf follows the same procedures. A negative member, *e.g.* -*j*, of the overflow filter represents that there had been an overflow on bucket *j*, but the child bucket, which is not both a leaf and the youngest child, was later merged back into bucket *j*. If bucket *j* is an initial or an intermediate address for a key, and the next intermediate address is its child bucket, then *j* is the final address for the key.

We released bucket 4 to the storage fool in Fig-4(b), leaving a hole in the address space. This is not a problem because bucket 4 is empty and need not be accessed anyhow. When another overflow occurs to bucket 2 in Fig-4(b), record 28 will be rehashed to a new child bucket 4, and *OF* [1] gets negated from -2 to 2.

4. Performance Characteristics

We analyzed the performance characteristics of filtered hashing in terms of space utilization, access time, and the size of the overflow filter. We also implemented the algorithm in the C language, ran various tests, and measured the performance figures to compare them with those of the analysis results.

4.1 Space Utilization

The behavior of data buckets in filtered hashing is very similar to the behaviors of leaf pages in dynamic hashing [5] and extendible hashing [6]. We can determine the average space utilization for filtered hashing from the analysis result of extendible hashing [7]. Assuming uniform distribution of the hashed values for the keys, the average number of buckets to store n records is $\dfrac{n}{b \times \ln 2}$, when a bucket holds up to b records. Since the minimum number of buckets to store n records is $\dfrac{n}{b}$, the average space utilization is $\ln 2 = 69.3\%$.

The length of the overflow filter in filtered hashing, L_{OF}, is the same as the number of overflow buckets, which is $\dfrac{n}{b \times \ln 2} - n_0$ on the average, where n_0 is the initial size of the file in buckets. This estimation turned out to be quite close to actual results as shown in Section 4.4.

4.2 Access Time

As described earlier, the number of disk accesses to retrieve a record is guaranteed to be one, whether successful or not. Thus the expected time to retrieve a record, $T_{retrieve}$, is:

$$T_{retrieve} = T_{cpu\_a} + T_{disk\_r} + T_{cpu\_r}$$

In the reverse order, T_{cpu_r} is the time required to read a record from a bucket after the bucket has been located on the disk. T_{disk_r} is the time required to locate a bucket on the disk, which is determined by the mechanical factors of the disk drive such as a rotational delay and a seek time. T_{disk_r} is typically on the order of 10 *milliseconds*, so $T_{disk\_r} \gg T_{cpu\_r}$.

T_{cpu_a} is the time required for the CPU to determine the address of a bucket by hashing the key and searching the overflow list:

$$T_{cpu\_a} = T_{hash\_fn} + T_{overflow} + T_{split\_fn} \times D_{overflow}$$

where T_{hash_fn} is the time to calculate a hash function, $T_{overflow}$ is the time to scan the overflow filter, T_{split_fn} is the time to calculate a split function, and $D_{overflow}$ is the average depth of overflows.

Time to scan the overflow filter and determine the final address of a key, $T_{overflow}$, is fast, even when there are many overflows on the path to locate a bucket. If we assume that the average *depth* of overflow is $D_{overflow}$, and that there are L_{OF} entries in the overflow filter, the number of entries to be examined appears to be $O\ (D_{overflow} \times L_{OF})$. However, the maximum number of entries to be examined is just L_{OF}. Since the overflow filter is maintained in the order of overflow occurrences, and no child bucket gets overflowed before its parent, no entry for a child bucket is ahead of the entry for its parent bucket. Thus we need to scan the overflow filter only once no matter what the depth of overflows is. Thus,

$$T_{cpu\_a} = T_{hash\_fn} + T_{check} \times L_{OF} + T_{split\_fn} \times D_{overflow}$$

where T_{check} is the time to check the value of an entry on the overflow filter, and $L_{overflow}$ is the average length of the overflow filter.

On a typical machine, T_{hash_fn}, T_{check}, and T_{split_fn} take a couple of instructions each, as discussed in Section 3.1. For $n \le n_0$, L_{OF} and $D_{overflow}$ are 0 or close to 0.

$$T_{cpu\_a} \approx T_{hash\_fn}$$

For a large n,

$$T_{cpu\_a} \approx T_{check} \times (\frac{n}{b \times \ln 2} - n_0)$$

Assuming that T_{check} takes about 5 instructions on a 10 MIPS machine, which is rather conservative,

$$T_{cpu\_a} \approx 0.5 microsec \times L_{OF}$$

T_{cpu_a} of 10 msec will be still smaller than T_{disk_r} for the overflow filter with as many as 20,000 entries.

The expected time to insert a record depends on whether it was necessary to split a bucket. T_{insert_1}, time to insert a record without a split, is:

$$T_{insert\_1} = T_{cpu\_a} + T_{disk\_r} + T_{cpu\_w} + T_{disk\_w}$$

where T_{cpu_w} and T_{disk_w} is the time required to write a bucket to the disk. Since $T_{disk\_r} \approx T_{disk\_w} \approx T_{disk}$, $T_{cpu\_a} \ll T_{disk}$, and $T_{cpu\_w} \ll T_{disk}$,

$$T_{insert\_1} \approx 2 \times T_{disk}$$

T_{insert_2}, time to insert a record with a split, is:

$$T_{insert\_2} = T_{cpu\_a} + T_{disk\_r} + b \times T_{split\_fn} \times D_{overflow} + (T_{cpu\_w} + T_{disk\_w}) \times 2$$

where b is the bucket size and $D_{overflow}$ is the average depth of overflows. Since $b \times T_{split\_fn} \times D_{overflow} \ll T_{disk}$,

$$T_{insert\_2} \approx 3 \times T_{disk}$$

Likewise, the expected time to delete a record depends on whether it was necessary to merge buckets after deleting a record. T_{delete}, time to delete a record without a merge, is the same as T_{insert_1}. Thus,

$$T_{delete\_1} \approx 2 \times T_{disk}$$

T_{delete_2}, time to delete a record with a merge, is more complex:

$$T_{delete\_2} = T_{delete\_1} + T_{merge}$$

where T_{merge} involves reading its parent bucket as described in Section 3.3, copying the records, if any, from the child bucket to its parent bucket, adjusting the overflow filter, and write the parent bucket back to the disk. Since CPU time for miscellaneous operations are negligible,

$$T_{merge} \approx T_{disk\_r} + T_{disk\_w} \approx 2 \times T_{disk}$$

which leads to $T_{delete\_2} \approx 4 \times T_{disk}$.

4.3 Size of the Overflow Filter

The size of each entry in the overflow filter is dependent on the the total size of a file. For a file with up to 32,767 buckets, each entry takes 2 bytes. For a bigger file, each entry may take up to 4 bytes, which can handle up to about 2×10^9 buckets or about $8 \times 10^{12} = 8$ Tera bytes for the bucket size of 4,096. But the size of the overflow filter depends on the number of overflows, not the size of the entire file. Hence the overflow filter is small enough to fit into the main memory for most applications. For example, the overflow filter of only 32 K bytes can accommodate up to 64 MBytes of overflow buckets assuming the bucket size of 4 K bytes.

4.4 Measured Results

We actually implemented the algorithm of filtered hashing in a C program, though the detailed description of the algorithm was omitted from this paper due to space limitation. We used a random number generator to simulate the key values, and ran the program with the n_0 vales of 10, 200, 500, and 1000 buckets each, where n_0 is the initial number of buckets in the file and the bucket size (b) is 10. Then we measured the performance figures such as space utilization, the length of the overflow filter, and the depth of overflows. The following figures show the test results obtained from these tests.

Fig-5. Lenght of the Overflow Filter

initial size	# of records	5000	6000	7000	8000	9000	10000
10	Expected	708	848	993	1141	1256	1393
	Measured	693	834	1001	1142	1264	1361
200	Expected	521	654	790	942	1096	1234
	Measured	516	649	776	939	1102	1229
500	Expected	229	347	484	631	779	936
	Measured	213	364	497	608	741	901
1000	Measured	0	0	0	0	0	0

The first graph in Fig-6 shows that space utilization is very close to 70%, as estimated in Section 4.1, and remains so over a wide range of changes. The table in Fig-5 and

96

Fig-6. Measured Results ($b = 10$)

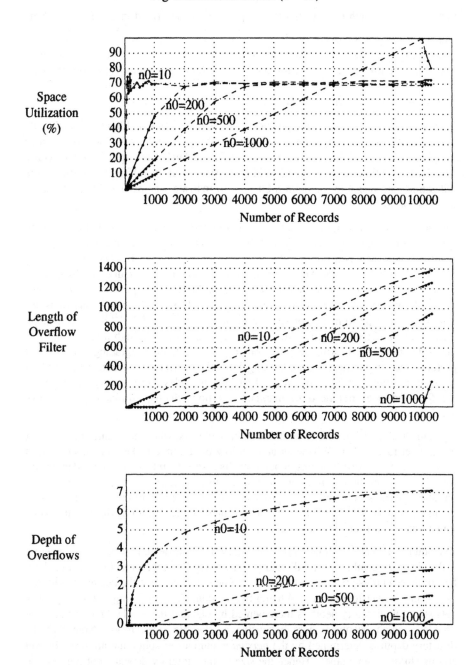

the second graph in Fig-6 show the length of the overflow filter, where the measured figures closely match the values of $\dfrac{n}{b \times \ln 2} - n_0$ as described in Section 4.1. Note that the length of the overflow filter remains 0 even after inserting 10,000 records when the file was reorganized with the initial size of 1000 blocks using a perfect hash function. The third graph shows the depth of overflows averaged over all the records.

5. Comparisons with Other Methods

In this section, we compare the performance characteristics of filtered hashing with other variable-size hashing schemes. Virtual hashing [8] doubles the file size when an overflow occurs, and the records in the overflowed bucket are split into two with a new hash function for the bigger address space. But it suffers from low space utilization, and needs to maintain a bit map to indicate whether each bucket had an overflow or not.

Linear hashing [9] also splits a bucket when an overflow occurs. But the bucket being split is not the one which encountered the overflow, but the one marked by the *split pointer* which increases one by one from the initial value of 0. The record which caused an overflow to a bucket is put into an overflow bucket chained to the original bucket, until the split pointer reaches the original bucket and splits all records in the chain of the original and the overflow buckets. There are several variations for achieving better performance or space utilization [10] [11] [12] [13] [14] [15] [16]. Though linear hashing extends the file size by one bucket at a time through maintaining only the split pointer, it still depends on overflow chains degrading the overall performance. In contrast, filtered hashing splits the overflowed bucket, not the bucket selected in a linear order. Thus filtered hashing provides more orderly expansion of the file, and does not need to maintain overflow chains, eliminating extra disk accesses.

Dynamic hashing [5] maintains an index on hashed keys, where each entry of the index is a pointer to a bucket. Whenever an overflow occurs in a bucket, the bucket is split into two, and the corresponding index entry is also split into two. The index entries form a forest of binary trees while undergoing a sequence of overflows. Some variations of the scheme were also proposed [17] [18]. The size of the forest depends on the number of buckets in the file. For a reasonably large file, going through the index forest usually costs an extra disk access.

Extendible hashing [6] [7] maintains a directory of 2^d entries on hashed keys, where d is the directory depth. Several directory entries may share the same bucket, and about half of those entries are changed to point to a new bucket when the bucket is split into two when an overflow occurs. When a bucket pointed to by a single directory entry gets split, the directory depth is incremented by one and the whole directory must be doubled, which becomes more expensive as the file size grows. Note that the directory depth is determined by the *maximum* number of splits that an initial bucket and its childrens encounter. Hence the size of the directory depends not only on the size of the entire file, but also on the worst case of overflow patterns. For example, the directory size of extendible hashing for the example of Fig-2(b) would be 48 entries $(= 3 \times 2^4)$, compared with 4 entries for filtered hashing.

While the dynamic and extendible hashing schemes maintain a directory structure for all the buckets in the file, filtered hashing stores only the addresses of the buckets that experienced overflows. Thus the filter is usually small enough to fit into the main memory, and the access time to retrieve a record can be guaranteed to be just one disk access as described in Section 4.2. The time to insert or delete a record is also bounded by between 2 and 4 disk accesses, while rearranging the directory structure in dynamic or extendible hashing can be very costly.

Another advantage of filtered hashing is its flexibility to reduce or even eliminate the overflow filter through reorganization, when convenient, using a new hash function h_0 with a larger file size n_0, as demonstrated by the example with the initial size n_0 of 1000 in Figures 5 and 6. Hence we can achieve excellent performance characteristics with high space utilization without maintaining a directory structure all the time. Even when a file is reorganized with extended or dynamic hashing, its directory size does not change much because it still depends on the size of the entire file. For the same example above, the directory size will be 1000 entries even for the perfect case of no overflow.

A method to maintain information in the main memory only for the overflowed buckets, not for all the buckets, has been proposed earlier [19]. The proposal uses perfect hashing to guarantee a single access retrieval by maintaining a key, a pointer to an overflow bucket, the number of overflow buckets, and a parameter of a perfect hash function in an internal table. It also relies on linear hashing to handle dynamic growth of the file. Compared with the proposal, filtered hashing is simpler, requires a smaller amount of information on overflow buckets, and handles dynamic growth and shrinkage of the file better.

Another types of dynamic hashing are based on the signature values and separators combined with linear hashing or spiral storage [20] [21]. Every bucket in a file is associated with a value called separator, and the table of separators is kept in the main memory for rapid access. When an overflow occurs to a bucket, the bucket is split by moving some records whose signature values are bigger than the separator value to be adjusted accordingly. Note that these schemes need to maintain the separator values for all the buckets, and they can suffer from clustering (in case of linear hashing), or degeneration (in case of spiral storage). Filtered hashing maintains the overflow filter only for the buckets that encountered overflows, handles the problem of non-uniform distribution better, and is more efficient in address calculations.

6. Conclusions

Filtered hashing is a new type of variable-size hashing scheme to combine useful characteristics of the directory and the directoryless schemes. Until there occurs an overflow, filtered hashing works in the same way as conventional fixed-size hashing, like a directoryless scheme. When an overflow or an underflow occurs, a bucket is split into two or merged with another, like directory schemes. Unlike directory schemes, filtered hashing does not require index entries for every bucket in a file. Only a list of overflow addresses, termed *overflow filter*, is maintained to represent the history of the changes that occurred to the file.

Since the overflow filter contains only the addresses of the buckets that encountered overflows, it is usually small enough to reside in the main memory even for a high degree of volatility. Then the number of disk accesses to retrieve a record is guaranteed to be just one, which is often difficult in other variable-size hashing schemes. The cost of inserting or deleting a record is also bounded by between 2 and 4 disk accesses. If the overflow filter grows too big due to excessive changes, the same hashing scheme can be applied recursively to the filter itself for a rapid access, as will be discussed elsewhere due to space limitation.

There are several variations for this scheme that can be considered to enhance the performance. For example, it is possible to maintain the overflow filter in a randomly accessible format. Various hashing methods are obvious candidates for this scheme, and filtered hashing itself can be applied recursively to the hashed filter using the *address* as the key (termed *recursive filtered hashing* or *filtered hashing with a filter-hashed filter*). For a higher space utilization, we may make the size of overflow buckets smaller than the regular buckets and use a weighted split function (*partial expansion*). We may also delay splitting a bucket by employing overflow chains, if an extra disk access is acceptable (*deferred splitting*). Discussions on the details of these enhancements are beyond the scope of this paper due to space limitation.

It is also possible to reorganize the file with a bigger address space at a convenient time to achieve the optimal performance of a static hashing, *e.g.* using a perfect hashing scheme [22] [23]. And the file continues to adapt to dynamic changes later on. Therefore, filtered hashing combined with periodic reorganization can provide optimal performance and high space utilization even when the size of the file dynamically grows or shrinks to a large degree.

References

1. V. Lum, P. Yuen, M. Dodd: *Key-to address transform techniques: A fundamental performance study on large existing formatted files*, Communications of ACM, Vol. 14, No. 4, Apr. 1971, pp. 228-239.

2. D. Severance, R. Duhne: *A Practitioner's Guide to Addressing Algorithms*, Communications of ACM, Vol. 19, No. 6, June 1976, pp. 314-326.

3. M. Ramakrishna: *Hashing in Practice, Analysis of Hashing and Universal Hashing*, ACM SIGMOD Record, Vol. 17, No. 3, Sep. 1988, pp. 191-199.

4. R. Enbody, H. Du: *Dynamic Hashing Schemes*, ACM Computing Surveys, Vol. 20, No. 2, June, 1988, pp. 85-113.

5. P. Larson: *Dynamic Hashing*, BIT, 18 (1978), pp. 184-201.

6. R. Fagin, J. Nievergelt, N. Pippenger, H. Strong: *Extendible Hashing - A Fast Access Method for Dynamic Files*, ACM Transactions on Database Systems, Vol. 4, No. 3, Sep. 1979, pp. 315-344.

7. H. Mendelson: *Analysis of Extendible Hashing*, IEEE Transactions on Software Engineering, Vol. 8, No. 6, Nov. 1982, pp. 611-619.

8. W. Litwin: *Virtual Hashing: A Dynamically Changing Hashing*, Proceedings of the Conference on Very Large Databases, 1978, pp. 517-523.

9. W. Litwin: *Linear Hashing: A New Tool For File And Table Addressing*, Proceedings of the Conference on Very Large Databases, 1980, pp. 212-223.

10. P. Larson: *Linear Hashing with Partial Expansions*, Proceedings of the Conference on Very Large Databases, 1980, pp. 224-232

11. P. Larson: *Performance Analysis of Linear Hashing with Partial Expansions*, ACM Transactions on Database Systems, Vol. 7, No. 4, Dec. 1982, pp. 566-587.

12. P. Larson: *Linear Hashing with Overflow-Handling by Linear Probing*, ACM Transactions on Database Systems, Vol. 10, No. 1, Mar. 1985, pp. 75-89.

13. K. Kawagoe: *Modified Dynamic Hashing*, Proceedings of ACM SIGMOD International Conference on Management of Data, May 1985, pp. 201-213.

14. J. Mullen: *Unified Dynamic Hashing*, Proceedings of the Conference on Very Large Databases, Aug. 1984, pp. 473-480.

15. K. Ramamohanarao, J. Lloyd: *Dynamic Hashing Schemes*, The Computer Journal, Vol. 25, No. 4, 1982, pp. 478-485.

16. K. Ramamohanarao, R. Sacks-Davis: *Recursive Linear Hashing*, ACM Transactions on Database Systems, Vol. 9, No. 3, Sep. 1984, pp. 369-391.

17. M. Scholl: *New File Organizations Based on Dynamic Hashing*, ACM Transactions on Database Systems, Vol. 6, No. 1, Mar. 1981, pp. 194-211.

18. E. Veklerov: *Analysis of Dynamic Hashing with Deferred Splitting*, ACM Transactions on Database Systems, Vol. 10, No. 1, Mar. 1985, pp. 90-96.

19. M. Ramakrishna, W. Tout: *DDynamic External Hashing with Guaranteed Single Access Retrieval*, Proceedings of the International Conference on Foundations of Data Organization and Algorithms, 1989, pp. 187-201.

20. P. Larson: *Linear Hashing with Separators - A Dynamic Hashing Scheme Achieving One-Access Retrieval*, ACM Transactions on Database Systems, Vol. 13, No. 3, Sep. 1988, pp. 366-388.

21. F. Cesarini, G. Soda: *A Dynamic Hash Method with Signature*, ACM Transactions on Database Systems, Vol. 16, No. 2, Jun. 1991, pp. 309-337.

22. R. Sprugnoli: *Perfect hash functions: A single probe retrieving method for static sets*, Communications of ACM, Vol. 20, No. 11, Nov. 1977, pp. 841-850

23. M. Ramakrishna, P. Larson: *File Organization Using Composite Perfect Hashing*, ACM Transactions on Database Systems, Vol. 14, No. 2, Jun. 1989, pp. 231-263.

Design and Implementation of DDH: A Distributed Dynamic Hashing Algorithm

Robert Devine

University of California at Berkeley
EECS Department, Computer Science Division
devine@cs.berkeley.edu

Abstract. DDH extends the idea of dynamic hashing algorithms to distributed systems. DDH spreads data across multiple servers in a network using a novel autonomous location discovery algorithm that learns the bucket locations instead of using a centralized directory.
We describe the design and implementation of the basic DDH algorithm using networked computers. Performance results show that the prototype of DDH hashing is roughly equivalent to conventional single-node hashing implementations when compared with CPU time or elapsed time. Finally, possible improvements are suggested to the basic DDH algorithm for increased reliability and robustness.

1 Introduction

Rapidly plunging hardware costs and increasing performance of CPUs and networks mean that future file and database systems are likely to be constructed as networked clusters of nodes. Algorithms should be devised to work in these environments. This paper describes the design and implementation of a distributed hashing algorithm.

Quick record retrieval is obviously crucial to overall file and database performance. The design of efficient retrieval algorithms has been a rich research area in computer science since the earliest days. Hashing algorithms can be classified as either static or dynamic. A static hash algorithm uses an constant sized hash table. A dynamic hash algorithm differs from a static hash algorithm because the table can grow and shrink from its initially allocated size to accommodate the continued insertion and deletion of records.

DDH (Distributed Dynamic Hashing) is an algorithm that gracefully expands and contracts without a central controller. A variable number of clients and servers participate in the

The performance of conventional, single-node hashing is determined by its CPU processing time and the number of I/Os needed. However for distributed hashing, the performance of messages must also be considered. Misdirected messages in DDH are possible but are shown to be minor if a local "hint" directory is used to provide a mapping of hash buckets to servers.

The paper is organized as follows: we present the design and implementation of DDH in sections 2 and 3, show the performance results in section 4, and conclude in section 5.

2 Goals for Distributed Hashing

The goals desired for distributed hash algorithms are listed below. High performance is of course a general goal. Other goals are certainly possible; Section 5 suggests several others. The above goals are used to evaluate and develop distributed algorithms. Section 3 tells how these goals are realized in DDH.

1. Location of distributed buckets and servers

   Two location requirements must be met. First a method is needed for locating candidate nodes that are eligible to participate in the distributed hash structure. The second requirement is to map a hash bucket to a server at run-time.

   If we restrict the selection of nodes to those that are within a few multiples of an access to a locally mounted disk, then all nodes that are within 50 milliseconds average network time away can be used. Nodes not on the same LAN can be used. From [3] it is shown that even many computers on the Internet wide area network have a mean response latency of under 50 milliseconds. While this fact argues for having a widely distributed hash tables, the concerns of administration boundaries and network overload (especially during bucket splits and merges) argue against extending a hash table distributed beyond the locally administered boundaries.

   A directory service can be used to identify which nodes can participate and converting their names to a network address. This information is relatively static because changes happen on a human time-scale as nodes are added or removed.

   Simple directory services are ill suited for dealing with the second requirement of tracking the rapidly changing bucket location information. Moreover if multiple directory services are used they must provide a consistent view of the bucket mappings. Because bucket splits and merges are happening at execution speed, the bucket directory problem must be handled dynamically.

2. Collision resolution

   There are several possible policies for handling filled buckets. The bucket could be temporarily expanded; records could overflow to an overflow bucket or a "buddy bucket" or the bucket can be immediately split.

   The effect of choosing one of the collision resolution methods is reflected in the overall performance and efficiency of the algorithm. When overflows are employed for a bucket that has a high rate of collisions, that bucket becomes unbalanced with respect to the average bucket. Alternately the policy of splitting evens out the load but may cause an imbalance in other ways such as an increased load on a single server.

   Expanding the bucket size is undesirable because it leads to more complex algorithms. Requiring permission before splitting means that agreement must be achieved using non-local information. Splitting immediately, while simpler, may cause complication in other areas, notably in the bucket location algorithm.

3. Load balancing across servers

   Ideally, no server is responsible for more than its proportional share of the total data size. This principle can be enforced by actively checking the local load level against the global load level and then performing adaptive load balancing to ameliorate hot spots. A naive approach would be to designate a load controller that partitions work among servers according to fairness criteria.

   The need for scalability obviates the naive approach. Any centralized solution would soon become a bottleneck as the hash table grows in size.

4. Parallel insertion and retrievals

   It is desirable to support multiple concurrent accesses to the same distributed hash table. Multiple readers can be easily supported because no changes are occurring. However, in a mixture of multiple readers and writers, the servers must institute a consistency control, such as locking to serialize access to its portion of the hash table.

   Each individual server should use the necessary consistency protocols to guarantee correctness when multiple clients are inserting records. In addition, if an insertion causes a split, the affected servers must mutually ensure consistency of their parts of the distributed table.

2.1 Previous Work

Multiple dynamic hashing methods have been proposed for single nodes with either a single processor [5, 2, 6] or with multiple processors [10].

LH* [7] is one proposal for a distributed hashing algorithm. It extends the notion of linear hashing [6] to allow multiple nodes in a network to participate in the same distributed data structure.

LH* is a directoryless algorithm like the single node version of linear hashing. It locates buckets through one of two algorithms based on the current split level and the bucket number. A client maintains what it thinks is the current split level and highest numbered bucket. Because the table can grow or shrink without the client knowing, the actual bucket may be located elsewhere.

As proposed in [7], LH* has some drawbacks:

First, each server has only one bucket. The limit is required for bucket location calculations. However, this can be easily overcome by using a logical server numbering scheme that maps to the actual server number (a round robin assignment would work fine). The larger problem is that a single bucket per server implies large buckets that result in a high cost to split a single bucket so each server should hold multiple, small buckets that are less expensive to split.

Second, splits must be ordered for the clients. Because the clients have no directory to allow unbalanced splitting, all splits are required to follow the bucket numbering order within each level. The bookkeeping of this ordering requires that a server send at least one more message than needed to just convey the split records. While the overhead of sending agreement messages with every split, the problem becomes most acute when dealing with failures. If the message controlling the ordering is lost or the server that owns the current split token crashes, all other servers are affected because they can not split until a new token is regenerated. This is analogous to the complexity of token ring networks compared to Ethernet.

Third, when multiple clients are inserting records there exists a timing window where it is possible that a client requires more than the expected maximum of two forwarding messages. If the client is slower than the rate of bucket splittings, the client's view of the LH* hash table will lag the actual configuration. While it is true that only two hash levels can exist at a single time, client actions are not time synchronous. Therefore it may see more than two versions of the hash table as it evolves. Each version may cause client addressing errors.

Fourth and most important, determining when a bucket can be split is not an autonomous decision that can be made by the affected server. The ordering of splits is imposed on the buckets to support the directoryless character. This restriction in inherent in LH* because of the need for all buckets to be determined from one of two bucket location functions. Several undesirable characteristics result from this. First, to strictly order the splits, the paper proposes a special split coordinator that participates in the bucket split operation. This is contrary to the goals of no load balance and high availability. Second is that buckets that are not allowed to immediately split must handle overflows locally. This leads to poorer performance and hot spots. Finally, because all buckets on a level must split before the next level can start to be split, this causes premature splitting of non-full buckets.

3 Distributed Dynamic Hashing

In this section, we introduce the design of DDH. The guiding philosophy for DDH is local autonomy. No changing global information guides the actions of individual servers; each server decides for itself when to split or merge buckets. Clearly some common, constant policy must be shared by all serves to avoid anarchy but the policy is constant can be easily coded into all servers. An interesting research question is what minimum level of shared policy is required yet still preserve a collaborative effort that is necessary for a distributed data structure.

A DDH server program runs at every server node that is participating in the distributed hash algorithm. It is responsible for controlling the storage of its portion of the entire table. Each server maintains the following information about each bucket: the bucket number, its split-level and the contents of the bucket. The server is responsible for handling all of the messages that a bucket may receive. This includes forwarding requests to another server, sending the appropriate response to a request and analyzing the replies to its own requests from other servers. Each DDH servers maintains a small local directory to store the bucket to server mapping. However, all DDH clients do not need to use such a directory but it is advantageous if they use one (performance results given in Section 4 show why).

A client calls the DDH library routines to do the insert or retrieve operation. A client program computes the hash key for the record, locates the *likely* bucket for that hash key, and then sends the request to the server that owns the bucket.

Each server maintains a directory containing location information about other server's buckets. The directory is not exact for remote buckets but gives likely location. Upon receiving any request concerning a data item from a client, the server determines if it is the correct recipient of the message by comparing the data item's key to the key range for its buckets. If the server discovers that it is not the right one, then it forwards the message to the correct recipient. Otherwise the operation is performed locally. A reply is sent from the server to the client indicating whether or not the operation was successful. The reply contains the current hash level of the bucket at which the operation was eventually performed. This allows the client to apply the DDH algorithm to update its local perception of the hash table.

3.1 Distributed Hash Table

The distributed hash table in DDH is a distributed main memory data structure composed of buckets spread over one or more servers. Each bucket holds up to some fixed number of records. It is not required that all servers use the same bucket size although There is one or more server processes per node, although it is expected that the usual arrangement is one server per node for the best performance. Client processes send requests to servers to insert or retrieve a record.

Bucket addressing is based upon binary radix trees, or *tries*. At split level N, the lowest order N bits are used to form the bucket number. As an example, suppose a record's key hashes to the value 0x81F0639C. Since 'C' hex is 1011 binary, if the current level is 1 then the bucket number is 1. If the level is 2 or 3, the bucket number is 3. And if the level is 4, the record must be in the bucket number 11 (= 'C' hex).

The syntax of bucket numbering is written as the pair (level, bucket number). When the algorithm begins there is a single bucket, numbered as bucket $(0,0)$, that matches all hash values. When it fills, its contents are split into two buckets by using bit 0 of the hash value; these are then buckets $(1, 0)$ and $(1, 1)$. In general, a level L bucket split uses bit L of the hash value to move records into its child buckets. When bucket (L, N) splits, it forms the children buckets $(L+1, N)$ and $(L + 1, N + 2^L)$.

Bucket and Server Location: Bucket location is described by the tuple *(number of servers, server distribution function, hash function, key, current hash table configuration)*. The first two items are defined for the entire table and must be known by all servers and clients. A client chooses the *hash function* that generates a *key* for each record. The fifth field, *current hash table configuration*, is changed with every insert or delete operation so it is known definitively only by the client and servers that were involved in the operation; all other nodes must discover the configuration.

A server when starting, knows its logical server number and the total number of servers. A fresh client without any location knowledge starts with the server for bucket (0, 0) because that is the only bucket whose existence is guaranteed. Thereafter a client progressively learns the current configuration by making requests that are either correct or are wrong but come back with the correct location information. The client sends requests to the server it believes owns the bucket but will adjust its directory if told that the guess was incorrect.

Two approaches are possible for the client to use the bucket-to-server mappings it has learned. First, a client can maintain a directory of mappings that it has learned from previous messages. Then future messages use this directory to select servers. Second, a client can use heuristics to guide guesses. For example, based upon the current average split level information a client has gleaned from previous message replies, a client can produce a reasonable guess by using that level for the next message. Performance trade-offs are compared in Section 4.

Likewise two approaches are possible to implement the address correction protocol. The client can have its incorrect guesses returned to it so that it has to retry a different server or the server can silently forward the message to the correct server. If it is the case that the client expects a reply within a bounded time else it will time-out and resend the message, then it is better for the client to retry to avoid time-outs caused by too long server forwarding. DDH chooses the method of requiring the server to forward misdirected messages.

Collision Resolution: When a bucket is filled, whether to split the bucket is entirely a local decision. Unlike Linear Hashing [6], no order of bucket splitting is necessary. Unlike Extensible Hashing [2], the entire table is not split as one operation. Splitting is an autonomous operation that does not require global knowledge. Skewed data can therefore be efficiently handled with the minimum number of split buckets and no special overflow areas.

The implementation of DDH practices an uncontrolled splitting policy. The splitting server sends a message to the new site server that will manage the new bucket. If this server accepts it, a series of messages are sent to the server with the split records. Multiple records are sent in the same split message as a performance optimization.

Load Balancing: There are only data servers in DDH unlike LH* that used an index or split manager. Because its buckets can be small, DDH achieves a fine-grained load sharing across servers. When starting, all requests go to bucket 0 but as the number of buckets increases, all servers soon get roughly the same number of buckets.

Parallel Operations: Multiple clients can insert and retrieve records in parallel with each other. From the viewpoint of message reception, all servers operate atomically. Clients do not see the internal state of servers where inconsistent operations may result. Rather, the consistency points are defined by servers as they send and receive messages. All server operations are locally serialized through complete processing of a message before starting another. Multiple servers synchronize their behavior when dealing with page splits.

3.2 DDH Networking Implementation

The three basic services offered by the DDH session layer implementation are packet encoding/decoding, retransmission, and response matching. As only simple data types are used, the packet is rebuilt each time it is sent.

Because it is unlikely that purely homogeneous clusters of systems would be using DDH, it was implemented as a portable session level service. All communication to the DDH servers uses the Internet User Datagram Protocol (UDP) [8] datagram service and messages are encoded in network byte order.

The DDH network protocol is designed to the request / response model. Requests messages are sent by clients to servers, and also by servers to other servers during bucket splits and merges. If the request is sent to the wrong server, the server puts the network address of the requester inside the packet and forwards it to the correct server. The receiving server uses this address to send back a reply directly to the requesting client. As network failures may cause one or more packets to be lost, all operations are self-contained and idempotent. Messages are retransmitted if no reply is received before a time-out.

Each packet consists of a fixed format header followed by a specified number of (key, value) pairs. Both the key and value are preceded by a short word containing the length. All integer values are converted if necessary before transport to the network byte order. The following request messages are supported: RETRIEVE, INSERT, DELETE, and SPLIT_BUCKET. Only servers send SPLIT_BUCKET requests other servers before performing a split or merge operation and to prepare it for a bulk data transfer using INSERT messages. These requests result in one of these responses: DUPKEY, ERROR, NOTFOUND, and SUCCESS.

4 Performance Experiments

To show the implementation of distributed hashing, the application of a phone service "white pages" lookup for finding a phone numbers is used. Given one of a large number of names, the phone number is returned. Up to 50,000 pairs of names and phone numbers were used. Each name was less than 32 bytes long and served as the key field.

We compare the performance of the following hashing packages:

1. DDH – the distributed hashing algorithm introduced in this paper
2. NDBM – the single node hashing package from AT&T [1]
3. SELYIT – the single node linear hashing package from [9]
4. GDBM – the single node dynamic hashing package from GNU freeware

4.1 Environment

Multiple DECstation 5000/133 workstations, an approximately 20 SPECmark machine, with ample memory (at least 16 megabytes) were used. The systems were running ULTRIX 4.2a, a variant of BSD UNIX. Each workstation communicated with either a 10 megabits/second Ethernet or a 100 megabits/second FDDI LAN.

Program execution was timed using the operating system's `getrusage()` system call to record actual resources used. The timer was started before any calls were made to the hash packages and stopped immediately afterwards to remove from consideration all of the normal process initialization overhead from the performance measurement. Tests were run twice to allow all code pages to be fetched from the disk so that no start-up overhead affected this area. and were run on idle systems at off hours to minimize any possible interference from the network. However, testing ran at the "multi-user" level rather than "single user" so that some interference from system level daemons running in the background was possible. It was necessary to run at the normal level so that the network could be used.

4.2 Time to Insert and Retrieve N Records

Records were loaded using the different hash packages. During the first phase of the test, every record in the test was read from an on-disk file, hashed, and inserted into the table. During the second phase, the records is reread and every record is retrieved. Note that there is a high probability of finding the record in memory for each of the single node hashing packages.

All times given below are the total time to insert and retrieve the same N records. The elapsed time needed to run the tests is the complete time needed to run the program from the shell prompt. The values for 30K, 40K, and 50K are not shown for GDBM because those times became quite large and would have dominated the graph.

The graph in Figure 1 shows that DDH is comparable to other hashing packages that operate in a single process on the same node. This experiment presented the disk-based hashing package in the best light because all disk blocks were likely to be in memory. Hence the only I/Os performed were during the flushing of blocks to disk. In contrast, the DDH numbers are both the best and the worst because the messages have to be sent to a remote node in either case.

There were several surprises in the performance results. First, the widely different elapsed times between the SelYit and the GDMB package are because the SelYit package did not flush its dirtied pages while the GDBM explicitly called `sync()` system call to flush its directory pages from the ULTRIX file system buffer cache to disk. In addition, the GDBM package used an extensible hashing algorithm [2] that doubled its directory size periodically. This explains the "knee" in the curves above the 10,000 name pairs point for GDBM. Finally, the user time for DDH is dwarfed by the system time with the ratio being roughly 1:4. If DDH were run on a system with operating system with higher performing messaging, the elapsed level would be lower.

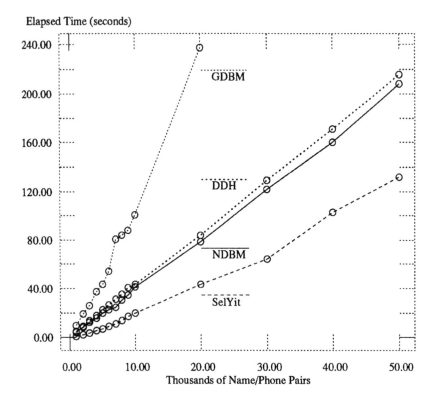

Fig. 1. Elapsed Time to Insert and Retrieve N Records

4.3 Bucket Location Strategies

The question of whether the DDH method of autonomous splitting causes the clients to make frequent addressing mistakes was examined. The experiments in this paper used a round-robin distribution to map buckets to servers but others are possible.

The number of server messages caused by addressing errors is also related to the number of split levels – i.e., because each bucket may have split to a new server, its current state is unknown unless a probe is made.

Three server locating strategies were compared. Table 1 shows the number of messages that result from addressing errors for a fresh client retrieving records from a 249 bucket hash table (9000 records stored in buckets holding a maximum of 64 entries) on 3 servers. The experiment used 3 servers because the value 3 a non-multiple of 2 and therefore causes every bucket split to send records to a different server.

The *heuristic* algorithms are based on a guess of the bucket's split level. The simple heuristic just uses the previous reply's split level to guess the next request's split level. The complex heuristic uses a *moving average* of all previous

Table 1. Bucket Addressing Errors

Strategy	Extra Messages for 249 buckets
Heuristic (simple)	1063
Heuristic (complex)	627
Incremental	62
Quick Start	9

replies so that the average would gradually converge on the actual size. Both heuristics assume that the hash table is reasonably well balanced. Like Linear Hashing [6], these are directoryless and neither store definite information about the whole hash table. Therefore they constantly makes the same mistakes and produce more errors than do the directory based strategies. Moreover, the mistakes made are more often because they result from individual record access unlike the directory strategies that use bucket granularity.

A client using the *Incremental Convergence* algorithm maintains a directory of definitive bucket locations the client receives from servers. Additionally, the location of a bucket can be inferred from the definitive knowledge of a sibling bucket. This strategy will incorrectly guess the bucket addresses about 25% (in the above table, 62/249 is approximately 25%) because of the four cases, it can correctly deduce two. When a bucket is authentically determined, it and its sibling are now known. That accounts for 50%. For remaining 50% buckets that it doesn't know about, in the worst case half will be located at the same node and half will be at a different node.

The *Quick Start* algorithm is similar to incremental convergence but a special probe message returns statistics about server 0's hash table when the client starts. The statistics are used to construct a complete directory so that the slow learning of the incremental strategy is avoided. While the resulting directory might not be completely accurate, it has the advantage of being mostly accurate and should some errors. This strategy made only a few bucket addressing errors because is able to completely guess the majority of the current directory by constructing a directory of the current depth. It is only wrong on the fringes where it had incorrectly assumed a higher split level.

For each of the above strategies, it is possible to propose examples that produce poor results. There are timing windows that would invalidate any previous knowledge and result in a miss on every bucket except bucket 0. However, real-world cases are unlikely to cause degenerative performance. Therefore the ability of a simple client directory produces very good results.

4.4 Number of Messages

Just as a main memory hashing is judged on the number of memory accesses and a disk based hash algorithm is judged on the number of I/Os it uses, a distributed hashing algorithm must show how many messages were used. This experiment found the average number of messages needed to insert or retrieve all records. DDH comes very close to the optimal of only two messages.

The number of messages is calculated as:

$$messages\_per\_request = request + reply + \varepsilon + \beta + \gamma \qquad (1)$$

The request and reply messages are the 2 normal user visible messages. The DDH message protocol requires an acknowledgment by the server for every client message received. Algorithms that assume reliable messages and only count the user visible messages fail to account for the low level acknowledgments used to enforce message reliability. Any low-level network messages are represented as ε and includes the messages invisible to user code such as low-level flow control, network name resolution messages, and message retransmissions. Since ε is unmeasuraable at the user level, it is not counted although it does affect performance. The effect of bucket splits is given by the β term which counts the number of bucket splits that occur between servers when a bucket fills. It is an inverse function of bucket size therefore it is advantageous to have the message size be slightly more than roughly half of the bucket size so that all of the migrated records can fit into one message.

Finally the γ term counts the addressing errors which are occurrences of forwarded messages between servers when a client asks the wrong server due to a change in the configuration of the distributed hash table. This is a non-linear function of number of servers and amount of data because a server can autonomously decide to split bucket while multiple clients are inserting or re-trieving records means that clients will have addressing errors. There are also addressing errors resulting from the period that a client is learning the current hash table. Section 4.3 measured these. Table 1 shows actual counts of address-ing errors. They are less than 1% of all messages when using the *Quick Start* algorithm.

The measured number of messages sent on average for every DDH request is 2.02 which is very close to the optimal message total of 2.

4.5   Network Performance

DDH used a synchronous request/response protocol for all of its communication using UDP messages. As a result, the network was the bottleneck. All perfor-mance monitoring showed that the CPU utilization rate was always in the low to mid 40% level for the client side. Of this amount, approximately 75% of the time was spent in system time as the kernel sent and received the UDP messages.

There is a common belief that because the raw speed of FDDI is 100 Mbps, it is 10 times faster in all dimensions than a 10 Mbps Ethernet. We found that FDDI produces only about 25% better response time. The proportion of user to system time was about 1:3 for FDDI as it was for Ethernet. This suggests that the network software layer is quite heavyweight.

To discover how the network performance affected the DDH performance, a comparison measurement was done using the ttcp network performance analysis tool. For the UDP protocol, by sending 80 byte packets to imitate the average message size used for DDH in the study, the CPU is nearly 100% busy. The workstations used in this study can send slightly under 800 UDP packets per second at its maximum. The ULTRIX kernel has a much higher code length for networking calls than it does for file system calls. By comparison, several thousand read and write calls per second are possible. Some modern microkernel OSs can perform a small-message RPC call in about a millisecond.

4.6 Multiserver Performance

One very strong advantage with distributed hashing is the ability to involve multiple servers to share the work load. A series of experiments were conducted to test the effect of adding more servers.

The first group of experiments quantify the speed-up of adding more servers. Speed-up means that increasing the available performance by N while keeping the workload constant should yield an N times speedup. Each record was inserted and then retrieved.

Table 2. Speed-up performance (elapsed time)

Records	1 Server / 1 Client	2 Servers / 1 Client	3 Servers / 1 Client
1000	6.2 seconds	5.5 seconds	7.0 seconds
2000	13.3	11.7	14.0
3000	19.1	16.8	20.1
4000	24.6	22.4	27.1
5000	30.5	28.5	33.6
6000	37.6	33.2	40.6
7000	44.0	38.7	46.3
8000	51.8	44.2	53.7
9000	56.8	50.9	63.0

Table 2 does not exhibit an increase of speed as one client uses one, two, or three servers. There is only marginal speed-up when using a second server. The most like explanation for the minimal speedup is that all messages are synchronous. Message throughput is still the bottleneck so that any added server capacity is unusable if the client waits.

The second group of experiments looked at the scale-up of increasing the workload commensurate with the increased available performance. Table 3 lists the resultant scale-up.

Table 3 shows that DDH has very good scalability when the load and capacity re both doubled. Based upon the DDH design, it seems very likely that scale-up exists when using higher multiples of server/client pairs. However those experiments where not performed so this remains unproven.

Table 3. Scale-up performance (elapsed time)

Records	1 Server / 1 Client	2 Servers / 2 Clients
1000	3.1 seconds	3.2 seconds
2000	5.9	6.1
3000	8.9	8.8
4000	13.9	12.8
5000	15.0	14.8
6000	19.1	19.0
7000	21.5	21.2
8000	25.8	24.4
9000	27.4	27.3

5 Conclusions and Future Work

With the growing number of networked systems that share information in a distributed manner, the argument for a distributed data structure is compelling. Freedom from single node limitations, easy scalability, and better overall performance are the goals. In comparison to a single-node hash table, a distributed table theoretically allows growth of the table to the composite size of all the workstation's memory before the hash table is forced to reside on disk.

DDH, a distributed dynamic hashing algorithm, was implemented on a group of workstations to quantify the benefit of using a distributed solution. The best environment for DDH is a group of servers under the same administrative control (either directly or indirectly) and have a "shared-nothing" architecture so that there is no interference between systems to diminish performance. Systems organized into *workstation farms* are likely the best match to the needs of DDH if they can provide network communication protocols with low latency.

Performance results show that it is comparable to other current implementations when measured with using CPU time or elapsed time. However, because DDH sends messages between systems, the network becomes the bottleneck. In our largest test that used 50,000 records, the test required approximately 200,000 network messages to insert and then retrieve all records. Because a single network message takes about 2 milliseconds elapsed time, even between fast workstations on the same Ethernet segment, the cumulative elapsed time is quite high. The cost of distributed access is better than a disk access, but far worse than a memory access.

The area of distributed data structures introduces several challenging research problems in the areas of concurrency control algorithm, server failure, and supporting variable number of servers. Since servers can fail, some method of using data redundancy or server redundancy should be employed [4]. However, the drawback is the increased complexity of dealing with replication or data consistency. The actual case may be more complex due to server failures that are not independent. Dynamic hashing freed hashing from the fixed sized hash tables. Distributed hashing expands hashing from a single node. The next logical step beyond is to allow for varying number of servers. The question is whether this is possible and still preserve retrieval using one message.

In summary, we find that DDH offers a useful approach for structuring distributed storage systems. DDH can prove to be useful when the data to be stored exceeds the size of a single system's memory. Because the network latency is less than the latency of a disk request, huge single table can be accessed from multiple servers with better performance. DDH is also more tolerant of skewed data than other dynamic hashing methods because it allows for bucket splitting on demand.

References

1. AT&T, DBM(3X), *Unix Programmer's Manual, System V.3*, pp. 506-8, 1985.
2. Ronald Fagin, Jurg Nievergelt, Nicholas Pippenger, and H. Raymond Strong, "Extensible Hashing – A Fast Access Method for Dynamic Files", *ACM Transactions on Database Systems*, Volume 4, No. 3, pp. 315-34, September 1979.
3. Richard Golding, "Accessing Replicated Data in a Large-Scale Distributed System", University of California at Santa Cruz technical report, June 1991.
4. H. I. Hsiao and David DeWitt, "Chained Declustering: A New Availability Strategy for Multiprocessor Database Machines", *Proceedings of the 6th International Conference on Data Engineering*, February 1990.
5. Per Larson, "Dynamic Hashing", *BIT*, 1978 Vol. 18(2), pp. 184-201.
6. Witold Litwin, "Linear Hashing: A New Tool for File and Table Addressing", *Proceedings of the 6th International Conference on VLDB*, October 1980.
7. Witold Litwin, Marie-Anne Niemat, and Donovan Schneider, "LH* – Linear Hashing for Distributed Files", *Proceedings of the 1993 ACM SIGMOD*. May 1993.
8. John Postel, "User Datagram Protocol", *USC/Information Sciences Institute*, Internet RFC 768, August 1980.
9. Margo Seltzer and Ozan Yigit, "A New Hashing Package for UNIX", *USENIX Conference Proceedings - Winter '91*, January 1991.
10. C. Severance, S. Pramanik, and P. Wolberg, "Distributed Linear Hashing and Parallel Projection in Main Memory Databases", *Proceedings of the 16th International Conference on VLDB*, Brisbane, Australia, 1990.

Performance Analysis of Superimposing-Coded Signature Files

Sam. Y. Sung

Department of Information Systems and Computer Science
National University of Singapore
Kent Ridge Road, Singapore 0511
e-mail: ssung@iscs.nus.sg

Abstract. Signature file has been shown as a very good filtering mechanism to reduce the amount of information that needs to be retrieved for a query. The main concern in the signature construction is to find the optimal signatrue weight to minimize the false drop probability. In this paper, a new formula of computing the false drop probability is presented. Different from previous works, our formula is based on the bit probability and which is independent of the signature size. Our formula is easier to analyze so that optimal solutions can be more adequately derived. Performance results show that our solutions are better than the solutions obtained before. Some interesting properties of the optimal solutions are also discussed.

1 Introduction

Signature files have been used in many areas such as text and document retrievals, to speed up searching in an editor, in differential files, multiattribute (partial match) retrievals, and so forth [2, 4, 5, 7, 8, 10, 11]. The signatrue file method works as follows: an abstraction (called *signatrue*) is associated with each object (an object can be formatted record or unformatted message); objects belong to the same block, such as a bucket or a document, will have their object signatures combined together to form a block signature. The block signatures are stored sequentially in a signatrue file. When a query is processed, a query signatrue is formed using the same encoding method that is used for forming object signatures; then the signature file, rather than the actual data file, is first examined for possible match between the query signatrue and block signatures. Each nonmatched block signature is identified and no need for further search on the corresponding actual block of data file since it can not possibly contain any qualifying objects.

A signature file has a storage overhead much smaller than that of an inverted file [3, 9]. Signature files can provide an almost tenfold speed-up over full-text scanning with only 10 percent space overhead [5]. Its simple file structure facilitates database maintenance. The ease of insertions and deletions makes it suitable for storage on optical disks, which can be written upon only a limited number of times. It can be easily applied with excellent results on parallel machines [6]. A prototype text retrieval system [13] using signature files on the

Connection Machines is expected to search a 15-gigabyte database in 3 minutes; 2 minutes are devoted to I/O activities, and 1 minute to computation.

The signatrues are constructed as follows. A database is considered *physically or logically* divided into a number of blocks, with each block consists of a number of formatted or unformatted objects. For a given block B, suppose it consists of m distinct objects; each object is associated with an *object signature* of n bits with exactly k bits set to 1. The integer n of an object signature S is called the **size** of the object signature, and k is called its **weight**. The creation of a signature from an object can be done from a lookup table or a perfect hash function if the pool of objects is small, or can be obtained by employing some good random hashing function if the pool is large. One place to choose a good hashing function is from the universal classes of hash functions described in [1]. Various techniques have been proposed for representing the block signature. Faloutsos and Christodoulakis [5] described some signature construction methods; these include Word Signatures, Superimposed Coding, Run Length Encoding, and Bit-block compression. Among the various compression techniques, superimposed coding method (denoted as SC method for short) has been widely used and shown to be an effective way of forming the signatures. With this method, the block signature is formed by superimposing (inclusive ORing) the object signatures. Compare with other compression methods, the superimposed coding has two distinctive advantages: first, this scheme always produces fixed-length block signatures, regardless of the number of objects within the block. Secondly, other compression techniques, although may be efficient in storage, they make query processing slower [5, 12], especially for partial match type of queries [2].

Under SC method, a block signature,S_b, is generated by superimposing all object signatures in that block. Therefore, the size of the block signature is also n, the same as the object signature. A query signature, S_q, is generated from the query Q in the same way as the block signature described above. A signature S_b is *qualified* if and only if for all bit positions in which S_q are set to 1, the corresponding bit position in S_b are also set to 1 (known as the inclusion condition, denoted as $S_q \subseteq S_b$).

The main problem for all signature files is they produce *false drops*; that is, the signature file may identify a block as one satisfying the query, but in fact, it is not. A precise definition of the false drop probability is computed over all possible queries and total number of blocks [3]. A simple, but accurate, approximation of the over-all false drop probability is to compute the false drop probability with respect to one given block and for single object queries [3].

For a block B with m distinct objects and signature size n, the false drop probability is monotonically decreasing as m decreases or n increases. When k increases, there are two conflicting effects on the false drop probability. One is that more bits in S_b are likely to be set to 1 and this will increase the false drop probability. On the other hand, more bits are probably set to 1 in S_q so that the false drop probability will decrease, Hence, one important optimization problem concerned in signature construction is to determine a balanced object weight k

such that the false drop probability is minimized. This is also our main concern in this paper.

The rest of the paper is organized as follows. In Sect. 2, we briefly described the SC method and some of the results from previous works. In Sect. 3, we give a new formula for computing false drop probability. Analytic and numerical optimal solutions are derived. Some performance analyses are done in Sect. 4. Concluding remarks are given in Sect. 5.

2 Description of the Superimposed Coding Method (SC)

The superimposed coding system works as follows. First, each object is mapped into a bit string of size n containing exactly k 1s and $n - k$ 0s. Suppose that a block B contains m distinct objects, then a block signature for b is formed by superimposing (inclusive ORing) the m object signatures. An example of this process is given in Figure 1. Note that SC method eliminates duplicates automatically. Since we only interest in noncommmon objects, from now on, we assume that the m objects in a block are distinct.

object	signature
Partial	01001000
Information	00011000
Retrieval	10010000
block signature	11011000

Fig. 1. An example of superimposed coding method. There are $m = 3$ objects in the The signature size is $n = 8$. It is assumed $k = 2$ bits set per object signature.

A query containing a single object is called a simple query. Otherwise, it is a composite query. A composite query can be represented in a canonical form by using conjunctive (AND) and disjunctive (OR) operations. A simple query has (query) signature created in the same way as an object signature. A conjunctive composite query containing multiple objects can be formed by superimposed coding method, same as the construction of a block signature.

If a block satisfies a query, then every bit position that is set in the query signature must also be set in the block signature. Thus to answer a query it is necessary to search for block signatures that match the query signature in this way.

It is possible that a block signature matches a query signature but the corresponding block does not satisfy the query. Such an occurrence is referred to as a *false drop*. False drops directly affect the number of block accesses (I/O time). Therefore, it is essential to reduce the false drop rate as much as possible.

A precise definition of the false-drop probability is given by [3].

Definition 1. False drop probability F_d is the probability that a block signature seems to qualify, *given that the block does not actually qualify*. Expressed mathematically,

F_d=Prob{signature qualifies | block does not}.

It has been shown[3] that to estimate F_d it is good enough to consider only the unsuccessful simple query search (i.e., the search object does not exist in the block).

Before we start the analysis of SC method, some notations and assumptions need to be given.

Notations:

F_d false drop probability
n signature size in bits (for both object signature and block signature)
m distinct objects in a block
k weight of an object; i. e. , the number of bits that is to be set to 1 in an object signature.

Assumptions:

1. only simple query is considered.
2. uniform distribution of occurrence and query frequencies.

Since queries concerned here are single object queries, a query signature has query weight, w_q, equal to k. The expected false drop probability F_d can be expressed as

$$F_d = \left(1 - \left(1 - \frac{k}{n}\right)^m\right)^k \tag{1}$$

The above formula can be seen from the following discussion: For a bit in the block signature to be set to 0, all m objects must set this bit to 0. The chance that a bit is set to 0 by an arbitrary single object is $1 - \frac{k}{n}$. Therefore, the probability that a bit position is set to 0 in the block signature is $(1 - \frac{k}{n})^m$. In other words, the probability that a bit is set to 1 is $1 - (1 - \frac{k}{n})^m$. A simple query has weight equal to k. A false drop occurs when all these k bits are set to 1. Therefore, the false drop probability is equal to $(1 - (1 - \frac{k}{n})^m)^k$.

From equation (1) one can see that the false drop probability F_d decreases monotonically as n increases, and increases monotonously as m increases. On the other hand, when k increases, F_d could be increasing or decreasing. The optimization problem in signature construction is defined as following: given that there are m objects per block, and that the size of the block signature is n, determine the object weight k that minimizes the false drop probability.

When m is large, from equation (1), the false drop probability can be approximated as

$$F_d = \left(1 - e^{-\frac{km}{n}}\right)^k \tag{2}$$

Stiassny [14] optimized the above formula (2) for k:

$$k_{opt} = \frac{n \ln 2}{m} \qquad (3)$$

where ln stands for the natural logarithm. In this case

$$F_d = \left(\frac{1}{2}\right)^{\frac{n \ln 2}{m}} \qquad (4)$$

3 A new Formula for False Drop Probability

In this section, we derive a new formula for estimating the false drop probability. Our formula is similar to formula (1), but more general and easy to be analyzed so that optimal solutions can be more adequately constructed.

First, we introduce some additional notations to be used.

Notations:

p   probability of a bit position in an object signature be set to 1.
p_b probability of a bit position in a block signature be set to 1.
p_q probability of a bit position in a query signature be set to 1.
w_b block weight; the total number of bits be set to 1 in a block signature.
w_q query weight; the total number of bits be sent to 1 in a query signature.

Notice that the three parameters p, p_b and p_q are bit-wise defined, therefore, they are independent of the signature size n. We call p, p_b and p_q the bit probabilities for object, block, and query, respectively. Or sometimes simply call them bit probabilities. The bit probabilities p_b and p_q can be derived from p as following:

$$p_b = 1 - (1-p)^m \qquad (5)$$

and

$$p_q = 1 - (1-p)^{m'} \qquad \text{where } m' \text{ is the number of objects in a query.} \qquad (6)$$

The relationships between the bit probabilities and weights are given below.

$$p = \frac{k}{n}, \; w_b = np_b, \text{ and } w_q = np_q \qquad (7)$$

Of course, the block weight and query weight obtained above in (7) are only expected values.

Under our assumptions, $m' = 1$ and p_q is equal to p. By a similar discussion as in derivation of formula (1), the false drop probability now can be derived as below

$$F_d = p_b{}^{w_q} = p_b{}^{np_q} = (1 - (1 - p)^m)^{np} \tag{8}$$

The optimization problem now is done with respect to p instead of k. Notice that unlike k, which is determined by two parameters n and m, p only depends on one parameter m. Consequently, the optimal solution of p in formula (8) is more easy to find than the optim al value k in (1). After we find the optimal solution for p, then we can use (7) to determine k.

Optimal solution:

Since the logarithm function is monotonically increasing, we can convert our original optimization problem into the following equivalent problem:

$$\min_{0<p<1} f(p) = \ln F_d = np \ln (1 - (1 - p)^m) \tag{9}$$

It is shown in Appendix A that the above problem has a unique solution existing at the point p where $f'(p) = 0$. Define $g(p) = \frac{f'(p)}{n} = \ln (1 - (1 - p)^m) + \frac{mp(1-p)^{m-1}}{1-(1-p)^m}$, we have two ways to find out the point p that is the root of $g(x)$, for $0 < x < 1$, and hencefore find the optimal solution for problem (9) stated above.

(1)*Analytical approach:*

Let

$$
\begin{aligned}
g(p) &= \ln (1 - (1 - p)^m) + \frac{mp(1-p)^{m-1}}{1-(1-p)^m} \\
&= \ln (1 - (1 - p)^m) + \frac{mp(1-p)^m}{(1-p)(1-(1-p))^m} \tag{10}
\end{aligned}
$$

For $m = 1$, solving equation (10) gives us the optimal bit probability $p_{opt} = \frac{1}{e} \approx 0.368$. In general case, it is not easy to find the exact analytic formula for the root of $g(x)$. A good approximation is to let $1 - (1 - p)^m = \frac{1}{2}$, so $(1 - p)^m = \frac{1}{2}$ and $p = 1 - (\frac{1}{2})^{\frac{1}{m}}$. Let us denote $p_a = 1 - (\frac{1}{2})^{\frac{1}{m}}$. Then we have

$$
\begin{aligned}
g(p_a) &= \ln \frac{1}{2} + \frac{mp_a}{1 - p_a} \\
&= -\ln 2 + \frac{m\left(1 - (\frac{1}{2})^{\frac{1}{m}}\right)}{(\frac{1}{2})^{\frac{1}{m}}} \\
&= -\ln 2 + m\left(\left(\frac{1}{2}\right)^{-\frac{1}{m}} - 1\right)
\end{aligned}
$$

$$= -\ln 2 + m \left(\left(1 + \ln \frac{1}{2} \left(-\frac{1}{m} \right) + \frac{1}{2} \left(\ln \frac{1}{2} \right)^2 \left(-\frac{1}{m} \right)^2 + \cdots \right) - 1 \right)$$

(Maclaurin series)

$$\approx -\ln 2 + m \left(\left(1 + \ln \left(\frac{1}{2} \right) \left(-\frac{1}{m} \right) \right) - 1 \right) \quad \text{(when } m \text{ is large)}$$

$$= 0 \tag{11}$$

Although p_a is close to p_{opt} when m is large, the difference between them becomes larger when m gets small. For instance, when $m = 1$, we have $p_a = \frac{1}{2}$, but $p_{opt} = \frac{1}{e} \approx 0.368$. This example shows the difference of p_{opt} and p_a in the case of small m is rather significant. The problem can be solved by using numerical approach described below.

(2)Numerical approach:

For fixed m, formula (10) is a one-variable nonlinear equation. One of the most widely used numerical methods of solving nonlinear equations is **Newton's method**.

$$x_{n+1} = x_n - \frac{g(x_n)}{g'(x_n)} \quad n = 1, 2, 3, \ldots$$

If starting from an initial points x_1 that is not too far from a root x, Newton's method is rapidly convergent. The convergence is defined as the successive *x-values* are sufficiently close, or the value of the function is sufficiently near zero; customarily, a specified tolerance is required.

In our problem, applying Newton's method to solve equation (10), we have

$$g(x) = \ln\left(1 - (1-x)^m\right) + \frac{mx(1-x)^{m-1}}{1-(1-x)^m},$$

and from Appendix A, we know $g'(x)$ can be simplified as

$$\frac{m(1-x)^{m-2}}{\left(1-(1-x)^m\right)^2} \left(2 - x - mx - (1-x)^m(2-x)\right).$$

Using p_a as the initial point, we get numerical solution for p_{opt}. A sample list of the optimal solutions is given in Table 3 of the next section.

4 Some Performance Analysis

The function value $g(p_a)$ in (11) is in fact slightly larger than 0. From the discussion of Appendix A, we know that the point p_a shall be somewhat greater than p_{opt}, where p_{opt} is the optimal solution; i.e., p_a is on the right side of p_{opt}.

The solution $p_a = 1 - \left(\frac{1}{2}\right)^{\frac{1}{m}}$ is a more accurate approximation than the solution $p_0 = \frac{\ln 2}{m}$, obtained before by Faloutsos [3], as shown in Table 1. This is because that $1 - \left(\frac{1}{2}\right)^{\frac{1}{m}} \leq \frac{\ln 2}{m}$, so both p_a and p_0 are on the right side of p_{opt}; but p_a is closer to p_{opt} than p_0 and therefore has better F_d value.

Table 1. Comparison of false drop probability $F_d(p) = (1 - (1 - p)^m)^{np}$ between $p_a = 1 - \left(\frac{1}{2}\right)^{\frac{1}{m}}$ and $p_0 = \frac{\ln 2}{m}$.

	n=4m		n=8m		n=16m		n=32m	
m	$F_d(p_a)$	$F_d(p_0)$	$F_d(p_a)$	$F_d(p_0)$	$F_d(p_a)$	$F_d(p_0)$	$F_d(p_a)$	$F_d(p_0)$
1	0.250000	0.361972	0.062500	0.131023	0.003906	0.017167	0.000015	0.000295
2	0.197080	0.213567	0.038841	0.045611	0.001509	0.002080	0.000002	0.000004
3	0.179793	0.186151	0.032325	0.034652	0.001045	0.001201	0.000001	0.000001
4	0.171270	0.174613	0.029333	0.030490	0.000860	0.000930	0.000001	0.000001
5	0.166202	0.168259	0.027623	0.028311	0.000763	0.000802	0.000001	0.000001
6	0.162845	0.164237	0.026518	0.026974	0.000703	0.000728	0.000000	0.000001
7	0.160457	0.161461	0.025747	0.026070	0.000663	0.000680	0.000000	0.000000
8	0.158673	0.159431	0.025177	0.025418	0.000634	0.000646	0.000000	0.000000
9	0.157289	0.157882	0.024740	0.024927	0.000612	0.000621	0.000000	0.000000
10	0.156184	0.156660	0.024393	0.024542	0.000595	0.000602	0.000000	0.000000
16	0.152471	0.152652	0.023248	0.023303	0.000540	0.000543	0.000000	0.000000
32	0.149397	0.149441	0.022319	0.022333	0.000498	0.000499	0.000000	0.000000
64	0.147867	0.147878	0.021865	0.021868	0.000478	0.000478	0.000000	0.000000
128	0.147104	0.147106	0.021639	0.021640	0.000468	0.000468	0.000000	0.000000
256	0.146722	0.146723	0.021527	0.021528	0.000463	0.000463	0.000000	0.000000
512	0.146532	0.146532	0.021472	0.021472	0.000461	0.000461	0.000000	0.000000

In practice, we need to select an integer for k such that $k \approx np_{opt}$ and $k > 0$. Therefore, a good selection for k is either $k = \lfloor np_{opt} \rfloor$ or $k = \lceil np_{opt} \rceil$. When m is large, since p_a is a good approximation to p_{opt}, we can assign $k = k_1 = \lfloor np_a \rfloor$ (and $k_1 = 1$ in case of $np_a < 1$) or $k = k_2 = \lceil np_a \rceil$. Because k_2 is larger than np_a, it always performs not better than np_a; and this is true as shown by Table 2. From Table 2, we can see k_1 performs better than k_2 in more cases; with k_2 is a better choice only when m is rather large ($m \geq 8$) and n is relatively small ($n \leq 8m$). It is interesting to notice that k_1 performs even better than $k = np_a$ in many cases.

We can use numerical analysis approach to find the exact optimal solution of (10). A list of the optimal bit probability is given in Table 3. It is shown in Table 3 that Newton's method converges fast.

Table 2. Comparisons among the three false drop probabilities F_0, F_1 and F_2, where $F_0 = (1 - (1 - p_a)^m)^{np_a}$ with $p_a = 1 - (\frac{1}{2})^{\frac{1}{m}}$, $F_1 = (1 - (1 - \frac{k_1}{n})^m)^{k_1}$ with $k_1 = \lfloor np_a \rfloor$ if $np_a \geq 1$ and $k_1 = 1$ if $np_a < 1$, and $F_2 = (1 - (1 - \frac{k_2}{n})^m)^{k_2}$ with $k_2 = \lceil np_a \rceil$

	n=4m			n=8m			n=16m		
m	F_0	F_1	F_2	F_0	F_1	F_2	F_0	F_1	F_2
1	0.250000	0.250000	0.250000	0.062500	0.062500	0.062500	0.003906	0.003906	0.003906
2	0.197080	0.191406	0.226284	0.038841	0.036636	0.040782	0.001509	0.001441	0.001663
3	0.179793	0.177491	0.193226	0.032325	0.031503	0.032467	0.001045	0.000990	0.001054
4	0.171270	0.171246	0.179591	0.029333	0.029176	0.032253	0.000860	0.000851	0.000921
5	0.166202	0.167698	0.172153	0.027623	0.027419	0.029637	0.000763	0.000752	0.000796
6	0.162845	0.165411	0.167471	0.026518	0.026328	0.028046	0.000703	0.000693	0.000723
7	0.160457	0.163814	0.164252	0.025747	0.025585	0.026979	0.000663	0.000655	0.000676
8	0.158673	0.162635	0.161904	0.025177	0.025046	0.026213	0.000634	0.000627	0.000643
9	0.157289	0.161730	0.160115	0.024740	0.024638	0.025637	0.000612	0.000607	0.000619
10	0.156184	0.161012	0.158707	0.024393	0.024318	0.025188	0.000595	0.000591	0.000600
16	0.152471	0.158635	0.154101	0.023248	0.023280	0.023747	0.000540	0.000542	0.000542
32	0.149397	0.156704	0.150426	0.022319	0.022460	0.022628	0.000498	0.000504	0.000498
64	0.147867	0.155756	0.148642	0.021865	0.022065	0.022094	0.000478	0.000478	0.000488
128	0.147104	0.155286	0.147763	0.021639	0.021871	0.021834	0.000468	0.000468	0.000477
256	0.146722	0.155052	0.147326	0.021527	0.021775	0.021705	0.000463	0.000463	0.000471
512	0.146532	0.154935	0.147109	0.021472	0.021727	0.021641	0.000461	0.000461	0.000468

Table 3. $F_d(p) = (1 - (1 - p)^m)^{np}$ where $n = 16m$. $p_a = 1 - (\frac{1}{2})^{\frac{1}{m}}$ and p_{opt} is the optimal numerical solution for bit probability, obtained by Newton's method using tolerance $\delta = 10^{-5}$ and initial point p_a.

m	p_{opt}	no. of iteration	p_a	$F_d(p_{opt})$	$F_d(p_a)$
1	0.367879	4	0.500000	0.002778	0.003906
2	0.239380	4	0.292893	0.001335	0.001509
3	0.177720	4	0.206299	0.000982	0.001045
4	0.141380	4	0.159104	0.000829	0.000860
5	0.117397	4	0.129449	0.000744	0.000763
6	0.100378	3	0.109101	0.000691	0.000703
7	0.087671	3	0.094276	0.000654	0.000663
8	0.077822	3	0.082996	0.000627	0.000634
9	0.069963	3	0.074125	0.000607	0.000612
10	0.063547	3	0.066967	0.000591	0.000595
16	0.040993	3	0.042397	0.000539	0.000540
32	0.021062	2	0.021428	0.000498	0.000498
64	0.010678	2	0.010772	0.000478	0.000478
128	0.005377	2	0.005401	0.000468	0.000468
256	0.002698	1	0.002704	0.000463	0.000463
512	0.001351	1	0.001353	0.000461	0.000461

In Table 3, we can see that p_{opt} seems decrease as m increases. This is true as shown in Theorem 1 of Appendix B.

From Theorem 1, we know that, for all m, $p_{opt,m} \leq p_{opt,1} = \frac{1}{e} \approx 0.368$.

Given a signature size of n and m objects in a block, alternatively, we may want to uniformly distribute the m objects into r regions (assume r is a factor of m) such that each region gets about $\frac{m}{r}$ objects; then allocating about $\frac{n}{r}$ bits to each region as its signature size. From Table 4, we can find that the larger r is, the worse the false drop probability is. The same argument is true for m is large, as shown by Theorem 2 in Appendix B. This suggests that if performance is the only factor to be concerned, then we should use as large signature size as possible and accommodate as many objects into a block as we can.

Table 4. $n = 1024$, $m = 64$ and r is a factor of m; i.e. $r = 1, 2, 4, \ldots, 64$. $p_{opt,r}$ is the optimal bit probability when $\frac{m}{r}$ objects in a block (note the solutions $p_{opt,r}$ can be found from Table 3).

$$F_r = F_d(p_{opt,r}) = \left(1 - (1 - p_{opt,r})^{\frac{m}{r}}\right)^{\frac{n p_{opt,r}}{r}}.$$

r	m/r	$p_{opt,r}$	F_r
1	64	0.010678	0.000478
2	32	0.021062	0.000498
4	16	0.040993	0.000539
8	8	0.077822	0.000627
16	4	0.141380	0.000829
32	2	0.239380	0.001335
64	1	0.367879	0.002778

We can easily extend formula (8) to the case of conjunctive composite query of 2 objects. For a query $q = q_1 \wedge q_2$, where q_1 and q_2 are simple queries, from equation (6) we have

$$p_q = 1 - (1 - p)^2 = 2p - p^2 = p(p - 2)$$

Let $p_{opt,q}$ be the optimal bit probability for query q, and $F_d(p_{opt,q})$ be the corresponding minimal false drop probability.

From (8), we have

$$\begin{aligned} F_d(p_{opt,q}) &= \left(1 - (1 - p_{opt,q})^m\right)^{n p_{opt,q}(2 - p_{opt,q})} \\ &\leq \left(1 - (1 - p_{opt,q_1})^m\right)^{n p_{opt,q_1}(2 - p_{opt,q_1})} \\ &= F_d(p_{opt,q_1})^{2 - p_{opt,q_1}} \end{aligned} \tag{12}$$

Since $p_{opt,q_1} \leq 0.368$, from the above formula (12), we have $F_d(p_{opt,q}) \leq F_d(p_{opt,q_1})^{1.632}$. When m is large, p_{opt,q_1} is near zero, and $F_d(p_{opt,q})$ is close to $F_d(p_{opt,q_1})^2$.

5 Concluding Remarks

One of the most important concerns in signature file construction is to minimize false drop probability. Previous studies of the false drop probability is to compute it directly on the signature weight, k, which is determined by the two parameters m and n. In this paper, we present a new formula to compute the false drop probability. Our formula is based on the bit probability that is independent of the parameter n, and therefore is much easy to derive optimal solutions. Numerical approach gives exact optimal solutions, and analytic formulas give simple but very accurate answers when m is large.

Performance analysis is discussed and some of the interesting results are summarized in the following:

1. the analytic solution obtained in this paper is better than previous result.
2. the optimal bit probability is a decreasing function with respect to the parameter m.
3. if performance is the only concern, it is not advisable to further group objects in a block into subblocks.

Our formula can be easily extended to handle more general type of queries. For 2 objects conjunctive queries, it is shown that the false drop probability is reduced almost quadratically.

Appendix A. Existence and Uniqueness of Optimal Solution

For a given $m > 0$, we show that there is a unique solution for the following problem:

$$\min_{0 < p < 1} f(p) = p \ln(1 - (1 - p)^m) \qquad (A.1)$$

We show that $f(p)$ has tow characteristics: (i) $f(p)$ is increasing for $1 > p \geq \frac{1}{m+1}$, and (ii) $f(p)$ is concave when $0 < p < \frac{1}{m+1}$.

(i) For $1 > p \geq \frac{1}{m+1}$.

$$f'(p) = \ln\left(1 - (1 - p)^m\right) + \frac{mp(1 - p)^{m-1}}{1 - (1 - p)^m}$$

$$= \left(-(1 - p)^m - \frac{1}{2}(1 - p)^{2m} - \frac{1}{3}(1 - p)^{3m} - \frac{1}{4}(1 - p)^{4m} - \ldots\right) + \frac{mp(1 - p)^{m-1}}{1 - (1 - p)^m}$$

$$= \frac{(1-p)^{m-1}}{1-(1-p)^m}((1-(1-p)^m)(-(1-p) - \frac{1}{2}(1-p)^{m+1} - \frac{1}{3}(1-p)^{2m+1}$$

$$-\frac{1}{4}(1-p)^{3m+1} - \ldots) + mp)$$

$$= \frac{(1-p)^{m-1}}{1-(1-p)^m}((-1+p+mp) + (1-\frac{1}{2})(1-p)^{m+1} + (\frac{1}{2} - \frac{1}{3})(1-p)^{2m+1}$$

$$+(\frac{1}{3} - \frac{1}{4})(1-p)^{3m+1} + \ldots)$$

$$> 0$$

(ii) For $0 < p < \frac{1}{m+1}$.

$$f''(p) = \frac{2m(1-p)^{m-1}}{1-(1-p)^m} - \frac{mp(m-1)(1-p)^{m-2}}{1-(1-p)^m} - \frac{m^2p(1-p)^{2m-2}}{(1-(1-p)^m)^2}$$

$$= \frac{m(1-p)^{m-2}}{(1-(1-p)^m)^2}(2(1-p)(1-(1-p)^m) - p(m-1+(1-p)^m))$$

$$= \frac{m(1-p)^{m-2}}{(1-(1-p)^m)^2}(2(1-p) - 2(1-p)^{m+1} - p(m-1) - p(1-p)^m)$$

$$= \frac{m(1-p)^{m-2}}{(1-(1-p)^m)^2}(2-p-mp-(1-p)^m(2-p))$$

$$\geq \frac{m(1-p)^{m-2}}{(1-(1-p)^m)^2}(2-p-mp-(1-mp+\frac{m(m-1)p^2}{2})(2-p))$$

$$= \frac{m(1-p)^{m-2}}{(1-(1-p)^m)^2}(mp-mp^2-m(m-1)p^2+\frac{m(m-1)p^3}{2})$$

$$> 0$$

From the above discussions, we know there exists a unique solution for the problem (A.1). Obviously, the optimal solution p satisfies $f'(p) = 0$.

Appendix B. Proofs of Theorems

Let $p_{opt,m}$ denote the optimal bit probability when there are m objects involved in a block.

Theorem 1. $p_{opt,m} > p_{opt,m+1}$ for $m = 1, 2, 3, \ldots$

Proof. To be simple, in this proof we use $p_1 = p_{opt,m}$. If we can show that

$$F_1 = \ln\left(1-(1-p_1)^{m+1}\right) + \frac{(m+1)p_1(1-p_1)^{m+1}}{(1-p_1)\left(1-(1-p_1)^{m+1}\right)} > 0$$

then, from appendix A, we can conclude that $p_1 > p_{opt,m+1}$
From (10), we know p_1 satisfying

$$\ln\left(1 - (1 - p_1)^m\right) + \frac{mp_1(1 - p_1)^m}{(1 - p_1)(1 - (1 - p_1)^m)} = 0$$

That is,

$$\frac{mp_1}{1 - p_1} = -\ln\left(1 - (1 - p_1)^m\right)\frac{1 - (1 - p_1)^m}{(1 - p_1)^m}$$

Therefore,

$$F_1 = \ln\left(1 - (1 - p_1)^{m+1}\right) + \frac{(m + 1)p_1(1 - p_1)^{m+1}}{(1 - p_1)(1 - (1 - p_1)^{m+1})}$$

$$= \ln\left(1 - (1 - p_1)^{m+1}\right) + \frac{m + 1}{m}(-\ln\left(1 - (1 - p_1)^m\right))\frac{(1 - (1 - p_1)^m)(1 - p_1)}{1 - (1 - p_1)^{m+1}}$$

since

$$\frac{(m + 1)(1 - (1 - p_1)^m)}{m(1 - (1 - p_1)^{m+1})}$$

$$= \frac{(m + 1)(1 - (1 - p_1))(1 + (1 - p_1) + (1 - p_1)^2 + \ldots + (1 - p_1)^{m-1})}{m(1 - (1 - p_1))(1 + (1 - p_1) + (1 - p_1)^2 + \ldots + (1 - p_1)^{m-1} + (1 - p_1)^m)}$$

$$= \frac{m(1 + (1 - p_1) + (1 - p_1)^2 + \ldots + (1 - p_1)^{m-1})}{m(1 + (1 - p_1) + (1 - p_1)^2 + \ldots + (1 - p_1)^{m-1}) + m(1 - p_1)^m}$$

$$+ \frac{1 + (1 - p_1) + (1 - p_1)^2 + \ldots + (1 - p_1)^{m-1}}{m(1 + (1 - p_1) + (1 - p_1)^2 + \ldots + (1 - p_1)^{m-1}) + m(1 - p_1)^m}$$

$$> 1 \quad (\text{because } m(1 - p_1)^m < 1 + (1 - p_1) + (1 - p_1)^2 + \ldots + (1 - p_1)^{m-1})$$

Thus,

$$F_1 > \ln\left(1 - (1 - p_1)^{m+1}\right) + (-\ln\left(1 - (1 - p_1)^m\right))(1 - p_1)$$

using Taylor's expansion on $\ln(1 - x) = -x - \frac{1}{2x^2} - \frac{1}{3x^3} - \ldots$, we have

$$F_1 > (-(1 - p_1)^{m+1} - \frac{1}{2}(1 - p_1)^{2m+2} - \frac{1}{3}(1 - p_1)^{3m+3} - \ldots) + ((1 - p_1)^{m+1}$$

$$+ \frac{1}{2}(1 - p_1)^{2m+1} + \frac{1}{3}(1 - p_1)^{3m+1} + \ldots)$$

$$> 0$$

Let $F_d(\frac{m}{r})$ denote the false drop probability for the case of $\frac{m}{r}$ objects in a block of size $\frac{n}{r}$. □

Theorem 2. *When m is large, and $1 \leq r \leq m$, then the false drop probability $F_d(\frac{m}{r})$ is increasing as r increases.*

Proof. From (8), we know the false drop probability $F_d(\frac{m}{r}) = (1 - (1 - p_{opt})^{\frac{m}{r}})^{\frac{np}{r}}$ where p_{opt} is the optimal solution. Since we assume m is large, p_{opt} can be approximated by $p = 1 - (\frac{1}{2})^{\frac{r}{m}}$. Let

$$
\begin{aligned}
f(r) &= (\frac{1}{n}) \ln F_d(\frac{m}{r}) \\
&\approx \frac{p}{r} \ln(1 - (1-p)^{\frac{m}{r}}) \\
&= (\ln 2)((\frac{1}{2})^{\frac{r}{m}} - 1)/r \\
&= (\ln 2)(\frac{r}{m} \ln(\frac{1}{2}) + (\frac{1}{2})(\frac{r}{m})^2 \ln(\frac{1}{2})^2 + \ldots)/r \quad \text{(Maclaurin series)} \\
&= (\ln 2)(\frac{1}{m} \ln(\frac{1}{2}) + (\frac{1}{2})(\frac{r}{m^2}) \ln(\frac{1}{2})^2 + \ldots)
\end{aligned}
$$

The above shows $f(r)$ increases as r increases, so is $F_d(\frac{m}{r})$. $\qquad\square$

References

1. Carter, L. J., Wegman, M. L.: Universal classes of hash functions. J. Comput. Syst. Sci.**18** (1979) 143-154
2. Du, H. C.: On the File Design Problem for Partial Match Retrieval. IEEE Trans. Software Engi. **SE-11, No. 2** (Feb. 1985) 213-222
3. Faloutsos, C., Christodoulakis, S.: Signature Files: An Access Method for Documents and Its Analytical Performance Evaluation. ACM Trans. Office Inf. Syst. **2, No. 4** (Oct. 1984) 267-288
4. Faloutsos, C., Christodoulakis, S.: Optimal Signature Extraction and Information Loss. ACM Trans. Database Syst.**12, No. 3** (Sept. 1987) 395-428
5. Faloutsos, C., Christodoulakis, S.: Description and Performance Analysis of Signature File Methods for Office Filing. ACM Trans. Office Inf. Syst. **5, No. 3** (July, 1987) 237-257
6. Lee, D. L.: A word-parallel, bit-serial signature processor for superimposed coding. Proc. of 2nd International Conference on Data Engineering, Los Angels. (Feb. 1986) 352-359
7. Lee, D. L, Leng, C. W.: Partitioned Signature Files: Design Issues and Performance Evaluation. ACM Trans. Inf. Syst.**7, No. 2** (Apr. 1989) 158-180
8. Lee, D. L, Leng, C. W.: A Partitioned Signature File Structure for Multiattribute and Text Retrieval. Proceedings of the 6th International Conference on Data Engineering (Los Angels, 1990) 389-397
9. Leng, C. W., Lee, D. L.: Optimal Weight Assignment for Signature Generation. ACM Trans. Database Sys.**17, No. 2** (June 1992) 346-373
10. Mullin, J. K.: A Second Look at Bloom Filters. Commun. ACM. **26, No. 8** (Aug. 1983) 57- 571

11. Ramakrishna, M. V., Ramos, E. A.: Optimal Distribution of Signatures in Signature Hashing. IEEE trans. Knowl. and Data Engi.**4, No. 1** (Feb. 1992) 83-88
12. Sacks-Davis, R., Kent, A., Ramamohanarao, K.: Multikey Access Methods Based on Superimposed Coding Techniques. ACM Trans. Database Syst. **12, No. 4** (Dec 1987) 655- 696
13. Stanfill, C., Kahle, B.: Parallel free-text search on the connection machine system. Commun. ACM **29, No. 12** (Dec. 1986) 1229-1239
14. Stiassny S.: Mathematical analysis of various superimposed coding methods. Am. Dic. **11, No. 2** (Feb. 1960) 155-169

Trie Methods for Representing Text

T. H. Merrett and Heping Shang

School of Computer Science, McGill University
Montréal, Qué. H3A 2A7
{tim shang}@cs.mcgill.ca

Abstract

We propose a new trie organization for large text documents requiring secondary storage. Index size is critical in all trie representations of text, and our organization is smaller than all known methods. Access time is as good as the best known method. Tries can be constructed in good time. For an index of 100 million entries, our experiments show size factors of less than 3, as compared with 3.4 for the best previous method. Our measurements show expected access costs of 0.1 sec., and construction times of 18 to 55 hours, depending on the text characteristics.

Our organization can also handle dynamic data, and we give new algorithms for inserting and deleting. It supports searches for general patterns, as well as a variety of special searches, such as proximity, range, longest repetitions and most frequent occurrences.

Key words and phrases: PATRICIA, pattern matching, secondary storage, text, trie.

1 Introduction

Digital trees [2] or tries [4] were used for text searching by Morrison [9] and exploited by Gonnet *et al.* [5, 6] for the implementation of the electronic version of the *New Oxford English Dictionary* (*New O.E.D.*).

Trie methods give search costs which are often proportional only to the length of the string being sought, and, in the worst case, to the height of the trie (which is expected to be logarithmic in the size of the text being searched). No other sublinear methods for pattern search in text are known, and for very large texts tries are indispensible.

A major difficulty with tries is that the index generated can be even larger than the text. For example, Morrison's index could approach eighteen times the size of the text. Recent work on tries has focussed on reducing the index size. The characteristics of actual text are important in this effort, and Section 2 describes measurements we have made on five representative large texts.

These statistics will help us show that index size is a significant problem, not just in the worst case, but for normal usage of languages such as English. This is true even for the methods used for the *New O.E.D.* Thus, in Section 3, we propose a still more compact trie representation. This requires special attention to the organization needed to store the trie on secondary storage.

In Section 4, we compare index sizes and access costs for our method and others. This comparison is done analytically, based on the statistics of Section 2.

Building a text index is potentially very slow when we are preparing for searches which could identify any byte in a large text. A construction method which allows the text to change dynamically could require one or more accesses to secondary storage *for each byte* of the text. As an example, the least time that could be expected for a 100 megabyte text on a disc costing 20 milliseconds per access works out to just under a month. True costs would be several times this. In Section 5, we overview techniques which are three orders of magnitude faster.

We have built our algorithms, and Section 6 shows experimental results for texts of about 1 megabyte in size. These are compared with analytical results based on the earlier statistics, and extrapolated to a 100 megabyte text.

Finally, we discuss some advanced searching applications using our trie, in Section 7.

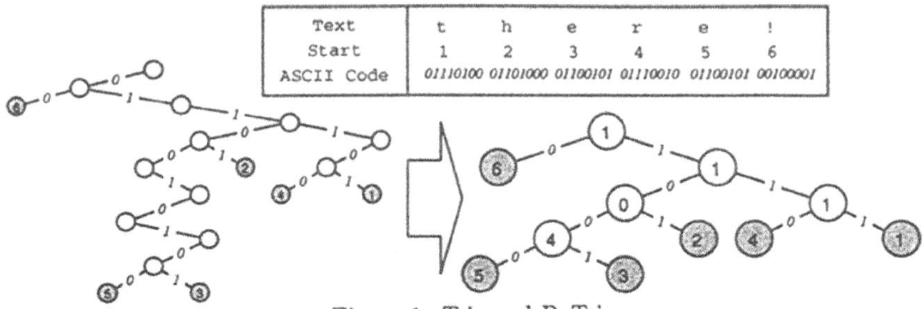

Text	t	h	e	r	e	!
Start	1	2	3	4	5	6
ASCII Code	01110100	01101000	01100101	01110010	01100101	00100001

Figure 1: Trie and PaTrie

2 Statistics on Text

2.1 Motivation

In our work, we follow Gonnet *et al.* in using semi-infinite strings, or *sistrings*. A sistring starts at some position in the text and runs all the way to the end of the text. (Sistrings are thus not really "semi-infinite", but, for 100 megabytes of text, they are effectively so.) A text consists of many sistrings. In this paper, we will usually assume that a search can find a string beginning at any byte of the text. Thus, if the text has N bytes, it will have N sistrings, the first one N bytes long, the second $N - 1$ bytes long, and so on. Sometimes — and this would require a much smaller index — we might ask to search for text strings beginning only at word starts. Since words average five characters in length and are delimited by blanks, such a text would have about $N/6$ sistrings.

We will use N for the size of the text in bytes, and n for the number of sistrings. We will usually set n to N in calculations, and will suppose $N = 100\text{M} = 2^{27} = \frac{1}{8}10^9$. These numbers are used for comparison with the *New O.E.D.* work of Gonnet *et al.*, which involves a text of 600 megabytes and $n = 119{,}000{,}000$ sistrings, each starting at a word. In most of our calculations, N appears only in a logarithm. For the *New O.E.D.*, $\lg N - \lg n = 3$ bits, which makes minor difference. Where the difference is significant, we also show results for $N = 600$ MB.

As an example, the text there! has six sistrings: there!, here!, ere!, re!, e!, and !.

A *trie* is a tree structure whose internal nodes are empty. The decision which way to branch from an internal node at depth d is made according to the value of the dth position in the seach string. For *binary* tries, which we shall exclusively consider, this is the dth bit, and the trie node offers two options: branch left if 0 else right. An example, for there!, is shown in Figure 1.

The leaf nodes contain pointers to the text. These are called "starts". A search for er would correspond to the ASCII code of this string, branching left on 0 and right on 1. Thus the code 0110010101110010 becomes the search *lrrllrlrlrrrllrl*, where *l* means "left" and *r* means "right".

Note that the starts are placed as high as possible in the trie, and that the trie does not continue below the levels at which a sistring is unambiguously identified in the text. Because the sistrings are "semi-infinite", there is no possibility of ambiguity.

We see that the trie may have to become quite deep to distinguish between similar sistrings. For the six sistrings in there!, we must go to ten bits to distinguish ere! from e!.

A *PaTrie* is a trie in which nodes with only single descendents have been left out. This gives a much shallower tree, but adds the cost of storing *height* or *skip* information at each internal node. Figure 1 shows skips: the number of bits to be skipped in the search string before finding the bit corresponding to the node. Skips are more compact to store than heights, but we shall also use the latter. The height of the internal node is the position in the search string of the corresponding bit. We shall use "depth" and "height" interchangably.

This paper is primarily about PaTries, but the statistics that follow will include tries, so that we can show that the cost of storing skips is more than offset by the reduced height.

With this introduction, we can examine and try to evaluate a simple implementation of PaTries. The quantities that we shall show to be needed by the evaluation will motivate the statistics of the remainder of this Section.

The implementation simply represents each internal node by two pointers and the skip information, and each leaf node by a start. For n sistrings, the tree has $2n - 1$ nodes, so each pointer requires $\lg 2n$ bits. Each start requires $\lg N$ bits to address the Nbytes of the text. And skips require an average number of bits which we do not yet know, but which cannot exceed $\lg 8N$ (because the longest chain in the trie cannot exceed the $8N$ bits of the text).

This identifies the *average skip size* as something we need to find out. Our statistics will show that this lies between 4.24 and 7.98 for the measured texts. Thus the size of this PaTrie index would be

$$\frac{1}{8} \left(2n \lg 2n + n \lg N + \left\{ \begin{array}{c} 4.24 \\ 7.98 \end{array} \right\} n \right) = \left\{ \begin{array}{c} 10.9 \\ 11.4 \end{array} \right\} n$$

for a 100 megabyte file: about eleven times the text size.

The cost of searching this index would be proportional to the *average and maximum PaTrie depth* in the expected and worst cases, respectively. These are also quantities which we must measure.

We will measure the above quantities for PaTries and also for tries, because our proposed implementation will be based on earlier work for tries, and we must show that the PaTrie is indeed better than the trie.

As an aside to the present discussion, but an item which will be important later, we mention two improvements to the above PaTrie implementation. The first saves us one pointer by storing the PaTrie in, say, preorder, so that left descendents will be immediate neighbours of their parent nodes and so need no pointer. (This improvement makes access slower, however.)

The second improvement uses *text pages* as the target of the starts, instead of individual bytes. If the text is stored in pages of $4K = 2^{12}$ bytes, the starts are shorter by 12 bits.

Both improvements together reduce the index size to

$$\frac{1}{8} \left(n \lg 2n + n \lg \frac{N}{4K} + \left\{ \begin{array}{c} 4.24 \\ 7.98 \end{array} \right\} n \right) = \left\{ \begin{array}{c} 5.9 \\ 6.4 \end{array} \right\} n$$

for a 100 megabyte file: about six times the text size.

2.2 Theoretical Distributions

Theoretical analyses of tries have been carried out by Knuth [7] Vol. III, Pittel [11], and Devroye [3]. Assuming that the sistrings are independently and uniformly distributed, they give the following results for the number of nodes, the average depth, and the maximum depth of tries and PaTries.

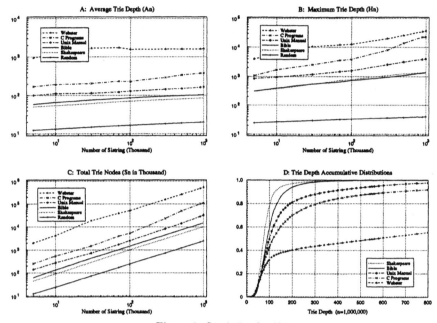

Figure 2: Statistics for Tries

Independent Random Sistring	Trie	PaTrie
S_n: Total Nodes	$n + n/\ln 2 = 2.44n$	$2n - 1$
A_n: Average Depth	$\lg n$	$\lg n$
H_n: Maximum Depth	$2 \lg n$	$\lg n$

Unfortunately, natural language text is not uniformly distributed. E is much more common than d in English. Nor is it independently distributed. Th is a more frequent combination than tz.

We must measure these quantities on actual texts. We will find that the theoretical values provide extreme lower bounds.

2.3 Measured Distributions

For five texts of 4.5 to 9.5 megabytes each, we picked 20 segments of 1Mbytes at random from each text, and constructed tries for all sistrings of each segment. The texts are: Shakespeare's *Complete Works*, as provided by Oxford University Press for NeXT Inc.; *The King James' Bible*, provided by ftp from akbar.cac.washington.edu; Section One of man pages for unix[tm] from Solbourne Computer Inc.; C source programs selected randomly from a departmental teaching machine; and *Webster's Ninth New Collegiate Dictionary*, as provided by NeXT Inc.

We calculated A_n and H_n for tries and PaTries. S_n is fixed at $2n - 1$ for PaTries, so we found it only for tries. For both tries and PaTries, we found the cumulative distribution of depths for $n = 1,000,000$ sistrings, that is, the proportion of nodes lying at or above a given depth in the tree. Finally, we found the cumulative distribution of skips for $n = 1,000,000$ sistrings, that is, the proportion of skips of size less than or equal to a given number of bits. This we used to estimate average skip sizes.

The results are plotted in Figures 2 and 3.

134

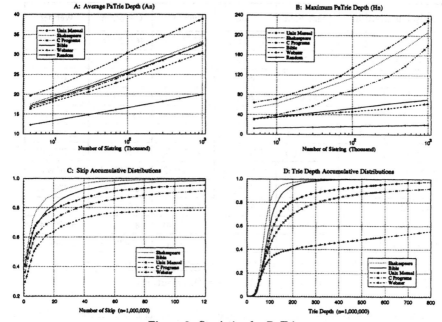

Figure 3: Statistics for PaTries

A qualitative inspection of these results shows that the texts fit a single ranking for S_n, A_n and H_n for tries and for skip sizes for PaTries. From best to worst:

Shakespeare's *Complete Works*
The King James' Bible
man pages from UNIX
C source programs
Webster's Ninth New Collegiate Dictionary

Webster was significantly worse than the others in all of these case. The reason is that we copied the dictionary redundantly from the NeXT by following all pointers, even if they lead to the same text. So our copy has many long, single repetitions. It is apparent that this is just what is bad for tries, but excellently handled by PaTries. So we expect Webster to behave well under PaTries, because it is effectively much shorter than the other texts, and that is what we find.

For H_n and A_n for PaTries, the rankings of the texts are almost consistent. The UNIX man pages are noticeably worse than the others. Webster is best, as expected, and, together with the Bible, has significantly lower maximum depth, H_n.

Where theory has given us results for independently and uniformly distributed text ("random"), we show them for comparison. They are much better than is possible with any of our actual texts.

The skip statistics are given in different form in Table 4. First, we show the maximum skip size found for each text, and its logarithm. Second, we show the percentage of skips of each of a given range of sizes (δ). Each of these ranges can be Huffman-encoded, giving a code length ρ. This added to a skip counter size, κ, can be weighted by δ and summed to give an expected skip size, ω. These give the best (Shakespeare) and worst (Webster) numbers used in Section 2.1 to calculate the index size.

Skip Distribution		Shakespeare	Bible	Unix Man	C Program	Webster
Largest Skip ⌈lg⌉		1519 (11)	1465 (11)	11067 (14)	46383 (16)	53540 (16)
ω = Σ δ* (κ + ρ)		4.24	4.79	5.36	6.55	7.98
skip	κ	δ (ρ)	δ (ρ)	δ (ρ)	δ (ρ)	δ (ρ)
0	0	30.85% (2)	30.26% (2)	27.82% (2)	24.29% (2)	20.39% (2)
1	0	14.06% (3)	10.95% (3)	13.50% (3)	11.85% (3)	9.35% (4)
2	0	4.64% (4)	4.19% (5)	5.18% (4)	4.36% (4)	3.73% (4)
3 .. 4	1	11.46% (3)	8.18% (3)	9.17% (3)	8.86% (4)	6.77% (4)
5 .. 8	2	15.65% (3)	14.61% (3)	12.21% (3)	11.54% (3)	11.84% (3)
9 .. 16	3	10.20% (3)	10.70% (3)	8.47% (3)	8.64% (4)	9.77% (4)
17 .. 32	4	7.54% (3)	10.67% (3)	7.66% (4)	8.97% (3)	8.48% (4)
33 .. 64	5	4.27% (5)	6.67% (4)	7.85% (4)	8.02% (4)	6.48% (4)
65 .. Largest	⌈lg(Larg)⌉	1.33% (5)	3.77% (5)	8.14% (4)	13.47% (3)	23.19% (2)

ω : average skip length (bits)   κ : skip length (bits)   δ : skip distribution   ρ : Huffmann code length

Figure 4: Table of Skip Distributions

Our experiments in Section 6 do not use techniques as sophisticated as those in Table 4. Instead, a five-bit counter is used for skip sizes of 30 or less, and a counter of maximum capacity (11–16 bits) is used for the rest. The ω used is shown in Table 14.

2.4   Parameter Fitting

Table 5 shows the results of regression fits to the data of Figures 2 and 3 for S_n, A_n and H_n. These numbers will be used in our comparisons in Section 4. (S_n for PaTries is always $2n - 1$.)

Table 6 shows the values of the regression formulae for 1 megabyte texts, and, for confirmation, the values actually measured on these texts. Only the maximum depth gives errors over 10%. (S_n for PaTreis is always 2M.)

Regressions on Measured Data	A_n (Average Depth)		H_n (Maximum Depth)		S_n (Total Nodes)
	Trie	PaTrie	Trie	PaTrie	Trie
Random	lg n	lg n	2 lg n	lg n	2.44n
Shakespeare	4.7 lg n - 8.0	2.1 lg n - 8.0	151 lg n - 1637	20.4 lg n - 212	10.2n - 13037
Bible	6.0 lg n - 13.7	2.0 lg n - 7.9	138 lg n - 1472	5.2 lg n - 33	15.1n - 32635
Unix Manual	8.5 lg n - 6.8	2.6 lg n - 12.4	425 lg n - 4886	22.5 lg n- 230	32.6n - 560816
C Program	28.5 lg n - 202.0	2.1 lg n - 9.5	2756 lg n - 37061	19.2 lg n - 219	111.4n - 3464685
Webster	68.1 lg n + 364.0	1.8 lg n - 6.5	4120 lg n - 50590	4.1 lg n - 21	529.1n + 58419

Figure 5: Table of Regression Fits

$n = 1,000,000$ Expected (Measured)	A_n (Average Depth)		H_n (Maximum Depth)		S_n (Total Nodes)
	Trie	PaTrie	Trie	PaTrie	Trie
Random	20	20	40	20	2.44 M
Shakespeare	86 (85)	34 (33)	1373 (1408)	195 (206)	10.2 (10.2) M
Bible	106 (105)	32 (32)	1279 (1383)	71 (71)	15.1 (15.1) M
Unix Manual	163 (168)	39 (39)	3585 (4022)	219 (230)	32.0 (32.9) M
C Program	366 (385)	32 (33)	17870 (22651)	164 (180)	107.9 (108.1) M
Webster	1721 (1622)	29 (30)	31528 (36955)	61 (63)	529.2 (531.8) M

Figure 6: Table Confirming the Regression

3 A Pointerless PaTrie

3.1 Motivation

In Section 2.1, we looked at one trie implementation, a tree with pointers. Removing one set of pointers saved significant space — about 3.5 times the text size. To motivate the following discussion, we now look at Gonnet's implementation, which has no pointers at all, and is not even a tree. ("Pointerless" refers to the absence of internal pointers in the tree structure. Starts, which are also pointers, are still needed.)

This is the PAT array implementation [6]. It stores nothing but starts, and so requires

$$(n \lg N)/8 = 3.4n \text{ bytes.}$$

The idea is to store these starts in lexicographical order of the sistrings they point to, and to use them for a binary search of the text.

This would seem to be the absolutely minimal index for addressing any character in a text. We find that it is not. The major consideration is that we cannot use the text paging improvement of Section 2.1 to reduce the start size. This is because the binary search must do a comparison with the text each time it looks up a start, and so the start must point to the starting byte of the text, not merely to a page. We will find a tree representation whose nodes are smaller than the 12 or so bits we lose on the starts by not paging the text.

Another drawback of the PAT array approach is that the text must be accessed each of the lg n times a start is looked up, and this is much more expensive than searching a well-made tree, with reference to the text only from the leaf nodes. For an index of 100M sistrings, this is 27 accesses to the text. In addition, we must access the PAT array, but in this case we can take advantage of storing it in pages on disk. If a page holds about $2^{10} = 1024$ starts, the last ten lookups of the PAT array will all be on the same page, so the cost will be only about 18 accesses to the PAT array. This is a total of 45 accesses.

For a disk with 20ms seek time on the average and 1μsec. per byte transfer time, supposing 4Kbyte text pages, 45 accesses cost just over one second.

This time can be halved by an idea which we have not seen suggested or worked out in the literature. We can save accesses to the text in the early part of the binary search by storing prefixes on each index page. For 100M sistrings and an alphabet of 2^7 printable characters, 14 bits can distinguish some $2^{14} = 16384$ different pages (which will thus each contain $2^{13} = 8192$ starts, needing about 27648 bytes). We can suppose that each choice of the binary search corresponds to a bit discrimination: this is true for random sistrings, and probably close for natural language sistrings in the early stages of the search. Thus, storing the 14 bits per index page (for a total of 28Kbytes extra for the index) saves us almost 14 accesses to the text.

Furthermore, the corresponding acesses to the index can be eliminated by storing only the prefixes in a master index, which can reside in RAM.

The resulting 14 accesses to 4Kbyte text pages, and one access to a 27Kbyte index pages costs

$$14 \times 24\text{ms.} + 1 \times 48\text{ms.} = 0.4 \text{ sec.}$$

Repeating this calculation with three characters stored per index page as a prefix gives 7 accesses to 4Kbyte text pages, and one access to an index page of $2^6 = 64$ starts or 216 bytes:

$$7 \times 24\text{ms.} + 1 \times 20\text{ms.} = 0.2 \text{ sec.}$$

for an overhead of 5.25 megabytes: the larger the prefix, and thus the smaller the index page, the better.

3.2   Orenstein's Pointerless Trie

The way to a compact PaTrie representation was shown by Orenstein [10], who represented ordinary tries with two bits per node. The first bit indicates the presence of a left descendent, and the second bit indicates the presence of a right descendent. These bits are stored breadth first in a bitstring. The position of the bits of either descendent, if it exists, of a node is easily calculated relative to the position of the node. For example, the bitstring corresponding to the trie for there! is 10110001111110010011100000001101100000: the root node has a left descendent only (10), which has two descendents (11), of which the first is a leaf (00) and the second has only a right descendent (01), etc.

All we have to add to this is a start for each leaf node, and we have a very compact representation of a trie. The starts may be abbreviated to point to a text page rather than the exact text byte.

If this were all, we would have to search this tree sequentially, because we must count on-bits in each level to determine the number of bits in the next level. The attractive part of Orenstein's approach is his partitioning mechanism. A certain number of levels of the trie are stored, as bitstrings, in a page which we shall call an *index page*, as opposed to the *text pages* discussed earlier. The upper levels fit on one page. The lower levels are grouped on pages so that there are levels of pages, too, and any level of the trie nodes is either entirely on or entirely off a level of pages.

Each page, p, contains two integers in addition to the bits for the nodes. *Tcount* counts the number of links coming from higher-level pages to pages to the left of p and on the same level. *Bcount* counts the number of links leaving those left neighbours for lower-level pages. With these two counters, appropriately stored, we can search this compact trie in a logarithmic number of accesses, with the sequential searches being confined to only the pages we access.

We adopt this method of organizing secondary storage, and describe it more precisely in Section 3.4.

Using a trie in this approach is potentially expensive. Our statistics for tries show us that the number of nodes in a trie ranges from $10.2n$ (for Shakespeare) to $529.1n$ (for Webster). The size of the index is 2 bits per node plus n starts, or

$$\frac{1}{8}\left(n \lg \frac{N}{4K} + 2\left\{\begin{array}{c} 10.2 \\ 529.1 \end{array}\right\} n\right) = \left\{\begin{array}{c} 4.4 \\ 134 \end{array}\right\} n \text{ bytes}$$

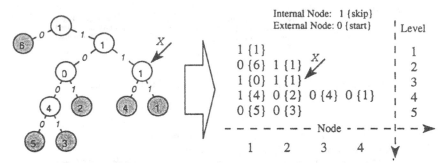

Figure 7: Bit String Representation for PaTries

for a 100 megabyte file. Thus, the index size is no smaller than PAT arrays, and can be immensely larger.

The search time will depend on the average and maximum trie depths, and we see from Section 2.4 that this is substantially higher for tries than for PaTries.

We proceed to see if we can adapt Orenstein's technique to PaTries, and if the result is worth while.

3.3   The Bit String Representation

In this section, we propose a new text index representation. Just as the pointerless trie can be represented with two bits per node, a pointerless PaTrie can be represented with one bit per node, plus, of course, a skip. The bit merely need tell us if the node has descendents or not, since any PaTrie node has either two descendents or none. That is, the bit is on for an internal node, and the associated integer is a skip, or it is off for an external node, and the associated integer is a start.

Figure 7 shows this representation for the text there!.

We can estimate the size right away, to see if it is worth going on. We must store n skips, n starts, and one bit for each of the $2n - 1$ nodes:

$$\frac{1}{8}\left(2n - 1 + n\lg\frac{N}{4K} + \left\{\begin{array}{c}4.24\\7.98\end{array}\right\}n\right) = \left\{\begin{array}{c}2.7\\3.1\end{array}\right\}n \text{ bytes}$$

for a 100M sistring index: about three times the text size, and always less than the PAT array. As with the earlier size calculations, the figures in braces are for Shakespeare and Webster, respectively, the best and worst cases.

Figure 7 illustrates the calculation to find the descendent of a node. Let l be the level and i be the number of internal nodes encountered within l. Then the descendents are at level $l + 1$: the left at position $2i - 1$ within $l + 1$; and the right at position $2i$. Thus, for X, shown, $(l, i) = (4, 2)$, because X is the second on-bit of level 4, and the descendents are bits 3 and 4 of level 5.

To do this, we must scan each level from beginning to end, counting internal nodes in variable inode. We need to know when a level ends. The total nodes in a level, tnode = 2×inode for the previous level. So we also count external nodes, enode, in a level, and reset the level when

$$\text{inode} + \text{enode} = \text{tnode}$$

So, as with Orenstein's method, we must scan the whole representation sequentially.

Algorithm 8 returns a child and its node position, and Algorithm 9 searches the trie for SearchKey, using ChildNode.

We discuss index paging and a way around this sequential access in the next section.

```
Type NodeLocation = Record
                    Page: ^IndexPage;                        {To an Index Page}
                    Level, Tnode, Height: Integer;           {Level Information}
                    Inode, Enode: Integer;                   {Node Position}
                    Case type: one Bit of
                      1: Skip: Integer;                      {Skip Counter}
                      0: Start: Integer                      {Start Counter}
                    End;
Procedure GetChild( LeftChild: Boolean; var CurrNode: NodeLocation);
  Var  ChildLevel, ChildPosition: Integer;
  Begin
    ChildLevel:= CurrNode.Level + 1;
    ChildPosition:= CurrNode.Inode * 2;
    If LeftChild then ChildPosition:= ChildPosition - 1;

    While CurrNode is not the child node do begin
      If CurrNode is the last node of the level then        {Inode+Enode ≠ Tnode}
        Begin CurrNode.Level:= CurrNode.Level + 1;           {Jump to Next Level}
              CurrNode.Tnode:= CurrNode.Inode * 2;           {Total Nodes of Next Level}
              CurrNode.Height:= CurrNode.Height + 1;         {Height of Next Level}
              CurrNode.Inode:= 0;  CurrNode.Enode := 0       {No Node Read in Yet}
        End;
      Read the next node from CurrNode.Page;
      If CurrNode.type = 1 then begin
        CurrNode.Inode:= CurrNode.Inode + 1;                 {CurrNode is an Internal Node}
        CurrNode.Height:= CurrNode.Height + CurrNode.Skip End
      Else CurrNode.Enode:= CurrNode.Enode + 1               {CurrNode is an External Node}
    End
End;
```

Figure 8: Algorithm for Finding a Child

```
Type NodeLocation = Record
                    Page: ^IndexPage;                        {To the Index Page}
                    Level, Tnode, Height: Integer;           {Level Information}
                    Inode, Enode: Integer;                   {Node Position}
                    Case type: one Bit of
                      1: Skip:  Integer;                     {Skip Counter}
                      0: Start: Integer                      {Start Counter}
                    End;
Function TrieSearch( SearchKey: Array of Bit): Boolean;
  Var  CurrNode: NodeLocation;
       IndexedKey: Array of Bit;
  Begin
    Read Trie root to CurrNode;                              {Search Starts from the Root}
    while CurrNode.type = 1 do                               {Stop If CurrNode is an External Node}
      If length of Searchkey >= CurrNode.Height then
        If Searchkey[CurrNode.Height] = 0 then               {SearchKey is not Exhausted Yet}
          GetChild( True, CurrNode)                          {Jump to the Left Child}
        Else GetChild( False, CurrNode)                      {Jump to the Right Child}
      Else GetChild( True, CurrNode);                        {Bits Beyond the Searchkey}

    IndexedKey:= Sistring pointed by CurrNode.start;         {Read in the Indexed Key}
    If SearchKey is a prefix of IndexedKey then              {Verify the Skipped Bits}
      TrieSearch:= True
    Else TrieSearch:= False
  End;
```

Figure 9: Algorithm for Searching the Trie

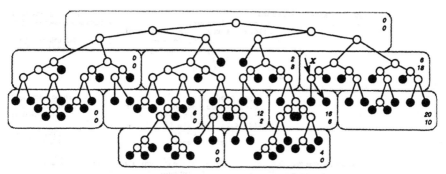

Figure 10: PaTrie with Index Paging

3.4   Index Paging

We are now concerned with partitioning the bit string for secondary storage. The method is the same as Orenstein's. Figure 10 shows an example where a level of pages corresponds to three levels of PaTrie nodes.

The example shows *Tcount*, the upper integer in each page, and *Bcount*, the integer below *Tcount*. *Bcount* is stored as shown in Figure 10, but *Tcount* in the page *above*. Each page thus has one *Bcount* and a set of *Tcounts*, together with pointers to the corresponding pages. For example, the page containing X will contain the *Tcounts* 6 and 20, and pointers to the pages below it that are shown with those *Tcounts*.

This structure is used to find, for example, the right child of X in the following way. *Bcount* is 18 and the right child of X is the second link out of the page. Thus we need a page whose *Tcount* is next below 18 + 2 = 20. The list of *Tcounts* on the page points us to the appropriate next page. Sequential scans were done only within the page, and at most one page per level is read.

Algorithm 11 spells this out. Figure 12 shows the data structure for the example of Figure 10.

The size for the index estimated above is out by less than a percent, with sufficiently large pages, due to the overhead of *Bcount*, *Tcount* and the page addresses. It is still smaller than the PAT array.

The access cost is A_n/k in the average case, where k is the number of node levels per page level, and H_n/k in the worst case. We find $k = 8$ corresponds to index pages of just over 1Kbyte. According to Section 2.4, this gives the following average access costs.

$$\frac{1}{8} \left(\left\{ \begin{array}{c} 1.8 \\ 2.6 \end{array} \right\} \lg n - \left\{ \begin{array}{c} 6.5 \\ 12.4 \end{array} \right\} \right) = \left\{ \begin{array}{c} 5.3 \\ 7.2 \end{array} \right\}$$

accesses for a 100M sistring index. For a disk with 20ms seek time on the average and 1μsec. per byte transfer time, this is a cost of from 0.11 to 0.15 sec. for a search for any character in the file. The two extreme cases above are Webster (best) and the UNIX manual (worst).

The worst case access costs are

$$\frac{1}{8} \left(\left\{ \begin{array}{c} 4.1 \\ 22.5 \end{array} \right\} \lg n - \left\{ \begin{array}{c} 21 \\ 230 \end{array} \right\} \right) = \left\{ \begin{array}{c} 11.2 \\ 47.2 \end{array} \right\}$$

accesses for a 100M sistring index. These correspond to 0.24 sec. and 0.99 sec., with the extremes again being given by Webster and the UNIX manual, respectively.

```
Type IndexPage = Record                                    { Index Page Structure }
              Bcount, M: Integer;              { M: number of connected Pages }
              Children: Array [1..M] of record
                            Tcount: Integer;             { Of children Pages }
                            Page: ^IndexPage           { To a child Index Page }
                        End;
              SubTrie: BitString                             { Bit String }
         End;
Type NodeLocation = Record
              Page: ^IndexPage;                        { To the Index Page }
              Level, Tnode, Height: Integer;          { Level Information }
              Inode, Enode: Integer;                     { Node Position }
              Case type: one Bit of
                  1: Skip: Integer;                        { Skip Counter }
                  0: Start: Integer                       { Start Counter }
              End;
Procedure GetPagedChild( LeftChild: Boolean; var CurrNode: NodeLocation);
  Var  ChildLevel, ChildPosition, i: Integer;
  Begin
     If  Children are in the same index page then GetChild( LeftChild, CurrNode)
     Else begin
        ChildPosition:= CurrNode.Inode*2 + CurrNode.Page->Bcount;
        If LeftChild then ChildPosition:= ChildPosition - 1;

        i:= 1;                                 {Children[i].Page will be the Entering Index Page}
        While CurrNode.Page->Children[i+1].Tcount < ChildPosition do i:= i + 1;

        ChildPosition:= ChildPosition - CurrNode.Page->Children[i].Tcount;
        CurrNode.Level:= CurrNode.Level + 1;        { Level # of the Entering Index Page }
        CurrNode.Tnode:= CurrNode.Page->Children[i+1].Tcount -
                  CurrNode.Page->Children[i].Tcount;     { # of First Level Nodes }
        CurrNode.Height:= CurrNode.Height + 1;          { Height of Next Level }
        CurrNode.Inode:= 0; CurrNode.Enode :=0;         { No Node Read in Yet }

        CurrNode.Page:= CurrNode.Page->Children[i].Page;
        Read CurrNode.Page into RAM, and read the first node into CurrNode;

        While CurrNode is not ChildPosition do begin       { Inode+Enode<>ChildPosition }
          Read the next node from CurrNode.Page->SubTrie;
          If CurrNode.type = 1 then begin
              CurrNode.Inode:= CurrNode.Inode + 1;      { CurrNode is an Internal Node }
              CurrNode.Height:= CurrNode.Height + CurrNode.Skip End
          Else CurrNode.Enode:= CurrNode.Enode + 1      { CurrNode is an External Node }
        End End
  End;
```

Figure 11: Algorithm to Find Child for Paged PaTrie

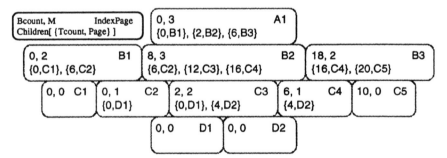

Figure 12: Data Structure for Paged PaTrie

4 Size and Access Comparisons

We summarize the size calculations made throughout earlier parts of the paper for various indexes. n is the number of sistrings, and the calculations all assume $n = 2^{27}$ and sistrings start at each byte. For timings, we assume a disk with 20ms. expected seek time and 1μsec. transfer time per byte. The text pages are 4Kbytes where applicable, and the index pages are 4Kbytes for PAT arrays and 1Kbytes for the Pointerless PaTrie.

PaTrie or Trie	Index Size	Access Average	Maximum
Pointer (PaTrie) (§2.1)	$5.9n\dots11.4n$		
PAT array (PaTrie) (§3.1)	$3.4n$	28 accesses 0.2 sec. (1 sec. by prev. methods)	
Pointerless Trie (§3.2)	$4.4n\dots134n$		
Pointerless PaTrie (§§3.3, 3.4)	$2.7n\dots3.1n$	$5.3\dots7.2$ $0.11\dots0.15$ sec.	$11.2\dots47.2$ $0.24\dots0.99$ sec.

Experiments in Section 6 will establish the validity of these analytical results.

5 Building the Pointerless PaTrie

This section treats very briefly the PaTrie construction algorithms detailed in [8]. These algorithms are adaptations to tries of similar methods given by Gonnet *et al.* [6] for PAT arrays. They differ mainly in the extensions we have made to include height (skip) information. In addition, we have devised an algorithm to handle dynamic texts.

For building the whole index, a dynamic algorithm is intrinsically slow, as we point out in Section 1. To build the whole PaTrie, we can do much better than the incremental algorithm by careful use of sorting. The approach is based on the fact that if we have an ordered set of sistrings, this is equivalent to the inorder traversal of the PaTrie. The PaTrie can be constructed from the ordered sistrings in one pass. The method is a special case of parsing expressions with operator precedence [1]. In particular, we have only binary "operators", and our tree is unique.

Sorting sistrings is more difficult than sorting fixed-length records. Here we refer to the methods of [6]. We followed two approaches.

The *prefix sort* simply sorts fixed-length prefixes of each sistring. This requires a large intermediate workspace. In our implementation, we used 50-byte prefixes, which, together with 4-byte starts, gives a multiplier of 54. Thus, 100M sistrings need a workspace of 5.4GB.

The *counter sort* includes *counters* in the initial runs, which tell us, for all previous runs, how many starts separate starts that are adjacent in the current run. This eliminates the prefixes, but still requires a workspace 16 times the number of sistrings: three counters and a start for each sistring.

6 Experimental Results

We built PaTries for one-, four-, and eight-megabyte extracts from each of our five texts, and measured access times, index sizes, and construction times. This section shows the comparisons of these results with calculations based on the considerations in this paper.

Text	Successful Searches			Unsuccessful
	Calculated (ms.) $n=100,000,000$		Measured (ms.) $n=1,000,000$	Measured (ms.)
Webster	160.18	113.84	116.10	102.43
Bible	175.35	123.86	121.40	115.58
C Programs	179.45	125.38	123.33	118.12
Shakespeare	185.26	131.19	125.67	116.72
UNIX man	219.70	152.76	145.45	144.40

Notes.

1. Calculations use $(A_n/8) \times 31$ ms.

2. A_n is from Table 5.

Figure 13: Access Time for PaTries

Text	ω	$N = n = 1,000,000$		$N = n = 4,000,000$		$N = n = 100,000,000$
		Measured	Calculated	Measured	Calculated	Calculated
Shakespeare	5.72	1.99MB	1.97MB	8.95MB	8.86MB	284.0MB
Bible	6.27	2.10MB	2.03MB	9.25MB	9.14MB	290.0MB
UNIX man	7.35	2.12MB	2.17MB	10.08MB	9.68MB	304.4MB
C Programs	8.60	2.39MB	2.33MB	10.59MB	10.30MB	320.0MB
Webster	9.91	2.47MB	2.49MB	10.95MB	10.96MB	336.4MB

Notes.

1. See Section 2.3 for discussion of ω.

2. Calculations use $n(2 + \lceil \lg N/4K \rceil + \omega)/8$

3. Calculations do not include $\approx 1\%$ counter overheads on index pages.

Figure 14: Table of Sizes of PaTries

6.1 PaTrie Searching

We measured access times for each of our texts for both successful and unsuccessful searches. Table 13 shows the results and the time we calculated for successful searches. The measured and calculated quantities differ by at most 2%. Note that we use 31 ms. as the multiplier instead of the ≈ 20 ms. of the rest of the paper: this is an adjustment to accommodate CPU processing. (Our disk actually has 13.5 ms. seek time and 0.5 μsec. transfer time.)

6.2 PaTrie Construction

The index sizes as estimated and as constructed are shown in Table 14. The discrepancy does not exceed 4%. We also show the estimated size for texts of 100M sistrings, one sistring per byte: we have not built indexes of this size.

Table 15 shows the costs of constructing PaTrie indexes by the two methods outlined in Section 5, the prefix sort and the counter sort techniques.

Measurement & Calculations for $N = n = 4M$						
	Shakespeare	Bible	UNIX	C Programs	Webster	Calc.
Prefix (minutes)	35	37	52	80	110	9
Counter (hours)	5.4	5.4	5.7	5.5	5.7	0.12
Extrapolations to $N = n \approx 8M$						
	Shakespeare	Bible	UNIX	C Programs	Webster	
Size (n_2)	6.7M	4.5M	7.5M	8M	8M	
$n_2 \lg n_2 / n_1 \lg n_1$	1.65	1.14	2.05	2.09	2.09	
Prefix	1.71	1.13	2.06	1.96	2.11	
Counter	1.69	1.14	2.14	2.09	2.16	
Extrapolations to $n = 100M$						
	Shakespeare	Bible	UNIX	C Programs	Webster	
Prefix (hours)	18	18	26	41	55	
Counter (days)	6.3	6.9	7.2	6.9	7.2	

Figure 15: Table of PaTrie Construction Times

The upper part of the table shows the times for 4,000,000 sistrings, starting at each byte. The measurements show times used by our algorithm running on a NeXT Cube (68030, 28MB RAM, 25 Mhz) and disk times of 13.5 msec. (average seek) and 0.5 μsec. (transfer per byte). For the prefix sort, which needs a workspace of 216MB, they range from 35 minutes (Shakespeare) to 1.83 hours (Webster). For the counter sort, which needs a smaller workspace of 64MB, the range is much tighter, from 5.39 to 5.68 hours. The calculations give I/O time only for the disk used. We see that the algorithms, especially the counter sort, is I/O bound, and the calculations give only a loose lower bound.

Therefore, the middle part of the table shows extrapolation factors, assuming the algorithm has complexity $O(n \log n)$. The extrapolation is from 4M sistrings to the size of the full texts, with a maximum of 8M. The upper line shows these sizes. The second row shows the calculated extrapolation factors. The lower two rows show the factors measured for prefix sort and for counter sort. For this doubling of the text, the extrapolation is good to 6%.

Finally, the bottom part of the table applies the extrapolation factors to a text of $n = 100,000,000$ sistrings. The results are essentially independent of N. For the prefix sort, which has an overhead of 5.4GB, the predicted times range from 17 to 55 hours. The counter sort requires only 1.6GB but takes 6.28 to 7.19 days.

7 Special Searching

Various searching problems are described by Gonnet *et al.* [6] and can be solved using their PAT array implementation. All of these problems can also be handled by our pointerless PaTrie. They include matching regular expressions by simulating the corresponding finite automaton on the trie or PaTrie. They also include proximity searching (*e.g.*, finding adjacent occurrences of t and h; finding longest repetitions (*e.g.*, e! and ere!); and finding most frequent strings of a given length or most common words of varying lengths.

8 Conclusions

We have presented a new implementation of PaTries for indexing very large text documents on secondary storage. We have shown that our implementation is 10% – 25% smaller than previous data structures. This difference is important since index size is crucial to the trie approach. Our access times are several times faster than the competitive trie index, and our method retains all the flexibility of other trie methods.

Building trie indexes may also be slow. The most recent report on the PAT array says it can be built over a weekend for the *New O.E.D.*. Our index takes 18 to 55 hours for a comparable text. We also present methods for dynamic tries, so that the text may change.

References

[1] A. V. Aho, R. Sethi, and J. D. Ullman. *Compilers Principles, Techniques, and Tools*. Addison-Wesley Publishing Co., Reading, MA, 1986.

[2] R. de la Briandais. File searching using variable-length keys. In *Proc. Western Joint Computer Conf.*, pages 295–8, San Francisco, March 1959.

[3] L. Devroye. A note on the average depth of tries. *Computing*, 28:367–371, 1982.

[4] E. H. Fredkin. Trie memory. *Communications of the ACM*, 3(9):490–9, Sept. 1960.

[5] G. H. Gonnet. Efficient searching of text and pictures. Technical Report OED-88-02, Centre for the New Oxford English Dictionary, University of Waterloo, Waterloo, Ont., Canada, 1988.

[6] G. H. Gonnet, R. A. Baeza-Yates, and T. Snider. Lexicograhic indices for text: Inverted files vs. PAT trees. Technical Report OED-91-01, Centre for the New Oxford English Dictionary, University of Waterloo, Waterloo, Ont., Canada, February 1991.

[7] D. E. Knuth. *The Art of Computer Programming*. Addison-Wesley Publishing Co., Reading, Mass., 1968–1973. Volumes I, II, III.

[8] T. H. Merrett and H. Shang. Trie methods for representing text. Technical Report TR–SOCS–93.3, McGill University, School of Computer Science, June 1993.

[9] D. R. Morrison. PATRICIA: Practical algorithm to retrieve information coded in alphanumeric. *Journal of the ACM*, 15:514–34, 1968.

[10] J.A. Orenstein. Blocking mechanism used by multidimensional tries. Unpublished Letter, February 1983.

[11] B. Pittel. Asymptotical growth of a class of random trees. *The Annals of Probability*, 13(2):414–427, 1985.

Estimation of False Drops in Set-valued Object Retrieval with Signature Files

Hiroyuki Kitagawa[*] Yoshiaki Fukushima[†§]
Yoshiharu Ishikawa[‡] and Nobuo Ohbo[*]

[*] Institute of Information Sciences and Electronics, University of Tsukuba
[†] Master's Program in Science and Engineering, University of Tsukuba
[‡] Doctoral Program in Engineering, University of Tsukuba
Tennohdai, Tsukuba, Ibaraki 305, Japan
E-mail: kitagawa,ishikawa,ohbo@dblab.is.tsukuba.ac.jp

Abstract. Advanced database systems have to support complex data structures as treated in object-oriented data models and nested relational data models. In particular, efficient processing of set-valued object retrieval (simply, set retrieval) is indispensable for such systems. In the previous paper [6], we proposed the use of *signature files* as efficient set retrieval facilities and showed their potential capabilities based on a disk page access cost model. Retrieval with signature files is always accompanied by mismatches called *false drops*, and it is very important in designing signature files to properly control the false drops.

In this paper, we present an in-depth study of false drops in set retrieval with signature files. We derive formulas estimating false drops in four types of set retrieval based on the "has-subset," "is-subset," "has-intersection," and "is-equal" relationships. Then we evaluate their validity by computer simulations. Simulation study is also done to investigate false drops in practically probable more complex situations.

1 Introduction

According to the recent expansion of the database application domain, requirements for the database system to handle complex data have been increasing. To meet the requirements, advanced data models such as nested relational data models [5, 8, 11] and object-oriented data models [9, 15] are investigated. Those models manipulate more complex data structures and, in particular, directly handle set values. Therefore, efficient set retrieval methods are necessary for database systems supporting those models. Although new indexing schemes such as the nested index and the multiindex [1, 12] considering the hierarchical structures in the complex data objects have been investigated, they are not designed to fully support set manipulation in general. We have proposed the use of *signature files* as efficient set retrieval facilities and showed their potential capabilities focusing on the retrieval with the set inclusion operator ($\subseteq$) [6].

Signature files were originally designed for text retrieval, where text blocks including a certain query word are retrieved [2, 3, 4]. Although applications of signature files to non-text object retrieval such as to the traditional record retrieval [10] and to the Prolog clause retrieval [14] were discussed, study on their capabilities in

---

[§] Current Affiliation: Open Systems Development Laboratories, NEC Corporation.

set retrieval has not been reported by other researchers to the best of our knowledge. Retrieval with signature files is always accompanied by mismatches called *false drops*. The number of false drops has a direct effect on the number of disk page accesses [6]. Therefore, it is important to estimate the false drops and to properly control them in the design of signature files.

In this paper, we present an in-depth study of false drops in set retrieval with signature files. Here, we consider the use of signature files in facilitating four types of set retrieval based on the "has-subset," "is-subset," "has-intersection," and "is-equal" relationships. In the analysis, we take distribution of cardinalities of retrieved sets into account. We derive probability-theoretic formulas estimating the false drops, and evaluate their validity by computer simulations. Moreover, we investigate false drops in practically probable more complex situations.

The paper is organized as follows: In Section 2, we give an overview of signature files and present their use in set retrieval based on the "has-subset," "is-subset," "has-intersection," and "is-equal" relationships. In Section 3, we derive formulas estimating false drops of the retrieval in two situations; (1) Uniform target cardinality, where retrieved sets have the same cardinality, and (2) Varying target cardinality, where their cardinalities follow the binomial distribution. In Section 4, we evaluate validity of those formulas by computer simulations. Simulation study is also done to investigate false drops in more complex situations. Section 5 is the summary and conclusion.

2 Set Retrieval with Signature Files

2.1 Set Retrieval Conditions

One of the typical data models supporting set values and their retrieval is the nested relational model [5, 8, 11]. Figure 1 shows a sample nested relation representing departments in a sales company. Attributes DNO and DNAME represent the department number and name, respectively. Each tuple is tagged with the tuple identifier (TID). SALES_ITEM is a *set attribute* and represents the set of sales items of each department. Tuple retrieval based on the SALES_ITEM attribute value, for instance SALES_ITEM $\supseteq$ {pen, pencil}, is an example of set retrieval investigated in this paper. In this case, each SALES_ITEM attribute value is called a *target set*, and {pen, pencil} is called a *query set*.

Although a number of nested relational algebras have been proposed, the selection operation in most of the nested relational algebras considers selection conditions including (some of) the following set comparison operators. Here, T and Q denote the target set and query set, respectively, and q denotes a simple value given in case of $T \ni q$.

1. $T \ni q$ (*has-element*): The target set has the simple value q as an element.
   Q1: Retrieve the departments that sell pencils.

2. $T \supseteq Q$ (*has-subset*): The target set has the query set as a subset.
   Q2: Retrieve the departments that sell both pens and pencils.

3. $T \subseteq Q$ (*is-subset*): The target set is a subset of the query set.
   Q3: Retrieve the departments that do not sell items other than pens, pencils, erasers, and cutters.

DEPT			
TID	DNO	DNAME	SALES_ITEM
			INAME
T1	314	stationery_1	pen
			pencil
			ink
T2	125	stationery_2	notebook
			eraser
			clip
			cutter

Figure 1 Example Nested Relation

4. $T \sqcap Q^*$ (*has-intersection*): The target set has intersection with the query set.
   Q4: Retrieve the departments that sell **erasers** or **staplers**.

5. $T \equiv Q$ (*is-equal*): The target set is equal to the query set.
   Q5: Retrieve the departments that sell only **pens**, **pencils**, and **ink**.

As $T \ni q$ is a special case of $T \supseteq Q$, we consider four types of set retrieval conditions $(T \supseteq Q, T \subseteq Q, T \sqcap Q, T \equiv Q)$ in the remaining part of this paper.

2.2 Use of Signature Files

Signature files were originally designed for text retrieval [2, 3, 4]. They require much smaller storage space than inverted files, and they can handle updates easily. A *signature* is a bit pattern formed for each data object and stored in the signature file. A typical query processing with the signature file is as follows: When a query is given, a *query signature* is formed from the query value. Then each signature in the signature file is examined over the query signature for potential match. If the signature satisfies a pre-defined condition implied by the query condition, the corresponding data object becomes a candidate that may satisfy the query. Such a data object is called a *drop*. The last step is the *false drop resolution*, and each drop is accessed and examined whether it actually satisfies the query condition. Drops that fail the test are called *false drops*, while the qualified data objects are called *actual drops*.

In set retrieval with signature files, a *target signature* is generated for each target set as shown in Figure 2. First, each element in a target set is hashed to a binary bit pattern called an *element signature*. All element signatures have F bit length, and m bits are set to "1". Then, a target signature is obtained by bit-wise OR-ing (*superimposed coding*) element signatures of all the elements in the target set. Pairs of such a target signature and a TID of the tuple including the target set are stored in the signature file as shown in Figure 3.

Queries mentioned in Subsection 2.1 are processed with the signature files in the following way.

---

* "$T \sqcap Q$" stands for "$T \cap Q \neq \phi$."

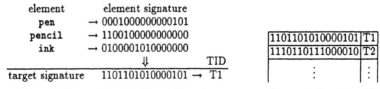

element	element signature
pen	→ 0001000000000101
pencil	→ 1100100000000000
ink	→ 0100001010000000
	⇓ TID
target signature	1101101010000101 → T1

Figure 2 Generation of a Target Signature

1101101010000101	T1
1110110111000010	T2
⋮	⋮

Figure 3 Signature File

1) A query signature is generated from the query set Q in the same way as the target signature.
2) The signature file is examined. Each target set becomes a drop if the following condition is satisfied.

   $T \supseteq Q$:   *query signature $\wedge$ target signature = query signature*[†].

   $T \subseteq Q$:   *query signature $\wedge$ target signature = target signature.*

   $T \sqcap Q$:   *weight(query signature $\wedge$ target signature) $\geq m$.*

   The number of bits set to "1" is called the *weight*, and the function *weight()* returns the weight.

   $T \equiv Q$:   *query signature = target signature.*

3) The drops in step 2) are retrieved and checked whether they actually satisfy the query condition (false drop resolution).

Figure 4 illustrates steps 1) and 2) in query processing of the query **Q2**. The tuple T1 becomes a drop because its satisfies the above condition for $T \supseteq Q$.

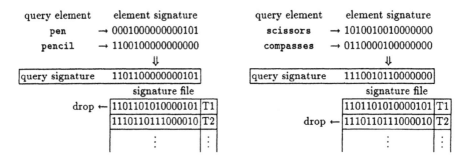

query element	element signature
pen	→ 0001000000000101
pencil	→ 1100100000000000
	⇓
query signature	1101100000000101

signature file

drop ←	1101101010000101	T1
	1110110111000010	T2
	⋮	⋮

Figure 4 Query Processing of **Q2**

query element	element signature
scissors	→ 1010010010000000
compasses	→ 0110000100000000
	⇓
query signature	1110010110000000

signature file

	1101101010000101	T1
drop ←	1110110111000010	T2
	⋮	⋮

Figure 5 False Drop

3   False Drop Probabilities

Figure 5 shows a case where false drops occur. The query with the condition $T \supseteq$ {scissors, compasses} is processed in this example. Although the tuple T2 does

---

[†] '$\wedge$' stands for bit-wise AND operation.

not satisfy this condition, it becomes a drop. Thus, it is a false drop. The false drop is due to the collision of element signatures and the superimposed coding method.

The frequency of false drop is usually measured in the *false drop probability*. The false drop probability Fd is defined as follows:

$$Fd = \frac{\text{false drops}}{N - \text{actual drops}}, \tag{1}$$

where N is the total number of target sets [3].

In set retrieval with signature files, the number of false drops is an important performance measure. Therefore, it is necessary to properly control the false drops. In this section, we derive mathematical formulas estimating false drop probabilities for the four types of queries mentioned in Section 2. As discussed in [3], we can derive those formulas assuming the case of unsuccessful search, where we have no actual drops.

3.1 Basic Considerations

Table 1 shows symbols used in our analysis. We make following assumptions related with the element signature generation.

1. The weight of an element signature is very small compared with the signature size ($m \ll F$).
2. The "1"'s are uniformly distributed in an element signature. Therefore, each bit position is set to "1" with the same probability.

From the assumption 2, each bit position in an element signature is set with the probability m/F. Therefore, the probability that a bit position b_t of a target signature is set to "1" is given by

$$p(b_t) = 1 - \left(1 - \tfrac{m}{F}\right)^{D_t} \approx 1 - e^{-\frac{mD_t}{F}} \quad (m \ll F).$$

Similarly, the probability that a bit position b_q of a query signature is set to "1" is given by

$$p(b_q) = 1 - \left(1 - \tfrac{m}{F}\right)^{D_q} \approx 1 - e^{-\frac{mD_q}{F}} \quad (m \ll F).$$

When the signature size F, the element signature weight m, the target set cardinality D_t, and the query set cardinality D_q are given, the expected values of the target signature weight $\bar{m}_t$ and the query signature weight $\bar{m}_q$ are expressed as follows.

$$\bar{m}_t = F \times p(b_t) \approx F(1 - e^{-\frac{mD_t}{F}}),$$
$$\bar{m}_q = F \times p(b_q) \approx F(1 - e^{-\frac{mD_q}{F}}).$$

The following formula giving the false drop probability for $T \ni q$ was derived in [3].

$$Fd_{\{T \ni q\}} = (p(b_t))^m \approx (1 - e^{-\frac{mD_t}{F}})^m. \tag{2}$$

When we consider this formula as a function of m, $Fd_{\{T \ni q\}}$ take the minimum value for

$$m = \frac{F \ln 2}{D_t} \quad (= m_{opt}) \tag{3}$$

[13]. We derive formulas giving false drop probabilities for $T \supseteq Q$, $T \subseteq Q$, $T \sqcap Q$, and $T \equiv Q$ taking these considerations as a starting basis.

Table 1. Symbols

symbol	definition
F	Signature size in bits
m	Element signature weight
D_t	Cardinality of a target set T
D_q	Cardinality of a query set Q
N	Total number of target sets in the database
V	Cardinality of the set element domain

3.2 Uniform Target Cardinality

In this subsection, we consider the case where all target sets have the same cardinality D_t. First, we derive equations used in later analysis. Let b_t^j $(1 \leq j \leq F)$ be the jth bit position of the target signature and b_q^j $(1 \leq j \leq F)$ be jth bit position of the query signature. For each i $(1 \leq i \leq F - m)$, the following equations hold:

$$Prob(b_t^1 = 0 \wedge \cdots \wedge b_t^i = 0) = \left(\frac{_{F-i}C_m}{_F C_m} \right)^{D_t}$$

$$= \left(\frac{(F-m)(F-m-1)\cdots(F-m-i+1)}{F(F-1)\cdots(F-i+1)} \right)^{D_t}$$

$$= \prod_{k=1}^{i} \left(1 - \frac{m}{F-k+1} \right)^{D_t}. \tag{4}$$

If $\frac{m}{F-k+1} \ll 1$ is satisfied for $1 \leq k \leq i$,

$$Prob(b_t^1 = 0 \wedge \cdots \wedge b_t^i = 0) = \left(1 - \frac{m}{F} \right)^{D_t} \left(1 - \frac{m}{F-1} \right)^{D_t} \cdots \left(1 - \frac{m}{F-i+1} \right)^{D_t}$$

$$\approx \left(1 - \frac{1}{F} \right)^{mD_t} \left(1 - \frac{1}{F-1} \right)^{mD_t} \cdots \left(1 - \frac{1}{F-i+1} \right)^{mD_t}$$

$$= \left(1 - \frac{i}{F} \right)^{mD_t}. \tag{5}$$

Similarly,

$$Prob(b_q^1 = 0 \wedge \cdots \wedge b_q^i = 0) = \prod_{k=1}^{i} \left(1 - \frac{m}{F-k+1} \right)^{D_q}. \tag{6}$$

If $\frac{m}{F-k+1} \ll 1$ is satisfied for $1 \leq k \leq i$,

$$Prob(b_q^1 = 0 \wedge \cdots \wedge b_q^i = 0) \approx \left(1 - \frac{i}{F} \right)^{mD_q}. \tag{7}$$

3.2.1 False Drop Probability Formulas

We derive formulas giving the false drop probabilities based on assumption that the weight of every target signature is equal to its expected value $\bar{m}_t$ and the weight of every query signature is equal to $\bar{m}_q$.

1) $T \supseteq Q$: A false drop occurs when the following condition holds for every bit position j $(1 \leq j \leq F)$:

$$b_t^j = 0 \quad \Rightarrow \quad b_q^j = 0.$$

As the number of "0"'s in the target signature is $F - \bar{m}_t \approx Fe^{-\frac{mD_t}{F}}$ by the above assumption, we can tell the false drop probability for $T \supseteq Q$ from equation (6) as follows:

$$Fd_{\{T \supseteq Q\}} = Prob(b_q^1 = 0 \wedge \cdots \wedge b_q^{F - \bar{m}_t} = 0) \approx \prod_{k=1}^{Fe^{-\frac{mD_t}{F}}} \left(1 - \frac{m}{F - k + 1}\right)^{D_q}.$$

If $\frac{m}{F-k+1} \ll 1$ holds for $1 \leq k \leq Fe^{-\frac{mD_t}{F}}$, we get from equation (7),

$$Fd_{\{T \supseteq Q\}} \approx (1 - e^{-\frac{mD_t}{F}})^{mD_q}. \tag{8}$$

Note that this formula coincides with formula (2) when $D_q = 1$, namely $T \ni q$. The formula (8) takes the minimum value for $m = m_{opt}$ given in (3).

2) $T \subseteq Q$: A false drop occurs when the following condition holds for every bit position j $(1 \leq j \leq F)$:

$$b_q^j = 0 \quad \Rightarrow \quad b_t^j = 0.$$

As the number of "0"'s in the query signature is $F - \bar{m}_q \approx Fe^{-\frac{mD_q}{F}}$ by the above assumption, we can tell the false drop probability for $T \subseteq Q$ from equation (4) as follows:

$$Fd_{\{T \subseteq Q\}} = Prob(b_t^1 = 0 \wedge \cdots \wedge b_t^{F - \bar{m}_q} = 0) \approx \prod_{k=1}^{Fe^{-\frac{mD_q}{F}}} \left(1 - \frac{m}{F - k + 1}\right)^{D_t}.$$

If $\frac{m}{F-k+1} \ll 1$ holds for $1 \leq k \leq Fe^{-\frac{mD_t}{F}}$, we get from equation (5),

$$Fd_{\{T \subseteq Q\}} \approx (1 - e^{-\frac{mD_q}{F}})^{mD_t}. \tag{9}$$

This formula take the minimum value for the following m:

$$m = \frac{F \ln 2}{D_q}.$$

3) $T \sqcap Q$: A false drop occurs when there exist at least m bit positions that satisfy the following condition:

$$b_q^j = 1 \quad \wedge \quad b_t^j = 1.$$

In other words, a false drop does not occur when there exist less than m bit positions that satisfy the above condition. Here, we make an additional assumption that each bit position in the target signature is set to "1" with probability $p(b_t)$ independently of other bit positions. Then the probability that there exist k bit positions that satisfy the above condition is given as follows:

$$_{\bar{m}_q}C_k p(b_t)^k (1 - p(b_t))^{\bar{m}_q - k}.$$

Therefore, the false drop probability for $T \sqcap Q$ is given by

$$Fd_{\{T \sqcap Q\}} = 1 - \sum_{k=0}^{m-1} {}_{\bar{m}_q}C_k p(b_t)^k (1 - p(b_t))^{\bar{m}_q - k}. \tag{10}$$

4) $T \equiv Q$: We consider the case where $D_t = D_q$. More general cases are considered in the next subsection. In this case, $\bar{m}_t = \bar{m}_q = \bar{m}$. Then, a target signature and a query signature may take $_FC_{\bar{m}}$ different bit patterns. A false drop occurs when the target signature is equal to the query signature. Hence, the false drop probability for $T \equiv Q$ is given as follows:

$$Fd_{\{T \equiv Q\}} = \tfrac{1}{_FC_{\bar{m}}}. \tag{11}$$

In this case, $_FC_{\bar{m}}$ takes the maximum value for $\bar{m} = F/2$. Therefore, the false drop probability takes the minimum for $m = m_{opt}$.

3.2.2 Revised False Drop Probability Formulas

In Subsection 3.2.1, we assumed that the weights of the target signature and the query signature are given by $\bar{m}_t$ and $\bar{m}_q$, respectively. Actually, this assumption does not hold, and the weight of the target signature, for example, varies even if F, m, and D_t are fixed. In this subsection, we revise the false drop probability formulas taking distribution of the target signature weight and the query signature weight into account. As in case of $T \sqcap Q$ in Subsection 3.2.1, let us assume that each bit position in the target signature and the query signature is set to "1" with probabilities $p(b_t)$ and $p(b_q)$, respectively, independently of other bit positions. Then the distribution of the target signature weight follows the binomial distribution, and the probability that the target signature weight is i is given by

$$p_t(i) = {}_FC_i p(b_t)^i (1 - p(b_t))^{F-i}.$$

Similarly, the probability that the query signature weight is i is given by

$$p_q(i) = {}_FC_i p(b_q)^i (1 - p(b_q))^{F-i}.$$

In the following, we derive revised false drop probability formulas for $T \supseteq Q$, $T \subseteq Q$, $T \sqcap Q$, and $T \equiv Q$. The effect of this revision is evaluated with simulation results in Section 4.

1) $T \supseteq Q$: If the target signature weight is i, the probability $f_{\{T \supseteq Q\}}(i)$ that the target set becomes a false drop is derived from equation (6) as follows:

$$f_{\{T \supseteq Q\}}(i) = Prob(b_q^1 = 0 \wedge \cdots \wedge b_q^{F-i} = 0) = \prod_{k=1}^{F-i} \left(1 - \tfrac{m}{F-k+1}\right)^{D_q}.$$

If $\frac{m}{F-k+1} \ll 1$ holds for $1 \le k \le F - i$, we get from equation (7)

$$f_{\{T \supseteq Q\}}(i) \approx \left(1 - \tfrac{F-i}{F}\right)^{mD_q} = \left(\tfrac{i}{F}\right)^{mD_q}.$$

As distribution of the target signature weight follows the binomial distribution, the false drop probability for $T \supseteq Q$ is given by

$$\begin{aligned} Fd_{\{T \supseteq Q\}} &= \sum_{i=1}^{F} p_t(i) f_{\{T \supseteq Q\}}(i) \\ &= \sum_{i=1}^{F} {}_FC_i (1 - e^{-\frac{mD_t}{F}})^i e^{-\frac{mD_t}{F}(F-i)} \left(\tfrac{i}{F}\right)^{mD_q}. \end{aligned} \tag{12}$$

2) $T \subseteq Q$: If the query signature weight is i, the probability $f_{\{T \subseteq Q\}}(i)$ that the target set becomes a false drop is derived from equation (4) as follows:

$$f_{\{T \subseteq Q\}}(i) = Prob(b_t^1 = 0 \wedge \cdots \wedge b_t^{F-i} = 0) = \prod_{k=1}^{F-i} \left(1 - \frac{m}{F-k+1}\right)^{D_t}.$$

If $\frac{m}{F-k+1} \ll 1$ holds for $1 \leq k \leq F - i$, we get from equation (5)

$$f_{\{T \subseteq Q\}}(i) \approx \left(1 - \frac{F-i}{F}\right)^{mD_t} = \left(\frac{i}{F}\right)^{mD_t}.$$

As distribution of the query signature weight follows the binomial distribution, the false drop probability for $T \subseteq Q$ is given by

$$
\begin{aligned}
Fd_{\{T \subseteq Q\}} &= \sum_{i=1}^{F} p_q(i) f_{\{T \subseteq Q\}}(i) \\
&= \sum_{i=1}^{F} {}_F C_i (1 - e^{-\frac{mD_q}{F}})^i e^{-\frac{mD_q}{F}(F-i)} \left(\frac{i}{F}\right)^{mD_t}.
\end{aligned}
\tag{13}
$$

3) $T \sqcap Q$: If the query signature weight is i, the probability $f_{\{T \sqcap Q\}}(i)$ that the target set becomes a false drop is given by

$$f_{\{T \sqcap Q\}}(i) = 1 - \sum_{k=0}^{m-1} {}_i C_k p(b_t)^k (1 - p(b_t))^{i-k}.$$

As distribution of the query signature weight follows the binomial distribution, the false drop probability for $T \sqcap Q$ is given by

$$
\begin{aligned}
Fd_{\{T \sqcap Q\}} &= \sum_{i=1}^{F} p_q(i) f_{\{T \sqcap Q\}}(i) \\
&= \sum_{i=1}^{F} {}_F C_i p(b_q)^i (1 - p(b_q))^{F-i} \left(1 - \sum_{k=0}^{m-1} {}_i C_k p(b_t)^k (1 - p(b_t))^{i-k}\right).
\end{aligned}
\tag{14}
$$

4) $T \equiv Q$: A false drop occurs if both the target signature weight and the query signature weight take the same value i, and the target signature is equal to the query signature. Therefore, the false drop probability for $T \equiv Q$ is given by

$$
\begin{aligned}
Fd_{\{T \equiv Q\}} &= \sum_{i=1}^{F} p_t(i) p_q(i) \frac{1}{{}_F C_i} \\
&= \sum_{i=1}^{F} {}_F C_i (1 - e^{-\frac{mD_t}{F}})^i (1 - e^{-\frac{mD_q}{F}})^i e^{-\frac{m(D_t+D_q)}{F}(F-i)}.
\end{aligned}
\tag{15}
$$

3.3 Varying Target Cardinality

In this subsection, we consider a case where the cardinality of the target set varies. Let a *set element domain* be a set from which each target set element is taken, and its cardinality be V. Here, we assume that each of the V elements in the set element domain appears in a target set with the same probability p. Then distribution of the target set cardinality follows the binomial distribution, and the average target set cardinality is given by $\bar{D}_t = pV$.

In this case, we can estimate the false drop probability with the following formula for each case of $T \supseteq Q$, $T \subseteq Q$, $T \sqcap Q$, and $T \equiv Q$:

$$Fd_{B,c} = \sum_{D_t=1}^{V} {}_V C_{D_t} p^{D_t} (1-p)^{V-D_t} Fd_c, \tag{16}$$

where c is a parameter indicating one of $\{T \supseteq Q\}$, $\{T \subseteq Q\}$, $\{T \sqcap Q\}$, and $\{T \equiv Q\}$, and Fd_c is the estimation formula of the false drop probability derived in Subsection 3.2 for each case. For example, the false drop probability for $T \supseteq Q$ using formula (8) is given as follows:

$$Fd_{B,\{T \supseteq Q\}} = \sum_{D_t=1}^{V} {}_V C_{D_t} p^{D_t} (1-p)^{V-D_t} (1 - e^{-\frac{mD_t}{F}})^{mD_q}$$

4 Simulation Study

In this section, we evaluate validity of estimation by the formulas derived in Section 3 by simulations. A number of physical signature file organizations have been proposed [2, 7]. In this study, we show the simulation results where parameter values are set assuming the bit-sliced signature file organization, since our previous work [6] showed advantages of the bit-sliced signature files in set retrieval. We set $M = 10000, V = 10000$, and $m = 2$. Simulation results with $D_t = 10$ and $D_t = 100$ are presented for four types of queries $T \supseteq Q$ (including $T \ni q$), $T \subseteq Q$, $T \sqcap Q$, and $T \equiv Q$. In the following discussion, we show simulation results comparing with estimates by the formulas derived in Section 3. In figures, we tag simulation results with sim, estimates by the formulas in Subsection 3.2.1 with est1, and estimates by the formulas in Subsection 3.2.2 with est2.

4.1 Uniform Target Cardinality

To check validity of the formulas derived in Subsection 3.2, we consider the case where the target sets have the same cardinality D_t.

1) $T \supseteq Q$: Figure 6 shows the simulation results, estimates by formula (8), and estimates by formula (12) for $D_t = 10$. Figure 7 shows the case of $D_t = 100$. We can see that (a) there is almost no difference between false drop probabilities given by formulas (8) and (12), and that (b) both formulas quite correctly estimate the actual false drop probabilities. In the following discussion, we use the simpler one, formula (8), to estimate the false drop probability for $T \supseteq Q$.

2) $T \subseteq Q$: Figure 8 shows the simulation results, estimates by formula (9), and estimates by formula (13) for $D_t = 10$. Figure 9 shows the case of $D_t = 100$. We can see that (a) the false drop probability given by formula (9) tends to be smaller than that given by formula (13), and that (b) the false drop probability given by (13) coincides well with the simulation results. Therefore, we can see that formula (13) gives more correct estimates of the false drop probability[‡].

[‡] In the cost analysis in [6], we used formula (9) to estimate the false drop probability for $T \subseteq Q$. However, the analysis is still valid, since the difference between estimates by (9) and (13) does not have a significant effect on the total cost.

156

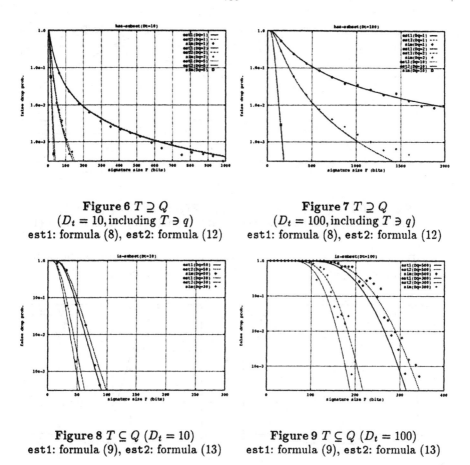

Figure 6 $T \supseteq Q$
$(D_t = 10, \text{including } T \ni q)$
est1: formula (8), est2: formula (12)

Figure 7 $T \supseteq Q$
$(D_t = 100, \text{including } T \ni q)$
est1: formula (8), est2: formula (12)

Figure 8 $T \subseteq Q$ $(D_t = 10)$
est1: formula (9), est2: formula (13)

Figure 9 $T \subseteq Q$ $(D_t = 100)$
est1: formula (9), est2: formula (13)

3) $T \sqcap Q$: Figure 10 shows the simulation results, estimates by formula (10), and estimates by formula (14) for $D_t = 10$. Figure 11 shows the case of $D_t = 100$. We can see that (a) the false drop probability given by (10) coincides well with the simulation results, and that (b) the false drop probability given by (14) does not fit the simulation results when D_q is too small. The latter phenomenon can be explained as follows. When D_q is very small, the query signature weight becomes mD_q in most cases. Therefore, the assumption for (14) that the distribution of the query signature weight follows the binomial distribution is not reasonable in such cases.

4) $T \equiv Q$: Figure 12 shows the simulation results, estimates by formula (11), and estimates by formula (15) for $D_t = 10$. Note that formula (11) can be used only when $D_t = D_q$. Figure 13 shows the case of $D_t = 100$. We can see that (a) the false drop probability given by (11) does not fit the simulation results for large D_t values, and that (b) the false drop probability given by (15) coincides well with the simulation results. Another simulation result indicates that (15) is not so reliable

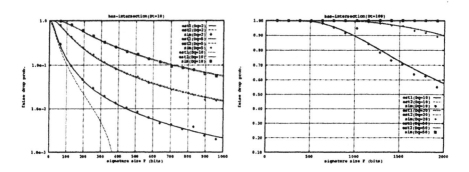

Figure 10 $T \sqcap Q$ ($D_t = 10$)
est1: formula (10), est2: formula (14)

Figure 11 $T \sqcap Q$ ($D_t = 100$)
est1: formula (10), est2: formula (14)

when D_t and/or D_q is too small. A remark similar to that for $T \sqcap Q$ will apply to such cases. However, we can use (15) for most probable D_t and D_q.

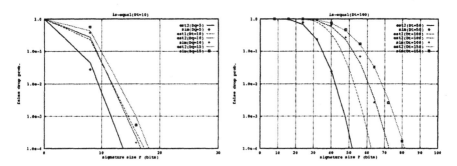

Figure 12 $T \equiv Q$ ($D_t = 10$)
est1: formula (11), est2: formula (15)

Figure 13 $T \equiv Q$ ($D_t = 100$)
est1: formula (11), est2: formula (15)

4.2 Alternative Processing Scheme for T ⊓ Q

As shown in Figures 10 and 11, the false drop probability for $T \sqcap Q$ is rather high. The reason is that the query signature generated with the superimposed coding has much chance of having more than m bit intersection with the target signature. To solve this problem, we can use another scheme to process queries of type $T \sqcap Q$. In the scheme, the steps 1) and 2) explained in Subsection 2.2 are modified as follows:

1) An element signature is generated for each element in the query set Q.
2) The signature file is examined. Each target set becomes a drop if any element signature generated in step 1) satisfies the following condition.

element signature $\wedge$ target signature = element signature.

query element1   element signature 1
eraser → 1010010000000000
query element2   element signature 2
stapler → 0010000010000100
signature file

1101101010000101	T1
1110110111000010	T2
$\vdots$	$\vdots$

drop ←

Figure 14 Query Processing of the Query **Q4**

Figure 14 illustrates query processing of the query **Q4** under this scheme.

If we ignore the probability of the hash collision in element signature generation, the false drop probability for $T \sqcap Q$ under this scheme is given by

$$Fd_{\{T \sqcap Q\}} = \sum_{i=1}^{D_q} Fd_{\{T \ni q\}} * (1 - Fd_{\{T \ni q\}})^{i-1} = 1 - (1 - Fd_{\{T \ni q\}})^{D_q}. \qquad (17)$$

By differentiating expression (17) with $Fd_{\{T \ni q\}}$, we get

$$\frac{\Delta Fd_{\{T \sqcap Q\}}}{\Delta Fd_{\{T \ni q\}}} = D_q(1 - Fd_{\{T \ni q\}})^{D_q - 1}.$$

Since $0 < Fd_{\{T \ni q\}} \leq 1$,

$$\frac{\Delta Fd_{\{T \sqcap Q\}}}{\Delta Fd_{\{T \ni q\}}} > 0.$$

Therefore, when $Fd_{\{T \ni q\}}$ takes the minimum value, namely $m = m_{opt}$, $Fd_{\{T \sqcap Q\}}$ also takes the minimum value.

Figure 15 shows the simulation results under this improved scheme, and estimates by formula (17) for $D_t = 10$. Note that formula (2) is used for $Fd_{\{T \ni q\}}$. Figure 16 shows the case of $D_t = 100$. We can see that estimates by (17) coincide well with the simulation results. In the following discussion, we suppose $T \sqcap Q$ is processed in this scheme.

4.3   Varying Target Cardinality

4.3.1   Uniform Element Occurrence Frequency

To check validity of estimation by the formulas derived in Subsection 3.3, we consider the case where each element in the set element domain appears in a target set with the same probability p. As discussed in Subsection 3.3, distribution of the target set cardinality follows the binomial distribution with the average $\bar{D}_t = pV$. In the following discussion, we tag estimates given by the formulas in Subsection 3.3 with est3 in the figures.

1) $T \supseteq Q$: Figure 17 shows the simulation results and estimates by formula (16) (formula (8) is used for $Fd_{\{T \supseteq Q\}}$ in (16)) for $\bar{D}_t = 10$. Figure 18 shows the case of $\bar{D}_t = 100$. For comparison, we also show the estimates by (8) with $D_t = \bar{D}_t$ in the figures. Estimates by (16) coincide with the simulation results. In $T \supseteq Q$, the false drop probability increases drastically as D_t becomes large. Therefore, formula (16) gives little larger estimates than formula (8), influenced by target sets with $D_t > \bar{D}_t$. However, there is no significant difference between estimates given by (8) and (16).

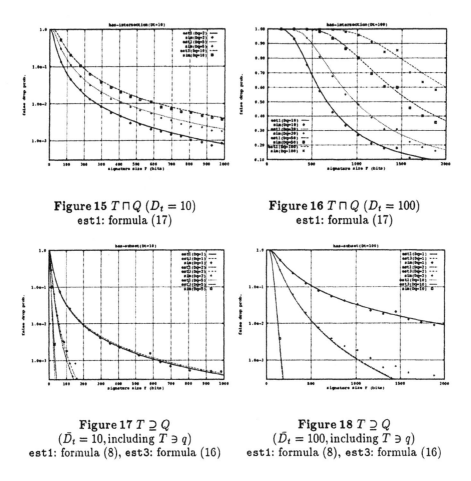

Figure 15 $T \sqcap Q$ $(D_t = 10)$
est1: formula (17)

Figure 16 $T \sqcap Q$ $(D_t = 100)$
est1: formula (17)

Figure 17 $T \supseteq Q$
$(\bar{D}_t = 10, \text{including } T \ni q)$
est1: formula (8), est3: formula (16)

Figure 18 $T \supseteq Q$
$(\bar{D}_t = 100, \text{including } T \ni q)$
est1: formula (8), est3: formula (16)

2) $T \subseteq Q$: Figure 19 shows the simulation results and estimates by formula (16) (formula (13) is used for $Fd_{\{T \subseteq Q\}}$ in (16)) for $\bar{D}_t = 10$. Figure 20 shows the case of $\bar{D}_t = 100$. For comparison, we also show the estimates by (13) with $D_t = \bar{D}_t$. Estimates by (16) coincide well with the simulation results. In $T \subseteq Q$, the false drop probability increases drastically as D_t becomes small. Therefore, formula (16) gives larger estimates than formula (13), influenced by target sets with $D_t < \bar{D}_t$. In case of $\bar{D}_t = 10$, distribution of the target set cardinality gives more influence than in case of $\bar{D}_t = 100$.

3) $T \sqcap Q$: Figure 21 shows the simulation results and estimates by formula (16) (formula (17) is used for $Fd_{\{T \sqcap Q\}}$ in (16)) for $\bar{D}_t = 10$. Figure 22 shows the case of $\bar{D}_t = 100$. For comparison, we also show estimates by (17) with $D_t = \bar{D}_t$. Estimates by (16) coincide well with the simulation results. In this case, there is no significant difference between estimates by (17) and (16).

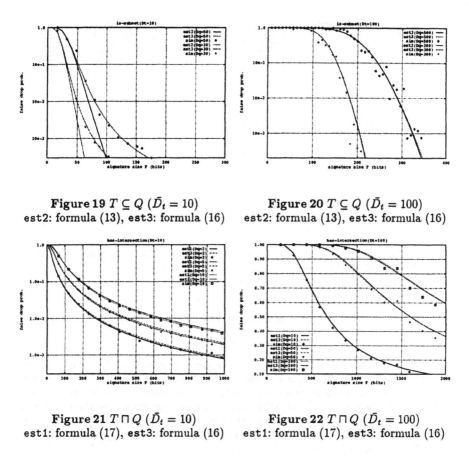

Figure 19 $T \subseteq Q$ $(\bar{D}_t = 10)$
est2: formula (13), est3: formula (16)

Figure 20 $T \subseteq Q$ $(\bar{D}_t = 100)$
est2: formula (13), est3: formula (16)

Figure 21 $T \sqcap Q$ $(\bar{D}_t = 10)$
est1: formula (17), est3: formula (16)

Figure 22 $T \sqcap Q$ $(\bar{D}_t = 100)$
est1: formula (17), est3: formula (16)

4) $T \equiv Q$: Figure 23 shows the simulation results and estimates by formula (16) (formula (15) is used for $Fd_{\{T \equiv Q\}}$ in (16)) for $\bar{D}_t = 10$. Figure 24 shows the case of $\bar{D}_t = 100$. For comparison, we also show estimates by (15) with $D_t = \bar{D}_t$. Estimates by (16) coincide well with the simulation results and there is no significant difference between estimates by (15) and (16).

4.3.2 Skewed Element Occurrence Frequency

In this subsection, we consider a more probable case in practice where elements in the set element domain do not have the same probability of occurrence in a target set. We assume that some elements in the set element domain are "hot spots," and have higher occurrence frequency than the others. The cardinality V of the set element domain is assumed to be 10000 here. We examine the following three cases.

Case 1. 100 elements in the set element domain have 100 times larger occurrence probability than the others.

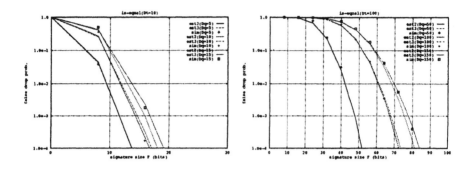

Figure 23 $T \equiv Q$ $(\bar{D}_t = 10)$
est2: formula (15), est3: formula (16)

Figure 24 $T \equiv Q$ $(\bar{D}_t = 100)$
est2: formula (15), est3: formula (16)

Case 2. 1000 elements in the set element domain have 100 times larger occurrence probability than the others.

Case 3. 3000 elements in the set element domain have 100 times larger occurrence probability than the others.

The average target set cardinality is given by

$$\bar{D}_t = p_h h + p(V - h),$$

where h is the number of elements with larger occurrence probability, p is the occurrence probability of regular elements in the set element domain, and $p_h = 100p$. For each of the above three cases, the p value is determined by the above equation with $\bar{D}_t = 10$. In Case 1, the experimental target sets generated for the simulation with $p = 5.0 \times 10^{-4}$ have the average cardinality $\bar{D}_t = 10.2$. Similarly, the average cardinalities in Cases 2 and 3 are $\bar{D}_t = 10.9$ ($p = 9.2 \times 10^{-5}$) and $\bar{D}_t = 12.2$ ($p = 3.3 \times 10^{-5}$), respectively.

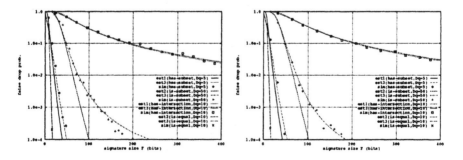

Figure 25 $h = 100, p_h = 100p$

Figure 26 $h = 1000, p_h = 100p$

Figure 25 shows the simulation results, estimates by formulas in Subsection 3.2, and estimates by (16) for four types of queries in Case 1. Figures 26 and 27 show the false drop probabilities in Cases 2 and 3, respectively. These figures show that estimates by (16) coincide well with the simulation results. Formula (16) was derived assuming that each element in the set element domain appears in a target set with the same probability. Therefore, the results here indicate that existence of hot spots does not have much effect on the false drop probability.

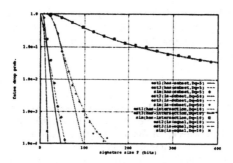

Figure 27 $h = 3000, p_h = 100p$

5 Summary and Conclusion

In this paper, we derived probability-theoretic formulas estimating false drop probabilities in set retrieval with signature files. We considered four types of retrieval conditions $T \supseteq Q, T \subseteq Q, T \sqcap Q$, and $T \equiv Q$. We evaluated their validity by computer simulations. The simulation results can be summarized as follows:

A) In case of uniform target set cardinality, formulas derived in Subsections 3.2 (and Subsection 4.2) well estimate the actual false drop probabilities. We can use formulas (8) for $T \supseteq Q$, (13) for $T \subseteq Q$, (17) for $T \sqcap Q$, and (15) for $T \equiv Q$. Note that we use the scheme in Subsection 4.2 for $T \sqcap Q$.

B) In case distribution of the target set cardinality follows the binomial distribution, formulas derived in Subsection 3.3 (and Subsection 4.2) well estimate the actual false drop probabilities. We can use formula (16) (with (8) for $T \supseteq Q$, (13) for $T \subseteq Q$, (17) for $T \sqcap Q$, and (15) for $T \equiv Q$). The simulation results show that we can get good estimates using just (8) for $T \supseteq Q$, (17) for $T \sqcap Q$, and (15) for $T \equiv Q$ even in this case.

C) We have not derived false drop probability formulas for more probable cases where the set element domain has some hot spots. The simulation results indicate that we do not make big mistakes in estimation substituting the set of formulas derived for the above case B) even though some hot spots may appear in the set element domain.

In this study, we have shown simulation results with parameters set assuming the bit-sliced signature file organization. Simulation study has been done for some other parameter sets, and we have checked that the formulas derived in this paper are also valid even in the context of the sequential signature file organization. We can use the formulas in many situations in the design of signature files to facilitate set retrieval in advanced database systems.

Acknowledgements

The authors are grateful to Prof. Yuzuru Fujiwara and Prof. Isao Suzuki for their encouragement to this research. They also thank many members of the database laboratory, University of Tsukuba, for fruitful discussion and collaboration.

References

1. E. Bertino and W. Kim, *"Index Techniques for Queries on Nested Objects,"* IEEE Trans. Knowledge and Data Engineering, Vol. 1, No. 2, June 1989, pp. 196-214.
2. W. W. Chang and H. J. Scheck, *"A Signature Access Method for the Starburst Database System,"* Proc. 15th VLDB, Amsterdam, The Netherlands, August 1989, pp. 145-153.
3. C. Faloutsos and S. Christdoulakis, *"An Access Method for Documents and Its Analytical Performance Evaluation,"* ACM Trans. Office Information Systems, Vol. 2, No. 4, October 1984, pp. 267-288.
4. C. Faloutsos and S. Christdoulakis, *"Description and Performance Analysis of Signature File Methods for Office Filing,"* ACM Trans. Office Information Systems, Vol. 5, No. 3, July 1987, pp. 237-257.
5. C. Fischer and S. Thomas, *"Operators for Non-First-Normal-Form Relations,"* Proc. IEEE COMPSAC 83, Chicago, November 1983, pp. 464-475.
6. Y. Ishikawa, H. Kitagawa, and N. Ohbo, *"Evaluation of Signature Files as Set Access Facilities in OODBs,"* Proc. ACM SIGMOD 1993, Washington, D.C., May 1993, pp.247-256.
7. A. Kent, R. Sachs-Davis, and K. Ramamohanarao, *"A Superimposed Coding Schema Based on Multiple Block Descriptor Files for Indexing Very Large Data Bases,"* Proc. 14th VLDB, Los Angeles, August 1988, pp. 351-359.
8. H. Kitagawa and T. L. Kunii, *"The Unnormalized Relational Data Model - For Office Form Processor Design,"* Springer-Verlag, 1989.
9. W. Kim, *"Introduction to Object-Oriented Databases,"* Computer Systems Series, The MIT Press, 1990.
10. R. Sacks-Davis and A. Kent, *"Multikey Access Methods Based on Superimposed Coding Techniques,"* ACM Trans. Database Systems, Vol12, No. 4, December 1987, pp. 655-698.
11. H. Schek and M. Scholl, *"The Relational Model with Relation-Valued Attributes,"* Information Systems, Vol. 11, No. 2, 1986, pp. 137-147.
12. J. Stein and D. Maier *"Associative Access Support in GemStone,"* in K. R. Dittrich, V. Dayal, and A. P. Buchmann (Eds.), On Object-Oriented Database Systems, Springer-Verlag, 1991, pp. 323-339.
13. S. Stiassny, *"Mathematical Analysis of Various Superimposed Coding Methods,"* American Documentation, Vol. 11, February 1960, pp. 155-169.
14. K. F. Wong and M. H. Williams, *"A Superimposed Codeword Indexing Schema for Handling Sets in Prolog Databases,"* Proc. 2nd International Symposium on Database Systems for Advanced Applications, Tokyo, Japan, April 1991, pp. 468-476.
15. S. Zdonik and D. Maier, (Eds.), *"Readings in Object-Oriented Database Systems,"* Morgan Kaufmann Publishers, 1990.

Data Structure and Algorithms for New Hardware Technology

Yahiko Kambayashi[1], Hiroki Takakura[1] and Shintaro Meki[2]

[1] Faculty of Engineering, Kyoto University
Sakyo, Kyoto 606-01 Japan
[2] Faculty of Computer Science, Okayama Prefecture University
Soja, Okayama 719-11 Japan

Abstract

New applications and new hardware/software technology are major factors to drive database research to new directions. In this paper we will discuss effects of up-to-date hardware technology to data structure and database algorithms. Historically in database file organization, utilization of sequential access and clustering of data are two important techniques to improve processing efficiency. Flash memory, which is believed to replace conventional disks for mobile application etc., can sequentially access only small amount of data compared with disks, and data clustering will not contribute to improve system performance. On the other hand, recently developed high-speed RAM contains cache memory which contributes to speed-up sequential access. We may be able to utilize special-purpose memory to improve database performance, such as content addressable memory and dual-port RAM. Most research on improvement of database performance using hardware was to develop hardware for relational database operations. Advanced flexible logic chips such as FPGA(Field Programmable Gate Array) can realize a circuit consisting of over 10,000 gates and connections in the circuit can be changed during system operation by modifying the contents of control SRAMs. We may be able to improve system performance by using FPGAs to realize bottle-neck portions of the database software. Such techniques can be applied especially to active and real-time database systems. Pipe-line processing is a special case of parallel processing and recently pipe-line processors for workstations have been developed. Although pipe-line processing is rather restrictive, it can be combined with concurrency control mechanisms rather easily. Optimization for pipe-line processing is also simpler than that for parallel/distributed systems. Use of pipe-line processors for database operations is also an important topic.

1 Introduction

In this paper we will discuss database research topics motivated from the recent progress of VLSI chips; memory chips and logic circuit chips. An ideal storage system can be designed by using various storage hardware to make use of their advantages. We need to know VLSI memory technologies for such a purpose. The following memory technologies are compared in this paper.

High-Speed DRAM
Flash Memory
Dielectric Thin Film Memory
Dual-Port RAM
Content Addressable Memory

Sequential access has been used to improve access efficiency in disk-based file organization. Semiconductor storage will also have sequential access property, but it is much different from disks. Such difference are discussed. We must modify file organization for disks in order to use semiconductor storage efficiently.

It is expected that flash memory will be used in mobile workstations etc., we will discuss how to use flash memory for secondary storage. One serious problem of flash memory is that the cost to erase is very much expensive (time required for erase operation is very long and the life time is determined by the number of erase operations). We have developed over-write operations to extend memory life. How to use over-write operations is discussed.

Dual-port-RAM which has two ports (direct I/O and serial output) can be used for back-up purpose also. Use of CAM (Content Addressable Memory) to find superclasses and subclasses in object-oriented databases is discussed.

As in database applications range of data size varies widely, we must consider this fact to design proper hardware. Since time required to input data is $O(n)$, it is no use to realize algorithm faster than $O(n)$, where n is the data size. Hardware processing is required for large n where software implementation takes too much time. To have large hardware, however, is very expensive. For sorting there are algorithms which require only $O(\log n)$ processors and $O(n)$ time, which seem to be optimum for database applications.

We will also discuss possibility of utilizing topics in logic design community to database research. FPGA can realize flexible hardware by writing connection information to SRAM. It can be used for active databases to improve efficiency of rule processing.

Finally pipe-line processing is discussed. Although pipe-line is a special case of parallel processing, it is suitable for database operations. Discussion on concurrency control, query optimization using commutative rules and implementation of database operations are given. By our implementation it is shown that vector processing is over 40 times faster than serial processing for three basic relational operations; select, project and join. Although our program is specially designed to utilize advantages of vector processors, it is expected that vector execution is over 10 times faster than serial execution of program carefully design for serial execution.

2 Basic Consideration on File Organization for Semiconductor Storages

Typical required properties for ideal database storages are as follows.

a. high-speed b. large capacity c. nonvolatile d. low cost
e. low power consumption f. long life time g. small size h. reliable

As there are no storage devices satisfying all the requirements, we need to combine more than one storage device. In order to select proper combination we need to consider 1) new memory technology and 2) requirements from new applications. Conventional database algorithms and file organizations are developed to utilize sequential access capability of disks. One of the serious questions on database file organization is as follows.

"Can we still use disk-based algorithms and file organizations for semiconductor storages?"

To find answer for this question, we need to compare characteristics of current database storages and semiconductor storages.

[Characteristics of Conventional Database Storages]

a) Two-level storage structure: A storage system consists of high-speed main memory and nonvolatile large-capacity disks (although there are multi-level systems, we will discuss two-level structures only for simplicity).

b) Characteristics of main memory: Cost is determined by the size of data access. Sequential access is not considered.

c) Characteristics of disks: Cost is determined by the following conditions.

   c-1) The number of disk access: Utilization of sequential access to reduce the total number of access is important.

   c-2) The total distance of disk head move: As the time required to move head from one track to another track is determined by the distance between the two tracks, cost is determined by the total of such distance.

   c-3) Required time for parallel processing: Data stored in different disks can be retrieved parallely. The required time determined by the longest retrieval among the parallel processes is considered to be the cost.

Especially use of sequential access is the most important factor, for example, B-trees[BaM72], consecutive retrieval files[Gho72], quasi-consecutive retrieval files[KaG85] (a required set of data must be distributed within a buffer size, and consecutive property is not required.), group commit procedures.

Let n be the number of data. Since in database applications n can be very large, even by parallel read we need $O(n)$ time to read the whole data. If we assume conventional two-level storage structure, access time can be regarded as in average k times of maim memory access time, if data in disks are required. Although most efficient algorithms are developed for main memory computation, they can be efficient too under two-level storage assumption. That is, main memory algorithms in time $O(n^i)$ are also $O(n^i)$ algorithms for two-level storage systems, since k is regarded as a constant. The value k is, however, very large. For example, the ratio between random access speeds of main memory and disks is 100 ns vs 10 ms = 1:100,000. The main purpose of algorithm design for two-level storages is to reduce k under cost conditions c-1) and c-2).

In the case of semiconductor files we can still use sequential access capability.

[Requirement of sequential access for semiconductor storages]

1) In order to reduce the number of digits to specify addresses, clustering of data is required. Data in each cluster should be retrieved sequentially.
2) In order to speed-up semiconductor storage, high-speed buffer can be attached. Sequential access is applied to the buffer.
3) For sequential access we only need to specify the start address and the length of data which will reduce overhead for data access, since address must be specified in every direct access.
4) Hardware to process large amount of data are designed to get input sequentially (see Section 5).

There are, however, the following differences.

[Difference of characteristics]

1) The speed difference between one sequential access and a set of direct access to retrieve the same set of data is not so much as that of disks.
2) The size of a block corresponding to one sequential access is smaller than that for disks.
3) The access speed difference between main memory and semiconductor files is much smaller than the access speed difference between main memory and disks.

Cost criteria (in characteristic of conventional database storages) c-1) and c-3) can be also used for semiconductor storage, although we need modification on block size, number of pointers etc. Optimization by clustering **c-2)** is not useful anymore. Thus results of papers utilizing clustering (minimization of the total distance of disk head move[Hus93]) may not be utilized. Actually if database systems use concurrency control (most systems do), clustering techniques may be useless unless special consideration is given, although there are many database papers using clustering techniques. The reason is as follows. If there are two sets of data, D_1 and D_2, to be retrieved together, then they will be assigned in two consecutive tracks. After read D_1, the concurrency control mechanism may interrupt the process (since during the time to access D_1 CPU becomes idle) and start another access to D_3 which may be stored in the track far from D_1. Head will move there and then when the system requires D_2 we need to move back the head. Thus clustering technique may improve the efficiency, but every time efficiency improvement is different. If a database system is used by many transactions, there will be no improvement.

One possible organization of semiconductor storage is shown in Fig. 1. It consists of several banks, which can work parallely. Data contents are transmitted to buffer for fast sequential access. Let h be the buffer size. We assign the first h data to Bank I, the second h data to Bank II, etc. Then during the access to Bank I, data is consecutive address in Bank II can be transmitted to the buffer. By this way sequential access for large amount of data can be realized. We can also utilize parallel processing capability of these memory banks.

We will summarize characteristics of several interesting memory chips.

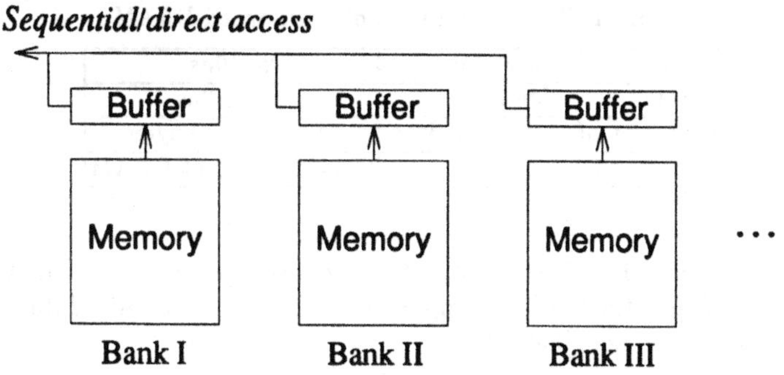

Sequential/direct access

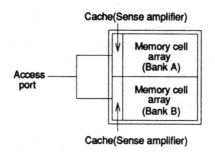

Fig. 1. Possible Organization of Semiconductor Storage

[High-Speed DRAM]

Since the bit cost of conventional SRAMs, used for cache, is very expensive compared with conventional memory devices, a system can rarely have a large cache. Recently, high-speed DRAMs, such as DRAMs based on Rambus, Synchronous DRAMs, Cache DRAMs or Enhanced DRAMs, have been produced. The basic structures of these DRAMs are similar, as shown in Fig. 2. Basically,

Fig. 2. Structure of High-Speed Memory

(Synchronous DRAM)

such a DRAM consists of memory cell arrays, which are the same as conventional DRAM and are divided into several blocks, and caches made of high-speed SRAMs or sense amplifiers. Each block has its own cache. All data in one cache can be accessed randomly. Furthermore, miss hit can be avoided by accessing caches alternatively, even if the size of required data exceeds the cache size. The specifications of high-speed DRAMs are shown in Table 1.

Table 1. The Specification of High-Speed DRAM

Access	Cache hit	2~10ns
cycle	Miss hit	30~100ns
Capacity of cache(/1MByte)		512bytes ~4kbytes
Chip cost		Close to Current DRAM

For conventional RAM we need not utilize sequential access, but for high-speed DRAM sequential access is important. We have to modify data structure suitable for main memory[LeC86].

[Nonvolatile Memory]

There are the following two kinds of nonvolatile memory chips available in the market.

Flash memory :

It's a version of EEPROM. We need to erase before write. Erase operation takes very long time and the life time is determined by the number of erase operations. Although there are restrictions, it is predicted the cost per bit will be go down rapidly. We will discuss how to use flash memory in Section 3.

Dielectric Thin Film Memory :

It is not yet popular as flash memory since the maximum capacity is still not big. Read/Write operations can be performed in 200 to 500 ns. The life time is determined by the total number of read/write, which is currently 10^8 or more. Ramtron International Corp. started to distribute 4-kbit chips from April 1992. 245-kbit chips are announced and samples will be available in 1994. In experimental lab. cells whose life time is over 10^{12} are developed. There is another type of memory whose life time is determined by the number of write (independent to read).

[Special Purpose Memory]

Dual-port-RAM :

It has two ports, one for random read/write and the other for sequential read, which was developed for display memory. Use of dual-port-RAMs is discussed in Section 4.

Functional Memory :

Functional memory is defined to be memory with embedded logic devices. The typical example is Content Addressable Memory(CAM). Use of CAM is also discussed in Section 4.

[Comparison of Memory Density]

Ratio of maximum capacities by currently available products is shown in Table 2. Since the structure for dielectric thin film memory is similar to DRAM, it is expected to catch up the density of SRAM.

In order to realize nonvolatile memory there are the following three choices.

Table 2. Comparison of Memory Density

SRAM	1
DRAM	4
Flash Memory	16
CAM	0.1
Dielectric Thin Film Memory	0.02

SRAM with battery-backup
Flash memory
Dielectric thin film memory

DRAM cannot be used since refresh operation consumes power while SRAM can keep its contents by back-up mode (with very little power). Even the capacity of dielectric thin film memory becomes comparable to that of SRAM, flash memory has much more capacity. Some developers of flash memory predicted that cost per bit is comparable to that of disks (currently 40 times). As recently disk cost is also decreasing rapidly, it is predicated that cost for 1 Mbyte will be less than $1 in 1996 even in the case of most expensive disk (1.8-inch disks). This tendency means that we need to develop a storage system consisting of various devices in order to satisfy the properties listed in the beginning of this section.

3   File Organization for Flash Memory

As flash memory is going to be used in mobile workstations[ImB92] in several years, we have to discuss whether current file organization for disks should be modified or not. In this section we will discuss characteristics of flash memory and file organization design.

3.1   Characteristic of Flash Memory

In order to rewrite contents of conventional electrical erasable ROM(EEPROM), the EEPROM must be pulled out from a system board and erased by an apparatus. Flash memory is a special kind of EEPROM, of which contents can be erased/written similar to conventional RAM. There are two kinds of flash memory, NAND type and NOR type. As NAND type can realize large chip density, we will discuss NAND type only in this section.

Since conventional EEPROMs have been manufactured through complicated process, it is difficult to realize large and cheap EEPROM. The manufacturing process of flash memory, however, is very similar to that of DRAM and the capacity (per unite area) of flash memory is four times as much as that of DRAM. Therefore the bit cost of flash memory is expected to become very low.

Fig. 3 shows a structure of NAND type flash memory[Tos92]. It consists of nonvolatile memory cell array and one data register. Both read and write operations for the cell array are performed through the data register. Typical characteristics of currently available flash memory are show in Table 3.

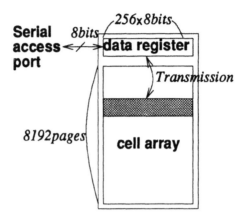

Fig. 3. Structure of Flash Memory

Table 3. Characteristics of Flash Memory

Register/Page size	256, 512 bytes
Block size	4 kbytes
Access cycle	60~100 ns
Data transfer rate Read	10 ~ 15 μs
(Register–cell array) Write	35~40 μs
Required time to erase	6~10 ms
Num. of erase ops.	~one million

- Each page can contain 256 bytes.
- There are 8192 pages in each cell array.
- Data register can contain the contents of one.
- Unit for one erase operation is one block (16 pages).

[Read operation for flash memory]

1) One of the pages in the cell array is selected.
2) Contents of the page are transmitted to the data register (it takes $10 \sim 15$ μs).
3) Through the serial port the contents of the data register can be read (each byte can be accessed in $60 \sim 100$ns). The time required to read the whole contents is 20 μs.

[Write operation for flash memory]

1) Select one page which was erased before (or never used).
2) Write to the data register (it will take 20 μs to write all the values in the data register).
3) Transfer the contents of the data register to the selected page and verify transferred data by comparing with register's data (self-verification)(totally 30 ~ 40 μs). These operations are automatically performed by flash memory just after all the values are stored in data register.

[Erase operation]

1) Select one block or the entire cell array.
2) Performs erase operation (6 ~ 10 ms).

In order to design a file structure we must consider the following characteristics.

Read:	Direct access$\cdots$20 μs in average.
	Sequential access$\cdots$30 μs for 256 bytes.
Write:	Sequential access$\cdots$60 μs for 256 bytes.
Write with erase:	Sequential access$\cdots$7 ms for 4 kbytes (one block).

Note that, in case of write with erase, there are not so much difference between sequential access to one block (4 kbytes) and that to the entire cell array.

There are the following two serious problems to use flash memory.

[Problems of flash memory]

1) Direct access for write operations: Even if we need to modify a few bytes, it is required to erase one whole block. Other data in the block must be rewritten.
2) Limitation of the number of erase operations: Currently the number is one million. If every block is erased in every one minute, flash memory can be used for two years. This may be acceptable for many applications since the battery life time of currently used battery-backed SRAM is about two years. For some applications we may have to erase each block in every one second. In such cases memory will last only for ten days.

Because of 1) we may need unnecessary erase, which will reduce the life time of the memory.

3.2   Methods to extend memory life

It is expected that the maximum number of erase operations will be getting bigger and bigger due to the improvement of the memory design. We expect that it will be very hard to make it infinite, so we need to find proper methods to reduce erase operations.

The physical structure of a memory cell of flash memory is shown in Fig. 4. If there are no charge at the floating gate, the cell is not conducting. Charge at the floating gate will generate n-channel path in the surface part of p-channel and the cell becomes conducting. By putting high voltage to the erase gate, charge at the floating gate will move to n-channel part and the generated n-channel will disappear. This corresponds to erase operation. As application of high voltage causes migration of materials which is the aging mechanism of the memory. We will develop over-write technique, which is write without erasure. If the contents of cells are (0010) and we over-write (0100) then the new contents will be (0110), which is actually OR of the two values. Note that contents of the memory is initially all 0's. Actually 1 and 0 are exchanged in real NAND type flash memory, but for simplicity we use this notation in this paper.

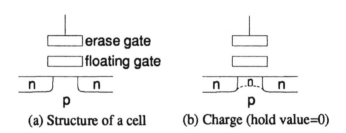

(a) Structure of a cell   (b) Charge (hold value=0)

Fig. 4. Internal Structure of Flash Memory

[**Over-write operation**]

(1) **Read:** Read the current values of the memory cells.
(2) **OR:** Perform OR operation between the values obtained by step (1) and the values to be written.
(3) **Store:** Write the value obtained by step (2) to the registers, which will be transmitted to the cells.
(4) **Self-verification:** Verify the values at step (3) and the current contents of the cells.

Since the cells automatically perform OR-operations, we need step (2) to ensure that the values written are identical to the cell contents. Otherwise at step (4) this write operation will be rejected, since self-verification is performed automatically. Thus steps (1) and (2) are required. If flash memory is used to backup main memory database, the before values are kept in the main memory part and thus step (1) is unnecessary.

Advantages of the over-write operations are as follows.

[Advantages of the over-write operation]

1. Since erase operation which requires 6~10 ms is not performed, the time required to write is very short.
2. It does not shorten the life time.

We need special coding, since by over-write we can only change 0 to 1 (not 1 to 0). Transition diagram for 3-bit encoding is shown in Fig. 5. As only change from 0 to 1 is permitted all the edge show direct change. Transitive change is also permitted. For example from (001) we can go to (101), (011) and (111).

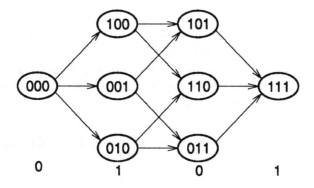

Fig. 5. Transition Diagram for 3-bit Encoding

If we assume that

0 is represented by (000), (101), (110), (011)
1 is represented by (100), (001), (010), (111)

then the value change $0 \rightarrow 1 \rightarrow 0 \rightarrow 1$ can be realized by over write operations over 3 bits.

If we use these 3 bits to represent addresses, the assignment shown in Fig. 6 is obtained.

Simple way to utilize overwrite operations is to reserve blank area at each page. Organization of one page is shown in Fig. 7.

1) One page is divided into several sections.
2) Each section consists of data part and link part. The initial values of the link part are all 0's.

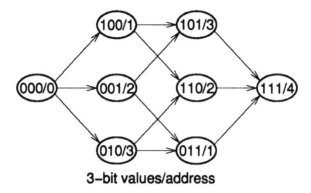

3-bit values/address

Fig. 6. Address Assignment for 3-bit Case

3) We assume that there are some number of reserved sections. If rewrite is required, find unused reserved section.

4) Write the new values to the new reserved section. Write the address of the section to the link part of the original data section. These writes are performed by overwrite operations.

Garbage collection is required after all the reserved section are used.

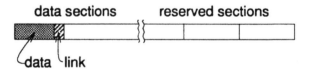

Fig. 7. Organization of a Page

If we use 3 bits for link part using the assignment shown in Fig. 6, we can link to four reserved sections; 1, 2, 3 and 4. By the first modification one of the reserved sections (1, 2 and 3) is assigned. Section 1 should be selected whenever it is not used. By the second modification one of the reserved sections (2, 3 and 4) is selected. Note that if we select 4 by the first modification we cannot select another reserved section. It is selected only when all other reserved sections are used.

3.3   Basic Consideration on File Organization Utilizing Flash Memory

In this section we will discuss how to use flash memory as secondary storage. First, characteristics of flash memory are summarized.

[Characteristics of flash memory]

1) Both read and write operations basically perform page access (sequential access).
2) If modification of data is required and erase operation is applied, the data before modification will be lost.
3) Erase operation is expensive, since it takes very long time and it will shorten the life time.

We will consider tree-structure indices for flash memory. The size of internal node is usually determined by the speed difference between direct access and sequential access. As sequential access is very much efficient for disks, in disk based indices each node is big whose size corresponds to the data volume retrieved by one sequential access. On the other hand, as there is no advantage to use sequential access in conventional main memory, binary trees are considered to be the best structure for such main memory. Since both high-speed RAM and flash memory have sequential access capability, each internal node should be bigger than that for binary trees.

For 2), we need to keep old data in some kind of nonvolatile memory or in flash memory. Keeping old values in flash memory is realized by dynamic address assignment.

[Basic dynamic address assignment]

1) Each block consists of data part and link part. Initial values of the link part are all 0's.
2) If there is a request to modify the block contents, a new block is assigned and new values are written in the new block.
3) The address of the new block is stored at the link part of the old block by overwrite operation.

This is a version of write-once memory[Mai82]. As it is very expensive to use one block every time there is some modification. By extending the method shown in Fig. 7, we can use block based version of overwrite method.

It should be noted that hot spot data are not suitable for flash memory. As hot spot data is only 10% of the whole data, we can use expensive nonvolatile memory such as battery-backed SRAMs and dielectric thin film memory.

Finally, we will discuss shortly on concurrency control for flash memory. The time required for write is very long since we need time-consuming erase operation. Compared with concurrency control developed for disk storage, we must consider the following conditions.

[Conditions to be considered in designing concurrency control for flash memory]

1) Unit of lock is different for each operation.

    read, overwrite : page

    erase, write   : block, entire cell array

2) Time required for each operation is distributed.

    read   : 30 μs for one page

    overwrite   : 60 μs for one page

    erase   : 6 $\sim$ 10 ms

    write for one block : 900 μs

If two-phase locking protocol is used, erase before write may not be serious. It consists of the following two steps.

a. lock phase: all required data should be locked.

b. unlock phase: after the completion of computation write operations are performed and then every lock is released.

For read operation, only beginning of locked period is used for read operations. For write operation, on the other hand, only the period before releasing the lock is used. The situations are shown in Fig 8(a), (b). In order to satisfy serializability lock period is very long, but only a part of period is used for real read/write operation. By this reason we can use two-phase locking protocol for overwrite and write with erase operations as show in Fig. 8(c), (d).

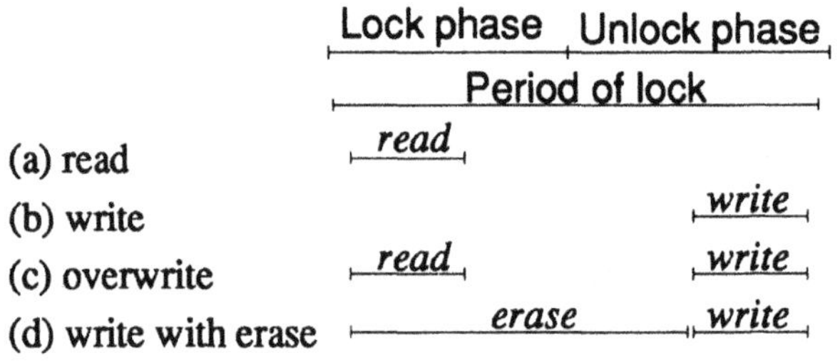

Fig. 8. Operation and Lock Period in Two-Phase Lock Protocol

There is no problem to realize overwrite operations which require both read and write operations. As erase operation is very long, we may have to extend the time for commit due the delay.

4 Use of Special-Purpose Memory

In this section we will discuss how to use memory for graphic displays and content-addressable memory.

4.1 Backup System Utilizing Dual-Port-RAM

In order to reduce overhead to get backup data, we can use memory chips developed for computer graphics, since they have two ports, one for read/write and the other for sequential read to display the contents of the memory.

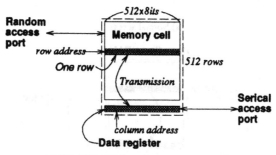

1-Mbit DRAM has four memory cells

Fig. 9. The Structure of Dual-Port DRAM

Fig. 9 shows the structure of dual-port-DRAM. Depending on the technology, there are dual-port-SRAM and dual-port-DRAM. As conventional RAMs dual-port-DRAM has big capacity. Dual-port-DRAM consists of RAM part and one data register. Contents of RAM can be accessed through random access port. From/To serial access port we can get/put data in the data register, of which contents were/will be transmitted from/to one selected row. 1-Mbit dual-port-DRAM consists of

4 RAMs of 512 × 512 bit
4 Data registers of 1 × 512 bit

Although 4 bits are retrieved parallely we need to read 512 times to get all the contents of the memory. The speed of random access port is the same as current DRAM and that of serial access port is very fast, e.g. 30 ns.

In a backup system, we use a random access port as an conventional main memory, and retrieve the backup data sequentially from the serial port. As normal access shown in Fig. 10(a), DM(Database Manager) accesses a random access port. During backup access shown in Fig. 10(b), DM accesses a random access port, too. When BRM(Backup Recovery Manager) accesses serial access port, one row data are transmitted from memory cells to serial port registers. After that, BRM starts to transmit the data to a disk. The advantage of this method is that DM must wait only when data are transmitted from memory cells to registers. The disadvantage is that we need a lot of checkpoints for recovery operations, i.e., the number of rows. For example, we need at least 512

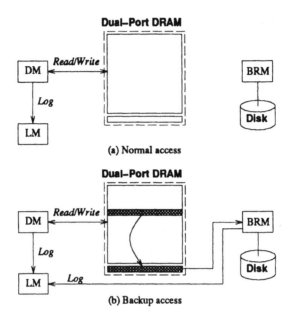

Fig. 10. Organization of Continuous Backup RAMs Using Dual-Port RAMs

data transmissions for 1 Mbit dual-port-DRAM. If there exist many checkpoints, BRM sends to LM(Log Manager) many logs which have the information about backup data. This increase the overhead of log management. For example, we assume that disk data transmit speed is 800[nsec/byte], and that a main memory is organized every 4 Mbytes block (each block uses 32 dual-port-DRAMs and 1byte consists of 2 DRAMs). We also assume that backup operations are performed in every block and that transmit operation from memory cell to register are done in all 32 DRAMs at one time. BRM send logs to LM every 6.6[msec] (= 800[nsec/byte] × 512[byte] × 16). We must take 512 logs per 6.6[msec].

Current dual-port-DRAMs cannot be used for backup systems, but dual-port-DRAMs for high definition TV can be used for such purposes by the following reasons.

In case of HDTV(High Definition Television), we assume that one frame is constructed in 33.3[msec] and has 1125 scan lines, and that one scan line has 1333 pixels (total number of pixels for one frame is 1500000 $\simeq$ 1333 × 1125) by Japanese NHK standard. We must use RAM whose read cycle of serial port is under 17.8[nsec]. This means that dual-port-DRAM needs to have faster serial access port. Although read cycle of serial access port becomes faster, disk data transmission speed is not fast enough. To deal with such large data quickly without conventional method, dual-port-DRAM needs faster random access port and larger serial access port register : e.g. 1333 bits to 1333 pixels.

When the capacity of serial port register became larger, we can reduce the number of logs which have the information about backup data. If dual-port-DRAM is developed for such a purpose, we can organize our backup system easily. In [KaT91] we have developed two-plane memory to simulate dual-port-RAM.

4.2 Use of Content Addressable Memory

The basic idea for Content Addressable Memory (CAM) is old [Sle56]. Currently there are some CAMs in the market. Basically the capacity of CAM is about one tenth of SRAM, which makes practical applications difficult. Usually when we need to process n data, we need at least $O(n)$ time to read the data. Using CAM only data necessary for computation can be selected and thus we can reduce the computation time. It is shown that problems in class NP can be solved in polynomial time by using enough amount of CAMs[TaT90].

Fig. 11 shows a basic structure of CAM.

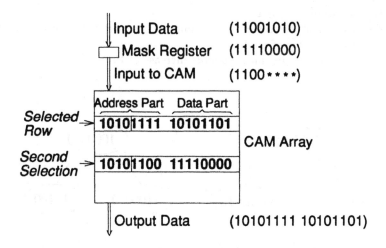

Fig. 11. Structure of Content Addressable Memory

CAM array is realized by RAM cells with exclusive OR function. There are two kinds of RAM cells, static and dynamic.

Input data (in this example, 11001010) is given to the mask register (selecting the first four bits) and only necessary bits (1100∗∗∗∗, ∗ means don't care) are selected. If data have identical values for the selected bits, they will be selected. Selected data can be obtained from the output terminal. If there are two or more selected data, they will be sent to the output terminal one by one.

Selection operation of relational databases is realized by CAM directly, although it is not easy to store a whole relation in CAM. Partial matching can be realized by adding a shift register.

[String search]

This is a partial-match string searcher. A set of words is stored in CAM. Input port is a shift register and the string to be checked is sequentially applied to the shift register. When a stored word appears in the register, output is produced from the CAM array. The input speed is 10 mega characters/sec by the implementation in [Yam87].

We will show two other applications.

[Finding a set of methods for a class in object oriented databases]

One advantage of object-oriented databases is use of method inheritance. If class hierarchy is complicated it is not easy to find all the methods corresponding to a given class. We can avoid path computation if we assign proper binary vectors to classes. Let v_i be the vector corresponding to class i.

(1) The length of each vector is the number of the class. Initial values of every v_i is $(00\cdots0)$.
(2) The i-th value of v_i is 1.
(3) If k-th value of the vector corresponding to a superclass of class i is 1, then put 1 to k-th value of v_i also.
(4) Apply (3) repeatedly, until no more increase of 1's.

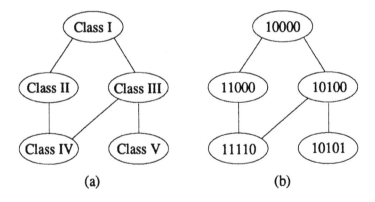

(a)   (b)

Fig. 12. Class Hierarchy and Its Corresponding Vector Hierarchy

Fig. 12 shows a class hierarchy and its corresponding vector hierarchy. By this representation, if class j is a subclass of class i and the k-th value of v_j is 0, then the k-th value of v_i is also 0. For example (see Fig. 12) class III (10100) has two subclasses class IV (11110) and class V (10101). If all the vectors are stored in CAM and input (1 * 1 * *) (it is obtained by converting 0 to * in the vector for class III) is applied, outputs are (10100), (11110) and (10101) corresponding to classes III, IV and V, respectively. By applying (*0 * 00) (corresponding to class III), superclasses are obtained (in this case class I and class III).

If we store pointers to the methods in the memory part of CAM, by applying the superclass search algorithm we can get all the methods applicable to the objects in the class.

[Finding a set of rules in active databases]

In ECA mechanism[Day88] if a set of conditions are satisfied, some action is required when some event occurs. There are cases when a lot of actions will be fired by an event. We may need to make a schedule in that case. If we assign each bit for each condition then the set of rules which may be fired can be obtained by CAM.

Data in CAM part consists of a condition vector, event pointer and action pointer, For example, assume that there are five conditions and one rule is as follows.

"If conditions 1 and 3 are satisfied, then action A is required when event E occurs."

Then the values in one row of CAM part are as follows.

10100, pointer for E, pointer for A.

If currently conditions 1, 3 are satisfied then we can get possible actions by giving (*0 * 00) to the input of the CAM. All the values whose condition sets are in {condition1, condition3} including the above can be obtained.

As there are many conditions, we need to use either (1) division of the condition set into small sets, or (2) usage of condition hierarchy. Details are omitted here. Furthermore, we need to handle coupling conditions, which is also omitted here.

If we have CAMs whose address part is 32 bits, then we can realize 320-bit CAM by combining 10 CAMs and some additional circuits. It may be enough for above applications.

5 Use of Hardware Circuits to Realize High-Performance Database Systems

Many relational database machines have been developed due to the following two reasons.

A. Relational database systems were too slow compared with network database systems.

B. Basic operations of relational databases are simple.

Due to the rapid progress of CPU chips, it is very hard to develop special-purpose hardware. Even if we design special-purpose hardware by the up-to-date chip technology, it will become obsolete when chips are ready to be produced.

Compatible speed-up may be obtained using up-to-date general purpose CPU chips. This is one of the major reasons why RISC (Reduced Instruction Set Computer) chips are popular, since developing time is much shorter than CISC (Complicated Instruction Set Computer) chips. As this trend is predicted to continue at least 10 more years, it is believed that development of special-purpose hardware is not worthwhile.

It is widely accepted that to develop cost effective database machines we should use multiple CPU's and large capacity main memory, both of which are available in the market. We should, however, note the following two points.

1) Recently very much advanced flexible logic chips are developed. In some kind of FPGA (Field Programmable Gate Array), a circuit consisting of more than 10,000 gates can be realized. Circuit connections are controlled by the contents of SRAM, so that circuits can be modified during the system operation. Although the speed is slower than conventional gate arrays, the difference is not big because the increase of delay is mainly caused by increase of connections length (gate speeds are not different). We believe a proper combination of FPGA with up-to-date CPU chips will solve some of the hardware development problems.

2) In most database machine projects, realization of high-speed database operations is the major objective. As database systems become completed (parallel, pipe-line, distributed) and also applications become complicated (multimedia, real-time), there are other bottle-necks like query optimization, integrity constraint checking, concurrency control, back-up and recovery.

Hardware realization of algorithms is called hardware algorithms. For database applications, we need to consider the following there kinds of problems.

I) Differences of characteristics between computer arithmetics and database operations must be considered.

II) Some kinds of database software bottle-neck can be solved by using hardware.

III) For applications like query optimizations we need to handle problems known as NP-complete.

For database applications we need to consider the following conditions. Let n be the maximum data size to be processed by a circuit and m be the input data size ($m \leq n$).

I-1) Wide distribution of data size: For example, a 64-bit multiplier usually handles numbers of 16 to 64 bits. For database applications, the number of data can be 1 to 1 million (upper bound is unlimited), for example.

I-2) Hardware realization is used for speed-up: For small number of data we can use software algorithms, so hardware realization is effective if the upper limit of the number of data handled by a circuit is large, although large circuits are expensive. For small number of data only a part of the circuit should be be utilized.

I-3) Sequential input and output: Since the data size is unlimited, inputs/outputs should be represented by a sequence of data blocks. Thus time required for input is $O(m)$. We can utilize sequential access capability of secondary storages.

I-4) Simultaneous data processing and input/output: Since time required for input/output is at most $O(n)$, database operations should be performed simultaneously with input/output operations. So it is not worth to use hardware realizing a database operation less than $O(n)$ and the delay time (the time required to get the first output data) is important.

I-5) Because the number of data can exceed any predetermined upper bound, we must handle the case when the number of data exceeds the bound of the circuit. The hardware algorithm is required to be combined with software easily for such cases.

Requirements for hardware due to I-2) are as follows.

I-2-1) Circuit size to handle n data must be much less than $O(n)$ except for required memory size. If the circuit size is proportional to n, we need a very large circuit for large n. The circuit size must be as small as possible (for example $O(\log n)$).

I-2-2) Even when a circuit to process n data for large n is prepared, we need to process small number of data by the same circuit. The circuit must be designed to process such small number of data efficiently.

I-2-3) We do not need circuits which can perform sort in less than $O(n)$ time, since we need $O(n)$ for data input.

There are two kinds of circuits; the total delay time is determined by the circuit size or by the data size. When we must handle the small number of data, the latter type is preferable. In the latter type we may be able to get the computation result immediately after the completion of the input since data input is performed sequentially and processing is realized concurrently with the data input. In hardware algorithm theory there are papers to realize sort in $O(\log n)$ time using a lot of hardware [Mul75]. Such kind of circuits cannot be used for database operations.

There can be the five kinds of one-dimensional circuits shown in Fig. 13(a), (b), (c), (d) and (e), which we call Type I, II, III, IV and V, respectively. There are other kinds of circuit configuration like trees and two-dimensional arrays [Tho77] which are omitted here.

As input and output terminals are located in the opposite sides of a circuit of Type I and II, the processing time required for such circuits is determined by the circuit size. In circuits of Type III, IV and V, we may be able to use a part of the circuit determined by the data size. Circuits of Type IV and V use bus lines for such purpose. For iterative arrays usually it is not preferable to have such broadcast lines, since the circuit size is not bounded. There are proposals to use such bus lines to improve effectiveness of communication among components[Yas82], [IwK89]. We will show examples of these circuits.

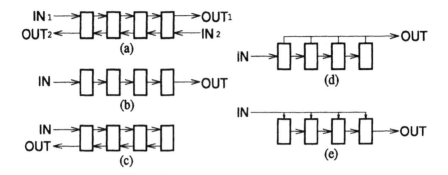

Fig. 13. One-Dimensional Structures

A systoric array-based join processor (Type I) [Kun80]: Tuples from two relations to be joined are given from IN1 and IN2, respectively. Tuples in the different relations will meet in the circuit and then values of the join attribute are compared. The circuit size is $O(n)$ to process at most n tuple relations and the delay time is also $O(n)$. Such kind of circuits are not suitable for database operations, since both circuit size and delay time are unacceptable for large n. For any $m \leq n$ the time required to process is constant.

Pipe-line sort-merge (Type II)[Tod78]: Fig. 14 shows an example of the sorter developed by Todd. As the processing requirement at each level of a tree to perform merge-join is identical, one processor is assigned for each level of the tree. The number of processors is $O(\log n)$ to sort n data, although the processor corresponding to the root of the tree requires $O(n)$ memory. There are many database machines utilizing this kind of sorters (for example, DBE of Toshiba, GREO of Mitsubishi) because of its circuit size. The delay time is always fixed to be $O(logn)$.

Sorter based on up-down counter[LeC81] (Type III): Lee et al., developed a sorter of Type III. Although the circuit size is $O(n)$, the sorted result is obtained immediately after the input is completed. Thus the delay is considered to be constant. Only the part of the circuit determined by the input data size is used.

Pipe-line heap sort[TaN80] (Type III): The circuit size is $O(\log n)$ and delay is $O(\log m)$. Although the circuit has ideal characteristics, it is not widely used since we must wait until the completion of sort before giving the next data set to the circuit (in [Tho83] it is shown that this sorter is patented by P.K. Armstrong, 1978).

Sorter with a bus line (Type IV): If we add a bus line to Todd's sorter, we can use the part of the sorter determined by the data size. When the whole data are sorted it is transmitted through the bus line if not occupied. As a result, the circuit size is $O(\log n)$ and the delay becomes $O(logm)$.

In [Tho83] various hardware sorters are compared. The quality of a sorter is given by (area) $\times$ (time)^2. The number of processors ranges from $\log n$ to

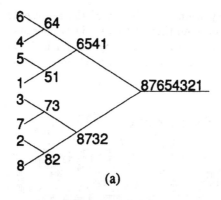

(a)

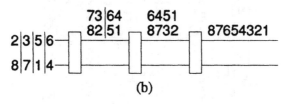

(b)

Fig. 14. Pipe-Line Merge Sorter

n^3. As discussed before, for database systems the number of processors is very important ("n^3 processors for large n" is not practical at all even if the value (area) $\times$ (time)^2 is small). There are three algorithms using $O(\log n)$ processors, merge sort, heap sort and bitonic sort.

In [BiD84] parallel sorting algorithms are summarized. They put emphasis on processing time. Major algorithms listed in Table 1 of the paper require at least n processors. These algorithms can be used for designing functional memory with sorting functions, but they may not be practical to sort large amount of data in database systems.

6 FPGAs and Applications

In this section we will discuss shortly on the possibility of hardware technology to improve database algorithms.

Programmable logic devices used to be rather simple. PLA (Programmable Logic Arrays) can realize a multiple-output three level (NOT-AND-OR) circuit (for example, see[Kam79]). By storing truth values, we can realize an arbitrary 20 variable function by 1M bit RAM (1M bit = 2^{20} bit). Recently much more advanced programmable logic devices are produced, called FPGA. We will discuss SRAM FPGA in this section.

LCA developed by Xilinx Inc. is one of the representative SRAM FPGA. Each LCA can contain more than 10^4 gates. LCA consists of a matrix of CLBs (Configurable Logic Block) as shown is Fig. 15. Each CLB can realize arbitrary circuit consisting of the gates inside of CLB. Connections among CLBs are real-

Switch matrix   IOB   CLB

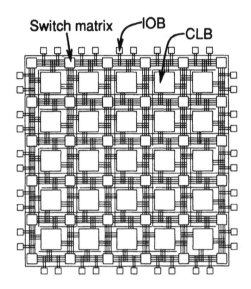

Fig. 15. Structure of SRAM FPGA

ized by vertical/horizontal bus lines. Connections between these two kinds of bus lines are realized by switch matrices. Interface parts for external inputs/outputs are realized by IOBs (input/output Block). CLBs, IOBs, and Switch Matrices are all controlled by the contents of SRAM. By changing the contents of the SRAM, the circuit connections are modified. We may be able to use nonvolatile memory, such as flash memory to control FPGA, since contents of SRAM may be lost by some accident.

If algorithm is implemented by FPGA it is processed in very short time. As FPGA offers flexibility previously not offered by hardware, we may be able to develop a program consisting of software and FPGA. FPGA can be used to speed-up bottle-neck part of software.

We will list some possible applications to databases.

[Logic Function]
    A set of logic functions can be easily realized by FPGA. There are semantic constraints which can be expressed by logic functions. Such constraints can be maintained by FPGA.

[Automaton]

Flexible automaton can be realized by FPGA. If we design a pattern matching machines[AhC75] for a given set of key strings, finding strings in a text will be efficiently realized. Each time a new set of key strings are given we must generate a new pattern matching machine. Different from CAM implementation, there is no limit of the lengths of key strings except for the gate limitation of FPGA. Furthermore, very general matching like "database * hardware" which can detect a part of the given text satisfying that 'Mdatabase" appears before "hardware".

[Petri Net]

Petri net can simulate a set of ECA rules in active databases. Because of timing problem it is very difficult to find conflicts among ECA rules, we need simulation to check. Petri net mode by FPGA realizes very fast operation and useful to simulate ECA rules. As ECA rules will be modified we need FPGA implementation.

BDD is a compact way to store truth value table of logic functions[Bry92]. Equivalence of logic functions can be determined easily. Currently all practical logic design procedures (for example, transduction procedure[MuK89] implemented by Fujitsu etc.) and logic simulators utilizes BDD. We can use BDD with FPGA to handle various logic functions.

7 Pipe-Line Processing for Database Operations

Although pipe-line processing is a special case of parallel processing, it is important to develop database algorithms for it by the following reasons.

1) Vector processors for workstations are currently developed by several companies to speed-up workstations.
2) Sequential access property of storage devices can be utilized efficiently.
3) The order of processing data is fixed for all processors in a pipe-line.

    3-1) If there is some accident, the process must start again. In general parallel system it is very hard to repeat the identical job due to critical timing problems. In pipe-line process it it very easy to repeat the job because of 3). We can reduce overhead for taking log.

    3-2) Combination of different operations can be realized. Data are applied in the same order to consecutive operations. We may be able to combine them (see Fig. 16).

    3-3) This property is especially suitable for concurrency control, where conflict of orders of data processed by operations is not permitted.

Pipe-line operations are also suitable for process in functional memory. In order to reduce communication cost data distribution approach is discussed[Kam84], which is designed by pipe-line approach.

Fig. 17(a) shows conventional pipe-line process for manufacturing line. If data are very big, to move data is expensive. It is rather easy to move processors

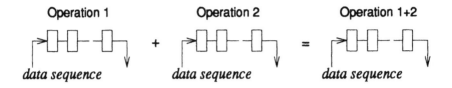

Fig. 16. Combination of Operations

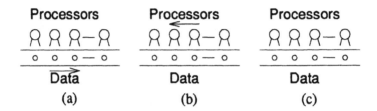

Fig. 17. Combination of Operations

in the opposite directions (see Fig. 17(b)). Instead of moving processors we can simulate the situation by changing functions of processors. For example, there are three consecutive processors performing functions f_1, f_2 and f_3. As data processed by f_1 (f_2) must be processed by f_2 (f_3) in the consecutive step, we can change the function of the left-most processor from f_1 to f_2 without moving processors or data. In this way we can avoid expensive data communication. This is called 'data distribution approach'. It is very similar to do the whole job by one processor, except that the orders of function applications are all same.

Currently we have a very serious problem for concurrency control. If a system has more than one processor (parallel systems, distributed systems), we have to use these processors simultaneously in order to improve efficiency. Concurrency control is developed for this purpose. Although concurrency control may improve efficiency, it imposes serializability constraint. As it is a global constraint, it is very hard to keep it. Efficiency may decrease by keeping such a global constraint. As a result concurrency control may not improve system performance. For example, in [KaK84] the problem of combining database systems with different concurrency control mechanisms is addressed. We first designed simulation approach (to simulate time-stamp ordering by two-phase locking protocol, etc.) to unify concurrency control mechanisms, but its approach turned out to be very much inefficient. In [KaK84] we took pipe-line approach under the assumption that there are not many global transactions in such cases. In both time-stamp ordering and two-phase locking protocol, the order of processing data is arbitrary and when there is conflict roll-back operations must be applied (in the case of two-phase locking protocol, conflict will cause dead-lock). Pipe-line approach enforces fixed order and thus roll-back is not required. Although it is believed that concurrency control by pipe-line has very little efficiency (special case of tree protocol[Sik80]), it has the following advantages.

1) Use of two kinds granularity:
   Although small granularity allows many transactions to operate in parallel, large system overhead to maintain locks is required. It is very difficult to determine proper granularity. If pipe-line process is applied to one attribute values in a relation, we need to maintain lock information in attribute level. Because operations are applied to tuples, concurrency of small granularity (lock on each tuple value) can be effectively achieved. Thus we can realize high concurrency with a little overhead to maintain locks.

2) Optimization:
   As discussed before we can improve efficiency by combining consecutive operations. Furthermore, by applying commutativity rule to operations we may be able to reduce the cost further.

We assume that there are the following basic operations; search, read, write and computation which are denoted by S, R, W and K, respectively. Let n be the number of tuples in relation P. We assume operations are applied to attribute values of the attribute A in P. Let V be a binary vector of length n. U is a vector of length n. Basic operations are as follows.

[Basic Operation on Attribute Values]

1) Search:
   $S(A, C, V)$: Find tuples satisfying that A-value satisfies condition C. The i-th value of V is 1 if and only if A-value of the i-th tuple satisfies condition C.

2) Read:
   $R(A, C, U)$: If A-value of i-th tuple satisfies condition C then (i, A-value of the i-th tuple)) is stored in U.
   $R'(A, V, U)$: If i-th value of V is 1 then (i, A-value of the i-th tuple) is stored in U.

3) Write:
   $W(A, C, U)$: If A-value of i-th tuple satisfies condition C and (i, _value_) is stored in U, the A-value is replaced by _value_.
   $W'(A, V, U)$: If i-th value of V is 1 and (i, _value_) is stored in U, replace A-value of i-th tuple by _value_.

4) Computation:
   $K(A, V, f, U)$: If i-th value of V is 1, (i, f(A-value of the i-th tuple) is stored in U.

In the above expressions if i-th value of U is (i, _value_), we can omit i for simplicity.

Read operation $R(A, C, U)$ is equivalent to a sequence $S(A, C, V)R'(A, V, U)$. Write operation $W(A, C, U)$ or $W'(A, V, U)$ must be applied after computing U. We will not discuss on optimization of expression by U.

The following sequence means that i-th value of the attribute B is increased by 10, when the i-th value of the attribute A is not less than 100.

$S(A, C, V)$: C is the condition $A \geq 100$.
$K(B, V, f(+10), U)$: If i-th value of V is 1 then $(i, (i$-th value of attribute $B)+10)$ is stored in U.
$W(B, V, U)$: If i-th value of V is 1 and there exists $(i, \underline{value})$ in U then i-th value of B is replaced by $\underline{value}$.

We can use commutativity rules. Some examples are as follows.

1) S, R and K are commutative.
2) $R(A, C_1, U_1)$ and $W(A, C_2, U_2)$ are commutative if $C_1 \cap C_2 = \emptyset$.
3) $W(A_1, C_1, U_1)$ and $W(A_2, C_2, U_2)$ are also commutative if $C_1 \cap C_2 = \emptyset$.

By applying commutativity rule we may get a sequence;

$$R(A, C_1, U_1) \; R(A_1, C_2, U_2) \quad (C_1 \neq C_2)$$

Then we can combine them into one operation by checking both C_1 and C_2 by one scan.

There are two measures to evaluate efficiency of pipeline algorithms.

[Vectorization ratio]

A vectorization ratio means the rate of operations executed by vector instructions to the whole operations in a program. Even in the case of running a program on vector processors, not all the operations of the program are executed by vector instructions and the rest is executed by scalar instructions. Vector processors won't achieve its high performance in the case that the vectorization ratio is low. For example, when vectorization ratio is only 50 percent, the total speedup, i.e. acceleration ratio, is at most twice, since the upper bound could be achieved if vector instructions require no execution time.

[Vector length]

Vector length is the length of operands of vector instruction. Since on starting vector instructions there are some overheads to start up the pipeline function units, they cannot be ignored unless the vector length is long enough. Roughly speaking, it should be larger than several hundreds to obtain the high performance of vector processors. Let us define **vector execution** as enabling pipeline function units to executable parts of a program by vector instructions, and **scalar execution** as disabling pipeline function units to execute whole of a program by scalar instructions. In order to evaluate the suitability of a program to vector processors, let us define **acceleration ratio** as the rate of the execution speed in vector execution to that in scalar execution. The ratio, then, is obtained by dividing CPU time of a program in scalar execution by that in vector execution. High acceleration ratio means that the program extracts the potential of vector processors sufficiently, and low one means that it doesn't. We consider an acceleration ratio about 10 to be high enough in the meaning above.

We have implemented relational operations for vector processors considering the two measures above. For evaluation, we selected the scalable Wisconsin benchmark[BiD83] to generate large relations. It is shown in Table 4.

Table 4. Attribute Specification of "Scalable" Wisconsin Benchmark Relations

Attribute Name	Range of Values	Order	Comment
unique1	0-(MAXTUPLES-1)	random	unique, random order
unique2	0-(MAXTUPLES-1)	sequential	unique, sequential
two	0-1	random	(unique1 mod 2)
four	0-3	random	(unique1 mod 4)
ten	0-9	random	(unique1 mod 10)
twenty	0-19	random	(unique1 mod 20)
onePercent	0-99	random	(unique1 mod 100)
tenPercent	0-9	random	(unique1n mod 10)
twentyPercent	0-4	random	(unique1 mod 5)
fiftyPercent	0-1	random	(unique1 mod 2)
uique3	0-(MAXTUPLES-1)	random	(unique1)
evenOnePercent	0,2,4,···,198	random	(OnePercent * 2)
oddOnePercent	1,3,5,···,199	random	(OnePercent * 2)+1
stringu1	—	random	candidate key
stringu2	—	sequential	candidate key
string4	—	cyclic	

It is easy to understand the meaning of the first thirteen integer attributes (unique1 through oddonepercent). Both two string attributes, stringu1 and stringu2, are computed from unique1 and unique2, respectively using a certain procedure. The last string attribute, string4, assumes four values in a cyclic manner. For details the readers should refer to the original paper[Dew91]. Since the number of the tuples of the original benchmark relation is ten thousands and is a little too small for our prototype system to show its performance, we scaled it up to have one hundred thousand tuples, which we call HUNDKTUP hereafter. We also used the relation APRIME as another relation of join query, which consists of the first ten thousand tuples of the relation HUNDKTUP.

To measure the essential performance of the system, the following queries are processed without indices.

Selection Query selects tuples with selectivity factor of 10 percent, i.e., it selects ten thousand tuples from the source relation HUNDKTUP.

Projection Query has a projection factor of 4 percent, eliminating 96 percent of the source relation HUNDKTUP as duplicates. Although the original projection query of the Wisconsin benchmark was intended to have a projection factor of 1 percent, it changed into 4 percent because the specification of the relation was modified. Then four thousands tuples are contained in the resulting relation.

Join Query is a simple join of the two relations HUNDKTUP and APRIME, where the size of APRIME is one tenth that of HUNDKTUP. Since each join attribute is unique, the result relation has the same number of tuples as that of APRIME.

Aggregate Query selects the minimum value of attribute uniquel. Although an index on it makes it possible to process the query by tracing it alone, in our experiment the query is processed by scanning all the tuples in the relation HUNDKTUP without indices.

In our implementation we use hash-base algorithm to perform equi-joins.

Table 5 shows time required to process the above four queries by scalar and vector execution by FACOM VP-2600 (512-Mbyte main memory, 5 GFLOPS) at Data Processing Center of Kyoto University. Acceleration ratios for three basic database operations (select, project, join) are all over 40. We expect vector execution is at least 10 times faster than serial execution, even if proper programs for serial execution are prepared.

Table 5. Benchmark Results

	CPU time (ms)		Acceleration
	Scalar execution	Vector execution	ratio
Selection	287	6	48
Projection	2280	52	44
Equijoin	616	15	41
Aggregation	27	2	13.5

8 Concluding Remarks

In this paper we discussed database research topics related to VLSI memory and circuit technology. We believe that this kind of research is very important as well as research topics motivated by new database applications stressed in [Sto93]. There are many hardware technologies which are not used any more, such as core memory, cryotorn[Sle56], bubble memory[LeC81], write-once optical disks[Mai82], etc. There are physical properties common in different technologies. For example, logic design technologies developed for relay circuits can be applied to cryotron and MOS gates (especially transfer gates). Structures of BDD are also similar to relay circuits. As the major motivation of database file organization is how to design ideal storage systems (high-speed, large capacity, nonvolatile, low cost, low power consumption, long life time, small size, reliable) for some specific applications under available hardware technology, we must watch hardware technology trends as well as database application trends.

There are many optimization problems in database research for which results from algorithm design can be utilized. We must not forget that the range of data size is very wide in database applications. From this standpoint most of hardware sorters discussed in [Tho83][BiD84] cannot be used for database applications because they require too many processors.

References

[AgJ89] R.Agrawal, H.V. Jagadish, "Recovery Algorithms for Database Machines with Nonvolatile Main Memory," Proc. of 6th Int. Workshop Database Machines, (Lecture Notes in Computer Science), Springer-Verlag, pp.269-285. June 1989.

[AhC75] A.V.Aho, M.J.Corasick, "Efficient String Matching: An Aid to Bibliographic Search," C.ACM, Vol.18, No.6, pp.333-340, June 1975.

[BaM72] R, Bayer, E.M. McCreight, "Organization and Maintenance of Large Ordered Indices," Acta Information, Vol.7, No.3, pp.173-189, 1972.

[BiD83] D.Bitton, D.J.Dewitt, C.Turbyfill," Benchmarking database systems: A systematic approach," Proceedings of the 1983 Very Large Database Conference, pp.8-19, 1983.

[BiD84] D.Bitton, D.J.DeWitt, D.K.Hsiao, J.Menon, "A Taxonomy of Parallel Sorting," ACM Computing Surveys, Vol.16, No.3, pp287-318, 1984.

[Bry92] R.E.Bryant, "Symbolic Boolean Manipulation with Ordered Binary-Decision Diagrams," ACM Computing Survey, Vol.24 No.3 September 1992, pp.293-318.

[Day88] U.Dayal, "Active Database Management Systems," Proc. 3rd Int. Conf. Data and Knowledge Base, pp.150-169, 1988.

[Dew91] D.J.Dewitt, "The Wisconsin Benchmark:Past, Present, and Future," The Benchmark Handbook, Morgan Kaufman, pp.119-165, 1991.

[Eic89] M.H.Eich, "Main Memory Database Research Directions," Proc. 6th International Workshop, IWDM'89, 1989, pp.251-268.

[Gho72] S.P.Ghosh, "File Organization: The Consecutive Retrieval Property," CACM, Vol.15, No.8, pp.802-808, 1972.

[Hus93] K.A.Hua, X.X.W.Su, C.M.Hua, "Efficient Evaluation of Traversal Recursive Queries," Proc. Int. Conf. Data Engineering, pp.549-558, April 1993.

[ImB92] T.Imielinski, B.R.Badrinath, "Querying in Highly Mobile Distributed Environments," Proc. 18th VLDB Conf., pp.41-52.

[IwK89] K.Iwama, Y.Kambayashi, "An O(log n) Parallel Connectivity Algorithm on the Mesh of Buses," Proceedings of the IFIP Congress, pp.305-310, August 1989.

[IwK93] K.Iwama, Y.Kambayashi, "A Simple Parallel Algorithms for Graph Connectivity," Journal of Algorithms (to appear).

[KaK84] Y.Kambayashi, S.Kondo, "Global Concurrency Control Mechanisms for a Local Network Consisting of Systems without Concurrency Control Mechanism," Proceedings of the AFIPS National Computer Conference, Vol.53, pp.31-39, July 1984.

[Kam79] Y.Kambayashi, "Logic Design of Programmable Logic Array," IEEE Transactions on Computers, Vol. C 28, No. 9, pp. 609-617, Sept. 1979.

[Kam84] Y.Kambayashi, "A Database Machine Based on the Data Distribution Approach," Proceedings of the AFIPS National Computer Conference, Vol.53, pp.613-625, July 1984.

[KaG85] Y.Kambayashi, S.P.Ghosh, "Query Processing Using the Consecutive Retrieval Property," in Query Processing in Database Systems, pp. 217-233, Springer-Verlag, 1985.

[Kam88] Y.Kambayashi, "Integration of Different Concurrency Control Mechanisms in Heterogeneous Distributed Databases," Proceedings of the Second International Symposium on Interoperable Information Systems (ISIIS ' 88), OHM Publishing Co., November 1988.

[KaT91] Y.Kambayashi, H.Takakura, "Realization of Continuously Backed-up RAMs for High-Speed Database Recovery," The 2nd International Symposium on DASFAA, pp.236-242, 1991.

[Kun80] H.T.Kung, P.L.Lehman, "Systoric (VLSI) Arrays for Relational Database Operations," Proc. of ACM SIGMOD, pp.105-116, 1980.

[LeC86] T.J. Lehman, M.J. Carey, "A Study of Index Structures for Main Memory Database Management Systems," Proc. of the 12th Int. Conf. on VLDB, 1986, pp.294-303.

[LeC81] D.T.Lee, H.Chang, C.K.Wong, "An On-Chip Compared/Steer Bubble Sorter," IEEE Trans. on Computers, C-30, pp.398-405, 1981.

[Mai82] D.Maier, "Using Write-One Memory for Database Storage," Proc. ACM PODS, pp.239-246, 1982.

[Mul75] D.E.Muller and F.P.Preparata, "Bounds to Complexites of Networks for Sortting and for Switching," JACM vol.22, no.2, April 1975.

[MuK89] S.Muroga, Y.Kambayashi, H.C.Lai, J.Culliney, "The Transaction Method - Design of Logic Network Based on Permissible Functions," IEEE Transactions on Computers. September 1989.

[OcI91] H.Ochi, N.Ishiura, S.Yajima, "Breadth-First Manipulation of SBDD of Boolean Functions for Vector Processing," Proceedings of 28th ACM/IEEE Design Automation Conference, pp.413-41, 1991.

[Sik80] A. Silberschatz, Z.Kedem, "Consistency in Hierarchical Database Systems," Journal of ACM, Vol.27, No.1, pp.72-80, 1980.

[Sle56] A.E.Slacle, H.O.MeMahon, "A Cryotron Catalog Memory System," Proc. of EJCC, pp.115-120, 1956.

[Sto93] M.Stonbraker, "Are We Polishing a Round Ball?," Panel at the International Conf. on Data Engineering, April 1993.

[TaN80] Y.Tanaka, Y.Nozaka, A.Masuyama, "Pipeline Searching and Sorting Modules as Components of a Data Flow Database Computer," Proc. of IFIP 80, October 1980.

[TaT90] T.Takagi, Y.Takenaga, S.Yajima, "Memory Parallel Computation Method and its Computation Power-The Third Approach to Realize Super Computers," Journal of IPSJ, Vol.31, No.11, pp.1565-1571, 1990 (in Japanese).

[Tho77] C.D.Thompson and H.T.Kung, "Sorting on a Mesh-Connected Parallel Computer," CACM vol.20,no.4, April 1977.

[Tho83] C.T.Thompson, "The VLSI Complexity of Sorting," IEEE Trans. on Computers, Vol.32, No.12, pp.1171-1184, Dec. 1983.

[Tod78] S.Todd, "Algorithm and Hardware for a Merge Sort Using Multiple Processors," IBM Journal of Research and Development, Vol. 22, No. 5, September 1978.

[Tos92] Toshiba, NAND E^2PROM, FT-TC584000P /F/Ft/FR, Data Sheet, June 1992.

[Uke93] R.L.Ukeiley, "Field Programmable Gate Arrays," PTR prentice-Hall, 1993.

[Ull80] J.D.Ullman, " Principles of database systems," Computer science Press, 1980.

[Yam87] H.Yamada, et.al., "A High-Speed String Search Engine," IEEE Journal of Solid-State Circuits, Vol.22, pp.829-834, Oct. 1987.

[Yas82] H.Yasuura, N.Takagi and S.Yajima, "The Parallel Enumeration Sortin Scheme for VLSI ," IEEE Trans, Comput., Vol.C-31, No.12, pp.1192-1201, December 1982.

Evaluation of Upper Bounds and Least Nodes as Database Operations

Joachim Biskup and Holger Stiefeling

Institut für Informatik, Universität Hildesheim
D-31113 Hildesheim, Germany

Abstract: We argue for supporting besides transitive closure two additional types of recursive queries in augmented relational database systems: the computation of upper bounds and least nodes in graphs that are persistently stored as database relations. We describe various algorithms for the evaluation of the specified query types. In essence, they vary in the kind of graph search, the search direction, the way how they prune search areas, and the way how they utilize intermediate results. Based on analytical results, we give a comparative assessment of the algorithms. The results of experiments substantiate our analytical findings.

1 Introduction

In recent years, a lot of work has been devoted to extending relational database systems by recursive query facilities. This task includes the design of an extended query language (e.g. [BRS90], [Ed90], [MS90]) and of corresponding evaluation algorithms. Many publications examine strategies for recursive queries in general (see [Ul89]). Others focus on special types. The transitive closure of a binary relation receives an important share of the latter group; selections and generalizations of the transitive closure attracted also attention (see [BiSt 88] for a general study and [KIC 92, Ja 92] for recent progress).

We suppose that the majority of recursive queries expected to be posed to an extended database system does not consist of general recursive queries. Instead, we consider queries delivering specific information on paths in graph structures more likely. Examining the requirements from various fields of knowledge engineering, we found that besides transitive closure and its selections two further types of such queries are prevailing, determination of upper bounds and least nodes (together with their symmetric counterparts lower bounds and greatest nodes).

More precisely, in many approaches to knowledge engineering the knowledge to be stored is represented by directed graphs. Their nodes model basic entities, and their edges express direct connections between two entities. Typical applications are the following. For a genealogy persons are modelled by nodes and parentage is reflected by edges. For a company departments and finer subunits are modelled by nodes and the relationships of interest are reflected by marked edges expressing the structure of ownership, reporting, etc.. For a communication network of any kind places are modelled by nodes and links are expressed by edges. For a concept hierarchy concepts are modelled by nodes and the relationship of subconcepts is expressed by edges. In many cases these graphs turn out to be acyclic or even trees or forests. And for ambitious applications these graphs tend to be rather large, say with many thousands of nodes. As an abstract illustration we will use the acyclic graph of Figure 1.1.

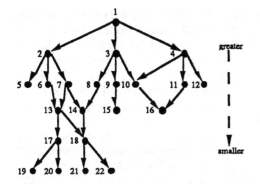

DAG	SOURCE	SINK
	1	2
	1	3
	1	4
	2	5
	2	6
	2	7
	⋮	⋮
	18	21
	18	22

Figure 1.1.   Figure 1.2.

Using the relational model of data directed graphs can conveniently be stored as binary database relations where an edge with source node i and sink node j corresponds to a tupel (i,j). For our abstract example we get the relation of Figure 1.2. Storing graphs as database relations we can take advantage of all facilities of relational database management systems, in particular management of secondary storage, persistency, transactions, integrity monitoring and high-level querying.

Whereas the three first mentioned facilities are sufficient for our purpose we would like that the integrity monitor supports various kinds of acyclicity as integrity constraints (which is beyond the scope of this paper) and that the query language allows specific types of recursive queries. For in the relational representation tuples (in the graphical form: edges) stand only for direct connections between entities whereas we need matching tuple sequences (in the graphical form: paths) to express indirect connections which are equally important for many applications. While sets of tuples, i.e. relations are a fundamental notion of relational databases, sets of matching tuple sequences have to be added by introducing the operation of transitive closure. This operation, however, requires recursion and is not expressible in the relational algebra.

Moreover, many applications do not simply consider paths (i.e. do not simply compute the transitive closure) but need to deal with two derived notions: upper, respectively lower bounds to a set of nodes and least, respectively greatest nodes with respect to the ordering defined by the set of paths. In our example applications bounds may have the following interpretations: for a genealogy a bound represents a common ancestor; for a company structure a bound may stand for a common owner or a common instance to whom reports must be delivered; for a network a bound stands for a commonly reachable place; for a concept hierarchy a bound expresses a common superconcept. Correspondingly least nodes can be interpreted as follows: for a genealogy a least node denotes a youngest person (among a given set of persons); for a company structure a least node may stand for a smallest subunit or an original source of reports; for a network a least node models a starting place; for a concept hierarchy a least node represents a most specific subconcept. Of course, both operations will often occur in combined form as least upper bound and greatest lower bound, respectively.

In our abstract example the nodes 13, 6, 7, 2, and 1 are upper bounds to the set of nodes {19, 20, 21, 22} where node 13 is a least upper bound. Sometimes we are only interested in bounds which are elements of some (previously determined) set of nodes.

For instance we can ask for all upper bounds to {19, 20, 21, 22} from which node 14 is reachable. As an answer we would now get the nodes 7, 2, and 1 (but not 13 and 6).

In [BRS90], the interested reader can find a more extended discussion on how to supply database support for the above mentioned applications and a proposal on how to extend SQL for a class of queries including upper bounds and least nodes. The present paper is concerned with evaluation strategies for these two fundamental queries which, as we argue, should be considered as basic database operations (besides the operations of the relational algebra and the transitive closure).

More precisely, as already indicated above, each binary (database) relation, say BinRel(Father,Son) on attributes Father and Son uniquely determines a directed graph $G=(V,E)$ with $V = \pi_{Father}(BinRel) \cup \pi_{Son}(BinRel)$ and $E = BinRel$, and vice versa. A node x is considered less than y, $y \neq x$, iff there exists a path from y to x. The first query type requires the specification of a graph BinRel (by a binary relation) and two node sets OfRel and ToRel (by unary relations) and then computes the upper bounds to ToRel in OfRel with respect to BinRel. The second query type requires the specification of a graph BinRel (by a binary relation) and a node set OfRel (by a unary relation) and then computes the least nodes in OfRel with respect to BinRel.

2 Definitions and basic approaches

For a *(finite directed) graph* $G = (V,E)$, where V is a finite set of nodes, and $E \subset V \times V$ is a set of edges, define

$succ[v] := \{w \mid (v,w) \in E\}$, the *direct successor set* of v, and
$pred[v] := \{w \mid (w,v) \in E\}$, the *direct predecessor set* of v.

The *transitive closure* of G is $G^+ = (V,E^+)$, where $E^+ = \{(v,w) \mid \exists$ path from v to w$\}$.

$succ^+[v] := \{w \mid (v,w) \in E^+\}$ denotes the *successor set* of v, and
$pred^+[v] := \{w \mid (w,v) \in E^+\}$ denotes the *predecessor set* of v.

(Direct) successor and (direct) predecessor sets are also called *adjacency sets*. When we want to leave open whether some adjacency set is a successor or predecessor set, we use ´adj´ as a fill-in for ´succ´ and ´pred.´ In virtue of the correspondence between binary relations and graphs all graph definitions carry over to binary relations.

Definition 2.1: Let BinRel be a binary relation with scheme BinRel(Father,Son), let OfRel and ToRel be unary relations with OfRel, ToRel $\subset$ V. We speak of a node x being *greater than* a node y, and y being *less than* x, iff there exists a path from x to y and $x \neq y$.

a) $Trcl(BinRel) := \{(x,y) \mid \exists$ path from x to y in BinRel$\}$.
b) $SelLeast(BinRel,OfRel) := \{x \in OfRel \mid \neg \exists y \in OfRel: x \neq y \land (x,y) \in Trcl(BinRel)\}$.
c) $SelUpperBounds(BinRel,OfRel,ToRel) := \{x \in OfRel \mid \forall y \in ToRel: (x,y) \in Trcl(BinRel)\}$.

There are two basic approaches to evaluate SelLeast(BinRel,OfRel) which are substantially refined lateron. The first approach is based on **forward searching**. For each starting node $SN \in$ OfRel we start a forward traversal of $succ^+[SN]$. If a node $w \neq$ SN in OfRel is encountered, then the traversal is stopped (because we have discovered that w is smaller than SN and thus SN is not a least node). If no such node is encountered, then SN is finally inserted into the result relation (because SN has been proven to be a least node). In our second query example the traversals for nodes 1, 2, 6, and 7 are stopped because another node of OfRel is encountered, namely 2, 6 or 7, 13, and 13, respectively. For node 13 the traversal is completed without encountering another node of OfRel and thus 13 is inserted into the result relation.

The second approach is based on **backward searching**. Now we initialize the result relation with OfRel and for each node $SN \in$ OfRel we start a backward traversal of $pred^+[SN]$. During the traversal any encountered node $w \in$ OfRel is deleted from the result (because we have discovered that it is greater than SN and thus not a least node). In our example, taking node 13 as first starting node we encounter nodes 6, 7, 2, and 1 as predecessors of 13 and thus delete them from the result relation. Then only node 13 remains in the result relation.

There are also two basic approaches to evaluate SelUpperBounds(BinRel,OfRel,ToRel) which are again substantially refined later on. The first approach is based on **forward searching**. For each node $SN \in$ OfRel we determine $succ^+[SN]$ by a forward traversal and finally check the condition ToRel $\subset succ^+[SN]$. If it holds, then SN is an upper bound to ToRel, otherwise it is not. In our third query example, considering for instance 7 as starting node we determine that $succ^+[7]=\{13,14,17,18,19,20,21,22\}$ and verify that this set covers $\{19,20,21,22\}$, and thus 7 is an upper bound. Considering, however, 8 as starting node we determine that $succ^+[8]=\{14,18,21,22\}$ and see that this set does not cover $\{19,20,21,22\}$, and thus 8 is not an upper bound.

The second approach is based on **backward searching**. Now we initialize the result relation Result with OfRel and successively delete elements for which we have discovered that they are not upper bounds to ToRel. More precisely, for each starting node $SN \in$ ToRel we determine $pred^+[SN]$ by a backward traversal and finally delete those elements of Result that have not been encountered, i.e. we compute Result $\cap pred^+[SN]$. Obviously the method can halt once Result has become empty. In our example, considering for instance 19 as starting node we determine that $pred^+[19]=\{17,13,6,7,2,1\}$ and thus nodes 3, 8, and 14 must be deleted from the result relation.

Given these straightforward basic approaches we have to investigate and finally to decide a number of questions, in particular:

1. Which kind of data structures should we use for storing adjacency sets and other program variables?
2. Which technique for the traversal of a graph is appropriate?
3. Which search direction is preferable?
4. Which options allow to cleverly avoid repeated traversal of parts of the graph?
5. How can we take advantage of integrity constraints like functional dependencies or acyclicity constraints?

Of course, these questions are potentially mutually dependent and thus hardly exhaustively answerable. Our results, however, will provide some concrete recommendations on how to solve them.

3 Graph interpretations

The main task of each evaluation method is the traversal of a graph, and the main part of operations on a graph consists of random accesses to adjacency sets by their key values, in general followed by a scan of the set or a merging operation. Thus, the data structure for the graph information shall provide a fast random access to adjacency sets and a fast sequential scan for the elements of an adjacency set.

This section specifies *graph interpretations* (*GIs* for short) as an appropriate class of data structures. They consist of two components, the access component and the graph component. The latter contains the adjacency sets of the graph $G = (V, E)$ as follows. Consider a node $x \in V$ which has the adjacency set $\{y_1,...,y_m\}$. This information, possibly augmented by a fixed number of *(node) tags* $t_1,...,t_s$ which store additional runtime information of evaluation procedures, is represented as an *(s-tagged) node element* which is a list $(x; m; t_1,...,t_s; y_{i1},...,y_{im})$ where $y_{i1},...,y_{im}$ is some ordering of the adjacency list. Then we call x a *key (node)* and $(y_{i1},...,y_{im})$ an *adjacency list.* We distinguish two types of adjacency lists. A list is called *sorted* iff $(y_{ij} < y_{ik} \Leftrightarrow j < k)$. If this condition is not preserved under updates, it is called *(potentially) unsorted*. For adjacency lists we use the same notation as for adjacency sets (succ[x], succ$^+$[x], pred[x], and pred$^+$[x]). In general, the type of the access component is not fixed in detail. However, for this paper we assume the access component to be implemented as a B$^+$-tree.

The graph component consists of leaf pages and optional overflow pages which contain the node elements. The leaves are arranged as a doubly chained list. There exists an overflow page for a leaf if and only if the leaf contains a single key and its node element does not fit into a single page. The overflow pages belonging to the same leaf are arranged as a chained list. There exists one node element for each key having a non-empty adjacency set, and they are located in a way that a forward-sequential scan of the leaves delivers the keys in ascending order.

A GI is called *degenerated (DGI for short)* if it contains only a single node element. We can consider any set of nodes as an adjacency list for some virtual, not really existing key node. Then, we can implement the set as a DGI. Furthermore, we employ conventional sequential and indexed files for unary relations. In some cases, they are required to be (canonically) sorted. Examining evaluation algorithms for the queries of Definition 2.1, b) and c) we assume OfRel and ToRel to be given as sequential or indexed files and BinRel as a GI, which we call 'Graph' in the sequel.

4 Graph traversal

For the traversal of a graph, we have two well-known techniques at our hands, the *breadth first search (bfs) method* and the *depth first search (dfs) method.* We mainly employ the bfs method. The basic breadth first search procedure operating on a globally given Graph can be sketched as follows:

```
     PROCEDURE  bfs (StartNode : node);
        VAR   S, S'  : set_of_nodes;
              v       : node;
     BEGIN
1)      S:= adj[StartNode]; S':= adj[StartNode];
2)      FOR  all v ∈ S' DO
3)           S':=S' - {v};
4)           S':=S' ∪ (adj[v] - S);
5)           S:=S ∪ adj[v];
6)      END;
     END bfs.
```

Just before the end of an execution of **bfs** the variable S contains the set adj^+[StartNode]. Of course in order to make this result accessible from outside of the procedure the variable S should actually not be local but suitably declared outside and maybe persistently stored. Using the data structures discussed in Section 3 we represent the sets S and S´ by sorted and unsorted DGIs respectively. Accordingly, line 1 describes the copying of the original direct adjacency list for StartNode into two copies of DGIs, lines 2 and 3 describe a scan of the unsorted list S´, and lines 4 and 5 the merging of S with adj[v] and the parallel appending of all new nodes to S´. In this implementation, S´ behaves like a queue. If its behaviour is changed to that of a stack, the traversal performs a dfs. We decided not to employ this iterative dfs method because, with respect to our applications, it has no beneficial features in comparison to the bfs method. A dfs traversal can also be programmed recursively. In this case, redundant traversals of subgraphs are avoided by tagging visited nodes. The procedure can do without any container for the transitive successors of the starting node. For, the information which guides the traversal is hidden in the recursive calling sequence. However, the procedure performs $|\{(y,z) \in E \mid y, z \in succ^+[\text{StartNode}]\}|$ accesses to node elements via the access component and just as many directly to node elements. In comparison, the bfs method performs only $|succ^+[\text{StartNode}]|$ accesses via the access component altogether (and so does the iterative dfs method). Obviously: $|succ^+[\text{StartNode}]| \leq |\{(y,z) \in E \mid y, z \in \{\text{StartNode}\} \cup succ^+[\text{StartNode}]\}|$. Nevertheless, the recursive dfs traversal is attractive because it has nice features which the bfs traversal has not. Its benefits are already pinpointed in [Ta72]. Due to the recursive calling sequence, information on the transitive successors can easily be made available for some node at the time when its visit is completed. Then, this information can be stored at the node and used furtheron during the traversal (for the same starting node or a subsequent starting node). Such a piece of information is for example the elementship of some transitive successor node in a given set. In conclusion, we employ the recursive dfs method (dfs-rec) only when we can make use of the features described above. The basic recursive dfs procedure operating on a globally given Graph can be sketched as follows:

```
         PROCEDURE dfs-rec (StartNode : node):
            VAR   S  :  set_of_nodes;
1)          PROCEDURE Visit (v : node);
                VAR   v  :  node;
            BEGIN
2)             S:=S ∪ {v};
3)             FOR all w ∈ adj[v] DO
4)                IF  w ∉ S THEN
5)                   Visit(w);
6)                END:
7)             END;
8)          END Visit;
         BEGIN
9)          S := ∅;
10)         Visit(StartNode);
         END dfs-rec.
```

Again, just before the end of an execution of **dfs-rec** the variable S contains the set adj^+[StartNode] and thus S should actually be suitably declared outside and maybe persistently stored. Using the data structures discussed in Section 3 we take Graph as 1-

tagged GI and employ the tags to represent S: for a node x the value 0 means "not_visited" and thus "not_member" of S, and value 1 means "visited" and thus "member" of S. Accordingly, line 9 describes the initialization of all tags with the value 0, line 2 describes the assignment of ´member´ to the tag of v, line 3 a scan of the direct adjacency list for v (in Graph), and line 4 a check whether the tag of w equals ´not_member.´

5 Evaluation algorithms

The above two procedures, bfs for breadth first traversal and dfs-rec for recursive depth first traversal, are the main tools for refining the basic approaches outlined in Section 2, forward searching and backward searching. Even using abstractions, full programs for a database environment (taking care of opening and closing scans, searching in access structures, and the page structure of storage) tend to be rather lengthy. Thus instead of presenting the full programs for all evaluation algorithms that have been studied by us we first classify our algorithms according to the two options given above, and then we specify some further essential subjects.

The algorithms LFL (SelLeastForwardLocal), LFSA (SelLeastForwardSophisticated-Acyclic), LBS (SelLeastBackwardSophisticated), and LBSPA (SelLeastBackwardSingle-PassAcyclic) compute SelLeast(BinRel,OfRel); the algorithms UBF (SelUpperBounds-Forward), UBB (SelUpperBoundsBackward), and UBBA (SelUpperBoundsBackward-Acyclic) compute SelUpperBounds(BinRel,OfRel,ToRel):

	bfs	dfs-rec
forward	LFL	LFSA
backward	LBS LBSPA	

	bfs	dfs-rec
forward	UBF	
backward	UBB UBBA	

As explained in Section 4, the recursive depth first search method has only a limited scope of applicability. Correspondingly we found it attractive only for the forward searching approach to evaluating SelLeast. But then, as for the other algorithms with suffix 'Acyclic', we assume the argument relation BinRel to be acyclic.

LFL is a straightforward implementation of the forward searching approach using breadth first traversals.

LFSA differs from LFL in three ways. First it employs depth first traversals. Second it stops a traversal or skips a subgraph when penetrating the search space of an already processed starting node. For this purpose we use a second (besides the first node tag required by the procedure dfs-rec) node tag with the following meaning:
$TAG2[v] = 0$ iff $succ^+[v] \cap OfRel = \emptyset$; $TAG2[v] = 1$ iff $succ^+[v] \cap OfRel \neq \emptyset$. $TAG2[v]$ is set when the call of Visit(v) has been completed, i.e. between lines 7 and 8 in the procedure dfs-rec. If lateron a traversal for some starting node reaches node v again, then that traversal can be totally stopped if $TAG2[v] = 1$, and it can skip the (repeated) call of Visit(v) otherwise. Third we cluster the checks for the general halting condition, $w \in OfRel$, for all elements w of a whole direct adjacency list succ[v].

Assuming acyclicity of the argument relation BinRel **LBSPA** implements the backward searching approach using a single full breadth first traversal. It is performed for a virtual starting node v2 the direct predecessor list of which is defined by merging the direct predecessor lists for all nodes in OfRel:

$$\text{pred}[v2] := \bigcup_{x \in \text{OfRel}} \text{pred}[x].$$

After completion of this full traversal the set of visited nodes $S = \text{pred}^+[v2]$ is subtracted from OfRel, i.e. we finally compute the result relation Result as Result := OfRel \ S. Thus all deletions of encountered nodes w, w ∈ OfRel, are clustered into the computation of this set difference.

LBS implements the backward searching approach without assuming acyclicity. It starts a breadth first traversal for each starting node SN in the result relation Result which initially contains OfRel. Since deletions from Result occur dynamically, the actual set of starting nodes is

$$\text{OfRelS} := \{ x \in \text{OfRel} \mid \neg \exists y \in \text{OfRel} : y < x \wedge x \in \text{pred}^+[y] \}.$$

The algorithm skips subgraphs when penetrating the search space of an already processed starting node. For this purpose we use a node tag with the following meaning:

$TAG[v] = 0$ iff   node v has not yet been visited;
$TAG[v] = 1$ iff   node v has already been visited.

$TAG[v]$ is set when leaving node v, i.e. between lines 1 and 2 of the procedure bfs for a starting node and between lines 3 and 4 otherwise. If lateron a traversal for some starting node reaches node v again, lines 4 and 5 of the procedure bfs are skipped. After each traversal, all encountered nodes except the starting node SN are deleted from the result relation. If there exists a cycle from SN to SN, an additional traversal is started to determine whether SN is a least node. If it is not, it is deleted as well. This is necessary because otherwise it may for several reasons be the case that SN is not deleted at all despite of not being a least node. The additional traversal is performed for a virtual node w(SN) the direct predecessor list of which is defined by pred[w(SN)] := Result \ {SN}. If SN is encountered, the traversal is stopped, and SN is deleted from the result relation. Otherwise, SN remains therein.

UBF is a rather straightforward implementation of the forward searching approach using breadth first traversals. It starts a forward traversal for each node SN in OfRel and counts the nodes in ToRel which are encountered. When the counter reaches |ToRel|, the traversal is stopped. SN is inserted into the result relation iff the counter reaches |ToRel|.

UBB is the straightforward implementation of the backward searching approach using breadth first traversals.

UBBA differs from UBB in the way that it stops a traversal and omits the corresponding deletions when a node in ToRel is encountered.

The interested reader should be able to state full programs for the evaluation algorithms using the informal descriptions given above (or should consult [St 91]). As a prerequisite it might be helpful to note that each algorithm is determined by the pertinent options for the essential topics listed below:

1) *Traversal method.*
2) *Search direction.*
3) *Data structures for the unary relations OfRel and ToRel.*
4) *Set of starting nodes.*
5) *Initialization of the result relation 'Result.'*
6) *Action at the end of each traversal.*

7) *Stopped traversals.* Some strategies stop individual traversals when some halting condition becomes TRUE. They perform checks for each newly encountered node, and upon success, perform a follow-up action.

a) *Kind of check:* In the case of bfs, the check is performed for each node w which is newly inserted into S. In the case of dfs-rec, it is performed for each node w in line 5 before Visit(w) is called. In each case, the membership of w in OfRel, OfRel - {StartNode}, ToRel, or {StartNode} is checked.

b) *Follow-up action:* The follow-up action can be the stop of the traversal or an incrementation of a counter and a subsequent stop if the counter reaches some limit. In the case of dfs-rec, we assume that a stop entails a deliberate retreat, i.e. tag values are still propagated.

c) *Check-mode:* Deviating from the checkpoints specified in a), checks can sometimes be performed clustered for a whole direct adjacency list. Then, the checkpoints change as follows. In dfs-rec, the direct adjacency list of v is checked between lines 2 and 3, and in bfs, it is checked during the merging in line 5. Accordingly, the check-mode can be either nodewise or listwise.

8) *Tags.*

Some further remarks to the data structures are necessary. Frequently, the following task has to be performed: For each node y contained in some adjacency list or in the difference of two adjacency lists, check whether y is contained in some unary relation Rel. In each case, the nodes are delivered by a scan of a sorted adjacency list. Now, if the number of nodes is large for a single scan, it is preferable to have Rel sorted and to perform the checks by a parallel scan on Rel. However, if it is small, it is preferable to have an index for Rel and to perform the checks via the access component. Therefore, whenever the above task is due, **we assume Rel to be both sorted and indexed** so that both procedures are applicable and the algorithms can decide how to proceed in dependence on the length of the adjacency list and the size of Rel.

6 Analysis

Basically the costs of the evaluation algorithms are determined by how often the most essential operations are performed by each algorithm:

a_1 denotes the number of **accesses to a GI (Graph) via the access component.** In bfs, they occur once for the starting node (line 1) and once for each $v \in S'$ (lines 4 and 5). In dfs-rec, they occur when for a fixed node v line 3 is executed the first time.

a_2 denotes the number of **accesses to an indexed file (OfRel or ToRel) via the access component.** They occur for each membership check (except those of the additional traversal in case of a cycle from SN to SN in LBS), and in the case of LBSPA and LBS, for each node in S when it is tried to be deleted from Result.

m denotes the number of **merging operations.** The operation occurs when lines 4 and 5 of bfs are executed with adj[v] ≠ ∅. This is once the case for each $v \in S'$ with nonempty adjacency list.

i denotes the number of **insertion calls** (including redundant attempts). A call occurs when a node is tried to be inserted into S in line 5 of bfs. This is the case for each node in adj[v].

r   denotes the number of **direct accesses to leaves or overflow pages of a GI** without requiring an access to the access component. They occur when line 3 of dfs-rec is executed for any but the first direct successor w of v.

In order to abreviate some formulas we will use the following notation. For a given GI containing the lists adj[x], $x \in S$ for some unary relation or adjacency list S, let $S^{>0} := \{ x \in S \mid \mid adj[x] \mid > 0 \}$.

6.1   SelLeast-algorithms

For **LFL** each bfs traversal is stopped if the halting condition (a node $w \neq SN$ in OfRel encountered) is fullfilled. Accordingly we define the reduced search space as follows:

$adjR1^{+}[x] :=$ the initial part of $adj^{+}[x]$ which is accessed by the scan in lines 2 and 3 (until the halting condition becomes true),

$adjR2^{+}[x] :=$ the contents of the adjacency list for x when the traversal for x stops.

Then we have:

$$a_1 = \mid OfRel \mid + \sum_{x \in OfRel} \mid succR1^{+}[x] \mid \qquad a_2 = \sum_{x \in OfRel} \mid succR2^{+}[x] \mid$$

$$m = \sum_{x \in OfRel} \mid succR1^{+}[x]^{>0} \mid \qquad i = \sum_{x \in OfRel} \sum_{y \in succR1^{+}[x]} \mid succ[y] \mid$$

For **LFSA** we consider the set of starting nodes OfRel as an adjacency list for some virtual node v1, ie. $succ[v1] := OfRel$, and according to the halting conditions for the dfs-rec traversals we define

$succI1[x] :=$ initial part of $succ[x]$ up to the first node (inclusively) in OfRel,

$$succI2[x] := \begin{cases} \varnothing & \text{if } succ[x] \cap OfRel \neq \varnothing \\ \text{initial part of } succ[x] \text{ up to the first node (inclusively)} \\ \text{which has a transitive successor in OfRel,} & \text{else} \end{cases}$$

$succS1^{+}[x] :=$ all nodes in dfs order for x up to the first node (inclusively) which has a direct successor node in OfRel, where the dfs order for starting node x denotes the order which is induced by the sequence in which the procedure Visit is called,

$$succS1^{+}[v1] := \bigcup_{x \in OfRel} succS1^{+}[x].$$

Then we have:

$$a_1 = \mid OfRel \mid + \sum_{x \in succS1^{+}[v1]} \mid succI2[x] \mid \qquad a_2 = \sum_{x \in succS1^{+}[v1]} \mid succI1[x] \mid$$

$$r = \sum_{x \in succS1^{+}[v1]} \mid succI2[x] \mid$$

For **LBSPA** recall that we employ a virtual starting node v2. Then we have:

$$a_1 = |\,OfRel\,| + |\,pred^+[v2]\,|$$

$$a_2 = |\,pred^+[v2]\,|$$

$$m = |\,OfRel^{>0}\,| + |\,pred^+[v2]^{>0}\,|$$

$$i = \sum_{y\,\in\,OfRel} |\,pred[y]\,| + \sum_{y\,\in\,OfRel} |\,pred[y]\,|$$

For **LBS** the starting nodes are taken from the result relation Result which is initialized by OfRel and considered as an adjacency list for some virtual node v3, i.e. pred[v3] := OfRel. Recall, however, that the actual set of starting nodes is

$$OfRelS := \{\, x \in OfRel \mid \neg\, \exists\, y \in OfRel : y < x \wedge x \in pred^+[y] \,\},$$

and according to the halting conditions for the bfs traversal we define

$$m(x) := \text{first element in } (succ^+[x] \cup \{x\}) \cap OfRel,$$

$$predS2^+[x] := \{ y \in pred^+[v3] \mid m(y) = x \},$$

$$predS3^+[x] := \bigcup_{y\,\in\,predS2^+[x]} pred[y],$$

$$OfRelC := \{ x \in OfRelS \mid x \in pred^+[x] \}.$$

Ignoring some negligible costs we have:

$$a_1 = |\,OfRelS\,| + \sum_{x\,\in\,OfRelS} |\,predS3^+[x]\,|$$

$$a_2 = \sum_{x\,\in\,OfRelS} |\,predS3^+[x]\,|$$

$$m = |\,pred^+[v3]^{>0}\,| - OfRelS\,|$$

$$i = \sum_{y\,\in\,pred^+[v3]\,-\,OfRelS} |\,pred[y]\,|$$

In the following our assessment mainly focusses on the value of a_1. For the cost terms a_2, m, and i are essentially determined by a_1 and often, the optimality of a_1 implies that of a_2, m, and i as well. Furthermore in the case that the main memory buffer runs short, a_1 and a_2 count the most expensive operation, and m and i incur no I/O costs at all, which then are considered decisive.

However, for SelLeastForwardSophAcyclic the values of a_1, a_2, m, and i are obviously not so closely related and in any case m(LFSA) = i(LFSA) = 0. Thus, when assessing the algorithms by their a_1 values, a **reduction factor** ρ has to be applied for SelLeastForwardSophAcyclic.

We make some observations which are not visible from the value of a_1.

a) If tags are employed by an algorithm, the required additional space slightly increases the size of the affected GI, and the page fault function stretches accordingly. We denote the arising additional costs as the **"tag overhead."**

b) For depth first graph traversals, special costs occur when scanning the direct successor list of node v in Visit (line 3). For, each access to an edge (v,w) may invoke a page fault. This is due to the fact that between two such operations a subgraph of arbitrary size may be traversed. The CPU time requirements (for the scan) are obviously not higher than those for a breadth first traversal. We call each access to an edge (v,w) in line 3 a "node return" and denote the additional I/O costs as the **"dfs overhead."** The dfs overhead depends on the size of the main memory buffer.

c) When the decision of the search direction is due (forward or backward), the main criterion would be the location (in the graph) of the nodes contained in OfRel. If $\sum_{x\,\in\,OfRel} |succ^+[x]| \ll \sum_{x\,\in\,OfRel} |pred^+[x]|$, the forward traversal methods are with high probability superior to backward traversal methods.

If $\sum_{x \in \text{OfRel}} |\text{succ}^+[x]| \gg \sum_{x \in \text{OfRel}} |\text{pred}^+[x]|$, the situation is vice versa. For acyclic graphs, it seems attractive to maintain some kind of **topological information** so that the values of

$$\sum_{x \in \text{OfRel}} |\text{succ}^+[x]| \quad \text{and} \quad \sum_{x \in \text{OfRel}} |\text{pred}^+[x]|$$

can be estimated. Data structures serving this purpose can be found in [LaDe89].

d) The value of a_1 is determined by two measures. The first one, called "**search domain**," describes a set of nodes which contains all nodes that might be accessed by an algorithm:

$$SD_{\text{OfRel}}^{\rightarrow} := \text{OfRel} \cup \bigcup_{x \in \text{OfRel}} \text{succ}^+[x] = \text{succ}^+[v1] \qquad \text{for forward traversal,}$$

$$SD_{\text{OfRel}}^{\leftarrow} := \text{OfRel} \cup \bigcup_{x \in \text{OfRel}} \text{pred}^+[x] = \text{pred}^+[v3] \qquad \text{for backward traversal.}$$

The second measure, called **redundancy measure**, is how often a node x of the search domain is accessed for some algorithm. We neglect accesses which occur during the traversals for the virtual nodes w(z). For some algorithm M, the measure is denoted by $rm_M(x)$.

Definition 6.1.: A path $p_1 = v_1, ..., v_m$ is *lexicographically less* than $p_2 = w_1,...,w_n :\Leftrightarrow \exists\ 1 \le i \le \min\{m+1,n\}: (\forall\ 1 \le j < i: v_j = w_j) \land (v_i < w_i \lor i = m+1)$. A path p from y to x is an *ll-path* $:\Leftrightarrow \forall$ paths $p' \ne p$ from y to x: p is lexicographically less than p'. Let $v_1, w_1 \in \text{OfRel}$. Then, two simple paths $p_1 = v_1,...,v_m$, x and $p_2 = w_1,...,w_n$, x, $p_1 \ne p_2$, are *terminal-disjunctive* : $\Leftrightarrow \exists\ 0 \le i \le \min\{m,n\}: (\forall\ 1 \le j \le i: v_j = w_j) \land ((\{v_{i+1},...,v_m\} \cap \{w_{i+1},...,w_n\} = \emptyset)$.

Theorem 6.1. [characterization of the **redundancy measures**]: Let $G = (V,E)$ be a(n acyclic) graph, and x be a node of the search domain.

i)
$$rm_{\text{LFL}}(x) = \begin{cases} 1 & \text{if } x \in \text{OfRel} \land x \notin \text{succR1}^+[x] \\ 2 & \text{if } x \in \text{OfRel} \land x \in \text{succR1}^+[x] \\ |\{y \in \text{OfRel} \mid x \in \text{succR1}^+[y]\}| & \text{if } x \notin \text{OfRel} \end{cases}$$

$$\le |\text{OfRel} \cap \text{pred}^+[x]| \qquad \text{if } x \notin \text{OfRel}$$

ii)
$$rm_{\text{LFSA}}(x) = \begin{cases} 1 & \text{if } x \in \text{OfRel} \\[1em] \begin{array}{l}\text{maximal count of ll-paths from some } y \in \text{OfRel to x so that they are} \\ \text{pairwise node-disjunctive excluding x and so that } x \in \text{succS1}^+[y], \\ \hfill \text{if } \text{succ}^+[x] \cap \text{OfRel} \ne \emptyset \land x \notin \text{OfRel}\end{array} \\[1.5em] \begin{array}{l}\text{maximal count of pairwise terminal-disjunctive paths from some } y \in \text{OfRel} \\ \text{to x so that for each edge (z,z') on any of these paths, } z' \in \text{succS1}^+[z], \\ \hfill \text{if } \text{succ}^+[x] \cap \text{OfRel} = \emptyset \land x \notin \text{OfRel}\end{array} \end{cases}$$

$$\le \begin{cases} \min\{|\text{pred}[x]|, |\text{OfRel} \cap \text{pred}^+[x]|\} & \text{if } \text{succ}^+[x] \cap \text{OfRel} \ne \emptyset \land x \notin \text{OfRel} \\ |\text{pred}[x]| & \text{if } \text{succ}^+[x] \cap \text{OfRel} = \emptyset \land x \notin \text{OfRel} \end{cases}$$

iii)
$$rm_{\text{LBSPA}}(x) = \begin{cases} 2 & \text{if } x \in \text{OfRel -ResultRel} \\ 1 & \text{else} \end{cases}$$

iv)
$$rm_{LBS}(x) = \begin{cases} |\{m(z)\,|\,z \in succ[x] \cap SD^{\leftarrow}\}| + 1 & \text{if } x \in OfRelS \\ |\{m(z)\,|\,z \in succ[x] \cap SD^{\leftarrow}\}| & \text{else} \end{cases}$$

$$\leq \begin{cases} \min\{|OfRelS \cap succ^{+}[x]|,\ |succ[x]|\} + 1 & \text{if } x \in OfRelS \\ \min\{|OfRelS \cap succ^{+}[x]|,\ |succ[x]|\} & \text{else.} \end{cases}$$

Proof: Part i) follows from the fact that for a fixed starting node y, y and the nodes of $succR1^{+}[x]$ are accessed.

The equation of part ii) for $succ^{+}[x] \cap OfRel \neq \emptyset \wedge x \notin OfRel$ follows from the fact that for a node x to be visited via a path p from a starting node y, the following conditions are necessary and sufficient: $x \in succS1^{+}[y]$, p is an ll-path, and there exists no ll-path to x which is not node-disjunctive and which has a lower starting node. The equation of part ii) for $succ^{+}[x] \cap OfRel = \emptyset \wedge x \notin OfRel$ follows from the fact that for a node x to be visited via a path p from a starting node y, the following conditions are necessary: $z' \in succS1^{+}[z]$ for each edge (z, z') on p, and there exists no lexicographically less path p' to x which is not terminal-disjunctive from p and which satisfies $z' \in succS1^{+}[z]$ for each edge (z, z') on p'. The inequalities of part ii) then follow from the definitions of node- and terminal-disjunctiveness.

Part iii) follows easily from the fact that accesses occur for each $x \in OfRel$ during the computation of pred[v2] and for each $x \in pred^{+}[v2]$ during the traversal.

Part iv) is proved by observing that for a fixed starting node y, y and the nodes of $succS3^{+}[y]$ are accessed, and by showing that there exists a one-to-one correspondence between $\{m(z)\,|\,z \in succ[x] \cap SD^{\leftarrow}\}$ and $\{y \in OfRelS\,|\,x \in predS3^{+}[y]\}$. ∎

It is interesting to observe that for the analysis of transitive closure algorithms the maximal count of node disjoint paths between two nodes, a concept closely related to our use of terminal-disjunctive paths, has proved to be an important complexity measure [Ja 92].

For some algorithm M we define the **search space** as:

$$SS_{M}^{\rightarrow} := \{x \in SD^{\rightarrow}\,|\,rm_{M}(x) \geq 1\}, \text{ and } SS_{M}^{\leftarrow} := \{x \in SD^{\leftarrow}\,|\,rm_{M}(x) \geq 1\}.$$

By Theorem 6.1, it holds: $SS_{LBSPA}^{\leftarrow} = SS_{LBS}^{\leftarrow} = SD^{\leftarrow}$. The backward traversal methods access each node of the search domain at least once, whereas the forward traversal methods often access only a proper subset. A node of the search domain is not accessed if it lies in the "search shelter" of another node. The search shelter depends on the traversal method (dfs or bfs). In the following Figure 6.1., node values are assumed to increase from the left to the right.

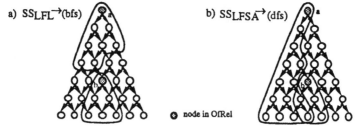

a) $SS_{LFL}^{\rightarrow}$(bfs)   b) $SS_{LFSA}^{\rightarrow}$(dfs)

⊗ node in OfRel

Figure 6.1.

We summarize the **advantages and disadvantages of the algorithms.** We take $SD^{\rightarrow}$ and $SD^{\leftarrow}$ respectively as a standard value for a_1 and list the sources for gains or losses against this standard.

We assume the following sources for losses to be of less significance:
- The repetitive accesses to "border" nodes when penetrating the search space of a different starting node (occurring for SelLeastForwardSophAcyclic and SelLeastBackwardSoph).
- The repetitive accesses to some distinguished starting nodes (occurring for SelLeastForwardLocal and SelLeastBackwardSinglePassAcyclic).
- The repetitive accesses to nodes during a traversal for the virtual starting node $w(x)$ (occurring for SelLeastBackwardSoph).

These assumptions are confirmed by experiments. We are left with the following phenomena:
- SelLeastForwardLocal and SelLeastForwardSophAcyclic gain from search shelters.

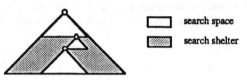

Figure 6.2.

- SelLeastForwardLocal suffers from overlappings of search areas, see Figure 6.3.
- SelLeastForwardSophAcyclic suffers from repetitive accesses to successor nodes for a fixed starting node, see Figure 6.4.

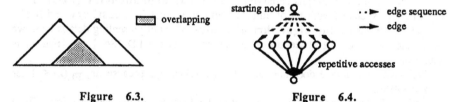

Figure 6.3.   **Figure 6.4.**

A first simple goal is to access **only nodes of the search domain.** A second goal is to perform **at most one access** to each node of the search domain. The former is easily achieved by each presented algorithm. The latter is achieved by none. SelLeastBackwardSinglePassAcyclic comes very near to it and accesses only nodes of OfRel - ResultRel twice. SelLeastBackwardSoph accesses "border" nodes of $\bigcup_{x \in OfRelS} predS3^{+}[x] - predS2^{+}[x]$, nodes of OfRelC, and successor nodes during the traversals for starting nodes $w(x)$ more than once. SelLeastForwardLocal contravenes the second goal because search areas for different starting nodes can overlap. SelLeastForwardSophAcyclic does as well because "border" nodes, which can be defined similar to those of SelLeastBackwardSoph, are accessed more than once, and repetitive accesses to successor nodes can even occur for a fixed starting node. However, the forward strategies achieve a third goal, that of not accessing nodes of the search shelters. Unfortunately, search shelters are defined relative to the traversal technique, which renders a comparison slightly more difficult. For the backward strategies, there does not exist any search shelters. From Theorem 6.1, ii), it follows that

- SelLeastForwardSophAcyclic suffers no losses from repetitive accesses to successor nodes in $SD^{\leftarrow} = pred^+[v3]$ for a fixed starting node because there exists at most one ll-path between two nodes.
- if $|E| / |V|$ is small, SelLeastForwardSophAcyclic suffers only minor losses from repetitive accesses to successor nodes for a fixed starting node because $rm_{LFSA}(x) \leq |pred[x]|$ for $x \in SD^{\rightarrow}$.

$E(|SD^{\leftarrow}|)$, the expected size of $SD^{\leftarrow}$, rapidly increases with the size of OfRel, in particular when $|E| / |V|$ is large (i.e. the graph has a high density). Thus, the second goal can only be contravened significantly if |OfRel| is small and $|E| / |V|$ is large.

Since **SelLeastForwardSophAcyclic** gains from search shelters, it is the **algorithm of choice for acyclic graphs** if not simultaneously |OfRel| and B are small and |E|/|V| is large. Inspired by realistic applications, we call $|E| / |V| \geq 3$ already "large."

If the graph is cyclic and |OfRel| is not too small, **SelLeastForwardLocal is the algorithm of choice** under those presented in Section 5, independently of the buffer size. This for us surprising result is based on the observation that for nearly all experiments $a_1(LFL) < a_1(LBS)$. We conjecture that for reasonable distributions the expected values, denoted by $E(.)$, actually satisfy $E(a_1(LFL)) \leq E(a_1(LBS))$. The reason for this result is that the gains from search shelters are in general higher than the losses from overlappings.

The remaining cases remained unclear. However, note that in these cases |OfRel| is always small and the amount of computation is not really large for either algorithm. Which values of |OfRel| can be considered "small" depends on the buffer size and the environment.

We also examined graphs satisfying **functional dependencies (FDs)**. They exhibited no special favouring of either algorithm, so that **SelLeastForwardSoph-Acyclic remained the algorithm of choice**. Without presenting details here, we only note the following observations for the case that the FD {Son} $\rightarrowtail$ {Father} is satisfied:

- SelLeastForwardLocal does not suffer from overlappings because $rm_{LFL}(x) \leq 1$ for $x \notin OfRel$.
- SelLeastForwardSophAcyclic does not suffer from repetitive accesses for a fixed starting node because $rm_{LFSA}(x) \leq 1$ for $x \in SD^{\rightarrow}$.
- For both algorithms, it is possible that there exist search shelters.

6.2 SelUpperBounds-algorithms

Recall the definitions of $adjR1^+[x]$ and $adjR2^+[x]$ for bfs traversals. Furthermore for the backward searching approach we define

$ToRelI \quad := \{x \in ToRel \mid \bigcap_{y \in ToRel, \ y <_s x} pred^+[y] \cap OfRel \neq \varnothing\},$
where $<_s$ refers to the scan sequence,

$ToRelS \quad := \{x \in ToRelI \mid (pred^+[x] \cap ToRel) - \{x\} = \varnothing\},$

$ResultRel := $ final state of Result.

Then the basic costs for our algorithms are summarized in the following table:

	UBF	UBB	UBBA
a_1	$\lvert OfRel \rvert +$ $\sum_{x \in OfRel} \lvert succR1^+[x] \rvert$	$\lvert ToRelI \rvert +$ $\sum_{x \in ToRelI} \lvert pred^+[x] \rvert$	$\lvert ToRelI \rvert +$ $\sum_{x \in ToRelI} \lvert predR1^+[x] \rvert$
a_2	$\sum_{x \in OfRel} \lvert succR2^+[x] \rvert$	——	$\sum_{x \in ToRelI} \lvert predR2^+[x] \rvert$
m	$\sum_{x \in OfRel} \lvert succR1^+[x] \rvert > q$	$\sum_{x \in ToRelI} \lvert pred^+[x] \rvert > 0$	$\sum_{x \in ToRelI} \lvert predR1^+[x] \rvert > 0$
i	$\sum_{x \in OfRel} \sum_{y \in succR1^+[x]} \lvert succ[y] \rvert$	$\sum_{x \in ToRelI} \sum_{y \in pred^+[x]} \lvert pred[y] \rvert$	$\sum_{x \in ToRelI} \sum_{y \in predR1^+[x]} \lvert pred[y] \rvert$

Table 6.2.

The intersection costs for SelUpperBoundsBackward and SelUpperBoundsBackward-Acyclic are in general insignificant because they only comprise $\lvert OfRel \rvert$ - $\lvert ResultRel \rvert$ deletions and $O(\sum_{x \in ToRelI} (\lvert OfRel \rvert + \lvert pred^+[x] \rvert))$ or $O(\sum_{x \in ToRelS} (\lvert OfRel \rvert + \lvert pred^+[x] \rvert))$ scan operations, respectively.

We first discuss **acyclic graphs**. For this class, SelUpperBoundsBackward can be discarded from the discussion because it is in general outperformed by SelUpperBounds-BackwardAcyclic. The cost formulas for the two remaining algorithms differ essentially only in two points.

- Where a term for SelUpperBoundsForward contains "OfRel," the corresponding one for SelUpperBoundsBackwardAcyclic contains "ToRelI."
- The halting conditions are different: Counter = $\lvert ToRelI \rvert$, in comparison to w $\in$ ToRel. With an increase in $\lvert ToRelI \rvert$, the likelihood of an early validation of the former condition decreases, whereas that of the latter increases. For, SelUpperBoundsForward must discover all nodes of ToRel, whereas SelUpperBoundsBackwardAcyclic must only discover a single node thereof.

For the frequent case $\lvert OfRel \rvert \geq \lvert ToRelI \rvert$ SelUpperBoundsBackwardAcyclic is clearly superior. It starts less traversals, one for each node in ToRelI $\subset$ ToRel, and its traversals are stopped earlier (on the average) than those of SelUpperBoundsForward since the corresponding halting condition is weaker.

For the general case we examine how the expected value of a_1 develops with an increase in $\lvert OfRel \rvert$ or $\lvert ToRelI \rvert$. To begin with, **assume ResultRel $\neq \varnothing$**. For SelUpperBoundsForward, $E(a_1)$ increases linearly with $\lvert OfRel \rvert$ and sublinearly with $\lvert ToRelI \rvert$, while for SelUpperBoundsBackwardAcyclic, it remains constant with an increase in $\lvert OfRel \rvert$ and increases sublinearly with $\lvert ToRelI \rvert$. To examine $\lvert OfRel \rvert \leq \lvert ToRelI \rvert$, we fix c ≤ 1 and consider $k = \lvert OfRel \rvert = c \cdot \lvert ToRelI \rvert$. Then, with an increase in k, $E(a_1(UBBA))$ starts from $\lvert E^+ \rvert / \lvert V \rvert$ for k / c = 1, increases sublinearly, and soon approaches $\lvert V \rvert$. We assume $E(a_1(UBBA))$ to be well-behaved in general. There is a strong evidence that always $E(a_1(UBBA)) \leq \lvert V \rvert$. For graphs which satisfy the FD {Father} $\rightarrow$ {Son}, this claim follows from Theorem 6.1. In contrast, $E(a_1(UBF))$ starts from slightly below $\lvert E^+ \rvert$ / $\lvert V \rvert$ for k = 1, increases sublinearly, and soon converges to the function $k \cdot \lvert E^+ \rvert / \lvert V \rvert$. Thus, for each c ≤ 1, there exists a **threshold k_c** so that **SelUpperBoundsForward is superior (on the average) for $k < k_c$** and SelUpperBoundsBackward-

Acyclic is superior (on the average) for $k > k_c$. For all graphs for which $E(a_1(UBBA))$ is non-decreasing with an increase in k, SelUpperBoundsForward is superior (on the average) at least for $|OfRel| = 1$. $a_1(UBF)$ can be estimated very well by the term $|OfRel| \cdot |E^+| / |V|$. If now, for a given graph, $E(a_1(UBBA))$ as a function of $|ToRel|$ can also be approximated well (either empirically or analytically), then the threshold can be estimated quite precisely. However, this judgement relies essentially on the assumption that ResultRel $\neq \emptyset$. In general, the decisive parameter is not $|ToRel|$ but $|ToRel|$. Unfortunately, $|ToRel|$ is not known when the decision of an algorithm is due, and its estimation is a difficult task since it is very sensitive to the graph structure and the node set OfRel. A removal of a single edge from the graph or a single node from OfRel can reduce $|ToRel|$ from a huge set to a singleton; even worse, the renaming of a single node can have the same result.

If it is not possible to approximate $E(a_1(UBBA))$ as a function of $|ToRel|$, we suggest to assume the costs to increase linearly with $|ToRel|$. Since $E(a_1(UBBA))$ is $|E^+| / |V|$ for $|ToRel| = 1$, and $|V|$ for $|ToRel| = |V|$, we get the cost function $c_{UBBA}(|OfRel|,|ToRel|) = |E^+| / |V| + (|ToRel|-1) (|V|^2- |E^+|) / (|V|\cdot(|V|-1))$. For SelUpperBoundsForward, we suggest to choose $c_{UBF}(|OfRel|,|ToRel|) = |OfRel| \cdot |E^+| / |V|$. Both choices slightly favour SelUpperBoundsBackward.

Finally, we consider **cyclic graphs**. Remind that we assume $E(a_1(UBBA)) \leq |V|$ for acyclic graphs, which often renders this algorithm by far superior to the remaining ones. Therefore we do not consider it worthwhile to compare SelUpperBoundsForward and SelUpperBoundsBackward. Instead, we prefer to discuss how **SelUpperBounds-BackwardAcyclic can be adapted to cyclic graphs**. There exist a whole variety of adaption techniques, e.g. the halting condition can be modified to $w \in$ ToRel $\wedge$ w < StartNode, which stops a traversal iff a transitive predecessor w < StartNode in ToRel is encountered. The problem is that it is not sufficient to intersect Result with the transitive predecessor sets for the greatest nodes of ToRel. However, it is sufficient to intersect it with the transitive predecessor sets for the greatest strongly connected components (sccs) which contain nodes of ToRel. Therefore, we recommend the following procedure. It combines two traversal techniques, the bfs traversal and the recursive dfs traversal. The latter is used to determine the greatest sccs which contain nodes of ToRel, and each time when such an scc is encountered, the former is used to compute its transitive predecessor set, which is then intersected with Result.

7 Experiments

We only outline the results of measurements from a large number of experiments performed for the SelLeast-algorithms. The experiments were conducted under UNIX on a SUN3/260 machine with 8MB main memory and 32MB swap space. The processes allocated a database buffer in the main memory and performed the paging from and to secondary storage themselves. The page and frame size was 1KB. It was also the unit of transfer between main memory and secondary storage. An LRU paging strategy was implemented which had the option to lock a small amount of pages in the buffer. Queries were evaluated by each algorithm on buffers of size B = 10KB and B = 5MB. The details of the experiments are documented in [St 91].

From the experiments we observed the following.

- Parameter a_1 is a decisive performance measure, and there is a close correlation between it and parameters a_2, m, and i.
- When applicable, **SelLeastForwardSophAcyclic is in general superior.**
- Excluding SelLeastForwardSophAcyclic, SelLeastForwardLocal is often superior.
- SelLeastForwardSophAcyclic and SelLeastBackwardSoph suffer from a small buffer more than the remaining algorithms. This is due to the tag overhead.
- SelLeastForwardSophAcyclic suffers from a small buffer even more than SelLeastBackwardSoph. This is due to the dfs overhead.
- There exist significant deviations from the average case.

8   Conclusions

We studied evaluation procedures for upper bounds and least nodes as database operations. We found that in the case of upper bounds, backward searching strategies perform in general better than forward searching ones, and that the situation is vice versa in the case of least nodes. For acyclic graphs, the algorithms SelLeastForwardSoph-Acyclic and SelUpperBoundsBackwardAcyclic proved superior over a wide range of applications, the former for SelLeast-queries and the latter for SelUpperBounds-queries.

9   References

[BRS 90] Biskup, J., Räsch, U., Stiefeling, H., An Extension of SQL for Querying Graph Relations, Computer Languages 15, 2, 1990, pp. 65-82.

[BiSt 88] Biskup, J., Stiefeling, H., Transitive Closure Algorithms for Very Large Databases, Proc. Int. Workshop on Graph-Theoretic Concepts in Computer Science, 1988, pp. 122-147.

[Ed 90] Eder, J., Extending SQL with General Transitive Closure and Extreme Value Selection, IEEE Trans. on Knowledge and Data Engineering 2, 4 (1990), pp. 381-390.

[Ja 92] Jakobsson, H., On Materializing Views and On-line Queries, Proc. 4th Int. Conf. on Database Theory, Berlin 1992, Lecture Notes in Computer Science 646, Springer, 1992, pp. 407-420.

[KIC 82] Kabler, R., Ioannidis, Y.E., Carey, M.J., Performance Evaluation of Algorithms for Transitive Closure, Information Systems 17,5, 1992, pp. 415-441.

[LaDe 89] Larson, P.A., Deshpande, V., A File Structure Supporting Traversal Recursion, Proc. ACM SIGMOD Int. Conf. on Management of Data, 1989, pp. 243-252.

[MS 90] Mannino, M.V., Shapiro, L.D., Extensions to Query Languages for Graph Traversal Problems, IEEE Transactions on Knowledge and Data Engineering 2,3 (1990), pp. 353-363.

[St 91] Stiefeling, H., Evaluation Strategies for a Subclass of Recursive Database Queries, Dissertation, Universität Hildesheim, 1991.

[Ta 72] Tarjan, R.E., Depth-First Search and Linear Graph Algorithms, SIAM J. Computing 1, 2, 1972, pp. 146-160.

[Ul 89] Ullman, J.D., Principles of Database and Knowledge-Base Systems, Vol. II, Computer Science Press, Rockville, MD, 1989.

A C++ Binding for Penguin: a System for Data Sharing among Heterogeneous Object Models*

Arthur M. Keller   Catherine Hamon

Stanford University, Computer Science Dept.
Stanford, CA 94305-2140

Abstract. The relational model supports the view concept, but relational views are limited in structure. OODBMSs do not support the view concept, so that all applications must share the same arrangement of object classes and inheritance. We describe the Penguin system and its support for the view concept. Each application can have its own arrangement of object classes and inheritance, and these are defined as views of an integrated, normalized conceptual data model, in our case the Structural Model. We define view-objects in a language-independent manner on top of the conceptual data model. These view-objects can be complex objects supporting a composite structure. We discuss the extension of Penguin to support PART-OF (reference) and IS-A graphs for composite view-objects. We also discuss the C++ binding to Penguin, where C++ code is generated for object classes corresponding to the view-objects along with basic operations on them (creation, query, navigate, browsing, and update).

1 Introduction

The relational model introduced by Codd [8] has found widespread acceptance. The model is successful because of its simple but powerful description and the ability to reorganize data upon retrieval according to the needs of the application program, rather than having to anticipate all application requirements in advance. Relational database design theory leads to the design of normalized data structures, which are mathematically elegant but can be inefficient for some applications. Object-oriented database management systems [2, 9, 19, 23] and extended relational database management systems [10, 18, 27] support a richer description of data in a manner more convenient for design and other applications. These systems either do not support the view concept, or their notion of views does not support object-orientation, such as inheritance.

One approach is to define a standard arrangement of object classes and inheritance for all applications in a given application area. For the reasons described in [33], we believe that this approach is bound to have limited success.

We believe that the "second application problem" will arise for object-oriented application development. Organizations that are convinced of the benefits of

---

* For information about the Penguin project, please write to Arthur M. Keller at the above address or ark@db.stanford.edu

object-orientation will develop a new application in a new object-oriented programming language using an object-oriented database management system as a persistent store. An arrangement of object classes and inheritance will be designed specifically for that application, and careful attention will be paid to encapsulation. This application will be successful, but it will not integrate with existing applications. A problem will arise when the organization attempts an encore, that is, when they attempt to develop a new application using the object paradigm that is to share data with the first application. The new development team will need to violate the encapsulation of the first applications arrangement of object classes in order to support the differing abstraction and navigation requirements of the new application. Thus, use of object-oriented databases will succeed the first time, but will succumb to the "second application problem" when attempting to integrate a second application.

Our approach is for the object classes, inheritance hierarchies, and encapsulation decisions to be application specific. We believe it is important to provide independence between the application view level and the conceptual level. We support data sharing among multiple applications using the object paradigm, by giving each application its own view, consisting of view-objects (object classes) and inheritance. The contribution of this paper is the extension of the object model proposed in [3] to support inheritance and reference.

The following is the structure of the remainder of this paper. We review the Structural Model we use for the integrated conceptual data model in section 2. In section 3, we present how an application view is defined, consisting of object classes with inheritance and references. In section 4, we discuss the generation of C++ code for an application view. In section 5, we describe the Penguin system and its architecture. Following this, we then describe our future plans and our conclusion.

2 Structural Model

The relational model provides a simpler model of data that facilitates database design and navigation. Database design theory (see [31], for example) shows how normalization is important for eliminating undesirable properties of a relational database design. However, the price paid for normalization is a scattering of data fragments in the entire database as the original structure is flattened. The Structural Model provides structural semantics missing from the relational model [32] and useful for the database design and view integration process. The structural model of a relational database is a formal semantic data model consisting of normalized relations and connections (representing relationships) among those relations. We use a directed-graph representation of a structural model of the database, where nodes correspond to relations and arcs to connections (see Figure 1).

Formally, a connection is specified by the connection type and a pair of source and destination relations. Three types of connections are used (see [3]); they

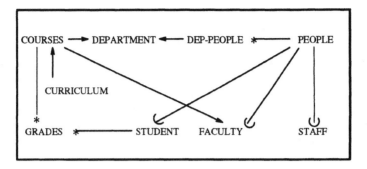

Fig. 1. Example of Structural Model.

correspond to precise integrity constraints, define the permissible cardinality of the relationships and encode the relationship semantics:

1. *Ownership connection* is a one-to-many relationship connecting a single parent tuple to zero or more child tuples dependent on the parent tuple. For example, the list of job skills for an employee is owned by the record for that employee. Two ownership connections may be used to represent an association between two entity sets, such as the grades relating students and the courses they take. We use —∗ to represent an ownership connection.

2. *Reference connection* is a many-to-one relationship from an entity set to an abstract entity set. For example, a course references the department offering that course. We use → to represent a reference connection. Note that both ownership and reference connections have the cardinality of many-to-one, but there is a semantic difference: The skill set for an employee is really a repeating group for that employee and was given a separate relation because of normalization, while courses represent their own abstract entity set.

3. *Subset connection* is a partial one-to-one relationship connecting a parent superset relation to a child subset relation. The IS-A relationship can be modeled by a subset connection from the child to the parent. We use the symbol —⊃ to represent a subset connection.

Note that many-to-many relationships are not modeled directly in the structural model but can be represented using combinations of the connections.

3 Defining Application Views

View-objects in Penguin define the windows that permit users to access and update tuples stored in different or overlapping subsets of normalized relations [5]. These windows organize the data into the objects useful to an application by reassembling the attributes scattered among different normalized relations into the attributes of an object class. The Penguin implementation of the view-object concept supports object-oriented access to shared information. Each view-object represents an object class for the programming language. They can refer to one or several existing view-objects to support a PART-OF hierarchy. They can also be organized into an inheritance graph that can support either single or multiple inheritance, as for an IS-A graph. In this section, we present the concept of view-object and describe how an application view can be built, consisting of object classes with inheritance and references.

3.1 View-Object Model

The view-object model proposed in [3] is based on the view-object concept introduced in [33] to support both abstract complex units of information and sharing of those units. In this model, a view-object is characterized by a name and a type. The name identifies the view-object, while the type specifies the hierarchical structure of view-object's instances. This structure is defined by a *template tree* whose nodes represent relations from the structural model, on which projections can be defined. The root of this tree represents a base relation called the *pivot relation* that will constitute the core component of the view-object. The remaining nodes represent the secondary relations that can be reached through different paths from the pivot relation in the graph defined by the structural model. Finally, an arc of the tree represents a path in the structural model between the relations located at the origin and the end of this arc. The semantics captured in the structural model through connections are thus kept at the view-object level.

The view-object model is based on a value-oriented approach since it uses the notions of hierarchical structures, and of set and records constructors. This model is similar to models based on the Nested Relational data model [1, 24, 25, 26] that permit the user to map complex objects to one nested relation. In the view-object model, relations are nested according to the hierarchical structure defined by the template tree. The major differences with the nested relational approach lay on the use of the Structural Model that enables us to build complex objects convenient for a specific application on top of the conceptual data model in a language-independent manner. Furthermore, a view-object model can exploit the three structural model concepts of aggregation, categorization and abstraction; integrity rules can thereby be more refined for view-objects than for nested relations [5].

We have extended the view-object model to support inheritance and reference among view-objects. The referential structure of a view-object defines the other view-objects that are reachable. Inheritance allows the user to reuse instance variables (i.e., attributes) and references from existing view-objects to design a new view-object. The result of the view-object definition contains the specification for the view-object but no actual data. The instantiation of a view-object is a separate process that fetches tuples from the underlying relational database and builds a hierarchical structure consisting of nested set of (sub)-tuples bound to the view-object. In this sense, a view-object is similar to an object class. Instantiation of a view-object will occur by a query or by navigation through object reference (e.g., PART-OF). In the remaining part of this subsection, we present the major concepts that support the different stages of the view-object definition.

Choosing the Pivot Relation. The notion of pivot relation is central to the view-object formalism. The tuples of the pivot relation have a one-to-one correspondence with the object instances in the view-object. Hence, the primary key of the pivot relation is the semantic key of the view-object. This requires all the key attributes to be included in the projection defined on the pivot relation. The semantic key of the object permits any given instance of the view-object to be uniquely identified. An instance of a view-object is generated from the outer join of the tuples of the corresponding relations. The hierarchical structure of each instance is in accordance with the view-object template tree.

Candidate Set. When a user selects a pivot relation, an important issue is to specify the "sphere of influence" for this pivot relation, that is, to specify which relations are near enough to the view-object's pivot relation that they should be presented to the user for inclusion in the view-object being defined. In Penguin, this is done by using an information-metric function that takes into account the type of each connection traversed and their combinations in a depth-first traversal of the tree (while avoiding cycles), and limiting the path length so that it does not exceed the threshold when measured using the information-metric function. For this purpose, all paths between two relations in the structural model are considered, independently on the direction of the arcs (connections) on the paths. The relations relevant for the pivot relation R are then kept in a *candidate set* that specifies the nodes of a subgraph $G(R)$ of the directed graph G_s defined by the structural model (see Figure 2(A)). The metric-function used in Penguin is described in [3], where a formal definition of a candidate set is also given. The purpose of the metric-function is to manage the scope of information presented to the user, as well as to reduce the size of the computation in defining a view-object.

Candidate Bag. Once a candidate set $G(R)$ is constructed, the problem arises that some relations in the candidate set may be reached using multiple paths from the pivot relation. The *candidate bag* for R contains all the relations of R's candidate set, the multiplicity of each relation Q in the bag being the number of valid paths from R to Q in $G(R)$. Relations contained in the candidate bag can be arranged in a unique hierarchical structure $T(R)$ called the candidate tree of R (see Figure 2(B) where *people* is replicated because there are two valid paths from the pivot relation *course* to the secondary relation *people*). Using a depth-first traversal of the candidate set graph starting at the pivot relation, we replicate the nodes of the graph for each path to create a tree. This operation is related to creating a spanning tree of a graph, where each node is retained but non-essential arcs are removed; here each arc is retained and nodes are replicated in order to create a tree. Note that we may traverse an arc in either direction, so that there are six connection types of interest (the three connections defined in

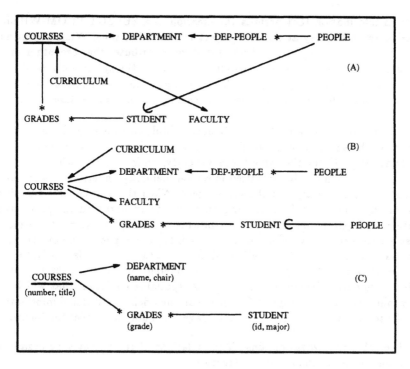

Fig. 2. Definition of a view-object: candidate set, candidate bag, and view-object.

the structural model, plus the three inverse connections obtained from traversal in the reverse direction). Thus, multiple copies of a non-pivot relation can be included in one view-object. The formal definition of a candidate bag and its transformation into a candidate tree is presented in detail in [3]. The candidate bag forms a *covering tree* of the candidate set.[2]

View-Object Template Tree. Once a pivot relation is chosen by the user, a unique candidate tree is generated by Penguin: It defines all possible configurations for a view-object template anchored on this pivot relation. The user defines a specific hierarchical structure for a view-object by selecting nodes (relations) and atomic attributes for each node (see Figure 2(C), the attributes selected for each node of the template tree are shown in parentheses). The subset candidate tree selected by the user is represented as a view-object template. However, a view-object template not only contains the relations for the object and the relationships among them, but also information on how to select and shape the view-object instances. The necessary joins and projections are only dependent on the object structure. Together, they define the *data access function* (DAF) for the object, that is computed at the view-object definition time. The DAF

---

[2] This name was suggested by Anne C. Elster of Cornell as the analog of a spanning tree.

contains information that permits the creation of a SELECT-FROM-WHERE block of an SQL query at the view-object instantiation time. While computing the DAF, the Penguin system checks for atomic attributes that are either missing or redundant—the atomic attributes must allow the system to identify the tuples for each relation comprising the view-object—and for relations that have not been chosen by the user but are necessary to the join expression.

Defining Inheritance of View-Objects. Multiple view-objects can be anchored on the same pivot relation and can have in common some nodes of the candidate tree. Using the inheritance property, view-objects anchored on the same pivot relation can be organized in a IS-A hierarchy. Inheritance in Penguin is used to define the type of the view-object. When the user chooses the pivot relation, he can inherit from existing view-objects anchored on the same pivot relation, and select one or more view-objects according to his needs. Some of these view-objects may belong to the same inheritance path; Penguin keeps in this case the most specialized view-object. In a case of multiple inheritance, a relation attribute of a tuple may appear in different inheritance sources and be defined differently. Penguin keeps the most specialized relation that will be finally inherited by the subtype.[3] The user can then define additional information specific to the new view-object. At this stage, Penguin guarantees the following:

- The subtype always contains all the relations of the parent type organized according to a similar nested structure.
- For each relation common to the two view-objects, the relation of the subtype must contain at least all the attributes of the corresponding relation of the parent type.
- The subtype always contains all the references of the parent type.

Thus, a view-object anchored on the pivot relation R can inherit relations and references defined in existing view-objects also anchored on R[4]. Additional information can be added such as new atomic attributes for the inherited relations, new relations coming from the candidate tree rooted on R, and new view-object references.

Defining References between View-Objects. A view-object anchored on R can refer to one or several view-objects whose pivot relation is contained in the candidate bag of R; it can also be itself the target of many references. Thus, the origin of a reference link is a view-object whose template tree contains a relation that serves as a pivot relation for the referenced view-object. This guarantees that, for a particular node's instance value in the referencing view-object, we

---

[3] Object instances created by an application program are created using the correct type. We envision that when data is fetched from the database, a test will be made to determine the correct type of the object to be instantiated. This test will be described declaratively or by a programmer-exit routine.

[4] It is also reasonable for an IS-A graph to include view-objects pivoted on a relation related by a subset connection to R.

can rapidly retrieve the corresponding instances attached to the referenced view-object and present them to the user according to their nested pattern. The user can therefore create a navigational structure convenient for an application, that is, view-object PART-OF graphs that make explicit the general data structure of the application. Navigation among view-objects is similar to navigation in the structural model or among object classes in C++.

3.2 Object Schema of an Application View

The view-object model enables users to build object schemas that are most convenient for different applications reusing the same collection of data. The semantics of shared data is captured in the structural model. View-objects represent hierarchically portions of the network described as a structural model and the relations that comprise them are composed through relational joins. For a specific application, the user defines complex object classes (view-objects) as well as IS-A and PART-OF classes graphs. The definition of an application view is language independent, because it is based on the structural model that plays the role of an integrated data model on top of the conceptual data model.

As stressed in [30], many problems come from the integration of database techniques and object-oriented programming languages. We argue that our approach must not only be seen as a means to favor data sharing among applications but also as a means of reconciling database and object-oriented approaches by keeping the best of each of them. In the following section, we present how Penguin generates language-specific code for the C++ binding to define the object classes describing the view-objects and basic operations on them (creation, navigate, browsing, and update).

4 Generating C++ Code for an Application View

C++ [28] appears to be a *de facto* standard in the object-oriented world, and a growing number of object-oriented databases offer this language to directly specify classes and methods. However, in these systems, a database is created from C++ classes, which can make the reusing of some parts of the database for other application programs difficult. The problem is that the design of an object class schema convenient for a particular application may not be convenient or easily extendable to support the requirements of future applications. This problem is particularly tricky because of the semantic richness of the object-oriented concepts and the limited experience the community has in integrated object schema from independently developed applications. The Penguin system uses another approach that consists in generating C++ classes convenient for each application, from an integrated structural model. An additional layer has thus been added to the Penguin system to make possible the automatic generation of C++ classes. These classes can be used in applications that want to access the data and then present it in the form of C++ objects.

4.1 Use of Two Layers for Mapping

In Penguin, the C++ mapping uses a two-layer approach to support sharing. In the lower layer, C++ classes are defined for each of the relations in the structural model, with the appropriate connections between classes. Each class is derived from one base relation and contains an attribute for each of the base relation's attributes in addition to an attribute for each connection or inverse connection involving the base relation. In the first case, the type of the attribute is a simple one (e.g., integer, real, char); in the second case, the type of the attribute corresponds to the name of a C++ subclass. For the relation classes, Penguin generates C++ methods responsible for instantiation, browsing and updating.

In the higher layer, C++ subclasses are created to define the view-object mapping. These subclasses make visible only those attributes and connections that the view-object preserves at its level. More precisely, to each view-object corresponds a collection of C++ subclasses, one subclass representing a relation involved in the view-object template. These C++ subclasses are actually organized into an aggregation hierarchy whose root is the subclass representing the pivot relation of the view-object; the remaining subclasses are located at the other nodes according to the view template tree defined by the user. Furthermore, the arcs of this C++ tree correspond to the connection attributes. We can note that the leaves of the tree actually represent subclasses that do not have connection attributes. Thus, there is a one-to-one mapping between the view-object template tree defined by the user and the corresponding C++ aggregation hierarchy created at the C++ layer.

In each subclass, simple attributes and connections are inherited from the class representing the entire relation. However, a subclass represents the information the user needs. For this purpose, *get* and *set* methods are defined for those attributes only; they permit the corresponding data to be accessed or updated. These methods are automatically generated by the Penguin system. C++ classes can be seen simply as structures generated for users to use in their programs. The user can specialize C++ classes and customize them for example by adding new attributes and new methods.

4.2 The Mapping Process

Since there are two levels of mapping, there are actually two mapping processes that occur. The first is the mapping of the semantic model onto C++ classes. This mapping creates a collection of classes that point to one another as needed to realize the connections between the relations. The mapping is done on a relation-by-relation basis and the class name corresponds to the relation name. Let us consider the structural model of Figure 1. We can get from this model the C++ classes named *courses*, *department*, *people*, *curriculum*, *grades*, *student*, *faculty*, and *staff*. For example, the class *courses* will be defined as shown in Figure 3(A).

```
class courses {

    protected:        /* only visible to subclasses */
                      /* attributes for columns: */
        int number ;
        char title[60] ;                           class courses_info : public courses {
        integer units ;                              public:
                      /* attributes for connections */      /* attributes of the relation courses */
        grades * c_grades ;  /* ownership */
        curriculum * c_curriculum ;  /* inverse reference */   int get_number() { return courses : : number ; }
        faculty * c_faculty ;  /* reference */           void set_number( int value ) { courses : : number = value ; }
        department * c_department ;  /* reference */       char * get_title() { return courses : : title ; }
                                                    void set_title( char * value ) { strcpy( courses : : title, value ) ; }
    public:
        get_relation_name() { return ("courses"); }          /* relation attributes of the relation courses */
             ...
}                                                   courses_info_grades * get_c_grades()
              (A)                                       { return (courses_info_grades *) courses : : c_grades() ; }
                                                    void set_c_grades( courses_info_grades * instance )
    object_name : courses_info                           { courses : : c_grades = instance; };

    1 courses                                       courses_info_department * get_c_department()
      Attributes : number, title                         { return (courses_info_department *) courses : : c_department() ; }
      2 grades                                      void set_c_department( courses_info_department * instance )
        Attributes : grade                               { courses : : c_department = instance ; };
        3 student
          Attributes : id, major                     ...
      2 department                                  }
        Attributes : name, chair                                    (C)
                  (B)
```

Fig. 3. C++ mapping for the relation *courses* and the view-object *courses-info*.

The second mapping process goes from the view-objects onto C++ classes that are subclasses of the classes defined for the semantic model. There is a starting point for each view-object: its root (i.e., its pivot relation). The class name corresponds to the view-object name. The view-object of Figure 2 has its template depicted in Figure 3(B). To each relation included in this view-object corresponds a C++ class whose name consists of the name of the view-object and the name of the relation. Each C++ class specifies *set* and *get* methods for the atomic and relation attributes that are visible in the corresponding relation. For example, Figure 3(C) shows part of the C++ specification for the view-object *courses-info*. Note that the *get* and *set* methods of the class *courses-info-grades* apply to the atomic attribute *grade* and the relation attribute *student*. Finally, the classes *courses-info-department* and *courses-info-student* access and update only atomic attributes that are respectively *name, chair*, and *id, major*.

4.3 C++ Level for Navigation, Query, and Update

The functions offered by Penguin to create, browse, and update view-object instances can be invoked by the C++ methods automatically generated during the mapping process. The methods *first, next, previous*, and *last* deal with the browsing of each view-object's instance. The methods *insert, delete*, and *replace* enable the user to insert, delete, or replace values that correspond to relations instances; they take into account update rules specific to each view-object and specified on it.

The *instantiate* method invokes the Penguin functions responsible for retrieving all the instances of a view-object. An instance of the view-object is then copied in the C++ objects organized according to the aggregate hierarchy defined by the instance of the C++ subclass. These C++ objects point to (sub)tuples values of the current view-object instance. Each call of a browsing operation returns a new view-object instance that replaces the previous one in the C++ structure.

5 Penguin Architecture

Since generality and portability are major objectives, the C programming language and the SQL language have been used to implement the Penguin system. The current implementation runs on UNIX with data stored in Ingres. Penguin also has been ported to Oracle. Penguin was originally written on VAX VMS using DEC's RDB.[5] Currently, this system has a four-layer architecture:

- The physical layer. Data are stored in relations in a relational database. This layer handles the storage requirements for Penguin.
- The relational layer. This layer is concerned with the semantic model that augments the relational model by adding connections between relations.
- The object layer. It corresponds to the view-object model. Penguin provides functions for creating, instantiating, updating, and browsing view-objects.
- The C++ layer. C++ classes are automatically generated by the Penguin system to provide a programmatic interface on top of Penguin for creating, instantiating, updating and browsing view-objects. This C++ mapping preserves the information-sharing features of Penguin.

The software components of the Penguin system have been defined in a modular way and are organized around six *agents*. The *call interface agent* creates a message-passing paradigm that provides interagent communications. The interaction between an application using Penguin (such as the generated C++ interface code), and the Penguin system is controlled by an *application interface agent*. In this section, we present the role of the four other agents and describe the module responsible for the C++ application generation.

5.1 Structural Model Agent

The *structural model agent* is responsible for the creation, the destruction and the display of connections between relations. The ownership, reference, and subset connections enable the user to capture all the potential links existing between data. This implies that a view-object template generated from the structural model defines a hierarchical structure that is complete for this view.

---

[5] Detailed documentation of the Penguin system is in [6]. A description of the theory of Penguin is contained in [5, 3]. Some other papers on the Penguin project are also in the bibliography [4, 20, 34, 35].

5.2 Template Generation Agent

This agent is responsible for the creation of a view-object template and the definition of the update, insert, and delete operations of the view. A template is defined as described in Section 3, generated from a candidate tree rooted on a pivot relation. Since the user can include any number of attributes for each relation in a view-object, this agent has to test for attributes that are either missing or redundant. The joins and projections that are necessary to get the view-object instances are dependent on the view-object structure and lead to the construction of the DAF for the view-object.

5.3 Object Instantiation Agent

This agent performs several tasks with the purpose of instantiating a view-object. It offers the user an Object Query Language [29] that has an SQL-like syntax and ensures the translation of a user object query into a relational SQL. Since the target of an object query is a view-object, the generated SQL query is based on the DAF of this view-object eventually augmented by additional predicates. This agent handles building the SQL query and passes it down to the Penguin database where the query is executed. The result is a collection of flattened tuples that are then organized into a hierarchical, nested, traversable structure according to the template tree. The resulting view-object instances are cached in main memory and bound to the corresponding view-object. The restructuring process, based on the approach developed in [21, 22], eliminates duplicate subtuples and null subtuples.

In the current Penguin system, each time a view-object is instantiated, the relevant instances are retrieved from the remote database and replace the old instances. By keeping the resulting tuples in the local memory for an extended period of time, we could reuse the cached tuples to locally answer queries and thereby avoid database accesses. To do that, we have defined a two-level client-side cache for composite objects mapped as views of a relational database[11]. The lower level of the cache contains the tuples from each relation that have been loaded into memory already. These tuples are linked together from relation to relation according to the joins of the structural model. This level of the cache is shared among all applications using the data on this client. The higher level of the cache contains composed objects of data extracted from the lower level cache. This cache uses the object schema of a single application, and the data is copied from the lower level cache for convenient access by the application.

5.4 Instantiation Navigation Agent

This agent is responsible for view-object instances browsing and updating. The browsing operations (*first, last, next, previous*) use the hierarchical structure of the nested sets of cached tuples. Navigation among view-object instances exploits the reference links defined between the view-objects. This agent also offers functions to perform instance modifications (delete, insert, and update).

It checks for consistency whenever a modification of a view-object instance is done. The integrity rules of semantic connections and the update rules specific to each view-object control the impact a user can have on the shared data of the underlying relations. The approach chosen to handle updating through view-objects [5] extends previous work on relational views [12, 13, 14, 16].

5.5 C++ Application Interface Generator

This module generates a C++ application interface from the structural model and an application view as described in section 4. A generic class *Root* common to the relation classes is created to specify generic methods that can be redefined at a lower level. A view-object is represented by an aggregate hierarchy of C++ classes whose root refers to the view-object's pivot relation.

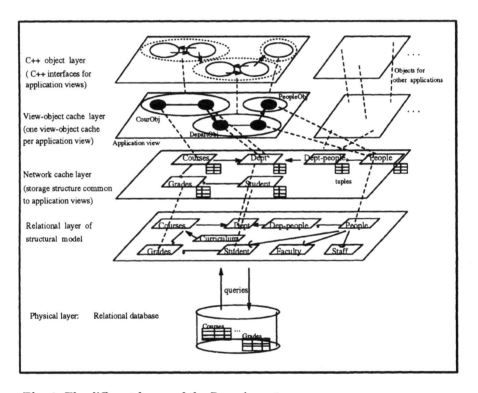

Fig. 4. The different layers of the Penguin system.

The C++ classes define the basic behavior (methods) of view-objects, that enables the user to create, browse and update view-objects instances. In this last case, C++ methods invoke Penguin functions that propagate changes in the cache and on the shared database. Cache consistency maintenance on the different client sides and client notification are part of ongoing research. Figure 4 shows an overview of the different layers in the Penguin system along these lines.

6 Ongoing and Future Work

We are currently using Penguin to demonstrate how independently developed applications with differing object schemas can be integrated. We have taken two applications with C++ object schemas, converted each of these schemas into a structural model, integrated the structural models, created a relational database to support these applications, and are now defining the object classes and porting the applications to use Penguin through these object classes.

We are also investigating new caching techniques using a predicate-based approach. This approach is important when objects are cached based on their contents, rather than by object ID. Our approach allows clients to cache data bound into the form convenient to the application, while minimizing communication with the server and supporting concurrency control. Our approach will allow queries to be executed locally if all data is available. As part of this research, we are investigating query languages that can be executed locally or decomposed into parts executable by a relational database to obtain data not available locally.

7 Conclusion

In this paper, we have explained how two fundamental concepts of the Penguin system aim at promoting data sharing between multiple object schemas and a relational model. Our approach allows the co-existence of legacy applications and databases using the relational model and new applications written using the object-oriented approach. Furthermore, our approach is compatible with object-view integration, a demonstration of which is in progress.

The first concept is the Structural Model that uses the concepts of aggregation, categorization and abstraction to explicitly express semantics relating normalized data. These connections specify precise integrity rules that are used to control the effects of view-object updates on the base relations. Both connections and inverse connections are considered when view-objects are created from the structural model. They are used to define the correct hierarchical arrangement of view-object's instances. The View-Object Model constitutes the second main component that allows the user to define application views consisting of view-objects organized into PART-OF and IS-A graphs. View-objects support the definition and the manipulation of complex data structures as well as data sharing between different applications.

Penguin generates C++ code defining the C++ structure and the basic behavior of an application view. This C++ mapping maintains the information sharing feature of Penguin and offers a high-level interface for data creation, browsing and update.

8 Acknowledgements

This effort was supported in part by the Microelectronics Manufacturing Science and Technology project as a subcontract to Texas Instruments on DARPA contract number F33615-88-C-5448 task number 9. The work of Catherine Hamon is supported by a postdoctoral fellowship supported by the French government.

The work reported herein was implemented by numerous students and visitors. Amelia Carlson implemented the generation of base C++ classes. Leonid Karasik implemented the specification of composite Penguin classes with inheritance and references, and generation of C++ class definitions. Tetsuya Takahashi defined and implemented the query system for the C++ binding. Tahir Ahmad, Larry Safran, and Srinivasan Venkatesan implemented other parts of the C++ binding for Penguin. Earlier development of the Penguin system includes work by Gio Wiederhold, Kincho Law, Thierry Barsalou, Niki Siambela, David Zingmond, Harvinder Singh, and Byung-Suk Lee, among others. We also thank Marianne Siroker for her assistance in the preparation of this paper.

References

1. S. Abiteboul and Bidoit. Non First Normal Form Relations: An Algebra Allowing Data Restructuring. *Journal of Computer and System Sciences*, December 1986.
2. T. Andrews and C. Andrews. Combining Language and Database Advances in an Object-Oriented Development Environment. *Proceedings of OOPSLA*, Orlando, Florida, 1987.
3. T. Barsalou. *View Objects for Relational Databases*. Ph.D. dissertation, Stanford University, March 1990, technical report STAN-CS-90-1310.
4. T. Barsalou and G. Wiederhold. Complex Objects For Relational Databases. *Computer Aided Design*, Vol. 22 No.8, Buttersworth, Great Britain, October 1990.
5. T. Barsalou, N. Siambela, A. M. Keller, G. Wiederhold. Updating Relational Databases through Object-Based Views. *ACM SIGMOD*, Denver, May 1991.
6. A. Carlson. *Penguin System Internal Maintenance Specifications*. Unpublished document, October 1992.
7. R. Cattell. *Object Data Management: Object Oriented and Extended Relational Systems*. Addison-Wesley, 1991.
8. E.F. Codd. A Relational Model of Data for Large Shared Data Banks. *CACM*, 13(6), June 1970.
9. O. Deux. The Story of O2. *IEEE Transactions on Knowledge and Data Engineering*, 2(1), March 1990.
10. L. Haas, W. Chang, G. Lohman, J. McPherson, G. Lapis, B. Lindsay, H. Pirahesh, M. Carey, and E. Shekita. Starburst Mid-Flight: As the Dust Clears. *IEEE Transactions on Knowledge and Data Engineering*, 2(1), March 1990.
11. C. Hamon and A. M. Keller. Two-Level Caching of Composite Object Views of Relational Databases. Submitted for publication, 1993.
12. A. M. Keller. *Updating Relational Databases Through Views*. Ph.D. dissertation, Stanford University, February 1985, technical report STAN-CS-85-1040.
13. A. M. Keller. The Role of Semantics in Translating View Updates. *IEEE Computer*, 19(1), January 1986.

14. A. M. Keller. Choosing a View Update Translator by Dialog at View Definition Time. *12th Int. Conf. on Very Large Data Bases*, Kyoto, Japan, August 1986.
15. A. M. Keller. Unifying Database and Programming Language Concepts Using the Object Model, (extended abstract). *Int. Workshop on Object-Oriented Database Systems*, IEEE Computer Society, Pacific Grove, CA, September 1986.
16. A. M. Keller and L. Harvey. *A Prototype View Update Translation Facility*. Report TR-87-45, Dept. of Computer Sciences, Univ. of Texas at Austin, December 1987.
17. A.M. Keller, R. Jensen, S. Agarwal. Persistence Software: Bridging Object-Oriented Programming and Relational Databases. *ACM SIGMOD*, 1993.
18. J. Kiernan, C. de Maindreville, and E. Simon. The Design and Implementation of an Extensible Deductive Database System. *SIGMOD Record*, September 1989.
19. W. Kim. *Introduction to Object-Oriented Databases*. The MIT Press, 1990.
20. K. H. Law, G. Wiederhold, T. Barsalou, N. Sambela, W. Sujansky, and D. Zingmond. Managing Design Objects in a Sharable Relational Framework. *ASME meeting*, Boston, August 1990.
21. B. S. Lee and G. Wiederhold. *Outer Joins and Filters for Instantiating Objects from Relational Databases through Views*. Center for Integrated Facilities Engineering (CIFE), Stanford University, Technical Report 30, May 1990.
22. B. S. Lee. *Efficiency in Instantiating Objects from Relational Databases Through Views*. Ph.D. dissertation, Stanford University, December 1990, technical report STAN-CS-90-1346.
23. D. Maier, J. Stein, A. Otis, and A. Purdy. Development of an Object-Oriented DBMS. *Proceedings of OOPSLA*, Portland, Oregon, 1986.
24. Z.M. Ozsoyoglu and L.Y. Yuan. A New Normal Form for Nested Relations. *ACM Transactions on Database Systems*, 12(1), 1987.
25. P. Pistor and F. Andersen. Designing a General NFNF Data Model with an SQL-Type Language Interface. *Twelfth International Conference on VLDB*, Kyoto, Japan, 1986.
26. M. A. Roth, H. F. Korth, and A. Silberschatz. Extended Algebra and Calculus for Nested Relational Databases. *ACM TODS*, 13(4), December 1988.
27. M. Stonebraker. Object Management in Postgres Using Procedures. *On Object-Oriented Database Systems*, Springer-Verlag, 1991.
28. B. Stroustrup. *The C++ Programming Language*. Addison-Wesley, 1986.
29. T. Takahashi and A.M. Keller. Querying Heterogeneous Object Views of a Relational Database. Submitted for publication, 1993.
30. D.C. Tsichritzis, T. Bogh. Fitting Round Objects into Square Databases. *OOPSLA*, New Orleans, 1989.
31. J. D. Ullman. *Principles of Database and Knowledge-Base Systems. Volume 1: Classical Database Systems*, Computer Science Press, 1988.
32. G. Wiederhold and R. ElMasri. The Structural Model for Database Design. *In Entity-Relationship Approach to System Analysis and Design*, North-Holland, 1980.
33. G. Wiederhold. Views, Objects and Databases. *IEEE Computer*, 19(12), 1986.
34. G. Wiederhold, T. Barsalou, and S. Chaudhuri. *Managing Objects in a Relational Framework*. Stanford Technical report CS-89-1245, January 1989, Stanford University.
35. G. Wiederhold, T. Barsalou, B. S. Lee, N. Siambela, and W. Sujansky. Use of Relational Storage and a Semantic Model to Generate Objects: The PENGUIN Project. *Database '91: Merging Policy, Standards and Technology*, The Armed Forces Communications and Electronics Association, Fairfax VA, June 1991.

Dynamic Selectivity Estimation for Multidimensional Queries

William I. Grosky, Junping Sun, and Farshad Fotouhi

Computer Science Department
Wayne State University
Detroit, Michigan 48202

Abstract. We have developed an adaptive selectivity estimation scheme for multidimensional queries which, experiments indicate, performs better than previously formulated non−adaptive methods when the distribution of the data is not known. Our approach uses a technique based on dynamic quantized spaces, a dynamic data structure developed for motion analysis in the field of computer vision. The objective of this research is to overcome the disadvantages of previously formulated non−adaptive, static methods which are relatively inaccurate in a dynamic database environment when the distribution of the data is not uniform. We have shown via many experiments that our approach is more flexible and more accurate in the computation of selectivity factors than both the equi−width and equi−depth histogram methods when the database is large and undergoes frequent update activity following a non−uniform distribution.

1 Introduction

Multidimensional queries are ubiquitous in non−standard databases which support geographical information processing, VLSI design, and CAD/CAM engineering applications, in addition to standard business and commercial applications. To support such queries, much research over the years has proposed such multidimensional index structures as the k-d tree [1], the R^+-tree [10], the grid file [6], and the hB-tree [4].

In order for a query optimizer to generate optimal access paths for answering multidimensional queries, accurate selectivity estimation must be accomplished. There are two broad types of selectivity estimation schemes. The first type utilizes various techniques of data sampling and an auxiliary data structure of minimal complexity [3,8]. This approach does access the database, but in a much more inexpensive fashion than would be the case if the various conditions were proposed as a normal query. However, even for a fixed database, if the conditions change then, depending on the nature of the change, the database might have to be resampled.

The second type of selectivity estimation scheme uses various sorts of histogram techniques to construct a statistical abstraction of the database [2,5]. Here, the database must be examined once in order to construct a more complex auxiliary data structure than is done in the previous scheme. Given a fixed database and the presence of this auxiliary data structure, the database need never be examined again, no matter what the conditions may be; the auxiliary data structure alone is consulted. The above papers develop the techniques of equi-width and equi-depth histograms to estimate selectivity factors, and it is shown that equi-depth histograms produce less of an error than equi-width histograms. An obvious disadvantage of these approaches is that they are not adaptive. When the database changes due to insertions, deletions, or modifications, especially if they follow a non-uniform distribution, the auxiliary data structure must then be rebuilt, with a possible need for reaccessing the entire database. Thus, it could be impractical to use static algorithms which are restricted by static accumulator array data structures, as the computational cost of data reorganization in these accumulator arrays will be extremely large, especially when a database has a large dimensionality and undergoes many updates, insertions, and deletions of a non-uniform nature.

The only way to avoid accessing the database is to design an adaptive selectivity estimation scheme with an auxiliary data structure which can be inexpensively updated in an incremental fashion as the database evolves. We have developed such a dynamic selectivity estimation scheme which, experiments indicate, performs better than the above non-adaptive methods for non-uniform data distributions. Our approach uses a technique similar to the dynamic quantized spaces of [7], which were developed for motion analysis in the field of computer vision. We have shown via many experiments that our approach is more flexible and more accurate in the computation of selectivity factors than both the equi-width and equi-depth histogram methods when the database is large and undergoes frequent update activity following a non–uniform distribution. Also, our technique is main-memory based and, as such, more efficient than secondary memory based index structures.

The organization of the remainder of our paper is as follows. Section 2 discusses existing static selectivity estimation methods and introduces our adaptive technique. Section 3 addresses our improvements to the data structure of [7], while in Section 4 we present the results of various experiments using our approach. Finally, Section 5 offers our conclusions.

2 Selectivity Estimation

In previous research on selectivity factor estimation for multidimensional queries, both the equi-width and equi-depth histogram methods have been shown to suffer some serious disadvantages. The equi-width histogram method produces erroneous results if the attribute values are not uniformly distributed. The reason for this estimation error is that space is equally divided and consequently the range of each equi-width histogram bin is fixed and of equal size during the estimation processing. There are two aspects to the problems of equi-width histogram estimation. One is that it is hard to predict the distribution of data in advance. Even for a uniform distribution of data in a particular region, it is often not possible to give a relatively accurate estimation of the selectivity in a larger region which includes the given one, especially when the data is clustered within the former region. The intervals of a histogram should be more finely divided in this clustering region, so that uniformity of allocation of point data attribute values in each bin can be achieved. This is what the equi-depth method tries to do. Another problem is that the equally divided and fixed range of bins can't reflect the dynamic behavior of a database. When frequent update activity occurs, an estimation schema based on the hypothesis of equally divided and fixed bin ranges will not be able to give a correct estimation of selectivity, particularly if a large number of insertions or deletions concentrate in some specific intervals of the histogram or in some specific bins. A reorganization of the data distribution in the various histogram bins then becomes inevitable in order to maintain the uniformity of data in the histogram so as to give a good estimation of selectivity factors.

We thus conclude that a variable and adaptive bin size is the critical focal point in any type of histogram approach. The equi-depth histogram method generates bins which are not of the same size. It tries to accomplish the equal distribution of attribute values in all bins along each dimension, whose intervals may vary with the distribution of data. However, even though the equi-depth histogram method gives, to some extent, the solution to the problem of skewed distribution of attribute values, it still has two problems from the point of view of computational cost. First, the cost of sorting the accumulator arrays in a multidimensional histogram is a function of the dimensionality and increases linearly as the dimensionality is increased. When the number of tuples or the number of data pages is very large, the total sorting cost becomes very large. Also, when a high frequency of updates, insertions, and deletions occurs in the database, the cost of reorganizing the data for the multidimensional histogram, which implies the resorting of all the accumulator arrays along each dimension, will be very costly.

The limitations or disadvantages of the previous static selectivity estimating methods gives a clear reason why we need to introduce a new dynamic selectivity estimating method to solve the problems mentioned above. In our approach, we use an adaptive data structure similar to a k–d tree [1] and to dynamically quantized spaces [7] to dynamically estimate the selectivity factors for multidimensional queries. This adaptive selectivity factor estimation method is different from both the equi-width and equi-depth histogram methods in that the size of each histogram bin is neither fixed nor of equal size during the process of histogram building, but rather adapts to the current data distribution. That is, it will dynamically reflect the database state at any given time as updates occur. Also, the size of each histogram bin will be dynamically readjusted to reflect the history of updates, insertions, and deletions, even when they are highly frequent and concentrated in particular intervals or bins. The adaptive behavior of our approach, which concerns when a histogram bin splits into multiple sub-bins and when a set of histogram bins merge into a super-bin, is governed by rules which seek to ensure that each bin has an approximately equal number of data points as well as that within each histogram bin, the data values are uniformly distributed. This will assure a relatively accurate estimation of selectivity factors for multidimensional queries at any given time.

In our approach, we use a data structure similar to a k-d tree as a hierarchical structure to store a histogram of attribute values in multidimensional space. There will be one such tree for each chosen set of attributes, each logical D-attribute tuple being interpreted as a D-dimensional point. A chosen set of attributes can comprise an individual relation, part of a relation, or part of a join of many relations. We call our data structure *SEDDS (selectivity estimation dynamic data structure).*

SEDDS is different from a k-d tree in the following respects. First, in the original k-d tree, there is no difference between an internal node and a leaf node. Both types of nodes are used to store a record which includes node range information, a discriminator value to be used in searching the tree, and pointers to descendent child nodes. In SEDDS, however, there is a structural difference between an internal node and a leaf node. Only leaf nodes correspond to histogram bins and, as such, are used to indicate in a gross way the distribution of data points which fall in the D-dimensional region covered by the given node. Instead of using a D-dimensional accumulator array to compute the multidimensional histogram, SEDDS uses D-dimensional bins to store the multidimensional histogram information, with one bin at each leaf node. All the bins in SEDDS will comprise the entire histogram in D-dimensional space. Second, the discriminator value is no longer cycled systematically. It could be any integer value between 1 and D for any node at any level. Finally, for the original k-d tree, all explicit attribute information related to each record is stored, while only implicit D-dimensional related histogram information is stored in the SEDDS nodes. That is, *SEDDS is an abstract of the data.* Each internal node has a discriminator value for search, insertion, or deletion, and pointers to its direct descendent child nodes. Each leaf node contains the count value of the point data in that region as well as a *count difference* vector, which indicates, for each dimension, the difference in count between points in the high half-space of the leaf node and points in the low half-space of the leaf node. This is the only record we have of the distribution of points in a particular bin. If a leaf node had a perfectly uniform distribution of data, each element of the difference vector for that node would be equal to zero. The value of a particular element of this vector for a given leaf node therefore indicates, in a very gross fashion, the non-uniformity of the data along the corresponding dimension in the D-dimensional region covered by the given leaf node. The low bound and high bound range values as well as a count are stored at internal nodes as well as at leaf nodes in SEDDS.

Using C notation, a SEDDS node is described as follows:

```
struct sedds_node {
            int node_type; float range[D][2]; float count;
            union {
                    struct {
                            int discriminator; float midpoint;
                            struct sedds_node *leftchild, *rightchild;
                    } internal;
                    float count_difference[D];
            } u;
}
```

The integer node_type indicates whether the node is an internal node or a leaf node. The D by 2 dimensional array range is similar to that in the original k-d tree. It stores the low bound and high bound values of that node along each dimension of D-dimensional space. The field count indicates the number of data points in the D-dimensional region covered by the given node. We note that due to the adaptive nature of our data structure, this field may take a non-integer value. If the node is an internal node, the variable discriminator gives the dimension for a search operation at that level. The value of midpoint will be used for dimension splitting and region partitioning. All leaf nodes are used as bins to store the D-dimensional histogram information as well as the range and count information, the latter two items also being stored at internal nodes. The leaf nodes represent adjacent D-dimensional subregions orthogonal to the attribute coordinate system, which comprise the entire D-dimensional range defined by the attributes of the given relation via its domains. The array count-difference indicates in a gross fashion the distribution of attribute values in each dimension for each leaf node bin.

The computation of the count difference vector value in each dimension is as follows. If the data point falls in the lower half-space along a given dimension, then the count difference value corresponding to that dimension will be −1 for that point, otherwise it will be +1. For example, suppose a node has a point data count value of 6. Then, if the count difference value count_difference[i] along some dimension i is 0, both the lower half-space and the upper half-space along that dimension have equal counts for that attribute value. Otherwise if count_difference[i] is, for example, +4, then 1 attribute value falls in the lower half-space along that dimension and 5 attribute values in the upper half-space.

From the above specification of SEDDS, we see that tuples lose their identity when inserted into this data structure. An important implication of this is that SEDDS cannot be used to detect duplicate keys or tuples; that is not its purpose. Duplicates must be detected as they normally are, through the mediation of an integrity checking module. SEDDS is designed to give a statistical profile of the database in the sense of heuristically determining how many tuples reside in certain volumes of tuple space, including duplicates if that is desired by the user. Its utility is that even when tuple identity is lost, it dynamically adjusts to insertions, deletions, and modifications to the database and gives quite good selectivity results, as we will see.

SEDDS supports the primitive operations of the insertion of a data point into a leaf node, the deletion of a data point from a leaf node, the split of a leaf node into two new leaf nodes, and merging one leaf node with its neighbor leaf nodes. Both split and merge operations try to achieve an equal count of data and a uniformity of distribution, through heuristic means. As we will show in Section 4, our split and merge rules give better performance than those of [7] when utilized in a database environment. The size of each bin corresponding to a D-dimensional region will be dynamically and adaptively adjusted during the histogram building or histogram updating process. For a given leaf node, if the value of count is too large or if the absolute value of count_difference[i] for some dimension i is too large, then that leaf node should be partitioned or split into two new leaf nodes, with each one covering half of the parent's range. The count of the old leaf node will be distributed to each child based on the value of count_difference[discriminator] where discriminator corresponds to the split-dimension. On the other hand, a leaf node should be merged with its neighboring leaf node(s) if the resultant merge operation will not generate too high a count and too large a count difference.

As previously mentioned, the goal of our algorithm is to have an approximately equal number of points in each bin and for the points in each bin to be uniformly distributed. There are 3 parameters associated with this goal: the optimum number of bins in the space (B_{target}), an indicator which tells us whether a bin is too full and should be split (α), and an indictor which tells us how non-uniform the distribution of the points within a bin should be allowed to be before we split it (β) [7].

If we want to have B_{target} bins and at a particular time we have p points, this tells us that we should have as close to p/B_{target} points per bin as possible. Call this quantity p_{target}. A particular bin, b, will be split if either [b → count] > α p_{target} or | [b → count_difference][i] | > β p_{target}, for some $1 \leq i \leq N$. The splitting dimension is the one with the maximal count difference, given by the count difference vector. For merging, let the neighbors of bin c in a given direction be c_1, ..., c_s. After the merge, each bin c_j expands and is called newc$_j$, for $1 \leq j \leq s$. See Figure 1 for an illustration where s = 6 and the merging is along dimension δ. Bin c will be merged along dimension δ with c_1, ..., c_s iff

1. For all $1 \leq j \leq s$, either [c$_j$ → count] $\leq \alpha$ p_{target} or | [b → count_difference][i] | > β p_{target}, for some $1 \leq i \neq \delta \leq N$.

2. | [newc$_j$ → count_difference][δ] | $\leq \beta$ p_{target} for all $1 \leq j \leq s$.

That is, after the merging, no split will occur along the merging dimension in any of the newly formed bins. The way we perform splitting and merging is quite different from that of [7] and will be discussed in the next section.

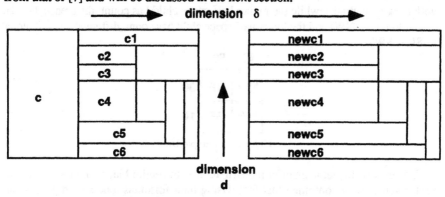

Fig. 1. Cellular Regions Previous to Merging and After Merging

3 New Split and Merge Rules for Our Dynamic Selectivity Estimation Scheme

The split and merge rules of [7] are heuristically formulated to give us a target number of bins, each with points which are uniformly distributed. In practice, however, we get more bins than the target and the points are not distributed uniformly within each bin. Taking into account the type of information which we keep in a SEDDS structure, we would consider the points in a bin uniformly distributed if the bin's count_difference vector consisted of all 0's. The weakness in the approach of [7] is that when formulating the split and merge rules, even though it is known that the actual distribution is non-uniform, by consulting the bias vector values, uniformity is assumed. Let us illustrate this via a 2-dimensional example. Consider a bin consisting of 100 points where count_difference[1] = 20 and count_difference[2] = 80. We would like to find the number of points in each quadrant of the bin. This will give us an approximation to the count_difference vectors of the two resulting bins after the given bin splits along the second dimension. Let NW, NE, SW, and SE represent the number of points in the northwest, northeast, southwest, and southeast quadrants of the bin, respectively. See Figure 2. Then, count_difference[1] = (NE + SE) − (NW + SW) and count_difference[2] = (NW + NE) − (SW + SE). We also have that NW + NE + SW + SE = 100. It is easily seen that NE + SE = 60, NW + SW = 40, NW + NE = 90, and SW + SE = 10. We cannot directly solve for NW, NE, SW, nor SE, but we can say something about their potential values. Given an ostensibly uniform distribution in the bin, NW + NE = 90 would seem to imply equal values for NW and NE of 45. This, however, would contradict the fact that NW + SW = 40. We never get a contradiction starting with the equation with the smallest right-hand side, however. This equation is SW + SE = 10, implying that SW = SE = 5. Using the other equations, we then get that NW = 35 and NE = 55. Thus, the child of the split bin corresponding to the higher half-space has a count field of 90 (NW + NE), while the child corresponding to the lower half-space has a count field of 10 (SW + SE). Both children have a count_difference[2] value of 0 (due to the uniformity assumption within each quadrant), while the higher half-space child has count_difference[1] = 20 (equal to NE − NW) and the lower half-space child has count_difference[1] = 0 (equal to SE − SW).

F i g . 2 . A Sample Bin

However, [7] assume a uniform distribution in the entire bin, even though the bias vector values may contradict that fact. Using their formulas, one would get similar values for the count fields of the higher half-space and lower half-space children of the split bin. Also, both children still would have a bias[2] value of 0. However, the bias[1] values of these children would be different. The higher half-space child would have bias[1] = 18 (90% of the original bias[1] value of 20, given that the higher half-space has 90% of the total points) and the lower half-space child would have bias[1] = 2.

Let us now illustrate merging. See Figure 3, which illustrates the merging of two sibling bins along dimension 1. Suppose bin 1 extends along [0,100) along dimension 1 and contains 100 points, while bin 2 extends along [100,150) and also has 100 points. For bin 1, assume count_difference$_1$[1] = 60 and count_difference$_1$[2] = 40, while for bin 2, let count_difference$_2$[1] = 80 and count_difference$_2$[2] = 20. The formulas of 15] assume a completely uniform distribution of data in each bin. Thus, for the merged bin, which extends along [0,150) and contains 200 points, they compute count_difference$_{new}$[1] = [100 + .25(100)] − .75(100) = 50, completely ignoring the fact that that bin 1 has 55 points in its higher half-space and 45 points in its lower half-space. Using this fact, we find that for the merged bin, count_difference$_{new}$[1] = [100 + .5(80)] − [20 + .5(80)] = 80.

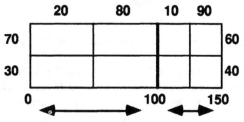

F i g . 3 . Merging Two Sibling Bins

For range queries also, we would use the count_difference vector in our calculations, while [7] does not. In higher dimensions, the differences produced by our approach would be magnified. In D dimensions, it would seem that we would have to estimate the number of points in each of the 2^D D-dimensional hyperquadrants, especially for our query estimation rules, which would take exponential time. We have, however, developed an algorithm which is $O(D^3)$. What is also important is that our rules consistently have given better results than the standard technique in all the experiments we have run, which we now describe. Note that in all these experiments, we have taken $\alpha = 1.2$ and $\beta = 0.6$, the same values as used in the experiments of [7].

We now present our approach. To simplify the following, we assume that D = 3; that is, our tuple population lies in 3-dimensional space. The equations which follow are easily generalized to higher dimensions. Suppose we have a database relation R with 3 real-valued attributes. In the SEDDS data structure R, suppose we have a bin b corresponding to a rectangular block $\mathcal{B}$. Along each of the three dimensions of $\mathcal{B}$, there is a low half-space and a high half-space. For example, $\mathcal{B}_{1,low}$, denotes the low half space along dimension 1, which, using Figure 4, we see is equal to region$_1$ ∪ region$_3$ ∪ region$_5$ ∪ region$_7$.

Now, bin b contains a count field, which is an estimate of the number of tuples of R contained within region $\mathcal{B}$. It also contains a count_difference vector of 3 elements, the jth value of which is an estimate as to the difference between the number of tuples of R contained in the high half-space of $\mathcal{B}$ along dimension j and the number of tuples of R contained in the low half-space of $\mathcal{B}$ along dimension j.

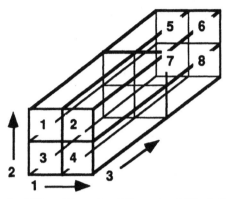

Fig. 4. A Three-Dimensional Example of Bin Splitting

Our New Split Rule. Suppose bin b splits into 2 sub-bins. This split should occur along the dimension having the largest count_difference value. Assume this is dimension s, where $1 \leq s \leq 3$. This split would produce 2 bins, $b_{s,low}$, corresponding to region $B_{s,low}$, and $b_{s,high}$, corresponding to region $B_{s,high}$. For each of these bins, we must compute a new count field and count_difference vector.

We can compute $[b_{s,low} \rightarrow count]$ and $[b_{s,high} \rightarrow count]$ by solving the following pair of simultaneous equations $[b_{s,high} \rightarrow count] + [b_{s,low} \rightarrow count] = [b \rightarrow count]$ and $[b_{s,high} \rightarrow count] - [b_{s,low} \rightarrow count] = [b \rightarrow count\_difference][s]$.

Along the split dimension s, we have little choice but to assume the data is uniformly distributed within each octant. This implies that $[b_{s,low} \rightarrow count\_difference][s] = [b_{s,high} \rightarrow count\_difference][s] = 0$.

The only quantities left to calculate remain $[b_{s,low} \rightarrow count\_difference][j]$ and $[b_{s,high} \rightarrow count\_difference][j]$ for $1 \leq j \neq s \leq 3$. This could easily be accomplished if we knew the number of tuples in each octant of bin b. This approach, however, would take time exponential in the size of the number of dimensions. Instead, we have developed a technique which has worst-case running time $O(D^3)$, where D is the number of dimensions. This technique essentially computes a disjoint covering of the set {region$_1$, ..., region$_{2D}$} of cardinality $O(D)$, where each element of the covering can be described by a D-element vector of elements from the set {low, high, *}, where * corresponds to *don't care* and where each region$_i$ which is an element of the same covering element has an equal number of tuples, which is also calculated. For example, for D = 3, a particular element of the disjoint covering might be (*,low,low), which corresponds to region$_3$ ∪ region$_4$. Along with this, we would also have calculated that each of the 2 regions has 7.5 tuples. Using this $O(D)$ cardinality disjoint covering we will be able to calculate the various needed count_difference quantities.

We will illustrate our approach through an example. If bin b split along dimension

j, $1 \le j \le 3$, we would have sub-bins $b_{j,low}$ and $b_{j,high}$. For any such j, we can calculate [$b_{j,low} \rightarrow$ count] and [$b_{j,high} \rightarrow$ count] in a similar fashion as above, by solving the following pair of simultaneous equations [$b_{j,high} \rightarrow$ count) + [$b_{j,low} \rightarrow$ count] = [$b \rightarrow$ count] and [$b_{j,high} \rightarrow$ count) − [$b_{j,low} \rightarrow$ count] = [$b \rightarrow$ count_difference][j]. This takes worst-case time complexity $O(D)$.

In 3 dimensions, we may then assume that we have [$b_{1,low} \rightarrow$ count], [$b_{1,high} \rightarrow$ count], [$b_{2,low} \rightarrow$ count], [$b_{2,high} \rightarrow$ count], [$b_{3,low} \rightarrow$ count], and [$b_{3,high} \rightarrow$ count]. We then sort this list in ascending order, which has worst-case time complexity $O(D \log D)$. Consider the following values for these quantities, [$b_{2,high} \rightarrow$ count] = 10 (count$_1$ + count$_2$ + count$_5$ + count$_6$ = 10), [$b_{3,low} \rightarrow$ count] = 20 (count$_1$ + count$_2$ + count$_3$ + count$_4$ = 20), [$b_{1,low} \rightarrow$ count] = 40 (count$_1$ + count$_3$ + count$_5$ + count$_7$ = 40), [$b_{1,high} \rightarrow$ count] = 60 (count$_2$ + count$_4$ + count$_6$ + count$_8$ = 60), [$b_{3,high} \rightarrow$ count] = 80 (count$_5$ + count$_6$ + count$_7$ + count$_8$ = 80), and [$b_{2,low} \rightarrow$ count] = 90 (count$_3$ + count$_4$ + count$_7$ + count$_8$ = 90), where count$_j$ is the number of tuples in region$_j$, for $1 \le j \le 8$.

In trying to find the values for count$_j$, $1 \le j \le 8$, we start with the equation with the smallest right-hand side, as mentioned previously for our 2-dimensional example. We then use the uniform distribution assumption and get that there are Size$_1$ = 2.5 tuples in each of #Regions$_1$ = 4 regions (in this case, region$_1$, region$_2$, region$_5$, and region$_6$, though at this point we don't actually have to know the identities of the individual regions), the union of these regions being described by the vector Regions$_1$ = (*,high,*). Thus, the regions yet to be considered are described by the vector RemainingRegions$_1$ = (*,low,*), corresponding to region$_3$ $\cup$ region$_4$ $\cup$ region$_7$ $\cup$ region$_8$.

The next equation to be considered concerns $b_{3,low}$. Now, $b_{3,low}$, corresponding to the vector (*,*,low), intersected with RemainingRegions$_1$ results in #Regions$_2$ = #Regions$_1$/2 = 2 new regions (in this case region$_3$ and region$_4$). Thus, each of these regions contain Size$_2$ = ([$b_{3,low} \rightarrow$ count] − Size$_1$ * number_of_regions(Regions$_1$ $\cap$ (*,*,low))) / #Regions$_2$ = ([$b_{3,low} \rightarrow$ count] − Size$_1$ * #Regions$_1$/2) / #Regions$_2$ = 7.5 tuples, the union of these regions is described by the vector Regions$_2$ = (*,low,low), and the regions yet to be considered are described by the vector RemainingRegions$_2$ = (*,low,high), corresponding to region$_7$ $\cup$ region$_8$.

Continuing in a similar manner, in worst-case time complexity $O(D^2)$ we find that of the $2^D = 2^3$ octants, there are 4 octants, corresponding to the region (*,high,*), each containing 2.5 tuples, 2 octants, corresponding to the region (*,low,low), each containing 7.5 tuples, 1 octant, corresponding to the region (low,low,high), containing 27.5 tuples, and 1 octant, corresponding to the region (high,low,high), containing 47.5 tuples. Using this information, we now show how to calculate $[b_{s,low} \rightarrow$ count_difference$][j]$ and $[b_{s,high} \rightarrow$ count_difference$][j]$ for $1 \leq j \neq s \leq 3$ in worst-case time complexity $O(D^2)$.

We note that in our example, the split dimension $s = 2$ since the absolute value of $[b_{j,high} \rightarrow$ count$] - [b_{j,low} \rightarrow$ count$]$ is maximized for $j = 2$. Thus, we must calculate $[b_{2,low} \rightarrow$ count_difference$][1]$, $[b_{2,low} \rightarrow$ count_difference$][3]$, $[b_{3,low} \rightarrow$ count_difference$][1]$, and $[b_{3,high} \rightarrow$ count_difference$][3]$. We show how to calculate $[b_{2,low} \rightarrow$ count_difference$][1]$, the other quantities being calculated in a similar fashion. Now, this quantity is equal to the cardinality of the regions included in (high,low,*) minus the cardinality of the regions included in (low,low,*). Using what we have calculated above, we may express this as

$$\sum_{i=1}^{4} [\text{number\_of\_regions}((\text{high,low},*) \cap \text{Regions}_i)$$
$$\text{number\_of\_regions}((\text{low,low},*) \cap \text{Regions}_i)] * \text{Size}_i,$$

which reduces to $(0 - 0) * 2.5 + (1 - 1) * 7.5 + (0 - 1) * 27.5 + (1 - 0) * 47.5 = 20$. Now, the calculation of each count_difference quantity has time complexity $O(D^2)$. There being $O(D)$ such quantities, this entire process has $O(D^3)$ time complexity.

Our New Merge Rule. Suppose bin c, corresponding to rectangular block $\mathcal{R}$, merges with bins $c^{(1)}, ..., c^{(n)}$, corresponding to rectangular blocks $\mathcal{R}^{(1)}, ..., \mathcal{R}^{(n)}$, respectively, along dimension δ, for $1 \leq \delta \leq D$, as shown in Figure 1a for $n = 6$. In this figure, the x-axis is dimension δ, while the y-axis is a generic dimension $d \neq \delta$. The resulting bin structure after the merge is as shown in Figure 1b. We must show how to calculate the count field and the count_difference vector for the bins $newc^{(1)}$, ..., $newc^{(n)}$, corresponding to rectangular blocks $new\mathcal{R}^{(1)}, ..., new\mathcal{R}^{(n)}$, respectively.

Again, our discussion will be for 3 dimensions. It easily generalizes for higher dimensions. Suppose we have a bin b corresponding to a rectangular block $\mathcal{B}$. We first show how to calculate an estimate for the number of tuples contained within a rectangular sub-block, S, of $\mathcal{B}$. As discussed in our new split rule, we first construct for $\mathcal{B}$ the sequences $\text{Regions}_1, ..., \text{Regions}_h$ and $\text{Size}_1, ..., \text{Size}_h$, where h is the size of each sequence. Suppose that $\mathcal{B}$ has bounding planes $x = x_1$ and $x = x_2 > x_1$, $y = y_1$ and $y = y_2 > y_1$, and $z = z_1$ and $z = z_2 > z_1$. Thus, $\mathcal{B}$ can be defined by the set of ordered triples $\{ <x,y,z> \mid x_1 \leq x < x_2, y_1 \leq y < y_2, \text{and } z_1 \leq z < z_2 \}$ and its volume is $(x_2 - x_1)(y_2 - y_1)(z_2 - z_1)$. For every rectangular sub-block, $\mathcal{B}_j$, of $\mathcal{B}$ corresponding to a particular Regions_j, for $1 \leq j \leq h$, one can write similar expressions. For example, the rectangular sub-block described by the vector (high, *, low) would correspond to the set of ordered triples $\{ <x,y,z> \mid (x_1 + x_2)/2 \leq x < x_2, y_1 \leq y < y_2, \text{and } z_1 \leq z < (z_1 + z_2)/2 \}$ and have volume $(x_2 - x_1)(y_2 - y_1)(z_2 - $

z_1) Assuming a uniform distribution of tuples within each $\mathcal{B}_j$ and given that $\{\mathcal{B}_1,$ ..., $\mathcal{B}_h\}$ is a disjoint covering of $\mathcal{B}$, we have that the number of tuples in $\mathcal{S}$ is

$$\sum_{i=1}^{h} \#Regions_i * Size_i * \frac{volume(\mathcal{B}_i \cap \mathcal{S})}{volume(\mathcal{B}_i)}.$$

We now indicate how to calculate [newc$^{(j)}$ → count], for $1 \leq j \leq n$ in D dimensions. Suppose that rectangular block $\mathcal{R}$ is described by the set of points $\{<p_1, ..., p_D> \mid p_{1,low} \leq p_1 \leq p_{1,high}, ..., $ and $p_{D,low} \leq p_D \leq p_{D,high}\}$, while rectangular block $\mathcal{R}^{(j)}$ is described by the set of points $\{<q_1, ..., q_D> \mid q_{1,low} \leq q_1 \leq q_{1,high}, ..., $ and $q_{D,low} \leq q_D \leq q_{D,high}\}$. Define rectangular block $\mathcal{R}^*$ by the set of points $\{<r_1, ..., r_D> \mid q_{k,low} \leq r_k \leq q_{k,high}$ for $1 \leq k \neq \delta \leq D$ and $p_{d,low} \leq r_d \leq p_{d,high}\}$. That is, $\mathcal{R}^*$ is the extension of $\mathcal{R}^{(j)}$ into $\mathcal{R}$ with respect to dimension δ. We note that $\mathcal{R}^*$ is a rectangular sub-block of $\mathcal{R}$, and thus the number of tuples in $\mathcal{R}^*$ can be calculated as above. We then have that [newc$^{(j)}$ → count] = [c$^{(j)}$ → count] + number_of_tuples($\mathcal{R}^*$). Since $\mathcal{R}^*$ and $\mathcal{R}^{(j)}$ are disjoint, we also have that, for $d \neq \delta$, [newc$^{(j)}$ → count_difference][d] = [c$^{(j)}$ → count_difference][d] + number_of_tuples($\mathcal{R}^*_{d,high}$) − number_of_tuples($\mathcal{R}^*_{d,low}$). Thus, the only quantity left to calculate remains [newb$^{(j)}$ → count_difference][δ].

Case 1: $p_{d,high} - p_{d,low} \leq q_{d,high} - q_{d,low}$

Consulting Figure 5, we see that [newc$^{(j)}$ → count_difference][δ] = [c$^{(j)}_{\delta,high}$ → count] + [c$^{(j)}_{\delta,low}$ → count] $* \omega/\xi$ − [c$^{(j)}_{\delta,low}$ → count] $* (1 - \omega/\xi)$ − number_of_tuples($\mathcal{R}^*$), where

$$\omega = \frac{q_{\delta,low} + q_{\delta,high}}{2} - \frac{p_{\delta,low} + q_{\delta,high}}{2} \text{ and } \xi = \frac{q_{\delta,low} + q_{\delta,high}}{2} - q_{\delta,low}.$$

Given that $q_{\delta,low} = p_{\delta,high}$, we get that

$$\frac{\omega}{\xi} = \frac{p_{\delta,high} - p_{\delta,low}}{q_{\delta,high} - q_{\delta,low}}.$$

Case 2: $p_{\delta,high} - p_{\delta,low} > q_{\delta,high} - q_{\delta,low}$

In a similar fashion, we get that [newc$^{(j)}$ → count_difference][δ] = [c$^{(j)}$ → count] + number_of_tuples(R$^*_{\delta,high}$) $* (1 - \omega/\xi)$ − number_of_tuples(R$^*_{\delta,low}$) − number_of_tuples(R$^*_{\delta,high}$) $* \omega/\xi$, where

$$\omega = \frac{p_{\delta,low} + q_{\delta,high}}{2} - \frac{p_{\delta,low} + p_{\delta,high}}{2} \text{ and } \xi = p_{\delta,high} - \frac{p_{\delta,low} + p_{\delta,high}}{2}.$$

Given that $p_{\delta,high} = q_{\delta,low}$, we get that

$$\frac{\omega}{\xi} = \frac{q_{\delta,high} - q_{\delta,low}}{p_{\delta,high} - p_{\delta,low}}.$$

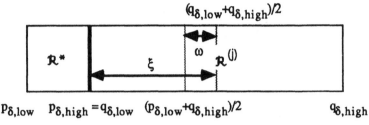

$$\frac{(q_{\delta,low}+q_{\delta,high})/2}{}$$

$$P_{\delta,low} \quad P_{\delta,high}=q_{\delta,low} \quad (P_{\delta,low}+q_{\delta,high})/2 \qquad q_{\delta,high}$$

Fig. 5 . Case 1 of Our Merge Example

4 Experiments

Our experiments concern the actual selectivity of a selection query. We build the tree incrementally using the approach of [7] for 100,000 tuples, each attribute being in the range [0,480]. For each 20,000 tuples inserted, we randomly generate 5,000 range queries and compute the mean difference between the estimated number of points satisfying the query and the actual number of points which satisfy it. We have calculated the Mean Query Bin Errors for uniformly and normally distributed data in 2, 3, and 5 dimensions. This is defined as MQBE = $[\Sigma(i = 1, ..., 5000)$ (|ActualQueryCount$_i$ − EstimateQueryCount$_i$ | / (5000 * ActualQueryCount$_i$). The 5,000 queries are represented by hyperrectangular regions whose dimensions are uniformly distributed in the range [1,480] and which are uniformly positioned in that part of the entire tuple space which results in the region being entirely contained within the tuple space. Figure 6 shows the Mean Query Bin Errors for uniformly and normally distributed data in 2 and 3 dimensions. The standard MQBE was calculated using the approach of [7], while the *enhanced MQBE* was calculated using our approach. The static scheme is the technique of [5] in which the uniform estimation scheme is used. (We note that the half-estimation scheme gave consistently worse results.) The static data structure was initially constructed after 10,000 tuples were inserted. The remainder of the tuples were then inserted into their appropriate bin by increasing the count field for that bin. We note that this static scheme didn't degrade over time, even under normal data distributions. However, we see that for these non-uniform distributions, especially in higher dimensions, our scheme is more accurate.

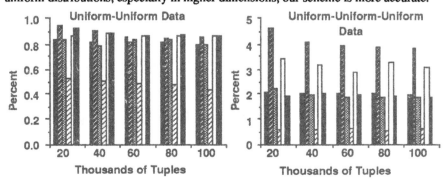

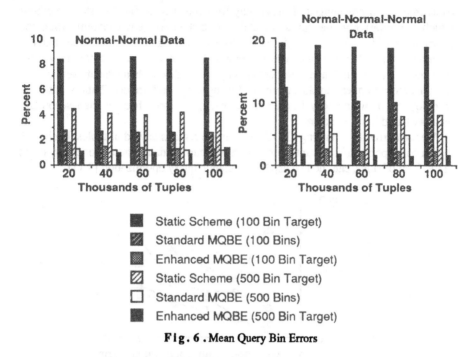

■ Static Scheme (100 Bin Target)

▨ Standard MQBE (100 Bins)

▨ Enhanced MQBE (100 Bin Target)

▨ Static Scheme (500 Bin Target)

☐ Standard MQBE (500 Bins)

■ Enhanced MQBE (500 Bin Target)

Fig. 6 . Mean Query Bin Errors

From these graphs, and other experiments we have done, the following intuitively plausible results hold:

1. For non-uniform data and in higher dimensions, as the number of target bins increases, the MQBE decreases.

2. The MQBE for our approach seems to be better for non-uniformly distributed data than for data which is uniformly distributed. Our approach has the ability to focus its attention on more dense data regions.

3. As the tuple space dimension increases, the MQBE increases.

4. For non-uniform data, our approach results in a smaller MQBE than the other approaches.

Figure 7 shows the number of splits and merges executed for the entire population of 100,000 tuples over various uniform and normal distributions. We see that the number of splits/merges ranges from 1 per 7 inserted tuples to 1 per 100 inserted tuples.

5 Conclusions

We have developed an adaptive selectivity estimation scheme for multidimensional queries which, experiments indicate, performs better than previously formulated non-adaptive methods when the distribution of the data is not known. Our approach uses a technique based on dynamic quantized spaces, a dynamic data structure developed for motion analysis in the field of computer vision. The objective of this research is to overcome the disadvantages of previously formulated non-adaptive, static methods which are relatively inaccurate in a dynamic database environment when the distribution of the data is not uniform. We have shown via many experiments that our approach is more flexible and more accurate in the computation of selectivity factors than both the equi-width and equi-depth histogram methods when the database is large and undergoes frequent update activity following a non-uniform distribution. Also, our technique is main-memory based and, as such, is more efficient than secondary memory based index structures.

We are currently extending SEDDS to manage regions devoid of tuples. Each such region corresponds to a semantic property of the current data. These properties, stated in the form of rules, can then be used for semantic query optimization [9,11].

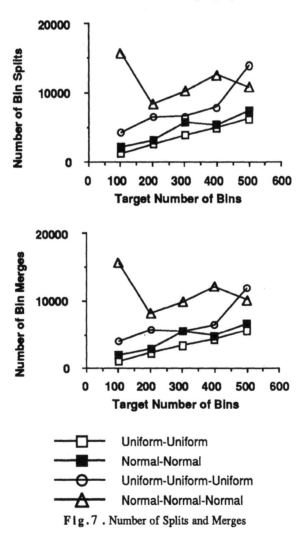

Fig.7 . Number of Splits and Merges

References

1. J.L. Bentley: Multidimensional Binary Search Trees in Database Applications. IEEE Transactions on Software Engineering SE-5, 333-340 (1979)
2. M.C. Chen, L. McNamee, and N. Matloff: Selectivity Estimation Using Homogeneity Measurement. Proceedings of the 6th International Conference on Data Engineering, Los Angeles, California, 304-310 (February 1990)
3. R.J. Lipton, J.F. Naughton, and D.A. Schneider: Practical Selectivity Estimation through Adaptive Sampling. Proceedings of the ACM–SIGMOD International Conference on Management of Data, Atlantic City, New Jersey, 1-11 (June 1990)
4. D.B. Lomet and B. Salzberg: A Robust Multi–Attribute Search Structure. Proceedings of the 5th International Conference on Data Engineering, Los Angeles, California, 296-304 (February 1989)
5. M. Muralikrishna and D.J. DeWitt: Equi–Depth Histograms for Estimating Selectivity Factors for Multi–Dimensional Queries. Proceedings of the ACM–SIGMOD International Conference on Management of Data, Chicago, Illinois, 28-36 (June 1988)
6. J. Nievergelt, H. Hinterberger, and K.C. Sevcik: The Grid File: An Adaptable Symmetric Multikey File Structure. ACM Transactions on Database Systems, 9, 38-71 (1984)
7. J. O'Rourke and K.R. Sloan, Jr.: Dynamic Quantization: Two Adaptive Data Structures for Multidimensional Spaces. IEEE Transactions on Pattern Analysis and Machine Intelligence, PAMI-6, 266-280 (1984)
8. S. Salza and M. Terranova: Evaluating the Size of Queries on Relational Databases with non–Uniform Distribution and Stochastic Dependence. Proceedings of the ACM–SIGMOD International Conference on the Management of Data, Portland, Oregon, 8-14 (June 1989)
9. S.T. Shenoy and Z.M. Ozsoyoglu: A System for Semantic Query Optimization. Proceedings of the ACM–SIGMOD International Conference on Management of Data, San Francisco, California, 181-195 (May 1987)
10. T. Sellis, N. Roussopoulos, and C. Faloutsos: R^+–Tree – A Dynamic Index for Multidimensional Objects. Proceedings of the 13th International Conference on Very Large Databases, Brighton, England, 507-518 (September 1987)
11. C.T. Yu and W. Sun: Automatic Knowledge Acquisition and Maintenance for Semantic Query Optimization. IEEE Transactions on Knowledge and Data Engineering, 1, 362-375 (1989)

Reducing Page Thrashing in Recursive Query Processing

Rakesh Agrawal and Jerry Kiernan

IBM Almaden Research Center
650 Harry Road, San Jose, CA 95120

Abstract. We introduce the problem of page thrashing in the semi-naive algorithm for computing recursive queries. We present techniques that take into consideration the system's paging behavior during query computation to reduce this page thrashing. We also propose a buffering strategy based on the Query Locality Set Model that reduces the total memory requirement of a recursive query. We present simulation results that demonstrate the effectiveness of our techniques, both in single and multi-user environments.

1 Introduction

Recursive query processing is the distinguishing feature of deductive database systems and several algorithms have been devised for evaluating recursive queries. The semi-naive algorithm [3] has emerged as the most widely used algorithm, and it has been implemented in almost all of the current deductive database system prototypes. The semi-naive algorithm computes a recursive query by successive iterations. Starting with a Δ table, initialized with the basis of recursion, a relational join is used in each iteration to compute a new Δ table from a Δ table computed in the previous iteration and from tuples in the base table. The computation terminates when no new tuple is generated in an iteration.

While recursive query processing has attracted large research interest, the system-level issues in the efficient implementation of recursive queries have not been adequately addressed. The future success of deductive databases hinges on addressing these issues and realizing their implementations in working systems. We review some of the system-oriented work in recursive query processing in Section 5.

In this paper, we introduce the problem of page thrashing in the semi-naive algorithm. We present techniques that take into consideration the system's paging behavior during query computation to reduce this page thrashing. In essence, we propose to delay composing some of the Δ tuples with the base table to maximize the use of in-memory base table pages. We present data structures for managing the delayed tuples. We also propose a buffering strategy based on the Query Locality Set Model [6] that reduces the total memory requirement of a recursive query. Simulation results demonstrate the effectiveness of our techniques, both in single and multi-user environments.

To keep the discussion concrete, we consider the Starburst implementation of the semi-naive algorithm. However, the problem we introduce and the solutions we propose are general, and are applicable to other implementations of the semi-naive algorithm. We discuss partial transitive closure computation expressed in the draft SQL3 standard as follows:

```
select * from
( select   src, dest  from Flights
  where   src='Paris' /*initialization subquery*/

  recursive union tc(src, dest)
  select   t.src, f.dest  from tc t, Flights f
  where   t.dest = f.src /*recursive subquery*/);
```

Flights is the base table and tc is the result table. This query finds all cities reachable from Paris by plane. The result of the initialization subquery is the basis of the recursion.

The remainder of the paper is organized as follows. In Section 2, we use the Starburst implementation of the semi-naive algorithm to illustrate the problem of page thrashing in the semi-naive algorithm. We also discuss how this problem is not specific to the Starburst implementation, but rather a general problem. In Section 3, we present the delayed semi-naive (DSN) algorithm and show how it reduces page thrashing. We also specify a buffering strategy for the DSN algorithm, based on the Query Locality Set Model. In Section 4, we present the results of simulation experiments that show the effectiveness of the DSN algorithm both in single-user and multi-user environments. We discuss related work in Section 5, and conclude with a summary in Section 6.

Unless indicated otherwise, we will use R to refer to the base table and tc to refer to the result table produced by the recursive query.

2   Standard Semi-Naive

To introduce the problem of page thrashing in the semi-naive algorithm, we briefly describe the Starburst implementation of the semi-naive algorithm. This implementation uses a data structure called *table queue* to store all intermediate Δ relations. A table queue [11] is an append-only table in which tuples are never updated in-place and new tuples are added at the end. A table queue is somewhat different from an ordinary table in that a table queue need not be fully instantiated before its contents can be accessed. A table queue can be scanned while tuples are being appended to it. It is possible that a cursor opened on a table queue gets a "temporary" end-of-file (EOF) response to a fetch, but then gets new tuples in response to future fetches if new tuples are added to the table queue after the return of EOF. A fetch of a cursor opened on an ordinary table does not return tuples added to the table after an EOF is returned. These features are of particular interest for recursive query processing because tuples corresponding to paths of length $i+1$ can be produced while tuples corresponding to paths of length i are being scanned.

The implementation of the semi-naive algorithm using table queues is shown in Figure 1. We will henceforth refer to it as the standard semi-naive (SSN) algorithm. Fields *src* and *dest* are the closure columns of the base table *R*. There is a B-tree index on the *src* column of *R*. The B-tree index stores distinct *(src, tid)* pairs. A *tid* encodes the page number of the corresponding tuple.

The table queue *tc* is initialized with the result of the initialization subquery. Recursive processing begins by opening a cursor over *tc* and obtaining the first tuple. Its *dest* field is used to access the B-tree index and the tids of matching tuples are extracted. The corresponding tuples are fetched from *R* using these tids. New tuples are appended to *tc* and sent to the next stage of query processing as well. If duplicate elimination is required, a temporary B-tree index is used over *tc* as a filter to detect and remove duplicates. This index is referenced before inserting a tuple into *tc* and sending it to the next stage of query processing.

```
procedure SSN (var tc: table queue, R: table);
  // tc is initialized with the resul of the initialization subquery
  // R is the base table having a B-tree index B on src
var
  P, Q : table;    C : cursor;    I : setOf tid;
begin
  let C = first tuple in tc;
  while C ≠ EOF do begin
    let I = iscan(B, C_dest);  let P = fetch(I);  let Q = π_{C_src, P_dest} | C_dest ⋈ P_src;
    append Q to tc;   let C = next tuple in tc;
  end
end
```

Fig. 1. The SSN algorithm

2.1 An Example

Consider the Flights table shown as a graph in Figure 2. The computation of cities reachable from Paris using the SSN algorithm is shown in Figure 3.

Table queue *tc* is initialized with the tuples in Flights having $src = Paris$. These are the first three tuples appearing in *tc*. Then the SSN procedure is applied. For each tuple in *tc*, tuples in Flights are scanned for matches between the *dest* value in the *tc* tuple and *src* value in Flights. Having found a match, a new tuple is composed using the *src* value in the *tc* tuple and the *dest* value in the Flights tuple. Thus, the first tuple in *tc*, namely *(Paris, Detroit)* is matched with the tuple *(Detroit, San Jose)* in Flights. The new tuple *(Paris, San Jose)* is produced and appended at the end of the table *tc*. This tuple is the fourth tuple in *tc*. The next two *tc* tuples are similarly processed. The process then continues with the next tuple in *tc*, which is *(Paris, San Jose)*. The cursor reaches the end of file marker in *tc* when all result tuples have been produced. The presence of a B-tree index on the *src* field of the Flights table allows a direct access to matching tuples in Flights.

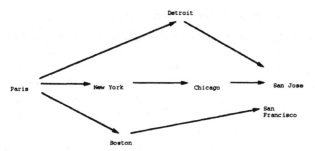

Fig. 2. The Flights graph

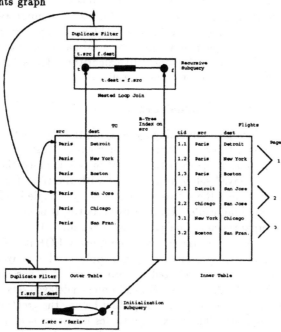

Fig. 3. Query evaluation using the SSN algorithm

2.2 The Problem of Page Thrashing

We illustrate the problem of page thrashing with a simple example. Let us reconsider the query given in the introduction, for finding cities reachable from Paris in the Flights table in Figure 2, and examine the paging behavior induced by this query. As shown in Figure 3, assume that the Flights table is stored on three pages: the first three tuples are stored on page 1, the next two on page 2, and the last two on page 3. Assume further that there is a single page available to buffer data pages of the Flights table. Then the minimum number of page faults incurred to buffer Flights in this operation would be three page faults. However, in this example, four page faults are incurred to buffer Flights while processing the query. Had we delayed processing the first tuple *(Paris, Detroit)* and processed it after processing the *(Paris, Boston)* tuple, the extra page fault would have been avoided.

2.3   Other Implementations of Semi-Naive

The semi-naive algorithm is generally thought of as consisting of distinct iterations. In iteration i, paths of length i are computed in a Δ_i relation, by composing paths of length $i - 1$ saved in Δ_{i-1} with the tuples in the base relation. From a cursory reading of Figure 1, it may appear that the SSN algorithm is different from the semi-naive algorithm. However, a little thought will convince the reader that the only difference is that the SSN algorithm is using one data structure, the table queue tc, to store all the Δ relations. Still, no tuple belonging to the Δ_i relation is generated before all the tuples belonging to the Δ_{i-1} relation have been generated. The use of table queues makes it easier to implement the semi-naive algorithm, but one could have also used a temporary table or a set of them for storing Δ relations. Thus, the problem of page thrashing is not limited to the Starburst implementation of the semi-naive algorithm; it is present in other implementations of the semi-naive algorithm. The solution we propose also applies to these implementations as well.

3   Reducing Page Thrashing

We propose to reduce page thrashing by delaying the composition of tuples that would match against tuples that are not in memory. Instead of performing a page fetch for an inner tuple in R that is not in the memory, the outer tc tuple is appended to a delayed set of tuples along with the tids of matching tuples. Hashing is used to select the set to which the delayed tuple is added. The page number of the matching tuple, obtained from its tid, is used as the hash value. We discuss the organization of delayed sets in Section 3.1.

The delayed sets are processed after a temporary EOF is reached on tc (i.e., when the cursor over tc produces no more tuples). The delayed set with the greatest number of tuples is selected for processing. It is possible to use other criteria for selecting the delayed set. For example, all delayed sets may be selected at this time. We may also select the delayed set having the greatest number of in-memory matching pages. The maximum tuples heuristic attempts to maximize the in-memory use of an R page. It is also likely contribute the greatest number of tuples to tc, that might match with in-memory R tuples.

New tuples produced by processing a delayed set are appended to tc. Processing then resumes by iterating over the new set of tuples in tc, producing new tuples by composing tc tuples with in-memory R tuples and delaying tc tuples that do not have matching R tuples in memory.

3.1   Management of Delayed Tuples

The intuitive model for delayed tuples is an array of sets of queued tuples along with matching tids. Each array element contains the set of delayed tuples that will match with tuples on the same page of R and stores the delayed tuples in the queue. We assume for ease of exposition that R tuples having an identical source value are stored on the same page.

Let D_n be the number of delayed sets. If D_n is less than the number of pages P_R in the base table R, then tc tuples matching with different pages of R will be mixed together in a delayed set. All the tuples in a delayed set that match with tuples on the same page of R are said to belong to the same group. If there is a large number of delayed sets, then there will be fewer groups of matching tuples per delayed set. The paging behavior over R will then be concentrated over few pages when a delayed set is processed. Conversely, if there is a small number of delayed sets, there will be more matching groups per set, and the paging behavior of R will be spread over more pages when a delayed set is processed. The disadvantage of having a large D_n is the wasted memory due to partially empty pages, the maximum number of partially empty pages being equal to D_n. The other disadvantage of having a large D_n is that the delayed set pages compete with the pages of R for memory.

The last page of each delayed set should be kept in memory since tuples are appended to the end of a set. Other pages of a set can be written out to disk if necessary. When the cursor iterates over these pages, they will be brought back into memory. If there is a single cursor iterating over tc, then a given page of a delayed set will be swapped to disk and fetched at most once. D_n is at most P_R and is at least one.

3.2 Delayed Semi-Naive

The algorithm that incorporates the above ideas is given in Figure 4. We refer to this algorithm as the DSN algorithm.

An Example

The evaluation presented in Figure 5 illustrates the optimization achieved by using the DSN algorithm. We again use the Flights table given in Figure 2. The table is assumed to be stored on three data pages as indicated on the right hand side of the Flights table. There is a B-tree index on the *src* field of Flights. Assume that we have a single memory page for caching tuples in the Flights table, and there are two delayed sets.

The initialization subquery sets the contents of tc to the three following tuples of Flights: {*(Paris, Detroit), (Paris, New York), (Paris, Boston)*}. The B-tree index is used to find the tids of the matching tuples, which in turn give the pages on which these tuples reside. Initially, no data page of the Flights table is in memory. Then, the initialization sub-query brings page 1 of the Flights table into memory.

The DSN procedure now attempts to match the first tuples in tc *(Paris, Detroit)* with a tuple in Flights using the B-tree index. Since the matching tuple in Flights *(Detroit, San Jose)* is on page 2 and this page is not in the memory, the tuple is delayed. This tuple along with the matching tids is copied to the delayed set that will match with tuples on page two. Similarly, the tuples *(Paris, New York)* and *(Paris, Boston)* are delayed. The first delayed set now contains one tuple and the second contains two tuples. At this point, no new result tuple has been produced and the temporary EOF marker has been reached in tc.

We now switch to processing a delayed set. The second delayed set is selected

```
procedure DSN (var tc: table queue, R: table);
  // tc is the result of the initialization subquery
  // R is the inner table having a B-tree index B on src
var
  P,Q : table;   D : setOf tables;   C,K : cursor;   I : setOf tids;

begin
  let C = first tuple in tc;
  while D ≠ ∅ or C ≠ EOF do begin
    while C ≠ EOF do begin
      let I = iscan(B,Cdest);
      if the page of R containing tuples
          corresponding to I is in memory then begin
        let P = fetch(I);   let Q = πCsrc,Pdest | Cdest ⋈ Psrc;   append Q to tc;
      end else begin
        let j = hash(page corresponding to I);
        append C,I to a delayed set Dj;
      end
      let C = next tuple in tc;
    end

    select the delayed set of tuples Di
        with the largest number of tuples;
    let K = first tuple in Di;
    while K ≠ EOF do begin
      let P = fetch(Ktids);   let Q = πKsrc,Pdest | Kdest ⋈ Psrc;
      append Q to tc;   let K = next tuple in Di;
    end
    free(Di);
  end
end
```

Fig. 4. The DSN algorithm

since it has the largest number of tuples. The first tuple *(Paris, New York)* in the delayed set causes page 3 of the Flights table to be brought into memory. This tuple is joined with the *(New York, Chicago)* tuple of Flights producing the tuple *(Paris, Chicago)*. Similarly, the tuple *(Paris, San Francisco)* is produced by matching the tuples *(Paris, Boston)* and *(Boston, San Francisco)*. Note that it is not necessary to access the index again since the tids of matching tuples are saved along with each delayed tuple. At this stage, the second delayed set has been processed, and it can be discarded.

Processing resumes over the tuple *(Paris, Chicago)* in tc. No in-memory tuple matches with this tuple and it is copied to the first delayed set of tuples. The next tuple in tc, *(Paris, San Francisco)*, does not match with any tuple in Flights. The first delayed set now contains the tuples *(Paris, Detroit)*, *(Paris, Chicago)* and EOF is reached in tc.

We now process the first delayed set. Page 2 of the Flights table is brought

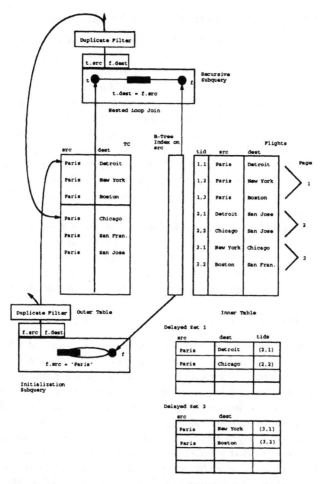

Fig. 5. Query evaluation using the DSN algorithm

into memory. Two tuples, namely *(Paris, San Jose)* and *(Paris, San Jose)* are produced as a result of processing this delayed set. The second duplicate tuple is eliminated by the duplicate elimination filter. Processing resumes in *tc*. Since the *(Paris, San Jose)* tuple in *tc* does not join with any tuple in Flights, EOF is reached in *tc*. All the delayed sets have also been processed. The algorithm terminates, causing a total of 3 page faults for the Flights table pages.

Note that in the standard semi-naive algorithm, there is a strict discipline in enlarging the result in one iteration, corresponding to breadth-first forward chaining. However, DSN is an opportunistic algorithm that uses memory residency to determine what tuples should be joined next.

3.3 Query Locality Set Model for the DSN Algorithm

The Query Locality Set Model (QLSM) [6] offers improvement over the LRU buffering strategy by considering "locality sets" for relational operations. QLSM can be used advantageously with the DSN algorithm.

The SSN algorithm has two locality sets: one for the outer tc table and the other for the inner base table R. The access to tc is sequential and requires a single buffer to read tuples. The cursor iterates over each tuple in a page. After all tuples in a page of tc have been processed, the page will not be referenced again and can therefore be swapped out. While the cursor is iterating over tc, tuples are appended at the end of tc. Thus, another buffer is required for tc to append tuples. If there is an index over the join column of the inner table R, the access to this table is random. The number of buffers for R should, therefore, be as large as possible.

In the DSN algorithm, additional buffers are needed for delayed sets. There should be at least one buffer for each delayed set. These buffers will be used when tuples are appended to the delayed sets. When we begin processing a delayed set, the buffer allocated for appending tuples to the delayed set can be used for reading tuples from that set since we will no longer append any tuple to it.

4 Experimental Verification

To assess the effectiveness of the DSN algorithm, we built a simulator for the SSN and DSN algorithms and performed several experiments in which we compute the successors of a given node. The simulator assumes a given number of available buffer pool pages. This number is varied in the experiments. At the start of each simulation, none of the data pages of the base table are assumed to be in memory. The simulator models the paging behavior of the result table tc, the base table R, and the delayed sets $D_1, \ldots, D_n$. For simplicity, the simulator does not model the paging of B-tree index pages. Both SSN and DSN access an equal number of index records, and the ordering of accesses to the B-tree induced by SSN has no particular advantage or disadvantage over DSN. We therefore expect the performance of the two algorithms to be comparable in this respect. The simulator also does not model the logging activity. The delayed sets are temporary data structures and the writing of delayed sets need not be logged.

4.1 Experimental Setup

We assume that a page is 4K bytes and that a tuple is 100 bytes and that 40 tuples fit on a page. There are four delayed sets, and the size of a tid is eight bytes. A delayed tuple also stores the tids of matching tuples and a trailing marker that is also eight bytes.

Data Sets

We considered both acyclic and cyclic data. We used trees to model acyclic data and cylinders [4] and random graphs to model cyclic data. Tuples in a dataset were clustered on the value of the source node. We assume no locality (such as topological ordering) in the data and the successors of a given node can be found on any data page with equal probability. No locality is achieved by generating nodes using random numbers and sorting the data in ascending source node value.

The outdegree of non-leaf nodes in the tree graphs is 2 and the depth is 12. The base table consisted of 8190 tuples.

Cylinders [4] are graphs such that the in-degree of nodes is equal to the outdegree of nodes. If the cylinder is acyclic, then root nodes and leaf nodes are the only exception to this rule. Cylinders have a fixed width, that is, the number of nodes at depth d and depth $d+1$ are equal. Cyclic cylinders are obtained from acyclic cylinders by creating arcs from leaf to root nodes. We synthesized cyclic cylinders having a depth of 682, a width of 6, and each node has two incoming and two outgoing arcs. The graph had 4092 nodes and a total of 8184 arcs.

Random graphs were generated using the procedure given in [1]. The graph generation procedure consisted of first determining for each node its out-degree, and then for each out-going arc from this node, its destination node. We ran experiment with graphs having 6500 nodes with the average outdegree of nodes being 4.

Buffering Policies

All the experimental results reported in this paper assume a buffering strategy based on QLSM for both SSN and DSN algorithms. We also carried out a set of experiments assuming LRU buffering for both SSN and DSN algorithms. In LRU buffering, there is a single buffer pool to store pages of the base table, the result table, and the delayed sets, and they all compete for buffer pages. Buffer pages were consumed until all available pages had been used. For replacing a page in memory, the buffer manager distinguished between clean and dirty pages. Dirty pages were result or delayed pages. Clean pages were pages in the base table or dirty pages that have previously been swapped to disk. Dirty pages had priority over clean pages for memory residency. A dirty page was swapped out by writing the memory copy to disk, whereas a clean page was swapped out by simply discarding the memory copy. Buffers used for a delayed set were freed back to the buffer pool once all tuples in that delayed set had been processed. We found in all cases, the QLSM implementations of SSN and DSN algorithms considerably outperformed their LRU counterparts, and we only present QLSM results.

As discussed in Section 3.3, the SSN algorithm has two locality sets: one for the outer tc table and the other for the inner base table R. We allocate two buffer pages for tc and the remaining buffers are used for pages of R. One additional buffer per delayed set is allocated in the DSN algorithm before allocating remaining pages to R. An LRU replacement policy is used to manage R and D locality sets. However, the replacement policy for tc takes into consideration whether the replacement is for a read or a write operation, and works as follows. If a *read* operation is requested, the "clean" page having the least usage recency is swapped out. If a *write* operation is requested, then the least recently used "dirty" page is swapped out. This policy was chosen to ensure that the "clean" page referenced by the cursor is not swapped out in favor of the last written page of tc.[1]

4.2 Single-User Experiments

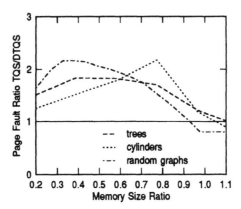

Fig. 6. Relative performance of SSN and DSN algorithms

Figure 6 compares the ratio of the total number of page faults with the SSN algorithm to the DSN algorithm for different memory sizes. The Y-axis is the ratio of the number of page faults observed with the TQS algorithm normalized with regards to the DTQS algorithm. The X-axis is the ratio of the size of the memory to the total size of R plus 2 pages required to buffer tc.

DSN outperforms SSN for the entire range of memory sizes until R completely fits in memory. For larger memories, the performance of DSN falls off slightly. This is because there is no paging of R, if R can fit in memory, and thus there is no advantage in delaying composition. Moreover, the disadvantage of delaying is that if a delayed set becomes large, it causes the delayed tuples to be written to disk and read back, degrading the relative performance of DSN. This drop in performance for large memory sizes can be avoided by modifying DSN to not delay tc tuples until all the buffers available to R have been used.

For small memory sizes, delaying helps but the delayed tuples compete with the base table pages for memory. Thus, on one hand, delaying improves the reuse of a base table page, but on the other hand, the number of base table pages that can be memory resident is reduced. The DSN algorithm performs best over the SSN algorithm for intermediate memory sizes.

---

[1] To see how this situation can arise, assume that no distinction is made between clean and dirty pages for page replacement and that LRU is used to manage buffer replacement within the locality set of tc. When processing tc tuples, one buffer is used for the cursor iterating over tc tuples, whereas the other buffer is used for appending result tuples to tc. When processing a delayed set, tuples are read from the delayed set, but appended to tc. This reduces the recency value of the page referenced by the cursor reading tuples from tc. If a new tc page needs to be written, the cursor's page will be swapped out instead of the last written page. When processing resumes over tc, the page referenced by the cursor has to be read back.

4.3 Page Size Experiments

In the next set of experiments, we studied the effect of page size on the relative performance of SSN and DSN algorithms. For each experiment, the available memory is set to 65% of the total number of pages needed to buffer R.

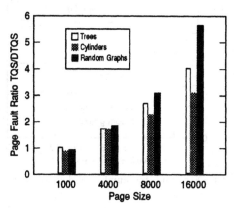

Fig. 7. Performance varying the page size

Figure 7 shows the relative performance of the SSN and DSN algorithms for different page sizes. For a fixed tuple size, varying the page size affects the number of tuples per page. When a page can hold a larger number of tuples, there is a greater probability that an in-memory page stores tuples that will match with tuples in tc or in a delayed set D_i (The maximum advantage that the DSN algorithm can have over the SSN algorithm is equal to the number of matching tuples per page). This effect results in a larger performance advantage of DSN over SSN. Inversely, the performance advantage is reduced for smaller page sizes. Note that the technology trend is toward larger page sizes.

4.4 Number of Delayed Sets Experiments

In the DSN algorithm, a page is reserved for each delayed set. The disadvantage of increasing the number of delayed sets is that it reduces the number of pages available for R. The advantage of having more delayed sets is clustering tuples according to pages of R. With more clusters, better locality can be achieved over R when delayed sets are processed.[2] We explored this trade-off in the next set of experiments.

Figure 8 shows the number of page faults for three types of graphs with memory sizes that were 30% and 65% of the number of pages required to buffer R. The figure shows that the trends for the number of page faults flatten out beyond 6 delayed sets. There, the increase in locality due to better clustering in

---

[2] Only tuples in tc are delayed. Tuples in a delayed set are matched with tuples in R in the order in which they appear in the delayed set. A possible optimization will be to sort the tuples of a delayed set according to the R pages with which they will join.

the delayed sets is balanced out by the reduction in memory available for the pages of R.

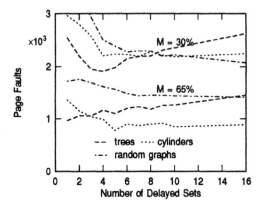

Fig. 8. Performance of DSN varying the number of delayed sets

4.5 Multi-User Experiments

Database systems are multi-user systems, and concurrent processes compete for pages in the buffer pool. A page brought into memory for use by one process can be swapped out by another process. The next set of experiments examined the effect of a multi-user environment on the performance of the DSN algorithm.

For these experiments, we assume that concurrent processes are computing the same recursive query over the same base table R, but each process maybe at a different stage in the computation. Pages of R are now shared. A page brought into memory by one process may be swapped out by another process, which in turn brings in a new page that might also be exploited by the former process. However, each process writes out its tc tuples and delayed tuples into private buffers. The greedy strategy for selecting a delayed set chooses the one having the greatest number of in-memory matching pages.

Concurrent processes affect what tuples are delayed. A tc tuple may have been added to a delayed set since the R page on which the joining tuple is found is not in the memory. This page is then brought into memory by a concurrent process. Thereafter, tc tuples joining with tuples on that page are no longer delayed. Conversely, a tc tuple may have found a matching R page in memory. This page is then swapped out by a concurrent process, and other tc tuples joining with this page will have to be delayed.

We simulated this environment assuming that a process cannot pin pages in memory for the entire query computation. While concurrent processes might be causing pages to be swapped in and out of memory, the performance accounting is done only from the point of view of one specific process, to be called the *current process*. Thus, the results show the impact concurrent processes have on the performance of the current one. The swapping activity of concurrent processes is modeled by inserting a random reference to a page of R by a concurrent process, following each reference to a page of R by the current process. This random reference may cause a page of R to be swapped out and a new page to be brought into the memory.

Figure 9 shows the performance results for trees, cylinders and random graphs. These results show that the performance advantage of DSN is even greater in a concurrent environment than in a single user environment.

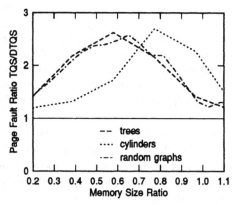

Fig. 9. Effect of a concurrent user

The SSN algorithm matches tc tuples in the order in which they appear, irrespective of the presence of the matching R tuples in the memory. The DSN algorithm, on the other hand, optimizes its usage of in-memory R pages by concentrating its activity on those pages that are in the memory. Thus, a process can take advantage of any pages brought into memory by other concurrent processes by concentrating its effort on those pages.

Concurrent Processes Executing Unrelated Queries

There may be concurrent processes that are executing queries over entirely different tables. Buffer management strategies proposed for relational database systems [12] suggest delaying the execution of the second query if the available memory is insufficient for it to run efficiently. Nevertheless, we expect the DSN algorithm to provide greater throughput than the SSN algorithm because it requires less memory to run efficiently. For example, from the results obtained for Figure 6 for trees, we find that the performance of DSN with a memory size of 200 pages (678 page faults) is roughly equal to that of SSN with a memory size of 280 pages (662 page faults).

5 Related Work

There have been several attempts to devise efficient algorithms for evaluating recursive queries (see [4] for a survey). Rewrite optimization techniques have also been developed that transform a given recursive query into a more efficiently computable form (see [13] for a discussion of several of these techniques). However, the system-level issues in the efficient implementation of recursive queries have not been adequately addressed.

The use of join indices was suggested in [14] for accelerating the join step in the evaluation of recursion, and the use of a hash-based join is proposed in [10]. A blocked nested loop join algorithm was found advantageous in [1]. The importance of efficient duplicate elimination in the evaluation of recursive queries was pointed out in [1]. This paper also addressed the issue of efficient movement of pages between disk and memory for transitive closure computation.

In [9], an access structure based on topological ordering has been proposed to enhance the performance of transitive closure queries over acyclic graphs. This organization has been extended to tolerate cyclic graphs and an index structure called *traversal index* has been proposed [2]. Locality arises from clustering nodes with their successors in such a way that data accesses become quasi-sequential. However, algorithms for updating the traversal index are fairly complex and expensive.

A technique for reducing page thrashing for non-recursive queries has been implemented in the DB2 DBMS [5]. Given an index on the join column of the inner table of a nested loop join, the algorithm works as follows. The index is accessed to obtain the tids of joining tuples in the inner table. Then, the page location of the corresponding tuples is determined. Tuples in the outer table and their matching tids are sorted in ascending page order of matching tids. Matching tuple in the inner table are fetched in ascending page order, therefore optimizing the number of tuples fetched per page.

A query behavior model for the relational operations, called the Hot Set Model, is proposed in [12]. It identifies the set of pages involved in a looping behavior as the *hot set*, and specifies that a query should be given a buffer large enough to hold the hot sets to run efficiently. This model is refined into a Query Locality Set Model (QLSM) in [6]. QLSM decomposes the reference pattern of a database operation into the composition of simple reference patterns, called locality sets. A different number of buffer pages may be associated with each locality set, and a different buffer management discipline can be selected for each set. The buffering strategy for the DSN algorithm is based on QLSM.

The HYBRIDTC algorithm [10] also attempts to optimize the usage of main memory when computing the transitive closure of a relation R. However, this algorithm differs from the DSN algorithm in the following respects. HYBRIDTC divides the base table R into n buckets. The assumption is that a bucket fits in the memory. An iteration in the HYBRIDTC algorithm resembles a depth-first search and consists in deriving all that can be derived with a single bucket. The DSN algorithm is essentially a breadth-first adaptive algorithm and has iterations in the same sense as the semi-naive algorithm. However, if tuples are delayed, the DSN algorithm will compute the result in more iterations than semi-naive. If a matching R tuple is not in the memory, the DSN algorithm delays the processing of the corresponding tc tuple, whereas the HYBRIDTC algorithm gets the tuple from the disk. If a matching R tuple is in the memory, the DSN algorithm appends the new tuple resulting from the join at the end of the table queue tc, whereas the HYBRIDTC algorithm immediately attempts to join the newly formed tuple with another tuple in R.

A conceptual framework for understanding fixed-point evaluation has been presented in [7]. Iterations induced by the standard description of the semi-naive algorithm are considered *systolic* in this framework. In systolic iterations, there is a strict discipline in enlarging the result in one iteration, corresponding to breadth-first forward chaining. However, iterations need not necessarily be systolic. In particular, iterations can be *pushy* in which a single iteration step computes more than prescribed by a systolic iteration. Examples of algorithms that use pushy iterations include the proposals in [10, 8]. Iterations can also be *sloppy* in which not all that should have been computed in an iteration step is in fact generated. No specific sloppy algorithm was proposed in [7]. The DSN algorithm proposed in this paper can be classified as an algorithm having sloppy iterations.

6 Summary

We introduced the problem of page thrashing in the semi-naive algorithm, and presented techniques for maximizing the in-memory usage of the base table and reducing page thrashing. The basic idea is to delay further composition of a generated result tuple if the matching base table tuple is not resident in memory. The resultant algorithm is an opportunistic algorithm that uses memory residency to determine what tuples should be joined next. We also proposed a buffering strategy for the algorithm, based on the Query Locality Set Model.

We presented simulation results that show the performance advantage of this algorithm using cyclic and acyclic graphs. The performance gain is greater when the available memory is large, but insufficient to hold the entire base table. Our techniques were found to be even more effective in a multi-user environment in which there are concurrent recursive queries over the same base table.

6.1 Future Work

Our experiments were focused on the paging behavior of the base table R, given that the memory size is insufficient to buffer R completely. A more elaborate set of experiments are required to also consider the paging behavior of the B-tree index over R, varying the number of buffer pages in its locality set. Throughout our experiments, we assumed that the locality set of the B-tree index is large enough to buffer it. Similarly, the size of the locality set for the B-tree index over tc, required for duplicate elimination, could also be varied.

Our experiments were limited to transitive closure queries with a single starting node. Further experiments might be conducted using multiple starting nodes, and computing full transitive closure. Comparisons might also be made with other algorithms that compute transitive closure and more general recursion.

We observe that the idea of delaying composition can be useful even for non-recursive joins. Further work is needed to confirm this conjecture and establish operating regions in which this technique can be effective.

Acknowledgements. We thank Shaul Dar, C. Mohan, Praveen Seshadri, and Jim Stamos for their comments on an earlier version of this paper.

References

1. Rakesh Agrawal, Shaul Dar, and H. V. Jagadish. Direct Transitive Closure Algorithms: Design and Performance Evaluation. *ACM Transactions on Database Systems*, 15(3):427–458, September 1990.

2. Rakesh Agrawal and Jerry Kiernan. An Access Structure for Generalized Transitive Closure Queries. In *Proc. 9th IEEE International Conference on Data Engineering*, Vienna, April 1993.

3. Francois Bancilhon. Naive Evaluation of Recursively Defined Relations. Technical Report DB-004-85, MCC, 1985.

4. Francois Bancilhon and Raghu Ramakrishnan. An Amateur's Introduction to Recursive Query Processing Strategies. In *Proc. ACM-SIGMOD International Conference on Management of Data*, pages 16–52, Washington, D.C., May 1986.

5. Josephine Cheng, Donald Haderle, Richard Hedges, Bala Iyer, Theodore Messinger, C. Mohan, and Yun Wang. An Efficient Hybrid Join Algorithm: a DB2 Prototype. In *Proc. 7th IEEE International Conference on Data Engineering*, Kobe, April 1991.

6. Hong-Tai Chou and David J. DeWitt. An Evaluation of Buffer Management Strategies for Relational Database Systems. In *Proc. 11th International Conference on Very Large Data Bases*, Stockholm, August 1985.

7. Ulrich Güntzer, Werner Kiessling, and Rudolf Bayer. On the Evaluation of Recursion in (Deductive) Database Systems by Efficient Differential Fixpoint Iteration. In *Proc. 3rd IEEE International Conference on Data Engineering*, pages 120–129, Los Angeles, February 1987.

8. Robert Kabler, Yannis E. Ioannidis, and Michael J. Carey. Performance Evaluation of Algorithms for Transitive Closure. *Information Systems*, 17(5):415–441, September 1992.

9. P.-A. Larson and V. Deshpande. A File Structure Supporting Traversal Recursion. In *Proc. ACM-SIGMOD International Conference on Management of Data*, pages 243–252, Portland, May-June 1989.

10. H. Lu. New Strategies for Computing the Transitive Closure of a Database Relation. In *Proc. 13th International Conference on Very Large Data Bases*, Brighton, September 1987.

11. John McPherson and Hamid Pirahesh. Table Queue Evaluation Strategy. Research Report, IBM Almaden Research Center, 1991.

12. Giovanni Maria Sacco and Mario Schkolnick. A Mechanism for Managing the Buffer Pool in a Relational Database System using the Hot Set Model. In *Proc. 8th International Conference on Very Large Data Bases*, pages 257–262, Mexico City, September 1982.

13. Jeffrey D. Ullman. *Principles of Database and Knowledge-Base Systems*, volume 2. Computer Science Press, 1989.

14. Patrick Valduriez and Haran Boral. Evaluation of Recursive Queries Using Join Indices. In *Proc. 1st International Conference on Expert Database Systems*, pages 197–208, Charleston, South Carolina, April 1986.

PANEL: Highways and Jukeboxes: A Revolution for Data Structures?

Witold Litwin (Chair)
University of Paris 6
visiting UCB & HP Labs

Isolated computers are becoming rare seldom. Most computers will interoperate with dozens or hundreds of others, through wire, or wireless, 100 Mbyte - Gigabit++/sec data highways. Broadcast capabilities will be a basic feature, especially on wireless nets. PCs will have hundreds of megabytes of RAM, often served by several CPUs, and new wonderful secondary and tertiary devices, like disk arrays and jukeboxes with robotic arms.

Does this environment generate new challenges for the foundations of data structures? For two decades, the main effort in this domain was geared towards a system that paired a small single-CPU RAM with a larger magnetic disk. This direction may seem by now explored, and over-explored to the point where any new paper in the area will be dull by definition. New challenges seem to involve issues like scalability over clusters of computers, large shared nothing RAM oriented structures, broadcast as a basic search primitive, graceful migration through a memory devices hierarchy, etc. New data structure schemes are needed, together with new tools for performance analysis. A number of new design constraints appear such as network bandwidth, network topology, reliability of new storage and transmission media, message cost per operation, storage/time to access cost ratio... These issues are clearly complex. One may argue however that the reward is data structures orders of magnitude larger and more powerful than ones we could imagine till now.

The panelists are known for their work in the domain of data organization, and are actively investigating the new area. They will present their views of the topic. The discussion, hopefully lively, and including the audience, should lead us to a better understanding of new research directions. We should also become more knowledgeable of the expected benefits, and of changes to the science of data structures that we used to know and teach.

Panelists

Tomasz Imielinski, Rutgers University
David Lomet, DEC Cambridge Research Lab
Marie-Ann Neimat, Hewlett-Packard Labs

The Sybase Replication Server Project

Yongdong Wang, Jane Chiao, Vasu Nori

Sybase Inc., 1650 65th St., Emeryville, CA 94608

Abstract. This paper describes the Sybase replication server, a log based database replication system that allows fine granularity data replication and continuously propagates update transactions from the primary copy of the data to the replicated copies. It uses a store and forward mechanism to provide fault tolerance in the propagation process. Its open system interface supports data replication among heterogeneous databases. An example was used to illustrate the role of the replication server in a data replication system.

1 Introduction

This paper describes the replication server project at Sybase. The replication server supports data replication in a distributed environment on a wide area network. It allows fine granularity data replication and continuously propagates update transactions from the primary copy of the data to the replicated copies. It uses a store and forward mechanism to provide fault tolerance in the propagation process. It also has an open system interface to support data replication among heterogeneous databases.

This work was motivated by the application requirements of data access in a networked distributed environment. In such an environment, the same data may be replicated at multiple sites for quick data access and for high data availability.

Since the late 70's, there has been a large number of publications on replicated data management [1, 3, 4, 6, 12, 14, 15]. Algorithms for maintaining replicated copies generally belong to two categories: tight (or strong) consistency and loose (or weak) consistency. The tight consistency algorithms guarantee that all available copies of a data object have the same value. While tight consistency is logically simple and works well for some applications, it increases transaction response time and may block updates when system failures occur.

In contrast, the Sybase replication server is based on the loose consistency approach. One copy of each data object is specified as the primary copy. Application transactions only update the primary copy of data. The updates are then propagated to other copies by the replication system. Although this approach does not guarantee tight consistency of all copies of the data, it provides an efficient way to maintain replicated data for applications that can tolerate loose consistency. Furthermore, when replicate copies are not available, applications can continue to update the primary copy of the data.

Several other commercially available systems support data replication [7]. DEC's VAX Data Distributor can periodically extract data from a primary database and either rebuild or update replicate databases. Although the replicate database is restricted to DEC's Rdb, the primary database can be Rdb, DB2, Oracle, or RMS or VSAM files [5]. AFIC's MSO uses a broadcast approach to replicate Sybase databases. It ensures tight consistency [2]. Oracle 7 supports real-time data replication using triggers, which ensures tight consistency. It also supports table snapshots which is similar to DEC's approach [11].

Compared to existing data replication systems that support loose consistency, the Sybase replication server is unique in several aspects:

- It supports continuous updates of replicate copies from the transaction log of the primary database. This idea is similar to the one used in remote backup systems [8, 9, 10, 13]. However, unlike those systems, the replication server supports row level granularity of replication.

- It supports replication of function executions.

- It maintains transaction semantics at the replicate sites. Transactions committed at the primary site are applied as transactions at the replicate sites in their original commit order. The data extraction and snapshot approach usually do not support this.

- It has an open system interface to support replication among heterogenous database systems. Users can also customize how transactions are applied at the replicate sites.

- It uses a store and forward approach to support recovery from system failures.

- It allows users to define logical routes to reduce message traffic on the network. If multiple replicate databases share the same route, only one copy of a message will be sent through the route.

The remainder of this paper is organized as follows. Section 2 describes the architecture of a data replication system using the replication server. Section 3 describes the important features of the replication server: fine granularity data replication, open system interface, and fault tolerance. Section 4 concludes the paper.

2 Replicated Data System Architecture

This section uses an example to illustrate the role of replication servers in a replicated data system. Figure 1 is a replicated data system with two replication servers RS1 and RS2. The two databases DB1 and DB2 contain primary data (maybe in addition to replicate data). They are called primary databases. The database DB3 contains only replicate data. It is called a replicate database. Each database is controlled by exactly one replication server. Updates to the primary copies are captured from the transaction log of a primary database by a log transfer manager (LTM). In Figure 1, DB1 and DB2 have log transfer managers LTM1 and LTM2 connected to them respectively. A log transfer manager reads the log records from the transaction log of a primary database, transforms them into replication server commands, and sends them to the replication server. The replication server determines which databases have replicate copies of the updated data and sends the update transactions to the replication servers controlling

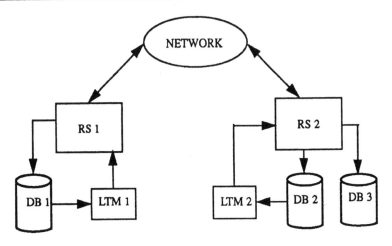

Figure 1. A Replicated Data System.

these databases. These update transactions are then applied to the databases to update the replicate copies of the data.

3 Replication Server Features

This section describes a subset of the important features that we have implemented in the replication server. These features distinguish the replication server from other data replication systems. While some individual features may have been explored in other systems, we believe the replication server is the first system that integrates all of them.

3.1 Fine Granularity Data Replication

The replication server allows data replication at the row level. A replicate site can request replicated data using a qualification similar to the *where* clause in an SQL select statement. Such a request is called a subscription. After a subscription request is processed by the replication server, the data is first downloaded and then all updates to the primary copy of the data meeting the qualification are propagated from the primary copy to the replicate copies. For large amount of data, users can also choose to copy the data to a replicate database manually and then inform the replication server that the initialization has been completed.

When an update to a primary copy is received by the replication server, it uses an efficient hash and range search algorithm to examine all subscriptions to determine which databases are interested in the update. It then groups log records into their original transactions and sends the transactions in their commit order to the replication servers controlling these databases. If one replicate database has several subscriptions that all include an updated row, only a single update command is sent to that replicate database. The replication server also allows users to define functions that can be replicated. When subsequent executions of these functions are received from the log transfer manager, the functions and their parameters are propagated instead of the end results of the function executions.

Row level subscription allows replicate sites to get only the updates that they are interested in. This reduces the network traffic and avoids unnecessary updates at the replicate sites.

3.2 Open System Interface

Almost all the other database replication systems we know of only work with proprietary databases (DEC's Data Distributor is an exception [5]). Although the replication server is being developed at Sybase, it has been designed independent of any data servers. In particular, it is not part of the Sybase SQL Server. It has an open system interface to database systems other than Sybase. The interface consists of two parts: one at the primary sites to accept the log records and another at the replicate sites to apply the replicated transactions.

At the primary site, the replication server has a documented, open interface language to accept update information. It is the responsibility of the log transfer manager to read the log records from the transaction log and transform them into the format understood by the replication server. The log transfer manager for any given primary database is system dependent because it must understand how to access the transaction log of the database or to use other means to capture the updates to the primary database. However, the replication server can communicate with log transfer managers for any databases so long as they support the commands expected by the replication server.

At the replicate site, the replication server provides a way for users to customize how a command should be applied to the replicate databases through either a language or a remote procedure call (RPC) interface. For heterogeneous databases, the users only need to provide a set of mappings that transform replication server commands to messages understood by the databases or gateways to the databases. We have successfully replicated data from a Sybase database to other relational databases and ISAM files.

The replication system architecture that makes the replication servers, the log transfer managers, and the data servers independent of each other gives it the flexibility to be interfaced to heterogeneous data servers. Instead of making the replication server work with a selected set of data servers, we provide an open system interface and the building blocks which can be used to achieve data replication among heterogeneous data servers.

3.3 Fault Tolerance

The replication server uses a store and forward mechanism to propagate messages from the primary database to other databases. Each log record from a primary database has a unique identifier. When a replication server sends a message to another replication server, the sender only deletes the message from its stable storage after the receiver has written the message into its stable storage. At the primary site, there is a protocol between the log transfer manager and the replication server. A log transfer manager will prevent the transaction log records from being truncated before they are sent and written into the stable storage of the replication server.

To prevent loss of updates due to single site media failure, the replication server provides a way for users to specify how long a message should remain in the stable storage of the sending replication server even after the receiving replication server has written the message into its stable storage. Of course, using mirrored disks for the stable storage of a replication server can further reduce the risk of losing data.

At the replicate site, there is a protocol between the replication server and databases. When a transaction from the replication server is committed, the unique identifier of the transactions's first command is recorded in the database. After a data server or replication server restart, the replication server queries the database for the last transaction committed. The replication server then starts applying transactions following the one committed. This will guarantee that the same transaction will never be applied more than once at a replicate site.

In the catastrophic event that the messages in a replication server's stable storage cannot be recovered from the sending sites after a media failure, the saved transaction logs of the primary databases can be replayed through the log transfer managers to the replication servers.

The replication server can be used to maintain a remote back up of a primary database. Due to the loose consistency nature of the replication server, such a back up system will be 1-safe [10].

4 Conclusion

This paper described the replication server project at Sybase. The replication server supports data replication in a distributed data system by providing fine granularity subscription, continuous and fault tolerant update of the replicate copies, and an open system interface for heterogeneous databases. It uses a log based approach and replicate transactions in their original commit order. We believe this project represents an important step towards providing practical solutions to data replication over a wide area network where maintaining tight consistency is too expensive and loose consistency is acceptable to applications.

Acknowledgments

We would like to thank Mark Deppe for his support and for reviewing this paper. The design and implementation of the replication server was achieved by the entire replication server project team at Sybase. The project also has several design partners who are Sybase users. We would also like to thank the anonymous referees for their comments that helped improve the presentation of this paper.

References

1. M.E. Adiba, B.G. Lindsay: Database Snapshots. Proceedings of 6th VLDB, 1980.

2. AFIC Computers: Multi Server Option For Sybase Systems. 1992.

3. P.A. Bernstein, N. Goodman: An Algorithm for Concurrency Control and Recovery in Replicated Distributed Databases. ACM Transactions on Database Systems 9, 4 (December 1984).

4. P.A. Bernstein, V. Hadzilacos, N. Goodman: Concurrency Control and Recovery in Database Systems. Addison-Wesley, 1987.

5. Digital Equipment Corporation: Software Product Description: VAX Data Distributor, V2.4. 1993.

6. A.R. Downing, I.B. Greenberg, J.M. Peha: OSCAR: A System for Weak-Consistency Replication. Proceedings of the Workshop on the Management of Replicated Data, 1990.

7. H. Edelstein: Replicating Data. DBMS, June 1993.

8. H. Garcia-Molina, et al: Two Epoch Algorithms for Disaster Recovery. Proceedings of 16th VLDB, 1990.

9. B. Goldring: Consistency Issues for Maintaining Copies from DBMS Transaction Logs. Seminar at University of Santa Clara, 1992.

10. J. Gray, A. Reuter: Transaction Processing: Concepts and Techniques. Morgan Kaufmann, 1993.

11. Oracle Systems: Oracle 7 Manuals. 1993.

12. C. Pu, A. Leff: Replica Control in Distributed Systems: An Asynchronous Approach. Proceedings of SIGMOD, 1991.

13. C.A. Polyzois, H. Garcia-Molina: Evaluation of Remote Backup Algorithms for Transaction Processing Systems. Proceedings of ACM SIGMOD Conference on Management of Data, 1992.

14. D. Skeen: Nonblocking Commit Protocols. Proceedings of ACM SIGMOD Conference on Management of Data, 1982.

15. Stonebraker: Concurrency Control and Consistency of Multiple Copies of Data in Distributed INGRES. IEEE Transactions on Software Engineering 5, 3 (May 1979).

Analogical Inferred Compensation Method for Heterogeneous Database Schema Mismatch and Its Application to Hypermedia Cooperative Work System

Shigeru Shimada, Toshihisa Aoshima and Tetsuzo Uehara

Central Research Laboratory, Hitachi, Ltd.
1-280 Higashi-koigakubo, Kokubunji-city, Tokyo, Japan

Abstract. Hypermedia Cooperative Work systems (HMCW) that simply use object-oriented databases have already been developed, but almost of them are not always regard to directly access stationary databases such as CD-ROMs and other conventional databases because of the need to convert to another media or to compensate for database schema mismatch. In order to solve these problems, we propose a new architecture with 3-level schema management to handle data in the heterogeneous database, and a dynamic schema mismatch compensation method based on an analogical inference mechanism. The effectiveness of this architecture and this method is established by using them in a practical hypermedia cooperative work environment: a patent information system.

1 Introduction

There is growing demand for a practical hypermedia cooperative work system (HMCW) to function as a cooperative data retrieval system between networks. Possible applications of HMCWs would be a patent information system in which users could append personal notes to the results of conditional retrievals of a patent database before distributing them, or a map/drawing information system in which residential maps and drawings are tagged for retrieval by related data.[1] Some practical HMCWs require direct access to patent data and residential maps stored on high-volume stationary databases such as CD-ROMs, and to patent reference and customer databases through a retrieval service in a heterogeneous database environment. From the user view point, HMCW requirements are summarized following three categories, and also problems and previous works are summarized on each category.

(1) Transparency of data location and media type

Generally HMCWs process various kinds of multimedia data, including text and graphics as well as vector codes for diagrams. These are defined as media "types" in this paper. And, the user should not have to know what type of media the data is in and where the exact location of media management facilities is; the processing should be transparent.

In order to realize this demand, there are many obstacles of data conversion. The processing involved in converting conventional media formats to object format is not simple. These obstacles are fundamental problems for realizing distributed databases. At present, by expanding relational databases, they have developed a method of dealing with distributed networks. Type transparency has also been addressed. Won, Kim, et. al., for example, have proposed a method by which OODBs can manipulate documents combining text and graphics.[2] And now, this demand also could be met satisfactorily using a standardizing distributed object management such as CORBA[3].

(2) Handling various retrieval formats

An easy-to-use system should support many diverse retrieval formats. But the retrieval formats depend heavily on the applications used, thus concrete analysis is difficult. Still, a single unified interface need a variety of View functions. It has been pointed out that the View functions in OODBs corresponding to varying viewpoints are generally weaker than those in relational databases.[4].

Although there are many approaches to conquer this weakness of view functions of OODBs, one of breakthroughs is compensation of database schema mismatch. W.Kent[5] points out that domain mismatch and schema mismatch problems must be resolved to manage media semantically under the heterogeneous database environment, but we treat multimedia which do not have clear properties, such as formal data which he treats in the object oriented database. On the other hand, to treat multimedia semantics, persistent multi-view function and analogical schema matching method[6][7] are proposed.
(3) Collaborative communication between users

Cooperative work support does not mean a mutual ability to use the media on each other's networks, but rather requires a communication mechanism for collaborating users to exchange ideas. Developing an asynchronous distributed cooperative work environment based on e-mail would be the first step in this direction.

Communicating ideas seems easy enough with a simple e-mail system, but the issue here is how workstations can easily exchange hypermedia, i.e. structured multimedia objects. Research is already under way into object lenses and other methods of sending structured objects.[8] However, is concerned with transmitting the contents of data objects in a common format along with additional local structured information, a field in which not enough work has yet been done.

In this paper, we focus on the second category of upper requirements and discusses how to manage media semantics and how to compensate schema mismatch under heterogeneous database environment for practical HMCWs.

2 Heterogeneous database environment for HMCW
2.1 A system model of HMCW

We propose a new system model of HMCW using a heterogeneous database illustrated in Fig.1. This system is composed that multimedia data is retrieved from lower DB servers and is displayed to upper client terminals. Especially DB servers are composed of stationary database servers such as CD-ROM server, text server and attribute RDB server. To aid development of HMCWs effectively, we have developed a media object management server, or MOM, capable of centralized management of data objects distributed in a system. The MOM is between the database server and the retrieval client, and uses a unified object model to manipulate and save into memory the semantic structure of multimedia data distributed among the database servers. Then next section presents a new architecture for MOM.

2.2 Three layer schema

Rather than converting everything to object format, as with conventional OODBs, our object-oriented system MOM is using a 3-layer schema architecture. This schema architecture is illustrated in Fig. 1 and explained below.
[Media schema]

This schema layer defines a one-to-one correspondence between the physical multimedia data and the software objects. Adopting the basic tools used by the CORBA distributed object management scheme, proposed by the Object Management Group (OMG)[3], permits multimedia data to be converted to object format and manipulated by an OODB. This layer solves obstacle(1) and mostly deals with persistent "entity objects".
[Semantic schema]

In order to handle multimedia data distributed among the layers as a single media

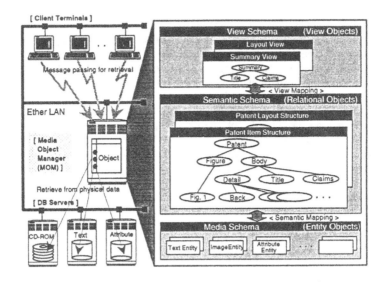

Fig. 1. Three layer schema in the heterogeneous database environment

object, like a map or patent, it is necessary to grasp the logical semantic links between object entities. Here, the logical semantic structure of, for example, the patent is often already provided along with the data itself by SMGL-format CD-ROM. Accordingly, this semantic schema can be considered as a schema structure that manages these static logical semantic structures. This layer solves obstacle(2) and primarily handles persistent "relational objects", which are statically linked to entity objects through semantic mapping.

[View schema]

This schema, unlike the static semantic schema, provides a logical semantic structure that permits the user to dynamically grasp multimedia data from an independent viewpoint. The objects handled here are view objects which use an analogical schema inference function to dynamically combine partial structures of semantic schema objects stored in static memory. The view schema composed of relational objects is dynamically linked according to domain through view mapping. And this layer will solve obstacles(2)(3) completely.

3 Schema mismatch compensation

3.1 A schema mismatch example and compensation

As already mentioned, we tried to construct a practical HMCW which directly treats static structured document data stored in stationary databases. The CD-ROM-format patent documents published by the Japan Patent Office have a structure which can be represented by a conventional book metaphor. For example as shown Fig. 2, the header of patent documents, {*Title, Number,Applied Date, Applicant, ...* } are laid out with specific text formatted with various fonts and sizes, and the body of the document {*Claims, Field of Invention, Prior Art, Composition of Embodiment, Drawings, ...* } is unified and classified by each item. Moreover, text areas and image areas are laid out on the same page. This structural information is embedded in the documents as tag information of the standard markup language (SGML)[10] form. Therefore, these static structured documents cannot provide a dynamic-structured document based on the various views from the applications that will be used as the communication unit of

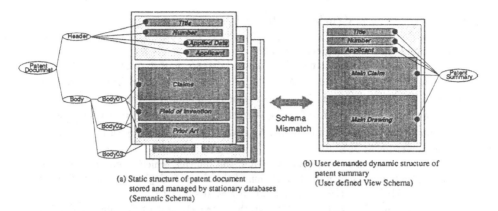

(a) Static structure of patent document
stored and managed by stationary databases
(Semantic Schema)

(b) User demanded dynamic structure of
patent summary
(User defined View Schema)

Fig. 2. A schema mismatch example in a patent information HMCW

HMCW. A patent information HMCW which manages a large number of patent documents does not use the full-specification items in the CD-ROMs but uses the partial items such as {*Title, Number, Applicant, Main Claim, Main Drawing*}, and it uses the summary as a communication unit, and this summary is newly laid out on one page.

In this study, we try to compensate dynamically this schema mismatch by using analogical inference as one of the view mapping functions of MOM.

3.2 Analogical inference mechanism
3.2.1 Object expression and formulation

In this paper, "object" is used as the general name for class objects and instance objects. Structure of objects describes the relationship between objects. Let us consider the expressive form that is used to process relationships easily between objects. List form is mainly the expression form which can be treated objects by a predicate logic programming language (such as prolog).

The list form of entity object E_i is as follows.

E_i = instance (SOIDi, InstanceName, ClassName, $Prop_{i1}$, $Prop_{i2}$, $Prop_{i3}$, ...).

where	InstanceName	: Character string given as entity name such as "Claims"
	SOID	: Semantic Object ID composed of object ID and surrogate
		object ID is 4 bytes of integer and surrogate indicate structure
	ClassName	: Character string given as class name
	$Prop_{ij}$ ...	: List of properties $Prop_{ij}$=(Property $Name_{ij}$, $Value_{ij}$)
		$Value_{ij}$ is 4 bytes integer.

On the other hand, the list form of relational object R_j is as follows.

R_j = Relation $Name_j$(SOIDj, Object Name1, [Object Name2], [$Prop_{j1}$,$Prop_{j2}$,$Prop_{j3}$, ...]).

where	Relation Name	: Character string given as relation name
		This relation name is one of {part_of, ako, is_a, func}
	Object Name1	: Character string given as first level class or instance name
	Object Name2	: Character string given as second level class or instance name
	[ ]	: Notation of possibility to be omitted

In order to simplify the formulation of analogical inference in the next section, we introduce the symbolic expression of object O_{ij} by using the above-defined list form expression, $O_{ij} = \{E_i, R_j\}$ (where i and j are not in order).

Normally, this object O_{ij} is assumed to be stored and managed in the semantic schema. Moreover, we define the symbolic expression of a rule which is formulated in the domain D_k, $\qquad$ $(O^k_{l1}, O^k_{l2}, \dots , O^k_{ln}) \rightarrow G^k_l$.

3.2.2 Formulation of analogical inference

The fundamental principle of analogical inference is that A_i $(1<i<n)$ is the fact formed in the domain D_1, and $(A_1, A_2, \dots , A_n) \rightarrow B$ is a rule formed in the domain D_1 regarding A_i. The following is the process of analogical inference. The unknown domain D_2 that attempts to acquire a rule from D_1 is determined. When A'_j $(1<j<m)$ is composed in the domain D_2, an analogy ϕ of A_i and A'_j is calculated. Unknown goal B' is acquired by rule conversion as $B\phi B'$ [12].

Then we expand the definition of rule and domain, which is given as *a priori* knowledge, into many sets in the formulation of the above analogical inference. The *l*-th rule is defined by $\qquad$ $(O^k_{l1}, O^k_{l2}, \dots , O^k_{ln}) \rightarrow G^k_l$; $(l = 1, \dots , L)$ under the domain D_k $(k=1,2, \dots ,K)$ which is one element of domain set D. This extension is caused by raising the accuracy of an inferred view object structure. These client requirements inferred from a single domain are not sufficiently precise because the client requirements depend on various applications. The reason is that a uniform analogical inference is made even if an analogy ϕ which is the supposition for analogical inference is extremely small.

In the above symbol definitions, the following are given as *a priori* knowledge. (1) A mapping rule, that is, object structures $\{O^k_{l1}, \dots , O^k_{ln}\}$ of semantic schema correspond with object processing method G^k_l using semantic schema in the domain set D. (2) Object structures $\{O'_1, \dots , O'_m\}$ of view schema in the new domain D'. Therefore, a new mapping rule which corresponds a view object to a object processing method G' will be determined by this analogical inference. This analogical inference procedure is composed of two processes, first process is that calculate similarity ϕ between two object structures, and second process is that infer new mapping rule on the view schema and compose new object processing method.

3.2.3 Calculation process of similarity

We explain the concrete process of calculating the similarity ϕ between the structure of an existing relational object $\{O^k_{l1}, \dots , O^k_{ln}\}$ which is the premise condition and the structure of unknown view object $\{O'_1, \dots , O'_m\}$. In this case, the similarity is calculated by changing a defined domain D_k, and determining the maximum similarity ϕ^k_M which has the local maximum value of each domain D_k.

(1) Similarity by distance among object properties

The values of properties given to objects are compared. The property of each object $\{O'_j\}$ which belongs to a view object is $\{Prop_{jp}\}$; $(j=1,m),(p=1,P)$ and the property of object $\{O^k_{li}\}$ which belongs to the domain D_k in the relational object stored in semantic schema is $Prop_{liq}$, $(l=1,L)$, $(i=1,n)$, $(q=1,Q)$. Therefore, similarity ϕ_p is given by the following formula, $\qquad$ $\phi_p = 1 / \Sigma(Prop_{jp} - Prop_{liq})^2$.

This ϕ_p becomes larger as the structure of both kinds of objects resemble each other.

(2) Similarity by distance among object structures

The structure distance among instances can be calculated by using the semantic object identifier SOID held in each instance [11]. The SOID of $\{O'_j\}$ which belongs to a view object is assumed to be $SOID_j$, and the SOID of $\{O^k_{li}\}$ which belongs to domain D_k

is assumed to be $SOID_{kfi}$, and the similarity ϕ_s is given by the following formula,

$$\phi_s = 1 \ / \ \Sigma(SOID_j - SOID_{kfi})^2.$$

For this ϕ_s, if the structure distance between both objects is small, this value increases.

Therefore, the similarity among final object structures is given by ϕ that is calculated from ϕ_p and ϕ_s of the two above-mentioned descriptions with weights w_1 and w_2 which control evaluation for similarity. $\phi = w_1\phi_p + w_2\phi_s$.

3.2.4 View schema composition

Based on the similarity ϕ between two object structures that is given by the above strategies, we explain the inference method which infers the conclusion part G' of the rule formed in the unknown domain D'. Initially, $\phi_M{}^k$ is assumed to be the maximum similarity which is calculated between the assumption part $(O^k{}_{l1}, ..., O^k{}_{ln})$ of the l-th rule in the domain D_k and the assumption part $(O'_1, ..., O'_m)$ of the rule formed in the unknown domain D'. The conclusion part G'_v of a rule formed in the unknown domain D' is obtained by the following inference process.

$$\frac{(O^k{}_{l1}, ..., O^k{}_{ln}) \to G^k{}_l < \text{rule conversion by } \phi_M{}^k >}{(O'_1, ..., O'_m), \quad \overline{(O'_1, ..., O'_m) \to G'_v} \quad < \text{inference by modus pones} >}{G'_v}$$

This series of inference process is performed on all domains D_k;(k=1, ..., K), the set of the conclusion part G'_v of each rule is obtained as $\{G'_v\}$. Finally, G' is obtained by using OR operator U_v, $\qquad G'=U_v\,G'_v$.

4 Evaluating the prototype applications

In this section, we evaluate a new architecture of the heterogeneous database system and a new schema mismatch compensation method based on analogical inference. Then we applied these new architecture and methods to the prototype patent information HMCW. Fig. 3 shows the display example of a user view which is retrieved patent information from heterogeneous database and modified as a compensated view adapting to user demanded schema structure. And moreover, this user view is able to be annotated by personal note information which is composed of icon and marker, and transferred to another users.

4.1 Evaluation of heterogeneous database architecture

To evaluate our proposed schema architecture, we will compare other architectures. The current research in schema architecture of object-oriented databases leads to the transfer of ANSI's three-level approach to an object-oriented approach for dynamic objects.[14][15] But this architecture requires explicit transformation of object structure and behavior, it is not always possible to transfer them under the heterogeneous environment. Our proposed schema architecture will be more natural for representing heterogeneous databases. However, dynamic view aspects are concealed in a schema mismatch compensation mechanism. To evaluate our proposed architecture more concretely, we explain the prototype that can retrieve patent information from CD-ROM servers with up to 100 CDs in which patent documents are stored on SGML format, and these documents can be transmitted to clients connected by TCP/IP via MOM. The prototype system can retrieve and display 10 pages of A4 sized documents in about 30 seconds. This time consists of the retrieval time of a CD by the CD-ROM server

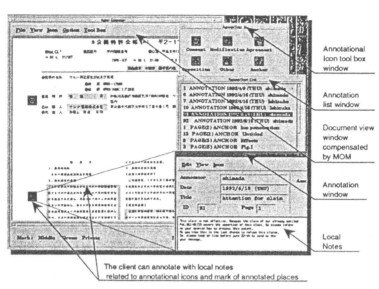

The window on the left of this figure shows a patent document retrieved and compensated by MOM. After marking the position of the problems, an annotation icon is selected from the tool box shown at the upper right, and a note is typed in the annotation window shown at the lower right. The window at center-right displays a complete list of the annotations added to this patent document.

Fig. 3. A display example of clients for patent information HMCW

(20 seconds), and the transmission time from the CD-ROM server to clients via MOM (10 seconds) which includes the media conversion time for displaying the X-window. This retrieval time was measured under an environment using a 76-MIPS UNIX workstation for the MOM, and 20-MIPS workstations for the clients. We feel that this response time of 30 seconds is not fast enough, but over 90% of this time consists of CD-ROM accessing and data transfer via TCP/IP. The contribution of MOM processing is under 10%. Therefore, we conclude that MOM processes the distributed media fast enough under this prototype environment. Also we expect that our proposed architecture will be evaluated more effectively if the speed of the CD-ROM driver and the data transmission rate become 10 times faster.

4.2 Evaluation of schema mismatch compensation

As already mentioned, in our proposed schema mismatch compensation method, the construction of relationships among objects is processed based on object properties. In particular, the sub process that gets the analogy between two objects resembles the process that makes uncertain relationships among instance objects which was formulated by K.Tanaka et. al.[9] as the fuzzy object base. However, with this fuzzy object base, it aims to retrieve an object itself based on fuzzy measurement. Our method aims to synthesize dynamically the new structured object using related objects by analogy.

On the other hand, the structure of patent documents which we use as the explanation examples are rather simple and most of the object properties are directly matched together among objects. Therefore in this situation, the method for getting an analogy is equivalent to the conventional method for sub-graph matching[13]. We have also used our proposed method on the problem of making a summary of residential maps[7]. In this case, the complexity of the object structure is 10 times greater than in the case of patent documents. Most of the properties do not directly match, but they relate to each other by a hierarchy of properties. Therefore, we confirm that our proposed method acts effectively to compensate schema mismatch in this complex object structure.

5 Conclusions

We have proposed a new semantic management method that allows an HMCW to use stationary databases under the heterogeneous environment. This method provides the following features:

(1) The management method has a three-level schema structure, consisting of a management schema at the standard distributed object management level, a semantic schema at the level of the actual media's fixed semantic structure, and a view schema at the level of the temporary semantic structure that matches the users' requirements. With this structure, it is easy to define and understand the semantic structure of stationary databases.

(2) An dynamic compensation mechanism for any schema mismatch between the schema required by the user and the static semantic schema of stationary databases is proposed by using analogical inference. This new mechanism broadens the range of user requirements to which the system can respond.

Also we developed an HMCW to demonstrate this MOM architecture: a patent information system that permits users to attach individual notes to the results of conditional data retrievals from high-volume patent document CD-ROMs. We used this to show how the MOM can be implemented.

In our future research, we will investigate the use of document data stored in SGML format or with very complicated structures. We will also attempt to strengthen the schema mismatch analogical inference function by increasing the amount of knowledge data provided in the form of templates.

References

[1] S. Shimada, K. Suzuki, Y. Yoshizawa and N. Chikada: "Object-Oriented Multimedia Annotation for Large-Scale Mapping System", Proc. Int. Symposium on Database Systems for Advanced Applications (DASFA'90), pp.315~319, (1991)

[2] D. Woelk, W. Kim, and W. Luther: "An Object-Oriented Approach to Multimedia Databases", ACM Trans. on Office Information Systems, vol. 4, No.1, pp. 311-325, (1986)

[3] OMG; "The Common Object Request Broker, Architecture and Specification": Draft 26 August 1991, (OMG Document No.91.8.1)

[4] K. Tanaka, N. Nishikawa, S. Hirayama and K. Nanba: "Query Pairs As Hyper-text Links, Proc. of the 7-th IEEE Data Engineering Conference, pp.456-463, Kobe Japan, April (1991)

[5] W. Kent: "Solving Domain Mismatch and Schema Mismatch Problems with an Object-Oriented Database Programming Language", Proc 17-th Int. Conf. on VLDB, pp147-160, Sept. (1991)

[6] D.A. Keim, K.C. Kim and V. Lum: "A Friendly and Intelligent Approach to Data Retrieval in a Multimedia DBMS", Proc. Int. Conf. on Database and Expert Systems Applications (DEXA'91), pp.102-111, Aug. (1991)

[7] S. Shimada and H. Matsushima: "Map Summarization using Analogical Matching of Schema", Proc. Int. Conf. on Database and Expert Systems Applications (DEXA'91), pp.339-344, Aug. (1991)

[8] K-Y. Lai, W. Malone and K-C. Yu: "Object Lense; A Spreadsheet for Cooperative Work", ACM Trans. on Office Information Systems, Vol. 6, No. 4, pp.332-353, (1988)

[9] K. Tanaka, S. Kobayashi and T. Sakanoue: "Uncertainty Management in Object Oriented Database Systems",Proc. Int.Conf.on Database and Expert Systems Applications(DEXA'91),pp.251-256,Aug. (1991)

[10] Eric van Herwijnen: "Practical SGML", Kluwer Academic Publishers, (1990)

[11] M. Toyoda, T Adachi and T. Ryu: "Semantic ID Method to Explain Complex Objects", Techical Report of IPS, Database System 91-4, pp.31-36, Nov. (1992), (in Japanese)

[12] Haraguchi, M.: "Analogical Reasoning Using Transformation of rules", Bull. Inform. Cybernetics, 22, pp. 1-8 (1986)

[13] Shi-kuo Chang: "Principles of Pictorial Information Systems Design",pp.146-171,Prentice Hall, (1989)

[14] G. Saake and R. Jungclaus: "Views and Formal Implementation in a Three-Level Schema Architecture for Dynamic Objects", Proc. 10th British National Conference on Databases, (BNCOD 10), pp.78-95, July (1992)

[15] M.A. Qutaishat, N. J. Fiddian and W.A. Gray: "Association Merging in a Schema Meta-Integration System for a Heterogeneous Object-Oriented Database Environment", Proc. 10 th British National Conference on Databases, (BNCOD 10), pp.9-226, July (1992)

A Survey of DBMS Research Issues in Supporting Very Large Tables

C. Mohan

Data Base Technology Institute, IBM Almaden Research Center
San Jose, CA 95120, USA
mohan@almaden.ibm.com

Abstract A number of interesting problems arise in supporting the efficient and flexible storage, maintenance and manipulation of large volumes of data (e.g., >100 gigabytes of data in a *single* table). Very large tables are becoming common. Typically, high availability is an important requirement for such data. The currently-popular relational DBMSs have been very slow in providing the needed support. To make it possible for RDBMSs to be deployed for managing many large enterprises' *operational* data and to support complex queries efficiently, these features are very crucial. We discuss some of the issues involved in improving the availability and efficient accessibility of partitioned tables via parallelism, fine-granularity locking, transient versioning and partition independence. We outline some solutions that have been proposed. These solutions relate to algorithms for index building, utilities for fuzzy backups, incremental recovery and reorganization, buffer management, transient versioning, concurrency control and record management.

1. Introduction

In this paper, we discuss some of the real-world problems which haven't received as much attention as they deserve from the data base research community. With the ever increasing levels of automation, process reengineering and the merger of large corporations (e.g., airlines, banks, etc.), the sizes of online data bases are increasing enormously. The requirements placed by such enterprises on their data base management systems (DBMSs) are testing the limits of those DBMSs. A significant number of the inadequately researched problems relate to supporting the efficient and flexible storage, maintenance and manipulation of large volumes of data (e.g., >100 gigabytes of data in a *single* table). While a classical DBMS like IMS Fast Path [GaKi85] exhibits some of these desired features, the currently-popular relational DBMSs have been very slow in providing such support. To make it possible for relational

---

™ DB2, DB2/2, DB2/6000, IBM and OS/2 are trademarks of International Business Machines Corp. NonStop SQL and Tandem are trademarks of Tandem Computers, Inc. DBC/1012 is a trademark of Teradata Corp.

DBMSs to be deployed for managing many large enterprises' *operational* data, these features are very crucial.

Even limits like at most 64GB of data can be stored in a *single* table are considered to be too severe and intolerable by some customers! Several DB2™ customers have many tables with millions of records in each table [IBM91]. The largest DB2 data base currently in production mode that we are aware of is the United Parcel Service's DIALS data base which contains 1.8 (about to reach 2.5) terabytes of package delivery data [Omer92, Youn93]! In [SFGM93], it has been mentioned that the four main SEQUOIA 2000 ES research groups collectively would like to store about 100 terabytes of data and that the EOS satellites would send 1 terabyte of data *each day* and all EOS data would have to be stored for 15 years (resulting in a 10 petabyte data base)! The current Teradata DBC/1012™ data base size limit is 8 terabytes [CaKo92].

As the popularity of DBMSs increases and the strategic value of protecting and using data is recognized by enterprises, more and more data residing in files is being moved under DBMSs, causing increases in data base sizes. RDBMSs became extremely popular primarily due to their ability to support ad hoc querying in a user-friendly manner. The latter has now enabled many new types of applications to become feasible without enormous expenses having to be incurred in programming the applications to retrieve the relevant data. Some of the applications which are driving up the demand for supporting very large tables are:

- Brokerage houses would like to maintain more and more of the past years' data on stock prices online to use in predicting future stock price changes based on the past data and information about some recent events which have a bearing on stock prices.

- Retail chains want to maintain online more and more of the current and past years' sales information to perform more long-term trend analyses and better forecasting of their inventory needs [CaKo92].

- Merger and globalization of many enterprises' operations (e.g., airlines, banks, credit bureaus, brokerage houses) cause even current data's (as opposed to historical data's) sizes to grow.

- Magazine publishers, mail order businesses and credit card companies want to keep online, for performing knowledge mining [AgIS93, CaKo92, FrPM91, KrIm91, Tsur90], vast quantities of data that they have accumulated about their customers' buying profiles.

- Globalization and increased popularity of package delivery services like UPS, Federal Express, etc., with their ability to quickly respond to queries about the status of deliveries, has caused a corresponding increase in the volume of data [Omer92, Youn93].

Supporting large tables does not involve just ensuring that the addressing scheme used in the DBMS is such that large tables could be created. For example, a 4-byte record identifier (RID) may allow only 64GB of data in a table. Just increasing the RID size to 6 or 8 bytes alone is not sufficient to *efficiently* support large tables. Many algorithms relating to the infrastructure of the DBMS would have to be replaced or enhanced to take into account properly the implications of managing very large tables. We discuss some of the issues involved in improving the availability and efficient accessibility of partitioned tables via parallelism, fine-granularity locking, transient versioning and partition independence. We outline some solutions that have been proposed, and in some cases, implemented. These solutions relate to algorithms for index building, utilities for fuzzy backups, recovery and reorganization, buffer management, transient versioning, concurrency control and record management. While system builders and some researchers have long recognized the value of and need for many of these features, the research community at large has not yet even begun to realize the degree of their importance [SiSU91].

2. Data Definition and Storage Management

In this section, we discuss problems relating to the data definition and storage management aspects of very large tables.

2.1. Partitioning of Tables

The bigger the table the more likely it is that accesses to the different parts of the table will be nonuniform. For this reason and also to make the large tables be manageable, it is important that the DBMS support the concept of *partitioning* a table. A partition consists of a subset of the records of a table. Typically, partitioning divides all the records of a table into disjoint subsets. Supporting partitioning would permit different partitions to be isolated from one another for performance, availability and other reasons. It would also allow I/O parallelism to be exploited easily and efficiently [PMCLS90], as has been done in DB2 V3 [Moha93a]. When partitioning is based on creation timestamps of records, a partition can also be the unit of *retiring* or migrating the data from online status (i.e., making the data go from online to offline status). For example, a user might want to keep online only data relating to the most recent 12 months. In this case, when a new month begins, the oldest month's data will be retired. Typically, partitioning will also allow different device types to be used for storing the different partitions. This way, the more frequently accessed data could be stored on faster devices and the less frequently accessed data could be stored on slower devices. This kind of support is provided by DB2 [CrHT90, HaJa84] and TPF [Scru87]. In DB2, a partition can be the unit of reorganization, backup (image copying), loading, unloading, starting/stopping of access, etc. Most other DBMSs which support partitioning of a table do so in the context of a *shared nothing* architecture: for example, Teradata DBC/1012 [CaKo92], NCR 3700 [WiCK93], NonStop SQL™ [Pong90], Gamma [DGSBH90] and Bubba [BACCD90].

2.1.1. Partitioning Specification

Different criteria could be used to specify how to partition the records of a table. The specification could be a declarative one based on key values or it could be a procedural one. In the case of the latter, a user exit (procedure) will be called when a record is inserted to determine the partition into which that record will be placed. With a procedural specification, *global* indexes (see below) would be needed to localize searches to only a subset of the partitions. In the case of declarative specifications, partitioning could be based on key ranges or hashing. DB2, NonStop SQL and Gamma support key ranges while DBC/1012, TPF and Gamma support hashing. With key range partitioning, if a range query involving the partitioning key were to be posed, then the DBMS could try to use the partitioning specification to limit the search to a *subset* of the partitions. With hashing, this would not be possible. Only for equality predicates, hashing would permit the DBMS to restrict the search to only one partition.

2.1.2. Indexing

For partitioned tables, an important design decision relates to how indexing is supported. The indexes can be local or global. With **local indexing**, all the keys in a particular index tree would relate to only the records stored in a given partition. Hence, for a particular indexing specification (e.g., index on C1 and C23), there will be as many index trees as there are partitions in the corresponding table. When a query involving a nonpartitioning indexed column is posed, the query must be broadcast to all the local indexes. Thus, local indexing does not allow the DBMS to restrict the search to only a subset of the partitions. When index entries contain record identifiers (RIDs) and a partition is reorganized, local indexing has the advantage that only that partition's index trees will be affected.

With **global indexing**, a single index tree is used and this tree will store the keys for all the records in all the partitions. When a query involving a nonpartitioning indexed column is posed, the query can make use of the global index and thereby allow the DBMS to possibly restrict the search to only a subset of the partitions. When a partition is reorganized, if the global index entries were to contain RIDs, then global indexing has the disadvantage that all the global index trees will be affected in widespread ways since the keys belonging to the reorganized partition can appear anywhere in those global indexes. Depending on the locking and logging approaches used for index data (see, e.g., [Moha90a, MoLe92]), global indexing could have many negative consequences.

DB2 stores the data records in a separate area and each index entry consists of a key value and the RID of the record containing that key value. DB2 does local indexing for the index on the partitioning key. For all other indexes, it does global indexing. DB2 does not permit the global index to be partitioned. DB2 requires that the partitioning key also be the clustering key. A more flexible approach would be to permit the latter to be different from the former.

NonStop SQL requires that all tables have a primary key and it stores all the data records of a table in a primary B^+-tree index. Each entry of this index consists of a primary key value and the corresponding record. Each entry of the other indexes (*secondary indexes*) on that table consists of a secondary key and the primary key of the record which contains that secondary key value. So the concept of a RID does not exist. Consequently, the primary index of a table can be reorganized independently without impacting the contents of the secondary indexes of that table. The restriction is that the primary key has to be unique and it cannot be updated. Furthermore, the records are clustered based on their primary key values and inter-table clustering is not possible. Both secondary and primary indexes can be partitioned based on key values.

In [ChMo93], we have presented a two-tier indexing method which supports local indexes and a *coarse* global index. This index method is suitable for transaction processing as well as for query processing. It not only is more efficient to maintain and use than the conventional methods, but it also exploits parallelism and is more versatile, scalable, and easier to migrate to for a nonpartitioning DBMS. The *coarse global index* contains one index entry for each key value present in a partition. Each global index entry consists of a key value and a partition number, where the partition number corresponds to the partition which contains that key value. There is only one such entry even if a particular partition has more than one record with the same key value. Of course, the same key value may be present in more than one partition. In that case, there will be as many global index entries with the same key value as there are partitions which contain records with that key value. Since the coarse global index does not contain RIDs, reorganization of a partition does not impact the contents of such a global index. To maintain the consistency between the local indexes and the coarse global index, efficient locking protocols are presented, which are designed to allow a high level of concurrent operation.

2.2. Storage Hierarchies

As the years go by, the number of levels in the storage hierarchy keep increasing. Traditionally, we have had main memory, magnetic disks and magnetic tapes. Now, we have page-addressable semiconductor memory like IBM's expanded storage, and volatile and nonvolatile cache memories in the disk controllers [CoKB89] and archival storage like optical disks and tapes. While main memory access times are of the order of nanoseconds, expanded storage requires tens of microseconds, magnetic disks require tens of milliseconds and optical drives take a few seconds. However big main memory might become, for the kinds of tables that we are considering, the size of main memory would not be big enough to hold all the data of a single table, let alone the whole data base! When we have very large tables, since much of the data in a table is likely to be accessed only very rarely, to minimize the cost of storage used for storing such data, we would like the DBMS to migrate data from the costlier media (e.g., magnetic disks) to cheaper media (e.g., optical/tape storage), and vice versa based on the access frequencies of the data [CaHL93, LoSa92, Ston91]. Many decisions have to be made in supporting such migrations. Some of the questions are:

- What criteria to use for migration from level to level and how to specify the criteria?

- What should the granularity of migration be?

  Traditionally, page is the unit of transfer between (volatile) main memory and (nonvolatile) magnetic storage.

  What is the appropriate unit for transfers between magnetic and archival stores?

- Should data be deleted from its original storage medium after it is migrated to another medium?

  If a page is brought into a main memory buffer pool, then it is made to continue to exist in magnetic storage also. This is necessary since main memory is volatile. We, probably, don't want to replicate data in magnetic and archival storage after it has been migrated from one medium to the other since both media are nonvolatile.

- Should the same index be used to index data stored on magnetic as well as archival storage [LoSa92, Ston87]?

- How should the query optimizer's cost formulas be modified to reflect the fact that an I/O to archival storage is much more expensive than an I/O to a direct access storage device like a magnetic disk?

2.3. Other Issues

The increased sizes of tables also make it more attractive to consider storing the data in a compressed form. There are several issues to consider here:

- What should the granularity of compression be? Should it be done at the page, record or field level?

- Which component of the system should do the compression/decompression? The disk controller or the DBMS? If it is the DBMS which does it, where in the DBMS should it be done? In the buffer manager or the record manager?

In order to improve the I/O bandwidth and to support parallel I/Os, the records of a single table need to be striped across multiple disks. Disk arrays can be used to accomplish this [PaGK88]. Many issues relating to their usage are still being studied [GrWa90].

Traditionally, RDBMSs have been quite primitive in their support for a table's schema's evolution (e.g., deleting a column, changing the definition of a column, etc.). Most changes to the schema of a table require unloading and reloading data. This would be very expensive for very large tables. Better methods for handling schema evolution have to be invented.

3. Data Manipulation

3.1. Buffer Management

The buffer manager of a DBMS needs to be carefully designed to deal with large tables, especially when the whole table cannot fit in memory. When a query requires a table scan or a complete range scan of an index defined on a very large table, unless the buffer manager has some sophisticated facilities, performance would be terrible. For attaining good response times and also to match processor and I/O speeds, especially when massive tables are being manipulated (e.g., via table scans), it is extremely important to use techniques like prefetching of data and multipage, asynchronous I/O operations, as is done in DB2 [TeGu84]. These techniques reduce I/O delays as well as CPU consumption relating to initiating I/Os and process switches.

Even when all the pages of an index do not have to be accessed, a *skip-sequential prefetching* technique [CHHIM91] can be used. While using this technique, we are more concerned with prefetching the *leaf* pages than the *nonleaf* pages since it is highly likely that the number of leaves examined will be significantly more than the number of nonleaves that are examined. The idea is to sort, if necessary, the list of keys to be looked up and then access the parents of leaf pages which contain those keys (using possibly a kind of "zig-zag" access described in [CHHIM91], but restricting the accesses at the lowest level of the tree to be at the parents of the leaf level) and identify the leaf pages which need to be accessed. Once we generate the list of *leaf* pages to be accessed, then we can initiate prefetches of those possibly logically discontiguous leaf pages. Note that there may be different ranges of logically *contiguous* leaf pages that need to read in from secondary storage. The skip-sequential prefetch technique would be better than a prefetch of all the pages of the index since it would avoid bringing into the buffer pool unwanted pages.

Accesses to data pages through unclustered indexes could also be converted into clustered accesses by postponing the accesses to the data until the qualifying record identifiers (RIDs) retrieved from the indexes are sorted [MHWC90]. By mapping different partitions of a table to different buffer pools, differential treatment with respect to memory residency can be provided to the different partitions' data. This is possible, for example, in DB2. For buffer replacement, sequentially prefetched data can be differentiated from randomly fetched data, as is done in DB2 [TeGu84]. This approach prevents a sequential scan from causing all the pages needed by random accessors (typically, OLTP transactions) to be replaced in the buffer pool. In DB2/2™ and DB2/6000™, when a page is being unpinned in the buffer pool, a weight (*love*, *unlove* or *hate*) is assigned to the page, based on the likelihood of the page being reaccessed, to achieve a similar effect.

Traditionally, decisions regarding prefetching of data or index pages are made by the query optimizer. In making such decisions, the optimizer considers only the data and/or index accesses needed to process a particular query. Unfortunately, this approach does not help those batch programs which use multiple SQL statements or repeated executions of the same SQL statements with different host variable values to post updates to a large number of records in some (e.g., clustering) key sequence. This classical processing is called *old master, new master* posting. To benefit from prefetching in such scenarios and also to avoid repeated traversals from the root to the leaves during index look-ups, DB2 V2R3 started caching some information about the most recent index and data page accesses. If possible, such cached information is made use of during future accesses of the same transaction. As a result, sequential or skip-sequential accesses are dynamically detected by the data manager and performance is optimized [HaSh92, IBM92].

3.2. Parallelism

To reduce the response time of ad hoc queries, especially when they access large tables, it is important to exploit parallelism [DeGr90, PMCLS90]. Parallelism would permit batch queries to be converted to interactive queries. Exploiting the power of multiple CPUs in a multisystem configuration can be done using the *shared disks* [DIRY89, MoNa91, MoNa92a, MoNa92b, MoNS91, Rahm91, Rahm93, ReSW89] or the *shared nothing* [BACCD90, CaKo92, DGSBH90, HSTMR91, MoSo90, WiCK93] architecture. In the shared nothing architecture, algorithms are needed for the online repartitioning of data in case the existing distribution is found to be inadequate. With large tables, such a repartitioning may be a very time-consuming operation. Hence, it is important to be able to support concurrently read and write accesses to the data being migrated.

Even if parallelism were to be exploited, complex queries involving very large tables may execute for a long time. It is possible that one or more systems might fail during that period. Under those conditions, it would very unfortunate if the queries that were in execution at the time of the failure(s) have to be aborted. A great deal of resource consumption that had taken place in many systems on behalf of such queries would go to waste. A concept like a *savepoint*, which is traditionally used (see [GMBLL81, MHLPS92]) while executing update transactions to support partial rollback capabilities, should be exploited to make such interrupted query executions restartable without losing most of the work already accomplished. This must be accomplished without penalizing query executions during normal (no-failure) circumstances, just as the traditional savepoints are very inexpensive. This would require extensions to the way files containing temporary tables are treated during restart recovery after a failure. Typically, during such a recovery, their descriptors are reset to indicate that those files do not contain anything useful. Since ad hoc query executions typically involve performing many sort operations, in this context, some of the ideas discussed in [MoNa92c] to make a long sort operation restartable are applicable.

Especially when the tables are very large, multiple query optimization becomes very attractive, if not absolutely necessary, to minimize the number of passes over the data. Credit card companies are interested in the simultaneous processing, during a single scan of information about their clients, of many SQL queries each of which is selecting customers who should receive promotional materials involving a particular product being offered for sale.

Parallelism is also very important for reducing the execution times of utilities to improve data availability, as we discuss in the section "4. Data Maintenance and Utilities".

3.3. More Powerful Operators

When the tables are very large, it is very likely that some users would be interested in extracting some information via random sampling of the data rather than by doing exhaustive search of all the data. The primary motivation for avoiding the latter would be to reduce the cost of performing the search. Some of the applications for sampling queries are financial auditing, quality control, marketing, epidemiology, and policy analysis of administrative data. The DBMS would have to be extended to support such search specifications and to implement them [OlRo89].

4. Data Maintenance and Utilities

4.1. High Availability

Increased reliance on DBMSs in critical day-to-day activities like billing, monitoring, call forwarding, CAD, CASE, etc. has increased the need for providing highly-available DBMS services. There is also increased competition in providing timely and wide-ranging services like credit reports on individuals from credit bureaus, credit verifications from point-of-sale (POS) terminals, etc. With the widespread adoption of relational DBMSs for various applications and the lure of online ad hoc query and report generation capabilities, there are increased user expectations with respect to response times. Planning in user organizations is also requiring more and more up-to-date operational data for implementing schemes like just-in-time (JIT) scheduling.

The consequences of the above trends are that (1) the cost of data unavailability is very high, and (2) more and more complicated and unanticipated queries are being posed. Some organizations, e.g., credit bureaus, are able to place more or less precise monetary values on the losses suffered by them when data is unavailable for a certain period of time based on the fact that they route requests for credit reports to a competing bureau during the time when their own data base is inaccessible. When automatic teller machines (ATMs) fail, this causes damage to the public relations image of the corresponding bank(s). Airlines, e.g., are trying to gain competitive advantages by making their frequent flyers' account information accessible readily via touch-tone telephones even during nonbusiness hours. Some of the stock exchanges are increasing their hours of operations thereby getting closer to round-the-clock stock sales.

4.1.1. Online Index Build

Higher availability cannot be equated just to the fact that the DBMS fails less frequently. Even when the DBMS does not fail, data availability may not be good if certain operations lock up vast quantities of data and make such data inaccessible to other operations. For example, in almost all the DBMSs, the creation of an index on a table causes at least an S lock to be obtained on the table, thereby preventing other transactions from modifying the table. Due to the unpredictability of ad hoc queries' data requirements, the need for building an index may arise anytime. When the index is being created for a large table, the index build may take many hours, and maybe even days, of processing and inability to update the table during that period may be unacceptable. It is for this reason that techniques like the ones described in [MoNa92c, SrCa91, Srin92] have been invented. Some of the problems involved in permitting an index build with concurrent updates are:

- Index and data may not be mutually consistent due to uncommitted updates being rolled back.

- Inconsistencies may be caused by race conditions between transactions' updates to data and a data scan by the index build utility.

Two algorithms, called NSF (*No Side-File*) and SF (*Side-File*), are presented in [MoNa92c]. They allow index builds concurrently with inserts and deletes of keys by transactions. NSF allows the index build utility, IB, to *tolerate* interference by transactions. That is, while IB is inserting keys into the index, transactions could be inserting and deleting keys from the same index tree. SF does not allow transactions to interfere with IB's insertion of keys into the index. In SF, the key inserts and deletes relating to the index still being constructed are maintained by the transactions in a *side-file* as long as IB is active. A side-file is an append-only (sequential) table in which the transactions insert tuples of the form <*operation, key*>, where *operation* is insert or delete. Transactions append entries without doing any locking of the appended entries.

IB does not do any locking of the data from which it extracts keys during its scan of the whole table. At the end, IB processes the side-file to bring the index up to date. [MoNa92c] also describes techniques for making the index-build operation restartable so that, in case a system failure were to interrupt the completion of the index-build operation, not all the work accomplished thus far is lost. In this context, algorithms are also presented for making a long sort operation restartable. They include algorithms for the sort and merge phases of sorting. The algorithms relating to sort have very general applicability, apart from their use in the current context of sorting keys for index creation.

4.1.2. Utilities

Traditionally, activities like creating indexes, loading data, reorganizing tables, etc. are performed during off-peak hours during what are called *batch windows*. Certain utility operations are executed only during certain times of the year (e.g, during some long holiday weekends). Even in DBMSs which are managing only small tables, problems like the above have become important since batch windows have begun to shrink due to the various trends that we discussed before. But, in a DBMS which manages large tables, even the durations of the traditional batch windows are not long enough to finish the above types of activities for very large tables within the time available [HaSh92]. Hence, other algorithms are needed which would permit utilities to do their jobs while the data is being subjected to normal read and write activities. It has been pointed out in [DeGr90] that loading, reorganizing or backing up a terabyte data base at a megabyte a second takes over 12 days and nights! Exploitation of parallelism to speed up some of the activities has become very important [Davi92]. DB2 V3 supports parallel processing of different partitions of a table by utilities.

When the currently-stored data in a table (or a partition) is being replaced with new data (i.e., a *load replace* operation), in order to speed up the process, instead of using the regular data manager record insert interface, some DBMSs produce directly page images with the new records in them and write them to disk. Since logging of the loaded data is being avoided, those DBMSs make copies of those pages as they are produced and write them to a backup file for use in case there is a need for media recovery after loading is completed. Since batch windows are shrinking, such techniques are necessary to guarantee reasonable completion times when large volumes of data are involved.

The above approach can also be used when more records are being added to the existing data in a table (i.e., a *load resume* operation) if it is acceptable to include the new records in pages which are appended to the end of the table's file. What this means is that any free space that currently exists in the file will not be made use of.

When a table (or a partition) is being reorganized in a batch fashion and that causes all its indexes to be reconstructed, then parallelism can be exploited during the sorting of the different indexes' keys and the subsequent building of the index trees.

4.1.3. Mixed Workloads

When ad hoc queries need to be executed with the isolation level of *repeatable read* (*degree 3 consistency* of System R [Gray78]), they could cause very undesirable interactions with short update transactions (the *bread and butter* applications) since the queries would hold S (share) locks on the accessed data for a very long time. Also, the query executions would be very expensive since fine-granularity locking may be used to provide high concurrency for the update transactions by minimizing conflicts amongst themselves. Since the queries access large volumes of data, fine-granularity locking would penalize them significantly by driving up their locking pathlength (CPU) costs very high. In the past, to avoid such interactions, two copies of a data base for which such a mix of workloads is likely to be executed were maintained: one main data base against which the short update transactions were executed and the other, an extracted version of the main data base, against which queries were issued with very little locking pathlength overhead. The latter copy was refreshed periodically from the former to bring it more up to date. The problems with this two-data-base approach are: it doubles the disk storage requirement and there would still be undesirable concurrency interferences when the refresh operation is performed. These problems make this approach infeasible, especially when the tables are very large. An alternative approach is the *transient versioning* of modified data so that the slightly older versions of the currently uncommitted or recently committed data can be read by queries without any locks having to be acquired [BoCa92, MoPL92, RaRe91]. This approach provides a transaction-consistent, albeit slightly out of date, view of the data.

If the complex query does not require a transaction consistent view of the data base and it is satisfied with the isolation level *cursor stability* (*degree 2 consistency* of System R), then a technique like *Commit_LSN* [Moha90b] can be used to drastically reduce the cost of locking for ad hoc queries. The Commit_LSN method is a much cheaper alternative to the traditionally-used locking approach for determining if a piece of data is in the committed state. The method takes advantage of the concept of a log sequence number (LSN) which is used in many systems. An LSN is recorded in each page of the data base to relate the state of the page to the log of update actions for that page [Gray78, MHLPS92]. The Commit_LSN method, which has been implemented in DB2 V3, uses information about the LSN of the first log record (call it *Commit_LSN*) of the *oldest* update transaction still executing in the system to infer that all the updates in pages with page_LSN *less than* Commit_LSN have been committed. Since we expect most of the data in a table, especially in the case of a large one, to be in the committed state at any given point in time, we would expect to find the above condition to be true for most of the pages in the table which the query accesses. Thus the Commit_LSN method significantly reduces locking overheads. In addition, the method may also increase the level of concurrency that could be supported. Many nontrivial applications of the Commit_LSN idea are described in [Moha90b], including its use in conjunction with index scans. It also allows certain predicate reevaluations which would otherwise become necessary [MHWC90] when multiple indexes are used for a single table access (*index AND/ORing*) to be avoided.

Of course, if a query does not mind reading uncommitted data, then it can be run with the isolation level *unlocked read* (*degree 1* consistency of System R). Even in this case, care is needed to ensure that the records returned to the user satisfy at least the local predicates involving that record's columns [Moha92].

4.1.4. Online Reorganization

Periodically, reorganizing the data of a table, index or a partition may be needed to

- Reestablish clustering property of data
- Reclaim unused space by better packing data
- Accommodate changed access requirements

One interesting problem for which completely satisfactory solutions are not yet available is: how to reorganize a table (or a partition of the table) while allowing concurrent read *and* update access to the data being reorganized by other transactions [SoIy93]? Some preliminary results are discussed in [SaDi92, Smit90]. Tandem's approach works only with tables which are stored in B^+-trees. Such a storage organization does not support inter-table clustering.

Another interesting problem is how to repartition a table without blocking concurrent updates to the table. Repartitioning may also involve splitting or merging some existing partitions. Release 2 of NonStop SQL provides support for splitting an existing partition into two partitions [Pong90]. During this operation, it permits only read access to the data in the partition being split.

Repartitioning may be needed to

- Accommodate changes in data access characteristics
- Deal with data access skew problems
- Improve data availability characteristics

DB2 V3 supports *partition independence* in that it permits different utilities to be operating against different partitions of a table concurrently. This allows parallelism to be exploited to reduce the time during which data is unavailable if, for example, multiple partitions have to be reorganized or restored from backups. It also permits SQL access to some partitions while other partitions are being operated on by utilities.

4.1.5. Failure Recovery

Some of the other problems which need to be tackled properly to provide high availability are:

• Fuzzy, *incremental* backup (image copying) of data with minimal pathlength and I/O overhead, and concurrency impact.

If a full backup of a table or a partition of a table is needed, then it would be much more efficient to do it by doing a device to device copy from the data base disk to the backup disk/tape than to do it through the DBMS and pay penalties like the following: buffer management overhead in terms of storage management, polluting the buffer pool with backed-up table's pages and possibly replacing more useful pages from the buffer pool, etc. An algorithm to do a device to device backup which can take advantage of device geometry is presented in [MHLPS92]. The algorithm is very unobtrusive since it does not lock any of the data being copied and it does not prevent the buffer manager from performing writes to the device from which copying is being done. Consequently, the data could be getting updated concurrently and the backup might have some uncommitted data. More efficient algorithms supporting incremental backups at the granularity of a page are proposed in [MoNa93]. With a large table, since only a small part of the table would be normally updated in the time period between the making of two backups of the table, it is important to be able to backup only the changed pages, rather than being required to always backup at the granularity of a table or a partition.

• Recovering damaged data at a fine-granularity, where the damage may be in the buffer pool version of the data due to a process failure or on disk due to a media problem.

Even if only a few pages of a table are damaged, many existing RDBMSs require restoring from a backup the whole data base or at least the whole table and then performing roll forward using the log. With very large tables, such a strategy is unacceptable from an availability and performance viewpoint. DB2 can recover even individual pages of a damaged table [Crus84]. This is possible since DB2 logs changes to all the pages of the data base. The way recovery is performed is pretty much like the way it is done during media recovery. In a system like System R which does not log, e.g., index changes, such a simple recovery is not possible. No efficient alternative to completely rebuilding the whole index currently exists for that system!

IMS Fast Path allows partitions to be replicated, thereby increasing data availability. Some other systems (e.g., NonStop SQL) support disk mirroring.

• Supporting deferred and selective restart so that a problem log record, data base page or some buggy code does not prevent restart recovery from completing, thereby delaying access to the rest of the data base. In a typical DBMS, if any actions of restart recovery cannot be completed due to some problem, then new transaction activity will not be allowed to begin until the problem is fixed.

DB2 allows restart recovery or normal transaction undo to proceed even if some device on which recovery needs to be performed is inaccessible [Crus84]. The table(s) on the device is placed in a *recovery pending* state and the range of log records to be applied is remembered. In the case of problems during the undo pass of recovery, DB2 is able to write *compensation log records* which describe the undo actions to be performed without actually performing those actions. DB2 also permits some phases of restart recovery to be skipped in case there are some problems which are unresolvable. The ARIES recovery method [MHLPS92, MoPi91, RoMo89] is capable of supporting deferred and selective restart. The details of the approach can be found in [MHLPS92].

• Allowing access by new transactions while restart recovery is in progress. This is an important problem since we are aware of some customers who very regularly produce many tapes worth of log records as a result of the execution of a *single transaction!* If a system failure were to occur when one such transaction is in execution, then restart recovery would take a long time and it may be unacceptable to prevent new transaction activity from beginning until restart recovery is completed.

A simple method which permits new transaction access even *during* restart recovery and which does not require any special hardware is described in [Moha93b].

• Minimize impact of system failures by providing hot standby support as in IMS/XRF [IBM87] and NonStop [Borr84].

• Efficient remote backup methods for providing recovery from disasters [GaPo90, Lyon90, MoTO93, Poly92].

4.2. High Performance

When large quantities of data are being manipulated using utilities, it is extremely important to assure good performance. For example, when additional data is being loaded into an already existing table, it should be possible to avoid having to log the insert activity. Those DBMSs which make utilities interact with the data manager component using the same interface that the SQL component uses may not be able to take advantage of the special properties associated with data manipulation via utilities. In contrast, DB2's utilities interact directly with the buffer manager, thereby improving performance. Even though logging may not be performed during the load, since a load operation may take a long time, it should still be possible to resume that load operation without too much loss of work in case system failure should interrupt the load operation. DB2's load utility supports these features.

To avoid repeated scans of large tables, it should be possible to gather statistics for query optimization purposes while loading the data. Even if the whole table is not being replaced with new data, but some additional data is being loaded into the table, it would be preferable to incrementally adjust the existing statistics to reflect the additional data, rather than having to recompute the statistics from scratch by accessing the old and the new data. By the same token, it should also be possible to take an backup copy of the data in a table as more data is being loaded into the table. Such a backup copy taken at the time of data loading (or soon after but before any updates are performed by transactions) would be necessary if no logging is being done of the records being loaded.

When a large number of records are loaded, it would not be very efficient to perform referential integrity checks [CEHH90] as each record is being inserted into the table since this would cause random accesses to the other tables involved in the constraints being checked. Also, there may be duplicate checks if, for example, multiple children of the same parent are being inserted. Hence, it would be preferable to perform the checks in a set-oriented manner by collecting all the relevant information from all the inserted records and postprocessing that information at the end of the load activity to eliminate duplicate checks. The checks may then be reordered to take advantage of clustered access to any indexes which might exist on the tables which have to be looked up [HaWa90]. If multiple referential constraints have to be checked, those checks could be done in parallel to reduce the total elapsed time for load.

5. Conclusions

In this paper, we discussed some of the problems relating to the management of very large tables. We believe that very large tables will become more common. Trends in the storage technology area make it economically feasible to have very large tables. But, for that to become a reality, DBMSs have to get ready by enhancing their infrastructure. There is ample scope here for many innovative solutions to be proposed. All aspects of data base management - e.g., query optimization, access methods, utilities, concurrency control, recovery - are affected by having to support very large tables efficiently and with high availability. Some of these areas (e.g., utilities) have traditionally not received as much attention as they deserve from the mainstream data base research community. Software developers who have had to deal with many of these problems in the context of DBMS products have very rarely published their solutions in the research literature. As a result, there has been a lack of awareness of the importance of understanding these problems and proposing good solutions for them.

Acknowledgements My thanks go to my colleagues in IBM Research and the IBM product divisions who have worked with me on many of the problems discussed in this paper. I would also like to thank Inderpal Narang for his comments on an earlier version of this paper.

6. References

AgIS93   Agrawal, R., Imielinski, T., Swami, A. *Mining Association Rules Between Set of Items in Large Databases*, **Proc. ACM SIGMOD International Conference on Management of Data**, Washington, D.C., May 1993.

BACCD90   Boral, H., Alexander, W., Clay, L., Copeland, G., Danforth, S., Franklin, M., Hart, B., Smith, M., Valduriez, P. *Prototyping Bubba, a Highly Parallel Database System*, **IEEE Transactions on Knowledge and Data Engineering**, Vol. 2, No. 1, March 1990.

BoCa92   Bober, P., Carey, M. *On Mixing Queries and Transactions Via Multiversion Locking*, **Proc. 8th International Conference on Data Engineering**, Tempe, February 1992.

Borr84   Borr, A. *Robustness to Crash in a Distributed Database: A Non Shared-Memory Multi-Processor Approach*, **Proc. 10th International Conference on Very Large Data Bases**, Singapore, August 1984.

CaHL93   Carey, M., Haas, L., Livny, M. *Tapes Hold Data, Too: Challenges of Tuples on Tertiary Store*, **Proc. ACM SIGMOD International Conference on Management of Data**, Washington, D.C., May 1993.

CaKo92   Carino, F., Kostamaa, P. *Exegesis of DBC/1012 and P-90 - Industrial Supercomputer Database Machines*, **Proc. 4th International PARLE Conference**, Paris, June 1992, Springer-Verlag.

CEHH90   Crus, R., Engles, R., Haderle, D., Herron, H. *Method for Referential Constraint Enforcement in a Database Management System*, **U.S. Patent 4,947,320**, IBM, August 1990.

CHHIM91   Cheng, J., Haderle, D., Hedges, R., Iyer, B., Messinger, T., Mohan, C., Wang, Y. *An Efficient Hybrid Join Algorithm: A DB2 Prototype*, **Proc. 7th International Conference on Data Engineering**, Kobe, April 1991. A longer version of this paper is available as **IBM Research Report RJ7884**, IBM Almaden Research Center, December 1990.

ChMo93   Choy, D., Mohan, C. *Locking Protocols for Two-Tier Indexing of Partitioned Data*, **IBM Research Report**, IBM Almaden Research Center, June 1993.

CoKB89   Cohen, E., King, G., Brady, J. *Storage Hierarchies*, **IBM Systems Journal**, Vol. 28, No. 1, 1989.

CrHT90   Crus, R., Haderle, D., Teng, J. *Method for Minimizing Locking and Reading in a Segmented Storage Space*, **U.S. Patent 4,961,134**, IBM, October 1990.

Crus84   Crus, R. *Data Recovery in IBM Database 2*, **IBM Systems Journal**, Vol. 23, No. 2, 1984.

Davi92   Davison, W. *Parallel Index Building in Informix OnLine 6.0*, **Proc. ACM SIGMOD International Conference on Management of Data**, San Diego, June 1992.

DeGr90   DeWitt, D., Gray, J. *Parallel Database Systems: The Future of Database Processing or a Passing Fad?*, **ACM SIGMOD Record**, Volume 19, Number 4, Decemeber 1990.

DGSBH90   DeWitt, D., Ghandeharizadeh, S., Schneider, D., Bricker, A., Hsiao, H.-I, Rasmussen, R. *The Gamma Database Machine Project*, **IEEE Transactions on Knowledge and Data Engineering**, Vol. 2, No. 1, March 1990.

DIRY89   Dias, D., Iyer, B., Robinson, J., Yu, P. *Integrated Concurrency-Coherency Controls for Multisystem Data Sharing*, IEEE Transactions on Software Engineering, Vol. 15, No. 4, April 1989.

FrPM91   Frawley, W., Piatetsky-Shapiro, G., Matheus, C. *Knowledge Discovery in Databases: An Overview*, In Knowledge Discovery in Databases, G. Piatetsky-Shapiro, W. Frawley (Eds.), The MIT Press, 1991.

GaKi85   Gawlick, D., Kinkade, D. *Varieties of Concurrency Control in IMS/VS Fast Path*, IEEE Database Engineering, Vol. 8, No. 2, June 1985.

GaPo90   Garcia-Molina, H., Polyzois, C. *Issues in Disaster Recovery*, Proc. IEEE Compcon Spring '90, March 1990.

GMBLL81 Gray, J., McJones, P., Blasgen, M., Lindsay, B., Lorie, R., Price, T., Putzolu, F., Traiger, I. *The Recovery Manager of the System R Database Manager*, ACM Computing Surveys, Vol. 13, No. 2, June 1981.

Gray78   Gray, J. *Notes on Data Base Operating Systems*, In Operating Systems - An Advanced Course, R. Bayer, R. Graham, and G. Seegmuller (Eds.), Lecture Notes in Computer Science, Volume 60, Springer-Verlag, 1978.

GrWa90   Gray, J., Walker, M. *Parity Striping of Disc Arrays: Low-Cost Reliable Storage with Acceptable Throughput*, Proc. 16th International Conference on Very Large Data Bases, Brisbane, August 1990.

HaJa84   Haderle, D., Jackson, R. *IBM Database 2 Overview*, IBM Systems Journal, Vol. 23, No. 2, 1984.

HaSh92   Hauser, D., Shibamiya, A. *Evolution of DB2 Performance*, InfoDB, Summer 1992.

HaWa90   Haderle, D., Watts, J. *Method for Enforcing Referential Constraints in a Database Management System*, U.S. Patent 4,933,848, IBM, June 1990.

HSTMR91 Hvasshovd, S., Saeter, T., Torbjornsen, O., Moe, P., Risnes, O. *A Continuously Available and Highly Scalable Transaction Server: Design Experience from the HypRa Project*, Proc. 4th International Workshop on High Performance Transaction Systems, Asilomar, September 1991.

IBM87   *IMS/VS Extended Recovery Facility (XRF): General Information*, Document Number GG24-3150, IBM, March 1987.

IBM91   *Database 2 - The Competitive Edge*, Document Number G520-6905-00, IBM, November 1991.

IBM92   *DB2 V2.3 Nondistributed Performance Topics*, Document Number GG24-3823, IBM, August 1992.

IyDi90   Iyer, B., Dias, D. *System Issues in Parallel Sorting for Database Systems*, Proc. 6th IEEE International Conference on Data Engineering, Los Angeles, February 1990.

KrIm91   Krishnamurthy, R., Imielinski, T. *Research Directions in Knowledge Discovery*, ACM SIGMOD Record, Volume 20, Number 3, September 1991.

LoSa89   Lomet, D., Salzberg, B. *Access Methods for Multiversion Data*, Proc. ACM SIGMOD International Conference on Management of Data, Portland, May 1989.

LoSa92   Lomet, D., Salzberg, B. *Rollback Databases*, Technical Report CRL 92/1, DEC Cambridge Research Laboratory, January 1992.

Lyon90   Lyon, J. *Tandem's Remote Data Facility*, Proc. IEEE Compcon Spring '90, March 1990.

MHLPS92 Mohan, C., Haderle, D., Lindsay, B., Pirahesh, H., Schwarz, P. *ARIES: A Transaction Recovery Method Supporting Fine-Granularity Locking and Partial Rollbacks Using Write-Ahead Logging*, **ACM Transactions on Database Systems**, Vol. 17, No. 1, March 1992. Also available as **IBM Research Report RJ6649**, IBM Almaden Research Center, January 1989; Revised November 1990.

MHWC90 Mohan, C., Haderle, D., Wang, Y., Cheng, J. *Single Table Access Using Multiple Indexes: Optimization, Execution, and Concurrency Control Techniques*, **Proc. International Conference on Extending Data Base Technology**, Venice, March 1990. An expanded version of this paper is available as **IBM Research Report RJ7341**, IBM Almaden Research Center, March 1990.

Moha90a Mohan, C. *ARIES/KVL: A Key-Value Locking Method for Concurrency Control of Multiaction Transactions Operating on B-Tree Indexes*, **Proc. 16th International Conference on Very Large Data Bases**, Brisbane, August 1990. A different version of this paper is available as **IBM Research Report RJ7008**, IBM Almaden Research Center, September 1989.

Moha90b Mohan, C. *Commit_LSN: A Novel and Simple Method for Reducing Locking and Latching in Transaction Processing Systems*, **Proc. 16th International Conference on Very Large Data Bases**, Brisbane, August 1990. Also available as **IBM Research Report RJ7344**, IBM Almaden Research Center, February 1990.

Moha92 Mohan, C. *Interactions Between Query Optimization and Concurrency Control*, **Proc. 2nd International Workshop on Research Issues on Data Engineering: Transaction and Query Processing**, Tempe, February 1992. Also available as **IBM Research Report RJ8681**, IBM Almaden Research Center, March 1992.

Moha93a Mohan, C. *IBM's Relational DBMS Products: Features and Technologies*, **Proc. ACM SIGMOD International Conference on Management of Data**, Washington, D.C., May 1993.

Moha93b Mohan, C. *A Cost-Effective Method for Providing Improved Data Availability During DBMS Restart Recovery After a Failure*, **Proc. 19th International Conference on Very Large Data Bases**, Dublin, August 1993. Also available as **IBM Research Report RJ8114**, IBM Almaden Research Center, May 1991.

MoLe92 Mohan, C., Levine, F. *ARIES/IM: An Efficient and High Concurrency Index Management Method Using Write-Ahead Logging*, **Proc. ACM SIGMOD International Conference on Management of Data**, San Diego, June 1992. A longer version of this paper is available as **IBM Research Report RJ6846**, IBM Almaden Research Center, August 1989; Revised June 1991.

MoNa91 Mohan, C., Narang, I. *Recovery and Coherency-Control Protocols for Fast Intersystem Page Transfer and Fine-Granularity Locking in a Shared Disks Transaction Environment*, **Proc. 17th International Conference on Very Large Data Bases**, Barcelona, September 1991. A longer version of this paper is available as **IBM Research Report RJ8017**, IBM Almaden Research Center, March 1991.

MoNa92a Mohan, C., Narang, I. *Efficient Locking and Caching of Data in the Multisystem Shared Disks Transaction Environment*, **Proc. International**

Conference on Extending Data Base Technology, Vienna, March 1992. Also available as IBM Research Report RJ8301, IBM Almaden Research Center, August 1991.

MoNa92b   Mohan, C., Narang, I. *Data Base Recovery in Shared Disks and Client-Server Architectures*, Proc. 12th International Conference on Distributed Computing Systems, Yokohama, June 1992. Also available as IBM Research Report RJ8685, IBM Almaden Research Center, March 1992.

MoNa92c   Mohan, C., Narang, I. *Algorithms for Creating Indexes for Very Large Tables Without Quiescing Updates*, Proc. ACM SIGMOD International Conference on Management of Data, San Diego, June 1992. A longer version of this paper is available as IBM Research Report RJ8016, IBM Almaden Research Center, March 1991.

MoNa93   Mohan, C., Narang, I. *An Efficient and Flexible Method for Archiving a Data Base*, Proc. ACM SIGMOD International Conference on Management of Data, Washington, D.C., May 1993.

MoNS91   Mohan, C., Narang, I., Silen, S. *Solutions to Hot Spot Problems in a Shared Disks Transaction Environment*, Proc. 4th International Workshop on High Performance Transaction Systems, Asilomar, September 1991. Also available as IBM Research Report RJ8281, IBM Almaden Research Center, August 1991.

MoPi91   Mohan, C., Pirahesh, H. *ARIES-RRH: Restricted Repeating of History in the ARIES Transaction Recovery Method*, Proc. 7th International Conference on Data Engineering, Kobe, April 1991. Also available as IBM Research Report RJ7342, IBM Almaden Research Center, February 1990.

MoPL92   Mohan, C., Pirahesh, H., Lorie, R. *Efficient and Flexible Methods for Transient Versioning of Records to Avoid Locking by Read-Only Transactions*, Proc. ACM SIGMOD International Conference on Management of Data, San Diego, June 1992. Also available as IBM Research Report RJ8683, IBM Almaden Research Center, March 1992.

MoSo90   Moore, M., Sodhi, A. *Parallelism in NonStop SQL Release 2*, Tandem Systems Review, Vol. 6, No. 2, October 1990.

MoTO93   Mohan, C., Treiber, K., Obermarck, R. *Algorithms for the Management of Remote Backup Data Bases for Disaster Recovery*, Proc. 9th International Conference on Data Engineering, Vienna, April 1993. Also available as IBM Research Report RJ7885, IBM Almaden Research Center, December 1990; Revised June 1991.

OlRo89   Olken, F., Rotem, D. *Random Sampling from B⁺-trees*, Proc. 15th International Conference on Very Large Data Bases, Amsterdam, August 1989.

Omer92   Omerza, R. *United Parcel Service DIALS Overview*, Proc. 4th Annual International DB2 User Group Conference, New York, May 1992.

PaGK88   Patterson, D., Gibson, G., Katz, R. *A Case for Redundant Arrays of Inexpensive Disks (RAID)*, Proc. ACM-SIGMOD International Conference on Management of Data, Chicago, May 1988.

PMCLS90   Pirahesh, H., Mohan, C., Cheng, J., Liu, T.S., Selinger, P. *Parallelism in Relational Data Base Systems: Architectural Issues and Design Approaches*, Proc. 2nd International Symposium on Databases in Parallel and Distributed Systems, Dublin, July 1990, IEEE Computer Society

Press. An expanded version of this paper is available as IBM **Research Report RJ7724**, IBM Almaden Research Center, October 1990.

Poly92   Polyzois, C. *Disaster Recovery for Transaction Processing Systems*, **PhD Thesis**, Princeton University, June 1992.

Pong90   Pong, M. *An Overview of NonStop SQL Release 2*, **Tandem Systems Review**, Vol. 6, No. 2, October 1990.

Rahm91   Rahm, E. *Recovery Concepts for Data Sharing Systems*, **Proc. 21st International Symposium on Fault-Tolerant Computing**, Montreal, June 1991.

Rahm93   Rahm, E. *Parallel Query Processing in Shared Disk Database Systems*, **Technical Report 1/93**, University of Kaiserslautern, March 1993.

RaRe91   Raghavan, A., Rengarajan, T.K. *Database Availability for Transaction Processing*, **Digital Technical Journal**, Vol. 3, No. 1, Winter 1991.

ReSW89   Rengarajan, T.K., Spiro, P., Wright, W. *High Availability Mechanisms of VAX DBMS Software*, **Digital Technical Journal**, No. 8, February 1989.

RoMo89   Rothermel, K., Mohan, C. *ARIES/NT: A Recovery Method Based on Write-Ahead Logging for Nested Transactions*, **Proc. 15th International Conference on Very Large Data Bases**, Amsterdam, August 1989. A longer version appears as **IBM Research Report RJ6650**, IBM Almaden Research Center, January 1989.

SaDi92   Salzberg, B., Dimock, A. *Principles of Transaction-Based On-Line Reorganization*, **Proc. 18th International Conference on Very Large Data Bases**, Vancouver, August 1992.

Scru87   Scrutchin, T. *TPF: Performance, Capacity, Availability*, **Proc. IEEE Compcon Spring '87**, San Francisco, February 1987.

SFGM93   Stonebraker, M., Frew, J., Gardels, K., Meredith, J. *The Sequoia 2000 Storage Benchmark*, **Proc. ACM SIGMOD International Conference on Management of Data**, Washington, D.C., May 1993.

SiSU91   Silberschatz, A., Stonebraker, M., Ullman, J. (Eds.) *Database Systems: Achievements and Opportunities*, **Communications of the ACM**, Volume 34, Number 10, October 1991.

Smit90   Smith, G. *Online Reorganization of Key-Sequenced Tables and Files*, **Tandem Systems Review**, Vol. 6, No. 2, October 1990.

SoIy93   Sockut, G., Iyer, B. *Reorganizing Databases Concurrently with Usage: A Survey*, **Technical Report TR 03.488**, IBM Santa Teresa Laboratory, June 1993.

SrCa91   Srinivasan, V., Carey, M. *On-Line Index Construction Algorithms*, **Proc. 4th International Workshop on High Performance Transaction Systems**, Asilomar, September 1991.

Srin92   Srinivasan, V. *On-Line Processing in Large-Scale Transaction Systems*, **PhD Thesis**, Technical Report 1071, University of Wisconsin at Madison.

Ston87   Stonebraker, M. *The Design of the POSTGRES Storage System*, **Proc. 13th International Conference on Very Large Data Bases**, Brighton, September 1987.

Ston90   Stonebraker, M. *Architecture of Future Data Base Systems*, **Data Engineering**, Volume 13, Number 4, Decemeber 1990.

Ston91   Stonebraker, M. *Managing Persistent Objects in a Multi-Level Store*, **Proc. ACM-SIGMOD International Conference on Management of Data**, Denver, May 1991.

TeGu84	Teng, J., Gumaer, R. *Managing IBM Database 2 Buffers to Maximize Performance*, IBM Systems Journal, Vol. 23, No. 2, 1984.
Tsur90	Tsur, S. *Data Dredging*, Data Engineering, Volume 13, Number 4, Decemeber 1990.
WiCK93	Witowski, A., Carino, F., Kostamma, P. *NCR 3700 - The Next Generation Industrial Database Computer*, Proc. 19th International Conference on Very Large Data Bases, Dublin, August 1993.
Youn93	Young, C. *A 1.4 Terabyte Database Faces Utilities*, Proc. 5th Annual IDUG North American Conference, Dallas, May 1993.

Partition-Based Clustering in Object Bases: From Theory to Practice

Carsten Gerlhof[1], Alfons Kemper[1], Christoph Kilger[2], Guido Moerkotte[2]

[1] Universität Passau, Lehrstuhl für Dialogorientierte Systeme,
Fakultät für Mathematik und Informatik, D-94030 Passau, Germany,
[gerlhof | kemper]@db.fmi.uni-passau.de
[2] Universität Karlsruhe, Fakultät für Informatik, D-76050 Karlsruhe, Germany,
[kilger | moer]@ira.uka.de

Abstract. We classify clustering algorithms into *sequence-based* techniques—which transform the object net into a linear sequence—and *partition-based* clustering algorithms. Tsangaris and Naughton [TN91, TN92] have shown that the partition-based techniques are superior. However, their work is based on a single partitioning algorithm, the Kernighan and Lin heuristics, which is not applicable to realistically large object bases because of its high running-time complexity. The contribution of this paper is two-fold: (1) we devise a new class of greedy object graph partitioning algorithms (GGP) whose running-time complexity is moderate while still yielding good quality results. (2) Our extensive quantitative analysis of all well-known partitioning algorithms indicates that no *one* algorithm performs superior for *all* object net characteristics. Therefore, we propose an *adaptable* clustering strategy according to a multi-dimensional grid: the dimensions correspond to particular characteristics of the object base—given by, e.g., number and size of objects, degree of object sharing—and the grid entries indicate the most suitable clustering algorithm for the particular configuration.

1 Introduction

Clustering of logically related objects on the same page is a very powerful optimization concept. Unlike other, more restricted models—e.g., the hierarchical model or the nested relational model—the object-oriented data models allow arbitrary object graphs. We distinguish between *sequence-based* and *partition-based* clustering. Under sequence-based clustering the object graph is transformed into a linear sequence of objects which is then sequentially assigned to pages. Under partition-based clustering the object graph is partitioned into object partitions that fit onto a single page. Tsangaris and Naughton [TN91, TN92] showed that the partition-based clustering is superior to sequence-based clustering. Unfortunately, the well-known partitioning algorithms—such as the Kernighan and Lin (KL) algorithm, which was the only one investigated in [TN91, TN92]—have a very high running-time complexity. This makes their application to realistically large object bases impossible.

Therefore, in this work we develop a new class of *greedy graph partitioning (GGP)* heuristics which have a moderate running-time complexity while still yielding good quality results. From the basic GGP heuristics we develop more sophisticated heuristics by incorporating a *look-ahead* with the possibility of rejecting less promising choices and a *new-chance* for those rejected choices at a later stage. Our extensive quantitative analysis—of which only a fraction could be covered in the paper—indicates that the quality of the (sophisticated) greedy partitioning is slightly inferior to the computationally complex algorithms, such as KL. However, the greedy heuristics are indispensable for two reasons:

1. They are extremely useful for pre-partitioning the cluster graph. These pre-partitions can then be improved using the computationally complex algorithms, e.g., KL.
2. For (realistically) large object bases the computationally complex algorithms cannot be employed because of their enormous running-time. In this case we can employ our greedy heuristic which is far better than the best known sequence-based algorithms—the *best-first* heuristics.

The above discussion leads to the conclusion that there is no *one* single cluster heuristics which is superior for *all* object base configurations. This motivates us to propose an *adaptable* cluster strategy according to a multi-dimensional grid: the dimensions correspond to particular characteristics of the object base—given by, e.g., number and size of objects, degree of object sharing—and the grid entries indicate the most suitable clustering algorithm for the particular configuration.

The rest of the paper is organized as follows. In Section 2 the cluster problem is defined and the related work is classified. Then, in Section 3 the well-known partitioning algorithms are reviewed and the basics of our greedy graph partitioning heuristics is introduced. In Section 4 two enhancements of the basic GGP heuristics are presented. Section 5 contains some of our extensive quantitative analysis of many different partition-based cluster heuristics. In Section 6 we derive the adaptable cluster strategy controlled by the multi-dimensional grid. Section 7 concludes the paper.

2 Clustering as a Graph Partitioning Problem

The clustering problem is closely related to the graph partitioning problem where some graph is to be partitioned into several disconnected subgraphs (partitions). The *object graph* (*OG*) is constructed considering objects as vertices and the inter-object references as directed edges [TN91]. Clustering algorithms partition the OG by assigning objects to equally sized pages. Instead of the OG clustering algorithms often use a more specific graph as input that is derived from the OG and/or from information about the applications' access behavior, e.g., access traces. We follow [TN91] and call this graph the *clustering graph* (*CG*). The vertices and edges of the CG are labeled with weights: vertex weights represent object sizes and edge weights represent the application's access behavior (higher weights denote that the start and terminal object of the edge are more often accessed in succession). For a given partitioning of the CG, the total weight of all edges crossing partition borders (i.e., page borders) are the *external costs* of this partitioning. The clustering problem is to find a partitioning of the CG such that the size of each partition, i.e., the total size of its objects, is less or equal the page size and the external costs are minimized.

There are two dimensions along which clustering algorithms can be classified: (1) the determination of the access patterns, i.e., edge weights, and (2) the algorithm that is applied to map objects into pages. Along the first dimension—the determination of the access patterns—*static* and *dynamic methods* can be distinguished. Along the second dimension we distinguish *sequence-based* from *partition-based* mapping algorithms.

2.1 Determination of the Access Patterns

Static methods are based on analyzing either the structure of the object base— e.g. static reference counts of objects[3] [Sta84]—or the access behavior of operations (that are part of the schema) [GKKM92a], or they require input from the database programmer, e.g., [Ben90, CDRS86]. *Dynamic methods* analyze the access trace of former database applications by monitoring the system [Sta84, HK89]. Usually, it is far more expensive to gather dynamic information on the access behavior of applications since this requires monitoring the applications. For a thorough discussion of the pros and cons of static versus dynamic access information see [GKKM92a]. In the remainder of this paper we assume the weights of the edges of the CG to be given—either by dynamic or static analysis.

2.2 Sequence-Based Mapping Algorithms

Sequence-based algorithms partition the CG by applying a graph traversal algorithm producing a linear sequence of all objects from the CG. This sequence of objects is then segmented—from left to right—into partitions. Sequence-based algorithms can be denoted in the style of a UNIX pipe consisting of the two steps *PreSort* and *Traversal*:

$$PreSort \mid Traversal$$

The *Traversal* component starts with some object and traverses all objects that are reachable from the start object and have not been visited before. After the current traversal is finished a new (unvisited) object is selected to start the next traversal. The *PreSort* method is used for sorting all objects, e.g. ordering by type [HZ87, Sta84, Ben90], ordering by decreasing dynamic reference counts[4] [HK89], and using some arbitrary ordering [Sta84, BKKG88]. The simplest *Traversal* algorithm maps objects into pages according to their position in the presort order [Sta84, HZ87]. Depth-first and breadth-first traversal algorithms for graphs were applied in [Sta84, BKKG88]. In Cactis [HK89] the

---

[3] The *static reference count* (SRC) of an object equals the number of references pointing to that object.

[4] The *dynamic reference count* (DRC) of an object equals the number of times the object is referenced by a sampling application.

usage of a best-first (BSTF) traversal algorithm is proposed. BSTF was the best *Traversal* algorithm in many comparison studys of clustering algorithms, e.g. [TN91, GKKM92a]. Therefore, in the remainder of this paper, we investigate only BSTF as the representative for sequence-based clustering.

2.3 Partition-Based Mapping Algorithms

Partition-based clustering algorithms segment the CG utilizing graph partitioning algorithms. In the literature graph partitioning algorithms for clustering were only considered in the work of Tsangaris and Naughton [TN91, TN92], where the algorithm by Kernighan and Lin (KL) was applied [KL70]. The clustering results obtained by the KL algorithm have been far superior to those obtained by sequence-based algorithms. Although the work of Tsangaris and Naughton lead the way to partition-based clustering their results were based on benchmarks run on a rather small object base where all objects were of uniform size. In practice there is a large diversity of object nets whose characteristics are essential for the performance and the cluster quality of partitioning algorithms: (1) The size of the object net which may range from a few hundred to hundreds of thousands of objects. (2) The size of the objects which may strongly vary. (3) The degree of sharing: there are tree-like object nets and others which exhibit a highly connected network strucure. It turns out that no one algorithm can be identified as superior in all (or even most of the) cases. Therefore, we investigate a wide range of partitioning algorithms for the clustering problem.

3 The Graph Partitioning Algorithms

According to [SM91] graph partitioning algorithms can be divided into two classes: *constructive partitioning* and *iterative improvement*. Constructive algorithms build a partitioning of a graph from the scratch; iterative algorithms start with some initial partitioning and repeatedly try to improve this partitioning. Iterative algorithms usually produce better results than constructive algorithms, but have a very large running-time compared to constructive algorithms. In the remainder of this section we sketch four graph partitioning algorithms known from the literature. Further, we describe the basics of our new greedy heuristics for graph partitioning—more sophisticated heuristics are developed in Section 4.

3.1 Iterative Algorithms

The Kernighan-Lin Heuristics. The Kernighan-Lin algorithm (KL) [KL70] was designed for the placement of VLSI chips—that is why KL is not well suited for clustering in object bases. The KL algorithm starts with an arbitrary partitioning of the CG and iterates over all pairs of partitions, trying to improve the partitioning by exchanging objects between the pair of partitions currently considered. Thus, the object sizes must not be strongly diverging for allowing objects to be swapped. While this may be true for VLSI applications, it is in general not true for object bases.

The Fiduccia-Mattheyses Heuristics. The graph partitioning algorithm by Fiduccia and Mattheyses (FM) [FM82] is derived from the KL algorithm. The main modification is that objects are *moved* across partition borders instead of being *swapped*. This modification allows for handling unbalanced partitions and non-uniform object sizes. On the other hand, swapping as employed in the KL heuristics, is advantageous in case of uniform size and nearly full pages—in this case no objects can be moved by the FM heuristics. Further, the FM heuristics is able to adapt the number of objects of the partitions, and even the number of partitions (if all objects are removed from some partition, the partition can be deleted). KL remains always stuck with the number of objects per partition and the number of partitions that was initially chosen.

Hierarchical Partitioning. The hierarchical partitioning algorithm (HP) is a combination of the KL and FM algorithms. The HP algorithm works as follows: All objects are assigned to one partition whose size is $P = 2^x * PageSize$ where x is chosen to be the smallest integer such that the total size of all objects is less than or equal to P. This partition is split such that the objects are distributed equally (by size) among both partitions. The resulting partitions are improved using the KL or the FM heuristics. This method is recursively applied until the size of every partition is below the page size. The idea that lead to the HP algorithm was taken from the work of Breuer [Bre77].

3.2 Constructive Algorithms

Optimum Partitioning of Trees. Lukes [Luk74] presents a pseudopolynominal-time algorithm for computing an optimum partitioning for the vertices of a tree, based on dynamic programming. The complexity of the algorithm is $O(n * B_{max}^2)$ where n is the number of vertices of the tree and B_{max} is the maximum number of objects per page.

The Greedy Graph Partitioning Heuristics. Because of the very good clustering results but poor running-time performance of known partition-based clustering algorithms, we have developed a new heuristics for graph partitioning, called *Greedy Graph Partitioning (GGP)*. The GGP algorithm was first proposed in [GKKM92a]. Graph partitioning is strongly related to subset optimization problems for which greedy algorithms often find good solutions very efficiently. The GGP algorithm is based on a simple greedy heuristics that was derived from Kruskal's algorithm for computing the minimum weight spanning tree of a graph [Kru56]. First, all partitions are inhabited by a single object only, and all partitions are inserted into the list *PartList*. For all objects o_1, o_2 connected by some edge in the CG with weight w_{o_1,o_2} a tuple (o_1, o_2, w_{o_1,o_2}) is inserted into the list *EdgeList*. All tuples of *EdgeList* are visited in the order of descending weights. Let (o_1, o_2, w_{o_1,o_2}) be the current tuple. Let P_1, P_2 be the partitions to which the objects o_1 and o_2 are assigned. If $P_1 \neq P_2$ and if the total size of all objects assigned to P_1 and P_2 is less than the page size the two partitions are joined.[5] Otherwise, the edge is merely discarded—and the partitions remain invariant. If e denotes the number of edges of the CG the running-time complexity of the GGP algorithm is $O(e \log e)$—the dominating factor is here the sorting of the list *EdgeList*.

4 New Heuristics for Greedy Graph Partitioning

In [GKKM92a] we have extensively benchmarked the GGP heuristics on various forms of CG's comparing it to several clustering strategies for object-oriented database systems. The performance of GGP indicated the best cost effectiveness in terms of running-time and clustering quality. In this section we present two heuristics that further improve the results of GGP:

1. *bounded look-ahead:* Before the partitions incident to the current edge, i.e., the edge with maximum weight, are being joined, a BSTF traversal is performed locally in order to look for better candidate partitions to be joined.
2. *new-chance:* If the bounded look-ahead heuristics finds potentially better candidate partitions the current edge is rejected. Rejected edges need be re-considered (triggered) if the condition that lead to the rejection changes.

We identify the enhanced GGP algorithm by GGPla (*GGP with look-ahead*). Subsequently, both improvements are discussed in more detail. The complete description of the algorithm GGPla can be found in [GKKM92b].

4.1 k-Look-Ahead

During each iteration the GGP algorithm takes the edge with maximum weight from the *EdgeList* and tries to join the partitions of the objects incident to that edge. Of course, this is not necessarily the best decision. Consider the example shown in Fig. 1. The CG is visualized in Fig. 1 (a); the maximum external costs are $EC_{\max} = 28$.[6] We assume uniform object sizes and a page capacity of 2 objects. Without look-ahead GGP decides to assign the objects o_2 and o_3 to the same partition resulting in a final partitioning with external costs of 18, visualized in Fig. 1 (b). Obviously, the optimum partitioning of this CG has only external costs of 10 (Fig. 1 (c)). The idea of the bounded look-ahead is to detect situations where it is advantageous to *reject* the current edge, i.e., the edge with maximum weight, and to consider other edges first. Subsequently, this rough outline of bounded look-ahead is detailed.

Consider the CG depicted in Fig. 2. The objects o_l and o_r have been assigned to the partitions P_l and P_r. Besides the edge (o_l, o_r) there are n external edges incident to o_l with weights $w_{l_1}, \ldots, w_{l_n}$ and m external edges incident to o_r with weights $w_{r_1}, \ldots, w_{r_m}$. Assume the next edge to be considered by GGP

---

[5] Partitions are represented as binary trees to accelerate the join operation.
[6] Squares denote objects, dashed boxes denote partitions.

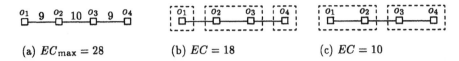

(a) $EC_{\max} = 28$ (b) $EC = 18$ (c) $EC = 10$

Fig. 1. An Example for Non-Optimal GGP Clustering

is (o_l, o_r) with weight w, which implies $w \geq \max\{w_{l_1}, \ldots, w_{l_n}, w_{r_1}, \ldots, w_{r_m}\}$. Further assume that the partitions P_l and P_r could be joined because their total size being less than or equal to the page size.

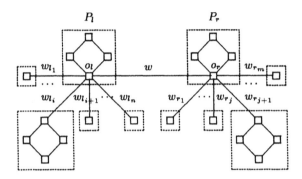

Fig. 2. Clustering Graph Before Analyzing the Edge (o_l, o_r)

To decide whether it is beneficial to join the partitions P_l and P_r (or not) we proceed in two steps:

1. We evaluate the potential gain in the case P_l and P_r are being joined and the resulting partition is being filled up to the maximum size. For that, a BSTF traversal is performed on the external edges of the CG starting at the objects $\{o_l, o_r\}$.[7] The traversal is terminated if either (1) the depth of the traversal exceeds some integer bound k, or (2) the total size of all partitions encountered (including P_l and P_r) exceeds the page size. Let $w_{l_1}, \ldots, w_{l_i}, w_{r_1}, \ldots, w_{r_j}$ be the weights of all edges accessed during the BSTF traversal. Then, $W_{\text{join}} = w + w_{l_1} + \ldots + w_{l_i} + w_{r_1} + \ldots + w_{r_j}$ denotes the potential gain in the case that the partitions P_l and P_r are being joined and the resulting partition were filled up completely using a BSTF traversal starting at the objects $\{o_l, o_r\}$.

2. We evaluate the effect of not joining P_l and P_r. To do so, we perform two BSTF traversals (on the external edges of the CG) starting at o_l (*left traversal*) and o_r (*right traversal*). The left (right) traversal is terminated as soon as the depth of the traversal exceeds k or when the total size of all partitions

---

[7] Note that the BSTF search inspects only paths that emanate from o_l and o_r—instead of inspecting all objects already in partitions P_l and P_r. Our experiments showed that the running-time becomes prohibitively large, otherwise.

encountered including P_l (P_r) exceeds the page size. Let W_{left} denote the total weight of all edges traversed by the left traversal, and let $\mathcal{P}_{\text{left}}$ denote the set of partitions encountered during the left traversal (including P_l). W_{left} denotes the gain that can potentially be achieved by GGP on the left part of the CG if the partitions P_l and P_r are *not* joined in the current stage of GGP. W_{right} and $\mathcal{P}_{\text{right}}$ are defined analogously for the right traversal.

Based on the definitions made above we can define two heuristics H1 and H2:

Heuristics H1: The edge (o_l, o_r) is **rejected**, i.e., P_l and P_r are not joined in the current stage of GGP, if either
- $W_{\text{left}} > W_{\text{join}}$ and the total size of all objects on pages in $\mathcal{P}_{\text{left}} \cup \{P_r\}$ exceeds the page size, or
- $W_{\text{right}} > W_{\text{join}}$ and the total size of all objects on pages in $\mathcal{P}_{\text{right}} \cup \{P_l\}$ exceeds the page size.

Heuristics H1 rejects the edge (o_l, o_r) if either the gain on the left part of the CG (rooted at o_l) or on the right part of the CG (rooted at o_r) is larger than the gain achieved by joining the partitions P_l and P_r.

Note, however, that by this heuristics the optimal partitioning of the CG shown in Fig. 1 is not found. This observation leads to the definition of

Heuristics H2: The edge (o_l, o_r) is **rejected**, i.e., P_l and P_r are not joined in the current iteration of GGP, if
- $W_{\text{left}} + W_{\text{right}} > W_{\text{join}}$ and the total size of all objects on pages in $\mathcal{P}_{\text{left}} \cup \mathcal{P}_{\text{right}}$ exceeds the page size.

Under heuristics H2, the total gain that can be potentially achieved by not joining the partitions P_l and P_r is compared to the gain potentially achieved by joining P_l and P_r. It is easy to see that the condition of H2 is always true if the condition of H1 is fulfilled—thus, H2 is a strengthening of H1. A similar heuristics that introduces more look-ahead into the Fiduccia-Mattheyses algorithm was proposed by Krishnamurthy [Kri84].

4.2 New-Chance

In this section we discuss the "fate" of edges that were rejected by the k-look-ahead heuristics. Rejected edges must not be removed from the *EdgeList* because they should be re-considered as soon as the condition leading to the rejection *changes*. Technically, in our implementation, edges are given a new chance by moving them to the end of the *EdgeList* when they are rejected.

The set of the external edges which has been visited in the k-look-ahead for some rejected edge e_r is called the *trigger-set* of e_r. Now let us assume that some edge e is considered and is not being rejected during the current iteration of GGP. Further assume that e is in the trigger-set of the rejected edge e_r. In this case the edge e_r is said to be *triggered*. After the join of the partitions incident to e the local situation in the CG that was responsible for rejecting the edge e_r has changed. In this new situation the edge e_r would possibly survive (i.e., not being rejected). Thus, we propose to retry any rejected edge when it is triggered.[8] Triggered edges are moved to the first position of the *EdgeList* as their weight is greater than or equal to the maximum of the weights of all edges that have not yet been considered.

5 Quantitative Analysis

In this section we investigate the quality of clustering algorithms (1) in terms of quality, i.e., external costs and (2) in terms of running-time. We decided to use the external costs of the partitioning to evaluate the quality of the clustering because this measure does not depend on the choice of the benchmark applications, the buffer size, the replacement policy, nor the working set window size. The experiments were carried out using a graph generator—that is part of our simulation workbench TEXAS.[9] The graphs used in the experiments consist of 10 *modules*, each constituting a highly connected subgraph. Every module is connected to one randomly selected module by an edge with minimal weight 1. The weights of the intra-module edges are uniformly distributed in the range $2, \ldots, 20$. We classify the characteristics of the examined clustering graphs according to five dimensions:

database cardinality	average number of objects per page	deviation of object sizes	degree of sharing	static reference count (SRC)

The cardinality of the database is the dominant factor of the running-time of the algorithms, whereas the remaining four parameters influence the quality of the partitionings generated by the algorithms. The degree of sharing is stated in % and determines the ratio of the number of shared objects to the total number of objects. We conducted experiments on many combinations of the five parameters. However, because of space restrictions in this paper, we discuss only the influence of the first four dimensions (omitting the SRC of shared objects) on the choice of the cluster algorithm—see [GKKM92b] for a more complete treatment. The following algorithms were measured: BSTF, GGP, GGPla, HP, Lukes and KL(x), FM(x) each with pre-partitioning produced by x, for $x \in \{$ GGPla, BSTF $\}$. The (iterative) algorithms KL(x) and FM(x) were run until no further improvement was achieved (or *maxint* was reached). To compensate for one major disadvantage of Lukes' algorithm (producing memory overflow when working on high trees) we limited the keeping of the best assignments of objects to partitions only up to the average number of objects per page.

5.1 Running-Time vs. Quality of Cluster Algorithms

The first experiment evaluates the cluster algorithms BSTF, GGP, GGPla, FM(GGPla), KL(GGPla), and HP in terms of (1) their partitioning quality—

---

[8] To avoid exhaustive searching we employ special data structures facilitating the direct access from the current edge to the set of triggered edges.

[9] The EXtensible Access Simulator for object bases.

that is, we compute the relative savings in external costs in relation to a random placement—and (2) their running-time dependent on the database cardinality. The algorithms worked on a scalable database of $n \leq 32$ modules—each constituting a random graph with 1000 objects and 4 edges per object on the average. Fig. 3 visualizes the results where the database size is plotted against the x-axis. In Fig. 3(a) the running-time is plotted against the y-axis, in Fig. 3(b) the relative savings of the obtained clustering to a random placement is plotted against the y-axis. The vertical (error) bars in the plots of Fig. 3 (b) visualize the standard deviation of the clustering results for the different graphs.

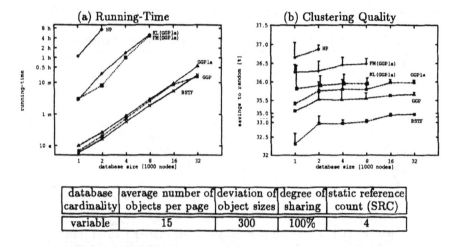

database cardinality	average number of objects per page	deviation of object sizes	degree of sharing	static reference count (SRC)
variable	15	300	100%	4

Fig. 3. Performance of Clustering Algorithms Dependent on the Database Size

The most important result of this experiment is that the running-times of the algorithms are drastically different. Whereas the constructive algorithms GGPla and GGP, and the sequenced-based technique BSTF are very fast (30 minutes for 32000 objects), the running-time of the iterative algorithms KL(GGPla), FM(GGPla), and HP is not acceptable for large databases. We limited the maximal running-time to 24 hours; Thus, HP is only feasible for small databases up to 2000 objects and KL/FM may be feasible for databases up to 8000 objects—if the long reorganization time is tolerable at all. Note, that even *small* differences in relative savings (the range is from 32% to 37%) exhibit enormous differences in absolute external costs—e.g., 40273 between BSTF and GGPla at a database cardinality of 32000 objects. The iterative algorithms HP, KL(GGPla), and FM(GGPla) exhibited the best partitioning results. Nevertheless, the results of the KL and FM heuristics strongly depend on the quality of the pre-partitioning. Utilizing a poor-quality pre-partitioning KL and FM cannot achieve such good results. Among the algorithms whose running-time is reasonably low GGP and GGPla performed best. The relative ordering of the algorithms—in running-time as well as in clustering quality—that was observed in this experiment remains stable in the majority of the experiments we conducted.

5.2 Changing the Partition Size

The number of objects per page has an important influence on the clustering results. Therefore, the page size is an effective tuning parameter in physical database design. Note, that varying the average object size instead of the page size would have the analogous effect. In the subsequent experiment we measure the performance of the clustering algorithms Lukes, HP, KL, FM, and GGPla under varying page sizes. Fig. 4 (a) visualizes the results for a tree-structured graph (sharing = 0) and Fig. 4 (b) visualizes the result for a graph with 50 % shared objects and an SRC of 11 for shared objects. All objects were of equal size. Thus, in this case our approximation of Lukes' algorithm is optimal.

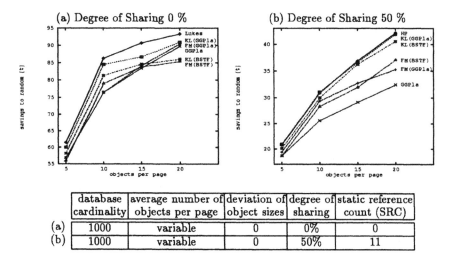

	database cardinality	average number of objects per page	deviation of object sizes	degree of sharing	static reference count (SRC)
(a)	1000	variable	0	0%	0
(b)	1000	variable	0	50%	11

Fig. 4. Influence of the Page Size on the Clustering Results

Lukes' algorithm achieves 93 % savings compared to random placement. The plot of the results of KL(GGPla) runs very close to this optimum—indicating that KL with the high quality pre-partitioning of GGPla is a good candidate for clustering trees of moderate size. The clustering results in Fig. 4 (b) range from 20 % to 40 % savings to random. Thus, if the degree of sharing is high and the page size is small, only small improvements can be achieved by clustering. With an increasing page size, the potential improvement by clustering increases, too.

5.3 Varying Object Sizes

Usually, the objects' sizes vary significantly—note, that the object net is composed of objects of many different types. E.g., there may be tuple-structured objects of just 50 bytes, whereas the size of set- or list-structured objects easily may even reach the page size. Fig. 5 (a) visualizes the results for a page capacity of 5 objects, and Fig. 5 (b) visualizes the results for a page size of 20 objects, both with 50 % sharing and SRC=11.

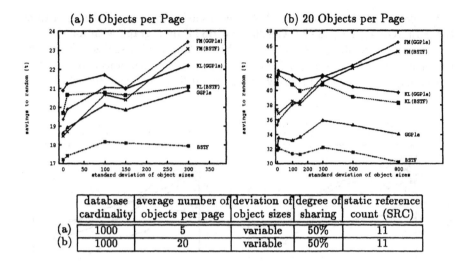

	database cardinality	average number of objects per page	deviation of object sizes	degree of sharing	static reference count (SRC)
(a)	1000	5	variable	50%	11
(b)	1000	20	variable	50%	11

Fig. 5. Performance of Clustering Algorithms Under Varying Object Sizes

The main observation is that the relative saving increase upon increasing the deviation of object sizes. The second result of this experiment is that FM performs better than KL if the object sizes vary substantially. Below a page capacity of 20 objects the break even point between KL and FM is at a standard deviation of object sizes of about 300 (Fig. 5 (b)). If the page capacity is only 5 objects per page on the average, the break even point is moved to a standard deviation of 150 (Fig. 5 (a)). To understand this result, consider Fig. 6. Neither KL nor FM can improve the partitioning of the graph depicted in Fig. 6 (a), where strong internal edges prevent from moving or swapping objects between the two partitions. If the number of objects decreases the probability of finding clustering subgraphs similar to those in Fig. 6 (b) and (c) increases. FM can improve the partitioning by moving a single object while KL cannot improve the partitioning as there are no pairs of objects to be swapped.

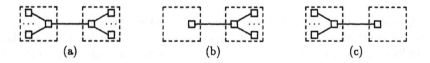

Fig. 6. Three Partitioning Problems

5.4 Degree of Sharing

The experiment in Section 5.2 already indicated that object sharing makes clustering more difficult. The next experiment is designed to investigate the influence of the degree of sharing on the clustering results. We measure the algorithms HP, KL(GGPla), KL(BSTF), GGPla, and BSTF on a graph with uniform object sizes and an SRC of 2 for shared objects. Fig. 7 (a) visualizes the results for a page capacity of 5, Fig. 7 (b) for a page capacity of 20 objects per page on the average. The degree of sharing varies from 0 % to 50 % (plotted against the x-axis).

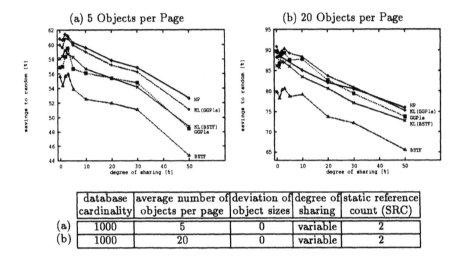

	database cardinality	average number of objects per page	deviation of object sizes	degree of sharing	static reference count (SRC)
(a)	1000	5	0	variable	2
(b)	1000	20	0	variable	2

Fig. 7. Performance of Clustering Algorithms Under Varying Degrees of Sharing

As expected, the plots of all algorithms show a steep decline as the degree of sharing increases. With 5 objects per page on the average the savings relative to random placement drop by about 10 %, with 20 objects per page even by 15 %. In both experiments, HP and KL(GGPla) yield the best clustering results among the algorithms tested.

6 The Case for Adaptable Algorithms

The results of the quantitative analysis presented in the previous section lead to the conclusion that no *one* algorithm performs superior for *all* object base configurations. Therefore, we derive a multi-dimensional grid: the dimensions correspond to particular characteristics of the object base configurations and the grid entries determine the best clustering algorithm for the particular configuration.

The grid is shown in Fig. 8. Three dimensions are visualized by the axes of the grid, i.e., the average number of objects per page, the standard deviation of the object sizes, and the degree of sharing. The fourth dimension, i.e., the size of the database in number of objects, is visualized by the coloring of the grid entries shown on the right hand side. Here, we distinguish three configurations: (1) a

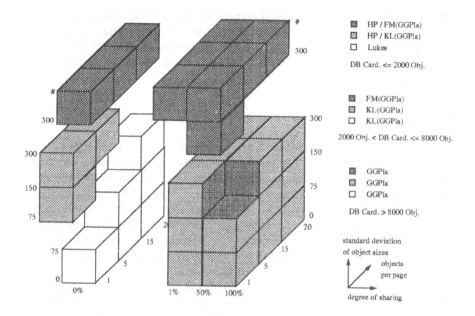

Fig. 8. Selecting the Best Clustering Algorithm

database with less than 2000 objects, (2) a database with more than 2000 and less than 8000 objects, and (3) a database with more than 8000 objects. For each configuration, the coloring (shading) of the grid indicates the most appropriate clustering algorithm. Subsequently, we briefly discuss the entries of the grid.

Let us start with the left hand side of the grid—representing a sharing of 0 %. In this case, the approximation of Lukes' algorithm is optimal if all objects are of equal size. Our experiments further indicate that the approximation of Lukes' algorithm yields good results as long as the ratio of the standard deviation of the object size to the average number of objects per page is small (white colored area). When this ratio increases other algorithms perform better than the approximation of Lukes, e.g., HP. We have found that beyond a database cardinality of 2000 objects Lukes' algorithm ran out of memory. That is why we propose to use KL/FM(GGPla) for medium cardinality and GGPla for large cardinality object bases even if the CG forms a tree. Next we investigate the right hand side of the grid, where the degree of sharing is greater than 0. If the database is of low or medium cardinality, i.e., below 8000 objects, KL(GGPla) or FM(GGPla) are the algorithms of choice: (1) Because KL is based on swapping objects, it is superior to FM if the standard deviation of the object size is small. (2) Beyond a standard deviation of around 300, FM achieves better results. For a database cardinality below 2000 objects HP can be used as an alternative to KL/FM (in the majority of the experiments we conducted HP produced the best results). When sharing is high, the page capacity is small, and the object sizes vary strongly (upper right grid corner), the FM heuristics is superior to KL because in this special case, moving objects achieves better results than swapping objects (see Section 5.3). Beyond a database cardinality of 8000 objects, the GGPla heuristics is the only method yielding acceptable cluster quality under reasonably low running-times.

7 Conclusion

Reconsider the title of this paper "Partition-Based Clustering in Object Bases: From Theory to Practice". The theory of partition-based clustering was developed by Tsangaris and Naughton [TN91]. They, in particular, proved the superiority of partition-based techniques over the sequence-based approaches. However, the hitherto known partition-based cluster approaches had to rely on the known computationally rather complex iterative partitioning algorithms, e.g., the Kernighan and Lin heuristics. Therefore, partition-based clustering was impractical for realistically large databases. Our greedy graph partitioning heuristics GGPla supplemented with the *look-ahead* and *new-chance* of once rejected choices has a much lower running-time complexity than the iterative algorithms. Nevertheless, the partitioning quality generated by GGPla is quite good compared to the computationally complex iterative partitioning heuristics and far better than sequence-based clustering algorithms. This makes the GGPla heuristics indispensable for two purposes:

1. As a pre-partitioning heuristics for small to medium cardinality object nets— on which iterative algorithms are then applied for improvement.
2. As the only applicable method on large cardinality object nets.

In conclusion, we therefore propose an adaptable clustering strategy which applies the most appropriate iterative partitioning method—in conjunction with a pre-partitioning by GGPla—on small to medium cardinality object nets and (pure) GGPla on large cardinality object nets. The adaptability is controlled by a multi-dimensional grid whose dimensions correspond to the object net characteristics which have to be established by, e.g., sampling the object base extension. The entries of the grid then determine the most appropriate cluster algorithm for the particular object base configuration.

Acknowledgement This work was partially supported by the German Research Council DFG under contracts Ke 401/6-1 and SFB 346.

We thank S. Fahrig his help in the implementation and extensive benchmarking of the various partitioning algorithms.

References

[Ben90]   V. Benzaken. An evaluation model for clustering strategies in the O₂ object-oriented database system. In *Proc. of the Int. Conf. on Database Theory (ICDT)*, pages 126–140. Springer-Verlag, 1990.

[BKKG88] J. Banerjee, W. Kim, S. J. Kim, and J. F. Garza. Clustering a DAG for CAD databases. *IEEE Trans. Software Eng.*, 14(11):1684–1699, Nov 1988.

[Bre77] M. A. Breuer. A class of min-cut placement algorithms. In *Proc. of the Design Automation Conference*, pages 284–290, 1977.

[CDRS86] M. Carey, D. DeWitt, J. Richardson, and E. Shekita. Object and file management in the EXODUS extensible database system. In *Proc. of the Conf. on Very Large Data Bases (VLDB)*, pages 91–100, Kyoto, Japan, Aug 86.

[FM82] C. Fidducia and R. M. Mattheyses. A linear-time heuristic for improving network partitions. In *Proc. of the Design Automation Conference*, pages 175–181, 1982.

[GKKM92a] C. Gerlhof, A. Kemper, C. Kilger, and G. Moerkotte. Clustering in object bases. Technical Report 6/92, Fakultät für Informatik, Universität Karlsruhe, D-7500 Karlsruhe, Jun 1992.

[GKKM92b] C. Gerlhof, A. Kemper, C. Kilger, and G. Moerkotte. Partition-based clustering in object bases: From theory to practice. Technical Report 92-34, RWTH Aachen, D-5100 Aachen, Dec 1992.

[HK89] S. E. Hudson and R. King. Cactis: A self-adaptive, concurrent implementation of an object-oriented database management system. *ACM Trans. on Database Systems*, 14(3):291–321, Sep 1989.

[HZ87] M. Hornick and S. Zdonik. A shared, segmented memory system for an object-oriented database. *ACM Trans. Office Inf. Syst.*, 5(1):70–95, Jan 1987.

[KL70] B. Kernighan and S. Lin. An efficient heuristic procedure for partitioning graphs. *Bell System Technical Journal*, 49(2):291–307, Feb 1970.

[Kri84] B. Krishnamurthy. An improved min-cut algorithm for partitioning VLSI networks. *IEEE Trans. on Comp.*, 33(5):438–446, 1984.

[Kru56] J. B. Kruskal. On the shortest spanning subgraph of a graph and the travelling salesman problem. *Proc. of the Amer. Math. Soc.*, 7:48–50, 1956.

[Luk74] J. Lukes. Efficient algorithm for the partitioning of trees. *IBM Journal of Research and Development*, 18:217–224, 1974.

[SM91] K. Shahookar and P. Mazumber. VLSI cell placement techniques. *ACM Computing Surveys*, 23(2):143–220, Jun 1991.

[Sta84] J. Stamos. Static grouping of small objects to enhance performance of a paged virtual memory. *ACM Trans. Comp. Syst.*, 2(2):155–180, May 1984.

[TN91] M. M. Tsangaris and J. F. Naughton. A stochastic approach for clustering in object bases. In *Proc. of the ACM SIGMOD Conf. on Management of Data*, pages 12–21, Denver, CO, May 1991.

[TN92] M. M. Tsangaris and J. F. Naughton. On the performance of object clustering techniques. In *Proc. of the ACM SIGMOD Conf. on Management of Data*, pages 144–153, San Diego, CA, Jun 1992.

An Algorithm for the Implementation of Replicated Tables

Brahma Dathan

Department of Computer Science, University of Wyoming, Laramie, WY 82071

Abstract. A table is an abstract data type that supports the three operations, *insert, delete,* and *find.* Such an ADT has wide applications in distributed databases and distributed file systems. In the last several years, several distributed systems that make use of tables have been implemented.

In this paper, we present a technique for the implementation of replicated tables. The technique assumes that the update operations, *insert* and *delete,* are performed by first updating the copy at one arbitrary site called the principal site and then propagating them to the others, called the subordinate sites. Our algorithm implements the update operations, *insert* and *delete,* in amortized time $O(\log n)$ at the principal site, but in amortized time $O(1)$ at the subordinate sites. The query operation, *find,* can still be done in worst-case time $O(\log n)$ at all the sites.

1 Introduction

A *table* is an extremely useful abstract data type (ADT) that supports the operations *insert,* which inserts a given element into the ADT, *delete,* which removes the element with a given key (for simplicity, we will assume that each element has a unique key) from the data structure, and *find,* which returns the contents of the element identified by a supplied key. Due to the ADT's great importance, a significant amount of effort has gone into the development of algorithms and data structures for its implementation. Major techniques include trees (e.g. binary search trees, AVL trees, 2-3 trees, B-trees) and hashing.

In this paper, we propose a technique for the implementation of tables in a distributed system. We assume that a copy of the table is maintained at more than one site, each site maintaining information about all of the elements in the ADT. Data replication is advantageous for two reasons. First, it provides fault tolerance by making the effects of site and communication failures on data availability less severe. Second, a local copy of the data at a site increases the potential for faster processing of queries at that site because the site does not have to send messages over communication links in order to retrieve information. (We will assume that the multiple computer systems do not share memory.)

We would like to note that over the past decade or so, some systems that maintain replicated tables have actually been constructed. Grapevine [1], which provides reliable mail service and authentication and access control mechanisms, maintains replicated tables of user names, group names, and their associated attributes. The ITC Distributed System [11] also uses tables for a similar purpose.

Clearinghouse [10], which supports a Yellow-Pages-like facility, uses a mapping mechanism from names (or sets of names) to sets of properties.

One chief issue related to the implementation of replicated tables, and in general any replicated ADT, is guaranteeing the "mutual consistency" of the multiple copies. Although many techniques have been developed to handle replicated data (see [3] for a survey), many distributed systems, including the ones mentioned above, use the following technique for manipulating and querying the data stored in the ADTs. A request for data modification, called an *update request*, (for example, inserting a new element), is made to one of the sites. This site, termed *principal site* in this paper, makes a local update and then transmits the update information to all the other sites, called *subordinate sites* in this work, which then perform their own local updates. Usually, a client performs a query by contacting a single site. We call this technique *principal copy algorithm*. The principal copy algorithm is a generalization of a technique called *primary copy algorithm* used in Distributed INGRES [12]. Both techniques have the virtue that invalid update requests are filtered at the source and will not result in increased communication and processor overheads.

In this regard, we note that Herlihy [6,7] has shown how to use the quorum consensus approach [5] for managing replicated ADTs. The focus of Herlihy's works is on the concurrency control aspects of replica management directed from a database point of view. He has, therefore, paid attention to the consistency of the ADTs by exploiting their type-specific properties.

Another concern in a replicated ADT is the data structures and algorithms employed at any given site for the ADT implementation. Given the fact that a *find* operation has a well known lower bound, a major consideration here should be to reduce the cost of the update operations, *insert* and *delete*. The cost of an update includes the processor overheads associated with the update at the multiple sites and the communication costs incurred when the update information is transmitted between the sites.

As mentioned earlier, the focus of the paper is on the development of algorithms and data structures for implementing a replicated table. We assume that the multiple copies of the table are are managed using the principal copy algorithm. Our algorithm implements the update operations, *insert* and *delete,* in amortized time[1] $O(\log n)$ (throughout the paper, we will use n to denote the number of elements in the table) at the principal site, but in amortized time $O(1)$ at the subordinate sites. The query operation, *find,* can still be done in worst-case time $O(\log n)$ at all the sites. The algorithm relies on an assumed synchronization mechanism, such as locking [4], which ensures that the updates occur in the same order at all of the sites.

It is appropriate at this stage to mention a technique suggested by Brown and Tarjan [2] and improved upon by Huddleston and Mehlhorn [8]. Brown and Tarjan showed how to reduce the amortized time to rebalance 2-3 trees for any "non-interacting" sequence of *insert* and *delete* operations. Using the notion of

---

[1] Informally, amortized time denotes the average of the "running times of operations in a sequence over the sequence." A more formal definition will be given later.

"fingers", they show how level-linked trees can be used to reduce the complexities of operations for certain applications. The result was extended by Huddleston and Mehlhorn for a-b trees where $a \leq \lfloor b/2 \rfloor$ for arbitrary sequences of *insert* and *delete* requests.

The results of [2,8] show that the complexities for insertion and deletion are still bounded by the time for searching that must precede any update. In the case of a table, the search can be expensive because the updates can be to arbitrary positions. In a replicated data structure that uses the principal copy algorithm, however, there is a potential to avoid such a search at the subordinate sites because the principal site performs the update first and should be able to provide crucial information to the subordinates enabling them to go about their updates faster. In our algorithm, the data structure is stored in several pieces of contiguous storage, which permits the principal site to supply the required information regarding the position where the insertion or deletion should occur.

The next section presents our technique. The paper concludes in Sect. 3.

2 The Technique

We first present an overview of our algorithms and data structures. All of the sites maintain identical copies of the data structure, which has three major parts. First, we have a set of $O(n/\log n)$ arrays (recall that n stands for the number of elements in the ADT), called *holders*, each of which has $O(\log n)$ cells. The n elements of the table are divided into groups of $O(\log n)$ elements and stored in the holders. The range of keys of the elements stored in any holder is unique. A second structure, called *holder identification table* (HIT), has $O(n/\log n)$ entries to store the identities and addresses of the holders. Finally, a third structure, called the *key range table* (KRT), is maintained to permit search operations to be done in $O(\log n)$ time.

When an *insert* request is submitted to it, the principal site searches the KRT to determine the holder that should receive the new element and inserts the element there. In most cases, the updates that will be required of the KRT or the HIT can be done in time $O(1)$. After the local update, the principal site transmits the *insert* request and the update information (key and data of the new element) to the subordinates. Piggy-backed on this message is the identity of the holder that should receive the new element. The subordinates use this information to retrieve the address of the affected holder from the HIT.

A deletion is processed in an analogous fashion.

The difficulty really arises when an update actually makes a holder contain more than or less than $O(\log n)$ elements. This would require a reorganization of the data structure and the central problem is to arrange matters so that such expensive operations are relatively far apart and the overheads associated with them can be amortized over the other operations.

We now proceed to a detailed description of the data structures.

2.1 Data Structures

The HIT and each holder are stored in contiguous storage (in main memory or, if so desired, in secondary storage). All entries in a holder (the HIT) have the same length. Clearly, given A, the starting address of any holder (the HIT), the contents of the ith entry can be obtained by accessing L locations starting at address $A + (i - 1)L$, where L is the length of an entry.

The above discussion implies that the holders and the HIT can be viewed as arrays, and for the sake of simplicity, we will do so throughout the paper.

It may seem that the $O(n/\log n)$ contiguous storage requirement for the HIT would require us to anticipate a maximum value for n, which in turn could waste storage or could place an upper limit on the maximum size to which the ADT can grow. Not so. As will become clear during later discussions, we acquire larger (smaller) pieces of contiguous storage as the size of the data structure increases (decreases), while previously-held storage is released.

Holders. Each site has a set of holders each of which is as an array. (Recall the earlier discussion.) Holders are denoted by h_1, h_2, etc., and $N(h_i)$ denotes the number of elements in holder h_i.

We define the following functions on the domain of non-negative integers.

$$MIN(n) = \begin{cases} 0 & \text{if } n = 0 \\ \lceil \log_2 n \rceil & \text{otherwise} \end{cases} . \tag{1}$$

$$MAX(n) = 2MIN(n) . \tag{2}$$

In a table that has n elements, the algorithm *attempts* to ensure that the maximum number of elements in a holder is between $MIN(n)$ and $MAX(n)$. However, a strict adherence to the above two extremes can be expensive. For example, consider a table with 64 elements, so $MIN(n) = 6$ and $MAX(n) = 12$. An insertion at this stage will cause $MIN(n)$ to increase by 1, so we need to make sure that for each holder h_i, $N(h_i) \geq 7$. This has a complexity of $O(n/\log n)$. A deletion with 65 elements in the ADT will change $MAX(n)$ from 14 to 12, requiring a check to ensure that $N(h_i) \leq 12$ for all holders h_i. Once again, this will be an expensive operation. Clearly, a sequence of alternating *insert* and *delete* with any value of n that is a power of 2 will foil our plan.

To overcome the problem, we introduce the notion of an *operating value*, denoted by n' and governed by the following rules.

1. If $n \leq 2$, then $n' = n$.
2. An *insert* operation will cause the operational value to change from n' to $2n'$ if and only if n, the number of elements after the insertion $= 3n'/2$.
3. A *delete* operation will cause a change in the operational value from n' to $n'/2$ if and only if n, the number of elements after the deletion $= n'/2$.

An example will make the idea clear. Assume that there are 32 elements in the system ($n = 32$). The operational value, n', will be 32 and will remain at 32 for all further insertions until n attains the value 48 because until then $n < 3n'/2 = 48$. With $n = 48$, n' becomes 64. It is easy to verify that from this point, a sequence of insertions will cause n' to change when the number of elements becomes 96. With $n = 48$, a sequence of deletions will not cause the operational value to decrease until $n = 32$ at which time $n' = 32$.

The algorithm to be discussed guarantees that in a table with n elements $N(h_i)$ is between $MIN(n')$ and $MAX(n')$ where n' is the operating value.

The following lemma is useful in proving the complexity of our algorithms.

Lemma 1. *Suppose an update operation changes the operational value to n'. Then, it will require at least $n'/2$ insert operations before the operational value will change again.*

Proof. Suppose when it changed to n', the operational value actually increased. Then, the number of elements $n = 3n'/4$. From its definition, we know that the operational value will not increase until n attains a value $3n'/2$. In this case, the minimum number of *inserts* required will be $3n'/2 - 3n'/4 = 3n'/4$. If the value of n' was attained by a reduction in the operational value, the value will remain at n' until the number of elements becomes $3n'/2$ requiring $n'/2$ updates. □

The next lemma shows that in any complexity expressed as a function of n' and n, n' may be replaced by n or vice-versa.

Lemma 2. *With $n \geq 1$ elements in the system, $2n/3 < n' < 2n$.*

Proof. First, consider the situation immediately after an update that changes the operational value. Any time the operational value changes to n' due to a *delete*, we have $n = n'$ after the decrease, so the result clearly is true. Similarly, when the operational value increases to n', $n = 3n'/4$, so the lemma holds again. It can now be verified that the result continues to hold until the operational value changes again either because of an *insert* or a *delete*. □

From Lemmas 1 and 2, it follows that the number of holders $NH(n) = C \times n/\lceil \log n \rceil$.

The minimum (or maximum) key value stored in h_i is denoted by MIN.h_i (or MAX.h_i). No holder h_j, $i \neq j$, stores a key k such that MIN.$h_i \leq k \leq$ MAX.h_i. As elements are inserted and deleted, the range of key values stored in a holder may change, but this range will remain unique. We arrange matters such that the MAX.$h_i <$ MIN.h_j for $i < j$.

We use the notation $h_i[j]$ to denote the jth cell of holder h_i. Each cell $h_i[j]$ has three parts: $h_i[j]$.ELEMENT that stores an element of the table and two indices, $h_i[j]$.SUCCESSOR and $h_i[j]$.PREDECESSOR, whose functions are now explained. Generally speaking, $h_i[j]$.SUCCESSOR is the index of that cell (within h_i) that contains the smallest element that is larger than $h_i[j]$.ELEMENT; if such an element does not appear in h_i, $h_i[j]$.SUCCESSOR has the special value *nil*. Similarly,

$h_i[j]$.PREDECESSOR is the index of the cell that contains the largest element that is smaller than $h_i[j]$.ELEMENT, if such an element exists and is stored in h_i and is *nil* otherwise.

Let there be m holders, h_1, ..., h_m. For any holder h_i, $2 \le i \le m - 1$, h_{i-1} and h_{i+1} are its *neighbors*. The neighbors of h_1 are h_2 and h_m, and the neighbors of h_m are h_1 and h_{m-1}. Neighbors are doubly linked, so that from any holder h_i we can access its neighbors in constant time.

Key Range Table (KRT). The Key Range Table is an AVL tree storing one node for each holder. (Please refer to Knuth [9] for a discussion on AVL trees.) Let N be a node of the AVL tree representing some holder h_i. Then, N stores MIN.h_i and MAX.h_i, either of which may be used as the key for ordering the nodes of the tree. The purpose of the KRT is to determine which holder should be used for servicing a specific *insert*, *delete*, or *find* request. Note that there are $O(n/\log n)$ elements in the KRT. Given a key, the KRT can be searched in $O(\log n)$ time to determine which holder might possibly contain the element.

The motivation behind using an AVL tree is the following. The AVL tree requires only $O(\log n)$ time to perform an update. In addition, as records are inserted and deleted from the holders, we will encounter situations when MAX.h_i and/or MIN.h_{i+1} will change for some existing holders h_i and h_{i+1}. These changes can be reflected in the KRT by modifying simply those AVL tree nodes that represent the affected holders. Since we ensure that MAX.h_i < MIN.h_{i+1} at all times, the changes to the KRT will require no reorganization, so can be performed in constant time. On the other hand, if a structure such as a 2-3 tree is used for implementing the KRT, the changes may require that the updates be propagated all the way to the root of the tree requiring $O(\log n)$ time.

Holder Identification Table (HIT). The HIT is an array of $NH(n)$ cells, one for each holder. $HIT[j]$ denotes the jth cell of the HIT. It stores the following information about some holder h_i.

1. The number of elements in h_i, denoted by $\#.h_i$.
2. MIN.h_i, the key value of the minimum element stored in h_i.
3. MAX.h_i, the key value of the maximum element stored in h_i.
4. A pointer that can be used to locate h_i in constant time. This is denoted by ADDRESS.h_i.
5. A pointer to the corresponding node in the KRT. (Recall that each holder is represented in the KRT by a tree node.) This pointer is denoted by KRT.h_i. The node at KRT.h_i maintains the index j.

It is important to observe that $HIT[j]$, the jth cell of the HIT, does not necessarily contain information about h_j, the jth holder. Each holder maintains a pointer to the HIT cell that points to it. Thus if the jth cell of the HIT stores information about holder h_i, a variable h_i.HIT, maintained by h_i, contains the index j, so that the HIT cell can be accessed in constant time after accessing h_i.

2.2 The Algorithm

We first show how an *insert* request is handled, first at the principal site and then at the subordinates.

Insertion of an Element. A site that receives an *insert* request from the external world performs the algorithm *PRINCIPAL_INSERT* shown in Fig. 1. It searches the KRT to determine the holder where the new element should be inserted and inserts it in the next available cell of the array that implements the holder. This is followed by a sequential search of the holder array to determine the indices of the smallest (or largest) element that is larger (or smaller) than the new element. Using these indices, the PREDECESSOR and SUCCESSOR fields of the newly-occupied cell are updated. If the new element is the smallest or the largest element of the holder, the appropriate HIT cell and KRT node are updated. These actions take $O(\log n)$ time.

Algorithm PRINCIPAL_INSERT
begin
    Receiver ← holder for insertion; % Obtained by searching the KRT.
    $\#.h_{Receiver}$ ← $\#.h_{Receiver}$ +1;
    $h_{Receiver}[\#.h_{Receiver}]$.Element ← E;
    S ← index of the holder cell storing the smallest element that is larger than E;
    P ← index of the holder cell storing the largest element that is smaller than E;
    $h_{Receiver}[\#.h_{Receiver}]$.Predecessor ← P;
    $h_{Receiver}[\#.h_{Receiver}]$.Successor ← S;
    if S $\neq$ **nil then**
        $h_{Receiver}[S]$.Predecessor ← $\#.h_{Receiver}$
    else
        update $Max.h_{Receiver}$ in the HIT cell and the KRT node of $h_{Receiver}$;
    if P $\neq$ **nil then**
        $h_{Receiver}[P]$.Successor ← $\#.h_{Receiver}$
    else
        update $Min.h_{Receiver}$ in the HIT cell and the KRT node of $h_{Receiver}$;
    if the operational value has changed **then**
        reorganize all holders
    else if $\#.h_{Receiver} > MAX(n')$ **then**
        reorganize $h_{Receiver}$ and one of its neighbors;
    send the message (INSERT, E, P, S, $h_{Receiver}$.HIT) to each subordinate site;
end;

Fig. 1. Algorithm to Insert an Element at the Principal Site

If the insertion increases the operational value, we reorganize the entire data structure by first creating $\lfloor n/\lfloor 1.25MIN(n') \rfloor \rfloor$ holders. All holders except h_1, h_2, and h_3 will contain $\lfloor 1.25MIN(n') \rfloor$ elements.

Holder h_1 will contain $\lfloor 1.25 MIN(n') \rfloor + \lfloor (n \bmod \lfloor 1.25 MIN(n') \rfloor)/3 \rfloor + \lfloor (n \bmod \lfloor 1.25 MIN(n') \rfloor) \bmod 3 \rfloor$ elements, whereas h_2 and h_3 will both contain $\lfloor 1.25 MIN(n') \rfloor + \lfloor (n \bmod \lfloor 1.25 MIN(n') \rfloor)/3 \rfloor$ elements. As in other situations, h_i will contain elements with keys that are smaller than the keys of h_{i+1}. The storage for the old holders is released. The whole operation has a complexity of $O(n)$.

As an example, consider the insertion of an element that causes n to be 384. It can be checked that n' would be changed to 512. Then, there will be 34 holders with h_1 containing 15 elements, h_2 and h_3 storing 14 elements each, and each of the other 31 holders storing 11 elements.

As the new holders are created, we allocate a contiguous area of size $O(n'/\log n')$ (use the new value of n') and enter the addresses and the other attributes of these holders in this area to create the new HIT. After the new HIT is created, we release the storage associated with the old HIT. These can be done in time $O(n/\log n)$.

The last step in the reorganization is the creation of the KRT. Since the key ranges appear in increasing order as we scan from the first holder to the last one, the tree creation can be done in time $O(n/\log n)$.

It should be clear that after the reorganization, all holders contain between $\lfloor 1.25 MIN(n') \rfloor$ and $\lfloor 1.75 MIN(n') \rfloor$ elements. This is a strategy to guarantee that a newly-created holder will have to have $O(\log n)$ update operations performed on it before it will have fewer than $MIN(n')$ or greater than $MAX(n')$ elements.

If the *insert* operation causes the holder h_i to have greater than $MAX(n')$ elements, then some reorganization is warranted. We now describe how this condition is handled.

Case 1: A neighbor, say h_{i+1}, has fewer than $1.75\ MIN(n')$ elements. Remember that the smallest element of h_{i+1} is greater than the largest element of h_i. Therefore, we transfer the largest element of h_i to h_{i+1}. This also requires adjusting MIN.h_{i+1} and MAX.h_i in the HIT. Using the pointers KRT.h_i and KRT.h_{i+1} in the HIT, we also adjust the key values of the nodes in the KRT. Observe that the relative order of the elements in the KRT does not change because MAX.h_i, the maximum key value stored in h_i, is still smaller than MIN.h_{i+1}, the smallest key value in h_{i+1}. Consequently, these changes in the nodes of the KRT will require no reorganization of the tree. It is also important to observe that no holder h_j stores a key k such that $k_1 \le k \le k_2$, where k_1 and k_2 are keys stored in some other holder h_i, $i \ne j$. Clearly, the operation can be done in time $O(1)$.

If h_{i-1} is chosen instead of h_{i+1}, the situation is analogous.

Case 2: Can not find a neighbor of h_i with fewer than $1.75\ MIN(n')$ elements. Pick one of the neighbors, say, h_{i+1}. Between them, h_i and h_{i+1} have at least $2MIN(n') + 1 + 1.75MIN(n') + x$ elements, where $x \le .25MIN(n')$. (Recall that $MAX(n') = 2MIN(n')$). Divide these elements into 3 sets as equally as possible. One-third of these elements that have the smallest key values are stored in h_i. Another one-third with the next higher key values are stored in h_{i+1}, and the rest are stored in a newly-created holder. There are at most $1 + 4\lceil \log n' \rceil$

elements, available in sorted order, and so each holder may be created in time $O(\log n)$. The existing elements of h_i and h_{i+1} in the HIT are updated to reflect the changes in their MIN, MAX, and # values. The corresponding KRT elements are also updated. The new holder will require the creation of a new cell in the HIT and the insertion of a new node in the AVL tree (implementing the KRT). These book-keeping functions on the KRT can be done in $O(\log n)$ time, and the HIT is updated in constant time. Thus the complexity of operations in this case is $O(\log n)$.

Actions at the Subordinate Sites. The last action taken by the principal site is to transmit the *insert* request to all of the other sites. In addition to the contents of the new element E, the message contains the index of the HIT cell that needs update, and the indices of the predecessor and successor elements of E. On receiving this message, a subordinate site performs essentially the same algorithm as in Fig. 1 with some minor differences that result in improved complexity. The site need not search the KRT to determine the value of RECEIVER because the HIT cell index supplied can be used to locate it. There is also no need to search the holder to find the predecessor and successor elements; they are already supplied. Thus, inserting the element can be done in constant time.

The latter actions, reorganizing the entire data structure, if $MIN(n')$ increases, or reorganizing $h_{Receiver}$ if it contains more than $MAX(n')$ elements are done exactly as at the principal site.

Notice that after the insertion is completed at all the sites, the data structure will be identical at all of the sites.

Deletion of an Element. When a site receives the *delete* request for an element E, it performs actions analogous to those for an element insertion. After using the KRT to locate the holder h_D containing E, the element itself is located by sequentially searching the holder. We then move the element in the last occupied cell of the holder array to the cell used by E. It is quite straightforward to update the predecessor and successor fields of all affected elements. After accessing the appropriate HIT cell, the value of $\#.h_D$ is decremented and any necessary changes to the values of MIN.h_D and MAX.h_D are made. Using the pointer from the HIT, any required changes to the KRT are also performed.

If the value of $MIN(n')$ changes as a result of the deletion, we reorganize the holders as in the case of *insert*.

The deletion may cause the holder h_i to hold less than $MIN(n')$ elements. In this case, we select 4 holders $h_j, h_{j+1}, h_{j+2}, h_{j+3}$, where one of the selected holders is h_i. For instance, we could pick h_{i-1}, h_i, h_{i+1}, and h_{i+2}.

Without loss of generality, assume that we have chosen h_i, h_{i+1}, h_{i+2}, and h_{i+3}. If h_{i+1} has more than $1.25MIN(n')$ elements, transfer the smallest element of h_{i+1} to h_i. Otherwise, if h_{i+2} has more than $1.25MIN(n')$ elements, transfer the smallest element of h_{i+2} to h_{i+1} and the smallest element of h_{i+1} to h_i. Otherwise, if h_{i+3} has more than $1.25MIN(n')$ elements, transfer the smallest element of h_{i+3} to h_{i+2}, the smallest element of h_{i+2} to h_{i+1}, and the smallest element of h_{i+1} to h_i. In all cases, we can update the HIT and the KRT in constant time. The complexity of this sub-case is $O(1)$. If none of the above is applicable, we divide the elements of h_i, h_{i+1}, h_{i+2}, and h_{i+3} as equally as possible into the three holders h_i, h_{i+1}, and h_{i+2}. Note that each of h_i, h_{i+1}, and h_{i+2} will have less than $1.75MIN(n')$ elements and at least $1.25MIN(n')$ elements. The holder creation will need $O(\log n)$ time. The KRT and the HIT are updated in constant time. The holder h_{i+3}, which is now empty, is deleted from the HIT in constant time and from the KRT in $O(\log n)$ time. The complexity of this sub-case is $O(\log n)$.

2.3 Complexity Analysis

Informally, when the entire data structure is reorganized because of a change in the operational value we are guaranteed from Lemma 1 and Lemma 2 that $O(n)$ updates would have preceded it. Thus, the cost of $O(n)$ for reorganization can be distributed over these updates to get an amortized time of $O(1)$ per update. Because of the fact that we have between $\lfloor 1.25MIN(n') \rfloor$ and $\lfloor 1.75MIN(n') \rfloor$ elements in any newly-created holder, we know that any reorganization that happens when a holder has a number of elements beyond the limits $MIN(n')$ or $MAX(n')$ would be the result of $O(\log n)$ updates. The cost of such a reorganization is $O(\log n)$ that can once again be attributed to these updates for an amortized time of $O(1)$ per update. All other updates take place in $O(\log n)$ time at the principal site and in constant time at the subordinates.

We now give a formal definition of amortized complexity, taken from [13]. The *potential* of a data structure in configuration D is a real number denoted by $\Phi(D)$. "The amortized time of an operation is $t + \Phi(D') - \Phi(D)$, where t is the actual time of the operation and D and D' are the configurations of the data structure before and after the operation, respectively." As shown by Tarjan [13], if the initial potential is zero and the potential is always nonnegative, the total time of a sequence of operations is never greater than the amortized time, which is therefore an upper bound on the total time.

Theorem 3. *The algorithm implements a replicated table with the following complexities. Principal Site: insert and delete: $O(\log n)$ amortized; Subordinate Site: insert and delete: $O(1)$ amortized; find: $O(\log n)$ at all of the sites.*

Proof. At the principal site, an update requires $O(\log n)$ time to search the KRT. At all of the sites, the reorganization that happens when the operational value changes has a complexity of $O(n)$ and is less than An' for some constant A. An insertion or deletion may require the creation or deletion of a holder and this activity will have a complexity of $O(\log n)$, which is less than $BMIN(n')$, where B is a constant.

We define the potential of the data structure in configuration D by $\Phi(D) = 4A(n'-u+1)+4Bv$, where n' is the operational value, u is the minimum number of *insert* operations required to change the operational value, and $v = \sum_{i=1}^{m} x_i$, where m is the number of holders and x_i is defined as below.

$$x_i = \begin{cases} \lfloor 1.25MIN(n') \rfloor - N(h_i) & \text{if } \lfloor 1.25MIN(n') \rfloor > N(h_i) \\ N(h_i) - \lfloor 1.75MIN(n') \rfloor & \text{if } \lfloor 1.75MIN(n') \rfloor < N(h_i) \\ 0 & \text{otherwise} \end{cases} \quad (3)$$

Initially, $n' = 0$, $u = 1$, and $v = 0$, so the potential is 0; at all times, $u \leq 3n'/4$ and $v \geq 0$, so the potential remains nonnegative.

Let us first examine the change in potential for updates. If it causes no reorganization whatsoever, in the worst case, an update operation may decrease the value of u by 1 and increase v by 1. So, the increase in potential may be at most $4A + 4B$.

The amortized cost of the operation at the principal site is then $O(\log n) + 4A + 4B = O(\log n)$. At all other sites, the cost is $O(1) + 4A + 4B = O(1)$.

If the operation is an *insert* that changes the operational value from $n'/2$ to n', the new potential is $4A(n' - 3n'/4 + 1) + 4B0$ (because $u = 3n'/4$ from the proof of Lemma 1) and the potential before the update is $4A(n'/2 - 1 + 1) + 4Bv$, so the difference is $-An' + 4A - 4Bv$. Adding the cost of the operation, which is $O(\log n) + An'$ at the principal site and An' at the others, we see that the amortized cost is $O(1)$ at all sites.

A *delete* that changes the operational value from $2n'$ to n' is analyzed as follows. The new potential is $4A(n' - n'/2 + 1) + 4B0 = 4A(n'/2 + 1)$ and the potential before the update is $4A(2n' - (n'/2 - 1) + 1) + 4Bv = 4A(3n'/2 + 2) + 4Bv$, so the difference is $-4A(n' + 1) - 4Bv$. Adding the cost of the operation to the change in potential, we find that the amortized cost is $O(1)$ at all sites.

Suppose the operational value does not change, but some holders are reorganized. Then, x_i will not increase for any holder and for h_i to which the update was directed, the value of x_i will change from $\lfloor 0.25MIN(n') \rfloor$ to 0. This means that if the potential before the update is $4A(n' - u + 1) + 4Bv$, the new potential is at most $4A(n' - (u - 1) + 1) + 4B(v - \lfloor 0.25MIN(n') \rfloor)$, so the change is $4A - BMIN(n')$. Adding this to the actual cost of the operation, we get an amortized cost of $O(1)$ at all sites. $\square$

3 Conclusions

In this paper, we developed a technique for implementing replicated tables in a distributed system. We looked at systems that perform updates at a single site and then transmit these updates to all of the other sites for modifications. Since query operations are executed by contacting a single site, all of the updates have to be propagated to all of the sites. While the overheads of our algorithm are, in the worst case, higher than using conventional mechanisms such as a 2-3 tree, its amortized complexities are better. Our algorithms are suitable when processor bottlenecks are of concern.

As far as the communication costs are concerned, the messages for transmitting the update require some extra fields, but their number and size are small. It is also important to note that the algorithm does not require any *additional* messages.

It is desirable to improve our technique in a couple of ways. First, it is an interesting question whether the complexity for the updates at the principal site can be improved to $O(\log n)$ even in the worst case. Second, our algorithm has the drawback that it is tied to the principal copy algorithm for replica management and that some form of synchronization is needed to ensure that the updates occur in the same order at all of the sites. If these requirements can be weakened, the algorithm would be more general and the updates would become more efficient.

References

1. Andrew D. Birrell, Roy Levin, Roger M. Needham, and Michael D. Schroeder. Grapevine: an exercise in distributed computing. *Communications of the Association for Computing Machinery*, 25(4):260–274, 1982.

2. M.R. Brown and R.E. Tarjan. Design and analysis of a data structure for representing sorted lists. *SIAM Journal on Computing*, 9:594–614, 1980.

3. S.B. Davidson, H. Garcia-Molina, and D. Skeen. Consistency in partitioned networks. *ACM Computing Surveys*, 17(3):346–370, September 1985.

4. K.P. Eswaran, J.N. Gray, R.A. Lorie, and I.L. Traiger. The notions of consistency and predicate locks in a database system. *Communications of the ACM*, 19(11):624–633, November 1976.

5. D.K. Gifford. Weighted voting for replicated data. In *Proceedings 7th ACM SIGOPS Symposium on Operating Systems principles*, pages 150–159, Pacific Grove, CA, December 1979.

6. M. Herlihy. Dynamic quorum adjustment for partitioned data. *ACM Transactions on Database Systems*, 12(2):170–194, June 1987.

7. M. Herlihy. A quorum-consensus replication method for abstract data types. *ACM Transactions on Computer Systems*, 4(1):32–53, February 1986.

8. S. Huddleston and K. Mehlhorn. A new data structure for representing sorted lists. *Acta Informatica*, 17:157–184, 1982.

9. D.E. Knuth. *The Art of Computer Programming Vol III: Sorting and Searching*. Addison Wesley, 1973.

10. Derek C. Oppen and K. Dalal, Yogen. The clearinghouse: a decentralized agent for locating named objects in a distributed environment. *ACM Transactions on Office Information Systems*, 1(3):230–253, 1983.

11. M. Satyanarayanan, John H. Howard, David A. Nichols, Robert N. Sidebotham, Alfred Z. Spector, and Michael J. West. The ITC distributed system: principles and design. In *Proceedings of the Twelfth Symposium on Operating Systems Principles*, pages 35–50, 1985.

12. M. Stonebraker. Concurrency control and consistency of multiple copies of data in distributed INGRES. *IEEE Transactions on Software Engineering*, 5(3):188–194, May 1979.

13. Robert E. Tarjan. Amortized computational complexity. *SIAM J. Alg. Disc. Meth.*, 6(3):306–318, April 1985.

Improved Traditional Mirror

Cyril U. Orji
Mark A. Weiss

School of Computer Science
Florida International University
Miami, Florida 33199
{orji,weiss}@scs.fiu.edu

Jon A. Solworth

Department of EECS (M/C 154)
University of Illinois at Chicago
851 S. Morgan, Rm 1120 SEO
Chicago, Illinois 60607-7053
solworth@parsys.eecs.uic.edu

Abstract

We propose a scheme for improving write performance in traditional mirrored disks using write caching. The technique uses write-only disk caches to improve write performance; a *write through* to disk for cached data and a write twice scheme to provide a highly fault tolerant system. The scheme is simple and can be readily integrated into existing systems with only low-level software redesign. Unlike some mirroring techniques, this technique maintains the semantics of traditional mirroring, allowing a disk to disk copy during recovery while improving write efficiency by almost a factor of 2 over traditional mirrors.

1 Introduction

Disk mirroring maintains a logical disk image on two physical disks. The two physical disks are called the *mirrored set*, and the disks in a mirrored set contain identical disk images. We refer to this scheme as *traditional mirroring* (TM) to distinguish it from other forms of mirroring.

Traditional mirroring improves reliability [1] and performance [2, 3] over a single disk system. Reliability is improved by replicating each component in the I/O subsystem. This allows continuous operation of the I/O subsystem even in the event of a single component failure. Performance improvements are derived from read requests. The improvements are of two types. The read rate is doubled since a read can be satisfied by any disk in the mirrored set. In addition, a read request is efficiently serviced using a nearest free arm scheduling algorithm. For a disk with n cylinders, traditional mirroring reduces the average seek distance of a read request to about $n/5$ cylinders [2]. This is in contrast to the average seek distance of about $n/3$ cylinders using a single disk. Intuitively, the 2 disk arms divide the total disk band into two regions.

Despite the improvements in read performance, TM does not improve the efficiency of small random writes. Since both disks must write a block, two randomly placed arms must seek to the same location. The (maximum) seek distance for a random write is increased to about $0.46n$ [2] instead of $0.33n$ in a single disk system. By batching writes as proposed in [14], disk mirroring with alternating deferred updates [12] achieves improved write performance even with increasing write ratio. However, this comes at the cost of reduced read efficiency since read requests do not take advantage of the two disk arms as suggested in [2].

Distorted mirror (DM) and *Doubly distorted mirror* (DDM) were proposed in [15, 16, 11] to address the write inefficiency in traditional mirror. Distorted mirror improves small write performance by almost a factor of 2 over traditional mirror by reducing two random writes to one. Doubly distorted mirror eliminates the random write achieving greater write efficiency. However, there are two major drawbacks to distorted and doubly distorted mirrors.

- The disks in the mirror set are not identical images, so that if one disk fails, a disk-to-disk copy can not be performed during recovery. The distortion map must be used to reconstruct the failed disk. This is an expensive operation and could seriously degrade performance during failure mode operation.

- The distorted and doubly distorted mirror use twice the meta information of traditional mirror. This must be in main memory for efficient use.

Caching improves read and write efficiency in I/O systems. However, there is a reliability issue whenever a volatile cache is used in I/O systems. Techniques for providing reliability such as the use of replication and a battery backed cache tend to significantly increase system cost. In a second approach, cache contents are periodically flushed to disk at regular intervals, but this has a negative effect of limiting write efficiency. The scheme we propose here uses a third technique for providing reliability, which is *writing through* to disk. Our contribution is to show how to write through at low cost.

In this paper we propose an improved traditional mirror (ITM) that uses a combination of caching, write through, and write twice schemes to improve the performance of traditional mirror. Write through is used so that when a block is placed or updated in cache, the block in the disk is also *immediately* updated. This technique is infrequently used because writing individual blocks synchronously to disk is expensive; but we show here how to make write through inexpensive. The advantages of this scheme are:

- The performance of small writes is improved using write-only disk cache and piggybacking techniques.

- Unlike distorted and doubly distorted mirrors, ITM does not require a distortion map. The disks in the mirror set are identical images thereby allowing a disk-to-disk copy during recovery as in TM.

- ITM and TM are fully compatible, and so can be seamlessly combined.

- ITM uses a write twice scheme to improve write performance with a write through strategy. This provides a high level of fault tolerance for the I/O subsystem.

The remainder of this paper is organized as follows. In Section 2 we describe the improved traditional mirror. In Section 3 we present the simulation model used in our study and discuss our evaluation methodology in Section 4. We present and discuss the simulation results in Section 5. In Section 6 we discuss recovery techniques for the improved traditional mirror and conclude the paper in Section 7.

2 The Improved Traditional Mirror

The improved traditional mirror design draws fundamentally from a previous work, write-only disk caches [14]. In a write-only disk cache, pending writes are placed in a non-volatile cache. These writes are either piggybacked by read requests or written in batch during block replacement, yielding a very low write cost per block.

Although write-only disk caches dramatically reduce the cost of small writes, they require a non-volatile cache. In this paper, we show how to remove this requirement by writing the block twice: the first time *backing up* the block to any free block on the disk (making it durable), and the second time piggybacking it to its final destination. If many free blocks are available for backups, the back up write can be made without a seek and with very little rotational latency.

2.1 Logical and Physical Address Spaces

The logical address space (L) of a disk in an ITM set is smaller than the physical address space (P) of the disk. Some disk blocks are designated as backup blocks, and they constitute the backup address space (B). Thus for the ITM, $P = L \cup B$ as opposed to the traditional mirror where $P = L$ (see Figure 1). Typically, we expect that $0.1P \leq B \leq 0.2P$, so that between 10% and 20% of the blocks are reserved for use as backups.

2.2 Allocation of Backup Blocks

We describe two techniques for allocating backup blocks – track and uniform allocation. But first we describe the data structures that support these allocation schemes.

SafeMap: The SafeMap contains an entry for each block backed up on disk. There is a SafeMap for each disk in the mirror set. SafeMap k has B entries for the B backup blocks on disk k. The ith entry in SafeMap k is the address of the data block backed up at the ith backup block of disk k.

BackupMap: This is a constant map which contains an entry for each address in B, sorted by physical address. The ith entry in BackupMap is the ad-

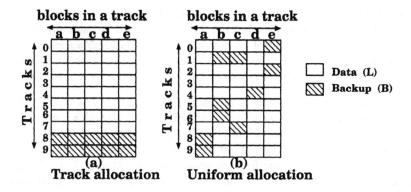

Figure 1: **Data and backup blocks in a cylinder**

dress of the ith block which is used for backups. There is one BackupMap for the mirror set.

FreeMap: This is a bit map of size B, with a 1 bit for each backup block in use and a 0 otherwise. There is a FreeMap for each disk in the mirror set.

2.2.1 Track Allocation

The track allocation strategy requires that each track is designated exclusively for either data or backup. An example is shown in Figure 1 (a) for a 20% backup allocation. Track allocation has the advantages that:

- It facilitates recovery. Blocks reserved for backup are easily identified during recovery. Given a logical backup address, it is straightforward to determine the physical block address. Consequently, this allocation policy does not require a BackupMap and a FreeMap since all information can be derived directly from the SafeMap.

- It allows data blocks to be contiguous in a cylinder facilitating sequential access. If the backup blocks are spread uniformly over all tracks in a cylinder, they tend to create "holes" that must be skipped during a sequential access.

2.2.2 Uniform Allocation

With uniform allocation the BackupMap is implemented to have the following properties:

- Legal backup blocks are *roughly* uniformly distributed among all disk blocks, but lack obvious patterns.

- The BackupMap can be easily constructed.

- An entry in the BackupMap can be checked relatively quickly. This of course implicitly implies that the BackupMap need not actually be stored in memory. The tradeoff is that access of a BackupMap entry will be orders of magnitude quicker than the check, but the check is more robust (since a BackupMap entry can be corrupted silently by a one-bit error).

Let M be the largest prime of the form $4k + 3$ which is less than P. Prime numbers are very common, and it is not difficult to find M, which is very close to P. The blocks that are reserved will be $B_i = i^2 (mod\ M)$, for $1 \leq i \leq B$. There are several points in order here. First, one must check that this indeed reserves B unique blocks. This follows from elementary number theory [7], if M is prime and $B_{i_1} = B_{i_2}$, then either $i_1 = i_2$ or $i_1 = M - i_2$ (modulo M). Since we assume that $i << P/2$, we can be assured that each i generates a unique B_i. Also, block zero can not be generated as a potential backup block. The algorithm can also be improved using techniques similar to quadratic probing in open addressing hash tables [17]. In our case, the observed distribution of the backup blocks is virtually indistinguishable from what would have been obtained by selecting B distinct blocks randomly. An example is shown in Figure 1 (b) for a 20% backup allocation.

However, our approach is more robust and fault tolerant than a straightforward random allocation. Given a candidate block X, one can efficiently determine if it is a legal backup block. This is because if M is a prime of the form $4k + 3$, a solution to $X \equiv Y^2 (mod\ M)$ is $Y = X^{(M+1)/4} (mod\ M)$. The other solution is $M - Y$. Thus, for a block X, we compute Y; if Y is larger than $M/2$, then we replace it with $M - Y$. At this point X is a legal backup block if and only if $1 \leq Y \leq B$.

2.3 Scheduling Algorithm

When a write is requested, the block is placed in cache and also immediately written through to a backup location on disk. Because backup blocks are located over the entire disk, in most cases writing through to disk is done without a seek and with minimum rotational latency. Later, the block is written to its proper address either by a block replacement policy or by a piggyback operation (See [14] for a discussion of piggybacking techniques).

When a read is requested, it is first checked whether the block is in cache, in which case no physical I/O is necessary. Otherwise, the read is scheduled using either a nearest free arm or, if no arm is free, earliest completion time algorithm. In addition to scheduling the read, any blocks in the cache which implicitly map to that track and which will be passed during the rotational latency are scheduled.

2.4 Block Replacement

Blocks in cache are of three types, *safe*, *clean* and *dirty*. A safe block is one that has been written to backup addresses on both disks but must still be written

No of cylinders	1000
Tracks per cylinder	20
Blocks per track	10
Block size	4 Kbytes
Average latency	8.33 ms
Average seek	13.50 ms
Seek cost function	nonlinear
Latency cost function	uniform

Table 1: **Disk parameters**

to its proper disk addresses. It is safe because it can be recovered even if the cache fails. A clean block is one that has been written to its proper disk address and hence can be deleted from the cache. Dirty blocks are blocks that have not been written to disk and hence are lost if the cache fails. Because of the write through policy, blocks are dirty in cache for only the time period needed to write them to backup locations at which time they become safe. This is usually in the order of milliseconds.

Any clean block in the cache can be deleted to make room for a new write. If there are no clean blocks, a block can be made clean by purging. The cylinder with the maximum number of dirty (or safe) blocks is always chosen to be purged. This yields a very low write cost per block. In [14] it was determined that using this technique about $2 \times b \times c$ blocks are always written out during a purge; b is the number of blocks per cylinder and c is the cache size as a ratio of disk size. For example, with a 2% cache and 200 blocks per cylinder, we expect an average of 8 blocks per purge.

2.5 Fault Tolerance

ITM achieves improved fault tolerance using a write through policy. Our simulation results show that the duration of blocks in cache before they are made safe is in the order of milliseconds. This compares very favorably to existing systems that use alternative techniques such as forced writes [8] to limit the duration of blocks in a volatile RAM. In ITM, once a write to a backup location is completed, system failures including the loss of a disk cache results in no loss of data. This is done without requiring non-volatile RAM for the disk cache.

3 Simulation Model

We wrote a simulator to compare the expected performance of the improved traditional mirror, and the traditional mirror. The disk parameters are summarized in Table 1.

In this experiment, no cache is used for the traditional mirror. In the improved traditional mirror, writes are cached and written through to backup addresses on disk. Read requests may be satisfied from the cache or by a physical I/O request.

There are three parameters in our model: cache size, backup factor and read ratio. The cache size is chosen as a percentage of the disk size. In this study 1% and 2% cache sizes were used[1]. The backup factor is the proportion of the disk reserved for backing up the contents of the volatile cache. In the current experiments, 20% backup factor was used. The read/write mix was varied from 0% read to 100% read in increments of 10%.

Requests are specified in terms of number of blocks. Different request sizes were simulated, however, in each simulation run, the request size is kept constant. Over the whole set of simulation runs, the request size grows by powers of two. The requests used in the experiments are uniformly distributed over the disk cylinders. Due to space limitations, we do not consider skewed distributions here.

The I/O system is modeled as a single-queue, single-server queuing system with an events scheduler and controller. The disk controller keeps mapped information on the disk blocks and determines which of the disks in the mirror set will service a request. The scheduler arranges the requests in service order and forwards the request to the appropriate disk.

4 Evaluation Methodology

Various metrics have been used in studies on disk I/O performance. For example, in [9], the read response time was used as the measure of performance, while in [13] write bandwidth was of primary concern. In this experiment, we consider the service time and response time for both read and write requests.

A write is declared completed once the data is safe, hence write response time is a measure of the time until a block is safe, since the cache is volatile. If there is always a clean block in cache, the write performance seen by the user is the time taken to complete the disk access. To service a mirrored write, the two disk arms are "rented" [5]. Using ITM, the "renting" frequency is doubled due to the write twice strategy, but this is more than compensated for by the fact that the "rental" cost is reduced by more than a factor of 2.

A read request is completed when the requested block is returned to the user. Since we considered only zero cost piggybacking for the second write, we do not expect piggybacking to have an effect on the read response time. Because our random workload does not exhibit spatial locality, the cache hit ratio is proportional to the size of the cache. Thus, the cache will not significantly impact the read request response time, since most read requests require a physical I/O.

Average read response is computed as the sum of the response times of all read misses divided by the number of read requests. The average service time

---

[1] For the size of disk used in the study, this is about 8 Mbytes and 16 Mbytes respectively

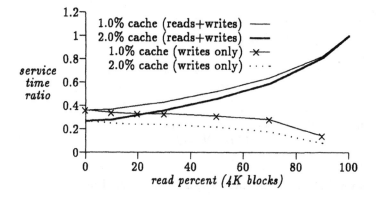

Figure 2: Single block service time ratio (ITM/TM) vs. read percent

is computed over all requests; a write request is serviced by both disks while a read request is serviced by a single disk.

5 Results

In this section the results obtained in simulating the traditional and improved traditional mirror schemes are presented. A 20% backup and track allocation scheme were used in all the ITM experiments. First the effect on single block requests is examined, and then the effect on multiple block requests is discussed. In both cases we examine the relative performance of the two schemes with respect to service time, and response time.

5.1 Single Block Write Time

Figure 2 shows the relative performance of ITM and TM on single random (4 Kbyte) block transfers for various read/write ratios. Two cache sizes, 1% and 2% are shown for the ITM. The read ratio is shown on the horizontal axis while on the vertical axis we show the ratio of the service times. The curves labeled *reads+writes* show values obtained by computing the service time over all requests, while the curves labeled *writes only* show the values obtained when only write requests are considered in a simulation run consisting of read and write requests. Each value on the vertical axis is obtained by dividing the ITM service time by the corresponding TM service time. Values less than 1.0 show where the ITM outperforms the TM. Thus for the range of parameter values used in our study, ITM outperforms TM since all vertical axis values are less than 1 (except for the 100% read).

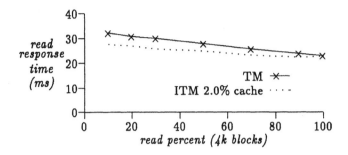

Figure 3: Single block read response time vs. read ratio

For the read+write curves, as the read ratio increases, the advantage of ITM over TM diminishes. For example, at a read ratio of 90%, Figure 2 shows that ITM has only about a 20% improvement over TM, while almost a 5-fold improvement over TM is observed at a read ratio of 0% with a 2% cache. The reason is that as the read ratio increases, both systems experience similar disk access patterns since almost every read request requires an explicit physical I/O. However, when only the write requests are considered, we see that ITM shows improved performance even with increasing read ratio. This is because writes are efficient in ITM and inefficient in TM. In addition some writes are piggybacked by the read requests in ITM and hence incur no costs.

5.2 Single Block Read and Write Response Time

The response time, or time it takes for a read operation to complete, depends on both the queuing time and on the minimum of the two service times; the response time for a write is the time until the block becomes safe. We separate read response time from write response time since an application is only delayed by read response time.

Figure 3 shows the single block read response time for the ITM and TM for various read/write ratios using a 2% cache for the ITM. ITM and TM show similar performance for a 100% read workload. For a read ratio ranging between 10% and 90%, ITM read response time shows improvements ranging between 34% and 5% over corresponding TM values. TM response time is more sensitive to the read/write ratio because writes are expensive in TM. The performance of both schemes tend to converge with increasing read ratio. ITM performance improvement is largest at high write ratios, where ITM shows up to a 34% response time improvement over TM.

Figure 4 shows the single block write response time for the ITM and TM for various read/write ratios using a 2% cache for the ITM. Because blocks are

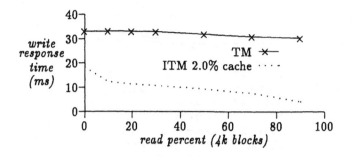

Figure 4: Single block write response time vs. read ratio

•

written efficiently through to disk, single block write response time for ITM is significantly more efficient than for TM. For the parameter values used in our simulation, no queuing time was involved, and for the ITM, writes are performed efficiently using the write through strategy. In any case, we believe that the write response time is a secondary issue. Since most systems perform writes asynchronously, their recovery mechanisms are dependent on the response time of the log [6, 4]. The response time of the log for ITM is identical to that of the traditional system.

For applications in which the write response time is too large, a small non-volatile memory can be used to hold the write requests temporarily until the blocks are backed up on disk. Note that this non-volatile memory is very small, on the order of a few blocks, as opposed to a large non-volatile disk cache required by a simple write-only disk cache.

5.3   Multi-block Service Time

In Figure 5 is shown semi-log graphs that compare the service times for the ITM against corresponding values for the TM for a 50% read/write mix and various request sizes. Values in the curves labeled *writes only* were obtained using data from only write requests over a simulation run. The *reads+writes* curves were obtained using data from both read and write requests.

There are two distinct size ranges in these experiments, small and large transfers. The size ranges are sensitive to the size of cache used for the ITM. For a 1% cache, ITM is superior from 1 to about 8 blocks (4 to 32 Kbyte transfers). For a 2% cache, the range is up to about 16 blocks (64 Kbyte transfers), Beyond this small transfer range, TM is better. Thus the size of cache determines the performance and also influences system cost.

The advantages of ITM for small writes are:

1. With sufficient backing store, the cost for the first write in the ITM is very small, since backup blocks are easily located.

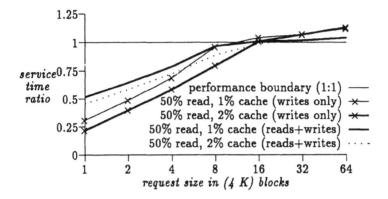

Figure 5: Multi block service time ratio (ITM/TM)

2. On average the cost for the second write is also small. Some blocks are piggybacked and hence written at no cost, the rest must be purged and this requires a seek, although in general a single seek time can be amortized over multiple writes.

Large block transfers in ITM incur a penalty over traditional mirror since the disk must do more track-to-track seeks as in traditional mirror and also must skip over the backup blocks.

The response time graphs are similar to the service time graphs and are not shown. Like the service time graphs, the response time graphs show two distinct performance regions; for single block transfers, ITM performance is superior to TM, however, for large transfers, TM is better. As with the service time, ITM incurs a penalty skipping backup sectors during transfers.

Figure 5 suggests that ITM may not be appropriate for very large sequential accesses. One possible solution is a hybrid which uses ITM for small writes and TM for large sequential writes. These schemes are completely compatible, and so can be seamlessly combined.

5.4 Disk Utilization

Although the write twice scheme increases the number of disk accesses, this does not necessarily translate to more work for the disk subsystem if the workload is dominated by single random block transfers. For example, Figure 6 shows the disk utilization variation with read/write ratio when the same workload (random single block transfers) is presented to the TM and ITM. Although the

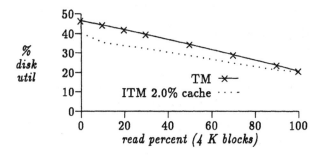

Figure 6: Disk utilization vs. read ratio

number of disk accesses observed in ITM was almost twice the number observed in TM, the disk utilization was consistently lower in ITM than in TM especially for write intensive workloads. For example, a 40% disk utilization was observed for the ITM with a 0% read (100% write), while a 47% utilization was observed for the TM for the same workload.

A number of conclusions can be drawn from this. The first is that for single block transfers, the ITM can support a higher throughput than the TM at the same disk utilization. The second is that for small reads and writes, the efficiency of disk access performance is a more important parameter than the number of disk accesses performed. In [10] the effective write ratio seen by a disk subsystem with a disk cache was studied, in terms of the number of accesses to disk. However, our study takes a different perspective to this problem and determines that for a workload dominated by single random block transfers the efficiency of disk access is probably a more critical consideration than the number of physical accesses to disk.

5.5 Effect of Block Size on Single Block Transfers

The performance of ITM is very sensitive to the block size and access size (for our studies, the block size and access size are equal). Figure 7 shows the relative performance of ITM and TM in single random block transfers for 2 Kbyte and 4 Kbyte block sizes. With a smaller block size (and hence more blocks per track), writing through to disk is more efficient since the chance of finding a free block increases with the number of blocks per track. Moreover, piggybacking becomes more efficient as more blocks can be transferred during piggyback operations.

However, with single random block transfers in TM, the only component of service time affected by a change in block size is the transfer time. The major components of the service time, seek and rotational latency are unaffected, hence TM is largely insensitive to changes in block size for single random block

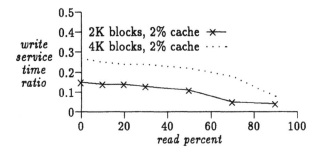

Figure 7: Single block service time ratio (ITM/TM) vs. read percent

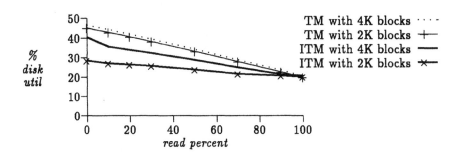

Figure 8: Disk utilization vs. read ratio

transfers. Consequently, the performance differences in Figure 7 are due to improved performance of the ITM for small block sizes.

Figure 8 is another way to show the impact of block sizes on the two schemes. With TM, the disk utilization for both block sizes is almost the same; however, for the ITM, a lower disk utilization is obtained for the smaller block size. The difference is more obvious for high write ratio, primarily as a result of the ease in locating free blocks.

6 System Recovery

We assume that the *SafeMaps* for the mirrored set are stored in the (non-volatile) disk controller cache. We consider two different failures and their effect on system recovery:

1. Disk failure, and
2. Cache failure.

If a disk fails, each block is directly accessible on the remaining disk as in the TM. Given this disk, a spare disk must be reconstructed from the remaining mirrored disk to restore mirroring protection. The cost of this operation is the same in both schemes since a direct disk-to-disk copy can be used.

Assume that Disk 1 in the mirror set has failed and a spare disk must be reconstructed from Disk 0. Once a disk failure is detected, the recovery algorithm is activated and the following actions take place during the reconstruction process.

- The map for the failed disk is considered obsolete and out of date.

- Write requests are performed *in place* in Disk 0 (the survivor disk) and the spare disk being reconstructed. The SafeMap for Disk 0 is updated if the block was previously backed up. The update essentially indicates the block is no longer backed up.

- Read requests may be directed to the spare disk if the block requested has been reconstructed, otherwise, they will be directed to Disk 0.

- A direct disk-to-disk copy is done as in TM.

- At the end of the disk copy operation, SafeMap for Disk 0 is copied to SafeMap for the reconstructed disk which now becomes Disk 1. Thus at the end of reconstruction, both disks contain identical data both in their logical and backup locations; hence their maps are also made identical.

Recovery from a failed disk is, therefore, identical as in TM except for the added cost of the NVRAM to store the maps. The size of the SafeMap is proportional to B, and for the disk parameters used in our simulation, this is about 320 Kbytes for the mirror set. If NVRAM costs about $500 per MB, this is about a $250 increase in cost for a 0.5 MB configuration to hold the maps.

In the case of cache failure, the data on each disk is uncorrupted and the SafeMaps are also safe (since we assume they are kept in NVRAM). The loss of cache does not result in data loss since all cache blocks are written through to disk. A higher level of fault tolerance can be achieved by using a few blocks of NVRAM to hold blocks until the disk access to make them safe is committed. Note that we are talking about one or two blocks of NVRAM and not NVRAM for the whole disk cache. Recovery process is similar to that of a failed disk. The recovery algorithm triggers the following actions:

- Write requests are performed *in place* on both disks and the SafeMaps updated if necessary.

- Read requests are processed by either disk; however, no blocks are piggy-backed since the cache is lost.

- When a new disk cache is installed, blocks are read from the backup locations on disk to cache. This is possible since the SafeMaps contain enough information on the backed up blocks and their backup addresses.

- Normal ITM operations resume after all backup blocks are read into the cache.

7 Conclusion

The improved traditional mirror provides an effective method for performing both small block reads and writes as well as large sequential transfers. However, the strength of ITM lies in small block transfers. For large sequential writes, TM outperform ITM. For improved traditional mirror we have shown that:
- Efficiency of single block transfers is significantly improved.

- Recovery is performed efficiently since a direct disk-to-disk copy is possible.

- A high level of fault tolerance is provided to the I/O subsystem with a write through strategy without degrading disk access performance.

The improved traditional mirror increases in importance as technological advances bring larger disk caches. Moreover, with large disk caches, more reads are satisfied in the cache, increasing the write ratio to disk. However, disk access performance in improved traditional mirror is very efficient and this increased write ratio does not pose a performance problem to the I/O subsystem.

Acknowledgements

One of the authors was supported in part by NSF Grant CCR-9208631. The authors thank the referees for their many useful comments.

References

[1] K. Bates and M. TeGrotenhuis. Shadowing Boosts System Reliability. *Computer Design*, April 1985.

[2] D. Bitton. Arm Scheduling in Shadowed Disks. In *Proceedings of the IEEE Computer Society International Conference (COMPCON)*, pages 132–136, San Francisco, California, February 1989.

[3] D. Bitton and J. Gray. Disk Shadowing. In *Proceedings of the International Conference on Very Large Data Bases*, pages 331–338, Los Angeles, California, September 1988.

[4] J. Gray. The Transaction Concepts: Virtues and Limitations. In *Proceedings of the International Conference on Very Large Data Bases*, pages 144–154, Cannes, France, September 1981.

[5] J. Gray and F. Putzolu. The 5 Minute Rule for Trading Memory for Disc Accesses and the 10 Byte Rule for Trading Memory for CPU Time. In *Proceedings of the International Conference of the ACM SIGMOD*, pages 395–398, San Francisco, California, June 1987.

[6] T. Haerder and A. Reuter. Principles of Transaction-Oriented Database Recovery. *ACM Computing Surveys*, 15 No. 4:287–317, December 1983.

[7] G. Hardy and E. Wright. *An Introduction to the Theory of Numbers*. Oxford Science Publications, Oxford, England, 1979.

[8] M. McKusick, W. Joy, S. Leffler, and R. Fabry. A Fast File System for UNIX. *ACM Transactions on Computer Systems*, 2 No. 3:181–197, August 1984.

[9] A. Narasimha Reddy. A Study of I/O System Organizations. In *Proceeding of 19th. International Symposium on Computer Architecture*, pages 308–317, May 1992. Also published as Computer Architecture News, Vol 20, No. 2.

[10] A. Narasimha Reddy. Reads and Writes: When I/Os Aren't Quite the Same. In *Proceeding of 25th. Hawaii Systems Conference*, January 1992.

[11] C. Orji and J. Solworth. Doubly Distorted Mirrors. In *Proceedings of the International Conference of the ACM SIGMOD*, pages 307–316, Washington D.C., May 1993.

[12] C. Polyzois, A. Bhide, and D Dias. Disk Mirroring with Alternating Deferred Updates. In *Proceedings of the International Conference on Very Large Data Bases*, Dublin, Ireland, 1993. To appear.

[13] M. Rosenblum and J. Ousterhout. The Design and Implementation of a Log-Structured File System. In *Proceedings of the Symposium on Operating Systems Principles*, Pacific Grove, California, October 1991.

[14] J. Solworth and C. Orji. Write-Only Disk Caches. In *Proceedings of the International Conference of the ACM SIGMOD*, pages 123–132, Atlantic City, New Jersey, May 1990.

[15] J. Solworth and C. Orji. Distorted Mirrors. In *First International Conference on Parallel and Distributed Information Systems*, pages 10–17, Miami, Florida, December 1991.

[16] J. Solworth and C. Orji. Distorted Mapping Techniques to Improve the Performance of Mirrored Disk Systems. *Distributed and Parallel Databases: An International Journal*, 1(1):81–102, 1993.

[17] M. Weiss. *Data Structures and Algorithm Analysis*. The Benjamin/Cummings Publishing Company Inc., Menlo Park, California, 1992.

Adaptive Load Balancing in Disk Arrays

Peter Scheuermann[1], Gerhard Weikum[2], and Peter Zabback[2]

[1] Dep. of Elec. Eng. and Computer Sc., Northwestern University, Evanston, IL 60208
[2] Dep. of Computer Science, ETH Zurich, CH-8092 Zurich, Switzerland

Abstract. Large arrays of small disks are providing an attractive approach for high performance I/O systems. In order to make effective use of disk arrays and other multi-disk architectures, it is necessary to develop intelligent software tools that allow automatic tuning of the disk arrays to varying workloads. In this paper we describe an adaptive method for data allocation and load balancing in disk arrays. Our method deals with dynamically changing access frequencies of files by reallocating file extents, thus "cooling down" hot disks. In addition, the method takes into account the fact that some files may exhibit periodical access patterns, and considers explicitly the cost of performing the "cooling" operations. Preliminary performance studies based on real-life I/O traces demonstrate the effectivity of this approach.

1 Introduction

1.1 Background and Problem

Large arrays of small disks (also known as RAIDs) provide an attractive alternative over large disks in terms of cost, volume and power [7, 13, 19]. In addition, disk arrays provide the potential for high performance I/O by exploiting the bandwidth of several disks to service a single logical request or multiple independent requests in parallel. The architectures that are being pursued range from disk arrays that appear as a single logical device to more conventional multi-disk systems based on loosely coupled small disks and standardized channel architectures [12]. The only assumption that we make in our work is that the operating system can access disks individually rather than bundling all disks together as a single logical device. In the following, we use the concise term "disk array" to include other loosely coupled multi-disk architectures as well.

In order to effectively exploit the potential for I/O parallelism in a disk array, files must be partitioned and distributed across disks. File striping or declustering [14, 15, 19, 20] is a technique for file organization which divides a file into runs of logically consecutive blocks (called "stripes") which are then spread across a number of disks in order to reduce the transfer time of a single request or to improve the throughput for multiple requests.

The degree to which the potential I/O parallelism of a disk array can be effectively exploited in an application depends on the placement of the application's data. The partitioning of a file determines the degree of parallelism in servicing a single request to the file, and the allocation of the file partitions onto disks determines the load balance in the array. Finally, the degree of intra-request parallelism and the load balancing together determine the throughput and the effective speed-up of requests.

The goal of our research on I/O parallelism is to develop algorithms and to build system software (i.e., a file manager and a low-level storage manager for advanced database systems) that can effectively exploit loosely coupled disks. Since the performance of a disk array depends critically on the placement of data, we have especially investigated algorithms for tuning the placement of files towards the workload characteristics of an application [22, 24, 25].

In principle, the data placement problem can be viewed as a file assignment problem, which has been intensively studied in many variants and is known to be NP-hard. Hence, viable solutions must be based on a heuristic approach. In the ample work reported on the file assignment problem [5, 26] such heuristics have been investigated only for the static case, that is, when all files are to be allocated at the same time and the access characteristics of the files are completely known in advance. Also, the issue of I/O parallelism in servicing a single request has been disregarded so far. In advanced data-intensive applications such as object-oriented database systems or multimedia storage servers, data placement methods must take into account the potential performance gains of intra-request parallelism as well as its overhead and deal with dynamic file allocations and deletions, with expansions or shrinkage of files, and with unpredictable changes in the access characteristics of existing files. Moreover, since the tuning of data placement should be automated and incorporated into the file manager or database system, practically viable algorithms for file partitioning and allocation must be invoked dynamically at low execution costs.

1.2 Contribution and Outline of the Paper

In this paper we describe an adaptive (i.e., "self-tuning") method for data allocation and dynamic load balancing in disk arrays. Its basic idea is to allocate and possibly migrate data such that the variance of the disk load in the array is minimized. This idea is generalized for workloads with periodic changes of their access characteristics by minimizing a "weighted" disk load variance over a specified time span, with weights proportional to the lengths of the time intervals with stable access characteristics. Such periodic changes do occur and are quite predictable, for example, in on-line transaction processing (OLTP) systems with batch processing during the night. The data migration, which we call "disk cooling", aims to move the data with the highest "temperature", that is, the ratio between the "heat" (i.e., access frequency) and the size of the data, from hot disks to colder disks while taking into account the cost of such migrations. This approach generalizes our previous work on disk load balancing [24] in that we consider the cost of data migration and can exploit foreknowledge of periodic changes of access characteristics. Further note that our previous work did not use an explicit objective function in its optimization heuristics.

The developed method has the following salient properties:

- It consists of modular building blocks that can be invoked independently; in particular, the algorithms for file allocation and disk load balancing can be used regardless of whether striping is employed or not. The allocation and load balancing algorithms are applicable also to parallel database systems in which relations or complex objects are partitioned based on attribute values [4, 6].
- It can take into account explicitly specified constraints on data placement for recovery, security and other administrative purposes.
- It uses simple but effective heuristics that incur only little overhead.
- Its constituent algorithms can be invoked on-line, i.e., concurrently with regular requests to existing files.
- It is beneficial for a variety of application classes, including OLTP, relational database systems, object-oriented database systems, network file servers, multimedia applications, and scientific applications.
- It is mostly motivated by the evolving disk array technology; however, it is applicable to all sorts of multi-disk architectures.

The work on disk load balancing in disk arrays reported in the literature has concentrated on static data placement [3, 26] and on improving the performance due to redundant data [9, 10, 11, 16, 17, 18]. Dynamic adaptation of the data allocation to evolving access characteristics with the goal of dynamic disk load balancing has not been addressed so far.

The rest of the paper is organized as follows. Section 2 presents our basic method for data allocation and load balancing, as developed in [24]. The load balancing is based on dynamic data migration from hot to cold disks, which we call disk cooling. Section 3 generalizes the load balancing method by considering predictable as well as unpredictable dynamic changes of access characteristics. Section 4 discusses preliminary results from two performance studies based on real-life I/O traces.

2 Basic Method for Data Allocation and Load Balancing

This section briefly reviews our previous work on data allocation and load balancing, which serves as the starting point for the generalized approach that is developed in this paper. We have designed and built an experimental file system called FIVE[3] [24], which incorporates low-overhead heuristic methods for tuning the placement of files on a disk array or conventional multi-disk system. These methods consist of a file partitioning algorithm based on striping [25] and a file allocation algorithm which aims to ensure good load balancing [24].

The partitioning algorithm allows that the striping unit can be chosen individually for each file or even portions of a file, so that files with different access characteristics (e.g., average request size) can be treated differently. We have developed a simple analytic model for heuristically determining the optimal striping unit of a file and the number of disks across which a file is spread [24, 25].

---

[3] FIVE stands for FIle system with adaptiVe Enhancements.

Our system allows relatively small striping units for files with very large request sizes and/or critical response time constraints, while using very coarse striping units for other files or even not striping other files at all because of throughput considerations [2, 7].

Having decided to partition and spread a file over a particular number of disks, all striping units of the file that would be mapped to the same disk are combined into a single allocation unit called an *extent*. We then have to select the disks on which the file extents are actually placed. When the various files have different access patterns, an intelligent decision is crucial for disk load balancing. Our system keeps track of a number of related statistics:

- the *heat* of extents and disks, where the heat is defined as the sum of the number of block accesses of an extent or disk per time unit, as determined by statistical observation over a certain period of time,
- and the *temperature* of extents, which is defined as the ratio between heat and size [3].

A simple but effective heuristic algorithm for the static allocation problem, where all files are to be allocated at the same time and the heat of each extent is known or can be estimated in advance, is discussed in [3]. The algorithm first sorts all extents by descending heat, and extents are allocated in this sort order. For each extent allocation, the algorithm selects the disk with the lowest accumulated heat among the disks that have not yet been assigned another extent of the same file.

We have extended this greedy algorithm so as to deal with dynamic allocations. In [24] we have developed a class of disk selection algorithms which provide a good compromise between access time minimization, load balancing and extra I/Os due to partial reorganization. If a certain disk is selected for allocation in a given strategy due to space or access time constraints, our algorithms also allow the invocation of a dynamic load balancing step, called *disk cooling*. This is basically a greedy algorithm which removes from the disk a number of extents in decreasing order of temperature and places them on the coolest disks which do not yet hold extents of the corresponding files. The temperature metric is used as the criterion for selecting the extents that are to be reallocated, because temperature reflects the benefit/cost ratio of a reallocation since benefit is proportional to heat (i.e., reduction of heat) and cost is proportional to size (of the reallocated extents).

3 Generalized Load Balancing

The basic method of the previous section allows for the various files to have different access patterns, but the access pattern of a given file is considered fixed in time. In practice, however, this is not the case; rather we encounter many environments in which the heat of the files changes over time, and, further, some files exhibit a periodical pattern of heat changes in applications with prescheduled operations.

As an example of the problem, consider the following scenario. In most OLTP systems for banking applications, the access characteristics during the day are significantly different from the access characteristics for the end-of-day batch processing during the night. Moreover, these periodic changes of access characteristics are well predictable. Table 1 shows an extremely simplified example of the daytime heat and night-time heat for a set of six files. Note that the 24-hour average heat is the same for all six files. Therefore, a vanilla placement of these files onto three disks, using our basic allocation method for static load balancing, could be as shown in Figure 1 (a). This placement appears well balanced over an entire 24-hour period. However, there are actually severe load imbalances for both the daytime period and the night-time period. A much better placement would be the one shown in Figure 1 (b). Obviously, to come up with such a placement (other than by chance), the allocation method has to be aware of the periodic heat changes of the files and needs to take into account the heat distribution in each of the two intervals.

Table 1. Example of files with periodic heat changes

	Daytime Heat (12 hours)	Night-time Heat (12 hours)	24-Hour Average Heat
File 1	10	0	5
File 2	8	2	5
File 3	6	4	5
File 4	4	6	5
File 5	2	8	5
File 6	0	10	5

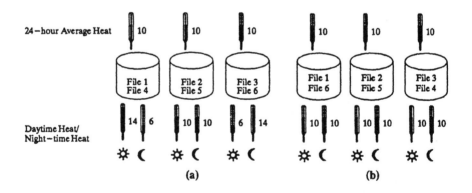

Fig. 1. (a) Unbalanced placement of files, (b) Balanced placement of files

To deal with this generalized load balancing problem, it becomes necessary to invoke a generalized disk cooling procedure periodically, with cooling decisions based on a generalized objective function that represents the variance of the disk heat in the array over a certain interval of time. We also need some bookkeeping to estimate the current heat of a file. Finally, we need to consider explicitly the cost of performing the cooling, which is not included in our earlier model. These three subproblems are discussed in the following three subsections.

3.1 Generalized Objective Function and Cooling Algorithm

We distinguish between Predictable Heat Files (PHF), which exhibit a periodical heat pattern over a given cycle, and Unpredictable Heat Files (UHF), for which we can observe only the current heat. For example, in an OLTP application with "canned" transactions, most files would be PHFs. On the other hand, in a multimedia archive of a news agency, most files would be UHFs since editors would typically access archived data in an unpredictable manner, depending on the latest news. In general, we aim to support any combination of PHFs and UHFs, including the special cases with PHFs or UHFs alone.

The optimization time span, TS, of the load balancing procedure can be chosen, as shown in Figure 2, as the maximum cycle of all the cycles of the PHFs. The union of the points in time where the individual PHFs change heat patterns induces a partition of TS into n time intervals. Thus, more formally we can define TS as the vector: $TS = [(t_1 - t_0), (t_2 - t_1), ...(t_n - t_{n-1})]$ and denote by interval j the interval of length $(t_j - t_{j-1})$. Let us also denote by $H(i, j)$ the heat of disk i in interval j. Correspondingly, the weighted disk heat of disk i over the time span TS is defined as:

$$WDH(i, TS) = \sum_{j=1}^{n} H(i, j) * (t_j - t_{j-1}).$$

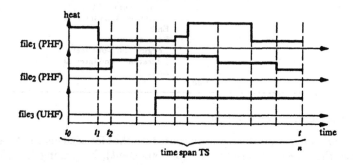

Fig. 2. Temporal heat changes of predictable-heat and unpredictable-heat files

Observe that the weighted heat of a disk i is composed of two components: WDH_P and WDH_U, where WDH_P is the heat due to the PHFs and WDH_U is the heat due to the UHFs. Since for UHFs we assume that the future behavior cannot be predicted, the best estimate we can make is that $WDH_U(i, j) = WDH_U(i, curr)$ for all intervals j following the current interval $curr$. Furthermore, note that both PHFs and UHFs may be dynamically allocated and deleted; hence, even if the load were originally balanced among the disks, it will be necessary later to perform a load balancing procedure. We use as an objective cost function to be minimized by our generalized load balancing procedure the Weighted Disk Heat Variance (*WDHV*) over the time span TS:

$$WDHV(H, TS) = \sum_{j=1}^{n} \sum_{i=1}^{D} (\bar{H}(j) - H(i,j))^2 * (t_j - t_{j-1})$$

where H is a matrix whose element in position (i,j) is $H(i,j)$

D = number of disks in the array

$\bar{H}(j) = \sum_{i=1}^{D} H(i,j)/D$

Note that, within each time interval, the total heat over all disks is constant for all possible allocations of the data, since the heat of each file is assumed to be constant within the interval. Thus, minimizing the disk heat variance really captures the intuitive goal of distributing the given load (which is constant) as evenly as possible. This goal implies minimizing disk queueing, which in turn is crucial for acceptable response time.

We will consider a number of heuristic strategies for generalized disk cooling. Let us define an action as a record with the components shown in Figure 3.

```
type action = Record
                  extent: Record
                             no: extent-id;
                             size : no-of-blocks;
                             heat: access-frequency;
                             End;
                  origin : disk-no;
                  target : disk-no;
                  read:   Record
                             begin: point-of-time;
                             duration: time-interval
                             End;
                  write:  Record
                             begin: point-of-time;
                             duration: time-interval
                             End;
              End;
```

Fig. 3. Definition of a cooling action

Our algorithm is basically a greedy procedure that for each consecutive action determines the extent to be removed (action.extent), by picking the disk with the highest weighted heat (action.origin) and then choosing the extent with the highest weighted temperature. We then determine to which disk the extent should be moved (action.target), by choosing the disk with the lowest weighted heat subject to some constraint. Let us denote by *WDHV'* the weighted disk heat variance over the time span TS after a given action is executed:

$$WDHV'(H, T, action) = \sum_{j=1}^{n} \sum_{i=1}^{D} (\bar{H}^*(j) - H^*(i,j))^2 * (t_j - t_{j-1})$$

where $H^*(i,j) = H(i,j)$ if $i \neq$ action.target or action.origin

$H^*(i,j) = H(i,j)$ + action.extent.heat if $i =$ action.target

$H^*(i,j) = H(i,j)$ − action.extent.heat if $i =$ action.origin

```
Generalized Disk Cooling Algorithm (GDC)
Input : D          – number of disks
        Matrix H   – H(i,j) is heat of disk D_i in interval j;
        Matrix T   – T(k,j) is the temperature of extent e_k in interval j;
        Vector TS  – intervals of time span;
        t_cur      – current point in life cycle;
Output : actions-to-do – list of cooling actions;
benefit = true;
actions-to-do = empty;
start-next-action= t_cur;
While benefit =true do
Step 0 : If trigger-condition = true then execute remaining steps;
Step 1 : Choose new extent and origin disk:
         action.origin = the disk with the highest weighted heat;
         action.extent.no = the extent on action.origin with the highest
                            weighted temperature;
Step 2 : Choose new target disk:
         action.target = the disk with the lowest weighted heat such that this disk
                         does not hold already an extent of the file to which
                         action.extent belongs;
Step 3: Estimate the cooling time:
        action.read.begin = the point in time at which the read phase of the cooling
                            action will start = start-next-action;
        action.read.duration = the time it takes to read action.extent from
                               action.origin into memory
        action.write.begin = start-next-action + action.read.duration
        action.write.duration = the time it takes to write action.extent onto action.target
Step 4: Determine the intervals m and n when action.read.begin and action.write.begin occur;
Step 5: Calculate E, the Extra-Weighted Disk Heat Variance due to action:
```

$$E = \sum_{i=1}^{D}(\bar{H}'(m) - H'(i,m))^2 * \text{action.read.duration} +$$

$$\sum_{i=1}^{D}(\bar{H}''(n) - H''(i,n))^2 * \text{action.write.duration};$$

```
Step 6: Compute WDHV, the current weighted disk heat variance, and WDHV', the weighted
        disk heat variance if action is to be executed;
Step 7: If WDHV - (WDHV' + E) > Epsilon
        then
                add action to actions-to-do
                start-next-action = start-next-action +
                action.read.duration + action.write.duration
        else benefit = false;
endwhile
```

Fig. 4. GDC algorithm

A high level version of the Generalized Disk Cooling algorithm (GDC) is given in Figure 4. In order to determine whether a given action is beneficial or not we have to consider not only the reduction in heat on the origin disk and the addition in heat on the target disk, but also the additional heat caused by the reorganization process itself as shown in Figure 5 (a). The cooling process is executed during two intervals of time, the first corresponding to the read phase of the action and the second corresponding to the write phase of the action. The read and write phases introduce an amount of additional heat on the origin and target disks which is computed by dividing the size of the extent to be moved by the corresponding duration of the phase.

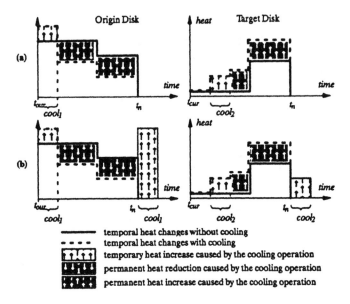

Fig. 5. (a) Cost and benefit of cooling, (b) adjustment of weighted heat variance

3.2 Heat Bookkeeping

The heat of a set of blocks (e.g., an extent or a disk) is the accumulated heat of its blocks. The heat of a block is the number of requests to the block per time unit. In our previous work, we assumed that this block heat can be measured in a sufficiently large, representative time interval (e.g., one hour) and remains relatively stable. In the case of files with dynamically changing heat, we obviously need a dynamic method for tracking the heat of the file's blocks. Our approach is to keep track of the last n requests to a block, using a "moving window" into the history of the block, as illustrated in Figure 6. This information, which can be collected fairly inexpensively, serves to estimate the average interarrival time of requests to the block. The heat of a block b is then estimated as the reciprocal of the average interarrival time of requests to the block, computed over the last n requests:

$$Heat(b) = \sum_{i=l-n+1}^{n} \frac{n}{t_i - t_{i-1}}$$

where t_l is the time of the last request to block b.

Extensive experiments with real-life I/O traces have shown that a value of $n = 20$ is sufficiently large to keep track of dynamic heat changes while eliminating stochastic noise. The experiments have also shown that the heat estimates are fairly insensitive with respect to the exact value of n.

To be able to control the overhead of the bookkeeping, our method can also record requests on a per extent basis rather than for each block individually. The heat estimate of an extent is updated with each request that accesses at least one

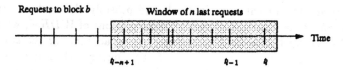

Fig. 6. Tracking the heat of a block

of the extent's blocks, and the heat estimation takes into account the number of accessed blocks within the extent. The details of this estimation are omitted here for brevity; the basic principle is identical to the block heat estimation method. Regardless of the granularity of the actual bookkeeping, the heat of any data granule that is larger than the bookkeeping granule can be estimated simply by summing up the heat of the constituent fine granules.

3.3 Estimating The Cost Of Cooling

The duration times of the read and write phases of an action can be calculated by making use of an M/G/1 queueing model with a non-preemptive prioritized server. We consider that our system consists of requests with two priorities: regular user requests have high priority, while the cooling requests have low priority. Cooling requests represent the read/write phases of the cooling actions. Let L_c denote the proportion of disk utilization due to cooling requests and L_r the proportion of disk utilization due to regular requests. Then, RT_c, the response time of a cooling request with a non-preemptive server is given by [8]:

$$RT_c = \frac{kLT}{(1-L)(1-L_r)} + T_c$$

where L is the total disk utilization ($L = L_c + L_r$), T is the average service time for requests of both priorities, T_c is the average service time for cooling requests and k denotes the time to finish the current request when a new one arrives. The distribution coefficient of the service time, k, is given by the Khintchine and Pollaczek equation as $k = \frac{1}{2} * \frac{E(T^2)}{T^2}$.

In an open queueing model, L_r, the disk utilization due to regular requests, can be calculated as: $L_r = T_r * \lambda_r$, where T_r is the average service time for regular requests and λ_r is the corresponding arrival rate. If we assume that the cooling request is currently performed on disk i and that it occurs during time interval m, then λ_r can be computed by using the formula:

$$\lambda_r = \frac{H(i,m)}{\bar{R}}$$

where $\bar{R}$ is the average request size.

Since cooling requests do not have an observable arrival rate, we shall estimate λ_c by the following upper bound :

$$\lambda_c \leq \frac{1}{(optimal\ service\ time\ for\ an\ average\ cooling\ request)}$$

In step 5 of the GDC algorithm we compute E, the Extra-Weighted Disk Heat Variance, by making use of the following approximation technique. In order to avoid splitting the current time interval, and possibly the next one (see Figure 5 (a)), and thus incurring expensive recalculations of $WDHV$, we add two "dummy" intervals to the load balancing cycle to account for the two cooling phases of the action, as shown in Figure 5 (b). During such a dummy interval the heat of each disk, except for the disk which is the subject of the cooling operation, is taken to be the same as the heat of the disk during the time interval when the corresponding cooling process started. Thus, the extra contributions to the $WDHV$ are computed as given below:

$H'(i,j) = H(i,j) +$ action.extent.size/action.action.read.duration for $i =$ action.origin
$H'(i,j) = H(i,j)$ otherwise
$H''(i,j) = H(i,j) +$ action.extent.size/action.write.duration for $i =$ action.target
$H''(i,j) = H(i,j)$ otherwise.

4 Performance Studies

The algorithms for file partitioning, file allocation, and dynamic load balancing (i.e., a simplified version of the GDC algorithm) are implemented in an experimental file system prototype [24]. This prototype, which is part of the COMFORT project [23], is implemented such that it can either manage real data on real hardware, or it can simulate the performance impact of virtual resources (especially disks) that are not available to us. In this section, we present simulation-based performance studies of the file allocation and load balancing algorithms, using an optimization time span with only one interval. Note that this is only a special case of the generalized load balancing problem, but already involves dynamic rebalancing because of unpredictable heat files. Performance studies of the general case with multiple-interval time spans and periodic heat changes are in preparation. The study of Subsection 4.1 is based on traces from file servers at the University of California at Berkeley [1]. The study of Subsection 4.2 is based on I/O traces from the OLTP system of a large Swiss bank (Union Bank of Switzerland).

4.1 File System Workload

The trace for this study contains approximately 320'000 requests to about 6'400 files, recorded during 24 hours.[4] About 4'800 out of these 6'400 files are allocated already at the beginning of the trace; the total size of these files (that were referenced in the trace) is about 3.5 GBytes. The trace itself contains about 1'600 dynamic file creations. Thus, this workload exhibits high dynamics with respect to allocations. In addition, the heat of the 4'800 pre-allocated files exhibits heavy changes in the 24-hour trace period. The average request size of the trace is 23 KBytes.

---

[4] This is basically trace 8 of [1]. Short-lived files (lifetime < 1 minute) are removed, since they would usually be memory-resident.

In our performance experiment, we treated all files as unpredictable heat files and assumed a single-interval optimization time span (of 24 hours, i.e., the entire trace period). The files were allocated on 16 disks of capacity 1.0 GBytes, using Round-robin as the basic allocation method. All files were striped with track-sized striping units.

During the experiment, we employed a simplified version of our cooling algorithm. Cooling was initiated whenever the heat of the hottest disk exceeded the average disk heat in the array by more than 1 percent. The heat of file extents was gathered dynamically, using the bookkeeping method described in Subsection 3.2.

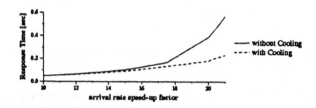

Fig. 7. Average response time [sec] with and without cooling

Figure 7 shows the results of this performance study. We compared our cooling algorithm with the vanilla Round-robin allocation method. To investigate the behavior of our algorithm at different load levels, we varied the arrival rate of the requests by "speeding up" the arrivals of the trace while retaining the relative interarrival times of the original trace. For example, a "speed-up factor" of 10 means that the 24-hour trace was executed on our simulation testbed within 2.4 hours. Figure 7 shows the average response time of the I/O requests with and without cooling, as a function of the arrival rate speed-up factor.

Under light load, the load imbalance in the array did not yet cause any significant queueing delays. Therefore, cooling did not have any impact at all. Under medium and heavy load, cooling was able to improve the load balance considerably, which led to a decrease of the average response time by a factor of 2.3 (at an arrival rate speed-up factor of 20).

Our cooling algorithm also coped well with the dynamic fluctuations in the load level of the workload. Figure 8 (a) shows the average response time as it varies over the time of the performance experiment (at a specific arrival rate speed-up factor of 20). The shape of the curves reflects the dynamics of the load. Especially during the load peak at the end of the trace, the cooling method achieves tremendous performance gains (by a factor of 5) due to better load balancing and, hence, reduced queueing.

Figure 8 (b) shows the frequency of the data migration steps invoked by our cooling method, varying over time. The figure shows that our algorithm was careful enough so as not to initiate too many cooling steps during the high-load

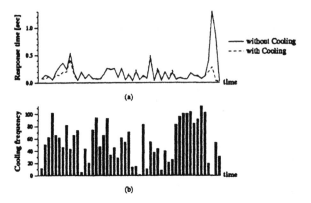

Fig. 8. Average response time and cooling frequency varying over time (at speed-up factor 20) for the file system workload

phases; rather the data migrations were performed mostly during the low-load phases, thus improving the load balance for the next high-load phase at low cost. This robustness is achieved by explicitly trading off the benefit of cooling versus its additional cost, as discussed in Section 3.

4.2 OLTP Workload

The database for this study consists of 166 pre-allocated files with a total size of 23 GBytes. The I/O trace contains approximately 550'000 I/O requests to these files, recorded during one hour. As in a typical OLTP application, most requests read or write a single block (of size 8 KBytes). The average request size is approximately 9 KBytes. This workload exhibits heavily skewed access frequencies both across files and within the hot files. In addition, the trace contains significant fluctuations in the access frequencies and in the overall arrival rate of requests.

As in the study of Section 4.1 we treated all files as unpredictable heat files. That is, even though all files were pre-allocated, we did not assume any advance knowledge of access frequencies. All files were striped across 24 disks (of capacity 1.0 GBytes), using track-sized striping units and Round-robin allocation.

As in Subsection 4.1, we compared the vanilla placement without cooling to our dynamic load balancing method based on cooling. The cooling method improved the average response time of the requests by approximately a factor of 1.1. At a first glance, this performance improvement may appear to be rather insignificant, but note that even more than in Section 4.1, the challenge of this workload was to react to the heavy load fluctuations.

Figures 9 (a) and 9 (b) show the average response time and the cooling frequency, as they vary during the processing of the trace (at a specific arrival

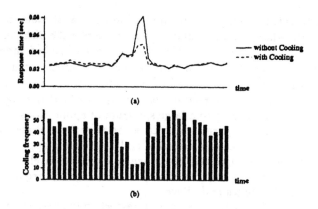

Fig. 9. Average response time and cooling frequency varying over time for the OLTP workload

rate speedup factor of 11). As Figure 9 (a) shows, the cooling method could not improve response time in the initial light-load phase, since the load imbalance of the vanilla method did not yet incur any severe queueing. However, the cooling method did collect heat statistics during this phase. This enabled the cooling method to rebalance the disk load by data migration. Then during the load peak (represented in Figure 9 (a) by the sharp increase of response time), the cooling method achieved a response time improvement by a factor of 1.7. Note that many OLTP applications have "soft" response time constraints such as ensuring a certain response time for 95 percent of the transactions. Thus, it is crucial to guarantee acceptable response time even during load peaks.

Similarly to Subsection 4.1, Figure 9 (b) demonstrates that the cooling method was careful enough to avoid many the data migration steps during the load peak.

5 Conclusion

We have developed a number of self-adapting procedures for load balancing in disk arrays geared towards environments where the files exhibit periodical access patterns. Our generalized disk cooling procedures make use of an objective function which represents the variance of the disk heat over a given time span. The duration times of the cooling actions are estimated making use of a queueing model, and these durations are then used to consider explicitly the costs of performing them and to determine whether they are beneficial or not. These generalized cooling procedures can be invoked any time that a certain trigger condition is met by our objective function.

Together with the algorithms for automatic file partitioning and allocation that we have developed earlier, these generalized cooling procedures form the basis of an integrated, intelligent software tool which is applicable to any multi-disk architecture where the operating system can access the disks individually. Our approach consists of modular blocks that can be invoked independently of each other; thus, the generalized load balancing procedures can be invoked regardless of whether striping is used or not, and they are applicable also to parallel database systems with relation- or object-based partitioning.

Our approach is applicable to a large spectrum of applications ranging from conventional "low-end" applications, such as relational database systems, to "high-end" applications, such as scientific and multimedia applications. Low-end applications require Gigabytes of storage and have relatively small request sizes; high-end applications may use Terabytes of storage and require maximum data rates of 100 Megabytes and above.

In addition, our approach scales up with respect to the performance requirements of an application and the available hardware resources. If certain applications require higher I/O rates or higher data rates, restriping of the affected files can be done on an individual basis, since our file partitioning strategy can assign different striping units to the various files. Similarly, if more disks are added to the array, restriping of the most crucial files allows us to take advantage of the additional resources. We are currently developing these procedures for global file reorganization and restriping. When dealing with large disks, the reorganization often is performed in place due to space restrictions [21]. As opposed to this approach, we are investigating a restriping algorithm that attempts to choose new disks for the reallocation in order to maximize the degree of parallelism between the read and write phases.

References

1. Baker, M.G., Hartman, J.H., Kupfer, M.D., Shirriff, K.W., and Ousterhout, J.K., "Measurements of a Distributed File System," Proc. of the Thirteenth ACM Symposium on Operating Systems Principles, 1991.

2. Chen, P.M. and Patterson, D.A.," Maximizing Performance in a Striped Disk-Array," Proc. of the 17th Int. Symposium on Computer Architecture, 1990.

3. Copeland, G., Alexander, W., Boughter, E., and Keller, T., "Data Placement in Bubba," Proc. ACM SIGMOD Int. Conf., 1988.

4. DeWitt, D.J. and Gray, J.N., "Parallel Database Systems: The Future of High Performance Database Systems," Communications of the ACM, Vol. 35, No. 6, 1992.

5. Dowdy, L.W. and Foster, D.V.," Comparative Models of the File Assignment Problem," ACM Computing Surveys, Vol. 14, No. 2, 1982.

6. Ghandeharizadeh, S. and DeWitt, D.J., "Hybrid-Range Partitioning Strategy: A New Declustering Strategy for Multiprocessor Database Machines," Proc. 16th Int. Conf. on Very Large Data Bases, 1990.

7. Gray, J.N., Horst B., and Walker, M., "Parity Striping of Disc Arrays: Low-Cost Reliable Storage with Acceptable Throughput," Proc. 16th Int. Conf. on Very Large Data Bases, 1990.

8. Highleyman, W., "Performance Analysis of Transaction Processing Systems," Prentice Hall, 1989.

9. Hsiao, H. and DeWitt, D.J., "Chained Declustering: A New Availability Strategy for Multiprocessor Database Machines," Proc. 6th IEEE Int. Conf. on Data Engineering, 1990.

10. Hsiao, H. and DeWitt, D.J., "A Performance Study of Three High-Availability Data Replication Strategies," Journal on Distributed and Parallel Databases, Vol. 1, No. 1, 1993

11. Holland, M. and Gibson, G.A., "Parity Declustering for Continuous Operation in Redundant Disk Arrays," Proc. 5th Int. Conf. on Architectural Support for Programming Languages and Operating Systems, 1992.

12. Katz, R.H.," High Performance Network and Channel-based Storage," Sequoia 2000 Technical Report #91/2, University of California at Berkeley, 1991.

13. Katz, R.H., Gibson, G.A., and Patterson, D.A., "Disk System Architectures for High Performance Computing", Proc. of the IEEE, Vol. 77, No. 12, 1989.

14. Kim, M.Y., "Synchronized Disk Interleaving," IEEE Transactions on Computers, Vol. C-35, No. 11, 1986.

15. Livny, M., Khoshafian, S., and Boral, H., "Multi-Disk Management Algorithms," ACM SIGMETRICS Int. Conf., 1987.

16. Muntz, R.R. and Lui, J.C., "Performance Analysis of Disk Arrays Under Failure," Proc. 16th Int. Conf. on Very large Databases, 1990.

17. Merchant, A. and Yu, P.S., "Design and Modeling of Clustered RAID," Proc. 22nd IEEE Int. Conf. on Fault-Tolerant Computing Systems, 1992.

18. Merchant, A. and Yu, P.S., "Performance Analysis of a Dual Striping Strategy for Replicated Disk Arrays," Proc. 2nd Int. Conf. on Parallel and Distributed Information Systems, 1993.

19. Patterson, D.A., Gibson, G., and Katz, R.H., "A Case for Redundant Arrays of Inexpensive Disks (RAID)," Proc. ACM SIGMOD Int. Conf., 1988.

20. Salem, K., and Garcia-Molina, H., "Disk Striping," Proc. 2nd Int. Conf. on Data Engineering, 1986.

21. Scheuermann, P., Park, Y.C. and Omiecinski, E., "A Heuristic File Reorganization Algorithm based on Record Clustering," BIT, Vol. 29, 1989.

22. Scheuermann, P., Weikum, G., and Zabback, P., "Automatic Tuning of Data Placement and Load Balancing in Disk Arrays," Database Systems for Next-Generation Applications — Principles and Practice, Advanced Database Research and Development Series (edited by W. Kim and Y. Kambayashi), World Scientific Publications.

23. Weikum, G., Hasse, C., Moenkeberg, A., Rys, R., and Zabback, P., "The COMFORT Project: Project Synopsis", Proc. 2nd Int. Conf. on Parallel and Distributed Information Systems, 1993.

24. Weikum, G., Zabback, P., and Scheuermann, P., "Dynamic File Allocation in Disk Arrays," Proc. ACM SIGMOD Int. Conf., 1991.

25. Weikum, G., and Zabback, P., "Tuning of Striping Units in Disk-Array-Based File Systems," Proc. 2nd Int. Workshop on Research Issues on Data Engineering: Transaction and Query Processing (RIDE-TQP), 1992.

26. Wolf, J., "The Placement Optimization Program: A Practical Solution to the Disk File Assignment Problem," Proc. ACM SIGMETRICS Int. Conf., 1989.

PANEL: Scientific Databases: Challenges to the Database Community

Robert Grossman (chair)
University of Illinois at Chicago, USA

Databases and object stores are being used more and more often to archive and analyze experimental scientific data. There are applications from a variety of disciplines, including global change, astronomy, high energy physics, and molecular biology.

The use of databases and stores for scientific applications is restricted however by limitations in current systems, including:

- the difficulty scaling current technology to support numerically intensive queries on 10's to 100's of gigabytes of data;
- the difficulty coupling database systems to hierarchical storage systems;
- the difficulty integrating databases and high performance computing environments.

The use of databases and stores for scientific applications is further restricted by inadequate understanding of several core issues, including:

- how to optimize queries involving derived data;
- strategies for replicating and distributing collections of complex objects of varying sizes;
- how to amortize the cost of several similar long duration queries;
- whether analysis of scientific data should be file based, table based, or object based;
- what to do when metadata requires its own metadata;
- how to develop a flexible and extensible scientific query language.

The panel consisted of application domain scientists and database scientists who discussed these and related issues.

Panelists

Yannis Ioannidis, University of Wisconsin
Edward May, Argonne National Laboratory
Ruth Pordes, Fermi National Accelerator Laboratory
Sakti Pramanik, Michigan State University

An Object-Oriented Office Space Description Model and an Office View Management Mechanism for Distributed Office Environment

Hideyuki Takada* and Yahiko Kambayashi

Integrated Media Environment Experimental Laboratory
Faculty of Engineering, Kyoto University, Sakyo, Kyoto, Japan

Abstract. In this paper, we define an object-oriented office description model and language for computer supported office work system, *VirtualOffice*, that we are currently developing to support cooperative work at offices. The system utilizes HyperCard-like user interface with underlying databases. The language provides the ability to describe layouts and functions of office space. Office view mechanisms to provide various views with users are also proposed based on the model. In addition, some examples of the prototype system of *VirtualOffice* are introduced.

1 Introduction

Due to the down-sizing of high performance computers and the progress of computer network technology, distributed computer systems have been used widely. In an office, each person has his/her own workstation which is connected to other workstations via a network, and works on his/her desk using it. As the use of distributed computer systems increases, the development of systems which support group work in a real office based on these computer systems becomes more and more important.

This kind of systems needs to support user-to-user interaction. Currently, communication equipment, such as telephones, FAX machines and TV phones are used to support human communication, and some of them are also connected to computer systems. Furthermore, various kinds of software, such as *file servers*, have been developed to allow the same data to be shared among multiple users. These systems have, however, focused on the user-to-computer interface, and thus user-to-user interaction is realized indirectly. So these systems are not sufficient for user-to-user interaction.

CAD(Computer Aided Design) database system is a database based approach for coordination among users. However, since these systems do not focus on the user-to-user interaction but on the management of shared data, users are not aware of what other users are doing during the design process. An electronic mail system and *phone* system on UNIX are known to support simple user-to-user interaction on a distributed computer system. But since these systems only send text-based messages from one user to other users, their functions are not enough for complete user-to-user interaction. Recently a lot of systems to support cooperative work on distributed computer systems, called *groupware*, have been developed. However, most of these systems focus on only a part of group work and there is a distinction between personal working space and group working space.

---

* Presently, Industrial Electronics and Systems Laboratory, Mitsubishi Electric Corporation.

We have developed a new type of system, *VirtualOffice*, that integratedly supports usual human office work between personal working space and group working space. *VirtualOffice* provides an environment where many office elements are virtualized in the computer system, and users can use these office elements through a user-friendly interface. Office layouts also visualize logical integrity constraints.

In real office environment, each worker constructs his/her own work space. To realize this function in a virtualized office space on a computer system, office space should be defined formally and a language to describe the office space is required.

In this paper, a formal model and a language to describe office space based on the object-oriented paradigm are proposed. In this model, all office elements are classified into four types. The system regards each element's type as a class. Each user can generate and place the class instances in the virtualized office space.

There are many users, many projects, and many office elements in a real office space. To realize this in a virtualized office space, various forms of views should be provided. In this paper, multi-view mechanisms for multi-user multi-project environment are presented from two points of security management and multi-project management.

A prototype system of *VirtualOffice* has been implemented using an interactive software tool. In this paper, some of the prototype system functions are introduced.

2 Basic Concepts of VirtualOffice

Distributed groupware systems focus on electronic conference based on multimedia processing technology, formal definition of task process and automatic classification using structured data. However these systems can only support each part of human cooperative work separately, and there exists clear separation between individual work and cooperative work. There are many cases when things that are processed in individual work also are used in group work. To support integration of personal work and group work is very important when a system supports *usual* office work.

VirtualOffice is a new type of the system for supporting usual human office work. In this Section, basic concepts of *VirtualOffice* are described.

2.1 Environment

VirtualOffice is assumed to be constructed on a distributed computer environment. Each person has his/her own workstation on his/her desk and does his/her work using his/her workstation. This use of computer systems has become popular with the down-sizing and down-pricing of high performance computers, in fact the UNIX systems and the Macintosh systems can easily be constructed in this form.

VirtualOffice takes the challenge of supporting usual human office work. Usual human work consists of both personal work and cooperative group work. Since conventional groupware systems have supported only cooperative work, users have to change their environment whenever they are going to do group work.

To support personal work and group work integratedly, *VirtualOffice* provides a *virtualized* office and an environment where a user can operate office elements as if they were *real* office elements with user-friendly interface. Each user can perform personal and group work simultaneously.

2.2 View Points

A lot of technology is required in order to virtualize an office space in computer systems. The following points have to be considered in *VirtualOffice*:

1. User-friendly interface
   User interface is very important for office systems because there may be office workers who are not familiar with computers. Because of this, the GUI (Graphical User Interface) is widely spread and used as interfaces for office automation systems. How to build a *good* user interface has to be considered also in *VirtualOffice*.
2. Intergration of the personal working space and the group working space
   There is a clear separation line between personal working space and group working space in current groupware systems. However, personal work and group work are done unitedly in a real office. How to unite personal work and group work should be considered related to the user interface.
3. Integration of communication equipment
   Integration of various kinds of communication equipment is required for supporting interaction. Currently, FAX modem systems and electronic mail systems are available, but these systems are used separately. In *VirtualOffice*, an environment where software for controlling the equipment connected to a computer are integrated as *virtual* equipment, is desirable. This gives user-friendly interface. For example, if there exists one type of software for controlling a FAX machine (a FAX modem) and another type for an electronic mail system, *VirtualOffice* provides an environment where these software can be integrated.
4. Coordination among multiple users
   Various functions for coordination among multiple users have to be supported for cooperative work. For example, someone who was asked to do some work wants to transfer it to another user. This kind of propagation needs to be handled.
5. Security Management
   By using computer networks, data can easily be shared among users. However, security management is a very important problem because secret data may exist. Since there are many people and various projects in an office space, the traditional form of security management is not enough. It should also be possible to combine the mechanism with the user interface.
6. Capability for constructing personal office space
   In a real office, people can arrange their own working space. To realize a function for arranging *virtual* working space, office space has to be defined formally, and a function for describing an office structure is needed.

In particular, functions which can be realized by using computer systems, but cannot be realized in a real office should be considered. Current groupware systems focus only on realizing a traditional form of work although it is implemented on computer systems.

Furthermore, although database technologies have contributed to store and share information in office systems, current groupware systems do not take advantage of database technology. Because applications of database technology have been found out to be very useful for building office information systems, database utilization is also considered in *VirtualOffice*.

In this paper, a formal model and a language for describing office space are defined in Section 3. This model gives *VirtualOffice* the capability of constructing personal office space. Office view management which realizes multiple views for supporting some of the above functions is also presented in Section 4. The user interface function is discussed in Section 5 by describing the implementation of a prototype system of *VirtualOffice*.

3 An Object-Oriented Office Description Model

In this section, a formal model and a language for describing office space are presented. The model is necessary for virtualizing office space in a computer, and the language is used for constructing personal office space and sharing it among multiple users.

3.1 A Data Model for Distributed Office Environment

The aim of *VirtualOffice* is to support usual human office work on distributed computer systems. Before defining a data model for describing the office space, required functions for distributed office environment are discussed.

The required functions are:

1. Communication capability between office elements
   There are many kinds of equipment and many tools in an office space which depend on each other. For example, a FAX machine depends on an address book in order to find the correct FAX number when sending a document to somewhere.
2. Location transparency of office elements
   When a user enters a virtualized office space, the same element in the office space should be accessible in the same way wherever he/she is. For example, when a user is in Tokyo and enters a virtualized office in Tokyo, a document in Kyoto should be accessible in the same way as it is in Kyoto if he/she wants to do so.

To satisfy these requirements, the object-oriented data model was selected. The object-oriented data model has the following features:

- Private data and public procedures (methods) are encapsulated as an object, data can be accessed only through the object's methods. The definition of an object type is called a *class*.
- A class can inherit the types of data and methods from other classes. This mechanism forms *class hierachies*.
- An object is created as an instance of a class.
- Each object has a unique ID.
- Computation proceeds by sending messages between object's methods.

Each office element can be regarded as an object and it can be distinguished from other office elements. This feature can support number 2 of the required functions above, because the object is referred to by a unique ID and can be accessed wherever the object is. Furthermore, the object-oriented computation model is suitable when realizing number 1 of the required functions, because the dependency among office elements can be performed by sending messages among objects.

For these reasons, the object-oriented data model is adopted for office space description.

3.2 An Office Description Model

3.2.1 Office Objects To define the structure of office space formally, elements in a real office are classified based on their properties.

Definition 3.1 Office elements are classified into four types as follows:
- *Space*
  An element which other elements can be put on, or can include other spaces. For example, rooms or document folders are *Space*.
- *Equipment*
  An element which realizes some functions. Equipment perform active actions. For example, FAX machines or telephones are *Equipment*.
- *Data*
  A form of information to be manipulated by *Equipment*. Data is created, modified, referred to or deleted by *Equipment*. Simple documents or documents with Figures are *Data*. *Data* are also stored in *Space*.
- *User*
  An element which enters a *Space* and manipulates *Data* by operating *Equipment* in the *Space*.

Each type defined in Definition 3.1 can be regarded as a class in the object-oriented data model because these office elements have attributes to represent the properties of the object, and methods to manipulate the attributes or to communicate with other objects.

Each type's methods have characteristic properties as shown in followings.

- Methods for Data
  Primitive methods such as *read, write, update* or access privilege control.
- Methods for Equipment
  Active methods to manipulate the data. For example, a FAX machine object communicates with the data object and reads the contents of it, then send the data using a FAX modem.
- Methods for Space
  Passive methods to manage the contents changed by user activities. For example, when the user *opens* a *Space* using the open command, methods of it display the contents included at the last closed time. Furthermore, it can control whether the objects included in it should be shown to a user or not.
- Methods for User
  These are not defined clearly because a *User* can be also a high-level *Equipment*. Although these definitions are required when coordination among users and programs are realized, they are not handled in this paper.

An example of a class hierarchy based on the above model is shown in Figure 3.1. A class *OfficeElement* which has basic attributes such as an object ID and an object name is defined as a super class of all classes. Each office element type is defined as an inherited class from *OfficeElement*, and each office element is defined as an inherited class from the office element type class it belongs to.

This classification is sufficient to define all elements of the office space. However it is also required to define objects which have the combined functions of two classes. For example, a FAX machine classified as *Equipment* may manage the sent and received documents. But the function for saving documents belongs to *Space* type. This problem can be solved by defining it as separate objects: one being *Equipment* and having the function for sending documents, and one being *Space* and managing the documents. However, these two classes should be re-defined as one class for realizing user-friendly interface.

From the reason described above, the following element type is defined:

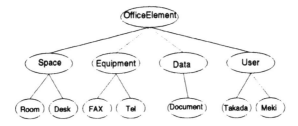

Fig. 3.1. Class hierachy representing office elements

Definition 3.2 A new element type which integrates two or more objects classified to different office element types is defined.
  − *Composite Element (CE)*
    An element which integrates the functions of different office element types, i.e. *Space, Equip, Data* and *User*. This element can not be defined by itself, it is described by specifying the corresponding classes.

Class hierarchies including *CE* is shown in Figure 3.2. The FAX machine mentioned above is defined as a *FAXMachine* inheriting from the *Folder* class and the *FAX* class. Another example is *TelwithAddressbook* which is defined as a class which inherits from the *Tel* class and the *Document* class.

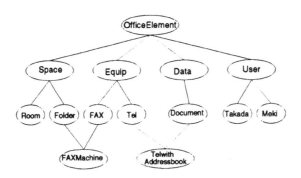

Fig. 3.2. Class hierarchies including complex elements

CE does not allow to integrate the functions which belong to the same office element type. In other works, a FAX machine class and a telephone class cannot be integrated in class level because the methods of each class are very similar and cannot be distinguished when they conflict by integrating their classes.

3.2.2 Office Structure In Section 3.2.1, classes for office elements which exist in an office space were defined. In this Section, a formal model to describe the office structure is defined.

In a real office space, there usually are some rooms in a building, and in each room there are documents and equipment. Spaces such as rooms can include other physical objects and manage the contents of the spaces. On the other hand, equipment such as telephones accomplish their active functions, but can not include other physical objects.

The structure of office space is defined based on the above fact.

Definition 3.3 The structure of office space is defined as follows.

$$Office \rightarrow Space$$
$$Space \rightarrow \{Space \mid Equipment \mid Data \mid User \mid CE\}^*$$

Definition 3.3 means that an office is *Space*, *Space* then can include other *Space, Equipment, data, User* and *CE*.

Each class has some attributes. For example, the room name for a *Space: room*, the telephone color and the location in the room for a *Equipment: telephone* etc. Each class also has some methods. However, the properties of the methods differ from each other as mentioned in Section 3.2.1.

3.2.3 Representation of Distributed Office Environment When this office description model is applied to distributed computer systems, each object can be placed anywhere. An example is shown in Figure 3.3. Each desk in Office A and Office B has two drawers, Drawer 1 and Drawer 2. However, there exists only one drawer in each office. This can be represented by describing that Desk in Office A includes Drawer 1 in Office A and Drawer 1 in Office B (named Drawer 2 in Office A), Desk in Office B includes Drawer 1 in Office B and Drawer 1 in Office A (named Drawer 2 in Office B). In this way, the same environment can be constructed in different office spaces, and users can access remote objects defined in the virtualized office space.

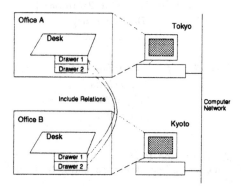

Fig. 3.3. Distributed office environment

3.3 An Office Space Description Language

In this Section, an *Office Space Description Language* is presented. It provides a way to describe office space and interchange the office space among users. Users can define his/her own office space using this office space description language and share it with other users.

Since it is not suitable to describe *User* in the language because *User* is an element type which uses this office description language, four elements, i.e. *Space, Equip, CE, Data* are described.

3.3.1 Syntax

Definition 3.4 The syntax of the office space description language is defined as follows.

$$Office \rightarrow PartsDef \cdot StructureDef$$

- Parts Definition Part
  This part relates to the variable definition parts of general programming languages.

$$
\begin{aligned}
PartsDef \rightarrow \ &(SpaceDef \\
&| \ EquipDef \\
&| \ CompElmDef)^* \\
SpaceDef \rightarrow \ &\textbf{SpaceDef} \ SpaceName \ \{ \\
&[SpaceAttribute] \\
&[SpaceMethod] \\
&\} \\
EquipDef \rightarrow \ &\textbf{EquipDef} \ EquipName \ \{ \\
&[EquipAttribute] \\
&[EquipMethod] \\
&\} \\
DataDef \rightarrow \ &\textbf{DataDef} \ DataName \ \{ \\
&[DataAttribute] \\
&[DataMethod] \\
&\} \\
CompElmDef \rightarrow \ &\textbf{CompElmDef} \ CompElmName \ \{ \\
&([SpaceName] \\
&| \ [EquipName] \\
&| \ [DataName])^* \\
&\}
\end{aligned}
$$

- Office Structure Definition Part
  This part defines the office structure using parts defined in the parts definition part.

$$
\begin{aligned}
StructureDef \rightarrow \ &SpaceInstance \\
SpaceInstance \rightarrow \ &SpaceName \ \{ \\
&[AttributeAssignment] \\
&(SpaceInstance
\end{aligned}
$$

$$
\begin{aligned}
& \mid \textit{EquipInstance} \\
& \mid \textit{CompElmInstance})^* \\
& \} \\
\textit{EquipInstance} \rightarrow\ & \textit{EquipName} \{ \\
& [\textit{AttributeAssignment}] \\
& \} \\
\textit{DataInstance} \rightarrow\ & \textit{DataName} \{ \\
& [\textit{AttributeAssignment}] \\
& \} \\
\textit{CompElmInstance} \rightarrow\ & \textit{CompElmName} \{ \\
& [\textit{AttributeAssignment}] \\
& \}
\end{aligned}
$$

3.3.2 Semantics The semantics of the office description language is as follows:

Parts Definition Part This portion defines the element types existing in virtualized office space as classes. In other words, this part determines the office elements which can be used in virtualized office space. For example, if a FAX machine is expected to be used, the attributes and the methods for the FAX machine have to be described. The name or the location can be regarded as the FAX machine's attributes, while database access or modem control can be regarded as its methods. The method description depends on the system in which the system is implemented. It may be a programming language such as C or Pascal, or high level language such as HyperTalk used in HyperCard on Macintosh.

Office Structure Definition Part This portion defines the office structure by combining the parts provided in the parts definition part. If an object is used in this part, an instance of the class defined in the parts definition part is created. This part should be able to be described by each user in order to define his/her own office space.

3.3.3 Utilization of the Office Space Description Language Using the office space description language, users can define their own office space. The parts definition part is provided by the system, since a description of attributes and methods is required, and it is difficult for low-end user to describe them. Each user needs to describe his/her own office space using parts provided in the parts definition part. In this way, it is possible to provide the environment where a user buys telephone and a document folder, put them on his/her desk and use them as if they were real office elements.

In addition, this office description makes it easy to interchange office space among users. Office space constructed by a user can be shared by other users with this language interface.

Furthermore, GUI to describe this language should be supported. This is because the user interface of the description of language is text-based and it is not suitable for low-end users.

4 Office View Management

4.1 Basic Concepts of Office View

In *VirtualOffice*, some functions which can be realized only in virtualized office space not in real office space are expected to be implemented because the advantages to use computers for supporting human work should be made use of. The followings are examples of such functions.

Shared Objects: Different from a real office, the same object can be shared by more than one space in the virtualized office. An example is a case when a document used by all members of one group can be put on each member's desk.

Virtual Space: In a real office, there are many cases when multiple projects are processed in one room. In *VirtualOffice*, however, a user can assign one room to each project he/she is working on by defining a *virtual* space using the office space description language. Then a user can work in the virtual rooms, where only documents required for the project are available.

Security Management: In a real office, a secret document can be put into a locked drawer so as not to be seen by other persons. However, the existence of the secret thing cannot be hidden in this way because a person who finds the locked drawer may suspect that there might be a secret thing in it. In *VirtualOffice*, a mechanism for hiding even the existence of a secret thing should be realized.

Since these functions can be realized by showing virtual data to users, they correspond to view management of database technology. In next section, view management mechanisms for two office element types, *Space* and *Equipment* is discussed.

4.2 View Management Mechanism for Office Space

According to the office definition described in Section 3.2.2, office space can be represented as a tree. A node means an object in the office space and an edge $n_i \rightarrow n_j$ represents that the space v_i includes the object n_j. A user belongs to one space node. Movement to another space can be realized by tracing the corresponding edge.

First, the office definition presented in Section 3.2.2 is extended for the *shared objects* described above. Then view management for *Space* is described from two points of security management and construction of personal environment. These ways of management provide *multiple views* of the same office space with users.

4.2.1 An Extended Office Description Model for Shared Objects As described above, office space can be represented by a tree based on the office description model. However there are many cases when one object such as a common document of a group is expected to be shared by multiple space such as a personal drawer of each member. To realize this requirement, new attributes are defined to an object. The attributes represent whether the object is a shared object or not, and specify the OID of the original object if the object is a shared object.

In this way, a tree representing an office space becomes a directed graph as shown in Figure 4.1.

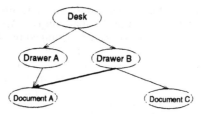

Fig. 4.1. A directed graph representing a shared object

4.2.2 Security Management Here, two types of security management are supposed.

1. A user can *use* or *access* an object or not.
2. A user can *see* an object or not.

A traditional mechanism for security management has supported the type 1 situations. The file permission mode in UNIX is an example of the type 1 situations and this mode can be managed by attributes of the file. However, this can not hide the existence of the file. Here, the way of realization of the type 2 is considered.

Suppose that a space s includes an object o, and o is shown to a user only when the user enters or opens s. To realize the type 2 of security management, the attribute to represent which user can see the object o is defined to the edge linking s to o [2].

An example is shown in Figure 4.2. A set of users (A, B) are assigned to the edge linking **Room** to **Desk** and a set of users (A, B, C) are assigned to the edge linking **Room** to **BookShelf**. Both **Desk** and **BookShelf** are shown when user A enters **Room**, while only **BookShelf** is shown when user C enters the room. In this way, even the existence of **Desk** is hidden from user C.

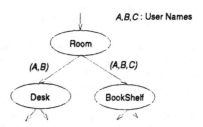

Fig. 4.2. Attribute of the edge for security management

---

[2] This set need not be represented directly, it is rather practical that the set is obtained by some operations such as comparing the security level.

To manage these attributes for the edge, an attribute representing a user name which owns the space is added to the space object. An access right attribute of an edge starting from a space object can be changed by the owner of the space object. The owner is responsible for specifying who can see an object in a space object and who can not see the object in the space object.

Figure 4.3 shows a more complicated case, assuming A is the owner of Desk. This figure represents the case when A wants to put Diary and Appointment into **Secret Folder** which nobody can see, but A wants to allow only B to see **Appointment**. Assigning sets of users to edges as shown in the figure, B can not see **Secret Folder** but can see **Appointment**. In this way, every user has his/her own view of the same office space.

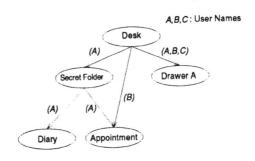

Fig. 4.3. A directed graph representing multi-user multi-view

The author calls this way of office view management *multi-user multi-view*.

4.2.3 Management of Personal Environment for Multiple Projects

Here a way of establishing a personal environment for multiple projects is presented. Like database can provide various views with a user, this way can change the view of office space according to user specifications.

Suppose that the same case as described in Section 4.2.2, where a *Space s* includes an object o. To realize view control for multiple projects environment, the attribute to represent which project is specified to o is defined to the edge linking s to o.

Consider an example in Figure 4.4. When a user in **Desk** specifies the project **P1**, **Telephone** and **BookShelf1** are shown, while **Telephone** and **BookShelf2** are shown when the user specifies the project **P2**.

This attribute for the edge should be able to be defined by the user owning the object.

Consider another example shown in Figure 4.5. If a user specifies the project *P1*, **Document P1** appears on the top of the **Desk** and **Document P2** is put into **Drawer**, while if a user specifies the project *P2*, **Document P2** appears and **Document P1** is put into **Drawer**.

As shown in this example, such a complicated but very useful view management can be supported. This is one mechanism for realizing multi-project management which recently has been discussed. The author calls this *multi-project multi-view*.

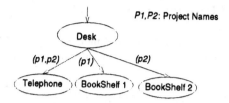

Fig. 4.4. Attribute of the edge for personal environment

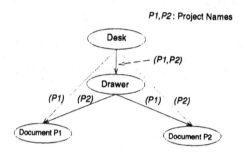

Fig. 4.5. A directed graph representing multi-project multi-view

5 Implementation of VirtualOffice

In this section, a prototype system of *VirtualOffice* implemented on an interactive software tool (ActivePage) is introduced. The ActivePage system provides the HyperCard-like environment where objects are managed in the object-oriented database system *Objectivity*.

5.1 Architecture of VirtualOffice on ActivePage

VirtualOffice's system is constructed as documents on ActivePage. *VirtualOffice* consists of the following three parts:

Public space This part has functions for shared space such as a room.
Personal space This part has functions for personal space such as a personal desk.
Shared database This part has functions of a database system storing shared data such as an address book or desk assignments.

Each part is realized as one document on ActivePage. The public space and the shared database are common among users. Personal space is created for each user by copying a template document. Each user can construct his/her office space using the GUI-based office description.

5.2 Concepts of User Interface

The user interface in *VirtualOffice* should be friendly. Since ActivePage provides an object-oriented user interface, most operations can be accomplished by using a mouse.

An example of public space in *VirtualOffice* is shown in left side of Figure 5.1. A desk is represented by a rectangle with a name and a user can enter the personal spaces by clicking on the desk. Since a name of a user using a workstation is shown in red, the office space state can be understood at a glance like in a real office.

An example of a personal space is shown in right side of Figure 5.1. Drawers can be opened and closed by clicking on them. Predefined classes of office elements based on the office description model are provided, and instances of the classes can be generated by selecting the class name included in the menu shown in the left side of Figure 5.2. Some kind of equipment, such as a FAX machine, or a telephone, are assumed to be connected to external interface. A user can use this kind of equipment by dragging and overlapping icons he/she wants processed by equipment.

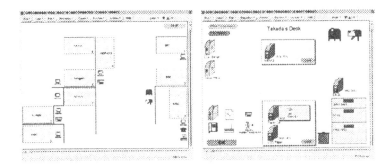

Fig. 5.1. An example of public space and personal space

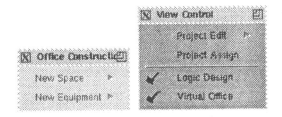

Fig. 5.2. Menus for defining office structure and office view

Such a user interface enables that users who are not familiar with computers can operate virtualized elements as if they were real things.

5.3 Office View Management

A mechanism for constructing personal environment is implemented on the prototype system of *VirtualOffice* using a user friendly interface.

The menu for defining multiple views is shown in the right side of Figure 5.2. First, a user has to define projects. This can be accomplished by selecting the *"New Project"* menu and typing a project name. If the user selects the *"Project Assign"* menu, the folder is displayed in the left side of the screen. For example, in Figure 5.1, since two projects *"VirtualOffice"* and *"Logic Design"* are defined, two folders with a character P are displayed. If the user wants to assign an object to the project, he/she only needs to drag the object icon to a corresponding project folder. Once an object is assigned to a project, the user can change the view of the personal space by specifying a project using the menubar. For example, if the folder *VOS Paper* shown in Figure 5.1 is assigned to the project *"VirtualOffice"*, this folder is displayed only when the user specifies this project.

5.4 Database Utilization

VirtualOffice utilizes database functions for security management and data sharing. A mechanism for security management is provided by the functions of the object-oriented database Objectivity in ActivePage, while a mechanism for data sharing is realized as an individual database constructed on ActivePage.

1. Security management
   Users can specify access rights to pages in an ActivePage's document. When a user creates a new page (i.e. a new working space), he/she can define the access right for this page, and specify who will be able to see this space and will not.
2. Data sharing
   Common data should be stored in database which can be accessed by all users. In *VirtualOffice*, address-data and a desk assignment table are stored in a database constructed on ActivePage. This database is made in the traditional form of a relational database except that data can be retrieved only by very primitive queries. The desk assignment table is referred to by the public space and the address database is referred to by FAX machines, telephones and e-mail systems realized in each personal space.

Security management for each office element such as telephones is not realized because ActivePage only supports the definition of access rights for documents and pages. Therefore the mechanism described in Section 4.2.2 is not supported. When this mechanism is implemented, data such as edge attributes should be stored in the database.

6 Conclusions

In this paper, a formal model for describing office space based on an object-oriented data model and an office space description language are proposed. This language provides an environment where each user can construct his/her own working space and share it with other users.

In addition, mechanisms for office view management are proposed using this office description model. The mechanisms to provide multi-user multi-view functionality for security management and multi-project multi-view functionality for personal working environment are described with some examples. These mechanisms enable to provide various views of the same office space.

In Section 5, implementation of a prototype of *VirtualOffice* is introduced. *VirtualOffice* is constructed on a GUI-based interactive software tool and provides an environment where users can do both personal work and group work integratedly. This prototype system supports only some basic functions that are required in *VirtualOffice*, because it is implemented on an existing tool. Although development of the system from the beginning to the end would take a large amount of time and many engineers, this type of system will be the mainstream for office information systems in the near future.

Acknowledgements

The authors would like to thank Matsushita Electric Industrial Corporation for supporting this research and providing the ActivePage system.

References

1. D.S.Batory, W.Kim: Modeling Concepts for VLSI CAD Objects, *ACM Transactions on Database Systems*, 10-3, (1985), 322-346.
2. C.A.Ellis, S.J.Gibbs, G.L.Rein : GROUPWARE: Some Issues and Experiences, *Communications of ACM*, 34-1 (1991), 39-58.
3. I.Greif, S.Sarin: Data Sharing in Group Work, *ACM Transactions on Office Information Systems*, 5-2 (1987) , 187-211.
4. H. Ishii: Design of Groupware, bit, 23-3 (1991), 273-283 (in Japanese).
5. H. Ishii: Trends of Groupware Technology, *Journal of IPS Japan*, 30-12 (1989) 1502-1508 (in Japanese).
6. H.Ishii: TeamWorkStation: Towards a Seamless Shared WorkSpace, *Proceedings of CSCW'90*, ACM, pp.13-26 (1990).
7. Y.Kambayashi, Q.Chen, T.Kunishima: Coordination Manager: A Mechanism to Support Cooperative Work on Database Systems, *Proceedings of The Second Far-East Workshop on Future Database Systems*, (1992), 176-185.
8. Kum-Yew Lai, Thomas W. Malone, Keh-Chiang Yu. :Object Lens:A "Spreadsheet" for Cooperative Work, *ACM Transactions on Office Information Systems*, 6-4 (1988), 332-353.
9. Stefik, M. et al.: Beyond the Chalkboard: Computer Supported For Collaboration and Problem Solving in Meetings, *Communications of ACM*, 30-1 (1987), 32-47.
10. Q.Chen, Y.Kambayashi: Coordination of Data and Knowledge Base Systems under Distributed Environment, *Proceedings of IFIP DS-5 Semantics of interoperable Database Systems*, (1992).
11. H.Tarumi: Groupware for Software Development, *Journal of IPS Japan*, 33-1 (1992) 22-31.
12. H.R. Tirri, J. Srinivasan, B. Bhargava: Integrating Distributed Data Sources Using Federated Objects, *Pre-Proceedings of International Workshop on Distributed Object Management*, (1992), 292-306.
13. K. Watabe, et al.: Multimedia Desktop Conference System: MERMAID, *Transactions of IPS Japan*, 32-9 (1991), 1200-1209.
14. K. Watabe, et al.: Distributed Multiparty Desktop Conference System: MERMAID, *Proceedings of CSCW'90*, (1990), 27-38.
15. Haiyan Xu: A Cooperative Transaction Model Handling Multiple Correctness Levels, *Proceedings of DASFAA'91*, (1991), 517-526.

Stamp Locking Method
for Multiversion Composite Objects

Wojciech Cellary, Waldemar Wieczerzycki

Franco-Polish School of New Information and Communication Technologies
ul. Mansfelda 4, 60-854 Poznań, Poland

Abstract. In this paper a new approach to locking multiversion composite objects is proposed, called the *stamp locking* approach. The main notion of this approach is a *stamp lock* defined as an extension of a classical lock in such a way that it contains the information about the position of locked nodes in the hierarchies concerned. The main advantage of this method is simple locking strategy following from the lack of intentional locks. To lock a hierarchy subtree it is sufficient to set one stamp lock only, whose node stamp identifies the subtree root. To determine stamp lock compatibility, it is sufficient to compare stamps that are particular identifiers of hierarchy nodes and subtrees. Advantages of the stamp locking method become particularly beneficial in the case of a database containing many versions of composite objects, whose composition structure is complex. This is a typical case of design databases where objects, being the artifacts of the design process, have usually many components available in many versions.

1 Introduction

Design databases have to provide such features as composite objects and multiversion objects. Composite objects are a natural way to model the structure of design artifacts. Versioning is required to memorize the history of object development during the design process, and object variants [1, 4, 6, 8]. Composition and versioning has to be efficiently combined with concurrency control. This problem cannot be solved by the use of concurrency control methods addressed to classical databases, because they do not concern semantic relationships between composite and component objects, and parent and child object versions. A concurrency control method has to take into account that some transactions accessing a composite object virtually access all its components. A transaction like this may conflict with another one that accesses the component object directly. The same concerns object versions. A transaction accessing an object version may, in some cases, virtually access all the versions derived from it and come into a conflict with another one accessing a derived object version directly.

It may seem that to solve this problem the classical hierarchical locking method may be adapted [5]. As is well known, the main notion of this method is a *granule*, being the lockable unit. Three types of granules are distinguished: the whole database, relations and tuples, which are vertices of the *granularity hierarchy*. When a particular granule is locked, all the granules nested in it (i.e., its successors in the granularity hierarchy) are locked implicitly. The concept of hierarchical locking is implemented by the use of *intentional locks*, which make it possible to detect the conflicts between transactions on a higher level of granularity hierarchy than the level where basic locks are set. The main rule of the hierarchical locking protocol is to set intentional locks on all the predecessors of a granule being basically locked.

Two attempts to adapt the classical hierarchical locking method to the requirements of objects are known from the literature [2,7]. Both of them were constructed for the general object-oriented databases. Both of them concern the composition hierarchy and the class inheritance hierarchy. None of them concerns the version derivation hierarchy. In [2] hierarchical locking is applied to two types of granules only: a class and its instances. The objects being components of a composition objects are locked explicitly by the basic locks. Their number is as big as the number of composite object components at any level of its composition hierarchy. In [7] hierarchical locking is applied to the class-instance hierarchy and the class inheritance hierarchy. Moreover, special lock types are available, used to lock the domains of composite object attributes identifying component objects. These locks are, however, very restrictive, considerably reducing the concurrency degree. When a lock like this is set by a transaction on a component object class, it excludes direct access of other transactions to all the instances of this class. Such an instance may only be accessed via composite reference of another composite object. In other words, two locks set on the same domain of an attribute of two different composite objects are compatible.

In fact it is difficult to adapt the classical hierarchical locking method to multiversion complex objects, because it was constructed under the assumption that there is one hierarchy only of the small depth. In design databases composition and version derivation hierarchies may be composed of hundreds levels. Thus, setting intentional locks from the root to a leaf of a hierarchy via hundreds intermediary nodes cannot be efficient. The approach proposed in [2] and [7] where classes are locked is still unsatisfactory.

In this paper a new approach to locking multiversion composite objects is proposed, called the *stamp locking* approach. It is free from the intentional locks. The main notion of this approach is a *stamp lock* defined as an extension of a classical lock in such a way that it contains the information about the position of locked nodes in both hierarchies. Thus, to lock related nodes or subtrees of nodes of one or both hierarchies it is sufficient to set a single stamp lock only.

The paper is organized as follows. In Section 2 the general concept of stamp locking methods is presented. In Sections 3 and 4 object versioning and object composition models are presented, respectively. In Section 5 the stamp locking method is described. Section 4 contains concluding remarks.

2 The Concept of Stamp Locking Methods

The concept of stamp locking methods is presented by the use of an abstract hierarchy of nodes (Fig. 1). The main idea is to extend the notion of a lock in such a way that it contains information on the position of a locked subtree in the whole hierarchy. The extended lock is called *stamp lock* and denoted *SL*.

A stamp lock is a pair:

$$SL = (lm, ns),$$

where *lm* denotes a *lock mode* and *ns* denotes a *node stamp*.

Lock modes describe the properties of stamp locks. They correspond to the lock modes used in the classical locking algorithms, namely, shared and exclusive lock modes. A node stamp is a sequence of numbers constructed in such a way that it makes it possible to determine all the node ancestors in the hierarchy. If a node is the *n*-th child of its parent whose node stamp is *p*, then the child node is stamped *p.n*. The root node is stamped *0*. For example, stamp lock $SL = (lm, 0.2)$ locks, in the *lm* mode, all the nodes composing the subtree rooted by the node stamped *0.2*. This subtree of nodes is called *stamp lock scope*. In Fig. 1, the scope of $SL = (lm, 0.2)$ is surrounded by the dashed line.

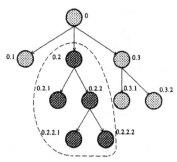

Fig. 1. An abstract hierarchy

Compatibility of two stamp locks is determined by the following rule:

Two stamp locks are compatible if and only if their lock modes are compatible, or their scopes have no common nodes.

Compatibility of lock modes is determined in a classical way: shared lock modes are mutually compatible, while exclusive lock modes are incompatible with both exclusive and shared lock modes. As follows from the above rule, in a case of incompatible lock modes, the corresponding stamp lock scopes have to be compared. Despite lock mode incompatibility, the stamp locks may be compatible, providing their scopes have no common nodes. All the possible relationships between the scopes of two stamp locks: SL_1 (dashed line) and SL_2 (dotted line) are given in Fig. 2. The scopes may be equal (Fig. 2a), different (Fig. 2b), the scope of SL_1 may include the scope of SL_2 (Fig. 2c), or the scope of SL_1 may be included in the scope of SL_2 (Fig. 2d).

Compatibility of stamp locks SL_1 and SL_2 may be summarized as follows: in cases a), c) and d) to be compatible the stamp lock modes have to be compatible, while in case b) stamp locks are always compatible, no matter if their lock modes are compatible or not.

To examine the relationship between the scopes of two stamp locks it is sufficient to compare their node stamps:

1. The scopes of two stamp locks SL_1 and SL_2 are equal (cf. Fig. 2a) if and only if their node stamps are identical;
2. The scope of a stamp lock SL_1 includes the scope of a SL_2 (cf. Fig. 2c) if and only if the node stamp of SL_1 is a head[1] of node stamp SL_2 ;
3. The scope of a stamp lock SL_1 is included in the scope of a SL_2 (cf. Fig. 2d) if and only if the node stamp of SL_2 is a head of node stamp SL_1 ;
4. The scopes of two stamp locks SL_1 and SL_2 are different (cf. Fig. 2b) if and only if cases 1,2 and 3 do not occur.

---

[1]Node stamp $ns_1 = a_1,a_2,...,a_m$ is a *head* of node stamp $ns_2 = b_1,b_2,...,b_n$ if and only if

$$m < n \wedge \bigvee_{i \leq m} a_i = b_i;$$

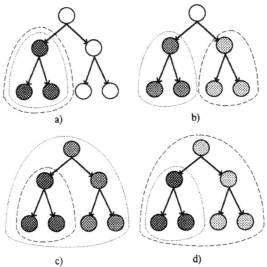

a)   b)

c)   d)

Fig. 2. Comparison of scopes of two stamp locks

To compare node stamps we define three operators.

Let $ns_1 = a_1, a_2, ..., a_m$ and $ns_2 = b_1, b_2, ..., b_n$ be two node stamps. We say that:

- node stamp ns_1 is different from stamp ns_2, denoted $ns_1 \;!= ns_2$, if and only if

$$m <> n \vee (m = n \wedge \underset{i \leq m}{\exists}\, a_i <> b_i)\,;$$

- node stamp ns_1 includes stamp ns_2, denoted $ns_1 >> ns_2$, if and only if

$$m > n \wedge \underset{i \leq n}{\forall}\, a_i = b_i\,;$$

- node stamp ns_1 is included in stamp ns_2, denoted $ns_1 <= ns_2$, if and only if

$$m \leq n \wedge \underset{i \leq m}{\forall}\, a_i = b_i\,;$$

As an example consider four node stamps $ns_1 = 0$, $ns_2 = 0.1$, $ns_3 = 0.1.2$ and $ns_4 = 0.2$ (cf. Fig. 2). Node stamp ns_2 includes stamp ns_1 ($ns_2 >> ns_1$), because ns_1 is a head of stamp ns_2. Node stamp ns_2 is included in stamp ns_3 ($ns_2 <= ns_3$), because ns_2 is a head of ns_3. Node stamps ns_2 and ns_4 are different ($ns_2 \;!= ns_4$), because their second elements are different. Note that from the fact that one node stamp does not include another one, we may not conclude that the first one is included in the second one. Node stamp ns_2 neither includes stamp ns_4, nor ns_4 includes ns_2 (cf. Fig 2 b).

Applying operators defined above to the node stamps composing two stamp locks, one may construct a logical rule which determines stamp lock compatibility. Considering all the stamp lock combinations it is possible to construct stamp lock compatibility matrix:

$$C_m : (SL_s, SL_r) \to R,$$

where R is a logical rule composed of operators defined above and node stamps, being their operands. Evaluating these rules makes it possible to determine the compatibility or incompatibility of locks compared. As an example consider the compatibility of two exclusive stamp locks:

$$SL_S = (X, ns_1) \text{ and } SL_r = (X, ns_2).$$

As we know, exclusive lock modes are incompatible. Thus, the compatibility of stamp locks SL_S and SL_r may be determined by the comparison of their scopes. The scopes must be different (cf. Fig. 2 b), that means node stamp ns_1 neither includes stamp ns_2, nor it is included in stamp ns_2. We may express it by the following rule:

$$r: \quad \neg (ns_1 <= ns_2) \wedge \neg (ns_1 >> ns_2).$$

If the rule r evaluates to *true*, then the stamp locks SL_S and SL_r are compatible.

The concept of stamp locking method proposed, may be extended for more then one hierarchy, providing they are orthogonal to each other, that means the hierarchies are composed of nodes of different types. To enable simultaneous locking in many orthogonal hierarchies it is necessary to extend the notion of the stamp lock in such a way, that it contains many node stamps, corresponding to different hierarchies. As a consequence, the notion of stamp lock scope is also extended, because each orthogonal hierarchy introduces its new dimension. It is also necessary to modify logical rules determining stamp lock compatibility.

In a case of two orthogonal hierarchies, the stamp lock definition has to be extended to the following triple:

$$SL = (lm, ns_1, ns_2),$$

where lm is a stamp lock mode, ns_1 and ns_2 are node stamps concerning the first and the second hierarchy, respectively.

To determine the compatibility of stamp locks concerning two orthogonal hierarchies we consider two following exclusive stamp locks:

$$SL_S = (X, ns_{1a}, ns_{2a}) \text{ and } SL_r = (X, ns_{1b}, ns_{2b}).$$

To decide if these locks are compatible or not, one has to compare their scopes in both hierarchies. The scopes have to be different in at least one hierarchy. We may express it by the following logical rule:

$$\neg (ns_{1a} <= ns_{1b}) \wedge \neg (ns_{1a} >> ns_{1b}) \quad \vee$$
$$\neg (ns_{2a} <= ns_{2b}) \wedge \neg (ns_{2a} >> ns_{2b}).$$

3 Object Versioning Model

The concept of stamp locking may be applied to different versioning models. In the paper we assume the database version approach, which was originally introduced in [3] as a new paradigm for maintaining consistency of versions in object-oriented databases, and which is currently under implementation for the O_2 object-oriented *DBMS*. The main concept of this approach is that of a *database version* which comprises a version of *each* multiversion object stored in the database. Some objects may be hidden in a particular database version by the use of the *nil* values of their versions. In the database version approach, a database version is a unit of consistency and versioning. It is a unit of consistency, because each object version contained in a database version must be consistent with the versions of all the other objects contained in it. It is a unit of versioning, because an object version cannot appear outside a database version. To create a new object version, a new database version has to be created, where the new object version appears in the context of versions of all the other objects and respects the consistency constraints imposed. Database versions are logically isolated from each other, i.e., any changes made in a database version have no effect on the others.

To operate on database versions, *dbv-transactions* are used, while to operate on object versions inside database versions, *object-transactions* are used. A dbv-transaction is used to derive a new database version, called a *child*, from an existing one, called its *parent*. To derive a child means to make a logical copy of all the object versions contained in the parent. Once created, the child database version evolves independently of its parent; also its parent is not prevented from evolving if it is admitted to by the application.

To efficiently implement database versions, and to avoid version value redundancy, database versions are organized as a tree reflecting derivation history, and are identified by *version stamps*. A version stamp, which is syntactically identical with node stamp (cf. Section 2), makes it possible to easily identify the path in the derivation tree from a given database version to the root, i.e., to identify all the ancestors of a given database version. A multiversion object is implemented as a set of object version values and a control data structure called *association table*. Each row of the association table of a multiversion object associates an object version value with one or several database versions. Some database versions are associated explicitly, i.e., their version stamps appear explicitly in the association table. Others are associated implicitly: if the version stamp of a database version does not appear in an association table, this means that it shares an object version value with its parent, which in turn may share it with its parent, etc. This rule gives an important advantage: to derive a new database version, it is sufficient to register its version stamp in the system. Just after derivation, this version stamp does not appear in any association table, so automatically the new database version shares version values of all the objects with its parent. As an example consider the database version derivation hierarchy given in Fig. 3. The multiversion database contains seven database versions stamped *0, 0.1, 0.1.1, 0.1.2, 0.1.3, 0.1.1.1* and *0.1.1.2* and two multiversion objects A and B. Object A, whose association table is given in Fig. 4a, appears in two versions: a_0 (nil version) and a_1, in database versions *0* and *0.1*, respectively. Version a_1 is shared by all the database versions composing the derivation subtree rooted by *0.1*. Object B, whose association table is given in Fig. 4b, appears in five versions: b_0, b_1, b_2, b_3 and b_4, in database versions *0, 0.1, 0.1.1, 0.1.3* and *0.1.1.2*, respectively. The database version *0.1.2* shares object version b_1 with the database version *0.1*, while database *0.1.1.1* shares version b_2 with database *0.1.1*.

To update shared version value in a database version d, the following simple algorithm is used. First, a new row is added to the association table, associating the new version value and the version stamp of the database version d. Then, in the original row concerning the old version value, the version stamp of d is replaced by the version stamps of those of its immediate successors (children) that do not explicitly appear in any row of the association table. In this way, all the successors of the database version d immediate and not which implicitly shared the old version value with database version d will continue to be associated with it. To illustrate this algorithm, assume a transaction T which updates object A in the database version *0.1.1* (Fig. 3). The modified association table is given in Fig. 5. The same algorithm is also used to create and delete objects in a database version. Creation of an object in a database version consists in updating its *nil* version value by a given one; deletion of an object in a database version consists in updating its value by *nil*. Creation of a new multiversion object in the database consists of the creation of its association table with one row associating the *nil* version value with the root database version.

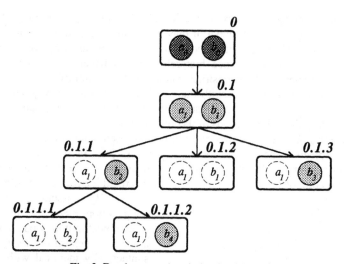

Fig. 3. Database version derivation hierarchy

Versions of object A	Version stamps
a_0	0
a_1	0.1

Versions of object B	Version stamps
b_0	0
b_1	0.1
b_2	0.1.1
b_3	0.1.3
b_4	0.1.1.2

a)   b)

Fig. 4. Association tables of objects A and B

Versions of object A	Version stamps
a_0	0
a_2	0.1.1
a_1	0.1, 0.1.1.1, 0.1.1.2

Fig. 5. Association table of object A

The versioning mechanism described above permits two object transactions addressed to two different database versions to run in parallel. They do not conflict and need not be serialized, even if both write the object version whose value is shared by both database versions addressed. This follows from the logical isolation of database versions: the update of a shared version value in one database version gives birth to a new one, while preserving the old one as explained above. Two object transactions addressed to the same database version are serialized in exactly the same manner as in a monoversion database.

4 Object composition model

The composition hierarchy reflects the *is-part-of* relationship between objects. Depending on a data model, it may be constructed in different ways. It may bind multiversion objects, object versions, classes or domains of composite attributes being subtrees of the inheritance hierarchy. In the paper we assume *restricted versioning* in which the composition hierarchy binds multiversion objects, i.e. multiversion composite objects with their multiversion components, which in turn may be composite as well. As a consequence, two versions of the same composite objects may only differ by versions of its components.

There are as many different composition hierarchies in an *OODB* as root composite objects. The stamp locking approach (cf. Section 2) requires one composition hierarchy. It may be easily obtained by the creation of a fictitious multiversion composite object whose components are all the root composite objects.

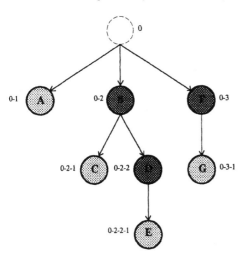

Fig. 6. Composition hierarchy

By assuming a single composition hierarchy, the position of an object in it may be identified by a single *composition stamp*, that is syntactically identical with the node stamp (cf. Section 2). To distinguish between version stamps and composition stamps we use hyphens instead of dots as stamp separators. An example of a composition hierarchy is shown in Fig. 6. The fictitious composite object is stamped *0*. Object *A*, which is simple, is stamped *0-1*. Composite object *B*, composed of objects *C*, *D* and *E* is stamped *0-2*. Finally, composite object *F*, composed of object *G* only, is stamped *0-3*. According to the semantics of a composition stamp, one may find all the objects which are composed directly or indirectly of a given object. For example, object *E* stamped *0-2-2-1* is a direct component of the object stamped *0-2-2*, i.e., object *D*, and indirect component of object stamped *0-2*, i.e., object *B*.

5 Stamp Locking Method for Multiversion Composite Objects

In this section we present a stamp locking method applied to two hierarchies: database version derivation and composition hierarchy. They are orthogonal, i.e. they do not contain the same nodes. The database version derivation hierarchy is constructed according to the rules presented in Section 3. To identify its single nodes, i.e. database versions, or the subtrees of its nodes, version stamps are used. The composition hierarchy is constructed according to the rules presented in Section 4. To identify its single nodes, i.e. multiversion objects, or the subtrees of its nodes, composition stamps are used. By the combination of these hierarchies the following lockable granules are distinguished:

1) the whole multiversion database,
2) a subtree of database versions,
3) a single database version,
4) a multiversion composite object,
5) a subtree of composite object versions,
6) a single composite object version,
7) a single multiversion object,
8) a subtree of object versions,
9) a single version of a single object.

The first three granules are related to the database version derivation hierarchy only. The last six granules are related both to the database version derivation hierarchy and the composition hierarchy. Granules 4), 5) and 6) provide locking a composite object with all its components. Of course, the object being locked may be a component of other objects. The granules 7), 8) and 9) provide locking a single object only, no matter if it is simple or composite.

A stamp lock is now defined as a triple:

$$SL = (lm, vs, cs),$$

where lm is a lock mode, vs is a version stamp of the database version subtree being concerned, and cs is a composition stamp of the object being locked.

Depending on the lock mode lm, stamp locks may be grouped in three following ways:

- exclusive and shared stamp locks;
- non-hierarchical and hierarchical stamp locks in the database version derivation tree. Non-hierarchical stamp locks provide composite object locking in a single database version, while hierarchical stamp locks provide composite object locking in a database version derivation subtree;
- non-hierarchical and hierarchical stamp locks in the composition tree. Non-hierarchical stamp locks provide locking objects without their components, while hierarchical provide locking objects together with all their components.

Eight stamp locks are distinguished:

(x, vs, cs),	(s, vs, cs),
(xc, vs, cs),	(sc, vs, cs),
(X, vs, cs),	(S, vs, cs),
(XC, vs, cs),	(SC, vs, cs);

where x means "exclusive", s means "shared", lock modes written in upper case mean "hierarchical in the database version derivation tree", while written in lower case mean "non-hierarchical in the database version derivation tree", lock modes with suffix *c* mean "hierarchical in the composition tree", while lock modes without suffix *c* mean "non-hierarchical in the composition tree".

Stamp locks *(x, vs, cs)* and *(s, vs, cs)* concern a single object whose composition stamp is *cs* in a single database version stamped *vs*.

Stamp locks *(X, vs, cs)* and *(S, vs, cs)* concern a single object whose composition stamp is *cs* in a subtree of database versions rooted by *vs*. In the particular case of *vs = 0*, locks *(X, 0, cs)* and *(S, 0, cs)* concern all the versions of an object *cs* contained in the database, i.e. they lock the whole multiversion object *cs*.

Stamp locks *(xc, vs, cs)* and *(sc, vs, cs)* concern a composite object whose composition stamp is *cs* together with all its components in a single database version stamped *vs*. In the particular case of *cs = 0*, locks *(xc, vs, 0)* and *(sc, vs, 0)* concern all the objects contained in a single database version, i.e. they lock a database version *vs*.

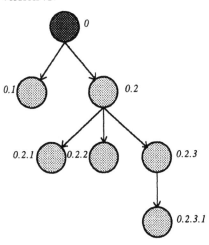

Stamp locks *(XC, vs, cs)* and *(SC, vs, cs)* concern a composite object whose composition stamp is *cs* together with all its components in a subtree of database versions rooted by *vs*. In the particular case of *vs = 0*, locks *(XC, 0, cs)* and *(SC, 0, cs)* concern all the versions of a composite object *cs* contained in the database, i.e. they lock the whole composite object *cs*. Moreover, if also *cs = 0*, locks *(XC, 0, 0)* and *(SC, 0, 0)* concern all the objects in all the database versions, i.e. they lock the whole multiversion database. As an example, consider the composition hierarchy given in Fig. 6, the database version hierarchy given in Fig. 7 and a stamp lock *(XC, 0.2, 0-2)*. It is hierarchical in both: the database version and the composition tree.

Fig. 7. Database version derivation hierarchy

Thus, it concerns the composite object *B* (whose composition stamp is *0-2*) with all its components, i.e. objects *C, D* and *E*, in the database version subtree rooted by *0.2*. The scope of the stamp lock considered is given in Fig. 8. For the purpose of simplicity, concerned subtrees of database derivation and composition hierarchies are depicted only. Object *B*, explicitly locked in the composition hierarchy, is locked explicitly in the database version *0.2* and implicitly in the database versions *0.2.1, 0.2.2, 0.2.3* and *0.2.3.1*. Objects *C, D* and *E*, implicitly locked in the composition hierarchy, are locked explicitly in the database version *0.2* and implicitly in the database versions *0.2.1, 0.2.2, 0.2.3* and *0.2.3.1*.

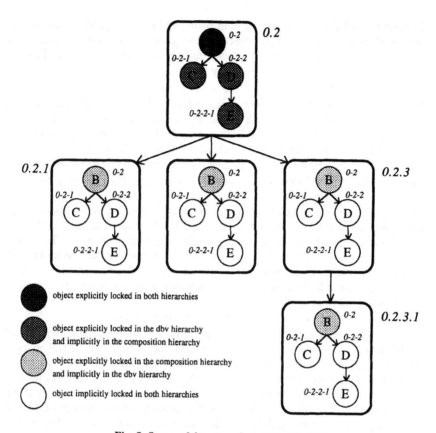

Fig. 8. Scope of the stamp lock (*XC, 0.2, 0-2*)

Shared stamp locks *S, s, SC, sc* are always compatible. All the other stamp locks are potentially incompatible. In the database version tree four stamp lock type combinations are possible: (non-hierarchical, non-hierarchical), (hierarchical, non-hierarchical), (non-hierarchical, hierarchical) and (hierarchical, hierarchical). Similarly, in the composition tree four stamp lock type combinations are possible. Because every pair of stamp locks concern simultaneously both hierarchies, 4x4 = 16 combinations of pairs: *(stamp_lock_granted, stamp_lock_requested)* have to be considered.

1. Both stamp locks are hierarchical in both trees: *XC* and *XC, SC* and *XC, XC* and *SC*. The scopes of these locks are subtrees of the database version tree and the composition tree. The scope intersection is empty if at least one of the following conditions is observed:
   - the composition subtree concerned by the first stamp lock does not include the composition subtree concerned by the second one, and vice versa, or
   - database version subtree concerned by the first stamp lock does not include the database version subtree concerned by the second one, and vice versa.

   The above conditions may be formalized in the form of the following rule:

   r1: $\neg (cs_1 \leq cs_2 \lor cs_1 >> cs_2) \lor \neg (vs_1 \leq vs_2 \lor vs_1 >> vs_2)$.

2. Both stamp locks are non-hierarchical in both trees: x and x, s and x, x and s. The scopes of these locks are single objects and single database versions. The scope intersection is empty if the stamp locks concern different objects or different database versions. It may be expressed by the following rule:

$$r2\text{: } cs_1 \mathrel{!=} cs_2 \ \lor vs_1 \mathrel{!=} vs_2$$

3. Both stamp locks are non-hierarchical in the composition tree and hierarchical in the database version tree: X and X, S and X, X and S. The scopes of these locks are single objects and subtrees of database version tree. The scope intersection is empty if the stamp locks concern different objects or the subtree of database versions concerned by the first stamp lock does not include the subtree concerned by the second one, and vice versa. It may be expressed by the following rule:

$$r3\text{: } cs_1 \mathrel{!=} cs_2 \ \lor \neg\, (vs_1 \leq vs_2 \lor vs_1 \gg vs_2).$$

4. Both stamp locks are hierarchical in the composition tree and non-hierarchical in the database version tree: xc and xc, xc and sc, sc and xc. The scopes of these locks are composition subtrees and single database versions. The scope intersection is empty if the composition subtree concerned by the first stamp lock does not include the composition subtree concerned by the second one, and vice versa, or the stamp locks concern different database versions. It may be expressed by the following rule:

$$r4\text{: } \neg\, (cs_1 \leq cs_2 \lor cs_1 \gg cs_2) \lor vs_1 \mathrel{!=} vs_2 \,.$$

5. The first stamp lock is non-hierarchical in the composition tree and hierarchical in the database version tree, while the second one is non-hierarchical in both hierarchies: X and x, X and s, S and x. The scope of the first stamp lock is a single object and a database version subtree, while the scope of the second one is a single object and a single database version. The scope intersection is empty if the stamp locks concern different objects, or the database subtree concerned by the first stamp lock does not include the database version concerned by the second one. It may be expressed by the following rule:

$$r5\text{: } cs_1 \mathrel{!=} cs_2 \ \lor \neg\, (vs_1 \leq vs_2).$$

6. The symmetric combination to the one presented above: first stamp lock is non-hierarchical in both trees, while the second one is non-hierarchical in the composition tree and hierarchical in the database version tree. The stamp lock compatibility may be expressed by the following rule:

$$r6\text{: } cs_1 \mathrel{!=} cs_2 \ \lor \neg\, (vs_2 \leq vs_1).$$

7. The first stamp lock is non-hierarchical in the composition tree and hierarchical in the database version tree, while the second one is hierarchical in both hierarchies: X and XC, X and SC, S and XC. The scope of the first stamp lock is a single object and a database version subtree, while the scope of the second one is a composition subtree and a database version subtree. The scope intersection is empty if at least one of the following conditions is observed:

- the object concerned by the first stamp lock is not a component of the object concerned by the second one, or
- the database version subtree concerned by the first stamp lock does not include the database version subtree concerned by the second one, and vice versa.

  It may be expressed by the following rule:

$$\textbf{r7:} \ \neg\,(cs_2 \leq cs_1) \lor \neg\,(vs_1 \leq vs_2 \lor vs_1 >> vs_2).$$

8. The symmetric combination to the one presented above. The stamp lock compatibility may be expressed by the following rule:

$$\textbf{r8:} \ \neg\,(cs_1 \leq cs_2) \lor \neg\,(vs_1 \leq vs_2 \lor vs_1 >> vs_2).$$

9. The first stamp lock is non-hierarchical in both hierarchies, while the second one is hierarchical in both hierarchies: x and XC, s and SC, s and XC. The scope of the first stamp lock is a single object and a single database version, while the scope of the second one is a composition subtree and a database version subtree. The scope intersection is empty if the object concerned by the first stamp lock is not a component of the object concerned by the second lock, or the database version concerned by the first stamp lock is not included in the database version subtree concerned by the second lock. It may be expressed by the following rule:

$$\textbf{r9:} \ \neg\,(cs_2 \leq cs_1) \lor \neg\,(vs_2 \leq vs_1).$$

10. The symmetric combination to the one presented above. The stamp lock compatibility may be expressed by the following rule:

$$\textbf{r10:} \ \neg\,(cs_1 \leq cs_2) \lor \neg\,(vs_1 \leq vs_2).$$

11. The first stamp lock is non-hierarchical in the composition tree and hierarchical in the database tree, while the second one is hierarchical in the composition tree and non-hierarchical in the database version tree: X and xc, X and sc, S and xc. The scope of the first stamp lock is a single object and a database version subtree, while the scope of the second one is a composition subtree and a single database version. The scope intersection is empty if the object concerned by the first stamp lock is not a component of the object concerned by the second lock, or the database version subtree concerned by the first stamp lock does not include the database version concerned by the first lock. It may be expressed by the following rule:

$$\textbf{r11:} \ \neg\,(cs_2 \leq cs_1) \lor \neg\,(vs_1 \leq vs_2).$$

12. The symmetric combination to the one presented above. The stamp lock compatibility may be expressed by the following rule:

$$\textbf{r12:} \ \neg\,(cs_1 \leq cs_2) \lor \neg\,(vs_2 \leq vs_1).$$

13. The first stamp lock is non-hierarchical in both hierarchies, while the second one is hierarchical in the composition tree and non-hierarchical in the database version tree: x and xc, x and sc, s and xc. The scope of the first stamp lock is a single object and a single database version, while the scope of the second one is a composition subtree and a single database version. The scope intersection is empty if the object concerned by the first stamp lock is not a component of the object concerned by the second lock, or the database versions concerned by the stamp locks are different. It may be expressed by the following rule:

$$\textbf{r13:} \ \neg\,(cs_2 \leq cs_1) \lor vs_1 \mathrel{!=} vs_2.$$

14. The symmetric combination to the one presented above. The stamp lock compatibility may be expressed by the following rule:

$$\textbf{r14:} \ \neg\,(cs_1 \leq cs_2) \lor vs_1 \mathrel{!=} vs_2.$$

15. The first stamp lock is hierarchical in both hierarchies, while the second one is hierarchical in the composition tree and non-hierarchical in the database version tree: XC and xc, SC and sc, SC and xc. The scope of the first stamp lock is a composition subtree and a database version subtree, while the scope of the second

one is a composition subtree and a single database version. The scope intersection is empty if one of the following conditions is observed:

- the composition subtree concerned by the first stamp lock does not include the composition subtree concerned by the second one, and vice versa, or
- the database version subtree concerned by the first stamp lock does not include the database version concerned by the second one.

    It may be expressed by the following rule:

$$\textbf{r15:} \quad \neg\,(cs_1 \leq cs_2 \vee cs_1 >> cs_2) \vee \neg\,(vs_1 \leq vs_2).$$

16.   The symmetric combination to the one presented above. The stamp lock compatibility may be expressed by the following rule:

$$\textbf{r16:} \quad \neg\,(cs_1 \leq cs_2 \vee cs_1 >> cs_2) \vee \neg\,(vs_2 \leq vs_1).$$

    The lock compatibility matrix is given in Fig. 9 (exclusive locks requested) and in Fig. 10 (shared locks requested). In the case of compatible stamp locks the word **true** is put to the respective matrix field. In the case of potentially incompatible stamp locks a reference to rules **r1, r2, ..., r16** is put, respectively for all 16 combinations of stamp lock types.

SL_s \ SL_r	$(X,\ vs_2,\ cs_2)$	$(x,\ vs_2,\ cs_2)$	$(XC,\ vs_2,\ cs_2)$	$(xc,\ vs_2,\ cs_2)$
$(X,\ vs_1,\ cs_1)$	r3	r5	r7	r11
$(x,\ vs_1,\ cs_1)$	r6	r2	r9	r13
$(XC,\ vs_1,\ cs_1)$	r8	r10	r1	r15
$(xc,\ vs_1,\ cs_1)$	r12	r14	r16	r4
$(S,\ vs_1,\ cs_1)$	r3	r5	r7	r11
$(s,\ vs_1,\ cs_1)$	r6	r2	r9	r13
$(SC,\ vs_1,\ cs_1)$	r8	r10	r1	r15
$(sc,\ vs_1,\ cs_1)$	r12	r14	r16	r4

Fig. 9. Lock compatibility matrix

SL_s \ SL_r	$(S, vs_2,\ cs_2)$	$(s, vs_2,\ cs_2)$	$(SC, vs_2,\ cs_2)$	$(sc,\ vs_2,\ cs_2)$
$(X,\ vs_1,\ cs_1)$	r3	r5	r7	r11
$(x,\ vs_1,\ cs_1)$	r6	r2	r9	r13
$(XC,\ vs_1,\ cs_1)$	r8	r10	r1	r15
$(xc,\ vs_1,\ cs_1)$	r12	r14	r16	r4
$(S,\ vs_1,\ cs_1)$	true	true	true	true
$(s,\ vs_1,\ cs_1)$	true	true	true	true
$(SC,\ vs_1,\ cs_1)$	true	true	true	true
$(sc,\ vs_1,\ cs_1)$	true	true	true	true

Fig. 10. Lock compatibility matrix

To illustrate the way of determining stamp lock compatibility consider two stamp locks: $SL_s = (X, vs_1, cs_1)$ and $SL_r = (X, vs_2, cs_2)$. Referring to the compatibility matrix given in Fig. 9 we find out that the compatibility of stamp locks considered is determined by the rule **r1**. The rule says that stamp locks SL_s and SL_r are compatible if they concern different objects (objects having different composition stamps) or their scopes in the database version tree are different.

The locking protocol does not depend on the size of a granule being locked and requires setting one stamp lock only. To illustrate this protocol assume a transaction T_1 which updates a composite object (together with its components) stamped 0-2-1 in a database version subtree rooted by 0.1 (cf. Fig. 11). It has to set the following stamp lock:

$$SL_1 = (XC, 0.1, 0\text{-}2\text{-}1).$$

The scope of SL_1 database version and composition hierarchies is surrounded by a dashed line. Now, assume transaction T_2 which updates all the objects in the database version subtree rooted by 0.2. It has to set the following stamp lock:

$$SL_2 = (XC, 0.2, 0).$$

As it follows from the evaluation of rule **r3**, stamp lock SL_2 is compatible with the stamp lock SL_1.

Finally, consider transaction T_3 which reads a single version of object 0-1 in database version 0.2.1. It has to set the following stamp lock:

$$SL_3 = (s, 0.2.1, 0\text{-}1),$$

which is compatible with the lock SL_1 set by T_1. It will not be granted, however, because of its incompatibility with the stamp lock SL_2 set by T_2. It follows from the evaluation of rule **r9**.

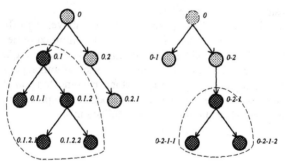

Fig. 11. Database version and composition hierarchies

6 Conclusions

The stamp locking method presented in this paper may be efficiently used in object-oriented databases to solve the problem of concurrent transaction execution. The main advantage of this method is simple locking strategy following from the lack of intentional locks, which is well adapted to deep hierarchies met in object-oriented databases. To lock a hierarchy subtree it is sufficient to set one stamp lock only, whose node stamp identifies the subtree root. To determine stamp lock compatibility, it is sufficient to compare stamp lock scopes. Advantages of the stamp locking method become particularly beneficial in the case of a database containing many versions of composite objects, whose composition structure is complex. This is a typical case of design databases where objects, being the artifacts of the design process, have usually many components available in many versions.

Future work will be focused on extensions of the method and relaxation of the assumptions made in this paper. The method needs an extension to be efficient when managing transactions modifying database schema and global queries. In the first case, dynamic changes to the class definition, e.g. adding or dropping an attribute, which are propagated to all its subclasses due to the inheritance property, require locking the modified class and all its subclasses, i.e. the whole inheritance subtree. In the second case, due to the search space of the global query which may encompass all the instances of a class, or all the instances of a class subtree, hierarchical locks concerning inheritance subtrees are also required. To solve these problems the stamp lock definition and locking strategy should concern the inheritance hierarchy in the same way as the composition and version derivation hierarchies.

Another extension of the method concerns directed acyclic graphs (*DAG*s) instead of trees, which is necessary in databases supporting multiple inheritance or shared composite references [7]. In this case, due to more then one direct predecessor of a node and, potentially, more then one root, we have to modify the way of the node stamp construction to ensure stamping unambiguity. Hierarchical locking of a subgraph containing nodes having more then one direct predecessor requires also extension of the locking algorithm.

The method should also be adapted for different composition and version derivation models. Some of them may lead to non-orthogonal hierarchies (*DAG*s), i.e. hierarchies sharing common nodes.

In parallel to method extensions mentioned above, the efficient way of its implementation is considered. One of the goals is to minimize time requirements of the method. It may be reached by comparing stamp locks requested only with potentially conflicting locks, instead of all the locks. Another goal is to minimize memory requirements for storing stamps, which become long in the case of deep hierarchies. It can be reached by the use of special compression techniques, e.g. storing differences between stamps instead of full stamps.

References

[1] Ahmed R., Navathe S.B., "Version Management of Composite Objects in CAD Databases", *Proc. ACM SIGMOD Conf.*, 1991.

[2] Cart M., Ferrie J. "Integrating Concurrency Control into Object-Oriented Database System", *EDBT Proc.*, Venice, Italy, 1990.

[3] Cellary W., Jomier G., "Consistency of Versions in Object-Oriented Databases", *Proc. 16th VLDB Conf.*, Brisbane, Aug. 1990, pp. 432-441.

[4] Chou H., Kim W., "A Unifying Framework for Version Control in CAD Environment", *12 VLDB Conf.*, Kyoto, Aug. 1986.

[5] Gray J. "Notes on Database Operating Systems", *Operating Systems: An Advanced Course*, Springer-Verlag, 1978.

[6] Hubel C., Kafer W., Sutter B., "Controlling Cooperation Through Design-Object Specification, a Database-oriented Approach", *Proc. of the European Design Automation Conf.*, Brussels, Belgium, 1992.

[7] Kim W., Bertino E., Garza J.F "Composite Objects Revisited", *Proc. ACM SIGMOD Conf.*, 1989.

[8] Zdonik S.B. "Version Management in an Object-Oriented Database", *Int. Works. on Advanced Programming Environments*, Norway 1986, pp. 139-200,

Queries on Structures in Hypertext

Tatsuo Minohara[†]   Ryuichi Watanabe[‡]
Mario Tokoro[†]

† Department of Computer Science, Keio University
3-14-1,Hiyoshi,Kohoku-ku,Yokohama,223,Japan
{minohara,mario}@mt.cs.keio.ac.jp

‡ Computers and Multimedia Department, Sony Corporation
Gotanda AN Building, 1-22-1, Higashi Gotanda,
Shinagawa-ku,Tokyo,141,Japan
ryuichi@sm.sony.co.jp

Abstract

In many existing hypertext systems, a navigation mechanism is provided as the main facility so that readers can search the contents. In order to expand the ability of searching, in this paper we propose a query mechanism to be used in addition to the ordinary navigation mechanism. We can express the advanced abilities of searching by combining the query mechanism with the navigation mechanism. These query expressions can be used to provide the user's point of view besides the designer's point of view, which was previously defined by the links among nodes. Especially, an environment that changes dynamically in correspondence with the user's navigation can be described when one uses our query mechanism. Since the mechanisms proposed in this paper are defined in a formal way, they can be applied to various practical hypertext systems.

1 Introduction

Current researches in hypertext systems have proposed various concrete realizations in which the predominant method of searching is navigation. In navigation, the user moves the focal point of the search from one node to another using links that were previously defined by the designer. Thus, it is difficult for the user to search a content outside the defined link environment, as is required in a string search. This problem was noted in [9]. Additionally, the query mechanism, which is used in ordinary relational databases, is also required in hypertext systems because ordinary relational database query is not supported in hypertext systems. Navigation is a search method that is most effective when unanticipated or ambiguous searches are required, and query is a search method that is most effective when explicit or exhaustive searches are required. Thus, it is easy to see that both methods of search are desirable in a hypertext system.

In this paper, we propose a rigorous framework whereby the query mechanism can be incorporated into hypertext system design. By using the query facility, users can create their own environment and point of view in a system that is outside of the predefined system of contents and links created by the system designer. For example, in the NoteCards system [18], the Guided Tour mechanism creates a new scenario for navigation that is based on the existing hypertext. The mechanism of view is essential to constructing a user oriented environment. Query allows the user to create various views of the system that represent different aspects of the hypertext, or the intentions of the user, or new navigation scenarios, because query can collect arbitrary elements stored in the hypertext. Which is the difference from database systems, that the views are fixed. In the hypertext systems, the user can navigate among the nodes, thus the point of view in the system changes dynamically according to the navigation of the user. In order to realize such views, we propose adding such a navigation oriented query mechanism to the the usual query mechanism currently used in the hypertext systems. We also focus on query expressions in which structural aspects of hypertexts are specified for information retrieval. In the hypertext systems, these are important because the relations among elements of information are explicitly expressed in the structures such as links. We propose a query mechanism by which one can specify structural aspects and contextual aspects simultaneously in a retrieval.

To present the advantages of queries, we start the design of our hypertext system by defining a considerable formal specification for the hypertexts in this paper. In many proposed hypertext systems, the formal specifications were not given. However, formal specification of a hypertext system is necessary to discuss the advantages of system architectures. We define our hypertext system formally by presenting two aspects: a structural aspect and an operational aspect. Since the semantic aspect of a hypertext, such as the kinds of links and the contents of nodes, depends on its application, we focus solely on the structural aspect. The structural aspect is general and independent of any application. On the operational semantics, we will focus on the navigation mechanism in this paper.

In Section 2, we describe our hypertext system by specifying the formal descriptions of structures and operations. In Section 3, we propose a syntax to express queries on our hypertext system and define its semantics. In Section 4, we show advanced query expressions that are based on the query as defined in the previous sections. We propose an integrated combination of query with navigation. In Section 5, we discuss related works by comparing them with our construction. Section 6 concludes this paper with a report of our current status.

2   A Formal Description of Hypertext

In the recent years, many researchers have proposed and implemented various hypertext systems. However, for most researchers, their main aim was to explore the vast possibilities of hypertexts. Only little research has been done concerning the formal specification of a hypertext system so that one can compare the functions of practical systems. In this section we give a formal description of a hypertext, so as to facilitate a more general discussion of a hypertext. This formalization will be done from a structural point of view.

2.1   Contents in Hypertext

A hypertext is usually made of nodes, blocks and links[5]. Other useful notions are anchors and bindings. Anchors increase the flexibility and expressive power of a hypertext[12]. Bindings are used to give users the ability to name an entity. Thus, a hypertext can be defined as a heterogeneous set of entities so that the entities in the hypertext have different structures.

Definition 1 (Entities and Hypertext) An entity is an intensional group, an extensional group, a node, a block, an anchor, a link, a name, a binding, an identifier, or a value. A hypertext $\mathcal{H}$ is a heterogeneous multiple set of all entities in a system. □

An arbitrary set of entities in a hypertext is defined as a group. Since a hypertext itself is a set of heterogeneous entities, a group in the hypertext can be a set of heterogeneous entities. By defining a group, we will be able to express an arbitrary set, such as a set of results of some queries and a set of entities that were collected without using queries. The former is called an intensional group and the latter is called an extensional group. Because a hypertext contains groups as elements, some entities may appear more than once, which is why we defined a hypertext as a multiple set.

Definition 2 (Group) A group G is a heterogeneous multiple subset of a hypertext $\mathcal{H}$. □

Nodes of hypertext are composed of indexed sequence of blocks and correspond on a one-to-one basis with windows. Sequences of blocks are manipulated by functions, such as append, insert, delete, concatenate, etc.

Definition 3 (Nodes) A node in the hypertext represents an indexed sequence of blocks. It is expressed by a tuple, $< id, b_1 \ldots b_n, a_1 \ldots a_n >$, where id indicates its unique identifier, $b_1 \ldots b_n$ and $a_1 \ldots a_n$ indicates sequence of blocks and their corresponding sequence of rhetoric attributes. Groups of nodes are denoted by the meta-variables, $N_1, \ldots, N_n$. Node entities are denoted by the meta-variables, $n_1, \ldots, n_n$. □

There are two types of blocks. One is *a primitive block* that represents a value, such as text, image, sound and animation. The other is *a compound block* that is composed from sequences of other blocks.

Definition 4 (Blocks) A block in the hypertext represents raw data or an indexed sequence of blocks. The former is called a primitive block and the latter is called a compound block. A primitive block is expressed by a tuple, $< id, v, a >$, where id indicates its unique identifier, v indicates a value, and a indicates an attribute. A compound block is expressed by a tuple, $< id, b_1 \ldots b_n, a_1 \ldots a_n >$, where id indicates its unique identifier, and $b_1 \ldots b_n$ and $a_1 \ldots a_n$ indicates sequence of blocks and their corresponding sequence of rhetoric attributes. Groups of blocks are denoted by the meta-variables, $B_1, \ldots, B_n$. Block entities are denoted by the meta-variables, $b_1, \ldots, b_n$. □

Rhetoric attributes hold information used for representing nodes and blocks, such as colors, font types, sizes, and locations. We explicitly treat such information in our structural model of hypertext, since these are essential for the hypertext. However, in this paper we do not specify the concrete types of rhetoric attributes, because we focus on the structures in hypertext.

Definition 5 (Rhetoric Attributes) A rhetoric attribute represents information used for presenting of nodes and blocks. A rhetoric attribute is expressed by a tuple, $< id, v >$, where id indicates its unique identifier, v indicates a value.

Anchors are attached to nodes or blocks in order to represent a point or a region in a hypertext. They are used to show the source or destination point of links, or simply as a means to record interesting information much in a manner of a book mark.

Definition 6 (Anchors) An anchor represents a point or a region in a hypertext to which a link is associated. An anchor is expressed by a tuple, $< id, G >$, where id indicates its unique identifier, G indicates a group of nodes or blocks. Anchor entities are denoted by the meta-variables, $a_1, \ldots, a_n$.
□

A link ties two anchors together with a directed arc, so that one can trace associated information efficiently. The source and destination points of a link must be anchors. An anchor can be attached to a group of nodes or blocks, so one can tie the following entities by using a link: 1)node-to-node, 2)node-to-block, 3)block-to-node, and 4)block-to-block.

Definition 7 (Links) A link is a directed arc that ties two anchors. A link is expressed by a tuple, $< id, k, s, d >$, where id is the unique identifier of the link, k indicates the kind of the link, s indicates the source anchor of the link, and d indicates the destination anchor of the link. Link entities are denoted by the meta-variables, $l_1, \ldots, l_n$.   □

There are various choices how one represents the kind of link. We simply define a kind is represented by a value in this paper. However, it is possible to represent a kind by a path expressions, e.g., "synonym.in.economics".

Each entity or group of entities can be named. A mapping from a name to a corresponding entity or a corresponding set of entities is called a binding. We suppose a simple global naming environment in this paper. Unlike other entities in a hypertext, a binding has no unique identifier, because names are assumed to be unique under this assumption.

Definition 8 (Bindings) A binding represents a mapping from a name to an entity or a group of entities. A binding is expressed by a tuple, $< name, e >$, where *name* indicates a unique name and e indicates an entity or a group of entities. Bindings are denoted by the meta-variables, $\beta_1, \ldots, \beta_n$.
□

An identifier is used for sharing an entity. The uniqueness of an identifier is managed by a hypertext system. A name is used for the convenience of users to specify an entity in a hypertext system. In order to represent the environment of bindings explicitly, we already defined the bindings as structures in a hypertext.

2.2   Example

Consider a hypertext-based Simple English Dictionary $\mathcal{H}$, in which each node represents a single word and has at least three blocks. The first block contains a title, the second contains a functional label, which is a part of speech, and the rest of the blocks represents the meanings of a word. Thus, a node representing a word has blocks in correspondence to the number of its distinct meanings. Every block in the sequence that represents a meaning contains a sequence of blocks, and each block contains a word. Then blocks taken together form a sentence that describes one meaning (See Figure 1). The notations in the following example are defined in the next section.

$$
\begin{aligned}
node &= \textit{each word} \\
node[1] &= \textit{title} \\
node[2] &= \textit{functional label (a part of speech)} \\
node[3[1 \sim w_1]] &= \textit{1st meaning} \\
node[4[1 \sim w_2]] &= \textit{2nd meaning} \\
&\vdots \\
node[m[1 \sim w_n]] &= \textit{n'th meaning, where m=n+2}
\end{aligned}
$$

Nodes and blocks in this dictionary can be linked to each other using five kinds of links. The kinds

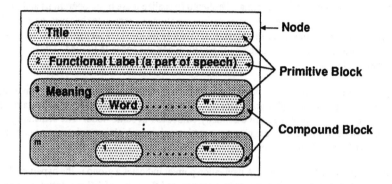

Figure 1: A node in Simple English Dictionary $\mathcal{H}$

of links provided are:

kind	source	destination	kind	source	destination
synonym	node	node	antonym	node	node
refer	node	node	explained	block	block

Suppose this dictionary $\mathcal{H}$ has the word *'easy'*. In an ordinary English dictionary, the entry for this word would look something like this (although this example is very simplified for the sake of clarity):

> **easy** *adj* **1** not difficult **2** free from pain **3** not much in demand

Then the corresponding node's and block's definitions are:

$$< n_1, b_1b_2b_3b_4b_5, a_{b1}a_{b2}a_{b3}a_{b4}a_{b5} >$$
$$< b_1, 'easy', a_1 >$$
$$< b_2, 'adjective', a_2 >$$
$$< b_3, b_{31}b_{32}, a_{b31}a_{b32} >$$
$$< b_{31}, 'not', a_{31} > < b_{32}, 'difficult', a_{32} >$$
$$< b_4, b_{41}b_{42}b_{43}, a_{b41}a_{b42}a_{b43} >$$
$$< b_{41}, 'free', a_{41} > < b_{42}, 'from', a_{42} > < b_{43}, 'pain', a_{43} > \ldots$$

Furthermore, if a synonym of the word *'easy'* also exists in this dictionary, such as *'effortless'*, and if its node identifier is n_2, then this relation is expressed by two anchors $< a_1, n_1 >$, $< a_2, n_2 >$ and one link $< l_1, 'synonym', a_1, a_2 >$.

2.3 Navigation on Hypertext

Various hypertext systems have been proposed and implemented using different approaches and different concepts, however for most of the hypertext systems, the basic operations are almost the same [5]. These operations are creation, destruction, modification, naming, and selection of entities, and navigation among nodes. We can define two operations applied on groups in a hypertext: adding an entity to a group and deleting. We should formalize these basic operations and establish their semantics. Rigorously, we should also define operations on sequences because we use indexed sequences to define the structures in a hypertext. We only focus on the navigation in this paper because we are discussing on the searching mechanism and the space is limited. Other operations were formalized in [20].

Navigation is the most ordinary way of accessing a hypertext. A user may choose an arbitrary link and traverse the nodes and blocks. This operation can be captured singly as a navigation from node to node, because all blocks are essentially embedded in some node. The semantics of this navigation can be formalized by defining a navigation pointer, which is a pointer to a node that the user's eyes are currently fixed upon.

Definition 9 (Navigation Pointer) A navigation pointer indicates a group in the hypertext $\mathcal{H}$. The special variable NP expresses the navigation pointer, and the value of NP is a group of identifiers associated with nodes in a group that the navigation pointer indicates. □

A navigation pointer can be considered a group of windows that display the contents of the nodes. Navigation is considered an operation by which the user moves around in a hypertext from a group of nodes to another group of nodes. It can be formalized as an operation that changes the value of the navigation pointer from a current group to a next group.

Definition 10 (Navigation) Navigation is an operation by which the value of NP is modified. If NP implies a node n and some appropriate anchor a is attached to n and some appropriate link l is defined on the source anchor a in $\mathcal{H}$, then the user can navigate from the node n to another group of nodes in which either node has the destination anchor a' of l through the link l. This operation is expressed by the **navigate()** function. As parameters for this function, the kind of the link l and the identifier of the anchor a are specified. The semantics of navigation is formally defined by the following two expressions:

$$\frac{n \in NP \quad \exists a \in anchors(n) \quad \exists l \in links(\exists kind, a, \exists a') \quad \textbf{navigate}(a, kind)}{NP = nodes(a')}$$

$$\frac{n \in NP \quad n \in implies(\exists b) \quad \exists a \in anchors(b) \quad \exists l \in links(\exists kind, a, \exists a') \quad \textbf{navigate}(a, kind)}{NP = nodes(a')}$$

In these expressions, the following functions are assumed:

- *nodes(a): Anchor → **Group of Nodes***
  returns a group of nodes with which the given anchor a is associated. Namely,

$$nodes(a) \equiv \{n \in Node \mid a = < id, G > \land n \in G\}.$$

- *implies(b): Block* → **Group of** *Nodes*
  returns a group of nodes in which the given block b is included. Namely,

$$
\begin{aligned}
implies(b) &\equiv \{n \in Node \mid n =< id, \ldots, b, \ldots > \\
&\quad \lor (n =< id, \ldots, \exists b' \ldots > \land b' \in includes(b))\} \\
includes(b) &\equiv \{b' \in Block \mid b' =< id, \ldots, b, \ldots > \\
&\quad \lor (b' =< id, \ldots, \exists b'' \ldots > \land b'' \in includes(b))\}.
\end{aligned}
$$

- *anchors(x): Node or Block* → **Group of** *Anchors*
  returns a group of anchors that are associated with the given node or block x. Namely,

$$
anchors(x) \equiv \{a \in Anchor \mid a =< id, G > \land x \in G\}.
$$

- *links(k, s, d): Kind* × *Anchor* × *Anchor* → **Group of** *Links*
  returns the set of links that are defined between the given source anchor s and the given destination anchor d and belong to the given kind k. Namely,

$$
links(k, s, d) \equiv \{l \in Link \mid l =< id, k, s, d >\}.
$$

$\square$

In the above expressions, two kinds of navigation are defined: navigation from a node to a node and navigation from a block to a node. We suppose the other two kinds of navigation: navigation from a node to a block and navigation from a block to a block. In these two kinds of navigation, the node in which the block associated with the destination anchor is implied is visited instead of the block, because the unit of navigation is a group of nodes.

We define a group of nodes and blocks instead of a single node or a single block for a navigation point. The aim of this approach is to represent group oriented navigation in addition to ordinary navigation. In group oriented navigation, multiple windows for nodes will appear in correspondence to a navigation. Such windows are semantically associated with each other in presentation of hypertext [18].

3 Query Expression

There are two kinds of formal descriptions for query. One of these uses an algebraic notation in which several algebraic operators are defined. The other uses a logical notation in which a query is described as a logical expression. Since the semantics of algebraic notation for query is often given by logical notation [7, 16], if we would adopt an algebraic notation, we should show both its logical notation and the semantics of the converted logical notation. Rigorously, the completeness and soundness of the defined set of algebraic operators should be shown on the converted logical notation. However, because of space limitations, we will adopt directly the logical notation in this paper. When practical implementation is required, we should define the algebraic operators in order to interpret queries efficiently. The logical notation defined in this section is similar to the one defined by Reiter [14]. We restrict the ability of expressiveness for queries to the level of relational calculus in this paper having a limited space, since the semantics of recursive queries requires more complex theories such as the fixed point theory [13, 19]. We sketch a simple query language with several examples in the following definitions. First, we will show definitions of syntax and then show model theoretical definitions of semantics.

3.1 Syntax of Query

In our simple query language, any query can be described using well formed formulae. In order
to define the semantics of our query language, we will use natural semantics [10] later. In natural
semantics, a non-terminated symbol that appears in the BNF notation is considered a class in the
syntax and a script written in the defined language is considered an instance. In the subsequent
definition, we often treat a non-terminated symbol as a class in the syntax.

3.1.1 Basic Components

Definition 11 (Literal) The literal of this language consists of the alphabetical and the numeric
characters and symbols. There are three kinds of literals in this language; variables are described
by alphabetical words, constants are strings or numerals or structured constants, and predicates are
names globally defined in the hypertext $\mathcal{H}$. The following meta-variables are used to denote an
instance of each class respectively:

$$Variable ::= x, y, z, \ldots \quad Constant ::= a, b, c, \ldots \quad Predicate ::= P, Q, R, \ldots$$

□

We assume the regular expressions commonly defined in the Unix operating systems can be used
for matching strings. For example, the string constant '.*tion' expresses words which terminate
with the letter 'tion' (e.g., 'definition', 'contribution', etc.). Besides the regular expressions, the
concatenate operator [] can be applied to string constants. For example, 'data' [] 'base' is evaluated
as 'database'.

Built-in Predicates are the special predicates defined previously and used to compare constants.
For example, the following operators are assumed in our language in order to compare integers or
compare strings in alphabetical order.

$$= \quad \neq \quad \leq \quad \geq \quad > \quad <$$

Definition 12 (Syntax for Terms) A node or a block stored in a hypertext $\mathcal{H}$ is specified by a term.
Constants and sequences and variables are also considered to be terms.

Term	::=	*Node Specification*
	|	*Block Specification*
	|	*Node Specification[Block Specification]*
	|	*Sequent Constructor*
	|	*Variable*
	|	*Constant*
Node Specification	::=	*Identifier Expression*
Identifier Expression	::=	*#(Cardinal Expression)*
	|	*Variable*
Block Specification	::=	*Block Index[Block Specification]*
	|	*Block Index*
Block Index	::=	*Cardinal Expression*
	|	*^ Cardinal Expression*
	|	*Cardinal Expression ~ Cardinal Expression*

Cardinal Expression	::=	*Integer Constant*
	|	*Variable*
	|	*Cardinal Expression* + *Cardinal Expression*
	|	*Cardinal Expression* − *Cardinal Expression*
	|	*Cardinal Expression* × *Cardinal Expression*
	|	*Cardinal Expression* ÷ *Cardinal Expression*
	|	− *Cardinal Expression*
	|	(*Cardinal Expression*)
Sequent Constructor	::=	[*Term*]
	|	[*Term*, . . . , *Term*]
	|	!(*Term*)
	|	*Term* ‖ *Term*

□

The syntax class of node specification is used to specify target nodes that are accessed by a query. In order to indicate a specific node, the identifier number of the node can be directly specified. For example, both #(5624) and #(703 × 8) indicate the same node.

The syntax of block specification can be used to extract several blocks from a node. For example, $a[24[5]]$ indicates the 5th block in the 24th block in the node a. In contrast with the syntax of block specification, by using the syntax of sequent constructor, a sequence consisting of entities is specified as a term. There are three kinds of operators to construct a sequence: sequent constructor, unfold operators, and catenate operators. Though the formal semantics of these operators are defined carefully later, we introduce several intuitive examples here. Assume a indicates a sequence: [*'Intuition'*, [*'noun'*], [*'immediate'*, *'understanding'*]] . When some operations are applied to a, the results are as follows:

Block Specification	$a[3[2]]$	=	*'understanding'*
Sequent Constructor	$[[a[1]], a[2]]$	=	[[*'Intuition'*], [*'noun'*]]
Unfold Operator	$!(a)$	=	[*'Intuition'*, *'noun'*, *'immediate'*, *'understanding'*]
Catenate Operator	$a[2] \parallel a[3]$	=	· [*'noun'* , *'immediate'*, *'understanding'*]

3.1.2 Logical Expression

Definition 13 (Syntax for Atomic Formulae) Any predicate in this language appears in the syntax of atomic formula. The number of arguments passing to a predicate corresponds to the arity of the predicate.

$$Atomic\ Formula \quad ::= \quad Predicate(Term, . . ., Term)$$

□

Abbreviation: When an atomic formula requires more than one argument, these arguments are considered a sequence of arguments. The atomic formula is syntactically replaced as follows:

$$p(t_1, . . ., t_n) \equiv p([t_1, . . ., t_n])$$

where $p \in Predicate$ and $t_1, . . ., t_n \in Term$.

For example, the binary relation =, that is one of built-in predicates, takes two arguments. Then, we describe the equality between two entities a_1, a_2 as $= (a_1, a_2)$. By using the example introduced in the previous section, we show the following several examples as atomic formulae, in which *title* = 1 and *functional label* = 2 and n denotes a node.

$$\leq (n[title], \text{`elephant'}) \qquad \neq (n[functional\ label], \text{`noun'})$$
$$= (n[title], \text{`.*tion'}) \qquad = (\text{`machine'}, n[3[1]])$$

Besides binary built-in predicates, named groups in the hypertext $\mathcal{H}$ can be specified as the predicate in an atomic formula. For example, if it is assumed that P indicates a subset of the simple English dictionary introduced in the previous section, then $P(x)$ denotes whether x is included in P.

Definition 14 (Syntax for Well Formed Formulae) In the following syntax, the scope of the variable introduced in a quantifier ($\forall$ or $\exists$) is limited syntactically in the following well formed formula.

Well Formed Formula	::=	*Atomic Formula*
	|	*(Well Formed Formula $\wedge$ Well Formed Formula)*
	|	*(Well Formed Formula $\vee$ Well Formed Formula)*
	|	*(Well Formed Formula $\rightarrow$ Well Formed Formula)*
	|	*$\neg$ Well Formed Formula*
	|	*($\exists$ Variable)(Well Formed Formula)*
	|	*($\forall$ Variable)(Well Formed Formula)*
	|	*($\exists$ Variable/Boundary)(Well Formed Formula)*
	|	*($\forall$ Variable/Boundary)(Well Formed Formula)*
Boundary	::=	*Predicate* □

For example, all of the following expressions are well formed formulae.

- $(\forall x / P)(\leq (x, 1000))$
  expresses whether all entities in the group P are less than 1000.
- $(\exists x)(Q(x) \rightarrow P(x))$
  expresses whether there is an entity which always belongs to a group P if it belongs to Q.

Abbreviation: When a boundary is specified in a quantifier, the well formed formula is substituted syntactically as follows.

$$(\forall x / \tau)(W) \quad \equiv \quad (\forall x)(\tau(x) \rightarrow W)$$
$$(\exists x / \tau)(W) \quad \equiv \quad (\exists x)(\tau(x) \wedge W)$$

where $x \in$ *Variable* and $\tau \in$ *Boundary* and $W \in$ *Well Formed Formula*.

3.1.3 Query Expression

Definition 15 (Syntax for Queries) A query is described by using the syntax of a qualifier.

Qualifier	::=	*<Constructor | Well Formed Formula>*
Constructor	::=	*Candidate*
	|	*[Candidate]*
	|	*[Candidate, ... , Canadidate]*
	|	*!(Candidate)*
	|	*Candidate || Candidate*
Candidate	::=	*Node Specification*
	|	*Node Specification/Boundary*
	|	*Block Specification*
	|	*Block Specification/Boundary* □

Abbreviation: If a boundary is specified in a candidate, it is substituted according to the following rule.

$$< x/\tau \mid W > \equiv < x \mid \tau(x) \wedge (W) >$$

where $x \in$ *Node Specification or Block Specification*, $\tau \in$ *Boundary*, and $W \in$ *Well Formed Formula*.

Because the syntax of a qualifier is used, it is possible to flexibly describe various queries. For example, the following advanced queries are naturally described in our query language.

- $Q \stackrel{\text{def}}{=} < x \mid (\exists i)((\exists j)(\geq (i,3) \wedge = (x[i[j]], \text{`animal'}))) >$
  searches the nodes in which the word 'animal' is included in the meanings.
- $< x[functional\ label] \mid = (x[title], \text{`dis.*'}) >$
  searches the functional labels of items in which titles start from the letter '*dis*'.
- $< x/Q \mid (\forall y)(\geq (x[title], y[title])) >$
  searches the last node in the dictionary order in the group Q.
- $< x \mid (\exists y)((\exists i)((\exists j)(\geq (i,3) \wedge = (y[i[j]], \text{`sing'}) \wedge = (x, y[i[j+1]])))) >$
  searches primitive blocks, each of which follows the word 'sing' from the explanations of all nodes.

3.2 Semantics of Queries in Hypertext

We begin to define the semantics of query by defining a domain that is a range of variable. We construct model theoretical semantics based on this domain. Because of the space limitations, we cannot show the proofs of the soundness and completeness of our semantics in this paper. However, if these are required, we will attach appendixes to this paper.

Definition 16 (Effective Domain) An effective domain D is defined as follows.

- D is a group of entities existing in $\mathcal{H}$, or
- D is a countably infinite or finite domain of constants, or
- D is a group of sequences, in which any element of each sequence belongs to some effective domain.

$c \in D$ denotes that a constant c belongs to an effective domain D. □

Since we must define a sound domain for the semantics of query, we introduce the concept of an effective domain that has extensional meaning. We do not assume nested groups, while but we do assume nested effective domains. In any effective domain, an element can be constructed from existing entities, constants, or sequences. Only the group of hypertext $\mathcal{H}$ can have a group as its direct element. In order to support structural queries, we introduce several pre-defined effective domains such as *Link* and *Anchor* in the next section. We now introduce several operations and relations for effective domains in order to use these operations and relations in subsequent definitions.

Definition 17 (Operations and Relations of Effective Domains) The union, product, and difference of effective domains are defined as follows. The results of these operations are also effective domains. The inclusion relation is also defined in the expressions below.

$$\forall x \in D \, \forall y \in E \vdash x \in D + E \, y \in D + E$$
$$\forall x \in D \, \forall y \in E \vdash x \parallel y \in D \times E$$
$$\forall x \in D \, \forall y \in E \vdash \text{if } x = y \text{ then } x \notin D - E \text{ else } x \in D - E$$
$$D \subseteq E \vdash \forall x \in D, x \in E$$

where $A \vdash B$ means 'B is deductive under A'. □

Abbreviation: This abbreviation is used to define the domain of arguments passed to a predicate.

$$\prod_{i=1}^{n} D_i \equiv (\ldots((D_1 \times D_2) \times D_3) \times \ldots) \times D_n$$

We introduce an interpretation of query in the next definition. This interpretation maps the notation of query into a extensional group of sequences (or nodes).

Definition 18 (Mapping and Interpretation) An *interpretation* of our query language $Q = (Literal, Qualifier)$ is expressed by a triple $I = (D, K, E)$, where

- D is an effective domain over which the variables in Q range,
- K is a mapping from constant literals to constants on D, and
  (i.e., for each $c \in Constant$, $K(c) \in D$)
- E is a mapping from the predicates in Q into a group of elements of D (i.e., for each $P \in Predicate$ with arity n, $E(P) \subseteq \prod_{i=1}^{n} D_i$). $E(P)$ is called the *extension* of P in the interpretation I.

The function ρ maps any variable that appears in a query into some constant in an appropriate effective domain. The ρ changes corresponding with the scope of variable. The ρ in a scope is called *variable environment*. The following expression means that a syntax of Q is interpreted as a meaning under a variable environment. When the additional assumption of environment, in addition to a variable environment, is required, it is expressed as the following second expression:

$$\vdash_\rho Syntax \Rightarrow_I Meaning$$
$$. Environment \vdash_\rho Syntax \Rightarrow_I Meaning \qquad \square$$

We embody the interpretation for each syntax rule. We have already given the interpretation in the previous definition for the literal in our language.

Definition 19 (Semantics of Term) In the definitions of interpretation as follows, we assume that each meta-variable belongs, respectively, to the following class of syntax.

$$i, i_1, i_2 \in Block\ Index \quad b \in Node\ or\ Block \quad a, a_1, a_2, \ldots, a_k, a_{k+1}, \ldots, a_{n-1}, a_n \in Term$$

Each meta-variable denotes a constant in the appropriate effective domain.

$$
\begin{aligned}
b = [a_1, \ldots, a_n] \vdash_\rho b[i] &\Rightarrow_I a_i \\
b = [a_1, \ldots, a_n] \vdash_\rho b[^\wedge i] &\Rightarrow_I [a_1, \ldots, a_{i-1}, a_{i+1}, \ldots, a_n] \\
b = [a_1, \ldots, a_n], i_1 \leq i_2 \vdash_\rho b[i_1 \sim i_2] &\Rightarrow_I [a_{i_1}, \ldots, a_{i_2}] \\
\vdash_\rho [a] &\Rightarrow_I [a] \\
\vdash_\rho [a_1, \ldots, a_n] &\Rightarrow_I [a_1, \ldots, a_n] \\
\vdash_\rho a_1 \,\|\, a_2 &\Rightarrow_I [a_1, a_2] \\
\vdash_\rho a_1 \,\|\, [a_2, \ldots, a_n] &\Rightarrow_I [a_1, a_2, \ldots, a_n] \\
\vdash_\rho [a_1, \ldots, a_{n-1}] \,\|\, a_n &\Rightarrow_I [a_1, \ldots, a_{n-1}, a_n] \\
\vdash_\rho [a_1, \ldots, a_k] \,\|\, [a_{k+1}, \ldots, a_n] &\Rightarrow_I [a_1, \ldots, a_n] \\
\vdash_\rho !(a) &\Rightarrow_I a \\
\vdash_\rho !([a]) &\Rightarrow_I a \\
\vdash_\rho !([a_1, \ldots, a_n]) &\Rightarrow_I [c_1 \,\|\, \ldots \,\|\, c_n] \\
&\quad where\ c_i = !(a_i)\ s.t.\ 1 \leq i \leq n
\end{aligned}
$$

$\square$

By using the concept of effective domain, we can show the model theoretical interpretation of our language in subsequent definitions.

Definition 20 (Semantics of Atomic Formulae) In the following definition, D_i denotes an effective domain corresponding to a constant c_i, and P is an instance of the syntax class *Predicate*. The two special values, **true** and **false**, are constants of Boolean effective domain.

$$[c_1, \ldots, c_n] \in P, P \subseteq \prod_{i=1}^{n} D_i \vdash_\rho P(c_1, \ldots, c_n) \Rightarrow_I \textbf{true}$$
$$[c_1, \ldots, c_n] \notin P, P \subseteq \prod_{i=1}^{n} D_i \vdash_\rho P(c_1, \ldots, c_n) \Rightarrow_I \textbf{false} \qquad \square$$

Even if some built-in predicate, such as =, appears in an atomic formula, we assume that it constructs a partial effective domain, which is a subdomain of the product. For example, $= (x_1, x_2)$ is considered an effective domain in which x_1 is always same to x_2.

Definition 21 (Semantics of Well Formed Formula) In the following definitions, W, W_1, and W_2 are instances of the syntax class *Well Formed Formula*. The meta-variables, ν, ν_1, and ν_2, denote Boolean constants (either **true** or **false**). The operators in *Meaning*: **and, or,** and **not** obey the ordinary logical semantics. D denotes an effective domain.

$$\textbf{and} \quad \frac{D \vdash_\rho W_1(e_1) \Rightarrow_I \nu_1 \quad D \vdash_\rho W_2(e_2) \Rightarrow_I \nu_2}{D \vdash_\rho W_1(e_1) \wedge W_2(e_2) \Rightarrow_I \nu_1 \textbf{ and } \nu_2} \quad \textbf{or} \quad \frac{D \vdash_\rho W_1(e_1) \Rightarrow_I \nu_1 \quad D \vdash_\rho W_2(e_2) \Rightarrow_I \nu_2}{D \vdash_\rho W_1(e_1) \vee W_2(e_2) \Rightarrow_I \nu_1 \textbf{ or } \nu_2}$$

$$\textbf{imply} \quad \frac{D \vdash_\rho W_1(e_1) \Rightarrow_I \nu_1 \quad D \vdash_\rho W_2(e_2) \Rightarrow_I \nu_2}{D \vdash_\rho W_1(e_1) \rightarrow W_2(e_2) \Rightarrow_I \textbf{not } \nu_1 \textbf{ or } \nu_2} \quad \textbf{not} \quad \frac{D \vdash_\rho W(e) \Rightarrow_I \nu}{D \vdash_\rho \neg W(e) \Rightarrow_I \textbf{not } \nu}$$

A well formed formula with the quantifier ($\forall$ or $\exists$) creates a new variable environment in which a variable in the quantifier has a local scope.

$$\textbf{forall} \quad \frac{\forall d \in D \vdash_\rho W(d) \Rightarrow_I \textbf{true}}{D \vdash_\rho (\forall x)W(x) \Rightarrow_I \textbf{true}} \quad \frac{\exists d \in D \vdash_\rho W(d) \Rightarrow_I \textbf{false}}{D \vdash_\rho (\forall x)W(x) \Rightarrow_I \textbf{false}}$$

$$\textbf{exists} \quad \frac{\exists d \in D \vdash_\rho W(d) \Rightarrow_I \textbf{true}}{D \vdash_\rho (\exists x)W(x) \Rightarrow_I \textbf{true}} \quad \frac{\forall d \in D \vdash_\rho W(d) \Rightarrow_I \textbf{false}}{D \vdash_\rho (\exists x)W(x) \Rightarrow_I \textbf{false}} \qquad \square$$

Definition 22 (Semantics of Query) In the following definition, S and D denote effective domains. The meta-variable x denotes a constant in an effective domain. y belongs to a syntax class *Constructor*. $W(x)$ is an instance of a syntax class *Well Formed Formula* with a parameter x.

$$\frac{S \subseteq D \vdash_\rho \forall x \in S, W(x) \Rightarrow_I \textbf{true} \quad S \subseteq D \vdash_\rho \forall x \in (D - S), W(x) \Rightarrow_I \textbf{false}}{D \vdash_\rho < y \mid W(y) > \Rightarrow_I S}$$

$$\square$$

We define the above semantics classically. The constructive definition may restrict implementations of query. This is why we avoid the constructive definition. Using the above definition, we now give the semantics of query in a hypertext $\mathcal{H}$ as follows.

Definition 23 (Query in Hypertext) When an instance q of the syntax class *Qualifier* is interpreted into S under the environment $\mathcal{H}$, the query described by q, which is issued in $\mathcal{H}$, is evaluated into S.

$$\frac{\mathcal{H} \vdash_\rho q \Rightarrow_I S}{\mathcal{H} \vdash_\rho \textbf{evaluate}(q) \Rightarrow_I S}$$

$$\square$$

We define the semantics of query as an operation of evaluation. The result of evaluation makes an extensional group temporally. We prove the completeness and soundness of the semantics of our query language in [20].

4   Advanced Queries

We show several advanced queries based on the query language defined in the previous section. There are three kinds of queries: a query in which both structural properties and contextual properties are specified, a query in which the order of blocks are specified, and a query that is sensitive to the current navigation point. In ordinary database systems, these queries cannot be explicitly described. In hypertext systems, such queries are essential because their information retrievals are considered searching on current structures.

4.1   Queries on Structures

We must define several groups and predicates so that one can specify the anchors and the links in a hypertext. For extension, we first define the following two special effective domains (namely groups).

- *Link*: is a group consisting of all existing links in a hypertext $\mathcal{H}$. Each element of this group is a 4 arity sequence, [*link id, kind, source anchor, destination anchor*].
- *Anchor*: is a group consisting of all existing anchors in a hypertext $\mathcal{H}$. Each element of this group is a 2 arity sequence, [*anchor id, entity id*]. The *entity id* is the identifier of an element of the group to which an anchor is attached.

Similarly to the relational calculus, the named groups can be used as predicates in query expressions. The number of passing arguments should be equal to the arity of the sequence in the group if a named group appears as a *Atomic Formulae*, while these arguments are not required if it appears in the syntax class *Boundary*. For example, the following query searches a group of nodes that are connected to a node named n through some kind of link.

$$A \stackrel{\text{def}}{=} < x \mid (\exists l)(\exists a)(\exists b)(\exists k)(Link(l, k, a, b) \land Anchor(a, n) \land Anchor(b, x)) >$$

Thus, we extend the ability of query so that it can support any entity in a hypertext $\mathcal{H}$. However, in order to treat a query more prudently, we discuss the result of a query. It is possible to construct several kinds of extensional group by a query as a result of evaluation. As homogeneous groups, there are four kinds of groups: groups consisting of nodes, groups consisting of blocks, groups consisting of links, and groups consisting of anchors. It is possible to construct heterogeneous groups by using the syntax of *Sequent Constructor* or the logical operator $\lor$ in the syntax of *Well Formed Formula*. For example, it is possible to construct a group consisting of nodes and anchors. In order to extract entities of the same kind from a heterogeneous group, we define the following effective domains besides *Anchor* and *Link*.

- *Node*: is a group consisting of all existing nodes in a hypertext $\mathcal{H}$.
- *Block*: is a group consisting of all existing blocks in a hypertext $\mathcal{H}$.

Note that we do not refer to the construction of these groups here. That is an issue of implementation. For example, the following query extracts nodes that have the title 'homogeneous' from a heterogeneous group G.

$$< x/G \mid Node(x) \land = (x[1], 'homogeneous') >$$

Thus, we provide tools shown above so that a group has various entities. In the following practical examples, the dictionary hypertexts are used. There are two kinds of links: 'database.synonym' and 'logic.antonym' mean the synonyms and the antonyms respectively in each research field. The next query searches pairs of nodes which are linked each other via both kinds of links. Namely, these words are synonyms in database but anonyms in logic.

$$< [x/Node, y/Node] \mid (\exists a_1)(\exists a_2)(\exists l_1)(\exists l_2)(Anchor(a_1, x) \wedge Anchor(a_2, y)$$
$$\wedge Link(l_1, 'database.synonym', a_1, a_2) \wedge Link(l_2, 'logic.antonym', a_1, a_2)) >$$

In the following example, the nodes to which some links are defined from the node whose title name is 'action'. Thus, both structural and contextual aspects can be specified in a query expression.

$$< x/Node \mid (\exists n)(\exists a_1)(\exists a_2)(\exists l)(\exists k)(Node(n) \wedge = (n[title], 'action')$$
$$\wedge Anchor(a_1, x) \wedge Anchor(a_2, y) \wedge Link(l, k, a_1, a_2)) >$$

4.2 Queries using Sequences

Besides groups, sequences are used to express the ordered elements. The order of elements can be specified by using indexes in a query expression. A query using sequences is considered a structural retrieval. In the previous section, we have shown a simple example which uses the sequence. Here we show more advanced examples. Before the examples, the two groups are defined as follows:

$$Noun \equiv < x[title] \mid Node(x) \wedge = (x[functional \ label], 'noun') >$$
$$Verb \equiv < x[title] \mid Node(x) \wedge = (x[functional \ label], 'verb') >$$

These groups mean the words that express nouns and verbs respectively in the dictionary hypertext. By using these groups, one can make illustrative sentences consisting of nouns and verbs. In the next example, new sequences are created by a query and each sequence is an illustrative sentence.

$$< ['A', n_1, v[]'s', 'a', n_2] \mid Noun(n_1) \wedge Noun(n_2) \wedge Verb(v) >$$

Such method can be applied to the meanings in the dictionary. The following example collects nodes having some sentences with 'queries' in the meanings.

$$< x/Node \mid (\exists i)(\exists j)(\exists v)(= (x[i[j]], 'queries') \wedge = (x[i[j + 1]], v) \wedge Verb(v) \wedge >= (i, 3)) >$$

4.3 Queries with Navigation

The difference between ordinary database systems and hypertext systems is that the latter has the operation *navigation*. Therefore, it is natural to express a query that is sensitive to the situation and the environment by using the navigation. In our definition, *NP* expresses the group on which the user focus in the current navigation. A query expression with *NP* is considered sensitive to navigation. Besides *NP*, we define a navigation closure *CNP* as follows for convenience. A navigation closure expresses a more broad region of navigation than *NP*. The result of a query using navigation closures or navigation points dynamically depends on the current navigation point.

Definition 24 (Navigation Closure) A *navigation closure* consists of the node pointed to by a navigation pointer and the links, anchors, and blocks attached to the node. The destination nodes that have some associated links are also included in the navigation closure. The navigation closure is denoted by $\lfloor NP \rfloor$ or *CNP*. □

In a more formal description, the navigation closure *CNP* is partially described by the following equation. Since the anchors attached to the transitive closure of blocks are not described in this equation, we use the symbol similar $\cong$, instead of the symbol equivalent $\equiv$. In our current query language, recursive queries cannot be described. Therefore, we cannot search the nested blocks transitively.

$$
\begin{aligned}
CNP \;\cong\; & < x \mid NP(x) \\
& \lor \; (\exists n)(Anchor(x, n) \land NP(n)) \\
& \lor \; (\exists i)(\exists n)(Block(x) \land = (n[i], x) \land NP(n)) \\
& \lor \; (\exists l)(\exists k)(\exists a)(\exists b)(\exists n)(Anchor(a, n) \land NP(n) \land (Link(x, k, a, b) \lor Link(x, k, b, a))) \\
& \lor \; (\exists l)(\exists k)(\exists a)(\exists b)(\exists n)(Anchor(a, n) \land NP(n) \\
& \quad\; \land (Link(l, k, a, b) \lor Link(l, k, b, a)) \land Anchor(b, x)) >
\end{aligned}
$$

The following example represents a group of nodes which are the neighbors to the node that a navigation pointer indicates, and their functional labels are *'adverb'*. A named group *CNP* is used as a predicate.

$$
< x/Node \mid CNP(x) \land = (x[\,functional\quad label\,], 'adverb') >
$$

Naturally navigation closures can be used multiply in a query. The next query represents the group of nodes that are neighbors to the navigation pointer and there is some kind of link between the neighbors.

$$
\begin{aligned}
< x \mid \; & (\exists y)(\exists z)(\exists a)(\exists b)(\exists l)(\exists k)(\\
& Node(x) \land Node(y) \land CNP(y) \land CNP(x) \\
& \land Anchor(a, x) \land Anchor(b, x) \land Link(l, k, a, b)) >
\end{aligned}
$$

5 Discussions

5.1 Structural Models and Queries for Hypertext

Formal descriptions for a hypertext have been proposed by several researchers. Tompa[17] proposes a data model that is based on hypergraphs[4]. In our definition of hypertext, since it is possible to have a group of nodes and blocks in an anchor, the hypergraphs are realized by using anchors. In Campbell's HAM[5], a powerful graph-based model is supported, and a query-like mechanism called a filter is proposed. However, this filtering mechanism can only be applied to attributes attached to contexts, nodes or links.

There are several approaches to realize hypertext systems on database systems. Schütt and Streitz take an approach that is similar to us [15]. The nodes and links are modeled by using objects that are tuples with identifiers. The query language is just based on SQL. Garg models hypertexts as a set of first order formulae [8], however his model only provides a linking between nodes, and does not include the semantics of navigation. Afrati generalizes Garg's model and suitably extends it to capture features such as structured nodes, and typed link with associated scripts [2]. His model provides a powerful query mechanism, that is only applicable to structures of the hypertext not to contexts. Beeri's model[3] is an extension of modal logic. Although his model provides the powerful query mechanism, his query mechanism is not combined with navigation mechanism. As we stated before query mechanism in itself is not suitable for representing the dynamic characteristics of the hypertext where users move among nodes. We believe our combination of query mechanism with navigation is the most natural way of representing the view in the hypertext. We define such navigation oriented view in [20]. In this paper, we describe the current navigation status by the navigation closure. It is possible to reflect the history of navigation on queries. In order to realize such history sensitive queries, we should prepare a navigation path that is a sequence of navigation points. We currently investigate various formulations to describe navigation paths.

5.2 Queries for Complex Structured Data

In this paper, we defined a query language which has expressiveness similar to that of relational calculus. In the research field of deductive databases, recursive query and stratified query that have negative atomic formula can be realized [13, 19]. For example, by using a recursive query, the transitive closure is easily expressed. We plan to extend the expressive power of our query language so that it can support these advanced queries. This will be quite natural and easy, since we have adopted a logic-based query language. Furthermore, we will give correct semantics to the extended language. Several advanced query languages were proposed in the field of deductive and object oriented databases [1, 6, 7, 11, 16]. In these query languages, a query is applied to a set of entities having complex structures, and entities are modeled by using the concept of object [1, 7, 16] or the concept of the complex term [6, 11], however we modeled entities mainly by using sequences that can be indexed. We consider that the access to a nested block from a node is more powerful than the access to a member from an object, since the access can be parametrized by using the index. We discuss whether we should adopt these high-order queries.

6 Conclusion

In this paper, we proposed adding a query mechanism to the usual navigation mechanism in hypertext systems in order to expand the user's ability to search the contents of a hypertext. By using this mechanism, environments that can change dynamically in accordance with the user's navigation can be described in query. We also defined advanced queries that can retrieve information from both structural and contextual aspects simultaneously in a hypertext system. The query language proposed in this paper is based on the formal semantics of relational calculus. It is applicable to the specifications of queries in many practical hypertext systems.

References

[1] *Abiteboul, S., and Grumbach, S.* COL: A Logic-Based Language for Complex Objects. In *Workshop on Database Programming Languages* (1987), pp. 253–276.

[2] *Afrati, F., and Koutras, C. D.* A Hypertext Model Supporting Query Mechanisms. In *Hypertext: Concepts, Systems and Applications*, N. Streitz, A. Rizk, and J. André, Eds., Cambridge University Press, Cambridge, UK, 1990, pp. 52–66. Proceedings of the European Conference on Hypertext.

[3] *Beeri, C., and Kornatzky, Y.* A Logical Query Language for Hypertext Systems. In *Hypertext: Concepts, Systems and Applications*, N. Streitz, A. Rizk, and J. André, Eds., Cambridge University Press, Cambridge, UK, 1990, pp. 67–80. Proceedings of the European Conference on Hypertext.

[4] *Berge, C. Graphs and Hypergraphs.* American Elsevier, New York, 1973.

[5] *Campbell, B., and Goodman, J. M.* HAM: A General Purpose Hypertext Abstract Machine. *Communications of the ACM 31*, 7 (July 1988), 856–861.

[6] *Chen, W., Kifer, M., and Warren, D. S.* HiLog as a Platform for Database Languages (or why predicate calculus is not enough). In *Proceedings of the 2nd International Workshop on Database Programming Languages* (1989), R. Hull, R. Morrison, and D. Stemple, Eds., Morgan Kaufmann Publishers, pp. 315–329.

[7] *Cluet, S., Delobel, C., Lécluse, C., and Richard, P.* Reloop, an Algebra Based Query Language for an Object-Oriented Database System. In *Proceedings of the 1st Conference on Deductive and Object-Oriented Databases* (1989), pp. 294–313.

[8] *Garg, P. K.* Abstraction mechanisms in hypertext. *Communications of the ACM 31*, 7 (July 1988), 862–870.

[9] *Halasz, F. G.* Reflections on NoteCards: Seven Issues for the Next Generation of Hypermedia Systems. *Communications of the ACM 31*, 7 (July 1988), 836–852.

[10] *Kahn, G.* Natural Semantics. In *Proceedings of 4th Annual Symposium on Theoretical Aspects of Computer Science* (1987), G. Goos and J. Hartmanis, Eds., Springer-Verlag, pp. 22–39. LNCS Volume 247.

[11] *Kifer, M., and Lausen, G.* F-logic: A higher-order language for reasoning about objects, inheritance and schema. In *Proceedings of the ACM Symposium on Principles of Database Systems* (1989), ACM Press, pp. 231–239.

[12] *Meyrowitz, N.* Hypermedia and the Desktop of Tomorrow. In *FRIEND21 Workshop* (October 1990).

[13] *Minker, J.*, Ed. *Foundations of Deductive Databases and Logic Programming*. Morgan Kaufmann Publishers, 1988.

[14] *Reiter, R.* "Towards a Logical Reconstruction of Relational Database Theory". In *On Conceptual Modelling*, M. L. Brodie, J. Mylopoulos, and J. W. Schmidt, Eds., Springer-Verlag, 1984, ch. 8, pp. 191–238.

[15] *Schütt, H., and Streitz, N. A. Hyper Base: A Hypermedia Engine based on a Relational Database Management System.* Arbeitspapiere der GMD 469, Gesellschaft für Mathematik und Datenverarbeitung mbH, July 1990.

[16] *Shaw, G., and Zdonik, S.* An Object-Oriented Query Algebra. In *Proceedings of the 2nd International Workshop on Database Programming Languages* (1989), R. Hull, R. Morrison, and D. Stemple, Eds., Morgan Kaufmann Publisher, pp. 103–112.

[17] *Tompa, F. W.* A Data Model for Flexible Hypertext Database Systems. *ACM Transactions on Information Systems 7*, 1 (January 1989), 85–100.

[18] *Trigg, R. H.* Guided Tours and Tabletops: Tools for Communicationg in a Hypertext Environment. *ACM Transactions on Office Information Systems 6*, 4 (October 1988), 398–414.

[19] *Ullman, J. D. "Principles of Database and Knowledge Base Systems"*. Vol. 1,2, Computer Science Press, 1988.

[20] *Watanabe, R. Query and Views in Hypertext.* Master's thesis, Keio University, Department of Computer Science, 1993. written in Japanese. English paper will appear.

Author Index

Springer-Verlag
and the Environment

We at Springer-Verlag firmly believe that an international science publisher has a special obligation to the environment, and our corporate policies consistently reflect this conviction.

We also expect our business partners – paper mills, printers, packaging manufacturers, etc. – to commit themselves to using environmentally friendly materials and production processes.

The paper in this book is made from low- or no-chlorine pulp and is acid free, in conformance with international standards for paper permanency.

Lecture Notes in Computer Science

For information about Vols. 1–660
please contact your bookseller or Springer-Verlag

Vol. 697: C. Courcoubetis (Ed.), Computer Aided Verification. Proceedings, 1993. IX, 504 pages. 1993.

Vol. 698: A. Voronkov (Ed.), Logic Programming and Automated Reasoning. Proceedings, 1993. XIII, 386 pages. 1993. (Subseries LNAI).

Vol. 699: G. W. Mineau, B. Moulin, J. F. Sowa (Eds.), Conceptual Graphs for Knowledge Representation. Proceedings, 1993. IX, 451 pages. 1993. (Subseries LNAI).

Vol. 700: A. Lingas, R. Karlsson, S. Carlsson (Eds.), Automata, Languages and Programming. Proceedings, 1993. XII, 697 pages. 1993.

Vol. 701: P. Atzeni (Ed.), LOGIDATA+: Deductive Databases with Complex Objects. VIII, 273 pages. 1993.

Vol. 702: E. Börger, G. Jäger, H. Kleine Büning, S. Martini, M. M. Richter (Eds.), Computer Science Logic. Proceedings, 1992. VIII, 439 pages. 1993.

Vol. 703: M. de Berg, Ray Shooting, Depth Orders and Hidden Surface Removal. X, 201 pages. 1993.

Vol. 704: F. N. Paulisch, The Design of an Extendible Graph Editor. XV, 184 pages. 1993.

Vol. 705: H. Grünbacher, R. W. Hartenstein (Eds.), Field-Programmable Gate Arrays. Proceedings, 1992. VIII, 218 pages. 1993.

Vol. 706: H. D. Rombach, V. R. Basili, R. W. Selby (Eds.), Experimental Software Engineering Issues. Proceedings, 1992. XVIII, 261 pages. 1993.

Vol. 707: O. M. Nierstrasz (Ed.), ECOOP '93 – Object-Oriented Programming. Proceedings, 1993. XI, 531 pages. 1993.

Vol. 708: C. Laugier (Ed.), Geometric Reasoning for Perception and Action. Proceedings, 1991. VIII, 281 pages. 1993.

Vol. 709: F. Dehne, J.-R. Sack, N. Santoro, S. Whitesides (Eds.), Algorithms and Data Structures. Proceedings, 1993. XII, 634 pages. 1993.

Vol. 710: Z. Ésik (Ed.), Fundamentals of Computation Theory. Proceedings, 1993. IX, 471 pages. 1993.

Vol. 711: A. M. Borzyszkowski, S. Sokołowski (Eds.), Mathematical Foundations of Computer Science 1993. Proceedings, 1993. XIII, 782 pages. 1993.

Vol. 712: P. V. Rangan (Ed.), Network and Operating System Support for Digital Audio and Video. Proceedings, 1992. X, 416 pages. 1993.

Vol. 713: G. Gottlob, A. Leitsch, D. Mundici (Eds.), Computational Logic and Proof Theory. Proceedings, 1993. XI, 348 pages. 1993.

Vol. 714: M. Bruynooghe, J. Penjam (Eds.), Programming Language Implementation and Logic Programming. Proceedings, 1993. XI, 421 pages. 1993.

Vol. 715: E. Best (Ed.), CONCUR '93. Proceedings, 1993. IX, 541 pages. 1993.

Vol. 716: A. U. Frank, I. Campari (Eds.), Spatial Information Theory. Proceedings, 1993. XI, 478 pages. 1993.

Vol. 717: I. Sommerville, M. Paul (Eds.), Software Engineering – ESEC '93. Proceedings, 1993. XII, 516 pages. 1993.

Vol. 718: J. Seberry, Y. Zheng (Eds.), Advances in Cryptology – AUSCRYPT '92. Proceedings, 1992. XIII, 543 pages. 1993.

Vol. 719: D. Chetverikov, W.G. Kropatsch (Eds.), Computer Analysis of Images and Patterns. Proceedings, 1993. XVI, 857 pages. 1993.

Vol. 720: V.Mařík, J. Lažanský, R.R. Wagner (Eds.), Database and Expert Systems Applications. Proceedings, 1993. XV, 768 pages. 1993.

Vol. 721: J. Fitch (Ed.), Design and Implementation of Symbolic Computation Systems. Proceedings, 1992. VIII, 215 pages. 1993.

Vol. 722: A. Miola (Ed.), Design and Implementation of Symbolic Computation Systems. Proceedings, 1993. XII, 384 pages. 1993.

Vol. 723: N. Aussenac, G. Boy, B. Gaines, M. Linster, J.-G. Ganascia, Y. Kodratoff (Eds.), Knowledge Acquisition for Knowledge-Based Systems. Proceedings, 1993. XIII, 446 pages. 1993. (Subseries LNAI).

Vol. 724: P. Cousot, M. Falaschi, G. Filè, A. Rauzy (Eds.), Static Analysis. Proceedings, 1993. IX, 283 pages. 1993.

Vol. 725: A. Schiper (Ed.), Distributed Algorithms. Proceedings, 1993. VIII, 325 pages. 1993.

Vol. 726: T. Lengauer (Ed.), Algorithms – ESA '93. Proceedings, 1993. IX, 419 pages. 1993

Vol. 727: M. Filgueiras, L. Damas (Eds.), Progress in Artificial Intelligence. Proceedings, 1993. X, 362 pages. 1993. (Subseries LNAI).

Vol. 728: P. Torasso (Ed.), Advances in Artificial Intelligence. Proceedings, 1993. XI, 336 pages. 1993. (Subseries LNAI).

Vol. 729: L. Donatiello, R. Nelson (Eds.), Performance Evaluation of Computer and Communication Systems. Proceedings, 1993. VIII, 675 pages. 1993.

Vol. 730: D. B. Lomet (Ed.), Foundations of Data Organization and Algorithms. Proceedings, 1993. XII, 412 pages. 1993.

Vol. 731: A. Schill (Ed.), DCE – The OSF Distributed Computing Environment. Proceedings, 1993. VIII, 285 pages. 1993.

Vol. 732: A. Bode, M. Dal Cin (Eds.), Parallel Computer Architectures. IX, 311 pages. 1993.

Vol. 733: Th. Grechenig, M. Tscheligi (Eds.), Human Computer Interaction. Proceedings, 1993. XIV, 450 pages. 1993.

Vol. 734: J. Volkert (ed.), Parallel Computation. Proceedings, 1993. VIII, 248 pages. 1993.

Vol. 735: D. Bjørner, M. Broy, I. V. Pottosin (Eds.), Formal Methods in Programming and Their Applications. Proceedings, 1993. IX, 434 pages. 1993.

Vol. 736: R. L. Grossman, A. Nerode, A. P. Ravn, H. Rischel (Eds.), Hybrid Systems. VIII, 474 pages. 1993.

Vol. 737: J. Calmet, J. A. Campbell (Eds.), Artificial Intelligence and Symbolic Mathematical Computing. Proceedings, 1992. VIII, 305 pages. 1993.